BIBLIOGRAPHY OF MEXICAN AMERICAN HISTORY

BIBLIOGRAPHY OF MEXICAN AMERICAN HISTORY

Compiled by Matt S. Meier

GP

GREENWOOD PRESS
Westport, Connecticut • London, England

Library of Congress Cataloging in Publication Data

Meier, Matt S.
  Bibliography of Mexican American history.

  Includes indexes.
  1. Mexican Americans—History—Bibliography.
I. Title.
Z1361.M4M414 1984   [E185.M5]   016.973'046872   83-18585
ISBN 0-313-23776-X (lib. bdg.)

Library of Congress Catalog Card Number: 83-18585
ISBN: 0-313-23776-X

First published in 1984

Greenwood Press
A division of Congressional Information Service, Inc.
88 Post Road West, Westport, Connecticut 06881

Printed in the United States of America

10 9 8 7 6 5 4 3 2 1

CONTENTS

PREFACE

Mexican American history has been studied and developed in a systematic, serious, and objective way only within the past decade and a half. It is therefore understandable that Mexican American bibliography, compared to bibliography in other fields of history, is just beginning to emerge from its infancy. Until recently United States historians have largely neglected materials dealing with this sizable and important minority group in American society. Yet these historical records, though ignored, have always been there, waiting to be put to use in writing the history of the Mexican American. Moreover, in the past fifteen years as much published material has been added to this store as was accumulated between the 1848 Treaty of Guadalupe Hidalgo and the middle 1960s.

The purpose of this bibliography, then, is to provide access to information necessary for a more sophisticated understanding of the Mexican American experience and its contribution to contemporary America. It is hoped that it will serve researchers, reference librarians, scholars, teachers, and students. Curriculum specialists and accessions librarians should find it a valuable resource for broadening their knowledge of, and improving their holdings in, the field of Chicano studies.

This is a comprehensive research bibliography for Mexican American history, partially and briefly annotated. It covers both primary and secondary works and includes general works, monographs, theses, dissertations, government documents, pamphlets, chapters from books, and journal articles. For the most part it excludes newspaper materials. The user should be aware, however, that since the late 1960s the New York Times has indexed articles under the heading "Minorities," with subheadings "Mexicans" and "Spanish-Speaking Groups." Similarly the Wall Street Journal has indexed articles since the early 1970s under the heading "Ethnic Groups" and since the beginning of the 1980s under "Minority Groups."

Mexican American history is understood to begin with the Treaty of Guadalupe Hidalgo in 1848, but its roots go back deeper in time to both Spain and Mexico. The bibliography attempts to include all historical works concerning Mexican Americans from 1848 to the present, as well as major studies dealing with the earlier historical periods. The overwhelming majority of listed items are in English; a few, authored by Mexican scholars, are in Spanish.

The terms Mexican American and Chicano are used interchangeably in the _Bibliography_. However, the reader will find that many other terms are used to refer to this ethnic group in the listed items. Among the most common are Hispano, Hispanic, Hispanic American, Spanish American, Latin American, Spanish-speaking, Mexican in the United States, and Raza. Some of these terms also are used more broadly for all people of Spanish or Latin American heritage.

The _Bibliography of Mexican American History_ is organized in twelve sections within two broad categories--one chronological and the other topical. The chronological divisions follow the widely accepted periodization that Professor Feliciano Rivera and I used in _The Chicanos: A History of Mexican Americans_ (Hill & Wang, 1972). The first three topical sections are devoted to important themes that run through the entire historical experience of the Mexican American, and the last three are bibliographic in nature. The sections in the order they appear in the bibliography are titled as follows: I. General Works; II. Colonial Period; III. Mexican Period; IV. Guadalupe Hidalgo to 1900; V. 1900 to World War II; VI. World War II to the 1980s; VII. Labor, Immigration, and the Border Region; VIII. Civil Rights and Politics; IX. Culture; X. Bibliographies and Guides; XI. Collections, Archives, and Libraries; XII. Journals. An author index and a selective subject index complete the work.

In order to prevent sections VII, VIII, and IX from becoming too unwieldy I have limited them to works that markedly overlap the chronological divisions or tend to be more descriptive than historical in their approach. To put it another way, a book on labor that falls totally within one chronological section has been placed in that section. Inevitably there is overlap from one section to another. It simply is not possible to compartmentalize history into any rigid chronological or topical framework. Where there is overlap of time or topic, I have tried to place works in those sections where they seem most pertinent and valuable. Sections II through IX are subdivided into three parts: Books, Theses, and Periodicals. Included in the Periodicals sections are appropriate chapters from survey works on such topics as immigration, civil rights, labor organization, and discrimination. The areas covered are detailed at the beginning of each section.

According to the 1980 census there are today approximately nine million Americans of Mexican heritage; they
constitute more than fifty percent of all Hispanic Americans, that is, of all Americans of Spanish or Latin American
heritage. Roughly one-half of these Mexican Americans live
in California and one-third in Texas; the remaining one-
sixth are scattered over the other forty-eight states. The
second largest minority in the United States, they have been
neglected or forgotten for most of this century—except when
they were perceived as a problem.

In recent decades new historical studies of the Chicano
experience have emerged; some of these are monographs
detailing specific aspects of that history, while others are
broader surveys. Section I includes a large body of mono-
graphic and periodical material dealing with the sweep of
Chicano history and other historical survey materials that
form a background to the creation of the Mexican people and
to their experience in the Southwest. Section II, on the
Colonial period of Mexican history, is necessarily selective
of the many excellent works on the historical and cultural
development of the mestizo; it also refers the user to two
valuable guides to publications on the period. Section III,
the Mexican Period, ends with the creation of the Chicano
through the incorporation of Mexico's northern frontier
region and its people into the United States. By the Treaty
of Guadalupe Hidalgo the United States acquired title to
about half of Mexico—nearly one million square miles.
Mexicans within this area were guaranteed their personal,
political, and property rights.

The second half of the nineteenth century, covered in
Section IV, witnessed a massive influx of Anglo-Americans
into the lands of these Mexican Americans. The loss of
grant lands, first in California and later in New Mexico,
provides an index to loss of power by the Spanish-speaking
peoples and to their subordination in an Anglo-dominated
society. Because Texas was settled so heavily by Anglos
from the old South with its racial prejudices and Protestant
fundamentalism, Mexicans in that state met with the greatest
hardship and hostility. By the end of the nineteenth century most Mexican Americans were to be found at the lowest
socioeconomic levels of American society. The scholarship
on this period centers largely on the themes of land loss by
Mexican Americans and of frontier and border violence.

The first half of the twentieth century, covered in
Section V, is dominated by a massive movement of Mexicans to
the United States, particularly from the 1910 Revolution to
the end of the prosperity decade of the twenties. Between
1910 and 1930 more than a million Mexicans came to the
United States—in one of the great migrations of history.
Although immigration and emigration statistics are unreli-
able, an estimated 300,000 Mexicans repatriated in the

thirties, and fewer than 25,000 "new" Mexican immigrants entered the United States during those depression years. Scholars have investigated and written about this population movement in some detail. However, little research and writing have been directed toward either the Chicano role in World War I or the late 1920s movement to bring Mexican immigration under the United States quota system established by Congress in 1921 and 1924.

Section VI, World War II to the 1980s, describes the important impact of the war and the bracero (imported Mexican labor) program on Mexican Americans. Moreover, it considers the topic of immigration--especially that of undocumented Mexicans--perhaps the most written-about issue in Chicano history. Lastly, this chapter includes the very important topic of Chicano social and political leadership, a subject that needs further scholarly investigation. Works on Cesar Chavez and the Delano grape strike form an important part of this section.

Section VII covers labor, immigration, and the border region, topics in which there has been considerable interest and, as a result, an abundance of articles, theses, and books. In addition, numerous government committees, agencies, and panels have produced useful reports, statistical tables, and other materials of value to the historian. This aspect of Chicano history has attracted considerable interest on the part of Mexican scholars.

Section VIII, on politics and civil rights, includes the subtopics of discrimination, segregation, and stereotyping. Much academic and even popular attention has been focused on these problems in the areas of education, housing, and politics; there has resulted considerable federal concern, leading to numerous official publications. Section IX, on culture, is a field of uneven scholarly activity. Some areas, like education, attracted early interest and research; others, like naturalization and acculturation, still await systematic historical study. However, there is a fair amount of sociologically oriented work on these topics. In recent years some writing on the history of Chicano literature and folk arts has appeared.

Each bibliographic item includes the name of the author, title of the work, city and publisher, and the date of publication. Periodical articles include author, title, periodical, number and date of issue, and the page numbers. Generally current names of institutions have been used to avoid confusion, for example, California State University, Northridge, rather than San Fernando Valley State College. The reader will find, of course, that some items are rich in historical information, while others offer a fairly thin gruel. Materials vary greatly in utility, completeness, and trustworthiness, but all are grist for the historian's mill. The usefulness of the bibliography is enhanced by brief

notations, especially where a title fails to indicate clear-
ly the content and coverage.

I believe the thesis-dissertation sections, which make
up about twenty percent of the bibliography, are of special
value, since much of the historical material and interpretation they contain is unavailable in regularly published
form. Although not completely historical in approach, a
number of early Mexican American theses and dissertations
from fields close to history are included. These are of
great value to the historian because many of them paint an
accurate picture of Mexican American and Mexican immigrant
status at the time the research was undertaken. A few even
include photographs of housing and other aspects of Chicano
life. Unless otherwise indicated, items listed in these
thesis sections are doctoral dissertations; most are available by purchase from Xerox University Microfilms. The
inclusion of a large number of master's theses is particularly helpful because most of them otherwise are difficult
to locate. They normally are available through interlibrary
loan. The reader should be aware that most theses, dissertations, and books--both general histories and monographs on
the Mexican American experience--include comprehensive
bibliographies or bibliographic essays.

ACKNOWLEDGMENTS _____

As with any undertaking of this type, the <u>Bibliography</u> is the sum of the work, help, and support of many people. For their moral and financial support, I wish to thank my department chairman, the director of Ethnic Studies at the University of Santa Clara, and my dean. I am indebted further to the University of Santa Clara for a President's Research Grant that helped defray some expenses incurred in this work.

I am particularly beholden to Professor Ellwyn Stoddard and to helpful librarians all over the Southwest. I owe a special debt I can never repay to Alice Whistler and Philip Warman of the Orradre Library at Santa Clara, who tracked down many elusive details of citations, and to Linda Campbell, who typed the manuscript with unfailing good humor. Beyond these there stands a small army of friends and well-wishers to whom I am grateful for acts of thoughtfulness and kindness far too numerous to mention. To them all I am greatly indebted.

Santa Clara, June 1983   Matt S. Meier

BIBLIOGRAPHY OF
MEXICAN
AMERICAN
HISTORY

I.
GENERAL WORKS

Books

Section I, General Works, includes books and articles
that survey the history of the Mexican American, the Spanish
heritage in the Southwest, general histories of the Chicana,
some important survey histories of the Southwest and state
histories, collections of documents and readings, and
historiographical articles.

1   Abbott, Carl. Colorado, A History of the Centennial
       State. Boulder: Colorado Association, 1976.
State history with limited reference to Mexican Americans.

2   Acuña, Rodolfo. America ocupada: los Chicanos y su lucha
       de liberacion. Mexico, D.F.: Ediciones Era, 1976.
A Spanish-language version of his Occupied America, 1972.

3   Acuña, Rodolfo. A Mexican American Chronicle. New York:
       American Book Co., 1971.
One of the best junior high school texts, with emphasis on
oppression of Chicanos.

4   Acuña, Rodolfo. Occupied America: A History of Chicanos.
       2nd ed. New York: Harper & Row Publishers, 1981.
Documents patterns of discrimination and repression.

5   Acuña, Rodolfo. Occupied America: The Chicano's Struggle
       Toward Liberation. New York: Harper & Row Publishers,
       1972.
Argues the theme of Chicano internal colonialism, from an
activist's viewpoint.

6   Acuña, Rodolfo. The Story of the Mexican Americans: The
       Men and the Land. New York: American Book Co., 1969.
An account of migrant workers' struggles; includes
biographical sketches of leaders.

7   Adams, Alexander B. The Disputed Lands: A History of the
        American West. New York: G. P. Putnam's Sons, 1981.
Covers the Far West from Alvar Nunez Cabeza de Vaca to the
Apache campaigns of the 1870s and 1880s.

8   Alford, Harold J. The Proud Peoples: The Heritage and
        Culture of Spanish-Speaking Peoples in the United
        States. New York: David McKay Co., 1972.
A popular history of all Hispanic American groups; good on
migrant workers.

9   Alsberg, Henry G., ed. Writers Program, New Mexico. New
        Mexico. A Guide to the Colorful State. New York:
        Hastings House, 1962.

10 Anderson, George B., ed. History of New Mexico, Its
        Resources and People. 2 vols. New York: Pacific
        States Publishing Co., 1917.
Volume one contains a complete list of Land Court decisions,
pp. 204-208.

11 Ashworth, Mary Herley, ed. Spanish-Speaking Americans
        in the U.S.A. New York: Friendship Press, 1953.
An early collection of articles.

12 Bakker, Elna. The Great Southwest. Palo Alto, Calif.:
        American West Publishing Co., 1972.
A general work, with some information on Chicanos.

13 Bancroft, Hubert Howe, ed. History of California. 7
        vols. San Francisco: History Co., 1884-1890.
        Reprint, 7 vols. Santa Barbara, Calif.: Wallace
        Hebberd Publishers, 1963-1970.

14 Bean, Walton. California: An Interpretive History. New
        York: McGraw-Hill Book Co., 1968.
A useful state history with some inclusion of Mexican
Americans.

15 Beck, Warren A. Historical Atlas of New Mexico.
        Norman: University of Oklahoma Press, 1962.

16 Beck, Warren A. New Mexico, A History of Four
        Centuries. Norman: University of Oklahoma Press,
        1962.
A valuable general survey with Hispano American material;
good on cultural conflict. An extensive bibliography.

17 Bentley, Harold W., comp. A Dictionary of Spanish Terms
        in English with Special Reference to the American
        Southwest. New York: Columbia University Press, 1932.

18   Bernard, Jacqueline. Voices from the Southwest. New
        York: Scholastic Book Services, 1972.
Biographies of Mexican American leaders, for the sixth grade
level.

19   Brown, Gertrude and Manuel Guerra. Our Mexican
        Heritage. Lexington, Mass.: Ginn & Co., 1972.
Primary school text with heavy emphasis on Mexican
background.

20   Burma, John H., ed. Mexican-Americans in the United
        States: A Reader. Cambridge, Mass.: Schenkman
        Publishing Co., 1970.
Sociological essays, some considered biased.

21   Burma, John H. Spanish-Speaking Groups in the United
        States. Durham, N.C.: Duke University Press, 1954.
Includes chapters on institutions, immigration, and labor.

22   Bustamante, Charles J. and Patricia L. Bustamante. The
        Mexican American and the United States. Mountain
        View, Calif.: Patty-Lar Publications, c1969.
A brief history, with biographies of prominent leaders.

23   Calvin, Ross. Sky Determines: An Interpretation of the
        Southwest. Albuquerque: University of New Mexico
        Press, 1965.
A popular synthesis with materials on the Mexican American.

24   Caughey, John W. California: A Remarkable State's Life
        History. 3rd ed. Englewood Cliffs, N.J.:
        Prentice-Hall, 1970.
Includes updated material on recent Chicano history.

25   Cleland, Robert Glass. From Wilderness to Empire: A
        History of California. New York: Alfred A. Knopf,
        1959.
Covers from 1542 to 1940; indicates Mexican American role.

26   Coan, Charles F. A History of New Mexico. 3 vols. New
        York: American Historical Society, 1925.
Has a good chapter on Spanish and Mexican land grants.

27   Connor, Seymour V. Texas: A History. New York: Thomas
        Y. Crowell Co., 1971.
A useful survey, balanced and comprehensive.

28   Cotera, Martha P. Diosa y Hembra: The History and
        Heritage of Chicanas in the U.S. Austin, Tex.:
        Information Systems Development, 1976.

29   Cotera, Martha P. Profile on the Mexican American
        Woman. Austin, Tex.: National Educational Laboratory,

        1976. Also published at Las Cruces: New Mexico State
        University, 1976.
Studies the Chicana from prehistory to present.

30 Cotera, Martha P. and Larry Hufford, eds. Bridging Two
        Cultures: Multidisciplinary Readings in Bilingual
        Bicultural Education. Austin, Tex.: National
        Educational Laboratory, 1980.
A series of excellent readings in the Mexican American
heritage.

31 Coy, Harold. Chicano Roots Go Deep. New York: Dodd,
        Mead & Co., 1975.
A general history of Mexican Americans; rather superficial.

32 Cruz, Frank J. Latin Americans: Past and Present.
        Boston: Houghton Mifflin Co., 1972.

33 Davis, Ellis A., ed. The Historical Encyclopedia of New
        Mexico. 2 vols. Albuquerque: New Mexico Historical
        Association, 1945.

34 De La Garza, Rudolph Z.; Anthony Kruszewski; and Tomas
        A. Arciniega, comps. Chicanos and Native Americans:
        The Territorial Minorities. Englewood Cliffs, N.J.:
        Prentice-Hall, 1973.
A collection of articles on Chicano political experiences.

35 De Leon, Nephtali. Chicanos: Our Background and Our
        Pride. Lubbock, Tex.: Trucha Publications, 1972.
An activist's brief personal interpretation of the Chicano
experience, with emphasis on Texas.

36 De Onis, Jose, ed. The Hispanic Contribution to the
        State of Colorado. Boulder, Colo.: Westview Press,
        1976.

37 Dinnerstein, Leonard and David M. Reimers. Ethnic
        Americans: A History of Immigration and Assimilation.
        2nd ed. New York: Harper & Row Publishers, 1982.
A brief general history, placing Mexican Americans in
context.

38 Dunn, Lynn P. Chicanos: A Study Guide and Source Book.
        San Francisco: R & E Research Associates, 1975.
A useful tool for teachers of Chicano studies.

39 Duran, Livie and Bernard Russell, eds. Introduction to
        Chicano Studies: A Reader. New York: Macmillan Co.,
        1973.
Some forty-seven topically arranged articles on historical
background, cultural problems, and adjustments. Includes a
list of Chicano periodicals.

40   Echevarria, Evelio and Jose Otero, eds. Hispanic
        Colorado: Four Centuries History and Heritage. Fort
        Collins, Colo.: Centennial Publications, 1976.

41   Eiseman, Alberta. Mañana is Now: The Spanish-Speaking
        in the United States. New York: Atheneum Publishers,
        1973.
An introduction to the Hispano experience at the junior high
school level.

42   Ellis, Richard N., ed. New Mexico Past and Present: A
        Historical Reader. Albuquerque: University of New
        Mexico Press, 1971.
A valuable collection; includes the 1911 New Mexico
constitution, and text of the Guadalupe Hidalgo Treaty.

43   Farish, Thomas E. History of Arizona. 9 vols. San
        Francisco: The Filmer Brothers Electrotype Co.,
        1915-1920.

44   Faulk, Odie B. Arizona: A Short History. Norman:
        University of Oklahoma Press, 1970.

45   Faulk, Odie B. Land of Many Frontiers: A History of the
        American Southwest. New York: Oxford University
        Press, 1968.
An able survey of Southwestern history from the sixteenth
century to the present.

46   Fehrenbach, T. R. Lone Star: A History of Texas and the
        Texans. New York: Macmillan Co., 1968.
An excellent survey which places Tejano history in context.

47   Fergusson, Erna. New Mexico: A Pageant of Three
        Peoples. 2nd ed. New York: Alfred A. Knopf, 1964.
Popular history with emphasis on the nineteenth century;
contrasts Anglo, Indian, and Mexican cultures.

48   Fergusson, Erna. Our Southwest. New York: Alfred A.
        Knopf, 1940.

49   Fergusson, Harvey. Rio Grande. New York: Alfred A.
        Knopf, 1933.
A well written journalistic history of New Mexico from the
1500s to ca. 1900.

50   Fernandez-Florez, Dario. The Spanish Heritage in the
        United States. Madrid: Publicaciones Españolas, 1965.
        Reprint, New York: Arno Press, 1980.

51   Forbes, Jack D., ed. Aztecas del Norte: The Chicanos of
        Aztlan. Greenwich, Conn.: Fawcett Publications, 1973.
A topically arranged collection of fairly short historical
articles, many contemporary to the events they describe.

Emphasis on the native American background.

52 Forbes, Jack D. Mexican-Americans: A Handbook for
      Educators. Berkeley, Calif.: Far West Laboratory for
      Educational Research and Development, 1967.
An early brief essay on Mexican American history; includes a
brief bibliography and description of some audio-visual
materials.

53 Foster, George M. Culture and Conquest: America's
      Spanish Heritage. New York: Wenner Gren Foundation
      for Anthropological Research, 1960.

54 Frantz, Joe B. Texas: A Bicentennial History. New
      York: W. W. Norton & Co., 1976.

55 Fritz, Percy S. Colorado, the Centennial State. New
      York: Prentice-Hall, 1941.

56 Fugate, Francis. The Spanish Heritage of the Southwest.
      El Paso: Texas Western Press, 1952.

57 Fulton, Maurice G., ed. New Mexico's Own Chronicle.
      Dallas, Tex.: B. Upshaw & Co., 1937.

58 Galarza, Ernesto. Dwellers of the Sunshine Slums:
      Mexican-Americans in the Southwest. Santa Barbara,
      Calif.: McNally & Loftin, 1964.

59 Galarza, Ernesto; Herman Gallegos; and Julian Samora.
      Mexican-Americans in the Southwest. Santa Barbara,
      Calif.: McNally & Loftin, 1970.
A concise contemporary overview with political and
sociological emphasis.

60 Garcia, George J., ed. Selected Reading Materials on
      the Mexican and Spanish American. Denver, Colo.:
      Commission on Community Relations, City and County of
      Denver, 1969.
Articles on the Mexican American experience by Mexican
Americans.

61 Garcia, Richard A. The Chicanos in America 1540-1974: A
      Chronology and Fact Book. Dobbs Ferry, N.Y.: Oceana
      Publications, 1977.
A useful tool for teachers, but outdated.

62 Garrison, George P. Texas: A Contest of Civilizations.
      Boston: Houghton Mifflin Co., 1903.

63 Gehlbach, Frederick R. Mountains, Islands, and Desert
      Seas: A Natural History of the U.S.-Mexican
      Borderlands. College Station: Texas A & M University
      Press, 1981.

Valuable for understanding the geography of the Borderlands
area from Texas to California.

64   Gilpin, Laura. The Rio Grande--River of Destiny. New
       York: Duell, Sloan and Pearce, 1949.
An historical interpretation of the river, land, and people.

65   Gomez, David F. Somos Chicanos: Strangers in Our Own
       Land. Boston: Beacon Press, 1973.
Emphasizes life in the barrio; largely socio-economic
history.

66   Gomez, Rudolph, ed. The Changing Mexican-American: A
       Reader. Boulder, Colo.: Pruett Publishing Co., 1972.
Contains nineteen general articles on the Chicano experience
and biographies of leaders.

67   Grebler, Leo; Joan W. Moore; and Ralph C. Guzman. The
       Mexican-American People: The Nation's Second Largest
       Minority. New York: Free Press, 1970.
An outstanding social science resource book for all aspects
of Mexican American life; includes an excellent
bibliography.

68   Haddox, John H. Los Chicanos: An Awakening People.   El
       Paso: University of Texas Press, 1970.
Brief essay describing the 1970 Chicano scene.

69   Hafen, LeRoy R. Colorado and its People. 4 vols. New
       York: Lewis Historical Publishing Co., 1948.
Detailed Colorado history by an outstanding western
historian.

70   Hafen, LeRoy R. Colorado: The Story of a Western
       Commonwealth. New York: Lewis Historical Publishing
       Co., 1970.

71   Hammond, George P. and Thomas C. Donnelly. The Story of
       New Mexico: Its History and Government. Albuquerque:
       University of New Mexico Press, 1936.
A balanced survey with some emphasis on the Hispanos of New
Mexico.

72   Hecht, Melvin E. and Richard W. Reeves. The Arizona
       Atlas. Tucson: Office of Arid Lands Studies,
       University of Arizona, 1981.
Maps and discussion of Spanish and Mexican traditions and
history.

73   Hedrick, Basil C. J.; Charles Kelley; and Carroll J.
       Riley, eds. The North Mexican Frontier: Readings in
       Archaeology, Ethnohistory, and Ethnography.
       Carbondale: Southern Illinois University Press, 1971.

74 Helm, June, ed. Spanish Speaking People in the United
       States. Seattle: University of Washington Press,
       1969.
An ethnological study of Mexican Americans.

75 Hernandez, Luis F. Aztlan: The Southwest and Its
       People. Rochelle Park, N.J.: Hayden Book Co., 1976.

76 Hispanic Influences in the United States. New York:
       Interbook, 1975.
Papers on Hispanic influences presented in a seminar at the
Spanish Institute, New York, 1974.

77 Hogan, William R. The Texas Republic: A Social and
       Economic History. Norman: University of Oklahoma
       Press, 1946.

78 Hollon, W. Eugene. The Southwest: Old and New. New
       York: Alfred A. Knopf, 1961.
An excellent broad survey, from the sixteenth to twentieth
century.

79 Horgan, Paul F. The Centuries of Santa Fe. New York:
       E. P. Dutton & Co., 1965.
Synthesizes Santa Fe's history from the seventeenth to the
twentieth centuries.

80 Horgan, Paul F. Great River: The Rio Grande in North
       American History. 2 vols. New York: Holt, Rinehart &
       Winston, 1954.
A Pulitzer prize-winning panoramic view of New Mexican
history. Volume I covers the colonial and Mexican periods;
volume II covers Anglo intrusion and conquest in the
nineteenth century.

81 Horgan, Paul F. The Heroic Triad: Essays in the Social
       Energies of Three Southwestern Cultures. New York:
       Holt, Rinehart & Winston, 1970.
Insightful essays on Mexican, Indian, and Anglo cultural
interaction.

82 Hundley, Norris, Jr., ed. The Chicanos. Santa Barbara,
       Calif.: American Bibliographical Center-Clio Press,
       1975.
Collection of historical essays originally published in The
Pacific Historical Review.

83 Hutchinson, William H. California: Two Centuries of
       Man, Land, and Growth in the Golden State. Palo Alto,
       Calif.: American West Publishing Co., 1969.

84 James, Daniel. Mexico and the Americans. New York:
       Praeger Publishers, 1963.
Discusses United States-Mexican relations; valuable for

border problems.

85 Jenkins, Myra E. and Albert H. Schroeder. A Brief
        History of New Mexico. Albuquerque: University of New
        Mexico Press, 1974.

86 Johnson, Francis White. A History of Texas and Texans.
        5 vols. Edited and updated by Eugene C. Barker.
        Chicago and New York: The American Historical Society,
        1914.
Includes biographies of important figures in Texas history.

87 Lamb, Ruth S. Mexican Americans: Sons of the Southwest.
        Claremont, Calif.: Ocelot Press, 1970.
Largely on period before 1850; a good bibliography.

88 Landes, Ruth. Latin Americans of the Southwest. New
        York: McGraw-Hill Book Co., 1965.
A brief survey, basically anthropological in approach.

89 Lavender, David. The Southwest. New York: Harper & Row
        Publishers, 1980.
Popular history with little emphasis on the Mexican
American.

90 Lelevier, Benjamin. Portfolio of Outstanding Americans
        of Mexican Descent. Menlo Park, Calif.: Educational
        Consulting Associates, 1970.

91 Loftis, Anne. California--Where the Twain Did Meet.
        New York: Macmillan Co., 1973.
Stresses minorities and race issues.

92 Lopez y Rivas, Gilberto. The Chicanos: Life and
        Struggles of the Mexican Minority in the United
        States. New York: Monthly Review Press, 1973.
Translation of his Mexican work published in 1971, with some
readings added.

93 Lopez y Rivas, Gilberto. Los chicanos: una minoria
        nacional explotada. Mexico, D.F.: Editorial Nuestro
        Tiempo, 1971.
Emphasizes Mexican emigration to the U.S.

94 Lopez y Rivas, Gilberto. Conquest and Resistance: The
        Origins of the Chicano National Minority. San
        Francisco: R & E Research Associates, 1979.

95 Ludwig, Edward W. and James Santibanez, eds. The
        Chicanos: Mexican American Voices. Baltimore, M.D.:
        Penguin Books, 1971.
A collection of topically arranged writings--many historical
in nature--reflecting mistreatment and injustice.

96   Lummis, Charles Fletcher. Flowers of Our Lost Romance.
        Boston: Houghton Mifflin Co., 1929.
Enumerates the Spanish contributions to Southwestern
culture.

97   Machado, Manuel A., Jr. Listen Chicano! An Informal
        History of the Mexican American. Chicago:
        Nelson-Hall, 1978.
A broad conservative interpretation of the Chicano
experience.

98   Maciel, David R., ed. La otra cara de Mexico: el pueblo
        chicano. Mexico, D.F.: Ediciones "El Caballito,"
        1977.
A collection of historical, economic, social, educational,
and cultural documents.

99   Maciel, David R. and Patricia Bueno, comps. Aztlan:
        historia del pueblo chicano (1848-1910). Mexico,
        D.F.: SepSetentas, 1975.
Contains nine articles by various historians, Anglo,
Chicano, and Mexican.

100 McWilliams, Carey. Al norte de Mexico: el conflicto
        entre "anglos" e "hispanos." Mexico, D.F.: Siglo
        Veintiuno, 1968.
The Spanish version of his North From Mexico.

101 McWilliams, Carey. The Mexicans in America: A
        Student's Guide to Localized History. New York:
        Teacher's College Press, Columbia University, 1968.
Provides a brief historical overview in a series on local
history.

102 McWilliams, Carey. North From Mexico. Philadelphia:
        J. B. Lippincott Co., 1949. Reprint, New York:
        Greenwood Press, 1968.
Pioneering work in Mexican American history by a journalist
who was involved in the early struggles by Chicanos and
Mexican immigrants.

103 Maldonado de Johnson, Carmen. A Probe into the Mexican
        American Experience; un examen sobre la experiencia de
        los mexico-americanos. New York: Harcourt Brace
        Jovanovich, 1973.

104 Mangold, Margaret M., ed. La Causa Chicana: The
        Movement for Justice. New York: Family Service
        Association of America, 1972.

105 Marinacci, Barbara and Rudy Marinacci. California's
        Spanish Place Names: What They Mean and How They Got
        There. San Rafael, Calif.: Presidio Press, 1980.
A chronological-historical description of California's

Spanish-Mexican heritage; not a dictionary of place names.

106   Martinez, Al. Rising Voices: Profiles of
        Hispano-American Lives. New York: New American
        Library, 1974.
A collection of short biographies of fifty-two outstanding
Spanish-speaking Americans, about half Mexican Americans.

107   Martinez, Elizabeth Sutherland and Enriqueta Longeaux y
        Vasquez. Viva La Raza! The Struggle of the
        Mexican-American People. New York: Doubleday & Co.,
        1974.
Documents political activities in the late nineteen sixties
and early seventies.

108   Martinez, Gilbert T. and Jane Edwards. The Mexican
        American: His Life Across Four Centuries. Boston:
        Houghton Mifflin Co., 1973.
A grade school survey with emphasis on the pre-Mexican War
period.

109   Martinez, Orlando. Viva Chicano! The Story of
        Mexicans in America. New York: Gordon Cremonesi,
        1979.

110   Martinez, Rafael. My House is Your House. New York:
        Friendship Press, 1964.
Reviews the cultural contribution of Spanish Americans to
the United States.

111   Martinez C., Hector. Yo chicano. Mexico, D.F.: B.
        Costa-Amic, 1976.
Analyzes community changes and acculturation since the
1950s.

112   Meier, Matt S. and Feliciano Rivera. The Chicanos: A
        History of Mexican Americans. New York: Hill & Wang,
        1972.
A wide-ranging historical survey presenting a Chicano
viewpoint while avoiding emotions.

113   Meier, Matt S. and Feliciano Rivera. Los Chicanos, una
        historia de los mexicano-americanos. Mexico, D.F.:
        Editorial Diana, 1976.
Spanish language version of The Chicanos.

114   Meier, Matt S. and Feliciano Rivera, comps. Dictionary
        of Mexican American History. Westport, Conn.:
        Greenwood Press, 1981.
A comprehensive research tool, indexed and cross referenced;
includes maps, tables, graphs, and charts, the Treaty of
Guadalupe Hidalgo and the Queretaro Protocol.

115 Meier, Matt S. and Feliciano Rivera, eds. Readings on
      La Raza. New York: Hill & Wang, 1974.
A collection of forty-six articles covering from 1900 to
1974 under six topical headings, with emphasis on
immigration and labor.

116 Meining, Donald W. Imperial Texas: An Interpretive
      Essay in Cultural Geography. Austin: University of
      Texas Press, 1969.

117 Meining, Donald W. Southwest: Three Peoples in
      Geographic Change 1600-1970. New York: Oxford
      University Press, 1971.
Analyzes the relations of Mexicans, Indians, and Anglos from
a historical geographic point of view.

118 Melville, Margarita B., ed. Twice a Minority: Mexican
      American Woman. St. Louis, Mo.: C. V. Mosby Co.,
      1980.
A collection of essays; includes bibliographic materials.

119 Mirande, Alfredo and Evangelina Enriquez. La Chicana:
      The Mexican-American Woman. Chicago: University of
      Chicago Press, 1979.
Socio-historical study of the Chicana and her changing role
in the family and community.

120 Moore, Joan W. Mexican-Americans: Problems and
      Prospects. Madison: University of Wisconsin Press,
      1966.
A brief overview of the Mexican American experience,
especially in the barrio.

121 Moore, Joan W. Los mexicanos de Los Estados Unidos y
      el movimiento chicano. Mexico, D.F.: Fondo de Cultura
      Economica, 1972.
Spanish language version of her Mexican-Americans (1970).

122 Moore, Joan W. with Alfredo B. Cuellar. Mexican
      Americans. Englewood Cliffs, N.J.: Prentice-Hall,
      1970.
A succinct history and socio-economic survey, with a chapter
on Chicano politics by Cuellar.

123 Moore, Joan W. with Harry Pachon. Mexican Americans.
      2nd ed. Englewood Cliffs, N.J.: Prentice-Hall, 1976.
A revision and updating of Moore's 1970 survey.

124 Moquin, Wayne and Charles Van Doren, eds. A
      Documentary History of the Mexican Americans. New
      York: Praeger Publishers, 1971.
Comprehensive collection of articles, mostly contemporary to
the events they describe, from the sixteenth to the

twentieth century, selected by Feliciano Rivera.

125   Mora, Magdalena and Adelaida R. Del Castillo, eds.
        Mexican Women in the United States: Struggles, Past
        and Present. Los Angeles: Chicano Studies Research
        Center, University of California, 1980.
Essays and addresses, with bibliographic references.

126   Moreno, Dorinda, ed. La Mujer: En Pie de Lucha. San
        Francisco: Espina del Norte, 1973.
Includes materials on the Chicana and other minority women.

127   Mosely, J. E., ed. The Spanish-Speaking Peoples of the
        Southwest. Indianapolis, Ind.: Council on
        Spanish-American Work, 1966.

128   Nava, Julian. Mexican Americans: A Brief Look at Their
        History. New York: Anti-Defamation League of the
        B'nai B'rith, 1970.
A forty-six page essay on the Mexican American experience.

129   Nava, Julian. Mexican Americans: Past, Present, and
        Future. New York: American Book Co., 1969.
Public school text; emphasizes the Mexican historical
background and includes short biographies.

130   Nava, Julian. Mexican Americans Today: In Search of
        Opportunity. Columbus, Ohio: Xerox Education
        Publications, 1973.

131   Nava, Julian, ed. Viva La Raza: Readings on Mexican
        Americans. New York: D. Van Nostrand Co., 1973.
A collection of sixty-eight selections, many extremely
brief.

132   Nava, Julian and Bob Barger. California: Five
        Centuries of Cultural Contrasts. Beverly Hills,
        Calif.: Glencoe Press, 1976.
Surveys California history with emphasis on cultural
conflict.

133   Newton, Lewis W. and Herbert P. Gambrell. Texas
        Yesterday and Today. Dallas, Tex.: Turner Co., 1948.
Social as well as political history; includes readings.

134   Nostrand, Richard L. Los chicanos: geografia historica
        regional. Mexico, D.F.: SepSetentas, 1976.
An excellent study in historical geography, with valuable
maps and tables.

135   Officer, James E. and Adela A. Stewart. Arizona's
        Hispanic Perspective. Phoenix: Arizona Academy, 1981.
Covers the Spanish-Mexican influence on Arizona from the
colonial period to the present.

136   Olson, James S. The Ethnic Dimension in American
        History. New York: St. Martin's Press, 1979.
Includes Mexican Americans; an accurate, but brief account.

137   Otero-Warren, Nina. Old Spain in Our Southwest. New
        York: Harcourt, Brace & World, 1936. Reprint,
        Glorieta, New Mex.: Rio Grande Press, 1962.

138   Pan American College. Inter-American Institute. The
        Role of the Mexican American in the Southwest.
        Edinburg, Tex.: Pan American College, 1969.
Six historical papers from a 1969 conference.

139   Pearce, Thomas M. New Mexico Place Names.
        Albuquerque: University of New Mexico Press, 1965.

140   Peixotto, Ernest C. Our Hispanic Southwest. New York:
        Scribner & Son, 1916.

141   Penuelas, Marcelino C. Cultura hispanica en Estados
        Unidos: los chicanos. 2nd ed. Madrid: Ediciones
        Cultura Hispanica, 1978.

142   Perrigo, Lynn I. The American Southwest: Its People
        and Cultures. New York: Holt, Rinehart & Winston,
        1971.
Revises and expands his 1968 survey; some Chicano materials
added. Good bibliography.

143   Perrigo, Lynn I. Texas and Our Spanish Southwest.
        Dallas, Tex.: Banks, Upshaw & Co., 1968.
Survey of southwestern history and culture emphasizing Texas
and Mexican contributions. Includes the Texas state
constitution.

144   Pinchot, Jane. Mexicans in America. Minneapolis,
        Minn.: Lerner Publications, 1973.

145   Pool, William C. A Historical Atlas of Texas. Austin,
        Tex.: Encino Press, 1975.

146   Powell, Lawrence Clark. Arizona: A Bicentennial
        History. New York: W. W. Norton & Co., 1976.

147   Prago, Albert. Strangers in Their Own Land: A History
        of Mexican Americans. New York: Four Winds Press,
        1973.
Brief, simplistic historical survey; junior high level.
Some emphasis on leadership.

148   Quintanilla, Guadalupe. Espiritu siempre eterno del
        mexico-americano. Washington, D.C.: University Press

of America, 1977.

149   Read, Benjamin M.   Illustrated History of New Mexico.
         Santa Fe: New Mexican Printing Co., 1912.   Reprint,
         New York: Arno Press, 1976.
A broad coverage of New Mexico history with emphasis on the
Spanish and Mexican periods.   Over 100 photographs.

150   Reeve, Frank Driver.   History of New Mexico.   3 vols.
         New York: Lewis Historical Publishing Co., 1961.

151   Reeve, Frank Driver.   New Mexico: Yesterday and Today.
         Albuquerque: Division of Government Research,
         University of New Mexico, 1946.
A short overview of New Mexican history.

152   Reeve, Frank Driver and A. A. Cleaveland.   New Mexico:
         Land of Many Cultures.   Boulder, Colo.: Pruett
         Publishing Co., 1969; 2nd ed., 1979.

153   Rendon, Armando B.   Chicano Manifesto: The History and
         Aspirations of the Second Largest Minority in America.
         New York: Macmillan Co., 1971.
A passionate activist interpretation of the Mexican American
experience.

154   Richardson, Rupert N.   Texas, the Lone Star State.   2nd
         ed.   Englewood Cliffs, N.J.: Prentice-Hall, 1958.

155   Richardson, Rupert N. and Carl C. Rister.   The Greater
         Southwest: The Economic, Social and Cultural
         Development of Kansas, Oklahoma, Texas, Utah,
         Colorado, Nevada, New Mexico, Arizona, and California
         from the Spanish Conquest to the Twentieth Century.
         Glendale, Calif.: Arthur H. Clark Co., 1934.

156   Rister, Carl Coke.   The Southwestern Frontier.
         Cleveland, Ohio: Arthur H. Clark Co., 1928.

157   Rivera, Feliciano.   A Mexican American Source Book.
         Menlo Park, Calif.: Educational Consulting Associates,
         1970.
A useful source book for history and social studies
teachers.

158   Robinson, Will Henry.   The Story of Arizona.   Phoenix,
         Ariz.: The Berryhill Co., 1919.

159   Rolle, Andrew F.   California: A History.   3rd ed.
         Arlington Heights, Ill.: AHM Publishing Corp., 1978.
Includes discussion of the Californios' land problems,
repatriation, and Cesar Chavez.

160   Rosaldo, Renato, et al. Chicano: The Beginnings of
       Bronze Power. New York: William Morrow & Co., 1974.

161   Rosaldo, Renato, et al. Chicano: The Evolution of a
       People. Minneapolis, Minn.: Winston Press, 1973; also
       Huntington, N.Y.: Krieger Publishing Co., 1976; 2nd
       ed., revised and updated, 1982.
Collection of readings, principally historical and
sociological.

162   The Saga of Texas, 1519-1965. 6 vols. Edited by
       Seymour V. Connor. Austin, Tex.: Steck-Vaughn Co.,
       1965.

163   Samora, Julian, ed. La Raza: Forgotten Americans.
       Notre Dame, Ind.: University of Notre Dame Press,
       1966.
Seven essays on Mexican American society by authorities in
various fields: history, politics, religion, etc.

164   Samora, Julian & Patricia Vandel Simon. A History of
       the Mexican-American People. Notre Dame, Ind.:
       University of Notre Dame Press, 1977.
A broad survey, apparently designed as a high school text.

165   Sanchez, George I. Forgotten People. Albuquerque:
       University of New Mexico Press, 1940.
A sympathetic account of pre-World War II Hispanos of New
Mexico by the dean of Mexican American scholars.

166   Sanchez, Rosaura and Rosa Martinez Cruz. Essays on La
       Mujer. Los Angeles: Chicano Studies Research Center,
       University of California, 1977.
Briefly surveys la Mexicana from Aztec times to the present.

167   Santos, Richard G. Texas and the Hispanic Southwest.
       San Antonio, Tex.: San Antonio I. S. D., 1969.

168   Scotford, John Ryland. Within These Borders: Spanish-
       Speaking Peoples in the U.S.A. New York: Friendship
       Press, 1953.

169   Servin, Manuel P., ed. An Awakened Minority: The
       Mexican-Americans. 2nd ed. Beverly Hills, Calif.:
       Glencoe Press, 1974.
Extensively revised second edition, more representative and
broader in coverage than the first edition.

170   Servin, Manuel P., ed. The Mexican Americans: An
       Awakening Minority. Beverly Hills, Calif.: Glencoe
       Press, 1970.
Sixteen historical essays, heavily twentieth century in
emphasis.

171   Shepherd, William R.   The Spanish Heritage in America.
      New York: International Telephone & Telegraph Corp.,
      1926.

172   Simmen, Edward, ed.   Pain and Promise: The Chicano
      Today.   New York: New American Library, 1972.
Historical and sociological articles covering the Mexican
American from 1900 to 1970.   Good bibliographic essay.

173   Simmons, Marc.   New Mexico: A Bicentennial History.
      New York: W. W. Norton & Co., 1977.
Winner of the 1977 History Award from the Border Regional
Library Association.   By one of New Mexico's outstanding
historians.

174   Sloan, Richard E.   History of Arizona.   4 vols.
      Phoenix, Ariz.: Record Publishing Co., 1930.

175   Smith, Michael M.   The Mexicans in Oklahoma.   Norman:
      University of Oklahoma Press, 1980.
Part of a series on immigrants in Oklahoma.

176   Sowell, Thomas.   Ethnic America: A History.   New York:
      Basic Books, 1981.
Chapter 10 is a brief description of the Mexican American
experience to the present.

177   Steiner, Stan.   La Raza: The Mexican American.   New
      York: Harper & Row Publishers, 1969.
Highly journalistic and impressionistic view of contemporary
Mexican Americans.

178   Stoddard, Ellwyn R.   Mexican Americans.   New York:
      Random House, 1973.   Reprint, Washington, D.C.:
      University Press of America, 1982.
An excellent socio-political and historical study
emphasizing the twentieth century.

179   Tebbel, John and Ramon E. Ruiz.   South by Southwest:
      The Mexican-American and His Heritage.   Garden City,
      N.Y.: Doubleday & Co., 1969.
A brief grade school survey, mostly about Mexican heritage.

180   Time-Life Books.   The Spanish West.   New York:
      Time-Life Books, 1976.

181   Trejo, Arnulfo D., ed.   The Chicanos: As We See
      Ourselves.   Tucson: University of Arizona Press, 1979.
Assembles essays by Chicano scholars in a variety of
disciplines.

182   Trimble, Marshall. Arizona: A Panoramic History of a
       Frontier State. Garden City, N.Y.: Doubleday & Co.,
       1977.

183   Twitchell, Ralph E. The Leading Facts of New Mexican
       History. 5 vols. Cedar Rapids, Iowa: Torch Press,
       1911-1917.
Provides a very useful chronicle, pro-Republican and
pro-Santa Fe Ring.

184   Twitchell, Ralph E. The Leading Facts of New Mexican
       History. Albuquerque, N. Mex.: Horn & Wallace, 1963.
Reproduction of vols. 1 & 2 of the five published in
1911-1917.

185   University of Arizona Faculty. Arizona, Its People and
       Resources. Tucson: University of Arizona Press, 1972.
Mostly historical and sociological essays by University of
Arizona faculty members.

186   Valdez, Luis and Stan Steiner, eds. Aztlan: An
       Anthology of Mexican American Literature. New York:
       Alfred A. Knopf, 1972.
A collection of readings, more historical than literary
despite the title.

187   Vega, Jose L. Nuestra America. Mexico, D.F.: Galve,
       S.A., 1969.
Stresses the contributions of Spain and Mexico to the
Southwest.

188   Vigil, James Diego. From Indians to Chicanos: A
       Socio-cultural History. St. Louis, Mo.: C. V. Mosby
       Co., 1980.
A high school or junior college level text.

189   Villanueva, Tino, comp. Chicanos: Antologia historica
       y literaria. Mexico, D.F.: Fondo de Cultura
       Economica, 1981.
A collection of articles, lectures, and literary works by
Mexican Americans.

190   Wagner, Nathaniel N. and Marsha J. Haug, eds.
       Chicanos: Social and Psychological Perspectives. St.
       Louis, Mo.: C. V. Mosby Co., 1971.

191   Wallace, Ernest and David M. Vigness. Documents of
       Texas History. Austin, Tex.: Steck Co., 1963.
A source book of 126 documents in Texas history, 1528 to
1961, arranged chronologically and introduced in context.

192 Waltrip, Rufus and Lela Waltrip. Mexican American
     Story. Boulder, Colo.: Shields Publishing Co., 1973.

193 Webb, Walter Prescott, ed. The Handbook of Texas.
     Austin: Texas State Historical Association, 1952.

194 Weber, David J., ed. Foreigners in Their Native Land:
     Historical Roots of the Mexican Americans.
     Albuquerque: University of New Mexico Press, 1973.
An excellent blend of the editor's introductory essays and
source materials; covers from 1800 to 1912.

195 Wellman, Paul. Glory, Gold and God. Garden City,
     N.Y.: Doubleday & Co., 1956.
Popular history of the Southwest.

196 Wertenbaker, Green Peyton. America's Heartland: The
     Southwest. Norman: University of Oklahoma Press,
     1949.

197 West, Stanley A. and June Macklin. Chicano Experience.
     Boulder, Colo.: Westview Press, 1979.

198 Williams, Jerry L. and Paul E. McAllister. New Mexico
     in Maps. Albuquerque: University of New Mexico Press,
     1982.
A comprehensive atlas of New Mexico. The maps present
historical data, population distribution, economic and other
information.

199 Winterburn, Rosa W. The Spanish in the Southwest. New
     York: American Book Co., 1903.

200 Wyllys, Rufus K. Arizona: The History of a Frontier
     State. Phoenix, Ariz.: Hobson & Herr, 1950.

201 Ybarra, Lea and Alex Saragoza. Nuestras Raices: The
     Mexican Community of the Central San Joaquin Valley.
     Fresno, Calif.: La Raza Studies, California State
     University, 1980.

I: Periodicals

202   Almaraz, Felix D., Jr.   "Spain's Cultural Legacy in
        Texas."   In The Texas Heritage, edited by Ben Proctor
        and Archie P. McDonald, pp. 5-17.   St. Louis, Mo.:
        Forum Press, 1980.
A brief historical sketch of the Spanish colonial period in
Texas.

203   Bernstein, Harry.   "Spanish Influence in the United
        States: Economic Aspects."   Hispanic American
        Historical Review 18:1 (Feb. 1938), 43-65.
Covers cattle-ranching, mining and agriculture.

204   Bushee, Alice H.   "Spanish Influence in the
        Southwest."   Hispania 6:3 (May 1923), 148-157.
A personal account of a visit to the Southwest, its missions
and pueblos.

205   Caughey, John W.   "The Spanish Southwest: An Example of
        Subconscious Regionalism."   In Regionalism in America,
        edited by Merrill Jensen, pp. 173-186.   Madison:
        University of Wisconsin Press, 1951.

206   Cortes, Carlos E.   "Mexicans."   Harvard Encyclopedia of
        American Ethnic Groups.   Cambridge, Mass.: Harvard
        University Press, 1980, pp. 697-719.
An excellent short comprehensive essay on the Mexican
American experience.

207   Corwin, Arthur M.   "Mexican American History: An
        Assessment."   Pacific Historical Review 42:3 (Aug.
        1973), 269-308.
Partially bibliographic essay on the state of Chicano
history.

208   De Leon, Arnoldo.   "Los Tejanos: An Overview of Their
        History."   In The Texas Heritage, edited by Ben
        Proctor and Archie P. McDonald, pp. 133-144.   St.
        Louis, Mo.: Forum Press, 1980.
A broad sketch of Tejano history going back to the colonial
era.

209   Estrada, Leobardo F., et al.   "Chicanos in the United
        States: A History of Exploitation and Resistance."
        Daedalus 110:2 (Spring 1981), 103-131.
An excellent broad overview from the mid-1800s to the
present; stresses discrimination and repression.

210   Galarza, Ernesto and Julian Samora.   "Chicano Studies:
        Research and Scholarly Activity."   Civil Rights Digest
        3:4 (Fall 1970), 40-42.

211   Garcia, Richard A.   "Chicano Intellectual History:
       Myths and Realities." Revista Chicano-Riquena 7:2
       (Spring 1979), 58-62.

212   Gomez-Quiñones, Juan. "Toward a Perspective on Chicano
       History." Aztlan 2:2 (Fall 1971), 1-49.
A broad scale periodization of Mexican history with an
evaluation of its 1971 state.

213   Guzman, Ralph C.   "Chicano Control of Chicano History:
       A Review of Selected Literature." California
       Historical Quarterly 52:2 (Summer 1973), 170-175.

214   Hilton, Ronald. "Is Intellectual History Irrelevant?
       The Case of the Aztecs." Journal of the History of
       Ideas 33:2 (April-June 1972), 337-344.

215   Hoffman, Abraham. "Where are the Mexican Americans? A
       Textbook Omission Overdue for Revision." History
       Teacher 6:1 (Nov. 1972), 143-150.
A survey of twelve college level U.S. history texts.

216   Johnson, James Wood. "Spanish America in the
       Southwest." Travel 80 (Nov. 1942), 13-17.

217   McNamara, Patrick H. "Mexican-Americans in the
       Southwest: Mexican American Study Project." America
       114 (March 12, 1966), 352-354.
Describes the University of California at Los Angeles Study
Project, which led to The Mexican American People, 1970,
item 67.

218   Marcella, Gabriel. "Spanish-Mexican Contributions to
       the Southwest." Journal of Mexican American History 1
       (Fall 1970), 1-15.

219   Martinez, Orlando. "Los Chicanos." Contemporary
       Review 237:1377 (Oct. 1980), 194-196.
A brief broad survey.

220   Navarro, Joseph. "The Conditions of Mexican-American
       History." Journal of Mexican American History 1 (Fall
       1970), 25-52.
A discussion of Chicano historiography with evaluation of
some of its literature.

221   Nostrand, Richard L. "Spanish Roots in the
       Borderlands." Geographical Magazine 52:3 (Dec. 1979),
       203-209.
Describes the legacy of Spain in the Southwest.

222   Onis, Federico de. "Espana y el sudoeste de los
       Estados Unidos." Revista Hispanica Moderna 9 (1943),
       186-190.

223   Onis, Federico de. "Spain and the Southwest." In
      Cultural Bases of Hemispheric Understanding Papers.
      Austin: Institute of Latin American Studies,
      University of Texas, 1942.

224   "Review Symposium [on] The Mexican American People.
      New York: Free Press, 1970." Social Science Quarterly
      52:1 (June 1971), 8-38.
Comments by five experts on this seminal work, item 67.

225   Rios-Bustamante, Antonio J. "A Contribution to the
      Historiography of the Greater Mexican North in the
      Eighteenth Century." Aztlan 7:3 (Fall 1976), 347-356.

226   Romano-V., Octavio I. "The Anthropology and Sociology
      of the Mexican-Americans: The Distortion of
      Mexican-American History." El Grito 2 (Fall 1968),
      13-26; also in Voices: Readings from El Grito . . .
      1967-1973, edited by Octavio Romano-V., pp. 43-56.
      Berkeley, Calif.: Quinto Sol, 1973.
Argues that stereotyping has led to misinterpretations.

227   Romano-V., Octavio I. "The Historical and Intellectual
      Presence of Mexican Americans." El Grito 2 (Winter
      1969), 32-47.
An essay on the Chicano experience, opting for cultural
pluralism rather than assimilation.

228   Sanchez, Corinne J. "Chicano Studies: A Challenge for
      Colleges and Universities." Civil Rights Digest 3:4
      (Fall 1970), 36-39.

229   Sanchez, George I. "Spanish-Speaking People in the
      Southwest--A Brief Historical Review." California
      Journal of Elementary Education 22 (Nov. 1953),
      106-111.

230   Shepherd, William R. "Spanish Heritage in America."
      Modern Language Journal 10 (Nov. 1925), 75-83.

231   Vigil, Ralph H. "The Hispanic Heritage and the
      Borderlands." Journal of San Diego History 19 (Summer
      1973), 32-39.

232   Vigil, Ralph H. "The New Borderlands History: A
      Critique." New Mexico Historical Review 48 (July
      1973), 189-208.

233   Weber, David J. "Mexico's Far Northern Frontier,
      1821-1854." Western Historical Quarterly 7:3 (July
      1976), 279-293.
An historiographical discussion calling for greater use of
Mexican sources for the early history of the Southwest.

234   Whitaker, Arthur P.   "The Spanish Contribution to
      American Agriculture."   Agricultural History 3 (Jan.
      1929), 1-14.

235   Worcester, Donald E.   "The Spanish-American Past: Enemy
      of Change."   Journal of Inter-American Studies 11
      (Jan. 1969), 66-75.

II.
COLONIAL PERIOD _____

Section II, Colonial Period (to 1821), is made up of works on the Spanish, Southwestern and Mexican Indian backgrounds, on the Spanish-Mexican exploration and conquest of the Southwest, on general Mexican history, and on missions and other institutions developed in the Southwest. It includes only major works on the general Spanish and Mexican Indian backrounds and the melding of these two cultures. Detailed bibliographies for this period, without particular emphasis on the development of the Mexican American, may be found in John F. Bannon, The Spanish Borderlands Frontier, 1513-1821, 1970, item 247, and in Michael C. Meyer and William L. Sherman, The Course of Mexican History, 1979, item 358.

236 Alba, Victor. The Mexicans, The Making of a Nation.
       New York: Praeger Publishers, 1967.
A broad survey history, as interpreted by a naturalized Mexican historian of Spanish birth.

237 Alessio Robles, Vito. Coahuila y Texas en la epoca
       colonial. Mexico, D.F.: Editorial Cultura, 1938.

238 Almaraz, Felix D., Jr. Tragic Cavalier; Governor
       Manuel Salcedo of Texas, 1808-1813. Austin:
       University of Texas Press, 1971.
Focuses on the Texas reaction to Miguel Hidalgo's 1810 revolution for independence from Spain.

239 Archibald, Robert R. The Economic Aspects of the
       California Missions. Washington, D.C.: Academy of
       American Franciscan History, 1978.

240 Ashford, Gerald. Spanish Texas: Yesterday and Today.
       Austin, Tex.: Jenkins Publishing Co., 1971.
Describes effects of Spanish-Mexican history on laws, government policy, social institutions, language, architecture, etc.

241   Bailey, Jessie Bromilow. Diego de Vargas and the
        Reconquest of New Mexico. Albuquerque: University of
        New Mexico Press, 1940.
The reimposition of Spanish control by Diego de Vargas,
1692-1696.

242   Bailey, Lynn R.   Indian Slave Trade in the Southwest.
        Los Angeles: Westernlore Press, 1966.

243   Bancroft, Hubert Howe. History of Arizona and New
        Mexico, 1530-1888. San Francisco: History Co., 1889.
        Reprints, Albuquerque, N. Mex.: Horn & Wallace, 1962;
        also New York: McGraw-Hill Book Co., 1967.

244   Bancroft, Hubert Howe. History of Mexico.   2 vols.
        San Francisco: History Co., 1883.

245   Bancroft, Hubert Howe. History of the North Mexican
        States and Texas. 2 vols. San Francisco: History
        Co., 1886-1889. Reprint, New York: McGraw-Hill Book
        Co., 1967.

246   Bandelier, Adolph F. The Discovery of New Mexico by
        the Franciscan Monk Friar Marcos de Niza in 1539.
        Translated and edited by Madeleine T. Rodack. Tucson:
        University of Arizona Press, 1981.

247   Bannon, John Francis. The Spanish Borderlands
        Frontier, 1513-1821. New York: Holt, Rinehart &
        Winston, 1970.
Synthesizes the colonial history of New Spain's (Mexico's)
northern frontier; includes a partially detailed and briefly
annotated bibliography.

248   Barreiro, Antonio. Ojeada sobre Nuevo Mexico. Santa
        Fe, N. Mex.: El Palacio Press, 1928. Reprinted in
        Three New Mexico Chronicles, item 270.
A view at the beginning of the Mexican period; originally
published in 1832.

249   Bean, Ellis P. Memoir of Colonel Ellis P. Bean,
        Written by Himself, About the Year 1816. Houston:
        Book Club of Texas, 1930.
The personal history of an American who fought in the 1810
Mexican revolution and later supported the Mexican
government in the 1836 Texas revolt.

250   Beilharz, Edwin A. Felipe de Neve, First Governor of
        California. San Francisco: California Historical
        Society, 1971.
Information on the early founding of California; emphasis on
Neve, not on common people.

251   Benson, Nettie L., ed. Report [of] Dr. Miguel Ramos de
       Arizpe. . . on . . . the Provinces of Coahuila, Nuevo
       Leon, Nuevo Santander, and Texas . . . . Austin:
       University of Texas Press, 1950.
Focuses on the northern frontier provinces at the end of the
Spanish period.

252   Berger, John A. The Franciscan Missions of California.
       Garden City, N.Y.: Doubleday & Co., 1941.
Divided into chapters on the individual missions.

253   Bernal, Ignacio. Mexico Before Cortez: Art, History
       and Legend. Garden City, N.Y.: Doubleday & Co., 1963.
A cultural history of the Aztecs and their predecessors, by
Mexico's outstanding anthropologist.

254   Bishop, Morris. The Odyssey of Cabeza de Vaca. New
       York: Appleton, 1933.
A good piece of popular history.

255   Blacker, Irwin R. and Harry M. Rosen. The Golden
       Conquistadores. Indianapolis, Ind.: Bobbs-Merrill
       Co., 1960.
Includes documents on the exploration of New Spain's
northern frontier.

256   Blackmar, Frank W. Spanish Colonization in the
       Southwest. Baltimore, Md.: Johns Hopkins University
       Press, 1890. Reprint, New York: Johnson Reprint Co.,
       1973.

257   Blackmar, Frank W. Spanish Institutions in the
       Southwest. Baltimore, Md.: Johns Hopkins University
       Press, 1891.
Tends to stress the negative side of Spanish
colonialization.

258   Bolton, Herbert E. Coronado, Knight of Pueblos and
       Plains. New York: Whittlesey House, 1949.
A classic work by the great historian of the American
Southwest.

259   Bolton, Herbert E. Rim of Christendom: A Biography of
       Eusebio Francisco Kino, Pacific Coast Pioneer. New
       York: Macmillan Co., 1936. Reprint, New York: Russell
       & Russell, 1960.
Covers the story of the early Spanish-Mexican occupation of
southern Arizona.

260   Bolton, Herbert E. Spanish Explorations in the
       Southwest, 1542-1706. New York: Charles Scribner's
       Sons, 1916.
Spanish source accounts of discovery and exploration.

261 Bolton, Herbert E. Texas in the Middle Eighteenth
     Century; Studies in Spanish Colonial History and
     Administration. Berkeley: University of California
     Press, 1915. Reprint, Austin: University of Texas
     Press, 1970.

262 Bosch-Gimpera, Pedro. La formacion de los pueblos de
       España. Mexico, D.F.: Imprenta Universitaria, 1944.
A seminal work by an outstanding Spanish anthropologist.

263 Bowden, J. J. Spanish and Mexican Land Grants in the
       Chihuahuan Acquisition. El Paso: Texas Western Press,
       1971.
Covers some twenty land grants in western Texas and adjacent
New Mexico.

264 Bowman, J. N. and Robert F. Heizer. Anza and the
       Northwest Frontier of New Spain. Los Angeles:
       Southwest Museum, 1967.
Describes the beginning of settlement in California.

265 Brayer, Herbert O. Pueblo Indian Land Grants of the
       "Rio Abajo," New Mexico. Albuquerque: University of
       New Mexico Press, 1939.

266 Brebner, John Bartlet. The Explorers of North America,
       1492-1806. Cleveland, Ohio: World Publishing Co.,
       1955.
A broad survey which includes the American Southwest.

267 Brinckerhoff, Sidney B. and Odie B. Faulk. Lancers for
       the King. Phoenix: Arizona Historical Foundation,
       1965.
Covers the colonialization of New Spain's northern frontier
in Arizona.

268 Brundage, Burr Cartwright. A Rain of Darts: The Mexica
       Aztecs. Austin: University of Texas Press, 1972.

269 Burland, Cottie A. The Gods of Mexico. New York: G.
       P. Putnam's Sons, 1967.
A brief but complete survey of Middle American religion,
mythology and culture; emphasis on Quetzalcoatl.

270 Carroll, H. Bailey and J. Villasana Haggard, trans.
       Three New Mexico Chronicles: The Exposicion of Pedro
       Bautista Pino, 1812; the Ojeada of Antonio Barreiro,
       1832; and the additions by Jose Agustin de Escudero,
       1849. Albuquerque, N. Mex.: Quivira Society, 1942.
       Reprint, New York: Arno Press, 1967.

271   Caso, Alfonso. The Aztecs, People of the Sun. Norman:
       University of Oklahoma Press, 1958.
A comprehensive description of Aztec civilization by an
outstanding Mexican archeologist and anthropologist.

272   Celiz, Fray Francisco. Diary of the Alarcon Expedition
       into Texas, 1718-1719. Translated by Fritz Leo
       Hoffmann. Los Angeles: Quivira Society, 1935.

273   Chapman, Charles E. A History of California: The
       Spanish Period. New York: Macmillan Co., 1921.
Still perhaps the best coverage of the period.

274   Chavez, Fray Angelico. My Penitente Land: Reflections
       on Spanish New Mexico. Albuquerque: University of New
       Mexico Press, 1974.
Includes material on the Penitentes and their organization
and practices.

275   Chavez, Fray Angelico. Origins of New Mexico Families
       in the Spanish Colonial Period. Santa Fe: Historical
       Society of New Mexico, 1954.

276   Chavez, Fray Angelico. Our Lady of the Conquest.
       Santa Fe: Historical Society of New Mexico, 1948.

277   Clinch, Byran J. California and Its Missions. San
       Francisco: Whitaker & Ray Co., 1904.

278   Clissold, Stephen. The Seven Cities of Cibola. New
       York: Clarkson N. Potter, 1961.
A popular history of the search in the Southwest for Cibola;
bibliography.

279   Cook, Sherburne F. The Conflict Between the California
       Indian and White Civilization. Berkeley: University
       of California Press, 1976.
Conclusions of an outstanding anthropologist after a
lifetime of study.

280   Cortes, Hernan. Letters from Mexico. Edited and
       translated by A. R. Pagden. New York: Grossman
       Publishers, 1971.
Cortes's five letters to Charles V, annotated and with maps.
Introduction by J. H. Elliot.

281   Covian Martinez, Vidal. Don Jose Bernardo Maximiliano
       Gutierrez de Lara . . . Ciudad Victoria, Tamaulipas,
       Mexico: Ediciones Siglo XX, 1967.
Life of an independence movement diplomat, insurgent leader
in Texas, and first Tamaulipas governor.

282   Dakin, Susanna Bryant. Rose, or Rose Thorn: Three
        Women of Spanish California. Berkeley, Calif.:
        Friends of the Bancroft Library, 1963.
Biographies of three women whose lives spanned Spanish and
Mexican California.

283   Day, A. Grove. Coronado's Quest; the Discovery of the
        Southwestern States. Berkeley: University of
        California Press, 1940. Reprint, Gloucester, Mass.:
        Peter Smith, 1964.
An excellent popular history of the Coronado expedition into
the Southwest, 1540-1542.

284   Diaz del Castillo, Bernal. The True History of the
        Conquest of Mexico. New York: Farrar, Straus &
        Cudahy, 1956.
The A. P. Maudslay translation of Bernal Diaz's account.

285   Dobyns, Henry F., ed. Spanish Colonial Frontier
        Research. Albuquerque, N. Mex.: Center For
        Anthropological Studies, 1981.
An anthology of nine articles which include land, trade, and
prehistory of Mexico's northern frontier.

286   Dobyns, Henry F. Spanish Colonial Tucson: A
        Demographic History. Tucson: University of Arizona
        Press, 1976.

287   Dominguez, Fray Francisco A. The Dominguez-Escalante
        Journal. Translated by Fray Angelico Chavez. Provo,
        Utah: Brigham Young University Press, 1976.
Journal of a 1776 journey from Santa Fe, through Colorado to
Utah, down the Colorado River, and back to New Mexico.

288   Donohue, John A., S.J. After Kino: Jesuit Missions in
        Northwestern New Spain 1711-1767. Rome: Jesuit
        Historical Institute, 1969.
Describes the second stage of Jesuit mission activity in
Pimeria Alta.

289   Dunne, Peter Masten, S.J. Pioneer Black Robes on the
        West Coast. Berkeley: University of California Press,
        1940.
Focuses on the early missionary efforts of the Jesuits in
northwestern New Spain.

290   Duran, Diego. The Aztecs; the History of the Indies of
        New Spain. Translated by Doris Heyden and Fernando
        Horcasitas. New York: Orion Press, 1964.
A sixteenth century account of Aztec civilization and
history by a Spanish missionary.

291   Dwinelle, John W. The Colonial History of San
        Francisco. San Francisco: Towne & Bacon, 1863.
Came out of John W. Dwinelle's advocacy of the city of San
Francisco's land claim.

292 Elliot, J. H. Imperial Spain, 1469-1716. New York:
        New American Library, 1966.
An excellent history of Spain at the age of discovery and
exploration.

293 Engelhardt, Zephyrin, O.F.M. Mission San Juan
        Bautista. Santa Barbara, Calif.: Mission Santa
        Barbara, 1931.
Part of a series on the California missions by the
Franciscan historian.

294 Englebert, Omer. The Last of the Conquistadors,
        Junipero Serra, 1713-1784. New York: Harcourt, Brace,
        1956.
Popular account of the Franciscan missioner in California.

295 Espinosa, Jose Manuel. Crusaders of the Rio Grande;
        The Story of Don Diego de Vargas and the Reconquest
        and Refounding of New Mexico. Chicago: Institute of
        Jesuit History, 1942.
Describes the resettlement after the 1680 Pope revolt of the
Pueblo Indians.

296 Ewing, Russell. Six Faces of Mexico. Tucson:
        University of Arizona Press, 1966.
An excellent series of six articles on the history, culture,
economy, etc. of Mexico. For background.

297 Faulk, Odie B. The Last Years of Spanish Texas,
        1778-1821. The Hague: Mouton & Co., 1964.
Focuses on Texas economic and social life circa 1800.

298 Fireman, Janet R. The Spanish Royal Corps of Engineers
        in the Western Borderlands: Instruments of Bourbon
        Reform, 1764 to 1815. Glendale, Calif.: Arthur H.
        Clark Co., 1977.
Good for a picture of changes in the Southwest on the eve of
Mexican independence.

299 Folsom, Franklin. Red Power on the Rio Grande: The
        Native American Revolution of 1680. Chicago: Follett
        Publishing Co., 1973.
Describes the Pueblo revolt led by Pope in New Mexico.

300 Forbes, Jack D. Apache, Navaho, and Spaniard. Norman:
        University of Oklahoma Press, c1960.
Emphasizes the history of southern Athapaskans and their
interaction with Spaniards, 1540-1698.

301   Garrett, Julia K. Green Flag Over Texas; A Story of
      the Last Years of Spain in Texas. New York: Cordova
      Press, 1939.
Covers the last years of Spanish authority; describes Anglo
American intrusion and filibustering.

302   Geiger, Maynard. Franciscan Missionaries in Hispanic
      California, 1769-1848: A Biographical Dictionary. San
      Marino, Calif.: Huntington Library, 1969.
Includes bibliographic materials.

303   Gerhard, Peter. The Northern Frontier of New Spain.
      Princeton, N.J.: Princeton University Press, 1981.
Contains a map and brief history of the regions of northern
New Spain; an excellent guide to sources of further
information on each area.

304   Ghent, W. J. The Early Far West, 1540-1850. New York:
      Tudor Publishing Co., 1936.

305   Gibson, Charles. The Aztecs Under Spanish Rule; a
      History of the Indians of the Valley of Mexico,
      1519-1810. Stanford, Calif.: Stanford University
      Press, 1964.
An excellent survey by an outstanding historian; extensive
bibliography.

306   Gladwin, Harold Sterling. A History of the Ancient
      Southwest. Portland, Maine: Bond Wheelright Co.,
      1957.
A survey and archeological history of the Indian cultures of
the Southwest.

307   Gladwin, Harold Sterling; Emil W. Haury; and E. B.
      Sayles. Excavations at Snaketown: Material Culture.
      Tucson: University of Arizona Press, 1965.
The archeology of the Hohokam Indians in southern Arizona.

308   Gomez Canedo, Lino. Primeras exploraciones y
      poblamiento de Texas, 1686-1694. Monterrery, N.L.,
      Mexico: Publicaciones del Instituto Tecnologico y de
      Estudios Superiores de Monterrey, 1968.

309   Hackett, Charles Wilson, ed. Historical Documents
      Relating to New Mexico, Nueva Vizcaya, and Approaches
      Thereto. 3 vols. Washington, D.C.: Carnegie
      Institution, 1923-1937.

310   Hackett, Charles Wilson, ed. New Spain and the
      Anglo-American West; Historical Contributions
      Presented to Herbert Eugene Bolton . . . . 2 vols. Los
      Angeles: Privately printed, 1932.

311   Hackett, Charles Wilson. Revolt of the Pueblo Indians
      of New Mexico and Otermin's Attempted Reconquest,
      1680-82. 2 vols. Albuquerque: University of New
      Mexico Press, 1942; reprint, 1970.

312   Hallenbeck, Cleve. The Journey of Fray Marcos de Niza.
      Dallas, Tex.: University Press, 1949.
A balanced interpretation of a controversial figure in the
early exploration of the Southwest.

313   Hallenbeck, Cleve. Land of the Conquistadores.
      Caldwell, Idaho: Caxton Printers, 1950.
Gives a complete picture of the early years of New Mexico.

314   Hallenbeck, Cleve. Spanish Missions of the Old
      Southwest. Garden City, N.Y.: Doubleday, Page & Co.,
      1926.
Includes good materials on daily life in the missions.

315   Hamill, Hugh. The Hidalgo Revolt: Prelude to Mexican
      Independence. Gainesville: University of Florida
      Press, 1966.
Probably the best account of the first stage of the revolt
for Mexican independence.

316   Hammond, George P. and Agapito Rey, eds. and trans.
      Don Juan de Oñate, Colonizer of New Mexico, 1595-1628.
      Albuquerque: University of New Mexico Press, 1953.
Excellent bibliographical material in footnotes to the
documents.

317   Hammond, George P. and Agapito Rey, eds. and trans.
      Narratives of the Coronado Expedition 1540-1542.
      Albuquerque: University of New Mexico Press, 1940.
Documents and bibliographic footnotes; includes the Fray
Marcos de Niza expedition, 1539.

318   Hammond, George P. and Agapito Rey. The Rediscovery of
      New Mexico, 1580-1594. Albuquerque: University of New
      Mexico Press, 1966.
Describes exploratory expeditions preceding settlement of
New Mexico by Juan de Oñate.

319   Hanke, Lewis. Aristotle and the American Indians; a
      Study in Race Prejudice in the Modern World. Chicago:
      Henry Regnery Co., 1959.
Stresses the early struggle for social justice in Spanish
America, emphasizing the moral aspects.

320   Hatcher, Mattie A., ed. The Opening of Texas to
      Foreign Settlement, 1801-1821. Austin: University of
      Texas Press, 1927.
Documents relating to efforts to hold Texas for Spain
against Anglo and other settlers.

321 Haury, Emil W. The Hohokam, Desert Farmers and
       Craftsmen: Excavations at Snaketown, 1964-1965.
       Tucson: University of Arizona Press, 1976.
Presents valuable additions to our knowledge of early Indian
culture in the Southwest.

322 Hedrick, Basil C. J.; J. Charles Kelley; and Carroll L.
       Riley, eds. The Mesoamerican Southwest. Carbondale:
       Southern Illinois University Press, 1974.
Discusses the relationship of Southwestern (U.S.) and
Meso-American Indian cultures.

323 Hewett, Edgar L. Ancient Life and the American
       Southwest. Indianapolis, Ind.: Bobbs-Merrill Co.,
       1930.

324 Hispanic-American Essays in Honor of Max Leon
       Moorehead. Edited by William S. Coker. Pensacola,
       Fla.: Perdido Bay Press, 1981.
Includes a chapter by Oakah L. Jones, Jr. on civil
settlements in colonial New Mexico.

325 Holmes, Jack D. L. Gayoso: The Life of a Spanish
       Governor in the Mississippi Valley, 1789-1799. Baton
       Rouge: Louisiana State University Press, 1965.
Problems of a Spanish governor in French-settled Louisiana.

326 Holmes, Maurice G. From New Spain by Sea to the
       Californias, 1519-1668. Glendale, Calif.: Arthur H.
       Clark Co., 1963.
Early West Coast exploration by Spaniards; includes a brief
bibliography.

327 Horgan, Paul. Conquistadores in North American
       History. New York: Farrar & Straus, 1963.
Popular history of Spanish exploration northward to 1810.

328 Hughes, Anne E. The Beginnings of Spanish Settlement
       in the El Paso District. Berkeley: University of
       California Press, 1914. Reprint, New York: Kraus
       Reprint Co., 1970.

329 Hutchinson, Cecil A. Frontier Settlement in Mexican
       California: the Hijar-Padres Colony and Its Origins,
       1769-1835. New Haven, Conn.: Yale University Press,
       1969.
Includes the efforts of Vice President Valentin Gomez Farias
to hold California to Mexico.

330 Jameson, J. Franklin, ed. Spanish Explorers in the
       Southern United States. New York: Scribner's, 1907.
Excellent survey by an outstanding historian.

331   John, Elizabeth A. H. Storms Brewed in Other Men's
      Worlds: The Confrontation of Indians, Spanish, and
      French in the Southwest, 1540-1795. College Station:
      Texas A & M University Press, 1975.

332   Jones, Oakah L., Jr. Los Paisanos: Spanish Settlers on
      the Northern Frontier of New Spain. Norman:
      University of Oklahoma Press, 1979.
An able overview of early Spanish-American settlement in the
Southwest; excellent bibliography.

333   Jones, Oakah L., Jr. Pueblo Warriors and Spanish
      Conquest. Norman: University of Oklahoma Press, 1966.
Covers conflicts and wars between the two groups;
bibliographic footnotes.

334   Jones, Oakah L., Jr., ed. The Spanish Borderlands--A
      First Reader. Los Angeles: L. L. Morrison, 1974.
A collection of secondary essays from the Journal of the
West.

335   Keffer, Frank M. History of San Fernando Valley.
      Glendale, Calif.: Stillman Printing Co., 1934.
Describes the development of the area immediately north of
Los Angeles, California.

336   Kenner, Charles L. A History of New Mexican-Plains
      Indian Relations. Norman: University of Oklahoma
      Press, 1969.
Covers from 1700 to 1880s; material on the Comancheros and
Ciboleros.

337   Kessell, John L. Friars, Soldiers, and Reformers:
      Hispanic Arizona and the Sonora Mission Frontier,
      1767-1856. Tucson: University of Arizona Press, 1976.
A vivid picture of the Sonora-Arizona mission frontier from
its Franciscan era beginnings to its decline.

338   Kessell, John L. Mission of Sorrows: Jesuit, Guevavi
      and the Pimas, 1691-1767. Tucson: University of
      Arizona Press, 1970.
Early Spanish-Mexican settlement in Pimeria Alta (Sonora and
southern Arizona).

339   Kinnaird, Lawrence, ed. Spain in the Mississippi
      Valley. 4 vols. Washington, D.C.: U.S. Government
      Printing Office, 1946-1949.
Sources in the Bancroft Library, University of California,
Berkeley.

340   Kirkpatrick, F. A. The Spanish Conquistadores.
      Cleveland, Ohio: World Publishing Co., 1962.
A broad coverage, including the Southwest.

341   Kocher, Paul H. California's Old Missions: The Story
       of the Founding of the 21 Franciscan Missions in
       Spanish Alta California, 1769-1823. Chicago:
       Franciscan Herald Press, 1976.

342   Lafora, Nicolas de. The Frontiers of New Spain;
       Nicolas de Lafora's Description, 1766-1768.
       Translated by Lawrence Kinnaird. Berkeley, Calif.:
       Quivira Society, 1958.
Account of Lafora's inspection of the northern frontier
presidios.

343   Laughlin, Ruth Barker. Caballeros. New York: D.
       Appleton & Co., 1931. Reprint, New York: Arno Press,
       1976.
A description of social life and customs in New Mexico.

344   Leon-Portilla, Miguel. Aztec Thought and Culture; A
       Study of the Ancient Nahuatl Mind. Translated by Jack
       Emory Davis. Norman: University of Oklahoma Press,
       c1963, 1971.
A translation of the author's La filosofia nahuatl.

345   Leon-Portilla, Miguel. The Broken Spears: The Aztec
       Account of the Conquest of Mexico. Boston: Beacon
       Press, 1962.
The conquest as viewed by the Aztecs, by the leading Nahua
scholar.

346   Livermore, Harold. A History of Spain. New York:
       Grove Press, 1960.
A standard work.

347   Loomis, Noel M. and Abraham P. Nasatir. Pedro Vial and
       the Roads to Santa Fe. Norman: University of Oklahoma
       Press, 1967.
Describes Vial's pioneering in the early 1790s of what later
became known as the Santa Fe trail.

348   Lopez de Gomara, Francisco. Cortes: The Life of the
       Conqueror by His Secretary. Translated by Lesley B.
       Simpson. Berkeley: University of California Press,
       1964.

349   Lowery, Woodbury. The Spanish Settlements Within the
       Present Limits of the United States, 1513-1561. New
       York: G. P. Putnam's Sons, 1901. Reprint, New York:
       Russell & Russell, 1959.
Emphasizes early settlements on Mexico's northern frontier.

350   McCaleb, Walter F. The Spanish Missions of Texas. San
       Antonio, Tex.: Naylor Publishing Co., 1954.

351   McCarty, Kieran. A Spanish Frontier in the Enlightened
      Age. Franciscan Beginnings in Sonora and Arizona,
      1767-1770. Washington, D.C.: Academy of American
      Franciscan History, 1981.
Describes difficulties which arose when Franciscans replaced
Jesuit missionaries in Pimeria Alta.

352   McDermott, John F., ed. The Spanish in the Mississippi
      Valley, 1762-1804. Urbana: University of Illinois
      Press, 1974.
A series of papers presented at a 1970 conference.

353   McGregor, John C. Southwestern Archaeology. Urbana:
      University of Illinois Press, 1965.
A broad survey of southwestern Indian cultures; good
bibliography.

354   Madariaga, Salvador de. Hernan Cortes, Conqueror of
      Mexico. New York: Macmillan Co., 1941. Reprint,
      Chicago: Henry Regnery Co., 1955.
Cortes's life, by the famous Spanish historian.

355   Mange, Juan Mateo. Unknown Arizona and Sonora,
      1693-1721, From the Francisco Fernandez del Castillo
      Version of Luz de tierra incognita. Tucson: Arizona
      Silhouettes, 1954.

356   Mason, Herbert Molloy. Missions of Texas. Birmingham,
      Ala.: Southern Living Books, 1974.
A brief popular history.

357   Menendez Pidal, Ramon. The Spaniards in Their History.
      New York: W. W. Norton & Co., 1966.
An interpretive history of Spain, by a noted Spanish
scholar.

358   Meyer, Michael C. and William L. Sherman. The Course
      of Mexican History. New York: Oxford University
      Press, 1979.
The first 300 pages are concerned with the Indian background
and the colonial period. Lists extensive bibliographic
materials in both English and Spanish.

359   Montoya, Juan de. New Mexico in 1602. Translated by
      George P. Hammond and Agapito Rey. Albuquerque, N.
      Mex.: Quivira Society, 1938. Reprint, New York: Arno
      Press, 1967.
Translation of Montoya's Relacion del descubrimiento del
Nuovo Mexico.

360   Moore, John Preston. Revolt in Louisiana: The Spanish
      Occupation, 1766-1770. Baton Rouge: Louisiana State

University Press, 1976.
Describes the difficulties Spain encountered trying to
establish control over formerly French Louisiana.

361 Moorhead, Max L. The Presidio: Bastion of the Spanish
    Borderlands. Norman: University of Oklahoma Press,
    1975.
Describes the important role played by the presidio in New
Spain's northern frontiers.

362 Morfi, Juan E. History of Texas, 1673-1779. 2 vols.
    Translated by Carlos E. Castañeda. Albuquerque, N.
    Mex.: Quivira Society, 1935. Reprint, New York: Arno
    Press, 1967.
An eighteenth century work by Fray Morfi describing the
Indians and missions in Texas.

363 Nasatir, Abraham P. Borderland in Retreat: From
    Spanish Louisiana to the Far Southwest. Albuquerque:
    University of New Mexico Press, 1976.
Describes Spain's loss of her northern claims.

364 Nentvig, Juan, S.J. Rudo Ensayo: A Description of
    Sonora and Arizona in 1764. Translated by Alberto
    Pradeau and Robert Rasmussen. Tucson: University of
    Arizona Press, 1979.

365 Padden, Robert C. The Hummingbird and the Hawk:
    Conquest and Sovereignty in the Valley of Mexico,
    1503-1541. New York; Harper & Row Publishers, 1967.
An excellent account of the first stage in cultural change
when Spaniard and Indian met.

366 Parsons, Francis B. Early 17th Century Missions of the
    Southwest; with Historical Introduction. Tucson,
    Ariz.: D. S. King, 1975.
A brief survey of missions in Arizona and New Mexico.

367 Peterson, Frederick A. Ancient Mexico. New York:
    Putnam, 1959.
Probably the best one volume history and description of the
Indian civilizations in Mexico.

368 Pino, Pedro B. Exposicion sucinta y sencilla de la
    provincia del Nuevo Mexico. Cadiz, Spain: Imprenta
    del Estado Mayor General, 1812. Reprinted in Three
    New Mexico Chronicles, item 270.
Pino was a Nuevo Mexicano delegate to the Spanish cortes at
the beginning of the nineteenth century.

369 Powell, Philip W. Soldiers, Indians, and Silver; the
    Northward Advance of New Spain, 1550-1600. Berkeley:
    University of California Press, 1952.
Scholarly account of advancing frontier settlement in

northern Mexico.

370   Prince, L. Bradford. Historical Sketches of New Mexico
      from the Earliest Records to the American Occupation.
      New York: Leggat Brothers, 1883.
Account by a territorial governor of New Mexico.

371   Ramos, Samuel. Profile of Man and Culture in Mexico.
      Translated by Peter G. Earle. Austin: University of
      Texas Press, 1962.
Describes and explains Mexican character and culture.

372   Richardson, Rupert N. and Carl C. Rister. The Greater
      Southwest. Glendale, Calif.: Arthur H. Clark Co.,
      1934.
Contains two chapters on Spanish expansion into the area.

373   Richman, Irving B. California Under Spain and Mexico.
      Boston: Houghton Mifflin Co., 1911.
Still has great historical value despite its age. A broad
survey.

374   Riesenberg, Felix, Jr. The Golden Road, the Story of
      California's Mission Trail. New York: McGraw-Hill
      Book Co., 1962.
A popular account of the California missions.

375   Roberts, Edward. With the Invader: Glimpses of the
      Southwest. San Francisco: S. Carson & Co., 1885.
Includes material on Spanish and Mexican periods; popular
history and travel.

376   Rowland, Leon. Los Fundadores. Fresno, Calif.:
      Academy of California Church History, 1951.
Lists alphabetically nearly 200 surnames of Spanish-Mexican
settlers in California, 1769 to 1785, with geneological
information on each.

377   Sanchez, Nellie Van de Grift. Spanish Arcadia. Los
      Angeles: Powell Publishing Co., 1929. Reprint, New
      York: Arno Press, 1976.
A colorful, romantic view of family life, social customs,
and economics in Spanish and Mexican California.

378   Sauer, Carl O. The Road to Cibola. Berkeley:
      University of California Press, 1932.
Describes the early movement up Mexico's west coast to the
Southwest.

379   Sauer, Carl O. and Donald Brand. Aztatlan: Prehistoric
      Mexican Frontier on the Pacific Coast. Berkeley:
      University of California Press, 1932.
Possible area of origin of the Aztecs.

380   Scott, Florence (Johnson.) Historical Heritage of the
      Lower Rio Grande; a Historical Record of Spanish
      Exploration, Subjugation and Colonization of the Lower
      Rio Grande Valley . . . together with the Development
      of Towns and Ranchos Under Spanish, Mexican and Texas
      Sovereignties, 1747-1848. San Antonio, Tex.: Naylor
      Publishing Co., 1937. Revised ed., Waco, Tex.: Texian
      Press, 1966.

381   Scott, Florence (Johnson.) Royal Land Grants North of
      the Rio Grande, 1777-1821. Rio Grande City, Tex.: La
      Retama Press, 1969.
Includes maps and bibliographic footnotes.

382   Sejourne, Laurette. Burning Water: Thought and
      Religion in Ancient Mexico. New York: Grove Press,
      1969.
Nahuatl mythology and religion, especially the cult of
Quetzalcoatl.

383   Sepulveda, Cesar. Tres ensayos sobre la frontera
      septentrional de la Nueva España. Mexico, D.F.:
      Editorial Porrua, 1977.
Discusses the Spanish role in the Anglo American Revolution
and the disintegration of Mexico's northern frontier.

384   Simmons, Marc. Spanish Government in New Mexico .
      Albuquerque: University of New Mexico Press, 1968.
Covers both history and government of the Spanish and
Mexican periods to 1848.

385   Simpson, Lesley Byrd. Many Mexicos. Berkeley:
      University of California Press, 1967.
Provides an excellent interpretive synthesis of the Mexican
colonial period.

386   Sonnichsen, Charles L. Pass of the North: Four
      Centuries on the Rio Grande. El Paso: Texas Western
      Press, 1968.
Popular history of the Rio Grande Valley; extensive
bibliography.

387   Soustelle, Jacques. The Daily Life of the Aztecs on
      the Eve of the Spanish Conquest. New York: Macmillan
      Co., 1962.
Perhaps the best description of Aztec culture and
civilization.

388   Spicer, Edward H. Cycles of Conquest: The Impact of
      Spain, Mexico, and the United States on the Indians of
      the Southwest, 1533-1960. Tucson: University of
      Arizona Press, 1962.
Focuses on the interrelations and conflict between Indian,
Mexican, and Anglo.

389   Sullivan, Ella C. and Alfred E. Lagle. The Story of
      the Old Spanish Missions of the Southwest. Chicago:
      Lyons & Carnahan, 1927.

390   Swadesh, Frances L. Los Primeros Pobladores. Notre
      Dame, Ind.: University of Notre Dame Press, 1974.
Covers early settlement in the New Mexico area.

391   Taylor, Virginia, ed. The Spanish Archives of the
      General Land Office of Texas. Austin, Tex.: Lone Star
      Press, 1955.
Includes a useful bibliography on Texas land grants.

392   Terrell, John Upton. Estevanico the Black. Los
      Angeles: Westernlore Press, 1968.
Popular history of Estevanico who accompanied Alvar Nuñez
Cabeza de Vaca.

393   Terrell, John Upton. Pueblos, Gods and Spaniards. New
      York: Dial Press, 1973.
A history of the Pueblo Indians and their interaction with
Spanish-Mexican explorers and settlers.

394   Thomas, Alfred B., trans. and ed. After Coronado:
      Spanish Exploration Northeast of New Mexico,
      1696-1727; Documents From the Archives of Spain,
      Mexico and New Mexico. Norman: University of Oklahoma
      Press, 1935.

395   Thomas, Alfred B., trans. and ed. Teodoro de Croix and
      the Northern Frontier of New Spain, 1776-1783.
      Norman: University of Oklahoma Press, 1941.
Translation of Comandante General Croix's report on the
northern border regions.

396   Twitchell, Ralph Emerson, comp. The Spanish Archives
      of New Mexico. Compiled and Chronologically Arranged
      With Historical, Genealogical, Geographical, and Other
      Annotations by Authority of the State of New Mexico.
      2 vols. Cedar Rapids, Iowa: Torch Press, 1914.
      Reprint, New York: Arno Press, 1976.
A collection of historical archival documents.

397   Twitchell, Ralph Emerson. Spanish Colonization in New
      Mexico in the Oñate and de Vargas Periods. Santa Fe:
      Historical Society of New Mexico, 1919.

398   Vaillant, George C. The Aztecs of Mexico. Garden
      City, N.Y.: Doubleday & Co., 1962.
Long the standard work on Aztec history and culture.

399   Villagra, Gaspar Perez de. A History of New Mexico.
      Los Angeles: Quivira Society, 1933. Reprint, Chicago:

Rio Grande Press, 1962.
A contemporary epic historical poem by Captain Villagra
covering the period from 1595 to 1610.

400   Wagner, Henry R.   Spanish Voyages to the Northwest
      Coast of America in the Sixteenth Century.   San
      Francisco: California Historical Society, 1929.
The most authoritative and detailed account by the
outstanding expert in the area.   With bibliographic notes.

401   Wagoner, Jay J.   Early Arizona: Prehistory to Civil
      War.   Tucson: University of Arizona Press, 1975.
A survey, with an extensive bibliography; includes material
on the Mexican era.

402   Warren, Harris Gaylord.   The Sword was their Passport,
      a History of American Filibustering in the Mexican
      Revolution.   Baton Rouge: Louisiana State University
      Press, 1943.
Popular history of the 1810-1821 filibusters in the
Texas-Louisiana area.

403   Weber, David J., ed.   New Spain's Far Northern
      Frontier; Essays on Spain in the American West,
      1540-1821.   Albuquerque: University of New Mexico
      Press, 1979.
A collection of essays and papers on the Spanish Southwest;
with a brief bibliography.

404   Weber, Francis J.   Catholic Footprints in California.
      Newhall, Calif.: Hogarth Press, 1970.
A collection of brief articles on the Catholic Church's
historic role.

405   Weddle, Robert S.   San Juan Bautista: Gateway to
      Spanish Texas.   Austin: University of Texas Press,
      1968.
A study of a transitional border area in the colonial
period.

406   Weddle, Robert S.   The San Saba Mission: Spanish Pivot
      in Texas.   Austin: University of Texas Press, 1964.

407   Whitaker, Arthur P.   The Spanish-American Frontier,
      1783-1795.   Lincoln: University of Nebraska Press,
      1969.

408   Wilcox, David R. and W. Bruce Masse, eds.   The
      Protohistoric Period in the North American Southwest.
      Tempe: Arizona State University, 1981.
Contains nineteen essays on the Indians of the Southwest
between 1450 and 1700 as they came into contact with
Europeans.   Excellent bibliographies.

409   Wilkinson, James. <u>Memoirs of My Own Time</u>. 3 vols.
        Philadelphia: Abraham Small, 1816. Reprint, New York:
        AMS Press, 1972.
Important for materials on Texas in the late 1700s. General
Wilkinson was American military governor of Louisiana and in
the pay of Spain at the same time.

410   Wolf, Eric R. <u>Sons of the Shaking Earth</u>. Chicago:
        University of Chicago Press, 1959.
Covers Indian history and culture in Middle America in an
outstanding fashion from an anthropological viewpoint.

411   Worcester, Donald E., trans. and ed. <u>Instructions for
        Governing the Interior Provinces of New Spain, 1786,
        by Bernardo de Galvez</u>. Berkeley, Calif.: Quivira
        Society, 1951.
A bilingual text of Viceroy Galvez's instructions to his
successor for governing the northern frontier region.

412   Zorita, Alonso de. <u>Life and Labor in Ancient Mexico</u>.
        Translated by Benjamin Keen. New Brunswick, N.J.:
        Rutgers University Press, 1963.
A somewhat idealistic picture of pre-conquest Mexico and its
decline under the Spaniards by a mid-1500s government
official.

II: Theses and Dissertations

413   Adams, David Bergen. "The Tlaxcalan Colonies of
        Spanish Coahuila and Nuevo Leon: An Aspect of the
        Settlement of Northern Mexico." Austin: University of
        Texas, 1971.

414   Ammons, Nancy C. "The Spanish Conquest of New Mexico
        in the Sixteenth and Seventeenth Centuries." Master's
        thesis. Norman: University of Oklahoma, 1931.

415   Bolkan, Thomas M. "Facundo Melgares and the Northern
        Frontiers of New Spain." Master's thesis.
        Albuquerque: University of New Mexico, 1965.
Includes information on land grants in the late Spanish and
early Mexican eras.

416   Brown, Lee Francis. "The Explorer, the United States
        Government, and the Approaches to Santa Fe: A Study of
        American Policy Relative to the Spanish Southwest,
        1800-1819." Chicago: Loyola University, 1972.

417   Charles, Ralph. "Development of the Partido System in
        the New Mexico Sheep Industry." Master's thesis.
        Albuquerque: University of New Mexico, 1940.

418   Christiansen, Paige Walrath. "Hugo Oconor:
        Spanish-Apache Relations on the Frontiers of New
        Spain, 1771-1776." Berkeley: University of
        California, 1960.

419   Coombs, Gary. "Migration Adaption: Indian
        Missionization in California." Los Angeles:
        University of California, 1975.

420   Cruz, Gilbert R. "Spanish Town Patterns in the
        Borderlands: Municipal Origins in Texas and the
        Southwest, 1610-1810." St. Louis, Mo.: St. Louis
        University, 1974.

421   Daniel, James M. "The Advance of the Spanish Frontier
        and the Despoblado." Austin: University of Texas,
        1955.

422   Garr, Daniel J. "Hispanic Colonial Settlement in
        California: Planning and Urban Development on the
        Frontier, 1769-1850." Ithaca, N.Y.: Cornell
        University, 1971.

423   Goodsel, Ruth. "California During the War of
        Independence, 1810-1822." Master's thesis. Berkeley:
        University of California, 1928.

424   Haggard, Juan Villasana. "The Neutral Ground Between
        Louisiana and Texas, 1806-1821." Austin: University
        of Texas, 1942.
Comprises a complete study of filibustering in the period.

425   Healey, Ettie Miriam. "The New Mexico Missions in the
        Middle Eighteenth Century." Master's thesis.
        Berkeley: University of California, 1922.

426   Hussey, John A. "The United States and the Bear Flag
        Revolt." Berkeley: University of California, 1941.

427   Kinnaird, Lawrence. "American Penetration into Spanish
        Territory to 1803." Berkeley: University of
        California, 1928.

428   Kyle, Clara Ethel. "The Re-Conquest of New Mexico,
        1680-1698." Master's thesis. Berkeley: University of
        California, 1926.

429   Larrey, Martin Fermin. "The Yuma Colorado Settlements,
        1775-1781." Master's thesis. Santa Clara, Calif.:
        University of Santa Clara, 1962.
Describes the efforts to link Alta California to central
Mexico by land.

430   Lewis, James A. "New Spain During the American
        Revolution, 1779-1783: A Viceroyalty at War." Durham,
        N.C.: Duke University, 1975.

431   Long, Stanton C. "Early Nineteenth Century El Paso."
        Master's thesis. Austin: University of Texas, 1953.
Covers life in El Paso, 1780-1830, with maps and documents.

432   Long, William W. "A History of Mining in New Mexico
        During the Spanish and American Periods." Master's
        thesis. Albuquerque: University of New Mexico, 1964.

433   Lynch, Margaret. "Colonial Texas as a Frontier
        Problem." Chestnut Hill, Mass.: Boston College, 1935.

434   McCollum, Dudley Foster. "Spanish Texas." New York:
        New York University, 1931.

435   Martin, John M. "Mission San Juan Bautista,
        California. The Cause and Effects of its Rise and
        Decline." Master's thesis. Santa Clara, Calif.:
        University of Santa Clara, 1933.

436   Myres, Sandra L. S. "The Development of the Ranch as a
        Frontier Institution in the Spanish Province of Texas,
        1691-1800." Fort Worth: Texas Christian University,
        1967.

437   Parraga, Charlotte M. N.   "Santa Fe De Nuevo Mexico: A
       Study of a Frontier City Based on an Annotated
       Translation of Selected Documents (1825-1832) from the
       Mexican Archives of New Mexico." Muncie, Ind.: Ball
       State University, 1976.

438 ·Reid, Archibald R.   "The Economic Development of the
       Hispanic California Missions." Albuquerque:
       University of New Mexico, 1975.

439   Walz, Vina E.   "A History of the El Paso Area,
       1680-1692." Albuquerque: University of New Mexico,
       1951.
Covers a period of rapid expansion as refugees from the Pope
revolt in New Mexico settled along the Rio Grande at the
ford.

440   Watson, Thomas Davis.   "Merchant Adventurer in the Old
       Southwest: William Panton, the Spanish Years,
       1782-1801." Lubbock: Texas Technological University,
       1972.

441   Wilson, Maurine T.   "Philip Nolan and his Activities in
       Texas." Master's thesis. Austin: University of
       Texas, 1932.
Gives an idea of early Spanish concern about U.S. intrusion
into Texas.

442   Wright, James L., Jr.   "English-Spanish Rivalry in
       North America, 1492-1763." Charlottesville:
       University of Virginia, 1958.

II: Periodicals

443   Adam, V. G.   "The Pious Fund." Historical Society of
       Southern California Annual Publications 4 (1889),
       228-233.
History of the fund originally set up to establish missions
in Baja California.

444   Adams, Eleanor B.   "Two Colonial New Mexican
       Libraries." New Mexico Historical Review 19 (April
       1944), 135-167.

445   Applegate, Frank.   "Spanish Colonial Arts." Survey
       66:3 (May 1, 1931), 156-157.

446   Aragon, Jane L.   "The People of Santa Fe in the
       1790s." Aztlan 7:3 (Fall 1976), 391-417.
Describes the organization of society and its growth at the
end of the century.

447   Archibald, Robert R.   "Acculturation and Assimilation
       in Colonial New Mexico." New Mexico Historical Review
       53 (July 1978), 205-217.

448   Archibald, Robert R.   "The Economy of the Alta
       California Missions, 1803-1821." Southern California
       Quarterly 58 (Summer 1976), 227-240.

449   Arizona Highways 48 (January 1972).
The entire issue is devoted to articles on the history and
culture of Indians of the Southwest; includes the Hohokam.

450   Bannon, John F., S.J.   "The Mission as a Frontier
       Institution: Sixty Years of Interest and Research."
       Western Historical Quarterly 10:3 (July 1979),
       303-322.
Includes an excellent bibliography.

451   Benson, Nettie L.   "A Governor's Report on Texas in
       1809." Southwestern Historical Quarterly 71 (April
       1968), 603-615.
Important because of the rising tensions on the
Texas-Louisiana border.

452   Bishko, Julian.   "The Iberian Background of Latin
       American History: Recent Progress and Continuing
       Problems." Hispanic American Historical Review 36
       (1956), 50-80.

453   Bloom, (Rev.) Lansing B., ed.   "Barreiro's Ojeada sobre
       Nuevo Mexico." New Mexico Historical Review 3 (1928),
       73-96.

454 Bloom, (Rev.) Lansing B. "The Vargas Encomienda." New
     Mexico Historical Review 14 (1939), 366-417.
Vargas was the reconqueror of New Mexico after the Pope
revolt of 1680.

455 Bolton, Herbert E. "The Mission as a Frontier
     Institution." American Historical Review 23 (October
     1917), 42-61.

456 Brand, Donald D. "The Early History of the Range
     Cattle Industry in Northern Mexico." Agricultural
     History 35 (1961), 132-139.

457 Brinckerhoff, Sidney B. "The Last Years of Spanish
     Arizona, 1786-1821." Arizona and the West 9 (Spring
     1967), 5-20.

458 Candelaria, Cordelia. "La Malinche, Feminist
     Prototype." Frontiers: A Journal of Women Studies 5:2
     (Summer 1980), 1-6.

459 Carlson, Alvar Ward. "Spanish Settlements on Indian
     Lands." El Palacio 84 (Winter 1978), 29-39.

460 Carlson, Alvar Ward. "Spanish-American Acquisition of
     Cropland Within the Northern Pueblo Indian Grants, New
     Mexico." Ethno History 22:2 (Spring 1975), 95-110.

461 Cheetham, Francis T. "The Early Settlements of
     Southern Colorado." Colorado Magazine 5 (1928), 1-8.

462 Coughlin, Magdalen C. S. J. "Boston Smugglers on the
     Coast (1797-1821): An Insight Into the American
     Acquisition of California." California Historical
     Society Quarterly 46:2 (June 1967), 99-120.

463 Cox, Isaac J. "Monroe and the Early Mexican
     Revolutionary Agents." American Historical
     Association Annual Report for the Year 1911 1 (1911),
     197-215.
Includes material on Jose Bernardo Gutierrez de Lara's
activities in Texas.

464 Davis, William R. "The Spanish Borderlands of Texas
     and Chihuahua." Texana 9:2 (1971), 142-155.
A brief survey of their history from 1528 to 1821.

465 Dominguez, Fray Francisco. "Letters of Fray Francisco
     Atanasio Dominguez." In The Missions of New Mexico,
     1776: A Description With Other Contemporary Documents.
     Translated by Eleanor B. Adams and Angelico Chavez,
     pp. 270-302. Albuquerque: University of New Mexico
     Press, 1956.

466   Donohue, John A., S.J. "The Unlucky Jesuit Mission at
       Bac." Arizona and the West 2 (Summer 1960), 127-139.

467   Downs, Fane. "Governor Antonio Martinez and the
       Defense of Texas from Foreign Invasion, 1817-1822."
       Texas Military History 7 (Spring 1968), 27-43.
Describes efforts of the last Spanish governor of Texas to
keep filibusterers out.

468   Faulk, Odie B. "Ranching in Spanish Texas." Hispanic
       American Historical Review 45 (May 1965), 257-266.

469   Forbes, Jack D. "Black Pioneers: The Spanish-Speaking
       Afroamericans of the Southwest." In Minorities in
       California History. Edited by George E. Frakes and
       Curtis B. Solberg. New York: Random House, 1971.

470   Garner, Van Hastings. "Seventeenth Century New
       Mexico." Journal of Mexican American History 4
       (1974), 41-70.
A critique of earlier interpretations of the Pope revolt,
especially those of France Scholes and Jack Forbes.

471   Garr, Daniel J. "A Rare and Desolate Land: Population
       and Race in Hispanic California." Western Historical
       Quarterly 6:2 (April 1975), 133-148.

472   Gentilcore, R. Louis. "Missions and Mission Lands of
       Alta California." Association of American Geographers
       Annals 51 (1961), 46-72.

473   Gerould, Katharine Fullerton. "New Mexico and the
       Backwash of Spain." Harper's 151 (July 1925),
       199-212.

474   Greenleaf, Richard A. "Atrisco and Las Ciruelas,
       1722-1769." New Mexico Historical Review 42 (Jan.
       1967), 5-25.

475   Greenleaf, Richard A. "Land and Water in Mexico and
       New Mexico, 1700-1821." New Mexico Historical Review
       47:2 (April 1972), 85-112.

476   Gronet, Richard. "The United States and the Invasion
       of Texas, 1810-1814." The Americas 25 (Jan. 1969),
       281-306.

477   Hackett, Charles W. "The Revolt of the Pueblo Indians
       of New Mexico in 1680." Texas Historical Association
       Quarterly 15 (Oct. 1911), 93-147.

478   Haggard, J. Villasana. "The Counter-Revolution at
       Bexar, 1811." Southwestern Historical Quarterly 43

(Oct. 1939), 222-235.
Part of the Mexican revolt for independence in Texas.

479   Hammond, George P., trans. and ed.   "Pimeria Alta After
      Kino's Time."   New Mexico Historical Review 4 (July
      1929), 220-238.
Describes the Sonora frontier in the early 18th century.

480   Haury, Emil W.   "First Masters of the American Desert,
      the Hohokam."   National Geographic 131:5 (May 1967),
      670-695.

481   Henderson, Harry M.   "The Magee-Gutierrez Expedition."
      Southwestern Historical Quarterly 55 (July 1951),
      43-61.

482   Hill, Joseph J.   "The Old Spanish Trail; A Study of
      Spanish and Mexican Trade and Explorations Northwest
      from Mexico to the Great Basin and California."
      Hispanic American Historical Review 4 (1921), 444-473.

483   Hill, Joseph J.   "The Pueblo Revolt of 1860."   New
      Mexico Magazine 58:6 (June 1980), 38-43.
A history of the New Mexico revolt with present day
photographs of the areas.

484   Jenkins, Myra E.   "Spanish Land Grants in the Tewa
      Area."   New Mexico Historical Review 47:2 (April
      1972), 113-134.
Discusses Spanish land grant policy and practice; by an
outstanding historian of New Mexico.

485   Kelley, Wilfrid D.   "Settlement of the Middle Rio
      Grande Valley."   Journal of Geography 54 (1955),
      387-399.

486   King, Grace.   "The Real Philip Nolan."   Louisiana
      Historical Society Publications, Proceedings and
      Reports, 1917 10 (1918), 87-112.
Describes early Anglo penetration into Texas at the end of
the 1700s.

487   Kramer, V. Paul.   "The Spanish Borderlands of Texas and
      Tamaulipas."   Texana 10 (Summer 1972), 260-272.

488   Lecompte, Janet.   "Don Benito Vasquez in Early Saint
      Louis."   Missouri Historical Society Bulletin 26:4
      (July 1970), 285-305.
Good for life of Spanish St. Louis, 1769-1804.

489   Lehmer, Donald J.   "The Second Frontier: The Spanish."
      In The American West: An Appraisal.   Edited by Robert
      G. Ferris.   Santa Fe: Museum of New Mexico Press,
      1963.

490   Lopez, Larry S., ed. "Sample Partido Contracts." New
      Mexico Historical Review 52 (April 1977), 111-116.
Illustrates the "crop" sharing arrangements in New Mexico
sheep raising.

491   McCaleb, Walter F. "The First Period of the
      Gutierrez-Magee Expedition." Texas Historical
      Association Quarterly 4 (Jan. 1901), 218-229.

492   McDonald, Archie P. "Anglo vs. Spaniard: Early
      Conflict." Military History of Texas and the
      Southwest 16:1 (1980), 23-32.
Covers the late 1700s and early 1800s, primarily in Texas.

493   Magalousis, Nicholas. "Missions, Military and the
      Spanish Crown." Chapman Quarterly (May 1981), 6-7.
Discusses reasons for the decline of California mission
Indian populations.

494   Marshall, C. W. "The Birth of the Mestizo in New
      Spain." Hispanic American Historical Review 19 (May
      1939), 161-184.
Describes the process of mestizage. About 300,000 Europeans
came to New Spain, 1519-1821, and few were women.

495   Matter, Robert A. "Mission Life in Seventeenth-Century
      Florida." Catholic Historical Review 67:3 (July
      1981), 401-420.

496   Mattison, Ray H. "Early Spanish and Mexican
      Settlements in Arizona." New Mexico Historical Review
      21:4 (Oct. 1946), 273-327.
Includes material on land grants in southern Arizona, most
awarded in the Mexican era of the 1820s.

497   Mayfield, Thomas, Jr. "Education in New Mexico During
      the Spanish and Mexican Periods." Research 2:3
      (1938), 99-106.

498   Parkhill, Forbes. "Colorado's Earliest Settlements."
      Colorado Magazine 34 (1957), 241-253.

499   Patrick, Elizabeth N. "Land Grants During the
      Administration of Spanish Colonial Governor Pedro
      Fermin de Mendinueta." New Mexico Historical Review
      47 (April 1972), 151-184.

500   Rios-Bustamante, Antonio J. "New Mexico in the
      Eighteenth Century: Life, Labor and Trade in La Villa
      de San Felipe de Albuquerque, 1706-1790." Aztlan 7:3
      (Fall 1976), 357-389.

501   Robinson, Willard B.   "Colonial Ranch Architecture in
       the Spanish-Mexican Tradition."   Southwestern
       Historical Quarterly 83:2 (Oct. 1979), 123-150.
Includes history of early ranching in Texas.

502   Scholes, France V.   "Juan Martinez de Montoya, Settler
       and Conquistador of New Mexico."   New Mexico
       Historical Review 19 (Oct. 1944), 337-342.

503   Schroeder, Albert H.   "Pattern Diffusion from Mexico
       into the Southwest After A.D. 600."   American
       Antiquity 31 (July 1966), 683-704.
Describes Middle American culture pattern diffusion from
southern Arizona.

504   Schroeder, Albert H.   "Unregulated Diffusion from
       Mexico into the Southwest Prior to A.D. 700."
       American Antiquity 30 (Jan. 1965), 297-309.
Describes the diffusion of a sedentary living pattern into
southern Arizona.

505   Servin, Manuel P.   "The Beginnings of California's
       Anti-Mexican Prejudice."   In his An Awakened Minority:
       The Mexican Americans, 1974, pp. 2-17, item 169.
Argues that racial/ethnic prejudice goes back to the Spanish
friars in the missions.

506   Shinn, C. H.   "Pioneer Spanish Families in California."
       Century 41 (1891), 377-389.
Emphasis on the Vallejo family in northern California.

507   Simmons, Marc.   "Settlement Patterns and Village Plans
       in Colonial New Mexico."   Journal of the West 3 (Jan.
       1964), 7-19.

508   Simmons, Marc.   "Spanish Attempts to Open a New
       Mexico-Sonora Road."   Arizona and the West 17 (Spring
       1975), 5-20.

509   Simmons, Marc.   "Tlascalans in the Spanish
       Borderlands."   New Mexico Historical Review 39 (1964),
       101-110.
Describes the important role of Tlaxcalan Indians of central
Mexico in Spanish northern frontier expansion.

510   Sizelove, Linda.   "Indian Adaption to the Spanish
       Missions."   Pacific Historian 22:4 (Winter 1978),
       398-402.
Limited to the Alta California missions.

511   Spicer, Edward H.   "Spanish-Indian Acculturation in the
       Southwest."   American Anthropologist 56 (1954),
       663-684.

512   Starnes, Gary. "The Spanish Borderlands of Texas and
       Coahuila." Texana 10:1 (1972), 20-29.

513   Stevens, J. Paul. "Changes in Land Tenure and Usage
       Among the Indians and Spanish Americans in Northern
       New Mexico." In Indian and Spanish American
       Adjustments to Arid and Semi-Arid Environments.
       Edited by Clark S. Knowlton, pp. 38-43. Lubbock:
       Texas Technological University, 1964.

514   Thomas, Alfred B., ed. "An Anonymous Description of
       New Mexico, 1818." Southwestern Historical Quarterly
       33 (1929-1930), 50-74.

515   Thomas, Alfred B. "Documents Bearing Upon the Northern
       Frontier of New Mexico" and "The Yellowstone River,
       James Long and Spanish Reaction to American Intrusion
       into Spanish Dominions, 1818-1819." New Mexico
       Historical Review 4:2 (April 1929), 146-177.
Two articles on early U.S. interest in the northern Mexican
frontier.

516   Van Ness, John R. "The Polvadera Grant: Hispanic
       Settlement in the Cañones Region." Spanish
       Borderlands Research 1 (1981), 79-84.
History of a 1766 land grant in northern New Mexico made to
Juan P. Martin.

517   Van Ness, John R. and C. M. Van Ness. "Introduction:
       Spanish Land Grants in New Mexico and Colorado."
       Journal of the West 19 (July 1980), 3-11.

518   Walker, Henry P. "William McLane's Narrative of the
       Magee-Gutierrez Expedition, 1812-1813." Southwestern
       Historical Quarterly 66:2 (Oct. 1962), 234-251; 66:3
       (Jan. 1963), 457-479; 66:4 (April 1963), 569-588.
A contemporary account of the Texas filibustering
expedition. Number 3 includes a list of the expedition's
members.

519   Warren, Harris Gaylord. "Jose Alvarez de Toledo's
       Initiation as a Filibuster, 1811-1813." Hispanic
       American Historical Review 20 (Feb. 1940), 56-82.
Has material on Jose Bernardo Gutierrez de Lara's activities
in Texas.

520   Weber, David J. "Spanish Fur Trade from New Mexico,
       1540-1821." The Americas 24:2 (Oct. 1967), 122-136.

521   Weiss, Lawrence D. "Modes of Production and Primitive
       Accumulation--Spanish New Mexico, 1600-1800."
       Southwest Economy and Society 3:1 (Fall 1980), 30-54.
A broad survey of trade development on the northern frontier

over two centuries.

522 West, Elizabeth H., trans. and ed. "Diary of Jose
     Bernardo Gutierrez de Lara, 1811-1812." American
     Historical Review 34:1 (Oct. 1928), 55-77; 34:2 (Jan.
     1929), 281-294.

523 Worcester, Donald E. "The Horses That Discovered
     America." Americas 13:4 (April 1961), 14-18.

524 Worcester, Donald E. "The Spread of Spanish Horses in
     the Southwest." New Mexico Historical Review 19
     (1944), 225-232.

525 Wyllys, Rufus K. "The Spanish Missions of the
     Southwest." Arizona Historical Review 6 (1935),
     27-37.

526 Zavala, Silvio. "The Frontiers of Hispanic America."
     In The Frontier in Perspective. Edited by Walker D.
     Wyman and Clifton B. Kroeber, pp. 35-58. Madison:
     University of Wisconsin Press, 1957.
Discusses and evaluates the frontier, emphasizing northern
Mexico.

III.
MEXICAN PERIOD _____

Books

Section III covers the period from Mexico's
independence in 1821 to the loss of its northern frontier
region in 1848 to the United States as a result of its
defeat in war. It includes works on the problems of Texas,
its revolt against the central Mexican government in 1836,
on independent Texas, the United States-Mexican War, and the
Treaty of Guadalupe Hidalgo. No attempt has been made to
include comprehensively the many books on the United
States-Mexican War; rather, emphasis has been placed on
borderland causes, developments, and results. For a
comprehensive bibliography on the war itself see Norman
Tuterow, <u>The Mexican-American War: An Annotated
Bibliography</u>, 1981, item 4214.

527 Alcaraz, Ramon. <u>The Other Side: Or, Notes for the
      History of the War Between Mexico and the United
      States</u>. New York: J. Wiley, 1850.
One of the earliest Mexican interpretations of the conflict
between the two countries.

528 Alessio Robles, Vito. <u>Coahuila y Texas desde la
      consumacion de la independencia hasta el tratado de
      paz de Guadalupe Hidalgo</u>. 2 vols. Mexico, D.F.:
      [N.P.], 1945-46.
Describes Mexico's northern frontier problems, including
land grants and Anglo immigration, 1821-1848.

529 Almonte, Juan N. <u>Noticia estadistica sobre Tejas</u>.
      Mexico: Ignacio Cumplido, 1835.
A member of the 1834 Mexico-U.S. boundary commission,
Almonte was active in conservative Mexican politics. See
item 839.

530   Arbuckle, Clyde. Santa Clara County Ranchos. San
      Jose, Calif.: Harlan-Young Press, 1968.

531   Austin, Stephen F. The Austin Papers. 2 vols. in 3.
      Edited by Eugene C. Barker. Washington, D.C.: U.S.
      Government Printing Office, 1924-1928.
Covers from 1789 to 1834. Valuable for the in-depth study
of the leading empresario in Texas.

532   Austin, Stephen F. Establishing Austin's Colony.
      Edited by David B. Gracy. Austin, Tex.: Pemberton
      Press, 1970.
Includes laws, contracts and orders of colonization.
Reprint of 1830 edition, Austin, Tex.: G. B. Cotten.

533   Austin, Stephen F. and Moses Austin. The Austin
      Papers. 3 vols. in 4. Edited by Eugene C. Barker.
      New York: AMS Press, 1982.
Reprint of the 1928 edition.

534   Austin, Stephen F. and Moses Austin. The Austin
      Papers, October 1834-January 1837. Vol. III. Edited
      by Eugene C. Barker. Austin: University of Texas
      Press, 1927.
Includes petitions, political addresses, proclamations,
memorials, and business memoranda.

535   Avina, Rose H. Spanish and Mexican Land Grants in
      California. San Francisco: R & E Research Associates,
      1973. Reprint, New York: Arno Press, 1976.
A 1934 master's thesis at the University of California,
Berkeley. Discusses land grant legislation and lists all
Mexican grants in California.

536   Bancroft, Hubert H. California Pastoral. San
      Francisco: The History Co., 1888.
Contains good material on society and economy in the Mexican
period.

537   Bancroft, Hubert Howe. California Pioneer Register and
      Index, 1542-1848. Baltimore, Md.: Regional Publishing
      Co., 1964.
Includes Spanish-Mexican settlers, 1769-1800; taken from
Bancroft's 7 volume History of California.

538   Bandini, Jose. A Description of California in 1828.
      Berkeley, Calif.: Friends of the Bancroft Library,
      1951. Included in item 680.
The work of a member of an important Californio family.

539   Barcena, Jose M. Recuerdos de la invasion
      norteamericana, 1841-1848. Mexico, 1947.
Gives an excellent Mexican perspective on the U.S. invasion

of Mexico and the Mexican War.

540   Barker, Eugene C.   Life of Stephen F. Austin, Founder
      of Texas, 1793-1836.   Nashville, Tenn.: Cokesbury
      Press, 1925.   Reprints, New York: Da Capo Press, 1968;
      Austin: University of Texas Press, 1971.
The standard work on Austin, his colony, and his relations
with the central government in Mexico City.

541   Barker, Eugene C.   Mexico and Texas, 1821-1835.
      Dallas, Tex.: P. L. Turner Co., 1928.   Reprint, New
      York: Russell & Russell, 1965.
Concerns itself with Anglo colonization in Texas and causes
of the Texas revolt in 1835.

542   Bartlett, John R.   Personal Narrative of Exploration
      and Incidents in Texas, New Mexico, California,
      Sonora, and Chihuahua.   2 vols.   Glorieta, N. Mex.:
      Rio Grande Press, 1965.

543   Bauer, K. Jack.   The Mexican War, 1846-1848.   New York:
      Macmillan Co., 1974.
By a specialist in the history of naval warfare; an
extensive bibliography.

544   Bauer, K. Jack.   Surfboats and Horse Marines: U.S.
      Naval Operations in the Mexican War, 1846-1848.
      Annapolis, Md.: United States Naval Institute, 1969.

545   Becker, Robert H.   Diseños of California Ranchos:
      Designs on the Land and Their Makers.   San Francisco:
      Book Club of California, 1969.
An outstanding collection of grant diseños, placed in
geographical and historical context.

546   Benson, Nettie L.   La diputacion provincial y el
      federalismo mexicano.   Mexico, D.F.: El Colegio de
      Mexico, 1955.

547   Berlandier, (Jean) Louis.   Journey to Mexico during the
      Years 1826 to 1834.   Austin: Texana Publishers, 1980.
Berlandier describes Texas frontier life just before
separation from Mexico.   He was a member of the Mexican
northeast border commission in the late 1820s.

548   Bidwell, John.   In California Before the Gold Rush.
      Los Angeles: Ward Ritchie Press, 1948.   Included in
      item 680.
A collection of articles by a pioneer of 1841, which were
published originally in Century Magazine, 1890-1891.

549   Bieber, Ralph P., ed.   Exploring Southwest Trails,
      1846-1854.   Glendale, Calif.: Arthur H. Clark Co.,
      1938.

The journal of the Mormon Battalion march, by Lt. Col. St.
George Cooke, and other journals and diaries.

550   Bieber, Ralph P. and LeRoy R. Hafen, eds. Southwest
        Historical Documents. 9 vols. Philadelphia:
        Porcupine Press, 1973.
A selection covering from 1821 to 1890.

551   Binkley, William Campbell. The Expansionist Movement
        in Texas, 1836-1850. Berkeley: University of
        California Press, 1925.

552   Binkley, William Campbell, ed. Official Correspondence
        of the Texas Revolution, 1835-1836. New York: D.
        Appleton-Century, 1936.

553   Binkley, William Campbell. The Texas Revolution.
        Baton Rouge: Louisiana State University Press, 1952.
A scholarly account of the process leading up to the Texas
revolt in 1835.

554   Bosch Garcia, Carlos. Historia de las relaciones entre
        Mexico y los Estados Unidos, 1819-1848. Mexico,
        D.F.: Universidad Nacional Autonoma de Mexico, 1961.
Interpretation by a modern Mexican historian.

555   Boyd, E. Popular Arts of Spanish New Mexico. Santa
        Fe: Museum of New Mexico Press, 1974.
Especially valuable for arts and crafts during the Mexican
period.

556   Brack, Gene M. Mexico Views Manifest Destiny,
        1821-1846; An Essay on the Origins of the Mexican War.
        Albuquerque: University of New Mexico Press, 1975.
Describes the angry Mexican reaction to aggressive U.S.
manifest destiny on both a popular and official level.

557   Brackett, R. W. A History of the Ranchos. San Diego,
        Calif.: Union Title Insurance and Trust Co., 1939.
Popular history of land development in California during the
Mexican era and beyond.

558   Brayer, Herbert O. Spanish and Mexican Land Grants.
        New York: Arno Press, 1974.
A reprint of four works on land grants in California, New
Mexico, and Colorado.

559   Brewerton, George D. Overland with Kit Carson: A
        Narrative of the Old Spanish Trail in '48. New York:
        Coward-McCann, 1930.

560   Brooks, Nathan C. A Complete History of the Mexican
        War, 1846-1848. Chicago: Rio Grande Press, 1965.

561 Caballeria y Collell, Juan. History of San Bernardino
     Valley: From the Padres to the Pioneers, 1810-1851.
     San Bernardino, Calif.: Times-Index Press, 1902.
     Included in item 680.

562 Callcott, Wilfrid H. Santa Anna: The Story of an
     Enigma Who Once Was Mexico. Norman: University of
     Oklahoma Press, 1936.

563 Canales, Jose T. Bits of Texas History in the Melting
     Pot of America. 2 vols. Brownsville, Tex.: [N.P.],
     1950-1957.
Volume II includes Spanish-Mexican contributions to the
colonization and independence of Texas.

564 Carnes, (Sister) Mary Loyola. The American Occupation
     of New Mexico 1821-1852. Albuquerque: University of
     New Mexico Press, 1939. Reprint, New York: Arno
     Press, 1976.
A sympathetic view of Nuevo Mexicano adjustment to Anglo
infiltration, conquest, and government.

565 Carroll, Horace B. The Texas Santa Fe Trail. Canyon,
     Tex.: Panhandle-Plains Historical Society, 1951.
Gives an account of the ill-fated 1841 Texan Santa Fe
expedition.

566 Carson, Christopher [Kit]. Kit Carson's Own Story as
     Dictated to Colonel and Mrs. D. C. Peters About
     1856-57. Edited by Blanche C. Grant. Taos, N. Mex.:
     [N.P.], 1926. Reprint, Taos, N. Mex.: Kit Carson
     Memorial Foundation, 1955.

567 Carter, Hodding. Doomed Road of Empire; the Spanish
     Trail of Conquest. New York: McGraw-Hill Book Co.,
     1971.
A broad survey of early Texas history; includes material on
Jose Bernardo Gutierrez de Lara.

568 Castañares, Manuel. Coleccion de documentos relativos
     al departamento de California. Mexico, D.F.: Imprenta
     de la Voz del Pueblo, 1845.

569 Castañeda, Carlos E., trans. & ed. The Mexican Side of
     the Texas Revolution (1836), by the Chief Mexican
     Participants. Dallas, Tex.: P. L. Turner Co., 1928 &
     1956. Reprints, Washington, D.C.: Documentary
     Publications, 1971; New York: Arno Press, 1976.
Contains contemporary eyewitness accounts including those of
Santa Anna, Gen. Vicente Filisola, and Gen. Jose Urrea.

570 Castañeda, Carlos E. Our Catholic Heritage in Texas,
     1519-1936. 7 vols. Austin, Tex.: Von Boeckmann-Jones

Co., 1936-1958. Reprint, New York: Arno Press, 1976.
The first six volumes of this panoramic study give a general
history of Texas to 1836. Excellent bibliographies in all
seven volumes.

571   Century of Conflict, 1821-1913. Incidents in the Lives
      of William Neale and William A. Neale, Early Settlers
      in South Texas. Edited by John C. Rayburn and
      Virginia Kemp Rayburn. Waco, Tex.: Texian Press,
      1966. Reprint, New York: Arno Press, 1976.
Reminiscences of Englishman William Neale and his grandson
provide insights on Texas-Mexico border difficulties in the
lower Rio Grande valley.

572   Chabot, Frederick C., ed. The Perote Prisoners: Diary
      of James L. Trueheart. San Antonio, Tex.: Naylor
      Publishing Co., 1934.
Concerns itself with the Texan survivors of the Mier
expedition of 1842.

573   Chamberlain, Samuel E. My Confession. New York:
      Harper Brothers, 1956.
Describes the experiences of an American in the U.S.-Mexican
War. Illustrates anti-Mexican feeling and prejudice.

574   Chidsey, Donald B. The War With Mexico. New York:
      Crown Publishers, 1968.

575   Clarke, Dwight L. Stephen Watts Kearny: Soldier of the
      West. Norman: University of Oklahoma Press, 1961.
Life of Gen. Kearny who took over New Mexico in 1846 and
went on to the conquest of California.

576   Cleland, Robert Glass. This Reckless Breed of Men; The
      Trappers and Fur Traders of the Southwest. New York:
      Alfred A. Knopf, 1950.

577   Colton, Walter. Three Years in California. New York:
      A. S. Barnes, 1854. Reprint, New York: Arno Press,
      1976.
A personal narrative of the 1846 conquest of California and
the ensuing years, by the first U.S. alcalde of Monterey.

578   Conmy, Peter T. A Centennial Evaluation of the Treaty
      of Guadalupe Hidalgo, 1848-1948. Oakland, Calif.:
      Oakland Public Library, 1948.
Gives a resume of what various U.S. historians have said
about the treaty, plus a brief history and description of
the treaty.

579   Conner, Palmer. The Romance of the Ranchos. Los
      Angeles: Title Insurance & Trust Co., 1939.

580   Connor, Seymour V. Adventure in Glory, 1836-1849.
         Austin, Tex.: Steck-Vaughn Co., 1965.
A popular historical account of the Texas revolt and
subsequent republic. Pro-U.S. and sympathetic to President
James Polk in treating the U.S.-Mexican War.

581   Connor, Seymour V. and Odie B. Faulk. North America
         Divided: The Mexican War, 1846-1848. Fair Lawn, N.J.:
         Oxford University Press, 1971.
The authors argue that the war resulted largely from
internal U.S. and Mexican politics.

582   Cooke, Philip St. George. The Conquest of New Mexico
         and California: An Historical and Personal Narrative.
         New York: Putnam, 1878. Reprint, New York: Arno
         Press, 1976.
Provides a most important American account of the U.S.
conquest of the north Mexican frontier.

583   Coulter, Thomas. Notes on Upper California: A Journey
         From Monterey to the Colorado River in 1832. Los
         Angeles: G. Dawson, 1951.

584   Cowan, Robert Granniss. Ranchos of California: A List
         of Spanish Concessions, 1775-1822, and Mexican Grants,
         1822-1846. Fresno, Calif.: Academy Library Guild,
         1956.
Includes maps and other supplementary materials.

585   Cutts, James Madison. The Conquest of California and
         New Mexico, by the Forces of the United States, in the
         Years 1846 and 1847. Albuquerque, N. Mex.: Horn &
         Wallace, 1965.
Includes estimates of the Mexican population of the
Southwest at the time.

586   Dakin, Susanna B. A Scotch Paisano in Old Los Angeles:
         Hugo Reid's Life in California, 1832-1852. Berkeley:
         University of California Press, 1939.
Life of one of the influential foreigners in Mexican
southern California.

587   Dana, Richard H. Two Years Before the Mast. New York:
         H. M. Caldwell Co., 1840. Numerous reprints.
Valuable for Dana's comments on economic and social
conditions in Mexican California.

588   Davis, William Heath. Sixty Years in California. San
         Francisco: A. J. Leary, 1889.
Good for the history and society of the Mexican period, and
beyond.

589   Dawson, Joseph M. Jose Antonio Navarro: Co-Creator of
         Texas. Waco, Tex.: Baylor University Press, 1969.
Biography of an important Tejano figure, a friend of Stephen
Austin.

590   Day, Donald. The Autobiography of Sam Houston.
         Norman: University of Oklahoma Press, 1954.
The role of a principal leader of the Texas revolt.

591   Des Montaignes, François. The Plains . . . North
         Mexico and Northwestern Texas. Edited by Nancy Alpert
         Mower and Don Russell. Norman: University of Oklahoma
         Press, 1972.
Memoranda made in the year 1845.

592   Duffus, Robert L. The Santa Fe Trail. New York:
         Longmans, Green, 1930. Reprint, Albuquerque:
         University of New Mexico Press, 1971.
Covers from the background history in the sixteenth century
to about 1880.

593   Edwards, Frank S. A Campaign in New Mexico with Col.
         Doniphan. Philadelphia: Carey & Hart, 1847. Reprint,
         Ann Arbor, Mich.: University Microfilms, 1966.
Shows anti-Mexican feeling of the times. Edwards was a
volunteer in Doniphan's command.

594   Emory, William H. Notes of a Military Reconnaisance
         from Fort Leavenworth in Missouri to San Diego in
         California. Washington, D.C.: Wendell & Van
         Benthuysen, 1848. Reprinted as part of item 753.
U.S. House of Representatives executive document No. 41,
31st Cong., 1st sess.

595   Ericson, Carolyn R. Nacogdoches-Gateway to Texas: A
         Biographical Directory, 1773-1849. Fort Worth, Tex.:
         Arrow-Curtis Printing Co., 1974.

596   Estergreen, M. Morgan. Kit Carson: A Portrait in
         Courage. Norman: University of Oklahoma Press, 1962.

597   Falconer, Thomas. Expedition to Santa Fe. New
         Orleans, La.: Lumsden, Kendall & Co., 1842.
Falconer was an English traveler and intellectual who went
on the Santa Fe expedition. Twelve pages.

598   Falconer, Thomas. Letters and Notes on the Texas Santa
         Fe Expedition, 1841-1842. Edited by Frederick W.
         Hodge. New York: Dauber & Pine Bookshops, 1930.
         Reprint, Chicago: Rio Grande Press, 1963.

599   Fergusson, Harvey. The Blood of the Conquerors. New
         York: Alfred A. Knopf, 1921. Reprints, New York:

Modern Age Books, 1937; New York: Arno Press, 1976.
A part of the Arno Chicano History series.

600 Fergusson, Harvey. Follwers of the Sun, A Trilogy of
     the Santa Fe Trail. New York: Alfred A. Knopf, 1937.
A popular and romantic view of the history of the Santa Fe
trail.

601 Field, Stephen J. Personal Reminiscences of Early Days
     in California, With Other Sketches. Washington, D.S.:
     [N.P.], 1893.

602 Figueroa, Jose. The Manifesto to the Mexican Republic.
     Oakland, Calif.: Biobooks, 1952. Also published as
     Manifesto to the Mexican Republic, Which Brigadier
     General Jose Figueroa, Commandant and Political Chief
     of Upper California, Presents on His Conduct and on
     That of Jose Maria de Hijar and Jose Maria Padres As
     Directors of Colonization in 1834 and 1835.
     Translated by C. Alan Hutchinson. Berkeley:
     University of California Press, 1978. Included in
     item 680.
Explains purposes and actions of the leaders of a
controversial colonization group in Mexican California.

603 Filisola, Vicente. Memorias para la historia de la
     guerra de Tejas. Mexico: Editora Nacional, S.A.,
     1952.
Reminiscences by one of Santa Anna's leading generals in the
conflict with Texas.

604 Foote, Henry S. Texas and Texans; or Advance of
     Anglo-Americans to the Southwest. 2 vols.
     Philadelphia: Thomas, Cowperthwait & Co., 1841.
Valuable for its contemporary view of the westward movement
and manifest destiny.

605 Francis, Jessie D. An Economic and Social History of
     Mexican California, 1822-1846: Volume I: Chiefly
     Economic. New York: Arno Press, 1976.
A 1935 thesis at the University of California, Berkeley;
extensive bibliography. Paints a realistic picture of
Californio efforts to develop a successful economy and
society.

606 Frazer, Robert W., ed. Over the Chihuahua and Santa Fe
     Trails, 1847-1848: George Rutledge Gibson's Journal.
     Albuquerque: University of New Mexico Press, 1981.
An eyewitness account of the north Mexican frontier by a
soldier in the invading U.S. army. It includes a preface,
notes, and other explanatory materials by the editor.

607   Fremont, John C. Memoirs of My Life. New York &
         Chicago: Belford, Clarke & Co., 1887.
Includes his expedition to Mexican California, 1845-1847,
and his actions there in the Bear Flag Revolt.

608   Fremont, John C. Report of the Exploring Expedition to
         the Rocky Mountains in the Year 1842 and North
         California in the Years 1843-1844. Washington, D.C.:
         Gales & Seaton, Printers, 1845.
This enthusiastic report did much to publicize California in
the Midwest and East.

609   Friend, Llerena B. Sam Houston: The Great Designer.
         Austin: University of Texas Press, 1954.
Biography of an important figure in the Texas revolt and
movement for independence.

610   Fuentes Diaz, Vicente. La intervencion norteamericana
         en Mexico. Mexico, D.F.: Imprenta Nuevo Mundo, 1947.

611   Fuller, John D. P. The Movement for the Acquisition of
         All Mexico, 1846-1848. Baltimore, Md.: Johns Hopkins
         University Press, 1936.

612   Garrard, Lewis H. Wah-To-Yah and the Taos Trail.
         Edited by Ralph P. Bieber. Glendale, Calif.: Arthur
         H. Clark, 1938.

613   Garrison, George P. Texas: A Contest of Civilizations.
         Boston: Houghton Mifflin Co., 1903.
Analyzes the Texas revolt of 1836 as primarily a cultural
conflict.

614   Garrison, Myrtle. Romance and History of California
         Ranchos. San Francisco: Harr Wagner Publishing Co.,
         1935.

615   Geary, (Rev.) Gerald J. The Secularization of the
         Calfiornia Missions. Washington, D.C.: Catholic
         University of America, 1934.
Covers the California missions from 1810 to 1846; emphasizes
secularization and its results.

616   Goetzmann, William H. Army Exploration in the American
         West, 1803-1863. New Haven, Conn.: Yale University
         Press, 1959.
Covers the numerous expeditions from Zebulon Pike to the
Civil War era.

617   Goodwin, Cardinal. John Charles Fremont, an
         Explanation of His Career. Stanford, Calif.: Stanford
         University Press, 1930.

618   Green, (Gen.) Thomas Jefferson. Journal of the Texian
      Expedition Against Mier; Subsequent Imprisonment of
      the Author; His Sufferings, and Final Escape From the
      Castle of Perote. New York: Harper, 1845.
A personal eye-witness account of the ill-fated 1843 Texan
expedition into Mexico.

619   Gregg, Josiah. Commerce of the Prairies. 2 vols.
      Norman: University of Oklahoma Press, 1966.
Includes descriptions of the people, culture, and government
in New Mexico and Chihuahua.

620   Griffin, John S. A Doctor Comes to California; The
      Diary of John S. Griffin, Assistant Surgeon with
      Kearny's Dragoons, 1846-1847. San Francisco:
      California Historical Society, 1943. Included in item
      753.

621   Griffin, John S. Los Angeles in 1849: A Letter from
      John S. Griffin, M.D. to Col. J. D. Stevenson, March
      11, 1849. Los Angeles: [Privately printed], 1949.

622   Grimes, Roy. Goliad: 130 Years After; Refugio and
      Guadalupe, Victoria, March 1836-1966. Victoria, Tex.:
      The Victoria Advocate, 1966.
A popular day by day account in the words of men who were at
these battles.

623   Grivas, Theodore. Military Governments in California,
      1846-1850. Glendale, Calif.: Arthur H. Clark Co.,
      1963.
Covers a critical five years in California's governmental
development.

624   Grow, William M. Spanish and Mexican Land Grants. San
      Francisco: Bancroft-Whitney Co., 1923.

625   Gulick, Charles A. and Katherine Elliot, eds. The
      Papers of Mirabeau B. Lamar. 6 vols. Austin, Tex.:
      A. C. Baldwin & Sons, 1921-1928.
Papers of an early president of the Texas Republic. Vol. I
includes material on Jose Bernardo Gutierrez de Lara.

626   Hafen, LeRoy R. and Ann W. Hafen. Old Spanish Trail:
      Santa Fe to Los Angeles. Glendale, Calif.: Arthur H.
      Clark Co., 1954.
Includes the diary of Antonio Armijo, who pioneered the
trail.

627   Hague, Harlan H. Road to California: The Search for a
      Southern Overland Route, 1540-1848. Glendale, Calif.:
      Arthur H. Clarke Co., 1978.

628   Hall, Frederick. History of San Jose and Surroundings,
         With Biographical Sketches of Early Settlers. San
         Francisco: A. L. Bancroft & Co., 1871.
Shows knowledge of and sympathy for Mexican society in
California.

629   Hammett, Arthur B. J.   The Empresario Don Martin de
         Leon. Waco, Tex.: Texian Press, 1973.
An expansion and revision of the 1971 work; includes
documents and commentary.

630   Hammett, Arthur B. J.   The Empresario Don Martin de
         Leon, the Richest Man in Texas. Kernville, Tex.:
         Braswell Printing Co., 1971.
Account of an important Texas land grant empresario in the
1820s and 1830s.

631   Hammond, George P.   The Larkin Papers. 11 vols.
         Berkeley: University of California Press, 1951-1964.
The papers of the first U.S. consul in Mexican California.

632   Hammond, George P.   The Treaty of Guadalupe Hidalgo,
         February Second, 1848. Berkeley, Calif.: Friends of
         the Bancroft Library, 1949.
The complete text of the treaty plus a long historical essay
on its development and ratification.

633   Hansen, Woodrow J.   The Search for Authority in
         California. Oakland, Calif.: Biobooks, 1960.
Describes mainly political events in Mexican California,
1821 to midcentury--the transition from Spain to Mexico, to
the United States.

634   Harding, George L.   Don Agustin V. Zamorano: Statesman,
         Soldier, Craftsman, and California's First Printer.
         Los Angeles: Zamorano Club, 1934. Reprint, New York:
         Arno Press, 1976.
Biography of the man who was comandante of Monterey
presidio, executive secretary of Alta California, and (1832)
acting governor.

635   Hart, James D.   American Images of Spanish California.
         Berkeley, Calif.: Friends of the Bancroft Library,
         1960.
A brief survey of the writing on Spanish and Mexican
California by 19th century Anglo visitor-writers.

636   Henson, Margaret Swett.   Juan Davis Bradburn: A
         Reappraisal of the Mexican Commander at Anahuac.
         College Station: Texas A & M University Press, 1982.
A revisionist look at the U.S.-born Mexican commander.

637   Hill, Joseph J.   History of Warner's Ranch and its
         Environs.   Los Angeles: [Privately printed], 1927.
The story of an important land grant ranch in southern
California.

638   Hogan, William R.   The Texas Republic: A Social and
         Economic History.   Austin: University of Texas, 1969.

639   Hollon, William E.   The Lost Pathfinder.   Norman:
         University of Oklahoma Press, 1949.
Tells the history of Zebulon Pike's expedition into Mexican
territory, 1806-1807.

640   Hopkins, H. C.   History of San Diego: Its Pueblo Land
         and Water.   San Diego, Calif.: City Printing Co.,
         1929.

641   Hughes, John T.   Doniphan's Expedition, Containing an
         Account of the Conquest of New Mexico.   Cincinnati,
         Ohio: U. P. James, 1847.   Reprint, Washington, D.C.:
         U.S. Government Printing Office, 1914.
Written by a member of Col. Alexander W. Doniphan's command.

642   Hutchinson, Cecil A.   Frontier Settlement in Mexican
         California: The Hijar-Padres Colony and Its Origin,
         1769-1835.   New Haven, Conn.: Yale University Press,
         1969.

643   Hutchinson, Cecil A.   The Mexican Government and the
         Mission Indians of Upper California, 1821-1835.
         Washington, D.C.: Academy of American Franciscan
         History, 1965.

644   James, Thomas.   Three Years Among the Indians and
         Mexicans.   Waterloo, Ill.: Office of the War Eagle,
         1846.   Reprints, Chicago: R. R. Donnelley, 1953; New
         York: Citadel Press, 1967.

645   Jarratt, Rie.   Gutierrez de Lara: Mexican Texan; The
         Story of a Creole Hero.   Austin, Tex.: Creole Texana,
         1949.   Included in item 1145.
Popular biography of a controversial figure on the
U.S.-Texas frontier, 1811-1821.   First governor of Mexican
Texas.

646   Jenkins, John H., ed.   Papers of the Texas Revolution,
         1835-1836.   10 vols.   Austin, Tex.: Presidial Press,
         1973.
An impressive document collection, from various archives.

647   Jimeno Casarin, Manuel.   Jimeno's Index to Land
         Concessions, From 1830 to 1845, and the "Toma de
         Razon," or Registry of Titles for 1844-45, in the

Archives of the Office of the Surveyor General of the
U.S. for California. San Francisco: Lee & Carl, 1858.

648   Johnson, Kenneth M. The Pious Fund. Los Angeles:
      Dawson's Book Shop, 1963.
The fund was established to help finance mission work and
helped support the Alta California missions.

649   Jones, Oakah L., Jr. Santa Anna. New York: Twayne
      Publishers, 1968.
Probably the best biography of the Napoleon of the West in
English.

650   Katz, Harney. Shadow on the Alamo. Garden City, N.Y.:
      Doubleday & Co., 1972.

651   Kendall, George W. Narrative of the Texan Santa Fe
      Expedition. London: Henry Washbourne, 1847. Reprint,
      Chicago: Lakeside Press, 1929.
Account by a New Orleans newsman who accompanied the
expedition in 1841.

652   Kirsch, Robert A. and William S. Murphy. West of the
      West; Witnesses to the California Experience,
      1542-1906. New York: E. P. Dutton & Co., 1967.
Includes material on the Mexican period by contemporaries.

653   Klein, Julius. The Making of the Treaty of Guadalupe
      Hidalgo, February 2, 1848. Berkeley: University of
      California, 1905.

654   LaFarge, Oliver. Santa Fe, Autobiography of a
      Southwest Town. Norman: University of Oklahoma Press,
      1959.

655   Lay, Bennett. The Lives of Ellis P. Bean. Austin:
      University of Texas Press, c.1960.
Includes Bean's role during the 1830s in the Texas revolt,
on the side of the Mexican central government.

656   Lederer, Lillian C. A Study of Anglo-American Settlers
      in Los Angeles County Previous to the Admission of
      California to the Union. San Francisco: R & E
      Research Associates, 1974.
Focuses on prominent settlers fitting into Spanish-Mexican
society; local attitudes toward them.

657   Lewis, Oscar,ed. California in 1846: Described in
      Letters from Thomas O. Larkin, "The Farthest West,"
      E. M. Kern, and "Justice." San Francisco: Grabhorn
      Press, 1934.

658 Lindheim, Milton. The Republic of the Rio Grande:
     Texans in Mexico, 1839-1840. Waco, Tex.: W. M.
     Morrison, 1964.
Has biographical sketches of the leaders, including Juan N.
Seguin and Antonio Canales.

659 Linn, John J. Reminiscences of Fifty Years in Texas.
     New York: D. & J. Sadlier & Co., 1883. Reprint,
     Austin, Tex.: Steck Co., 1935.

660 Livermore, Abiel A. The War with Mexico Reviewed.
     Boston: American Peace Society, 1850. Reprint, New
     York: Arno Press, 1976.
An analysis of the various causes, political, social, and
psychological, of the war.

661 Loomis, Noel M. The Texas-Santa Fe Pioneers. Norman:
     University of Oklahoma Press, 1958.

662 Lord, Walter. A Time to Stand. New York: Harper,
     1961.
A detailed popular history of the Alamo defense by Tejanos
and Anglo Texans.

663 Lowrie, Samuel H. Culture Conflict in Texas,
     1821-1835. New York: Columbia University Press, 1932.
     Reprint, New York: AMS Press, 1967.
Describes Anglo-Mexican conflict, especially over slavery,
as an important causative factor in the Texas revolt.

664 Lozano, Ruben R. Viva Tejas: The Story of the
     Mexican-born Patriots of the Republic of Texas. San
     Antonio, Tex.: San Antonio & Houston Southern Literary
     Institute, 1936.
A fifty-page popular history stressing the importance of
Tejano contributions.

665 Lukes, Edward A. DeWitt Colony of Texas. Austin,
     Tex.: Jenkins Publishing Co., 1976.
Covers the Green DeWitt colony, 1825 to 1836; has an
excellent bibliography.

666 McCutchan, Joseph D. Mier Expedition Diary: A Texan
     Prisoner's Account. Edited by Joseph M. Nance.
     Austin: University of Texas Press, 1978.
A twenty-year old Texan's experience on the Mier expedition
in 1843.

667 McDonald, Archie P. The Mexican War: Crisis for
     American Democracy. Lexington, Mass.: D. C. Heath &
     Co., 1970.

668 McKittrick, Myrtle M. Vallejo, Son of California.
         Portland, Ore.: Binford & Mort, 1944.
Biography of an important northern Californio, Mariano
Vallejo, who helped the early Anglo settlers.

669 McLean, Malcolm D., ed. Leftwich's Grant, 1823-1826.
         Vol. 2. Fort Worth: Texas Christian University Press,
         1975.
Story of an early empresario grant in Texas.

670 McLean, Malcolm D., ed. May Through October 10, 1830,
         Tenoxtitlan, Dream Capital of Texas: Papers Concerning
         Robertson's Colony in Texas. Vol. 4. Arlington:
         University of Texas, 1977.

671 McLean, Malcolm D., ed. The Nashville Colony
         1826-1830. Vol. 3. Fort Worth: Texas Christian
         University Press, 1976.

672 McLean, Malcolm D., ed. The Texas Association,
         1788-1822. Vol. I. Fort Worth: Texas Christian
         University Press, 1974.
Papers regarding the Robertson colony, 1788-1822.

673 McLean, Malcolm D., ed. The Upper Colony. Vol. 5.
         Arlington: University of Texas Press, 1978.
Covers the Robertson colony from Oct. 1830 through March 5,
1831.

674 Magoffin, Susan Shelby. Down the Santa Fe Trail and
         Into Mexico: the Diary of Susan Shelby Magoffin,
         1846-1847. New Haven, Conn.: Yale University Press,
         1962.
Includes materials on the U.S.-Mexican War, as well as
social history of Mexico's northern frontier.

675 Manning, William R. Early Diplomatic Relations Between
         the United States and Mexico. Baltimore: Johns
         Hopkins Press, 1916.
Good for the first two decades of Mexican national
independence.

676 Marti, Werner H. Messenger of Destiny. San Francisco:
         John Howell Books, 1960.
Recounts the activities of Lt. Archibald Gillespie in the
U.S. conquest of California.

677 Martinez, Antonio Jose. Ecsposicion que el Presbitero
         Antonio Jose Martinez, cura de Taos de Nuevo Mexico,
         dirije al Gobierno del Exmo. Sor. General D. Antonio
         Lopez de Santa Ana. Proponiendo la civilisacion de
         las naciones barbaras que son al contorno del
         Departamento de Nuevo Mexico. Taos, N. Mex.: J.M.B.,
         1843. Included in item 694.

678   Maverick, Samuel A. Notes on the Storming of Bexar in
      the Close of 1835. Edited by Frederick Chabot. San
      Antonio, Tex.: Artes Graficas, 1942.

679   Medina Castro, Manuel. El gran despojo: Texas, Nuevo
      Mexico, California. Mexico, D.F.: Editorial Diogenes,
      1971.

680   Mexican California. Anthology with an introduction by
          Carlos E. Cortes. New York: Arno Press, 1976.
Contents: Frances Smith, The Architectural History of
Mission San Carlos Borromeo, California, 1921. Jose
Bandini, A Description of California in 1828, 1951. Thomas
Coulter, Notes on Upper California. A Journey from Monterey
to the Colorado River in 1832, 1951. Jose Figueroa, The
Manifesto to the Mexican Republic, 1952. George Tays,
Governor Mariano Chico's Report to the Mexican Government,
1933. John Bidwell, In California Before the Gold Rush,
1948. William Carey Jones, Report on the Subject of Land
Titles in California, 1850. Juan Caballeria, History of San
Bernardino Valley: From the Padres to the Pioneers, 1902.

681   Miller, Thomas L. The Public Lands of Texas,
          1519-1970. Norman: University of Oklahoma Press,
          1972.
A broad survey of the land question in Texas.

682   Moorhead, Max L. New Mexico's Royal Road; Trade and
          Travel on the Chihuahua Trail. Norman: University of
          Oklahoma Press, 1958.
Based largely on Mexican sources; excellent description of
trade on the northern frontier.

683   Mora, Joseph Jacinto. Californios, the Saga of the
          Hard-Riding Vaqueros, America's First Cowboys. Garden
          City, New York: Doubleday & Co., 1949.
Popular history of the California ranch cattle industry, to
the end of the Mexican period.

684   Morrow, William W. Spanish and Mexican Private Land
          Grants. San Francisco: Bancroft-Whitney Co., 1923.
          Reprinted as part of Spanish and Mexican Land Grants,
          New York: Arno Press, 1974. Item 558.
Covers grants in California, New Mexico, and Colorado.

685   Morton, Ohland. Teran and Texas. Austin, Tex.: Texas
          State Historical Association, 1948.
Manuel Mier y Teran proposed settling Mexicans in Texas in
the 1820s to offset Anglo influence.

686   Moyano Pahissa, Angela. El comercio de Santa Fe y la
          guerra del '47. Mexico, D.F.: Secretaria de Educacion

Publica, 1976.
A Mexican scholar's view of the Santa Fe trade and the war with the United States.

687 Myers, John M. The Alamo. New York: E. P. Dutton & Co., 1948.
A jingoistic journalistic account of the Alamo siege and its background.

688 Nackman, Mark E. A Nation Within a Nation: The Rise of Texas Nationalism. Port Washington, N.Y.: Kennikat Press, 1975.
Covers Anglo Texan and Mexican federalist interaction; a good bibliography.

689 Nance, Joseph M. After San Jacinto: The Texas-Mexican Frontier, 1836-1841. Austin: University of Texas Press, 1963.
Covers an important period and area of continuing conflict with Mexico after Texas independence.

690 Nance, Joseph M. Attack and Counterattack--The Texas-Mexican Frontier, 1842. Austin: University of Texas Press, 1964.

691 Navarro, Jose Antonio. Apuntes historicos interesantes de San Antonio de Bexar. San Antonio, Tex.: Imprenta de A. de Siemering y Cia., 1869.
The views of the Tejano "co-creator of Texas." See item 589.

692 Nevins, Allan. Fremont, the West's Greatest Adventurer. 2 vols. New York: Harpers, 1928.
The standard biography of the Pathfinder and California's first U.S. senator.

693 Newell, Chester. History of the Revolution in Texas, Particularly of the War of 1835-36. New York: Arno Press, 1975.
Reprint of a contemporary (1838) account.

694 Northern Mexico on the Eve of the United States Invasion: Rare Imprints Concerning California, Arizona, New Mexico, and Texas, 1821-1846. Edited with an introduction by David J. Weber. New York: Arno Press, 1976.
Contains: Jean Louis Berlandier, Caza del Oso y Cibolo, en el nor-oeste de Tejas, 1844. Juan N. Almonte, Noticia estadistica sobre Tejas, 1835. Juan N. Seguin, Personal Memoirs of John N. Seguin, 1858. Manuel de Jesus Rada, Proposicion hecha al soberano congreso general de la nacion por el diputado del territorio de Nuevo Mexico, 1829. Antonio Jose Martinez, Esposicion que el presbitero Antonio Jose Martinez . . ., 1843. El Historiador [Antonio Jose

Martinez], Historia consisa del cura de Taos Antonio Jose
Martinez, 1861. Pedro Sanchez, Memorias sobre la vida del
presbitero Don Antonio Jose Martinez, 1903. Ignacio Zuñiga,
Rapida ojeada al estado de Sonora, 1835. Mariano Guadalupe
Vallejo, Ecsposicion que hace el comdanante (sic) general de
la Alta California al gobernador de la misma, 1837. Manuel
Castañares, Coleccion de documentos relativos al
departamento de California, 1845. Manuel Payno, Puerto de
Monterey, Alta California, 1845.

695   Oberste, William H. Texas Irish Empresarios and Their
       Colonies: Power & Hewetson, McMullin & McGloin,
       Refugio-San Patricio. Austin, Tex.:
       Von-Boeckmann-Jones Co., 1953.

696   Oliva, Leo E. Soldiers on the Santa Fe Trail. Norman:
       University of Oklahoma Press, 1967.

697   Olmstead, Virginia L., comp. and trans. New Mexico
       Spanish and Mexican Censuses, 1790-1823-1845.
       Albuquerque, N. Mex.: Geneological Society, 1975.
Includes data on occupations, ages, etc.

698   Ord, Angustias de la Guerra. Occurrences in Hispanic
       California. Translated and edited by Francis Price
       and William H. Ellison. Washington, D.C.: Academy of
       American Franciscan History, 1956.
A contemporary account by a Californiana who married a U.S.
Army doctor.

699   Origins of the Mexican War: A Documentary Sourcebook.
       2 vols. Edited by Ward McAfee and J. Cordell
       Robinson. Salisbury, N.C.: Documentary Publications,
       1982.
A collection of 110 documents showing the darker side of
U.S. westward expansion.

700   Pattie, James O. The Personal Narrative of James O.
       Pattie of Kentucky. Edited by Timothy Fling.
       Chicago: R. R. Donnelley, 1930.
Travels through the Southwest, especially California, in the
mid-1820s.

701   Peña, Jose Enrique de la. With Santa Anna in Texas: A
       Personal Narrative of the Revolution. Translated and
       edited by Carmen Perry. College Station: Texas A & M
       University Press, 1975.
Also available in the original Spanish under the title, La
rebelion de Texas, manuscrito inedito de 1836 por un oficial
de Santa Anna. Salisbury, N.C.: Documentary Publications,
1982.

702   Peña y Reyes, Antonio de la, ed. Algunos documentos
       sobre el tratado de Guadalupe y la situacion de Mexico

durante la invasion americana. Mexico, D.F.:
Secretaria de Relaciones Exteriores, 1930.
A collection of Mexican documents relating to the treaty and
its ratification.

703 Perales, Alonso S. El Mexicano Americano y la politica
del sur de Texas. San Antonio, Tex.: [Artes
Graficas?], 1931.
A brief account of Anglo-Tejano relations over 35 years.

704 Pico, Pio. Don Pio Pico's Historical Narrative.
Edited by Martin Cole and Henry Welcome. Glendale,
Calif.: Arthur H. Clark Co., 1973.
As dictated to Thomas Savage (for H. H. Bancroft) in 1877.
Pico was governor of Mexican California.

705 Pletcher, David M. The Diplomacy of Annexation: Texas,
Oregon, and the Mexican War. Columbia: University of
Missouri Press, 1973.
Probably the best interpretive account of the annexation of
Texas and the causes of the war with Mexico. An impartial
detailed survey of the war's origins which neither condemns
nor justifies the conduct of the two countries.

706 Rada, Manuel de Jesus. Proposicion hecha al soberano
Congreso General de la Nacion por el diputado del
Territorio de Nuevo Mexico (Proposal Made to the
Sovereign General Congress of the Nation by the
Representative From New Mexico). Mexico, D.F.:
Imprenta de C. Alejandro Valdes, 1829.
Concerns the problems on Mexico's northern frontier at the
beginning of independence.

707 Ramirez, Felipe T., ed. Leyes fundamentales de Mexico,
1808-1957. Mexico, D.F.: Editorial Porrua, 1957.
Includes legislation dealing with the Anglo settlements in
Texas.

708 Ramirez, Jose F. Mexico During the War With the United
States. Edited by Walter Scholes. Columbia:
University of Missouri Press, 1950.
Ramirez's letters and documents, originally published in
Mexico in 1905. The author (1804-1871) was an important
historian and politician who participated in the war and
treaty of Guadalupe Hidalgo.

709 Read, Benjamin M. Guerra mexico-americana. Santa Fe,
N. Mex.: Compania Impresora del Nuevo Mexico, 1910.

710 Red, (Rev.) William Stuart. The Texas Colonists and
Religion, 1821-1836. Austin, Tex.: E. L. Shettles,
1924.
Covers Protestant activities in Texas during the period.

711   Reynolds, Matthew G. Spanish and Mexican Land Laws,
       New Spain and Mexico. St. Louis, Mo.: Buxton &
       Skinner, 1895.

712   Rhoades, Elizabeth R. Foreigners in Southern
       California During the Mexican Period. San Francisco:
       R & E Research Asociates, 1971.
A 1924 thesis done at the University of California,
Berkeley.

713   Rippy, J. Fred. Joel R. Poinsett, Versatile American.
       Durham, N.C.: Duke University Press, 1935.
Includes Poinsett's efforts to acquire part of Texas for the
United States.

714   Rives, George L. The United States and Mexico,
       1821-1848. 2 vols. New York: C. Scribner's Sons,
       1913.
Argues that the United States and President James Polk were
guilty of aggressive attitudes and actions against Mexico.

715   Roa Barcena, Jose M. Recuerdos de la invasion
       norteamericana, 1846-1848. 3 vols. Mexico, D.F.: J.
       Buxo y Cia., 1883. Reprint, Mexico, D.F.: Imprenta de
       V. Agüeros, 1901, 1902.
Outstanding account of the U.S.-Mexican War, from the
Mexican viewpoint.

716   Robinson, Alfred. Life in California. New York: Wiley
       & Putnam, 1846. Reprint, New York: De Capo Press,
       1969.
One of several reprints of this well known work. Includes
material on the Indians, missions, Californios, and early
Anglo settlers.

717   Robinson, William W. Land in California: The Story of
       Mission Lands, Ranchos, Squatters, Mining Claims,
       Railroad Grants, Land Scrip and Homesteads. Berkeley:
       University of California Press, 1948; reprint, 1979.
An interesting survey of land history down to the present.
Includes a chapter on the land problems of San Francisco and
Los Angeles.

718   Ross, Calvin. Lieutenant Emory Reports. Albuquerque:
       University of New Mexico Press, 1951; paperback
       reprint, 1968.
Notes on Emory's western reconnaissance in 1846.

719   Salado Alvarez, Victoriano. Como perdimos California y
       salvamos Tehuantepec. Mexico, D.F.: Editorial Jus,
       1968.
Journalistic history written circa 1907 and 1908.

720   Sanchez, Jose M. Viaje a Texas--en 1828-1829, diario
       del Teniente D. Jose Maria Sanchez, miembro de la
       Comision de Limites. Mexico, D.F.: Papeles
       Historicos, 1939.

721   Sanchez, Nellie Van de Grift. Spanish and Indian Place
       Names of California: Their Meaning and Their Romance.
       San Francisco: A. M. Robertson, 1930. Reprint, New
       York: Arno Press, 1976.

722   Sanchez Lamego, Miguel A. The Second Mexican-Texas
       War, 1841-1843. Translated by Joseph Hefter.
       Hillsboro, Tex.: Hill Junior College Press, 1972.
Includes Gen. Adrian Woll's 1842 expedition against San
Antonio and the attempted Texas retaliation against Mier,
Tamaulipas; plus documents.

723   Sanchez Lamego, Miguel A. The Siege and Taking of the
       Alamo. Santa Fe, N. Mex.: Press of the Territorian,
       1968.
Interpretation by a Mexican military historian.

724   Santa Anna, Antonio Lopez de. The Eagle: The
       Autobiography of Santa Anna. Austin, Tex.: Pemberton
       Press, 1967.

725   Santa Anna, Antonio Lopez de. The Mexican Side of the
       Texas Revolution. For full reference see item 569.

726   Santleben, August. A Texas Pioneer. Edited by I. S.
       Affleck. New York: Neale Publishing Co., 1910.
Describes his life as a freighter on the Chihuahua trail.

727   Santos, Richard G. Santa Anna's Campaign Against
       Texas, 1835-1836; Featuring the Field Commands Issued
       to Major General Vicente Filisola. Waco, Tex.: Texian
       Press, 1968. 2nd ed., rev. Salisbury, N.C.:
       Documentary Publications, 1982.
Field commands of Antonio Lopez de Santa Anna to General
Vicente Filisola, with comments and explanation by the
editor.

728   Schroeder, John H. Mr. Polk's War: American Opposition
       and Dissent, 1846-1848. Madison: University of
       Wisconsin Press, 1973.
Stresses the widespread (early) unpopularity of the war in
the United States.

729   Seguin, Juan Nepomuceno. Personal Memoirs of John N.
       Seguin, From the Year 1834 to the Retreat of General
       Woll from the City of San Antonio, 1842. San Antonio,
       Tex.: Ledger Book & Job Office, 1858. Included in
       item 694.

Seguin, a friend of Stephen Austin, recounts his
difficulties after Texas independence.

730 Sellers, Charles Grier. James K. Polk, Continentalist,
     1843-1846. Princeton, N.J.: Princeton University
     Press, 1966.
Vol. II of Polk's biography covers the years leading up to
the U.S.-Mexican War.

731 Shumate, Albert. Francisco Pacheco of Pacheco Pass.
     Stockton, Calif.: University of the Pacific, 1977.
Biography of a member of an important Californio landowning
family.

732 Sibley, George Champlain. The Road to Santa Fe: The
     Journal and Diaries of George Champlain Sibley and
     Others Pertaining to the Surveying and Marking of a
     Road From the Missouri Frontier to the Settlements of
     New Mexico, 1825-1827. Edited by Kate L. Gregg.
     Albuquerque: University of New Mexico Press, 1952.

733 Sibley, Marilyn McAdams. Travelers in Texas,
     1761-1860. Austin: University of Texas Press, 1967.

734 Smith, George W. and Charles Judah. Chronicles of the
     Gringos: The U.S. Army in the Mexican War, 1846-1848.
     Albuquerque: University of New Mexico, 1968.

735 Smith, Justin H. The Annexation of Texas. New York:
     Baker and Taylor Co., 1911. Reprint, New York: Barnes
     & Noble, 1941.

736 Smith, Justin H. The War With Mexico. 2 vols. New
     York: Macmillan Co., 1919. Reprint, Gloucester,
     Mass.: Peter Smith, 1963.
Defends President Polk's actions and blames Mexican vanity
and pride as causes of the war. Includes over 400 pages of
documentation.

737 Stephenson, Nathaniel W. Texas and the Mexican War.
     New Haven, Conn.: Yale University Press, 1920.
     Reprint, New York: United States Publishing
     Association, 1971.
A monograph in the Chronicle of America series.

738 Stapp, William P. The Prisoners of Perote: Containing
     a Journal Kept by the Author, Who Was Captured by the
     Mexicans at Mier, December 25, 1842, and Released from
     Perote, May 15, 1844. Philadelphia: G. B. Zieber,
     1845. Reprint, Austin: University of Texas Press,
     1977.

739 Sutter, Johann A. New Helvetia Diary: A Record of
     Events Kept by John A. Sutter and His Clerks at New

Helvetia, California From September 9, 1845 to May 25,
1848. San Francisco: Grabhorn Press, 1939.

740   Talbot, Theodore. Soldier in the West; Letters of
      Theodore Talbot During His Services in California,
      Mexico, and Oregon, 1845-53. Edited by Robert V. Hine
      and Savoie Lottinville. Norman: University of
      Oklahoma Press, 1972.
Talbot was a member of the 1843 Fremont expedition.

741   Thompson, Joseph A., O.F.M. El Gran Capitan: Jose de
      la Guerra. Los Angeles: Cabrera & Sons, 1961.
The life of a prominent Santa Barbara Californio who was a
rival to Gov. Luis Argüello.

742   Tinkle, Lon. Alamo. New York: New American Library,
      1967. Original title: Thirteen Days to Glory; the
      Siege of the Alamo. New York: McGraw-Hill Book Co.,
      1958.
A popular historical account of the Mexican victory at the
Alamo.

743   Tinnery, Thomas D. Mexican War Diary of Thomas D.
      Tinnery. Edited by D. E. Livingston-Little. Norman:
      University of Oklahoma Press, 1970.

744   Tolbert, Frank X. The Day of San Jacinto. New York:
      McGraw-Hill Book Co., 1959. Reprint, Austin, Tex.:
      Pemberton Press, 1969.

745   Tompkins, Walker A. Old Spanish Santa Barbara; From
      Cabrillo to Fremont. Santa Barbara, Calif.: McNally &
      Loftin, 1979.

746   Tompkins, Walker A. Santa Barbara's Royal Rancho.
      Berkeley, Calif.: Howell-North, 1960.

747   Treaties and Other International Acts of the United
      States of America. Edited by Hunter Miller.
      Washington, D.C.: U.S. Government Printing Office,
      1931-1948.
Vol. V contains the Treaty of Guadalupe Hidalgo with part of
its history. Vol. VI includes the Gadsden Treaty and its
history.

748   Trueba, Alfonso. California, tierra perdida. Mexico,
      D.F.: Editorial Jus, 1958.

749   Twitchell, Ralph Emerson. The Conquest of Santa Fe,
      1846. Truchas, N. Mex.: Tate Gallery, 1967.
Has details of the U.S. conquest and occuption of New
Mexico, 1845-1848.

750   Twitchell, Ralph Emerson. The History of the Military
      Occupation of the Territory of New Mexico, From 1846
      to 1851 by the Government of the United States
      Together With Biographical Sketches of Men Prominent
      in the Conduct of the Government of That Period.
      Denver, Colo.: The Smith-Brooks Co., 1909. Reprints,
      Chicago: Rio Grande Press, 1963; New York: Arno Press,
      1976.
A U.S. view of the conquest and the Taos revolt; with
eighteen short biographies of prominent Anglos and Nuevo
Mexicanos.

751   Ulibarri, Richard O. American Interest in the Spanish
      Southwest, 1803-1848. San Francisco: R & E Research
      Associates, 1974.
Includes discussion of manifest destiny and racism.

752   Underhill, Reuben L. From Cowhides to Golden Fleece.
      2nd ed. Stanford, Calif.: Stanford University Press,
      1946.
Covers California from 1832 to 1858; based on U.S. Consul
Thomas Larkin's correspondence.

753   The United States Conquest of California. Anthology of
      primary sources with an introduction by Carlos E.
      Cortes. New York: Arno Press, 1976.
Contains Oscar Lewis, ed., California in 1846, 1934; William
H. Emory, Notes of a Military Reconnaissance, from Fort
Leavenworth in Missouri, to San Diego, in California, 1848;
and John S. Griffen, A Doctor Comes to California: The Diary
of John S. Griffin, Assistant Surgeon with Kearny's
Dragoons, 1846-1847, 1943.

754   Valades, Jose C. Mexico, Santa Anna y la guerra de
      Texas. Mexico, D.F.: Editores Mexicanos Unidos, 1965.
Account of the Texas revolt by an important Mexican
historian.

755   Vallejo, Mariano Guadalupe. Ecsposicion que hace el
      Comdanante [sic] General de la Alta California al
      Gobernador de la misma. Sonoma, Calif.: [Privately
      printed], 1837.
Also included in item 694.

756   Van Nostrand, Jeanne. A Pictorial and Narrative
      History of Monterey, Adobe Capital of California,
      1770-1847. San Francisco: California Historical
      Society, 1968.

757   Vazquez de Knauth, Josefina. Mexicanos y
      norteamericanos ante la guerra del 47. Mexico, D.F.:
      Secretaria de Educacion Publica, 1972.
A recent work on the causes of the U.S.-Mexican War by an

important modern Mexican historian.

758 Vestal, Stanley. The Old Santa Fe Trail. Boston:
      Houghton Mifflin Co., 1939.
A popular historical account of the development of the Santa
Fe trail.

759 Vigness, David Martell. The Revolutionary Decades;
      1810-1836. Austin, Tex.: Steck-Vaughn Co., 1965.
Covers Texas history during the independence movement and
under Mexican rule. Includes maps.

760 Webb, James J. Adventures in the Santa Fe Trade,
      1844-1847. Glendale, Calif.: Arthur H. Clark Co.,
      1931.

761 Weber, David J., comp. The Extranjeros: Selected
      Documents From the Mexican Side of the Santa Fe Trail,
      1825-1828. Santa Fe, N. Mex.: Stagecoach Press, 1967.
Includes a brief but excellent history of New Mexico to
1848.

762 Weber, David J. The Mexican Frontier, 1821-1846: The
      American Southwest Under Mexico. Albuquerque:
      University of New Mexico Press, 1982.
A comprehensive view of the borderlands frontier from a
Mexican perspective. Includes an excellent bibliographical
essay, pp. 377-407.

763 Weber, David J., ed. Northern Mexico on the Eve of the
      United States Invasion: Rare Imprints Concerning
      California, Arizona, New Mexico, and Texas, 1821-1846.
      New York: Arno Press, 1976.
Includes items 706, 729 and 755.

764 Weber, David J. The Taos Trappers: The Fur Trade in
      the Far Southwest, 1540-1846. Norman: University of
      Oklahoma Press, 1971. Reissued in paperback, 1980.
Includes material on the impact of Anglo fur traders on
Spanish-Mexican economy and society.

765 Weems, John E. To Conquer a Peace: The War Between the
      U.S. and Mexico. Garden City, N.Y.: Doubleday & Co.,
      1974.

766 Weinberg, Albert K. Manifest Destiny. Chicago:
      Quadrangle Books, 1963.

767 White, Joseph. A New Collection of the Laws . . . of
      Mexico and Texas. Philadelphia: T. & J. W. Johnson,
      1839.

768   White, Michael C. California All the Way Back to 1828.
        Los Angeles: Dawson's Book Shop, 1956.
Reminiscences of White as taken down by Thomas Savage for
H. H. Bancroft, 1877.

769   Williams, Amelia W. and Eugene C. Barker, eds. The
        Writings of Sam Houston, 1813-1863. 8 vols. Austin:
        University of Texas Press, 1938-1943.
Documents of one of the top leaders in the Texas revolt and
independence movement.

770   Wilson, Iris H. William Wolfskill (1798-1866):
        Frontier Trapper to California Ranchero. Glendale,
        Calif.: Arthur H. Clark Co., 1965.

771   Wishart, David J. The Fur Trade of the American West,
        1807-1840: A Geographical Synthesis. Lincoln:
        University of Nebraska Press, 1979.
Good for early American penetration of Mexico's northern
frontier region.

772   Woodman, David, Jr. Guide to Texas Emigrants. Boston:
        M. Hawes, 1835.
Pamphlets issued by the Galveston Bay and Texas Land Company
which controlled the Zavala, Burnet, and Vehlein grants.

773   Woodward, Arthur. Lances at San Pascual. San
        Francisco: California Historical Society, 1948.
Describes the 1846 battle in which Californios defeated U.S.
forces under Stephen W. Kearny.

774   Wright, Doris M. A Yankee in Mexican California: Abel
        Stearns, 1798-1848. Santa Barbara, Calif.: W.
        Hebberd, 1977.
Stearns, who became an influential merchant and rancher,
reached California in the middle years of the Mexican
period.

775   Zollinger, James P. Sutter, the Man and His Empire.
        New York: Oxford University Press, 1939.

II : Theses and Dissertations

776   Alexander, Gladys M.   "The Position of Texas in the
      Relations Between the United States and Mexico."
      Master's thesis. Denton: North Texas State
      University, 1942.

777   Baker, George Towne, III.   "An Exposition Addressed to
      the Supreme Government by the Commissioners who Signed
      the Treaty of Peace with the U.S." Master's thesis.
      Fullerton: California State University, 1966.
Gives the Mexican reasons for accepting the Treaty of
Guadalupe Hidalgo.

778   Barker, Bernice.   "The Texas Expedition to the Rio
      Grande in 1842." Master's thesis. Austin: University
      of Texas, 1929.
Describes part of the continuing Texas-Mexican conflict
after Texas independence, the Meir expedition.

779   Berge, Dennis E.   "Mexican Response to United States'
      Expansionism, 1841-1848." Berkeley: University of
      California, 1965.

780   Bloomquist, Leonard.   "California in Transition . . .,
      1830-1850." Master's thesis. Berkeley: University of
      California, 1943.
Covers mission secularization, the development of ranching,
and the changes from Mexican to American political
institutions.

781   Bork, Albert.   "Nuevos aspectos del comercio entre
      Nuevo Mexico y Misuri, 1822-1846." Mexico, D.F.:
      Universidad Nacional Autonoma de Mexico, 1944.
A Mexican perspective on the Santa Fe trade.

782   Bromilow, Jessie.   "Don Pio de Jesus Pico." Master's
      thesis. Los Angeles: University of Southern
      California, 1931.
Describes the public life of Pico as landowner, cattleman,
and politician, 1801-1848.

783   Brown, Lee F.   "The Explorer, the United States
      Government and the Approaches to Santa Fe . . ."
      Chicago: Loyola University, 1972.

784   Brown, Thomas A.   "An Episode in United States Foreign
      Trade: Silver and Gold, Santa Fe and St. Louis,
      1820-1840." Muncie, Ind.: Ball State University,
      1974.

785   Cason, Ina Wilson.   "The Bent Brothers on the
         Frontier." Master's thesis. Albuquerque: University
         of New Mexico, 1939.
Describes the extraordinary role of Charles Bent and his
brothers on the U.S. southwestern frontier in the late
Mexican period.

786   Cassidy, Joseph E.   "Life and Times of Pablo de la
         Guerra, 1819-1874." Santa Barbara: University of
         California, 1977.
Pablo de la Guerra owned a large ranch in northern
California; later he was elected state senator.

787   Childers, Laurence.   "Education in California under
         Spain and Mexico, and under American Rule to 1851."
         Master's thesis. Berkeley: University of California,
         1930.
Covers mission and other schools and the decline of mission
schools under Mexican rule.

788   Cottrell, Dorothy.   "Texas Reprisals Against New Mexico
         in 1843." Master's thesis. Albuquerque: University
         of New Mexico, 1934.
Gives details of the continuing conflict between the
Republic of Texas and Mexican New Mexico as a result of the
Texan Santa Fe expedition.

789   Crisp, James E.   "Anglo-Texan Attitudes Toward the
         Mexican, 1821-1845." New Haven, Conn.: Yale
         University, 1976.

790   Cunningham, Robert E.   "James Treat and his Mission to
         Mexico." Master's thesis. Austin: University of
         Texas, 1950.
Includes conditions in Texas and Mexico; covers Treat's
mission to Mexico in 1839 and his involvement in Texas
affairs.

791   Downs, Fane.   "The History of Mexicans in Texas,
         1820-1845." Lubbock: Texas Technological University,
         1970.
Discusses cooperation between Anglo and Mexican Texans.

792   Estep, Raymond.   "The Life of Lorenzo de Zavala."
         Austin: University of Texas, 1942.
Has material on Zavala's empresario colony in Texas and his
role as a Mexican federalist.

793   Farrand, Andrew.   "Cultural Dissonance in
         Mexican-American Relations: Ethnic, Racial, and
         Cultural Images and the Coming of War, 1846." Santa
         Barbara: University of California, 1979.

794   Faugsted, George, Jr.   "The Chilenos in the California
       Gold Rush." Master's thesis. Santa Clara, Calif.:
       University of Santa Clara, 1963.

795   Florstedt, Robert F. "The Liberal Role of Jose Maria
       Luis Mora in the Early History of Independent
       Mexico." Austin: University of Texas, 1950.
One of the leading early 19th century Mexican liberal
reformers, Mora was concerned with secularization of the
missions.

796   Fritz, Naomi. "Jose Antonio Navarro." Master's
       thesis. San Antonio, Tex.: St. Mary's University,
       1941.
Tells the life of the "co-creator of the Texas Republic."

797   Gant, N. A. "A History of Texas Boundary Disputes."
       Master's thesis. Greeley: University of Northern
       Colorado, 1930.

798   Gomez, Fernando Chacon. "The Intended and Actual
       Effect of Article VIII of the Treaty of Guadalupe
       Hidalgo: Mexican Rights Under International and
       Domestic Law." Ann Arbor: University of Michigan,
       1977.

799   Graebner, Norman. "The Treaty of Guadalupe Hidalgo:
       Its Background and Formation." Chicago: University of
       Chicago, 1950.
Presents an American viewpoint, largely to the exclusion of
Mexican attitudes and views.

800   Gutierrez, Ramon. "Marriage, Sex and the Family:
       Social Change in Colonial New Mexico, 1690-1846."
       Madison: University of Wisconsin, 1980.
Sees considerable changes in Nuevo Mexicano society during
the Mexican period, 1821-1846.

801   Hinojosa, Gilbert M. "Settlers and Sojourners in the
       'Chaparral': A Demographic Study of a Borderlands Town
       in Transition, Laredo, 1775-1870." Austin: University
       of Texas, 1979.

802   Hruneni, George A. "The Diplomatic Mission of Joel
       Roberts Poinsett to Mexico." Master's thesis. Santa
       Clara, Calif.: University of Santa Clara, 1967.
Describes the early years of U.S.-Mexican antagonism in the
1820s.

803   Jones, Frances S. "Diplomacy--Rio Grande, 1842-1848."
       Master's thesis. San Antonio, Tex.: St. Mary's
       University, 1938.

804   Lawrence, Eleanor. "The Old Spanish Trail from Santa
         Fe to California." Master's thesis. Berkeley:
         University of California, 1930.
Describes the opening and use of the trail, 1832-1848, its
conditions, and decline.

805   Leonard, Glen M. "Western Boundary-making: Texas and
         the Mexican Cession, 1844-1850." Salt Lake City:
         University of Utah, 1970.

806   Luce, W. Ray. "Samuel Brannan, Speculator in Mexican
         Lands." Master's thesis. Provo, Utah: Brigham Young
         University, 1968.
Discusses the role of a prominent Mormon settler in
California lands.

807   McGrath, (Sister) Paul of the Cross. "Political
         Nativism in Texas, 1825-1860." Washington, D.C.:
         Catholic University of America, 1930.

808   McKee, James Reese. "Kit Carson: Man of Fact and
         Fiction." St. Louis, Mo.: St. Louis University, 1977.

809   McReynolds, James M. "Family Life in a Borderland
         Community: Nacogdoches, Texas, 1779-1861." Lubbock:
         Texas Technological University, 1978.

810   Meldrum, George Weston. "The History of the Treatment
         of Foreign and Minority Groups in California
         1830-1860." Stanford, Calif.: Stanford University,
         1949.
Covers the policies of the Mexican and United States
governments toward foreigners, and their treatment.

811   Miles, Robert. "An Examination of Article II of the
         Treaty of Guadalupe Hidalgo." Master's thesis. El
         Paso: University of Texas, 1972.
Article II deals with the reestablishment of constitutional
government in areas occupied by the U.S. forces.

812   Miller, Mervyn. "A History of the Secularization of
         the Missions of California." Master's thesis.
         Stockton, Calif.: College of the Pacific, 1932.
Describes the opening of mission lands to private ownership.

813   Milligan, James C. "Jose Bernardo Gutierrez de Lara,
         Mexican Frontiersman, 1811-1841." Lubbock: Texas
         Technological University, 1975.
The activities of a fascinating figure in the history of the
Texas-Tamaulipas frontier.

814   Minge, Ward A. "Frontier Problems in New Mexico
         Preceding the Mexican War, 1840-1846." Albuquerque:

University of New Mexico, 1965.
Contains much material on the role of Governor Manuel
Armijo.

815   Moore, Richard.   "The Role of the Baron de Bastrop in
        the Anglo-American Settlement of the Spanish
        Southwest." Master's thesis. Austin: University of
        Texas, 1932.
Concerns the critical role of the baron in the Stephen
Austin colony in Texas.

816   Morrison, Raymond.   "Luis Antonio Argüello, First
        Mexican Governor of California." Master's thesis.
        Los Angeles: University of Southern California, 1938.
Gives a brief biography of Argüello as explorer, soldier,
etc., 1784-1830.

817   Palm, Rufus A., Jr.   "New Mexico Schools from
        1581-1846." Master's thesis. Albuquerque: University
        of New Mexico, 1930.

818   Parraga. Charlotte M. N.   "Santa Fe de Nuevo Mexico: A
        Study of a Frontier City Based on an Annotated
        Translation of Selected Documents (1825-1832) from the
        Mexican Archives of New Mexico." Muncie, Ind.: Ball
        State University, 1976.

819   Pilant, James.   "Guadalupe Hidalgo: Article X and the
        Protocol." Master's thesis. Santa Clara, Calif.:
        University of Santa Clara, 1971.
An investigation of the U.S. Senate reaction to the Treaty.

820   Robins, Jerry D.   "Juan Seguin." Master's thesis. San
        Marcos: Southwest Texas State University, 1962.
Gives an excellent account of Seguin's role in the early
development of Anglo settlement in Texas.

821   Sandoval, David A.   "Trade and the 'Manito' Society in
        New Mexico, 1821-1848." Salt Lake City: University of
        Utah, 1978.

822   Smith, Marian.   "Pio Pico, Ranchero and Politician."
        Master's thesis. Berkeley: University of California,
        1928.
Biography 1801-1845, emphasizes his role as a rancher,
revolutionary leader, and governor.

823   Tatum, Inez.   "Mexican Missions in Texas." Master's
        thesis. Waco, Tex.: Baylor University, 1938.

824   Taylor, Margery.   "A Study of the Attitudes of
        Anglo-American Immigrants to Texas 1820-1835."
        Master's thesis. Abilene, Tex.: Hardin-Simmons
        University, 1963.

825   Tays, George. "Revolutionary California: The Political
      History of the Mexican Period, 1822-1846." Berkeley:
      University of California, 1932.
A detailed study of the disorder and unrest which brought on
the decline of missions and trade.

826   Tijerina, Andrew A. "Tejanos and Texas: The Native
      Mexicans of Texas, 1820-1850." Austin: University of
      Texas, 1977.

827   Tyler, Daniel. "New Mexico in the 1820's: The First
      Administration of Manuel Armijo." Albuquerque:
      University of New Mexico, 1970.

828   Urbina, Manuel, II. "The Impact of the Texas
      Revolution on the Government, Politics, and Society of
      Mexico, 1836-1846." Austin: University of Texas,
      1976.

829   Valle, Rosemary Keupper. "Medicine and Health in Alta
      California Missions, 1769-1833, as Examplified by a
      Study of Mission Santa Clara de Asis." San Francisco:
      University of California, 1973.

830   Vigness, David Martell. "The Lower Rio Grande Valley,
      1836-1846." Master's thesis. Austin: University of
      Texas, 1948.

831   Vigness, David Martell. "The Republic of the Rio
      Grande: An Example of Separatism in Northern Mexico."
      Austin: University of Texas, 1951.
Investigates the important role of federalism on the Mexican
northeastern frontier.

832   Vincent, Gwendolyn M. "The Runaway Scrape of the Texas
      Revolution: The Return and Effect on the
      Participants." Master's thesis. Abilene, Tex.:
      Hardin-Simmons University, 1976.

833   Welch, Vernon E. "Las Vegas and the Adjacent Area
      During the Mexican Period." Master's thesis. Las
      Vegas: New Mexico Highlands University, 1950.
Early history of the New Mexican area east of Santa Fe.

834   Werne, Joseph R. "Guadalupe Hidalgo and the Mesilla
      Controversy." Kent, Ohio: Kent State University,
      1972.

III: Periodicals

835   Aguirre, Yjinio F. "Echoes of the Conquistadores:
      Stock Raising in Spanish-Mexican Times." Journal of
      Arizona History 16 (Autumn 1975), 267-286.

836   Almaraz, Felix D., Jr. "Aspects of Mexican Texas: A
      Focal Point in Southwestern History." Red River
      Valley Historical Review 2:3 (Fall 1975), 363-379.

837   Almaraz, Felix D., Jr. "Governor Antonio Martinez and
      Mexican Independence in Texas: An Orderly Transition."
      Permian Historical Annual 15 (1975), 45-54.

838   Almaraz, Felix D., Jr. "Historical Origin of the
      Mexican in Texas: An Interpretation." Austin: Office
      of Bilingual and International Education, Texas
      Education Agency, 1968.

839   Almonte, Juan Nepomuceno. "Statistical Report on Texas
      [1835]." Translated by Carlos E. Castañeda.
      Southwestern Historical Quarterly 28 (1924-1925),
      177-222.
Almonte was appointed member of an 1834 commission to
establish the Texas-Louisiana boundary. See item 529.

840   Atherton, Lewis E. "Disorganizing Effects of the
      Mexican War on the Santa Fe Trade." Kansas Historical
      Quarterly 6 (1937), 115-123.

841   Aubury, Samuel E. "The Private Journal of Juan
      Nepomuceno Almonte, February 1-April 16, 1836."
      Southwestern Historical Quarterly 48 (1944), 10-32.
Almonte took part in the Mexican government's effort to
defeat the Texas rebels, fighting both at the Alamo and at
San Jacinto.

842   Bacarisse, Charles A. "The Union of Coahuila and
      Texas." Southwestern Historical Quarterly 61 (Jan.
      1958), 341-349.
Discusses this issue so important to Anglo and Mexican
Texans in the 1820s.

843   Barker, Eugene C. "Land Speculation as a Cause of the
      Texas Revolution." Texas Historical Association
      Quarterly 10:1 (July 1906), 76-95.
Includes a discussion of the land laws and grants of
1834-1835.

844   Barker, Eugene C. "Native Latin American Contributions
      to the Colonization and Independence of Texas."
      Southwestern Historical Quarterly 46 (Jan. 1943),
      317-335.

845   Barton, Henry W.   "The Anglo-American Colonists Under
      Mexican Militia Laws." Southwestern Historical
      Quarterly 65 (July 1961), 61-71.

846   Berge, Dennis E.   "A Mexico Dilemma: The Mexico City
      Ayuntamiento and the Question of Loyalty, 1846-1848."
      Hispanic American Historical Review 50 (May 1970),
      229-256.
The problems of government under U.S. military control.

847   Berger, Max.   "Education in Texas During the Spanish
      and Mexican Periods." Southwestern Historical
      Quarterly 51 (July 1947), 41-53.

848   Bidwell, John.   "Life in California Before the Gold
      Discovery." Century 41:2 [new series, 19] (Dec.
      1890), 163-183.
Bidwell entered California in 1841 as a leader of the first
organized U.S. immigrant group.

849   Bieber, Ralph P.   "The Southwestern Trails to
      California in 1849." Mississippi Valley Historical
      Review 12 (1925), 342-375.

850   Binkley, William Campbell.   "New Mexico and the
      Texan-Santa Fe Expedition." Southwestern Historical
      Quarterly 27 (1923), 85-107.

851   Bloom, John Porter.   "New Mexico Viewed by
      Anglo-Americans, 1846-1849." New Mexico Historical
      Review 34:3 (July 1959), 165-198.

852   Bloom, (Rev.) Lansing B.   "The Chihuahua Highway." New
      Mexico Historical Review 12 (1937), 209-216.

853   Bloom, (Rev.) Lansing B.   "The Governors of New
      Mexico." New Mexico Historical Review 10:2 (April
      1935), 152-157.

854   Bloom, (Rev.) Lansing B.   "Ledgers of a Santa Fe
      Trader." El Palacio 14 (1923), 133-136.
The ledgers of merchant Manuel Alvarez.

855   Bloom, (Rev.) Lansing B.   "New Mexico Under Mexican
      Administration, 1821-1846." Old Santa Fe 1:1-4 (July
      1913-April 1914), 3-49, 131-175, 235-287, 347-368;
      2:1-4 (July 1914-April 1915), 3-56, 119-169, 223-277,
      351-380.

856   Brack, Gene M.   "Mexican Opinion, American Racism, and
      the War of 1846." Western Historical Quarterly 1:2
      (April 1970), 161-174.

857   Brack, Gene M.   "Mexican Opinion and the Texas
        Revolution." Southwestern Historical Quarterly 72:2
        (Oct. 1968), 170-182.

858   Broadhead, G. C. "The Santa Fe Trail." Missouri
        Historical Review 4 (1909-1910), 309-319.

859   Brown, Dee. "Along the Santa Fe Trail." American
        History Illustrated 15:6 (Oct. 1980), 8-13.
Covers the history of the trail until about 1880.

860   Burton, Estelle Bennett. "The Taos Rebellion." Old
        Santa Fe 1:2 (Oct. 1913), 176-209.
Argues that there is no historical evidence that Fr. Antonio
Martinez took an active part in the revolt.

861   Coalson, George O. "Texas Mexicans in the Texas
        Revolution." In The American West: Essays in Honor of
        W. Eugene Hollon. Edited by Ronald Lora. Toledo,
        Ohio: University of Toldeo, 1981.

862   Connor, Seymour V. "Attitudes and Opinions About the
        Mexican War, 1846-1970." Journal of the West 11
        (April 1972), 361-366.

863   Cox, Isaac Joslin. "Education Efforts in San Fernando
        de Bexar." Southwestern Historical Quarterly 6 (July
        1902), 27-63.
An excellent survey of the education of Tejanos.

864   Cox, Isaac Joslin. "The Louisiana-Texas Frontier."
        Texas Historical Association Quarterly 10:1 (July
        1906), 1-75.

865   Cox, Isaac Joslin. "Opening the Santa Fe Trail."
        Missouri Historical Review 25 (Oct. 1930), 30-66.

866   Crampton, C. Gregory. "Utah's Spanish Trail." Utah
        Historical Quarterly 47:4 (Fall 1979), 361-383.
Highlights the Utah part of the Old Spanish Trail from Santa
Fe to Los Angeles.

867   Cuello, Jose. "Beyond the 'Borderlands' is the North
        of Colonial Mexico: A Latin-Americanist Perspective to
        the Study of the Mexican North and the United States
        Southwest." Proceedings of the Pacific Coast Council
        on Latin American Studies 9 (1982), 1-24.
Defines the complex nature of Borderlands history and
describes some of its historiography.

868   "Efficient Yanqui Empresarios and the Colonizing of
        Texas." Life 46 (April 20, 1959), 82-83.

869   Estep, Raymond. "Lorenzo de Zavala and the Texas
       Revolution." Southwestern Historical Quarterly 58
       (Jan. 1954), 322-335.
Excellent for relations between the Anglo Texans and Mexican
federalists.

870   Fremont, John C. "Conquest of California." Century 19
       (1890-1891), 917-928.

871   Garrison, George P., ed. "The Prison Journal of
       Stephen F. Austin." Texas Historical Association
       Quarterly 2 (Jan. 1899), 183-210.
Written while he was imprisoned in Mexico City in 1834.

872   Gates, Paul W. "California's Embattled Settlers."
       California Historical Quarterly 41 (June 1962),
       99-130.
Refers to a number of Anglo recipients of Mexican land
grants; views the land issue from the Anglo settlers
viewpoint.

873   Gates, Paul W. "Carpetbaggers Join the Rush for
       California Land." California Historical Quarterly 56
       (Summer 1977), 98-127.

874   Gates, Paul W. "The Fremont-Jones Scramble for
       California Land Claims." Southern California
       Quarterly 56 (Spring 1974), 13-44.

875   Gates, Paul W. "The Land Business of Thomas O.
       Larkin." California Historical Quarterly 54 (Winter
       1975), 323-344.

876   Gates, Paul W. "Public Land Disposal in California."
       Agricultural History 49 (Jan. 1975), 158-178.

877   Goetzmann, William H. "The United States-Mexican
       Boundary Survey, 1848-1853." Southwestern Historical
       Quarterly 62 (1958-1959), 164-190.

878   Goodrich, James W. "Revolt at Mora, 1847." New Mexico
       Historical Review 47:1 (Jan. 1972), 49-60.
A part of the Taos revolt in New Mexico after U.S. takeover.

879   Graebner, Norman A. "The Mexican War: A Study in
       Causation." Pacific Historical Review 49 (August
       1980), 405-426.

880   Graf, LeRoy P. "Colonizing Projects in Texas South of
       the Nueces, 1820-1845." Southwestern Historical
       Quarterly 50 (April 1947), 431-448.
Explains why the efforts were unsuccessful in this critical
northeastern Mexican area.

881   Greenleaf, Cameron and Andrew Wallace. "Tucson:
        Pueblo, Presidio, and American City: A Synopsis of its
        History." Arizoniana 3:2 (Summer 1962), 18-27.
A brief general history of Tucson down to 1887.

882   Griswold del Castillo, Richard. "The Del Valle Family
        and the Fantasy Heritage." California History 59
        (Spring 1980), 2-15.
Describes the mostly 19th century history of Ventura County
Del Valle family and especially of Reginaldo del Valle.

883   Hafen, LeRoy R., ed. "[Antonio] Armijo's Journal of
        1829-30: The Beginning of Trade Between New Mexico and
        California." Colorado Magazine 27 (April 1950),
        120-131.

884   Hafen, LeRoy R. "Mexican Land Grants in Colorado."
        Colorado Magazine 4 (May 1927), 71-93.

885   Hale, Charles A. "The War With the United States and
        the Crisis in Mexican Thought." The Americas 14
        (1957), 153-173.

886   Haley, J. Evetts. "The Comanchero Trade."
        Southwestern Historical Quarterly 38 (Jan. 1935),
        157-176.
Describes the largely illegal trade between Mexican and
Anglo traders and the southern plains Indians.

887   Haley, J. Evetts. "Pastores del Palo Duro." Southwest
        Review 19 (1933-1934), 279-294.
Describes cattlemen and sheepherder conflicts.

888   Hall, G. Emlen. "Juan Estevan Pino, 'se los coma': New
        Mexico Land Speculation in the 1820s." New Mexico
        Historical Review 57:1 (Jan. 1982), 27-42.
Concerns lands in northern New Mexico.

890   Handman, Max S. "San Antonio: The Old Capital City of
        Mexican Life and Influence." Survey 66 (May 1931),
        163-166.

891   Hawgood, John A. "The Pattern of Yankee Infiltration
        into Mexican Alta California, 1821-1846." Pacific
        Historical Review 27 (Feb. 1958), 27-37.
Discusses the differences between pre- and post-1840
immigrants from the U.S.

892   Henderson, Mary V. "The Iturbide Revolution in the
        Californias." Hispanic American Historical Review 2:2
        (1919), 188-242.
Describes the impact of Mexican independence on Alta and
Baja California.

893   Henderson, Mary V. "Minor Empresario Contracts for the
         Colonization of Texas, 1825-1834." Southwestern
         Historical Quarterly 31 (April 1928), 295-324; 32
         (July 1928), 1-28.
Covers twenty-four minor empresario contracts.

894   Hornbeck, David, Jr. "Land Tenure and Rancho Expansion
         in Alta California, 1784-1846." Journal of Historical
         Geography 4:4 (Oct. 1978), 371-390.
Includes maps.

895   Hutchinson, C. Alan. "General Jose Antonio Mexia and
         His Texas Interests." Southwestern Historical
         Quarterly 82 (Oct. 1978), 117-142.
Mexia was a Mexican federalist and empresario with Lorenzo
de Zavala.

896   Hutchinson, C. Alan. "Mexican Federalists in New
         Orleans and the Texas Revolution." The Americas 14
         (1957), 1-47.

897   Hutchinson, C. Alan. "The Mexican Government and the
         Mission Indians of Upper California, 1821-1835". The
         Americas 21 (1965), 335-362.

898   Huth, Tom. "Echoes Along the Santa Fe Trail."
         Historic Preservation 32:2 (Mar.-Apr. 1980), 36-43.
A brief history of the trade along the trail.

899   Johnson, Kenneth M. "Baja California and the Treaty of
         Guadalupe Hidalgo." Journal of the West 11 (April
         1972), 328-347.

900   Kelly, Edith L. and Mattie A. Hatcher, eds. "Tadeo
         Ortiz de Ayala and the Colonization of Texas,
         1822-1833." Southwestern Historical Quarterly 32:1
         (July 1928), 74-86; 32:2 (Oct. 1928), 152-164; 32:3
         (Jan. 1929), 222-251; 32:4 (April 1929), 311-343.

901   Kluck, Frederick and Sandra Beyer. "A French Account
         of the Texan-Santa Fe Expedition." Greater Llano
         Estacado Southwest Heritage 10:3-4 (Fall-Winter
         1980-1981), 4-8.

902   Labadie, Nicholas D. "Let Us Attack the Enemy and Give
         Them Hell." American West 5:3 (May 1968), 26-34.
Eyewitness account of the battle of San Jacinto.

903   Lambert, Paul F. "The Movement for the Acquisition of
         All Mexico." Journal of the West 11 (April 1972),
         317-327.
Describes the various factions in the United States
supporting or opposing the movement.

904 Langum, David J. "Californios and the Image of
     Indolence." Western Historical Quarterly 9:2 (April
     1978), 181-196.

905 Laumbach, Verna. "Las Vegas Before 1850." New Mexico
     Historical Review 8 (Oct. 1933), 241-264.

906 Lavender, David. "The Mexican War: Climax of Manifest
     Destiny." American West 5:3 (May 1968), 50-64.

907 Lawrence, Eleanor F. "Mexican Trade Between Santa Fe
     and Los Angeles, 1830-1848." California Historical
     Society Quarterly 10:1 (March 1931), 27-39.
A brief history of trade via the Old Spanish Trail.

908 Lecompte, Janet S. "The Independent Women of Hispanic
     New Mexico, 1821-1846." Western Historical Quarterly
     12:1 (Jan. 1981), 17-35.
Contrasts the image from court records with Anglo
stereotypes of Nuevo Mexicanas as dominated and passive.

909 Lecompte, Janet S. "Manuel Armijo and the Americans."
     Journal of the West 19:3 (July 1980), 51-63.
The relations of New Mexican governor Armijo with Anglo
traders, trappers, and settlers. Controverts George
Kendall's biased view of Armijo; presents him as a
responsible and able official.

910 Lecompte, Janet S. "Manuel Armijo's Family History."
     New Mexico Historical Review 48 (July 1973), 251-258.

911 Lord, Walter. "Myths and Realities of the Alamo."
     American West 5:3 (May 1968), 18-25.

912 Lyon, Fern. "The First Gold Rush in the West." New
     Mexico Magazine 58:2 (Feb. 1980), 24-27, 43-45.
Describes a rush to Dolores Spring south of Santa Fe in
1829.

913 Maciel, David R. "Comments on North America Divided:
     The Mexican War, 1846-1848." Aztlan 2:2 (Fall 1971),
     173-177.
Argues that the war still needs an unbiased scholarly
interpretation, rejecting the book's thesis that blame for
the war lay on both sides equally. See item 581.

914 McLemore, S. Dale. "The Origins of Mexican American
     Subordination in Texas." Social Science Quarterly 53
     (March 1973), 656-670.

915 McMurtrie, Douglas C. "The History of Early Printing
     in New Mexico." New Mexico Historical Review 4 (Oct.

1929), 372-409.
Covers 1834-1860; includes the Abreu-Martinez press.

916 McMurtrie, Douglas C. "El Payo de Nuevo Mejico." New
       Mexico Historical Review 8:2 (April 1933), 130-138.
A Nuevo Mexico newspaper of 1845.

917 McWilliam, Perry. "The Alamo Story: From Fact to
       Fable." Journal of the Folklore Institute 15:3
       (Sept.-Dec. 1978), 221-233.
A revisionist debunking of Alamo myth.

918 Mahood, Ruth. "The Coronel Collection." Los Angeles
       County Museum Quarterly 14 (Autumn 1958), 4-7.
Antonio Coronel was an important southern Californio leader.

919 Marshall, Thomas Maitland. "Commercial Aspects of the
       Texas-Santa Fe Expedition." Southwestern Historical
       Quarterly 20 (1917), 242-259.

920 Martinez, L. Pascual. "Rev. Antonio Jose Martinez."
       LULAC News 5 (Sept. 1938), 3-6.

921 Mawn, Geoffrey P. "Framework for Destiny: San Franisco
       1847." California Historical Quarterly 51 (Summer
       1972), 165-178.
Land in San Francisco, especially laying out of streets.

922 Mawn, Geoffrey P. "A Land Guarantee: The Treaty of
       Guadalupe Hidalgo or the Protocol of Queretaro."
       Journal of the West 14 (Oct. 1975), 49-63.
Discusses an enduring controversy about interpretation of
the treaty.

923 May, Florence. "The Penitentes." Natural History 38
       (Dec. 1936), 435-438.
Describes the various practices of the Penitentes,
especially during Holy Week. Includes two photographs.

924 Miller, Thomas L. "Mexican Texans at the Alamo."
       Journal of Mexican American History 2 (Fall 1971),
       33-44.
Deals primarily with Texas land warrants given to families
of the Tejanos who fought at the Alamo.

925 Miller, Thomas L. "Mexican Texans in the Texas
       Revolution." Journal of Mexican American History 3
       (1973), 105-130.
Basically a list with brief information about each person.

926 Moore, Ike H. "The Earliest Printing and First
       Newspaper in Texas." Southwestern Historical

Quarterly 39:2 (Oct. 1935), 83-99.

927 Moore, R. Woods. "The Role of the Baron de Bastrop in
     the Anglo-American Settlement of the Spanish
     Southwest." Louisiana Historical Quarterly 31 (July
     1948), 606-681.
The baron was extremely important in the Anglo movement into
Texas.

928 Moorehead, Max L. "Notes and Documents [Mexican Report
     of the American Invasion of New Mexico]." New Mexico
     Historical Review 26 (Jan. 1951), 68-82.

929 Moorehead, Max L. "Spanish Transportation in the
     Southwest, 1540-1846." New Mexico Historical Review
     32 (1957), 107-122.

930 Morrison, Raymond K. "Luis Antonio Argüello: First
     Mexican Governor of California." Journal of the West
     2 (April & July 1963), 193-204, 347-361.

931 Morton, Ohland. "Life of General Don Manuel de Mier y
     Teran as it Affected Texas-Mexican Relations."
     Southwestern Historical Quarterly 47 (July 1943),
     29-47; (Oct. 1943), 120-142; (Jan. 1944), 257-267; 48
     (July 1944), 51-66; (Oct. 1944), 193-218; (April
     1945), 499-546.
Mier y Teran was sent to study the Texas situation after the
Fredonia revolt of 1826.

932 Murphy, Lawrence R. "The Beaubien and Miranda Land
     Grant, 1841-1846." New Mexico Historical Review 42
     (Jan. 1967), 27-47.
The early history of the land grant that later became the
controversial Maxwell Land Grant.

933 Nackman, Mark E. "Anglo-American Migrants to the West:
     Men of Broken Fortunes: The Case of Texas, 1821-1846."
     Western Historical Quarterly 5:4 (Oct. 1974), 441-455.

934 Noggle, Burl. "Anglo Observers of the Southwest
     Borderlands, 1825-1890: The Rise of a Concept."
     Arizona and the West 1 (1959), 105-131.

935 Northrop, Marie E., ed. "The Los Angeles Padron of
     1844." Historical Society of Southern California
     Quarterly 42 (1960), 360-417.

936 Nostrand, Richard L. "Mexican Americans Circa 1850."
     Association of American Geographers Annals 65 (1975),
     378-390.

937 Oates, Stephen B. "Los Diablos Tejanos: The Texas
     Rangers in the Mexican War." Journal of the West 9:4

(Oct. 1970), 487-504.

938   Officer, James E.   "A Note on the Elias Family of
      Tucson."   Arizona and the West 1 (Winter 1959),
      378-380.

939   Ogden, Adele.   "Hides and Tallow: McCullock, Hartnell,
      and Company, 1822-1828."   California Historical
      Society Quarterly 6 (Sept. 1927), 254-265.
Describes the early years of the trade that became the
backbone of the Mexican Alta California economy.

940   Perrigo, Lynn I., trans.   "New Mexico in the Mexican
      Period as Revealed in the Torres Documents."   New
      Mexico Historical Review 29 (Jan. 1954), 28-40.

941   Presley, James.   "Santa Anna in Texas: A Mexican
      Viewpoint."   Southwestern Historical Quarterly 62:4
      (April 1959), 489-512.

942   Rather, Ethel Z.   "DeWitt's Colony."   Texas Historical
      Association Quarterly 8 (Oct. 1904), 95-102.
A description of one of the more important Anglo empresario
groups in Texas.

943   Reeve, Frank D., ed.   "The Charles Bent Papers."   New
      Mexico Historical Review 29:3 (July 1954), 234-239;
      31:3 (July 1956), 251-253.

944   Reeves, Jesse S.   "The Treaty of Guadalupe-Hidalgo."
      American Historical Review 10 (1904-1905), 309-324.
Focuses on Nicholas P. Trist's role in developing the
treaty.

945   Reynolds, Curtis R.   "The Deterioration of
      Mexican-American Diplomatic Relations, 1833-1845."
      Journal of the West 11 (April 1972), 213-224.

946   Rivera, Feliciano.   "A Chicano View of the Treaty of
      Guadalupe Hidalgo."   In Minorities in California
      History.   Edited by George E. Frakes and Curtis B.
      Solberg, pp. 41-42.   New York: Random House, 1971.
Argues that the treaty guarantees cultural as well as
religious and civil rights.

947   Robinson, Cecil.   "Flag of Illusion; the Texas
      Revolution Viewed as a Conflict of Cultures."
      American West 5:3 (May 1968), 10-17.

948   Romero, Cecil V., ed.   "Apologia of Presbyter Antonio
      J. Martinez."   New Mexico Historical Review 3:4 (Oct.
      1928), 325-346.

949   Ruiz, Ramon E. and Mario T. Garcia.   "Conquest and
        Annexation."   The New Scholar 7:1&2 (1978), 237-254.

950   Sanchez, Armand J. and Roland M. Wagner.   "Continuity
        and Change in the Mayfair Barrios of East San Jose."
        San Jose Studies 5:2 (May 1979), 6-20.
Outlines the early history of San Jose, California.

951   Sanchez, Jose Maria.   "A Trip to Texas in 1828."
        Southwestern Historical Quarterly 29 (April 1926),
        249-288.
Translated by Carlos E. Castañeda.   Sanchez was a member of
the boundary commission sent to Texas.

952   Servin, Manuel P.   "The Secularization of the
        California Missions: A Reappraisal."   Southern
        California Quarterly 47 (June 1965), 133-149.
Counters the pro-Fransiscan interpretation of most
historians--but mildly.

953   Southwestern Historical Quarterly 37:1-4 (July
        1933-April 1934).
The entire volume is devoted to a study of the siege of the
Alamo and its defenders.

954   Stoller, M. L.   "Grants of Desperation, Lands of
        Speculation: Mexican Period Land Grants in Colorado."
        Journal of the West 19 (July 1980), 22-39.
Centers on grants to Gervasio Nolan, the Beaubiens,
Guadalupe Mirande and Ceran St. Vrain.

955   Sully, John M.   "The Story of the Santa Rita Mine."
        Old Santa Fe 3 (April 1916), 133-149.
Useful for study of the New Mexican economy during the
Mexican period.

956   Tays, George, ed.   "Pio Pico's Correspondence with the
        Mexican Government, 1846-1848."   California Historical
        Society Quarterly 13 (June 1934), 99-149.
Relations of the last Mexican governor of Alta California
and Mexico City.

957   Timmons, W. H.   "The El Paso Area in the Mexican
        Period, 1821-1848."   Southwestern Historical Quarterly
        84 (July 1980), 1-28.

958   Townley, John M.   "El Placer: A New Mexico Mining Boom
        Before 1846."   Journal of the West 10 (June 1971),
        102-115.

959   Trulio, Beverly.   "Anglo-American Attitudes Toward New
        Mexico Women."   Journal of the West 12 (April 1973),
        229-239.

960   Tyler, Daniel. "Anglo-American Penetration of the
         Southwest: The View from New Mexico." Southwestern
         Historical Quarterly 75 (Jan. 1972), 325-338.
Ties in the events in Texas to attitudes and views of Nuevo
Mexicanos.

961   Tyler, Daniel. "Governor Armijo and the Tejanos."
         Journal of the West 12 (Oct. 1973), 589-599.
Argues that Manuel Armijo stirred up anti-Texan feeling to
make Nuevo Mexicanos forget his sometimes arbitrary rule.

962   Tyler, Daniel. "Governor Armijo's Moment of Truth."
         Journal of the West 11:2 (April 1972), 307-316.
Discusses the question of Manuel Armijo's failure to fight
the invading U.S. forces in 1846 and concludes it probably
resulted from his desire for self-preservation rather than
bribery.

963   Tyler, Daniel. "Gringo Views of Governor Manuel
         Armijo." New Mexico Historical Review 45 (Jan. 1970),
         23-46.

964   Tyler, Daniel. "The Mexican Teacher." Red River
         Valley Historical Review 1 (Fall 1974), 207-211.
Brief but good for education in the Southwest during the
Mexican era.

965   Tyler, Daniel. "The Personal Property of Manuel
         Armijo, 1829." El Palacio 80 (Fall 1974), 45-58.

966   Vallejo, Mariano Guadalupe. "Ranch and Mission Days in
         Alta California." Century 41:2 [new series 19] (Dec.
         1890), 183-192.

967   Van Hook, Joseph O. "Mexican Land Grants in the
         Arkansas Valley." Southwestern Historical Quarterly
         40:1 (July 1936), 58-75.

968   Walter, Paul A. Jr. "The First Civil Governor of New
         Mexico Under the Stars and Stripes." New Mexico
         Historical Review 8 (1933), 98-129.

969   Weber, David J. "American Westward Expansion and the
         Breakdown of Relations Between 'pobladores' and
         'indios barbaros' on Mexico's Far Northern Frontier,
         1821-1846." New Mexico Historical Review 56:3 (July
         1981), 221-238.
Argues that weapons and new markets led to the decline of
relations within the north Mexican frontier.

970   Weber, David J. "Failure of a Frontier Institution:
         The Secular Church in the Borderlands under
         Independent Mexico, 1821-1846." Western Historical

Quarterly 12:2 (Apr. 1981), 125-143.

971   Weber, David J.   "Mexico and the Mountain Men,
      1821-1828." Journal of the West 8:3 (July 1969),
      369-378.

972   Weber, David J., ed. and trans.   "An Unforgettable Day:
      Facundo Melgares on Independence." New Mexico
      Historical Review 48 (Jan. 1973), 27-44.

973   Wetmore, Alphonso.   "Santa Fe Trade and Santa Fe
      Trail." Missouri Historical Review 8 (1914), 177-197.

974   Wilcox, Sebron S.   "Laredo During the Texas Republic."
      Southwestern Historical Quarterly 42 (October 1938),
      83-107.
Laredo remained a Mexican town outside the control of the
Texas Republic.

975   Williams, Amelia.   "A Critical Study of the Siege of
      the Alamo and of the Personnel of its Defenders."
      Southwestern Historical Quarterly 37 (July 1933),
      1-44.

976   Williams, Amelia.   "Siege of the Alamo." Southwestern
      Historical Quarterly 36:4 (April 1933), 251-287.

977   Wollenberg, Charles.   "Ethnic Experiences in California
      History: An Impressionistic Survey." California
      Historical Quarterly 50 (Sept. 1971), 221-233.
Places the Mexican experience in the context of the broader
immigrant experience.

978   Woodward, Arthur, ed.   "Benjamin David Wilson's
      Observations on Early Days in California and New
      Mexico." Historical Society of Southern California
      Annual Publication 16 (1934), 74-150.

979   Young, Otis E.   "The Spanish Tradition in Gold and
      Silver Mining. Arizona and the West 7 (Winter 1965),
      299-314.
An excellent description of early mining technology.

IV.
GUADALUPE HIDALGO
TO 1900

Books

   This section, on the second half of the nineteenth
century, is especially concerned with the Penitentes of New
Mexico, an organization which became a religious and
political focal point in this period, with general histories
of the Texas Rangers, with rancho histories and land grant
problems, and with materials on Anglo ascendency in the
Southwest. While some land grant materials appear in other
sections, particularly the colonial and Mexican periods, the
bulk of them are in Section IV because of the overwhelming
importance that validation of grants assumed during this
time period. This section also includes some important
general works on "scientific racism," which affected
attitudes towards Mexican Americans even though it was
directed primarily at Blacks.

980 Adams, Emma H. To and Fro in Southern California; With
     Sketches in Arizona and New Mexico. Cincinnati, Ohio:
     W. M. B. C. Press, 1887. Reprint, New York: Arno
     Press, 1976.
Originally these sketches of Mexican American life derived
from a series of letters to various eastern newspapers.

981 Alianza Federal de las Mercedes. Spanish Land Grant
     Question Examined. Albuquerque, N. Mex.: [Privately
     printed] 1966.
Focuses on communal grants in northern New Mexico. Included
in item 1223.

982 Arizona, Historical Records Survey. The 1864 Census of
     the Territory of Arizona. Phoenix: Historical Records
     Survey, 1938.
Gives vital statistics from the 1864 territorial census;
includes many Mexicans who were incorporated into the United

983 Arnold, Elliott. The Time of the Gringo. New York:
     Alfred A. Knopf, 1953.

984 Ashbaugh, Carolyn. Lucy Parsons. Chicago: Kerr
     Publishing Co., 1976.
The life of Lucia Gonzalez Parsons, wife of one of the
Haymarket Square (1886) anarchist scapegoats, who was very
active in the U.S. labor movement in the late 1800s.

985 Baca, Manuel C. de. Historia de Vicente Silva, sus
     cuarenta bandidos, sus crimenes y retribuciones. Las
     Vegas, N. Mex.: La Voz del Pueblo, 1896.
Silva was a well-known New Mexican bandit in the late 1800s.

986 Baca, Manuel C. de. Vicente Silva and His Forty
     Bandits. Translated by Lane Kauffmann. Washington,
     D.C.: E. McLean, 1947.
Translation of Baca's 1896 work.   Item 985.

987 Barrera, Mario. Race and Class in the Southwest: A
     Theory of Racial Inequality. Notre Dame, Ind.:
     University of Notre Dame Press, 1979.
Interpretation of a modern Chicano scholar.

988 Barret, O. D. The Mora Grant of New Mexico.
     Washington, D.C.: R. O. Polkinhorn & Son, 1884.

989 Barrows, Henry D. The Lugo Family of California. Los
     Angeles: Historical Society of Southern California,
     1914.
Land problems of an important southern Californio family.
Included in item 1147.

990 Bartlett, John R. Personal Narrative of Explorations
     and Incidents in Texas, New Mexico, California,
     Sonora, and Chihuahua, Connected with the United
     States and Mexican Boundary Commission, During the
     Years 1850, '51, '52, and '53. 2 vols. New York: D.
     Appleton & Co., 1854. Reprint, Chicago: Rio Grande
     Press, 1965.

991 Bell, Horace. On the Old West Coast: Being Further
     Reminiscences of a Ranger, Major Horace Bell. Edited
     by Lanier Bartlett. New York: William Morrow & Co.,
     1930. Reprint, New York: Arno Press, 1976.
Good for California customs and social life post-Guadalupe
Hidalgo. Describes the decline of Californio society.

992 Bell, Horace. Reminiscences of a Ranger; Or Early
     Times in Southern California. Los Angeles: Yarnell,
     Caystite & Mathes, 1881. Reprint, Santa Barbara,
     Calif.: W. Hebberd, 1927.
Southern California in the 1850s to 1880s.

993   Bender, Averam B. The March of Empire: Frontier
       Defense in the Southwest, 1848-1860. Lawrence:
       University of Kansas Press, 1952. Reprint, New York:
       Greenwood Press, 1968.
A 1932 doctoral dissertation at Washington University, St.
Louis, Mo. Includes an extensive bibliography.

994   Bidwell, John. Echoes of the Past About California.
       New York: Clark Boardman Co., 1928.

995   Bowman, Lynn. Los Angeles, Epic of a City. Berkeley,
       Calif.: Howell-North Books, 1974.
Includes an eleven-page bibliography.

996   Brackett, R. W. The History of San Diego County
       Ranchos. 5th ed. San Diego, Calif.: Union Title
       Insurance Co., 1960.

997   Brackett, R. W. A History of the Ranchos; the Spanish,
       Mexican, and American Occupation of San Diego County
       and the Story of the Ownership of the Land Grants
       Therein. San Diego, Calif.: W.P.A. Federal Writers
       Project, 1939.

998   Braddy, Haldeen. Mexico and the Old Southwest. Port
       Washington, N.Y.: Kennikat Press, 1971.
A chatty, episodic, journalistic history of the border
region.

999   Bradfute, Richard Wells. The Court of Private Land
       Claims. The Adjudication of Spanish and Mexican Land
       Titles, 1891-1904. Albuquerque: University of New
       Mexico Press, 1975.
An excellent survey of the Court's work in New Mexico,
Colorado, and Arizona.

1000   Brayer, Herbert O. William Blackmore: The
       Spanish-Mexican Land Grants of New Mexico and
       Colorado, 1863-1878. 2 vols. Denver, Colo.: Bradford
       Robinson Printing Co., 1949.
Probably the most detailed land grant history.

1001   Brent, Joseph Lancaster. The Lugo Case: A Personal
       Experience. New Orleans, La.: Searcy & Pfaff, 1926.
A prominent Californio family's land problems.

1002   Brewer, William H. Up and Down California in
       1860-1864. 3rd ed. Berkeley: University of
       California Press, 1966.

1003   Browne, John R. Adventures in the Apache Country.
       New York: Harper & Bros., 1868. Reprint, Tucson:

University of Arizona Press, 1974.

1004   Browne, John R. A Tour Through Arizona, 1864, or
        Adventures in the Apache Country. Tucson: Arizona
        Silhouttes, 1950.
A reprint of Adventures in the Apache Country.

1005   Burns, Walter N. The Robin Hood of El Dorado. New
        York: Coward-McCann, 1932.
Historical romance based on the Joaquin Murieta story.

1006   Caballeria y Collell, Juan. History of the City of
        Santa Barbara, California, From Its Discovery to Our
        Own Day. Translated by Edmund Burke. Santa Barbara,
        Calif.: F. de P. Gutierrez, 1892.

1007   Cabeza de Baca, Fabiola. We Fed Them Cactus.
        Albuquerque: University of New Mexico Press, 1954.
        Also in item 1663.
Tales of the "old days," 1848-1910.

1008   The California Outlaw: Tiburcio Vasquez. Compiled by
        Robert Greenwood. Los Gatos, Calif.: Talisman Press,
        1960. Reprint, New York: Arno Press, 1974.
Life of the famous Californio outlaw, often portrayed as an
example of social banditry. Includes a contemporary account
by George Beers.

1009   Camarillo, Alberto. Chicanos in a Changing Society:
        From Mexican Pueblos to American Barrios in Santa
        Barbara and Southern California, 1848-1930.
        Cambridge, Mass.: Harvard University Press, 1979.
Principally the history of Santa Barbara's Mexican
community. A slight expansion of the author's 1975 thesis,
Los Angeles: University of California.

1010   Canales, Jose T., ed. Bits of Texas History in the
        Melting Pot of America. 2 vols. Brownsville, Tex.:
        [N.P.], 1950-1957.

1011   Canales, Jose T. Juan N. Cortina Presents His Motion
        for a New Trial. San Antonio, Tex.: Artes Graficas,
        1951.

1012   Carson, James H. Early Recollection of the Mines, and
        a Description of the Great Tulare Valley. Stockton,
        Calif.: Published to accompany the steamer edition of
        the "San Joaquin Republican," 1852.

1013   Castillo, Pedro and Alberto Camarillo, eds. Furia y
        Muerte: Los Bandidos Chicanos. Los Angeles: Chicano
        Studies Center, University of California, 1973.
A study in social banditry.

1014   Caughey, John Walton. Gold is the Cornerstone.
        Berkeley: University of California Press, 1948.
        Republished with new title: The California Gold Rush.
        Berkeley: University of California Press, 1975.

1015   Chandler, Alfred N. Land Title Origins, A Tale of
        Force and Fraud. New York: Robert Schalkenbach
        Foundation, 1945.

1016   Chase, Allan. The Legacy of Malthus: The Social Costs
        of Scientific Racism. New York: Alfred A. Knopf,
        1977.
An excellent broad account of the myths and the reality of
racism.

1017   Chavez, Angelico. But Time and Chance: The Story of
        Padre Martinez of Taos, 1793-1867. Santa Fe, N. Mex.:
        Sunstone Press, 1981.
Biography of Antonio Jose Martinez whose life spanned the
Spanish, Mexican, and American eras. A corrective to the
views of Paul Horgan, item 1103.

1018   Clappe, Louise A. (Smith). The Shirley Letters from
        the California Mines. New York: Alfred A. Knopf,
        1949.
Has interesting material on Sonorans in the gold rush.

1019   Cleland, Robert Glass. The Cattle on a Thousand
        Hills: Southern California, 1850-1870. San Marino,
        Calif.: Huntington Library, 1941; 2nd ed. (to 1880),
        1951; reprinted, 1964.
Includes the American-Mexican cultural conflict in addition
to economic and social development. The land grant problem.

1020   Cleland, Robert Glass. The Irving Ranch of Orange
        County, 1810-1950. San Marino, Calif.: Huntington
        Library, 1952.
Traces the history of the ranch from its land grant
beginnings.

1021   Clendenen, Clarence C. Blood on the Border: The
        United States Army and the Mexican Irregulars. New
        York: Macmillan Co., 1969.
Has material on Juan N. Cortina and Francisco Villa.

1022   Coe, Wilbur. Ranch on the Ruidoso; the Story of a
        Pioneer Family in New Mexico, 1871-1968. New York:
        Alfred A. Knopf, 1968.

1023   Cook, James H. Fifty Years on the Old Frontier.
        Norman: University of Oklahoma Press, 1957.
Includes material on the Nuevo Mexicano figure, Elfego Baca.

1024   Cookridge, E. H. [Edward Spiro.] The Baron of
       Arizona. New York: John Day Co., 1967.
Relates the history of James Addison Reavis' fraudulent land
claim.

1025   Cosio Villegas, Daniel. The United States versus
       Porfirio Diaz. Lincoln: University of Nebraska Press,
       1963.
An excellent coverage of border problems by the late giant
of Mexican historians.

1026   Cosulich, Bernice. Tucson. Tucson: Arizona
       Silhouettes, 1953.
The history of a frontier border town.

1027   Coy, Owen Cochran. Gold Days. Los Angeles: Powell
       Publishing Co., 1929.
A history of the California gold discoveries and conflict in
the mines; bibliography.

1028   Crichton, Kyle S. Law and Order Ltd.: The Rousing
       Life of Elfego Baca of New Mexico. Santa Fe: New
       Mexican Publishing Corp., 1928. Reprint, New York:
       Arno Press, 1974.
Written from Baca's recollections and with his
collaboration.

1029   Crocchiola, Stanley F. L. [pseud. F. Stanley]. The
       Civil War in New Mexico. Denver, Colo.: World Press,
       1960.
Emphasizes the New Mexican volunteers and has a list of
them--overwhelmingly Mexican Americans.

1030   Crocchiola, Stanley F. L. Desperados of New Mexico.
       Denver, Colo.: World Press, 1953.

1031   Crocchiola, Stanley F. L. Giant in Lilliput: The
       Story of Donaciano Vigil. Pampa, Tex.: Pampa Print
       Shop, 1963.
The life of an important Nuevo Mexicano political leader who
spanned the Mexican and U.S. periods.

1032   Crocchiola, Stanley F. L. The Grant That Maxwell
       Bought. Denver, Colo.: World Press, 1952.

1033   Crosby, Elisha O. Memoirs of Elisha O. Crosby:
       Reminiscences of California and Guatemala from 1849 to
       1864. San Marino, Calif.: Huntington Library, 1945.

1034   Cue Canovas, Agustin. Los Estados Unidos y el Mexico
       olvidado. Mexico, D.F.: B. Costa-Amic, 1970.
       Reprint, New York: Arno Press, 1976.
A study of the Treaty of Guadalupe Hidalgo and the postwar
loss of land by Mexican Americans, by a prominent Mexican

historian.

1035   Dale, Edward E. The Range Cattle Industry; Ranching
        on the Great Plains From 1865-1925. Norman:
        University of Oklahoma Press, 1960.

1036   Dana, Juan F. Blond Ranchero. Los Angeles: Dawson's
        Book Shop, 1960.
Recollections of a Santa Barbara rancher whose mother was a
Carrillo.

1037   Dana, Samuel T. and Myron Krueger. California Lands.
        Narbeth, Pa.: Livingston Publishing Co., 1958.

1038   Darley, (Rev.) Alexander M. The Passionists of the
        Southwest; Or, the Holy Brotherhood. A Revelation of
        the Penitentes. Pueblo, Colo.: [N.P.], 1893.
        Reprint, Glorieta, N. Mex.: Rio Grande Press, 1968.
Includes photographs of Penitente activities; by a
Protestant minister who was anti-Penitente. Included in
item 1177.

1039   Dary, David. Cowboy Culture: A Saga of Five
        Centuries. New York: Alfred A. Knopf, 1981.
Of some value in tracing the expansion of the
Spanish-Mexican cattle industry into the Southwest.

1040   Davis, John L. The Texas Rangers; Their First 150
        Years. San Antonio: Institute of Texan Cultures,
        University of Texas, 1975.

1041   Davis, Richard Harding. The West From a Car-Window.
        New York: Harper, 1892.
Late 19th century West as seen by a famous journalist.

1042   Davis, William Heath. Seventy Five Years in
        California. San Francisco: J. Howell, 1929; 3rd ed.,
        1967.
Recollections of California from the 1830s to the end of the
century.

1043   Davis, William Watts Hart. El Gringo, or New Mexico
        and Her People. New York: Harper & Bros., 1857.
        Reprint, Santa Fe, N. Mex.: Rydal Press, 1938.
An excellent picture of Santa Fe society circa 1855 as seen
through the eyes of the U.S. attorney for the Territory of
New Mexico.

1044   De Aragon, Ray J. Padre Martinez and Bishop Lamy.
        Las Vegas, N. Mex.: Pan-Am Publishing Co., 1979.
The story of conflict between the first "Anglo" bishop and
the leading Nuevo Mexicano clergyman.

1045   De Leon, Arnoldo. Apuntes Tejanos. Ann Arbor, Mich.:
       University Microfilms International, 1978.
Newspaper articles from various Texas newspapers, 1855-1900;
material on Juan N. Cortina, Jose A. Navarro, the Cart War,
El Paso Salt War, Teresa Urrea, and Pedro Jaramillo.

1046   De Leon, Arnoldo. The Tejano Community, 1836-1900.
       Albuquerque: University of New Mexico Press, 1981.
The first political, economic, and social history of Mexican
Americans in Texas during the nineteenth century. It
includes chapters on politics, urban and rural labor,
education, religion, and daily life; and it advances the
thesis that Tejanos developed a culture that grew out of
both their Mexicanidad and their residence in the U.S.

1047   Defouri, (Rev.) James H. Historical Sketch of the
       Catholic Church in New Mexico. San Francisco:
       McCormick Bros., 1887.

1048   Delano, Alonzo. Life on the Plains and Among the
       Diggings. Auburn, N.Y.: Milner, Orton & Mulligan,
       1854. Reprint, New York: Readex Microprint, 1966.
Good for an easterner's picture of life in the mines.

1049   Dillon, Richard H. Fool's Gold: The Decline and Fall
       of Captain John Sutter of California. New York:
       Coward-McCann, 1967.

1050   Dobie, James Frank. A Vaquero of the Brush Country.
       Dallas, Tex.: Southwest Press, 1929. Various reprints
       including Boston: Little, Brown & Co., 1943, 1946, and
       1949.
Describes frontier and ranch life in the late 1800s;
includes Ranger material.

1051   Donaldson, Thomas. The Public Domain: House
       Miscellaneous Document 45, 47th Cong., 2nd sess.
       Washington, D.C.: U.S. Government Printing Office,
       1884.
Covers the public land system and its history.

1052   Duffus, Robert L. The Santa Fe Trail. New York:
       Longmans, Green and Co., 1930. Reprint, Albuquerque:
       University of New Mexico Press, 1971.

1053   Dumke, Glen S. The Boom of the Eighties in Southern
       California. San Marino, Calif.: Huntington Library,
       1944.
The boom that helped bring an end to Californio cultural
resistance in the South.

1054   Dunbar Ortiz, Roxanne A. Roots of Resistance: Land
       Tenure in New Mexico, 1680-1980. Los Angeles: Chicano

Studies Center, University of California, 1980.
A Marxian economic interpretation of land conflict; a 1974
thesis.

1055   Du Puy, William A. Baron of the Colorados. San
        Antonio, Tex.: Naylor Publishing Co., 1940.
The fictionalized story of James A. Reavis' land fraud
attempt.

1056   Durham, George. Taming the Nueces Strip: The Story of
        McNally's Rangers. Austin: University of Texas Press,
        1962.
Describes the development of the Texas Rangers under Captain
L. H. McNally.

1057   Ebright, Malcolm. The Tierra Amarilla Grant: A
        History of Chicanery. Santa Fe, N. Mex.: Center for
        Land Grant Studies, 1980.
Explains how this northern New Mexico grant was despoiled.
Includes an appendix of documents relating to the grant.

1058   Ellis, Richard N., ed. New Mexico Historic Documents.
        Albuquerque: University of New Mexico Press, 1975.
Includes documents from 1821 to 1941, especially the 1911
constitution with amendments to 1974.

1059   Ellison, Joseph. California and the Nation,
        1850-1869; A Study of the Relations of a Frontier
        Community with the Federal Government. Berkeley:
        University of California Press, 1927.

1060   Eno, Henry. Twenty Years on the Pacific Slope;
        Letters of Henry Eno from California and Nevada,
        1848-1871. Edited by W. Turrentine Jackson. New
        Haven, Conn.: Yale University Press, 1965.
A valuable picture of frontier life and customs.

1061   Evans, George W. Mexican Gold Trail, the Journal of a
        49er. Edited by Glenn Dumke. San Marino, Calif.:
        Huntington Library, 1945.

1062   Faulk, Odie B. Destiny Road: The Gila Trail and the
        Opening of the Southwest. Fair Lawn, N.J.: Oxford
        University Press, 1973.
Contains information about Esteban Ochoa (1831-1888), the
Arizona transportation king and civic leader.

1063   Faulk, Odie B. Too Far North--Too Far South: The
        Controversial Boundary Survey and the Epic Story of
        the Gadsden Purchase. Los Angeles: Westernlore Press,
        1967.
Perhaps the best account of the Gadsden Purchase Treaty of
1853.

1064   Fernandez, Jose Emilio. Cuarenta años de legislador:
        biografia del senador Casimiro Barela. Trinidad,
        Colo.: [N.P.], 1911. Reprint, New York: Arno Press,
        1976.
The life of the father of the Colorado state constitution.

1065   Ferrier, William W. Ninety Years of Education in
        California, 1846-1936. Berkeley, Calif.: Sather Gate
        Book Shop, 1937.
Contains material for Chicano education history.

1066   Fisher, Anne B. The Salinas: Upside-down River. New
        York: Farrar & Rhinehart, 195.
History of Spanish-Mexican settlers in the Salinas valley
from mission days to World War II.

1067   Forbes, Robert H. Crabb's Filibustering Expedition
        into Sonora, 1857. Tucson: Arizona Silhouettes, 1952.
The history of an important filibuster in northern Sonora in
1857.

1068   Ford, John S. Rip Ford's Texas. Austin: University
        of Texas Press, 1963.

1069   Foster, Stephen C. El Quacheno: How I Want [sic] to
        Help Make the Constitution of California--Stirring
        Historical Incidents. Los Angeles: Dawson's Book
        Shop, 1949. Included in item 1147.

1070   French, William. Some Recollections of a Western
        Ranchman. London: Methuen & Co., 1927. Reprint, New
        York: Argosy-Antiquarian Books, 2 vols., 1965.
Has material on Nuevo Mexicano folk hero Elfego Baca.

1071   Fulton, Maurice G. History of the Lincoln County War.
        Edited by Robert N. Mullin. Tucson: University of
        Arizona Press, 1968.
The story of the most famous cattlemen's war in New Mexico,
1878.

1072   Garber, Paul N. The Gadsden Treaty. Philadelphia:
        University of Pennsylvania Press, 1923.

1073   Gates, Paul W., ed. California Ranchos and Farms,
        1846-1862: Including the Letters of John Quincy Adams
        Warren of 1861, Being Largely Devoted to Livestock,
        Wheat Farming, Fruit Raising, and the Wine Industry.
        Madison: State Historical Society of Wisconsin, 1967.
Good material on California agriculture early in the
American period.

1074   Gerstacker, Friedrich. Scenes of Life in California.
        San Francisco: J. Howell, 1942.
Has good material on racism in the gold mines.

1075   Giffen, Helen S., ed. The Diaries of Peter Decker:
       Overland to California in 1849 and Life in the Mines,
       1850-1851. Georgetown, Calif.: Talisman Press, 1966.

1076   Gil, Mario. Nuestros buenos vecinos. Mexico, D.F.:
       Azteca, 1964.
Discusses the problems of Mexicans in the Southwest after
1848 and also border problems.

1077   Gillet, James B. Six Years With the Texas Rangers:
       1875-1881. New Haven, Conn.: Yale University Press,
       1925.

1078   Gillingham, Robert Cameron. The Rancho San Pedro; the
       Story of a Famous Rancho in Los Angeles County and of
       Its Owners the Dominguez Family. Los Angeles:
       Dominguez Estate Co., 1961.

1079   Gobineau, Joseph Arthur compte de. The Inequality of
       Human Races. Translated by Adrian Collins. New York:
       G. P. Putnam's Sons, 1915.
An early work of scientific racism (originally published in
1853-1855) by a prominent authority who influenced American
thinking.

1080   Goetzmann, William H. Exploration and Empire. New
       York: Alfred A. Knopf, 1966.
Covers scientists and explorers in the West, 1805-1900.

1081   Grant, Madison. The Passing of the Great Race; or the
       Racial Basis of European History. New York: Charles
       Scribner's Sons, 1916.
This influential work went through numerous revised editions
and was extremely important in shaping American views on
racial equality.

1082   Graves, Jackson A. My Seventy Years in California,
       1857-1927. Los Angeles: Times-Mirror Press, 1927.

1083   Gregg, Andrew K. New Mexico in the Nineteenth
       Century: A Pictorial History. Albuquerque: University
       of New Mexico Press, 1968.
Presents an excellent balance of Indian, Mexican, and Anglo
heritage.

1084   Gregg, Robert D. The Influence of Border Troubles on
       Relations Between the U.S. and Mexico, 1876-1910.
       Baltimore, Md.: Johns Hopkins University Press, 1937.
       Reprint, New York: Da Capo Press, 1970.

1085   Griggs, George. History of the Mesilla Valley; or,
       the Gadsden Purchase. Las Cruces, N. Mex.: Bronson

Printing Co., 1930.
A miscellaneous collection of materials on the Mesilla
Valley.

1086 Griswold del Castillo, Richard A. The Los Angeles
      Barrio, 1850-1890: A Social History. Berkeley:
      University of California Press, 1979.
Includes bibliography, charts, tables, and maps. Based on
his 1974 dissertation.

1087 Guinn, James M. A History of California and an
      Extended History of Los Angeles and Environs. Los
      Angeles: Los Angeles Historic Record Co., 1915.

1088 Harris, Benjamin Butler. The Gila Trail: The Texas
      Argonauts and the California Gold Rush. Norman:
      University of Oklahoma Press, 1960.

1089 Hatcher, Mattie A. Letters of an Early American
      Traveler--Mary Austin Holley, Her Life and Her Works.
      Dallas, Tex.: Southwest Press, 1933.

1090 Havinden, M. A. and Celia M. King, eds. The Southwest
      and the Land. Exeter, Devon, Great Britain:
      University of Exeter, 1970.

1091 Hayes, Benjamin. Pioneer Notes From the Diaries of
      Judge Benjamin Hayes, 1849-1875. Los Angeles: McBride
      Printing Co., 1929. Reprint, New York: Arno Press,
      1976.
An important source for studying southern California early
in the American period.

1092 Heizer, Robert F. and Alan J. Almquist. The Other
      Californians. Berkeley: University of California
      Press, 1971.
Describes prejudice and racism in attitudes toward
minorities under Spain, Mexico, and the United States to
1920.

1093 Henderson, Alice Corbin. Brothers of Light: The
      Penitentes of the Southwest. New York: Harcourt Brace
      & Co., 1937.
Describes Penitente Holy Week observances. Included in item
1177.

1094 Hendricks, George. The Bad Man of the West. San
      Antonio, Tex.: Naylor Publishing Co., 1941.
Includes Nuevo Mexicano outlaws.

1095 Hertzog, Peter. A Directory of New Mexican
      Desperados. Santa Fe, N. Mex.: Press of the
      Territorian, 1965.

1096   Hill, Joseph J. History of Warner's Ranch and Its
        Environs. Los Angeles: [Privately printed], 1927.

1097   Hobsbawn, Eric. Bandits. New York: Dell Publishing
        Co., 1969.
The classic theory of social banditry.

1098   Hoffman, Ogden. Reports of Land Cases Determined in
        the U.S. District Court for the Northern District of
        California . . . (1853-1858). San Francisco: Numa
        Hubert, 1862.

1099   Hofstadter, Richard. Social Darwinism in American
        Thought. Philadelphia: University of Pennsylvania
        Press, 1944. Reprint, London: Oxford University
        Press, 1945. Revised, Boston: Beacon Press, 1955.
An outstanding work; describes the adaption of Darwin's
theories in biology to society and economic life. By
definition almost, racial minorities were held to be
inferior.

1100   Hollon, William E. The Great American Desert Then and
        Now. New York: Oxford University Press, 1966.

1101   Holmes, Jack Ellsworth. Politics in New Mexico.
        Albuquerque: University of New Mexico Press, 1967.
Includes material on Thomas B. Catron and the Santa Fe ring.
Covers from about 1900 to 1963.

1102   Horgan, Paul. The Habit of Empire. Santa Fe, N.
        Mex.: Rydal Press, 1938.

1103   Horgan, Paul. Lamy of Santa Fe: His Life and Times.
        New York: Ferrar, Straus, & Giroux, 1975.
A somewhat pro-Lamy biography of the Southwest's first
bishop. Describes his problems with the Nuevo Mexicano
clergy.

1104   Horn, Calvin. New Mexico's Troubled Years: The Story
        of the Early Territorial Governors. Albuquerque, N.
        Mex.: Horn & Wallace, 1963.

1105   Hoyle, M. F. Crimes and Career of Tiburcio Vasquez.
        Hollister, Calif.: Evening Free Lance, 1927.
A popular account of the famous California bandit's career.

1106   Hughes, W. J. Rebellious Ranger. Norman: University
        of Oklahoma Press, 1964.
Has material on Juan N. Cortina.

1107   Hunt, Robert Lee. A History of Farm Movements in the
        Southwest, 1873-1925. College Station: Texas A & M
        University Press, 1935.

1108   Hutchinson, William H.   A Bar Cross Man.   Norman:
        University of Oklahoma Press, 1956.
A history of Elfego Baca, folk hero of New Mexico.

1109   Jackson, Joseph H.   Bad Company.   New York: Harcourt
        Brace & Co., 1949.
Popular history of western banditry, with details of the
Murieta legend's development.

1110   Jaramillo, Cleofas M.   Shadows of the Past.   Santa Fe,
        N. Mex.: Seton Village Press, 1941.
Includes descriptive material on the Penitentes and Fr.
Antonio J. Martinez; mostly reminiscences and customs.

1111   Jones, William Cary.   Land Titles in California.
        Report on the Subject of Land Titles in California,
        made in Pursuance of Instructions from the Secretary
        of State and the Secretary of the Interior, by William
        Cary Jones: Together with a Translation of the
        Principal Laws on That Subject and Some Other Papers
        Relating Thereto.   Washington, D.C.: Gideon & Co.,
        1850.
Beyond land titles, a broad social survey of Hispanic
California.   Jones was fluent in Spanish and acted as
special agent for President Millard Fillmore.

1112   Jones, William Carey.   Letters of William Carey Jones,
        in Review of Attorney General Black's Report to the
        President of the United States, on the Subject of Land
        Titles in California.   San Francisco: Commercial Steam
        Book and Job Printing Establishment, 1860.

1113   Juan N. Cortina: Two Interpretations.   Edited by
        Carlos Cortes.   New York: Arno Press, 1974.
An anthology of two works on Juan N. Cortina: Charles W.
Goldfinch, Juan N. Cortina 1824-1892: A Re-Appraisal, 1949,
item 1295, and Jose T. Calanles, Juan N. Cortina Presents
His Motion for a New Trial, 1951, item 1011.

1114   Keleher, William A.   The Fabulous Frontier; Twelve New
        Mexico Items.   Santa Fe, N. Mex.: Rydal Press, 1945.
        Reprint, Albuquerque: University of New Mexico Press,
        1962.
Good for Santa Fe ring and Thomas B. Catron.

1115   Keleher, William A.   The Maxwell Land Grant--A New
        Mexico Item.   Santa Fe, N. Mex.: Rydal Press, 1942.
The history of the most important Mexican era grant,
originally made to Guadalupe Miranda and Carlos Beaubien in
1841.

1116   Keleher, William A.   Memoirs: 1892-1969: A New Mexico
        Item.   Santa Fe, N. Mex.: Rydal Press, 1969.
Personal reminiscences which include two chapters on Elfego

Baca, with photographs; by an excellent amateur local
historian.

1117   Keleher, William A.   Turmoil in New Mexico, 1846-1868.
        Santa Fe, N. Mex.: Rydal Press, 1952.
Largely a history of the American conquest and of Indian
wars.

1118   Keleher, William A.   Violence in Lincoln County
        1869-1881.   Albuquerque: University of New Mexico
        Press, 1957.
The story of the Lincoln County cattlemen's war.

1119   Kusz, Charles L.   The Gringo and Greaser, by Peter
        Hertzog.   Santa Fe, N. Mex.: Press of the Territorian,
        1964.
Excerpts from the newspaper, the Gringo and Greaser,
1883-1884.

1120   La Farge, Oliver.   Santa Fe; the Autobiography of a
        Southwestern Town.   Norman: University of Oklahoma
        Press, 1959.

1121   Lamar, Howard Roberts.   The Far Southwest, 1846-1912:
        A Territorial History.   New Haven, Conn.: Yale
        University Press, 1966.   Reprint, New York: W. W.
        Norton & Co., 1970.
An outstanding political history; material on the Santa Fe
ring and Nuevo Mexicano political participation.

1122   Lang, Aldon S.   Financial History of the Public Lands
        in Texas.   Waco, Tex.: Baylor University, 1932.
The Baylor Bulletin, vol. 35:3.

1123   Larralde, Carlos.   Mexican American Movements and
        Leaders.   Los Alamitos, Calif.: Hwong Publishing Co.,
        1976.
A series of biographical essays on various leaders of
Chicano movements, 1848 to 1976; especially valuable for
Teresa Urrea and Emma Tenayuca.

1124   Larson, Robert W.   New Mexico Populism: A Study of
        Radical Protest in a Western Territory.   Boulder:
        Colorado Associated University Press, 1974.
Includes materials on the White Caps and Caballeros de
Labor.

1125   Larson, Robert W.   New Mexico's Quest for Statehood,
        1846-1912.   Albuquerque: University of New Mexico
        Press, 1968.
An expansion of his 1961 dissertation at the University of
New Mexico.

1126   Lathrop, Barnes F. Migration into Texas, 1835-1860.
        Austin: Texas State Historical Association, 1949.

1127   Latta, Frank F. Joaquin Murrieta and His Horse Gang.
        Santa Cruz, Calif.: Bear State Books, 1980.
Popular history.

1128   Lea, Tom. The King Ranch. 2 vols. Boston: Little,
        Brown & Co., 1957.
Describes Mexican influence on Anglos in Texas; volume two
has information on Juan N. Cortina.

1129   Lockwood, Frank C. Life in Old Tucson, 1854-1864.
        Los Angeles: Ward Ritchie Press, 1943.

1130   Lowie, Robert H. The History of Ethnological Theory.
        New York: Farrar & Rinehart, 1937.
Views of an outstanding American ethnologist, a specialist
in Indian cultures, especially those of the United States.

1131   Luebke, Frederick C., ed. Ethnicity on the Great
        Plains. Lincoln: University of Nebraska Press, 1980.
Concerns Mexicans as well as other ethnic groups.

1132   Lugo, Jose del Carmen. Vida de un ranchero. San
        Bernardino, Calif.: San Bernardino County Museum
        Association, 1961.
Problems of a southern Californio landowner, as told to
Thomas Savage, for H. H. Bancroft.

1133   Lummis, Charles F. The Land of Poco Tiempo. New
        York: Charles Scribner & Sons, 1893. Reprint,
        Albuquerque: University of New Mexico Press, 1966.
Chapter IV has material on the Penitentes and their
practices.

1134   Lummis, Charles F. Some Strange Corners of Our
        Country: The Wonderland of the Southwest. New York:
        Century Co., 1892.

1135   McCall, George A. New Mexico in 1850: A Military
        View. Edited by Robert W. Frazer. Norman: University
        of Oklahoma Press, 1968.

1136   McCarty, Frankie. Land Grant Problems in New Mexico.
        Albuquerque, N. Mex.: Albuquerque Journal, 1969.

1137   McCarty, John L. Maverick Town: The Story of Old
        Tascosa. Norman: University of Oklahoma Press, 1946.

1138   Maciel, David R. El proceso historico del pueblo
        chicano, 1848-1910. Mexico, D.F.: SepSetentas, 1974.
Broad survey of the early history of the Chicano.

1139   McLoughlin, Emmet. Famous Ex-Priests. New York: Lyle
       Stuart, 1968.
Includes a chapter on Fr. Antonio Jose Martinez of Taos, New
Mexico and his difficulties with Bishop Lamy.

1140   Martin, Jack. Border Boss: Captain John R.
       Hughes--Texas Ranger. San Antonio, Tex.: Naylor
       Publishing Co., 1942.

1141   Martinez, Antonio Jose. Historia consisa del cura de
       Taos Antonio Jose Martinez. Taos, N. Mex.: Imprente
       de Vicente F. Romero, 1861.

1142   Mayo, Morrow. Los Angeles. New York: Alfred A.
       Knopf, 1933.
A popular history; little on the Mexican American after
1900.

1143   Melendy, Howard Brett and Ben F. Gilbert. Governors
       of California, Burnett to Brown. Georgetown, Calif.:
       Talisman Press, 1965.

1144   The Mexican Experience in Arizona. With an
       introduction by Carlos E. Cortes. New York: Arno
       Press, 1976.
Contains: George Griggs, History of the Mesilla Valley or
the Gadsden Purchase, 1930. James Colquhoun, The Early
History of the Clifton-Morenci District, 1924. George
Barker, Pachuco: An American-Spanish Argot and Its Social
Functions in Tucson, Arizona, 1950.

1145   The Mexican Experience in Texas. With an introduction
       by Carlos E. Cortes. New York: Arno Press, 1976.
Contents: Rie Jarratt, Gutierrez de Lara: Mexican Texan: The
Story of a Creole Hero, 1949. Report of the Mexican
Commission on the Northern Frontier Question, 1875. Lyle
Saunders, The Spanish-Speaking Population of Texas, 1949.

1146   The Mexican Texans. San Antonio: Institute of Texan
       Cultures, University of Texas, 1971.
Also issued in Spanish with the title Los mexicanos texanos.

1147   Mexicans in California After the U.S. Conquest.
       Anthology with introduction by Carlos Cortes. New
       York: Arno Press, 1976.
Eight selections, almost all dealing with southern
California. Contents: John S. Griffin, Los Angeles in 1849:
A Letter from John S. Griffin, M.D. to Col. J. D. Stevenson,
March 11, 1849, 1949. Stephen Clark Foster, El Quacheno:
How I Want to Help Make the Constitution of
California--Stirring Historical Incidents, 1949. Joseph
Lancaster Brent, The Lugo Case: A Personal Experience, 1926.
W. W. Robinson, People Versus Lugo: Story of a Famous Los

Angeles Murder Case and Its Amazing Aftermath, 1962. Mario
T. Garcia, Merchants and Dons: San Diego's Attempt at
Modernization, 1850-1860, 1975. Charles Hughes, The Decline
of the Californios: The Case of San Diego, 1846-1856, 1975.
San Bernardino County Flood Control District, Agua Mansa and
the Flood of January 22, 1862: Santa Ana River, 1968. Terry
E. Stephenson, Don Bernardo Yorba, 1963.

1148   Mexico. Comision Pesquisidora de la Frontera del
       Norte. Report of the 1873 Commission on the Northern
       Frontier. New York: Baker & Godwin, 1875.
Translation of a Mexican government commission report.

1149   Mexico. Secretaria de Relaciones Exteriores.
       Correspondencia diplomatica relativa a las invasiones
       del territorio mexicano por fuerzas de los Estados
       Unidos de 1873 a 1877. Mexico, D.F.: Imprenta de
       Ignacio Cumplido, 1878.
Mexican complaints to the United States government about
U.S. Army border crossings.

1150   Miller, Robert Ryal. Arms Across the Border: United
       States Aid to Juarez During the French Intervention in
       Mexico. Philadelphia: American Philosophical Society,
       1973.
Details a part of the reciprocal influence of Mexicans and
Mexican Americans.

1151   Miller, Thomas L. Bounty and Donation Land Grants of
       Texas, 1835-1888. Austin: University of Texas, 1967.

1152   Miller, Tom. On the Border: Portraits of America's
       Southwestern Frontier. New York: Harper & Row, 1981.

1153   Mills, George T. and Richard Grove. Lucifer and the
       Crucifer: The Enigma of the Penitentes. Colorado
       Springs, Colo.: Taylor Museum, 1956.
A brief account of the Penitentes which includes
photographs.

1154   Mills, William W. Forty Years at El Paso, 1858-1898:
       Recollections . . .   Chicago: W. B. Conkey Co., 1901.

1155   Montagu, Ashley. The Idea of Race. Lincoln:
       University of Nebraska Press, 1965.
Discusses racial theories and the fallacy of race.

1156   Moore, (Rev.) Frank L. The Penitentes of New Mexico.
       New York: Congregational Home Mission Society, [n.d.].
A contemporary late 19th century account by a
Congregationalist missionary.

1157   Moore, (Rev.) Frank L. Souls and Saddlebags: The
       Diaries and Correspondence of Frank L. Moore, Western

Missionary, 1888-1896. Denver, Colo.: Big Mountain
Press, 1962.

1158 Morefield, Richard H. The Mexican Adaption in
American California, 1846-1875. San Francisco: R & E
Research Associates, 1971.
Reprint of his 1955 master's thesis at the University of
California, Berkeley.

1159 Morrell, W. P. The Gold Rushes. Chester Springs,
Pa.: Dufour, 1968.
Contains an excellent description of the Mexican
contribution to mining in the American West.

1160 Nadeau, Remi. The Real Joaquin Murieta: Robin Hood
Hero or Gold Rush Gangster. Corona del Mar, Calif.:
Trans-Anglo Books, 1974.
Probably the best historical examination of the Joaquin
Murieta story.

1161 Newmark, Harris. Sixty Years in Southern California,
1853-1913. New York: Knickerbocker Press, 1916.
Reprints, Boston: Houghton Mifflin Co., 1930; Los
Angeles: Zeitlin & Ver Bruggs, 1970.

1162 Oden, Bill Arp. Early Days on the Texas-New Mexico
Plains. Edited by J. Evetts Haley. Canyon, Tex.:
Palo Duro Press, 1965.
Describes ranch life in Anglo Texas and the "Little Texas"
area of eastern New Mexico.

1163 Olmstead, Frederick Law. A Journey Through Texas; Or,
A Saddle-Trip on the Southwestern Frontier. New York:
Dix, Edwards & Co., 1857. Reprint, New York: Burt
Franklin, 1969.
A description of the southwestern frontier in Texas just
before the Civil War.

1164 Osgood, Ernest S. The Day of the Cattleman.
Minneapolis: University of Minnesota, 1929. Reprint,
Chicago: University of Chicago, 1957.
A good history of the cattleman's frontier moving out of
central Texas after the Civil War; however, there is little
mention of the Mexican roots of the industry.

1165 Otero, Miguel A., I. Address to the People of New
Mexico. Santa Fe, N. Mex.: [n.p.], 1860.

1166 Otero, Miguel A., II. My Life on the Frontier,
1864-1882: Incidents and Characters of the Period When
Kansas, Colorado, and New Mexico Were Passing Through
the Last of Their Wild and Romantic Years. Vol. I.
New York: Press of the Pioneers, 1935.
Otero, member of a leading Nuevo Mexicano family, played an

important political role in New Mexico.

1167 Otero, Miguel A., II. My Life on the Frontier,
      1882-1897: Death Knell of a Territory and Birth of a
      State. Vol. II. Albuquerque: University of New
      Mexico Press, 1939.
Volume II includes New Mexico's Hispano politics, with
discussion of the Penitentes, White Caps, and Santa Fe ring.

1168 Otero, Miguel A., II. My Nine Years as Governor of
      the Territory of New Mexico, 1897-1906. Vol. III.
      Edited by Marion Dargan. Albuquerque: University of
      New Mexico Press, 1940.

1169 Otero, Miguel A., II. Otero: An Autobiographical
      Trilogy. Reprint of vols. I-III. New York: Arno
      Press, 1974.
Anthology of the three autobiographical volumes, by Miguel
Otero II, governor, businessman, banker and Nuevo Mexicano
leader.

1171 Padilla, Jose Leon. History of the Las Vegas Grant:
      Containing a Correct Literal Translation of the
      Original Spanish Papers. East Las Vegas, N. Mex.: J.
      A. Caruth, 1890.

1172 Paredes, Americo. With His Pistol in His Hand.
      Austin: University of Texas Press, 1958.
The corrido de Gregorio Cortez (1875-1916), a Tejano symbol
of conflict between Anglo and Mexican and of a double
standard of justice.

1173 Paul, Rodman W. California Gold: The Beginning of
      Mining in the Far West. Cambridge, Mass.: Harvard
      University Press, 1947. Reprint, Lincoln: University
      of Nebraska Press, 1965.

1174 Paul, Rodman W. The Mining Frontiers of the Far West,
      1848-1880. New York: Holt, Rinehart & Winston, 1963.

1175 Pearson, Jim Berry. The Maxwell Land Grant. Norman:
      University of Oklahoma Press, 1961.
A history of the Beaubien-Miranda grant which was acquired
by Lucien B. Maxwell, and later sold to speculators.

1176 Peavy, Charles D. Charles A. Siringo, A Texas Picaro.
      Austin, Tex.: Steck-Vaughn Co., 1967.

1177 The Penitentes of New Mexico. Edited by Carlos
      Cortes. New York: Arno Press, 1974.
An anthology of: Alex[ander] M. Darley, The Passionists of
the Southwest, or, the Holy Brotherhood, 1893. Alice Corbin
Henderson, Brothers of Light: The Penitentes of the
Southwest, 1937. Dorothy Woodward, The Penitentes of New

Mexico, 1935.

1178   Perkins, William. Three Years in California: Journal
       of Life at Sonora, 1849-1852. Edited by Dale Morgan
       and James Scobie. Berkeley: University of California
       Press, 1964.
Makes reference to Mexicans and Californios in the mines.

1179   Peterson, Richard H. Manifest Destiny in the Mines: A
       Cultural Interpretation of Anti-Mexican Nativism in
       California. 1848-1853. San Francisco: R & E Research
       Associates, 1975.
A reprint of his 1965 master's thesis at San Francisco State
University.

1180   Pierce, Frank C. A Brief History of the Lower Rio
       Grande Valley. Menasha, Wis.: George Banta Publishing
       Co., 1917.

1181   Pillsbury, Dorothy L. No High Adobe. Albuquerque:
       University of New Mexico Press, 1950.
Popular historical sketches which were originally written
for the Christian Science Monitor.

1182   Pillsbury, Dorothy L. Roots in Adobe. Albuquerque:
       University of New Mexico Press, 1959.
A collection of articles on New Mexican social life and
customs, first published in the Christian Science Monitor.

1183   Pillsbury, Dorothy L. Star Over Adobe. Albuquerque:
       University of New Mexico Press, 1963.
Describes Santa Fe social life circa 1890.

1184   Pitt, Leonard. California Controversies. Glenview,
       Ill.: Scott Foresman & Co., 1968.

1185   Pitt, Leonard. The Decline of the Californios: A
       Social History of the Spanish Speaking Californians,
       1846-1890. Berkeley: University of California Press,
       1966.
Outstanding pioneer monograph on the Mexican American in
California after the Mexican War. Based on his 1958
dissertation.

1186   Poldervaart, Arie W. Black-Robed Justice. A History
       of the Administration of Justice in New Mexico from
       the American Occupation of 1846 Until Statehood in
       1912. Santa Fe: Historical Society of New Mexico,
       1948. Reprint, New York: Arno Press, 1976.
Volume 13 of Publications in History, the Historical Society
of New Mexico. Each chapter is devoted to an individual
chief justice.

1187   Pomeroy, Earl S. The Territories and the United
       States, 1861-1890: Studies in Colonial Administration.
       Philadelphia: University of Pennsylvania Press, 1947.
Describes well the territorial system in New Mexico and
Arizona.

1188   Poston, Charles D. Building a State in Apache Land.
       Tempe, Ariz.: Aztec Press, 1963.
Good for the Gadsden Purchase and a description of Arizona
after the Treaty of Guadalupe Hidalgo.

1189   Powell, Donald M. The Peralta Grant: James Addison
       Reavis and the Barony of Arizona. Norman: University
       of Oklahoma, 1960.
An excellent account of the infamous Reavis land claim case.

1190   Powell, H. M. T. The Santa Fe Trail to California,
       1849-52; the Journal and Drawings of H. M. T. Powell.
       Edited by Douglas S. Watson. San Francisco: Book Club
       of California, 1931.
Describes and depicts both the Santa Fe trail and the route
from Santa Fe on to California.

1191 Powers, Stephen. Afoot and Alone. Hartford, Conn.:
       Columbia Book Club, 1872.
Covers Arizona, New Mexico, and southern California in the
post-Civil War period.

1192   Rambo, Ralph. Trailing the California Bandit Tiburcio
       Vasquez. San Jose, Calif.: Rosicrucian Press, 1968.

1193   Ramirez, Emilia Schunior. Ranch Life in Hidalgo
       County After 1850. Edinburg, Tex.: New Santander
       Press, 1971.

1194   Ramsdell, Charles W. Reconstruction in Texas.
       Gloucester, Mass.: P. Smith, 1964.

1195   Ridge, John Rollin. [pseud. Yellow Bird.] The Life
       and Adventures of Joaquin Murieta, the Celebrated
       California Bandit. 3rd ed. San Francisco: Frederick
       MacCrellish & Co., 1871. Reprint, Norman: University
       of Oklahoma Press, 1955.
A largely legendary account, originally published in 1854.

1196   Rippy, J. Fred. The United States and Mexico. New
       York: Alfred A. Knopf, 1926.
Based on his 1920 dissertation at the University of
California, Berkeley. Good for the period, 1848-1860.

1197   Rister, Carl Coke. Robert E. Lee in Texas. Norman:
       University of Oklahoma Press, 1946.

1198   Rister, Carl Coke. The Southwestern Frontier,
        1865-1881. Cleveland: Arthur H. Clark Co., 1928.

1199   Robinson, William W. People Versus Lugo: Story of a
        Famous Los Angeles Murder Case and Its Amazing
        Aftermath. Los Angeles: Dawson's Book Shop, 1962.
A part of the story of the despoiling of Californios' lands.

1200   Robinson, William W. Ranchos Become Cities.
        Pasadena, Calif.: San Pasqual Press, 1939.

1201   Rodriguez, Jose Maria. Memoirs of Early Texas. San
        Antonio, Tex.: Passing Show Printing Co., 1913.
        Reprint, San Antonio, Tex.: Standard Printing Co.,
        1961.

1202   Rojas, Arnold R. California Vaquero. Fresno, Calif.:
        Academy Library Guild, 1953.

1203   Rojas, Arnold R. The Vaquero. Charlotte, N.C.:
        McNally & Loftin, 1964.
Reminiscences of life on Californio ranchos.

1204   Rosenbaum, Robert J. Mexicano Resistance in the
        Southwest: The Sacred Right of Self-Preservation.
        Austin: University of Texas Press, 1981.
Includes the Maxwell grant, border violence, the White Caps,
and El Partido del Pueblo Unido. Concentrates on the time
period, 1870-1900.

1205   Ross, Ivy Belle. The Confirmation of Spanish and
        Mexican Land Grants in California. San Francisco:
        R & E Research Associates, 1974.
Reprint of her 1928 master's thesis at the University of
California, Berkeley. Includes mission secularization, the
U.S. Land Commission, and U.S. land policy.

1206   Royce, Josiah. California From the Conquest in 1846
        to the Second Vigilante Committee in San Francisco: A
        Study of American Character. Boston: Houghton Mifflin
        Co., 1892. Reprint, Santa Barbara, Calif.: Peregrine
        Publishers, 1970.

1207   Salmon, D. E. and Ezra Carman. Sheep Industry of the
        United States. Washington, D.C.: U.S. Department of
        Agriculture, Government Printing Office, 1892.

1208   Salpointe, (Rev.) Jean Baptiste. Soldiers of the
        Cross. Notes on the Ecclesiastical History of New
        Mexico, Arizona, and Colorado. Banning, Calif.: St.
        Boniface's Industrial School, 1898.
Account by the successor to Jean Baptiste Lamy and second
(American) bishop of the New Mexico diocese.

1209   Samora, Julian; Joe J. Bernal; and Albert Peña.
        Gunpowder Justice: A Reassessment of the Texas
        Rangers. Notre Dame, Ind.: University of Notre Dame
        Press, 1979.
A critical revisionist view of the Texas Rangers, offsetting
the favorable views of Walter Prescott Webb. See item 1252.

1210   Sanchez, Pedro, ed. Memorias sobre la vida del
        Presbitero Don Antonio Jose Martinez. Santa Fe, N.
        Mex.: Compañia Impresora del Nuevo Mexico, 1903.

1211   Sanchez, Pedro, ed. Recollections of the Life of the
        Priest Don Antonio Jose Martinez. Translated by Ray
        John de Aragon. Santa Fe, N. Mex.: Lightening Tree
        Press, 1978.

1212   Schaefer, Jack. Heroes Without Glory. Boston:
        Houghton Mifflin Co., 1965.
Includes a chapter on folk hero Elfego Baca.

1213   Secrest, William B. Joaquin: Bloody Bandit of the
        Mother Lode, the Story of Joaquin Murieta. Fresno,
        Calif.: Saga-West, 1967.
A popular history of Joaquin Murieta by a California
historian.

1214   Secrest, William B. Juanita: The Only Woman Lynched
        in the Gold Rush Days. Fresno, Calif.: Saga-West,
        1967.
Describes the lynching of Josefa at Downieville, California.

1215   Shinn, Charles H. Graphic Description of Pacific
        Coast Outlaws. San Francisco: R. R. Patterson, 1887.
Covers California bandits, 1850-1870.

1216   Shinn, Charles H. Mining Camps, a Study in American
        Frontier Government. Edited by Rodman W. Paul. New
        York: Harper & Row Publishers, 1965.
Describes the gold discoveries and life in California mining
camps.

1217   Shrinkle, James D. Fifty Years of Roswell History,
        1867-1917. Roswell, N. Mex.: Hall-Poorbaugh Press,
        1964.

1218   Simmons, Marc. The Little Lion of the Southwest, a
        Life of Manuel Antonio Chaves. Chicago: Swallow
        Press, 1973.
Recounts the life of this Nuevo Mexicano frontiersman,
Indian fighter, and businessman.

1219   Siringo, Charles A. Riata and Spurs; the Story of a
        Lifetime Spent in the Saddle as Cowboy and Ranger.

Boston: Houghton Mifflin Co., 1927.

1220 Sonnichsen, Charles L. The El Paso Salt War, 1877.
      El Paso, Tex.: C. Hertzog, 1961.
The story of an important economic and cultural border
conflict.

1221 Sonnichsen, Charles L. Ten Texas Feuds. Albuquerque:
      University of New Mexico Press, 1957.
Includes the El Paso Salt War.

1222 Sorrentino, Giuseppe M., S.J. Dalle Montagne Rocciose
      al Rio Bravo. Naples, Italy: Casa Editrice Federico &
      Ardia, [1948].
Has material on the Mexican Americans in the Southwest.

1223 Spanish and Mexican Land Grants. Edited by Carlos
      Cortes. New York: Arno Press, 1974.
Includes William Morrow, Spanish and Mexican Private Land
Grants, 1923; Herbert Brayer, William Blackmore: The
Spanish-Mexican Land Grants of New Mexico and Colorado,
1863-1878, 1949; and Alianza Federal, Spanish Land Grant
Question Examined, 1966.

1224 The Spanish Texans. San Antonio: Institute of Texan
      Cultures, University of Texas, 1972.
See also item 1146.

1225 Stephenson, Terry E. Don Bernardo Yorba. Los
      Angeles: Glen Dawson, 1941; reprint, 1963.
Member of an important old Californio family whose founder
had come with Gaspar de Portola.

1226 Stratton, Porter A. The Territorial Press of New
      Mexico, 1834-1912. Albuquerque: University of New
      Mexico Press, 1969.

1227 Sunseri, Alvin R. Seeds of Discord: New Mexico in the
      Aftermath of the American Conquest, 1846-1861.
      Chicago: Nelson-Hall, 1979.
Based on his 1973 dissertation. An excellent piece of
research and writing.

1228 Tate, Bill. The Penitentes of the Sangre de Cristos:
      An American Tragedy. Truchas, N. Mex.: Tate Gallery,
      1967.

1229 Taylor, Morris F. O. P. McMains and the Maxwell Land
      Grant Conflict. Tucson: University of Arizona Press,
      1979.
Reverend McMains was opposed to the land company and
pro-settler.

1230   Treadwell, Edward.   The Cattle King: The Story of
          Henry Miller.   Fresno: California Valley Publishers,
          1967.
A history of land acquisition and cattle ranching.

1231   Truman, Ben C.   Life, Adventures and Capture of
          Tiburcio Vasquez, the Great California Bandit and
          Murderer.   Los Angeles: Los Angeles Star Office, 1874.
A contemporary journalistic account.

1232   Tuttle, Charles R.   History of the Border Wars.
          Chicago: C. A. Wall & Co., 1874.

1233   Twitchell, Ralph Emerson.   Old Santa Fe; the Story of
          New Mexico's Ancient Capital.   Santa Fe: Santa Fe New
          Mexican Publishing Co., 1925.   Reprint, Chicago: Rio
          Grande Press, 1963.
Includes material on the Santa Fe ring and its leaders.

1234   Ulibarri, Sabine.   Mi abuela fumaba puros/ My Grandma
          Smoked Cigars.   Berkeley, Calif.: Quinto Sol, 1977.
Personal reminiscences of Ulibarri's growing up in Tierra
Amarilla country.

1235   U.S., Congress, House, 31st Cong., 1st sess.
          California and New Mexico: Message from the President
          of the United States.   January 21, 1850.   House
          Executive Document No. 17.   Washington, D.C.: U.S.
          Government Printing Office, 1850.   Reprint, New York:
          Arno Press, 1976.
Includes government reports, correspondence, and documents
from the period 1846 to 1849.

1236   U.S., Congress, House, 36th Cong., 1st sess.
          Difficulties on Southwestern Frontier.   House
          Executive Document No. 52.   Washington, D.C.: U.S.
          Government Printing Office, 1860.

1237   U.S., Congress, House, 36th Cong., 1st sess.   New
          Mexico--Private Land Claims . . ., Documents . . .,
          February 10, 1860.   House Executive Document No. 14,
          Serial 1047.

1238   U.S., Congress, House, 36th Cong., 1st sess.   To
          Confirm Certain Land Claims in the Territory of New
          Mexico, April 2, 1860.   House Report No. 321, Serial
          1068.

1239   U.S., Congress, House, 37th Cong., 2nd sess.   Private
          Land Claims in New Mexico . . . The Reports of the
          Surveyor General and Papers in Four Private Land

Claims in New Mexico, May 16, 1862. House Executive
Document No. 112, Serial 1137.

1240 U.S., Congress, House, 45th cong., 2nd sess. El Paso
      Troubles in Texas. House Executive Document No. 93,
      Serial 1809. Washington, D.C.: U.S. Government
      Printing Office, 1877-1878.
Concerns the Salt War of 1877 in Texas.

1241 U.S., Congress, Senate, 43rd Cong., 2nd sess.
      Conditions of the Records and Documents of Mexico
      Relating to the Land Now Embraced Within the
      Territories of Arizona and New Mexico, Also to Their
      Place of Custody and Deposit and to the Method of
      Procuring Authentic Transcripts of Such Records and
      Documents, December 10, 1874. Senate Executive
      Document No. 3, Serial 1629.

1242 Van Ness, John R. and Christine M. Van Ness, eds.
      Spanish and Mexican Land Grants in New Mexico and
      Colorado. Manhattan, Kans.: Sunflower State
      University Press, 1980.
A collection of lectures and essays on land grant history of
the New Mexico area.

1243 Vickery, Joyce C. Defending Eden: New Mexican
      Pioneers in Southern California, 1830-1890.
      Riverside, Calif.: Riverside Museum Press, 1977.
A history of settlement in the San Bernardino valley,
California.

1244 Vigil, Diego. Early Chicano Guerrilla Fighters. La
      Mirada, Calif.: Advanced Graphics, 1974.
Discusses whether they were social bandits or merely
bandits.

1245 Vigil, Maurilio E. Los Patrones: Profiles of Hispanic
      Political Leaders in New Mexican History. Washington,
      D.C.: University Press of America, 1980.
A series of short biographies of prominent Nuevo Mexicanos
from 1848 to the present.

1246 Wagoner, Jay J. Arizona Territory, 1863-1912: A
      Political History. Tucson: University of Arizona
      Press, 1970.

1247 Wagoner, Jay J. The History of the Cattle Industry in
      Southern Arizona, 1540-1940. Tucson: University of
      Arizona Press, 1952.
Places emphasis on the U.S. period after the Gadsden
Purchase Treaty of 1853.

1248   Wallace, Ernest.   Texas in Turmoil, 1849-1875.
          Austin, Tex.: Steck-Vaughn Co., 1965.

1249   Wallace, Susan Arnold (Elston).   The Land of the
          Pueblos.   New York: J. B. Alden, 1888.
The territorial governor's wife, Mrs. Lew Wallace, discusses
Santa Fe women workers.

1250   Warner, Louis H.   Archbishop Lamy: An Epoch Maker.
          Santa Fe: Santa Fe New Mexican Publishing Co., 1936.
An early account of the Rev. Lamy and the quarrel between
him and Father Antonio Jose Martinez.   See also items 1017
and 1103.

1251   Waters, Frank.   To Possess the Land: A Biography of
          Arthur Rochford Manby.   Chicago: Sage Books, 1974.
Includes material on land grants in Taos County, New Mexico.

1252   Webb, Walter P.   The Texas Rangers: A Century of
          Frontier Defense.   Boston: Houghton Mifflin, 1935.
          Reprint, Austin: University of Texas Press, 1965.
A favorable view of the rangers, with materials on Juan N.
Cortina and the Mexican American border dwellers.   See item
1209.

1253   Weber, Francis J.   A Biographical Sketch of Right
          Reverend Francisco Garcia Diego y Moreno, First Bishop
          of the Californias, 1785-1846.   Los Angeles: Borromeo
          Guild, 1961.

1254   Weber, Francis J.   Francisco Garcia Diego,
          California's Transition Bishop.   Los Angeles: Dawson's
          Book Shop, 1972.
An expansion of the author's 1961 account.

1255   Weigle, (Mary) Marta.   Brothers of Lights, Brothers of
          Blood: The Penitentes of the Southwest.   Albuquerque:
          University of New Mexico Press, 1976.
Probably the best interpretation of the Penitente
brotherhood.   Includes an excellent bibliographic essay and
a collection of documents in the appendixes.   Reviewed
before publication by the Hermano Supremo of the Penitentes.

1256   Weigle, (Mary) Marta.   The Penitentes of the
          Southwest.   Santa Fe, N. Mex.: Ancient City Press,
          1970.
Based on her doctoral research at the University of
Pennsylvania.

1257   Wellman, Paul I.   The Trampling Herd.   New York:
          Garrick & Evans, 1939.
Describes Arizona outlaws and difficulties of the
territory's Mexican population.

1258   Westphall, Victor. The Public Domain in New Mexico,
       1854-1891. Albuquerque: University of New Mexico
       Press, 1965.
An excellent survey of land grant issues in New Mexico.

1259   Westphall, Victor. Thomas Benton Catron and His Era.
       Tucson: University of Arizona Press, 1973.
The biography of a leading member of the Santa Fe ring.

1260   Wheeler, Kenneth W. To Wear a City's Crown: The
       Beginnings of Urban Growth in Texas, 1836-1865.
       Cambridge, Mass.: Harvard University Press, 1968.

1261   Williams, Elgin. The Animating Pursuits of
       Speculation: Land Traffic in the Annexation of Texas.
       New York: Columbia University Press, 1949.
A Columbia University thesis on land problems in early Texas
state history.

1262   Wollenberg, Charles, ed. Ethnic Conflict in
       California History. Los Angeles: Tinnon-Brown, 1970.
Talks given in a 1968 University of California, Berkeley
lecture series. Chapter 7 is a brief history of the Chicano
as farm worker and chapter 8 deals wih the political
coalition of Chicanos and Blacks.

1263   Wood, Raymond F. Mariana La Loca, "Prophetess of the
       Cantua" and Alleged Spouse of Joaquin Murrieta.
       Fresno, Calif.: Fresno County Historical Society,
       1970.
Local historical lore.

1264   Woodman, Lyman. Cortina, Rogue of the Rio Grande.
       San Antonio, Tex.: Naylor Publishing Co., 1950.
A popular biography of Juan N. Cortina and his border
activities.

1265   Wright, Arthur A. The Civil War in the Southwest.
       Denver, Colo.: Big Mountain Press, 1964.
Includes descriptions of the campaigns and battles.

IV: Theses and Dissertations

1266   Airey, Guy. "The Texas Mexican Border, 1861-1866."
        Master's thesis. Beaumont, Tex.: Lamar University,
        1971.

1267   Akers, Toma. "Mexican Ranchos in the Vicinity of
        Mission San Jose." Master's thesis. Berkeley:
        University of California, 1931.
Covers the decline of the rancho in California from 1843 to
1891.

1268   Allen, R. H. "The Influence of Spanish and Mexican
        Land Grants in the Agricultural History of
        California." Manuscript. Berkeley: Giannini
        Foundation, University of California, 1932.

1269   Almaguer, Tomas. "Class, Race, and Capitalist
        Development: The Social Transformation of a Southern
        California County, 1848-1903." Berkeley: University
        of California, 1979.

1270   Arellano, Anselmo. "Don Ezequiel C. de Baca and the
        Politics of San Miguel County." Master's thesis. Las
        Vegas: New Mexico Highlands University, 1974.
E. Cabeza de Vaca (1864-1917) was an important Nuevo
Mexicano political leader; in 1916 he was elected governor.

1271   Ash, Bette G. "The Mexican Texans in the Civil War."
        Master's thesis. Commerce: East Texas State
        University, 1972.

1272   Ash, George Rickard, Jr. "Frontier Authority:
        Authority in the New Mexico-Arizona Territories."
        Tucson: University of Arizona, 1973.

1273   Bailey, David T. "Stratification and Ethnic
        Differentiation in Santa Fe, 1860 & 1870." Austin:
        University of Texas, 1975.

1274   Baydo, Gerald R. "Cattle Ranching in Territorial New
        Mexico." Albuquerque: University of New Mexico, 1970.

1275   Bennett, Clarice. "A History of Rancho La Brea to
        1900." Master's thesis. Los Angeles: University of
        Southern California, 1938.
Describes the Rocha land grant and litigation over title in
the American period.

1276   Bents, Doris W. "The History of Tubac, 1752-1948."
        Master's thesis. Tucson: University of Arizona, 1949.
Tubac was an important presidio and settlement on the
Sonoran frontier. After the Gadsden Purchase Treaty (1853)

it became a part of the United States.

1277   Blew, Robert W. "Californios and American
        Institutions: A Study of Reactions to Social and
        Political Institutions." Los Angeles: University of
        Southern California, 1973.

1278   Bowden, J. J. "Private Land Claims in the Southwest."
        6 vols. Dallas, Tex.: Southern Methodist University,
        1969.
An extremely comprehensive law dissertation.

1279   Briggs, A. K. "The Archeology of 1882 Labor Camps on
        the Southern Pacific Railroad, Val Verde County,
        Texas." Master's thesis. Austin: University of
        Texas, 1974.

1280   Brown, Robert B. "Guns Over the Border: American Aid
        to the Juarez Government during the French
        Intervention." Ann Arbor: University of Michigan,
        1951.
Summarizes the various aid attempts.

1281   Carroll, Declan F. "The Sisters of Loretto, Pioneer
        Educators." Master's thesis. Lexington: University
        of Kentucky, 1937.
Includes the nuns' important role in southwestern education
in the second half of the 19th century.

1282   Caughey, John W. "Early Federal Relations With New
        Mexico." Master's thesis. Berkeley: University of
        California, 1926.

1283   Cervantes, Alfonso. "Border Raiding, Internal
        Conflict and the Mexican Image." Master's thesis.
        San Antonio, Tex.: St. Mary's University, 1970.

1284   Colton, Ray C. "The American Civil War in the Western
        Territories of New Mexico, Arizona, Colorado and
        Utah." College Park: University of Maryland, 1954.

1285   Cordova, Alfred G. "Octaviano Ambrosio Larrazolo, The
        Prophet of Transition in New Mexico: An Analysis of
        His Political Life." Master's thesis. Albuquerque:
        University of New Mexico, 1950.
The life of an important Mexican American leader, 1859-1930.
He was elected governor of New Mexico in 1918 and a decade
later was elected to the United States Senate.

1286   Coronel, Antonio F. "Cosas de California."
        Manuscript. Berkeley: Bancroft Library, University of
        California.
Antonio Coronel (1817-1894) was a prominent Los Angeles
civic and political leader.

1287   Crudup, Robert E.   "The Gadsden Purchase."   Master's
       thesis.   Stillwater: Oklahoma A & M University, 1933.

1288   Daddysman, James W.   "The Matamoros Trade 1861-1865."
       Morgantown: West Virginia University, 1976.

1289   Dominguez, Arnold.   "A Historical Study of Rancho San
       Juan Cajon de Santa Ana and its Owners Until 1857."
       Master's thesis.   Los Angeles: University of Southern
       California, 1950.
Describes the Ontiveros family's development of the rancho,
1833-1857, from the late Mexican era into the early American
period.

1290   Evans, James L.   "The Indian Savage, the Mexican
       Bandit, the Chinese Heathen--the Popular Stereotypes."
       Austin: University of Texas, 1968.

1291   Fichandler, Joseph B.   "The Porfirian Response to the
       Mexican Migrant Phenomenon and the Problems of the
       Mexican Community in the United States, 1876-1911."
       Manuscript.   Storrs: University of Connecticut, 1976.

1292   Finch, Gail H.   "The Anglo-American Regime in New
       Mexico, 1846-1861."   Master's thesis.   Norman:
       University of Oklahoma, 1936.

1293   Galindo Alvirez, Jose.   "Latin American Methodism in
       the Southwest."   Master's thesis.   Beaumont, Tex.:
       Lamar University, 1962.
Describes the efforts of Methodist missionaries to make
converts among Mexican Americans.

1294   Ganaway, Loomis Morton.   "New Mexico and the Sectional
       Controversy, 1846-61."   Nashville, Tenn.: Vanderbilt
       University, 1941.

1295   Goldfinch, Charles W.   "Juan N. Cortina, 1824-1892: A
       Reappraisal."   Master's thesis.   Chicago: University
       of Chicago, 1949.

1296   Goldstein, Marcy G.   "Americanization and
       Mexicanization: The Mexican Elite and Anglo-American
       in the Gadsden Purchase Lands, 1853-1880."   Cleveland,
       Ohio: Case Western Reserve University, 1977.

1297   Graf, LeRoy P.   "The Economic History of the Lower Rio
       Grande Valley, 1820-1875."   Cambridge, Mass.: Harvard
       University, 1942.

1298   Graves, Donald.   "Fence Cutting in Texas, 1883-1885."
       Master's thesis.   El Paso: University of Texas, 1962.
Presents one phase of Anglo-Mexican American conflict in the

Southwest. The activities of the Caballeros de Labor and
the White Caps grew out of this unrest.

1299   Gwin, Adeline. "A History of San Elizario, Texas."
       Master's thesis. El Paso: University of Texas, 1950.

1300   Halla, Frank L., Jr. "El Paso, Texas, and Juarez,
       Mexico: A Study of a Bi-Ethnic Community, 1846-1881."
       Austin: University of Texas, 1978.

1301   Hammons, Nancy Lee. "A History of El Paso County,
       Texas to 1900." Master's thesis. El Paso, Tex.:
       College of Mines and Metallurgy, 1942.

1302   Hanchett, William F. "Religion and the Gold Rush,
       1849-54: The Christian Churches in the California
       Mines." Berkeley: University of California, 1952.

1303   Hannon, Ralph L. "The Gadsden Purchase, 1854-1884: An
       Historical Geographic Justification." Master's
       thesis. Tempe: Arizona State University, 1966.

1304   Harris, Marilyn. "Arizona Land Grants: Cases Which
       Appeared Before the Court of Private Land Claims
       1891-1904." Master's thesis. San Diego, Calif.: San
       Diego State University, 1961.
Includes the Peralta grant and Reavis' confession of fraud.

1305   Hastings, Virginia M. "A History of Arizona During
       the Civil War, 1861-1865." Master's thesis. Tucson:
       University of Arizona, 1943.

1306   Heffernan, Violle C. "Thomas Benton Catron."
       Master's thesis. Albuquerque: University of New
       Mexico, 1940.
The life of one of the leading land lawyers and landowners
of New Mexico in the late 1800s.

1307   Helpler, Robert D. "William Watts Hart Davis in New
       Mexico." Master's thesis. Albuquerque: University of
       New Mexico, 1941.
Davis was a U.S. attorney, the territorial secretary, and
acting governor between 1853 and 1857.

1308   Henniker, Helen Blom. "The Beginnings of Nativism in
       California, 1848-1852." Master's thesis. Berkeley:
       University of California, 1948.
Survey of anti-Mexican and anti-Chinese feeling in the early
years of U.S. rule.

1309   Hornbeck, David, Jr. "Spatial Manifestations of
       Acculturative Processes in the Upper Pecos Valley, New
       Mexico, 1840-1880." Lincoln: University of Nebraska,
       1974.

Includes diagrams, tables, and maps.

1310 Hovious, JoAnn. "Social Change in Western Towns: El
      Paso, Texas, 1881-1889." Master's thesis. El Paso:
      University of Texas, 1972.

1311 Hughes, Charles W. "The Decline of the Californios?
      The Case of San Diego, 1846-1856." Master's thesis.
      San Diego, Calif.: San Diego State University, 1974.
Argues that San Diego Californios underwent no economic or
social decline in the decade after the U.S.-Mexican War.

1312 Irby, James A. "Line of the Rio Grande: War and Trade
      on the Confederate Frontier: 1861-1865." Athens:
      University of Georgia, 1969.

1313 Jenkins, Robert L. "The Gadsden Treaty and
      Sectionalism: A Nation Reacts." State College:
      Mississippi State University, 1978.

1314 Johnson, Emmet E. "New Mexico in the War of the
      Rebellion, 1860-61." Master's thesis. Las Vegas: New
      Mexico Highlands University, 1934.

1315 Jones, Ollie. "Rancho Santa Margarita y las Flores."
      Master's thesis. San Diego, Calif.: San Diego State
      University, 1957.
Describes the rancho's ownership and development from 1841
to 1941.

1316 Kenny, Wm. Robert. "History of the Sonora Mining
      Region of California, 1848-1860." Berkeley:
      University of California, 1955.
Describes social and economic conditions, morals, crime,
justice and nativism.

1317 Kerr, Homer L. "Migration into Texas, 1865-1880."
      Austin: University of Texas, 1953.

1318 Kitchen, Carr P. "Mexican Depredations on the Lower
      Rio Grande Valley, 1835-1885." Master's thesis.
      Waco, Tex.: Baylor University, 1933.

1319 Lee, Lawrence F. "Los Hermanos Penitentes." B.A.
      thesis. Albuquerque: University of New Mexico, 1910.
A description of the history and activities of the
Penitentes organization. Parts reprinted in El Palacio,
1920.

1320 Leopard, Donald B. "Joint Statehood, 1906." Master's
      thesis. Albuquerque: University of New Mexico, 1958.
Describes a part of the New Mexico-Arizona statehood
movement and its failure.

1321   McDowell, Archie M. "The Opposition to Statehood
        Within the Territory of New Mexico, 1888-1903."
        Master's thesis. Albuquerque: University of New
        Mexico, 1939.

1322   McGinty, Ruth. "Spanish and Mexican Ranchos in the
        San Francisco Bay Region." Master's thesis.
        Berkeley: University of California, 1921.
Describes rancho development and the problems of transition
to the U.S. period.

1323   Masters, Mary J. "New Mexico's Struggle for
        Statehood, 1903-1907." Master's thesis. Albuquerque:
        University of New Mexico, 1942.

1324   Miller, Robert Ryal. "Mexican Secret Agents in the
        United States, 1861-1867." Berkeley: University of
        California, 1960.
Describes Benito Juarez's agents and their activities and
relations with Mexican American communities in the
Southwest.

1325   Mitchell, Richard G. "Joaquin Murieta: A Study of
        Social Conditions in California." Master's thesis.
        Berkeley: University of California, 1927.
Study of Mexican-Anglo friction and the problem of outlaws,
based heavily on J. R. Ridge, item 1195.

1326   Neri, Michael C. "Hispanic Catholicism in
        Transitional California: The Life of Jose Gonzales
        Rubio, O.F.M., 1804-1875." Berkeley, Calif.: Graduate
        Theological Union, 1974.

1327   Orum, Thomas T. "The United States and Mexico,
        1861-1865." Master's thesis. Tucson: University of
        Arizona, 1967.
Focuses on border problems during the U.S. Civil War.

1328   Ottaway, Harold N. "The Penitente Moradas of the
        Taos, New Mexico Area." Norman: University of
        Oklahoma, 1975.

1329   Park, Joseph F. "The History of Mexican Labor in
        Arizona during the Territorial Period." Master's
        thesis. Tucson: University of Arizona, 1961.
An important pioneering work on Mexican labor in the
Southwest.

1330   Paulus, Lena. "Problems of the Private Land Grants in
        New Mexico." Master's thesis. Pittsburgh, Pa.:
        University of Pittsburgh, 1933.

1331   Pearson, Jim Berry. "A New Mexico Gold Story--The
        Elizabethtown-Red River Area." Austin: University of

Texas, 1955.

1332 Pitt, Leonard M. "The Foreign Miners' Tax of 1850: A
      Study of Nativism and Anti-nativism in Gold Rush
      California." Master's thesis. Los Angeles:
      University of California, 1955.
Has good detail on Foreign Miners' Tax and its repeal.

1333 Prestwood, Nadine. "The Social Life and Customs of
      the People of El Paso, 1848-1910." Master's thesis.
      El Paso: University of Texas, 1949.

1334 Ramirez, Nora E. "The Vaquero and Ranching in the
      Southwestern United States, 1600-1970." Bloomington:
      Indiana University, 1979.

1335 Rebord, Bernice A. "A Social History of Albuquerque,
      1880-1885." Master's thesis. Albuquerque: University
      of New Mexico, 1947.

1336 Riley, John D. "Santos Benavides: His Influence on
      the Lower Rio Grande, 1823-1891." Fort Worth: Texas
      Christian University, 1976.
Details the life of a prominent Tejano who was active during
the Civil War era and after in Laredo.

1337 Robertson, James. "From Alcalde to Mayor: A History
      of the Changes From the Mexican to the American Local
      Institutions in California." Berkeley: University of
      California, 1908.
Decribes the transition in politics and government at the
local level.

1338 Rodgers, William M. "Historical Land Occupance of the
      Upper San Pedro River Valley Since 1870." Master's
      thesis. Tucson: University of Arizona, 1965.
The San Pedro River in southeast Arizona runs northward into
the Gila River.

1339 Rogan, Francis E. "Military History of New Mexico
      Territory During the Civil War." Salt Lake City:
      University of Utah, 1961.

1340 Rowley, Ralph Alcorn. "United States Acquisition of
      the Spanish Borderlands: Problems and Legacy."
      Albuquerque: University of New Mexico, 1975.

1341 Shearer, Ernest C. "Border Diplomatic Relations
      Between the United States and Mexico, 1848-1860."
      Austin: University of Texas, 1939.

1342 Sluga, Mary E. "The Political Life of Thomas Benton
      Catron, 1896-1921." Master's thesis. Albuquerque:

University of New Mexico, 1941.
Benton was a leader of the Santa Fe ring and a prominent New Mexico lawyer.

1343   Smith, Cecil B.   "Diplomatic Relations Between the United States and Mexico Concerning Border Disturbances During the Diaz Regime, 1876-1910." Master's thesis. Austin: University of Texas, 1928.

1344   Sotomayor, Elsie. "Historical Aspects Related to the Assimilation and Acculturation of the Mexican American People, 1848-1920." Master's thesis. Fullerton: California State University, 1977.

1345   Standart, (Sister) M. Collette. "The Sonoran Migration to California, 1848-1856." Master's thesis. San Rafael, Calif.: Dominican College, 1974.

1346   Stapleton, Ernest S., Jr. "The History of the Baptist Missions in New Mexico, 1849-1860." Master's thesis. Albuquerque: University of New Mexico, 1954.

1347   Stensvagg, James T. "Clio on the Frontier: History and Society in the Mexican Cession, 1847-1930." Albuquerque: University of New Mexico, 1978.

1348   Stout, Joseph A., Jr. "The Last Years of Manifest Destiny: Filibustering in Northwestern Mexico, 1848-1862." Stillwater: Oklahoma State University, 1971.

1349   Tapay, Audry. "Las Vegas, 1890-1900; A Frontier Town Becomes Cosmopolitan." Master's thesis. Albuquerque: University of New Mexico, 1943.

1350   Telling, Irving, Jr. "New Mexican Frontiers: A Social History of the Gallup Area, 1881-1901." Cambridge, Mass.: Harvard University, 1953.

1351   Valencia, Francisco. "New Almaden and the Mexican." Master's thesis. San Jose, Calif.: San Jose State University, 1977.
The New Almaden mercury mines were active from the mid-1800s to the 1880s. Many Mexican miners were employed.

1352   Vowell, Jack C. "Politics at El Paso: 1850-1920." Master's thesis. El Paso, Tex.: Western College, 1952.
Includes good coverage of the El Paso Salt War, 1866-1877.

1353   Wagers, Jerard. "The History of Agricultural Labor in California Prior to 1880." Master's thesis. Berkeley: University of California, 1957.

1354   Waldrip, William I. "New Mexico During the Civil
        War." Master's thesis. Albuquerque: University of
        New Mexico, 1950.

1355   Ward, Charles F. "The Salt War of San Elizario."
        Master's thesis. Austin: University of Texas, 1932.
More commonly referred to as the El Paso Salt War,
1866-1877.

1356   Watkins, Lucy R. "Mexican Colonization in the United
        States Border, 1848-1858." Master's thesis.
        Berkeley: University of California, 1912.

1357   Webster, Michael G. "Texas Manifest Destiny and the
        Mexican Border Conflict, 1865-1880." Bloomington:
        Indiana University, 1972.

1358   Westphall, Victor. "History of Albuquerque
        1870-1880." Master's thesis. Albuquerque: University
        of New Mexico, 1947.

1359   Whalen, Norman M. "The Catholic Church in Arizona,
        1820-1870." Master's thesis. Tucson: University of
        Arizona, 1964.

1360   White, Katherin H. "The Pueblo de Socorro Grant." El
        Paso: University of Texas, 1961.

1361   Willoughby, Roy. "The Range Cattle Industry in New
        Mexico." Master's thesis. Albuquerque: University of
        New Mexico, 1933.

1362   Wilson, Thomas R. "William Walker and the
        Filibustering Expedition to Lower California and
        Sonora." Master's thesis. Austin: University of
        Texas, 1944.

1363   Woodward, Dorothy. "The Penitentes of New Mexico."
        New Haven, Conn.: Yale University, 1935.
Included in item 1177.

IV: Periodicals

1364 Acuña, Rudolph F. "Ignacio Pesqueira: Sonoran
      Caudillo." Arizona and the West 12:2 (Summer 1970),
      139-172.
Material on the Henry Crabb filibuster in 1857. Crabb had
married into a Mexican American family which had land claims
in Sonora.

1365 Aguirre, Yjinio F. "The Last of the Dons." Journal
      of Arizona History 10:4 (Winter 1969), 239-255.
A reminiscence and history of the Aguirre family, active in
Southwestern freighting--with photographs.

1366 Albrecht, Elizabeth. "Esteban Ochoa: Mexican-
      American Businessman." Arizoniana 4:2 (Summer 1963),
      35-40.
A brief biography of an important Arizona freighter,
1831-1888. As Arizona legislator and as mayor of Tucson he
worked to defend the interests of La Raza.

1367 Allen, R. H. "The Spanish Land Grant System as an
      Influence in the Agricultural Development of
      California." Agricultural History 9:3 (July 1935),
      127-142.

1368 Almaraz, Felix, Jr. "The Historical Heritage of the
      Mexican American in 19th Century Texas, An
      Interpretation." In The Role of the Mexican American
      in the History of the Southwest: Conference of
      Inter-American Institute, Pan American College, pp.
      12-23. Edinburg, Tex.: Pan American College, 1969.

1369 Antony, (Rev.) Claudius. "Kit Carson, Catholic." New
      Mexico Historical Review 10:4 (Oct. 1935), 323-326.
Carson married into a Taos Nuevo Mexicano family and became
a spokesman for pro-Anglo Nuevo Mexicanos.

1370 Applegate, Hetty. "Hermanos Penitentes." Southwest
      Review 17 (1931), 100-107.

1371 Archibald, Robert. "Cañon de Carnue: Settlement of a
      Grant." New Mexico Historical Review 51 (Oct. 1976),
      313-328.

1372 Ashkenazy, Irwin. "The Angels Join the Union."
      Westways 71:12 (Dec. 1979), 18-21, 80.
Describes Californios' celebration of Christmas, 1850.

1373 Atencio, Tomas C. "The Human Dimensions in Land Use
      and Displacement in Northern New Mexico Villages." In
      Indian and Spanish American Adjustments to Arid and
      Semi-Arid Environments. Edited by Clark S. Knowlton.

Lubbock: Texas Technological University, 1964.

1374 "Atrisco: A 17th Century Spanish Landgrant into the
      20th Century." By the Westland Development Co., Inc.
      La Luz 9:3 (March 1981), 12-14.
A brief history of the Atrisco grant from 1680 to the
present.

1375 Austin, Mary. "Trail of Blood: An Account of the
      Penitent Brotherhood of New Mexico." Century 108 (May
      1924), 35-44.

1376 Baldwin, P. M. "A Short History of the Mesilla
      Valley." New Mexico Historical Review 13:3 (July
      1938), 314-324.

1377 Bandini, Helen E. "Our Spanish American Families."
      Overland Monthly 26 (1895), 9-31.
Gives a sympathetic view of the Californios by a member of
the group.

1378 Barrows, June. "A Vermonter's Description of a Sunday
      in Los Angeles, California, in 1852." Vermont History
      38:3 (Summer 1970), 192-194.

1379 Binkley, William Campbell. "The Question of Texan
      Jurisdiction in New Mexico Under the United States."
      Southwestern Historical Quarterly 24 (July 1920),
      1-38.
Discusses Texas's claim to all of the New Mexican area east
of the Rio Grande River.

1380 Blackburn, George M. and Sherman L. Richards. "A
      Demographic History of the West: Nueces County, Texas,
      1850." Prologue 4 (1972), 3-21.
Uses census data to show impact of Anglo migration on the
Tejano community.

1381 Blew, Robert W. "Vigilantism in Los Angeles,
      1835-1874." Southern California Quarterly 54:1
      (Spring 1972), 11-30.

1382 Bowden, J. J. "The Texas-New Mexico Boundary Dispute
      Along the Rio Grande." Southwestern Historical
      Quarterly 63:2 (Oct. 1959), 221-237.

1383 Boyd, E. "The Third Order of St. Francis and the
      Penitentes of New Mexico." In Popular Arts of Spanish
      New Mexico, by E. Boyd, pp. 440-483. Santa Fe: Museum
      of New Mexico Press, 1974, item 555.

1384 Brackenridge, R. Douglas. "Presbyterian Missions to
      Mexicans in Texas in the Nineteenth Century." Journal

of Presbyterian History 49 (Summer 1971), 103-132.

1385   Bradfute, Richard W. "The Las Animas Land Grant,
        1843-1900." Colorado Magazine 47 (Winter 1970),
        26-43.

1386   Brinckerhoff, Sidney. "The Last of the Dons."
        Journal of Arizona History 10 (Winter 1964), 239-255.

1387   Brumgardt, John R. and William D. Putney. "San
        Salvador: New Mexican Settlement in Alta California."
        Southern California Quarterly 59 (Winter 1977),
        353-364.

1388   California, Office of the Surveyor General.
        "Corrected Report of Spanish and Mexican Grants in
        California, Complete to August 1, 1890." In Report of
        the Surveyor-General of the State of California, from
        August 1, 1888 to August 1, 1890, pp. 41-59.
        Sacramento, 1890.
Updates the register of land grants in California made by
Spanish or Mexican authorities. The report records
approximately 600 grants.

1389   California, Office of the Surveyor General.
        "Corrected Report of Spanish and Mexican Grants in
        California, Complete to February 25, 1886." In Report
        of the Surveyor General of the State of California
        from August 1, 1884, to August 1, 1886. Appendix to
        the Journal of the California Senate and Assembly of
        the 27th session, pp. 11-29. Sacramento, 1887.

1390   California, Office of the Surveyor General. "Report
        of Spanish or Mexican Grants in California, prepared
        by James S. Stratton." In Report of the Surveyor
        General of the State of California, from August 1,
        1879 to August 1, 1880. California, Legislature,
        Appendix to the Journals of the California Senate and
        Assembly of the 24th session, pp. 33-54. Sacramento,
        1881.
A list of land grants, organized by county.

1391   Cameron, William R. "Rancho Santa Margarita of San
        Luis Obispo." California Historical Society Quarterly
        36 (March 1957), 1-17.

1392   Campa, Arthur L. "Chile in New Mexico." New Mexico
        Business Review. University of New Mexico,
        Albuquerque (April 1934), 60-63.

1393   Carlson, Alvar W. "New Mexico's Sheep Industry,
        1850-1900: Its Role in the History of the Territory."
        New Mexico Historical Review 44:4 (Jan. 1969), 25-49.

1394   Carr, Ralph.   "Private Land Claims in Colorado."
       Colorado Magazine 25 (1948), 10-30.

1395   Chavez, Fray Angelico.   "The Penitentes of New
       Mexico." New Mexico Historical Review 29:2 (April
       1954), 97-123.

1396   Clum, John P.   "Santa Fe in the '70s." New Mexico
       Historical Review 2 (Oct. 1927), 380-386.

1397   Coerver, Don M.   "From Mortoritos to Chamizal: The
       U.S.-Mexican Boundary Treaty of 1884." Red River
       Valley Historical Review 2 (Winter 1975).

1398   Coffery, Frederic A.   "Some General Aspects of the
       Gadsden Treaty." New Mexico Historical Review 8
       (1933), 145-164.

1399   Cortes, Carlos E.   "El bandolerismo social chicano."
       In Aztlan: Historia del pueblo chicano, 1848-1910.
       Edited by David Maciel and Patricia Bueno, pp.
       111-122.   Mexico, D.F.: SepSetentas, 1975.   Item 99.

1400   Cortes, Carlos E.   "The Chicanos--A Frontier People."
       Agenda 10:1 (Jan.-Feb. 1980), 16-21, 42.

1401   Cortes, Enrique.   "Mexican Colonies During the
       Porfiriato." Aztlan 10 (Fall 1979), 1-14.
Includes efforts of Porfirio Diaz's government to repatriate
Mexicans from the United States.

1402   Cumberland, Charles C.   "Border Raids in the Lower Rio
       Grande Valley." Southwestern Historical Quarterly 57
       (Jan. 1964), 285-309.

1403   Dargan, Marion.   "New Mexico's Fight for Statehood,
       1895-1912, "I: The Political Leaders of the Latter
       Half of the 1890s and Statehood." New Mexico
       Historical Review 14:1 (Jan. 1939), 1-33; "II: The
       Attitude of the Territorial Press (1895-1901)."   14:2
       (April 1939), 121-142; "III: The Opposition Within the
       Party (1888-1890)."   15:2 (April 1940), 133-187; "IV:
       The Opposition Within the Territory During the
       Nineties."   16:1 (Jan. 1941), 70-103; "V: The
       Silencing of the Opposition at Home."   16:4 (Oct.
       1941), 379-400; "VI.: Advertising the Backyard of the
       United States."   18:1 (Jan. 1943), 60-96; "VII: The
       Part Played by the Press in the Southwest."   18:2
       (April 1943), 148-175.

1404   De Leon, Arnoldo.   "Wresting a Competence in
       Nineteenth Century Texas: The Case of the Chicanos."
       Red River Valley Historical Review 4 (1979), 52-64.

1405 Destruction of Spanish and Mexican Archives in New
      Mexico by United States Officials. [Santa Fe, 1870].
A four page reprint from the Santa Fe Weekly Post describing
the cavalier attitudes of early U.S. officials toward the
archival records. The University of California's Bancroft
Library has a copy.

1406 Dobie, J. Frank. "The Mexican Vaquero of the Texas
      Border." Southwestern Political and Social Science
      Quarterly 8 (June 1927), 15-26.

1407 Dobson, John M. "Desperados and Diplomacy: The
      Territory of Arizona v. Jesus Garcia, 1893." Journal
      of Arizona History 17 (1976), 137-160.

1408 Donnell, F. S. "When Texas Owned New Mexico to the
      Rio Grande." New Mexico Historical Review 8 (1933),
      65-75.
The issue of Texas claims to the eastern half of New Mexico.

1409 Dugan, Frank H. "The 1850 Affair of the Brownsville
      Separatists." Southwestern Historical Quarterly 61:2
      (Oct. 1957), 270-287.

1410 Dunham, Harold H. "Coloradians and the Maxwell
      Grant." Colorado Magazine 32 (April 1955), 131-145.

1411 Dunham, Harold H. "New Mexico Land Grants with
      Special Reference to the Title Papers of the Maxwell
      Grant." New Mexico Historical Review 30:1 (Jan.
      1955), 1-22.

1412 Dunham, Harold H. "Spanish and Mexican Land Grants in
      the Southwest." In The Hispanic Contribution to the
      State of Colorado. Edited by Jose de Onis. Boulder,
      Colo.: Westview Press, 1976.

1413 Dysart, Jane. "Mexican Women in San Antonio,
      1830-1860: The Assimilation Process." Western
      Historical Quarterly 7 (Oct. 1976), 365-375.

1414 Ebright, Malcolm. "The Embudo Grant: A Case Study of
      Justice and the Court of Private Land Claims."
      Journal of the West (July 1980), 74-85.
Argues against Richard Bradfute's view that the Court of
Private Land Claims was relatively fair in its decisions.

1415 Ebright, Malcolm. "The San Joaquin Grant: Who Owned
      the Common Lands? A Historical-legal Puzzle." New
      Mexico Historical Review 57:1 (Jan. 1982), 5-26.
Describes the history of a 19th century Rio Arriba, New
Mexico land grant.

1416   Egan, Ferol. "Twilight of the Californios." American
       West 6:2 (March 1969), 34-42.
Includes a number of excellent photographs.

1417   Egenhoff, Elizabeth L. "The Elephant as They Saw It:
       A Collection of Contemporary Pictures and Statements
       on Gold Mining in California." Centennial Supplement
       to the California Journal of Mines and Geology 45
       (Oct. 1949), 1-128.

1418   Ellis, Bruce T. "Fraud Without Scandal: The Roque
       Lovato Grant and Gaspar Ortiz y Alarid." New Mexico
       Historical Review 57:1 (Jan. 1982), 43-62.

1419   Ellison, William H., ed. "'Recollections of
       Historical Events in California, 1843-1878.' by
       William A. Streeter." California Historical Society
       Quarterly 18 (March 1939), 64-71; (June, 1939),
       157-179; (Sept. 1939), 254-278.

1420   Espinosa, Gilberto. "About New Mexico Land Grants."
       Albuquerque Bar Journal 7 (Sept. 1967), 5-15.

1421   Espinosa, Gilberto. "New Mexico Land Grants." The
       State Bar of New Mexico Journal 1 (Nov. 1, 1962),
       3-13.

1422   Espinosa, Jose Manuel, ed. "Memoir of a Kentuckian
       [Samuel Ellison] in New Mexico, 1848-1884." New
       Mexico Historical Review 13:1 (Jan. 1938), 1-13.

1423   Faulk, Odie B. "Projected Mexican Colonies in the
       Borderlands, 1852." Journal of Arizona History 10
       (1969), 115-128.
Proposal of Juan N. Almonte to save northern Mexico from
further U.S. expansionism.

1424   Foscue, Edwin J. "Historical Geography of the Lower
       Rio Grande Valley of Texas." Texas Geographic
       Magazine 3:1 (1939), 1-15.

1425   Francis, E. K. "Padre Martinez, a New Mexican Myth."
       New Mexico Historical Review 31:4 (Oct. 1956),
       265-289.
Father Antonio Martinez, the priest of Taos, was a leading
figure in New Mexican history from the late 1820s to his
death in 1867.

1426   Friend, Llerena B. "W. P. Webb's Texas Rangers."
       Southwestern Historical Quarterly 74:3 (Jan. 1971),
       293-323.
A critique of Webb's view and interpretation of the Texas
rangers.

1427   Gallego, Hilario. "Reminiscences of an Arizona
        Pioneer." Arizona Historical Review 6 (Jan. 1935),
        75-81.
Deals with Arizona history from ca. 1850 to 1900, including
the Gadsden Purchase and Apache-settler conflict.

1428   Ganaway, Loomis Morton. "New Mexico and the Sectional
        Controversy, 1846-1861." New Mexico Historical Review
        18:2-3 (April-July 1943), 113-147, 205-246.
The slavery issue found Nuevo Mexicanos somewhat divided.

1429   Garcia, Mario T. "The Californios of San Diego and
        the Politics of Accommodation." Aztlan 6 (Spring
        1975), 69-85.
Describes the background to the decline of southern
Californios, which the author ties in with loss of their
lands.

1430   Garcia, Mario T. "The Chicana in American History:
        The Mexican Women of El Paso, 1880-1920: A Case
        Study." Pacific Historical Review 49 (May 1980),
        315-337.
Includes description of the kinds of jobs that Chicanas
held; a preliminary study. Argues that the history of
Chicano workers is only half told until the Chicana
contribution is studied.

1431   Garcia, Mario T. "Merchants and Dons: San Diego's
        Attempt at Modernization, 1850-1860." Journal of San
        Diego History 21 (Winter 1975), 52-80.

1432   Garcia, Mario T. "Racial Dualism in the El Paso Labor
        Market, 1880-1920." Aztlan 6:2 (Summer 1975),
        197-218.

1433   Gates, Paul W. "Adjudication of Spanish-Mexican Land
        Claims in California." Huntington Library Quarterly
        31 (May 1958), 213-236.

1434   Gates, Paul W. "The California Land Act of 1851."
        California Historical Society Quarterly 50 (Dec.
        1971), 395-430.

1435   Gates, Paul W. "Pre-Henry George Land Welfare in
        California." California Historical Society Quarterly
        46 (June 1967), 121-148.

1436   Gonzales, Jovita. "Folk-Lore of the Texas-Mexican
        Vaquero." In Texas and Southwestern Lore. Edited by
        J. Frank Dobie. Austin: Texas Folklore Society, 1927.
        Reprint, Dallas: Southern Methodist University Press,
        1967.

1437 Gonzalez Navarro, Moises. "Los braceros en el
      porfiriato." In Estudios Sociologicos. Mexico, D.F.:
      Quinto Congreso Nacional de Sociologia, 1964.

1438 Greer, Richard A. "Origins of the Foreign-born
      Population of New Mexico During the Territorial
      Period." New Mexico Historical Review 17:4 (Oct.
      1942), 281-287.

1439 Griswold del Castillo, Richard. "La Familia Chicana:
      Social Changes in the Chicano Family of Los Angeles,
      1850-1880." Journal of Ethnic Studies 3:1 (Spring
      1975), 41-58.

1440 Griswold del Castillo, Richard. "Myth and Reality:
      Chicano Economic Mobility in Los Angeles, 1850-1880."
      Aztlan 6 (Summer 1976), 151-171.

1441 Guinn, James M. "The Sonoran Migration." Historical
      Society of Southern California Annual Publications 8
      (1909-1910), 31-36.

1442 Hall, G. Emlen. "Giant Before the Surveyor General:
      The Land Career of Donaciano Vigil." Journal of the
      West 19:3 (July 1980), 64-73.
Vigil (1802-1877) was active in New Mexico government from
the late 1830s until the end of the 1860s.

1443 Hall, Martin H. "Native Mexican Relations in
      Confederate Arizona, 1861-1862." Journal of Arizona
      History 8 (1967), 171-178.
Describes degrees of Mexican Americans' loyalty to their new
country early in the Civil War when the Confederacy
dominated Arizona.

1444 Halleck, Henry W. "Report on California Land Grants."
      In California Message and Correspondence, 1850.
      United States Congress, House Executive Document No.
      17. Washington, D.C.: U.S. Government Printing
      Office, 1850.
Halleck was Secretary of State in California's military
government. His 1850 report argued that most Mexican land
claims were invalid.

1445 Harby, Lee C. "Mexican-Texan Types and Contrasts."
      Harpers 81 (July 1890), 229-246.
An early discussion of the development of Spanish-speaking
border towns on the United States side.

1446 Hargis, Donald. "Native Californians in the
      Constitutional Convention of 1849." Historical
      Society of Southern California Quarterly 26:1 (March
      1954), 3-13.

1447   Haskett, Bert. "History of the Sheep Industry in
        Arizona." Arizona Historical Quarterly 7 (July 1936),
        3-49.

1448   Herring, Patricia R. "A Plan for the Colonization of
        Sonora's Northern Frontier: The Paredes Proyectos of
        1850." Journal of Arizona History 10 (1969), 103-114.
An effort to avoid further U.S. expansion after Guadalupe
Hidalgo, and especially the Gadsden Purchase.

1449   Hittell, John S. "Mexican Land Claims in
        California." Hutching's Illustrated California
        Magazine 2 (1857-1858), 442-448.

1450   Hornbeck, David. "Mexican-American Land Tenure
        Conflict in California." Journal of Geography 75:4
        (April 1976), 209-221.

1451   Hornbeck, David and Mary Tucey. "The Submergence of a
        People: Migration and Occupational Structure in
        California, 1850." Pacific Historical Review 46 (Aug.
        1977), 471-484.
Describes the impact of Anglo migration into California on
the Californio population's occupational pattern; several
maps.

1452   Hughes, Charles. "The Decline of the Californios: The
        Case of San Diego, 1846-1856." Journal of San Diego
        History 21 (Summer 1975), 1-31.

1453   Hyde, Arthur E. "The Old Regime in the Southwest."
        Century 63 (March 1902), 690-701.
Describes the conflict between Anglos and Mexican Americans.

1454   Jackson, Joseph H. "The Creation of Joaquin
        Murieta." Pacific Spectator 2 (Spring 1948), 176-181.
An early critique of the Murieta legend.

1455   Jackson, W. T. "The Chavez Land Grant: A Scottish
        Investment in New Mexico, 1881-1940." Pacific
        Historical Review 21 (Nov. 1952), 349-356.
Illustrates the European investment in Mexican land grant
claims.

1456   Jenkins, Myra E. "The Baltasar Baca Grant: History of
        an Encroachment." El Palacio 61 (1961), 47-64; 68
        (1968), 87-105.
Describes the serious problem of expansion of claims in New
Mexican land grant history.

1457   Journal of the West 19:3 (July 1980).
The entire issue is devoted to Spanish and Mexican land
grants in New Mexico and Colorado.

1458   Juarez, Jose Roberto. "La iglesia catolica y el
        chicano en sur Tejas, 1836-1911." Aztlan 4 (Fall
        1973), 217-255.

1459   Julian, George W. "Land Stealing in New Mexico."
        North American Review 145 (July 1, 1887), 2-31.
Julian was surveyor general for the New Mexican Territory in
the second half of the 1880s.

1460   Julian, George W. "Redemption of New Mexico."
        Magazine of Western History 10 (1889), 238-246.

1461   Keleher, William A. "Law of the New Mexico Land
        Grant." New Mexico Historical Review 4 (Oct. 1929),
        350-371.

1462   Kenny, Wm. Robert. "Mexican-American Conflict on the
        Mining Frontier, 1848-1852." Journal of the West 6
        (Oct. 1967), 582-592.
Describes the anti-Mexican attitudes and actions in the
California gold rush that led to the Foreign Miners' Tax.

1463   King, William F. "El Monte: An American Town in
        Southern California, 1851-1866." Southern California
        Historical Quarterly 53 (Dec. 1971), 317-332.

1464   Knapp, Frank A., Jr. "A Note on General Escobedo in
        Texas." Southwestern Historical Quarterly 55 (Jan.
        1952), 394-401.
General Mariano Escobedo (1826-1902) was a political refugee
in the 1870s as result of his anti-Porfirista stance.

1465   Knowlton, Clark S. "Causes of Land Loss Among the
        Spanish Americans in Northern New Mexico." Rocky
        Mountain Social Science Journal 1 (1963), 201-211.

1466   Knowlton, Clark S. "Culture Conflict and Natural
        Resources." In Social Behavior, Natural Resources,
        and the Environment. Edited by William Burch, et al.,
        pp. 109-145. New York: Harper, 1972.
Describes the loss of land grants in New Mexico largely as
the result of cultural differences and resultant conflict.

1467   Knowlton, Clark S. "Patron-peon Pattern Among the
        Spanish-Americans of New Mexico." Social Forces 41
        (Oct. 1962), 12-17.
An abstract of a complex historical development that began
in the colonial period.

1468   Knowlton, Clark S., ed. "Spanish and Mexican Land
        Grants in the Southwest." Social Science Journal 13
        (1976), 3-64.

1469   Knowlton, Clark S.   "The Town of Las Vegas Community
       Land Grant: An Anglo-American Coup d'Etat." Journal
       of the West 19:3 (July 1980), 12-21.
Describes how the grant was lost to its inhabitants through
a legal fiat in 1902.

1470   Lamar, Howard R.   "Land Policy in the Spanish
       Southwest, 1846-1891: A Study in Contrasts." Journal
       of Economic History 22:4 (Dec. 1962), 498-515.
Studies the differences in devising government policies for
land questions in New Mexico as compared to California and
Texas. Includes the Maxwell grant.

1471   Lamar, Howard R.   "Political Patterns in New Mexico
       and Utah Territories, 1850-1900." Utah Historical
       Quarterly 28:4 (Oct. 1960), 363-388.
Largely the story of the Santa Fe ring and its political
activities.

1472   Lamar, Howard R.   "The Reluctant Admission: The
       Struggle to Admit Arizona and New Mexico to the
       Union." In The American West: An Appraisal. Edited
       by Robert G. Ferris. Santa Fe: Museum of New Mexico
       Press, 1963.

1473   Larson, Robert W.   "The White Caps of New Mexico: A
       Study of Ethnic Militancy in the Southwest." Pacific
       Historical Review 44 (May 1975), 171-185.
Ties the White Caps in with the Knights of Labor and
describes the role of Juan Jose Herrera.

1474   Lo Buglio, Rudecinda A.   "California Private Land
       Claim Records." Spanish-American Geneologist 31-34
       (1979), 544-555.
Briefly discusses the 621 California land claims available
on microfilm from the National Archives.

1475   Lo Buglio, Rudecinda A.   "Spanish and Mexican Land
       Records." Spanish-American Geneologist 21 (Jan.
       1976), 372-392; 22 (June 1976), 412-417; 27-30 (1978);
       31-34 (1979), 577-581.
The Spanish-American Geneologist also contains oral history
recollections, and family records.

1476   Lopez, Ruben E.   "The Legend of Tiburcio Vasquez."
       Pacific Historian 15:2 (Summer 1971), 20-30.
A general account of the California bandit Tiburcio Vasquez
including some oral history and folk history.

1477   Love, Clara M.   "History of the Cattle Industry in the
       Southwest." Southwestern Historical Quarterly 19
       (April 1916), 370-399; 20 (July 1916), 1-18.

1478   Lugo, Jose Del Carmen. "Life of a Rancher."
       Historical Society of Southern California Quarterly 32
       (Sept. 1950), 185-236.
A translation of Lugo's dictation to Thomas Savage in 1877,
item 1132.

1479   McBride, James D. "The Liga Protectora Latina: A
       Mexican-American Benevolent Society in Arizona."
       Journal of the West 14:4 (Oct. 1975), 82-90.
Describes the founding and development of one of the oldest
Mexican American mutualist societies in the Southwest, 1914
to 1920s.

1480   McCornack, Richard B. "Porfirio Diaz en la frontera
       texana, 1875-1877." Historia Mexicana 5:3 (Jan.-March
       1956), 373-410.
Describes the troubled Texas border and the activities of
the U.S. government to prevent unneutral acts. Based on
U.S. archival materials.

1481   McCourt, Purnee A. "The Conejos Land Grant of
       Southern Colorado." Colorado Magazine 52 (Winter
       1975), 35-51.

1482   McKain, Walter C., Jr. and Sara Miles. "Santa Barbara
       County Between Two Social Orders." California
       Historical Society Quarterly 25 (Dec. 1946), 311-318.
Argues that many Californios became acculturated into the
post-Gudalupe Hidalgo Anglo culture.

1483   "The Man Who Wrote the Colorado Constitution." La Luz
       1 (June 1972), 50-53.
Senator Casimiro Barela was the principal Hispano Colorado
political leader in the second half of the nineteenth
century.

1484   Martinez, Oscar. "On the Size of the Chicano
       Population: New Estimates, 1850-1900." Aztlan 6
       (Spring 1975), 43-67.
Revises upward by about one third the earlier estimates of
Mexican American population; includes tables of population
estimates.

1485   Mattison, Ray H. "The Tangled Web: The Controversy
       Over the Tumacacori and Baca Land Grants." Journal of
       Arizona History 8:2 (Summer 1967), 71-90.
An excellent illustration of land grant problems--and their
solutions.

1486   Mawn, Geoffrey P. "A Land Grant Guarantee: The Treaty
       of Guadalupe Hidalgo or the Protocol of Queretaro."
       Journal of the West 14:4 (Oct. 1975), 49-63.
Argues that the treaty of Guadalupe Hidalgo, and not the
Protocol, guarantees the validity of legitimate Mexican and

Spanish land grants.

1487   Maxwell, Grant. "Course of Empire." New Mexico
       Magazine 16 (Oct. 1938), 18-19, 34, 36, 38.
Describes the Mesilla takeover by the U.S. in 1854.

1488   May, Ernest R. "Tiburcio Vasquez." Historical
       Society of Southern California Quarterly 29:3-4
       (Sept.-Dec. 1947), 122-135.
A brief life of the famous California brigand.

1489   Mead, Martha D. "Colonel Jose Francisco Chaves. A
       Short Biography of the Father of the New Mexico
       Statehood Movement." Greater Llano Estacado Southwest
       Heritage 8:4 (Winter 1978-1979), 13-21.

1490   Metzgar, Joseph V. "The Atrisco Land Grant,
       1692-1977." New Mexico Historical Review 52 (Oct.
       1977), 269-296.

1491   Meyer, Doris L. "The Language Issue in New Mexico,
       1880-1900: Mexican-American Resistance Against
       Cultural Erosion." Bilingual Review/Revista Bilingue
       4:1-2 (Jan.-Aug. 1977), 99-106.

1492   Miller, Robert Ryal. "Californians Against the
       Emperor." California Historical Society Quarterly 37
       (Sept. 1958), 192-214.
Story of Placido Vega's mission, 1864-1865, to help the
Liberal revolt against the Emperor Maximilian.

1493   Miller, Robert Ryal. "Gaspar Sanchez Ochoa: A Mexican
       Secret Agent in the United States." The Historian 23
       (May 1961), 316-329.

1494   Miller, Robert Ryal. "Matias Romero, Mexican Minister
       to the United States During the Juarez-Maximilian
       Era." Hispanic American Historical Review 45:2 (May
       1967), 228-245.
Some material on the recruiting of Mexicans in the United
States with leads to other materials.

1495   Miller, Robert Ryal. "Placido Vega: A Mexican Secret
       Agent in the United States." The Americas 19 (Oct.
       1962), 137-148.

1496   Miller, Thomas L. "The Texas Court of Claims,
       1856-1861." Agricultural History 34 (Jan. 1940),
       35-40.

1497   Montgomery, Robert H. "Keglar Hill." Survey 46:3
       (May 1, 1931), 171, 193-195.
Concerns Keglar Hill, a Texas cotton community "invaded" by
Mexican laborers in the 1880s.

1498   Morefield, Richard H. "Mexicans in the California
        Mines, 1848-53." California Historical Society
        Quarterly 35:1 (March 1956), 37-46.
Describes Californio and Mexican miners' difficulties with
Anglos and their being pushed into less attractive aspects
of mining.

1499   Morris, Leopold. "The Mexican Raid of 1875 on Corpus
        Christi." Texas Historical Association Quarterly 4
        (1900-1901), 128-139.

1500   Mosely, Edward H. "The Texas Threat, 1855-1860."
        Journal of Mexican American History 3 (1973), 89-104.
Describes filibustering and other activity threatening
Mexican border residents.

1501   Newman, Simeon H., III. "The Santa Fe Ring: A Letter
        to the New York Sun [1875, by Simeon Harrison
        Newman]." Arizona and the West 12:3 (Autumn 1970),
        269-288.

1502   Nostrand, Richard L. "The Hispanic-American
        Borderland: Delimitation of an American Culture
        Region." Association of American Geographers Annals
        60 (1970), 638-661.

1503   Nostrand, Richard L. "The Hispanic American
        Borderland." In Chicano: The Evolution of a People,
        pp. 23-25. Edited by Renato Rosaldo, Robert Calvert
        and Gustav Seligman. Minneapolis, Minn.: Winston
        Press, 1973. Item 161.

1504   Officer, James. "Historical Factors in Interethnic
        Relations in the Community of Tucson." Arizoniana 1
        (Fall 1960), 12-16.

1505   Otis, Raymond. "Medievalism in America." New Mexico
        Quarterly 6 (1936), 83-90.
Describes the Penitentes' organization in upper New Mexico.

1506   Padilla, Fernando V. "Early Chicano Legal
        Recognition: 1846-1897." Journal of Popular Culture
        13 (Winter 1979), 564-574.

1507   Paul, Rodman. "The Spanish-Americans in the
        Southwest, 1848-1900." In The Frontier Challenge:
        Responses to the Trans-Mississippi West. Edited by
        John Clark, pp. 31-56. Lawrence: University of Kansas
        Press, 1971.

1508   "Los Penitentes." La Luz 6:3 (March 1977), 11-15.

1509   Pilcher, J. E.   "Outlawry on the Mexican Border."
       Scribner's 10 (1891), 78-86.

1510   Pitt, Leonard.   "The Beginnings of Nativism in
       California."   Pacific Historical Review 30 (Feb.
       1961), 23-38.
A description of the Foreign Miners' Tax during the
California gold rush and attendant developments.

1511   Prince, L. Bradford and J. N. Irwin.   "Claims to
       Statehood."   North American Review 156 (1893),
       346-358.
Prince was territorial governor of New Mexico and a leader
in the Santa Fe Ring.

1512   Puckett, Fidelia M.   "Ramon Ortiz: Priest and
       Patriot."   New Mexico Historical Review 25 (Oct.
       1950), 265-295.
The life of an important figure in later nineteenth century
New Mexican history.

1513   Rasch, Philip J.   "The People of the Territory of New
       Mexico vs. the Santa Fe Ring."   New Mexico Historical
       Review 47 (April 1972), 185-202.

1514   Rippy, J. Fred.   "Anglo-American Filibusters and the
       Gadsden Treaty."   Hispanic American Historical Review
       5 (May 1922), 155-180.
Describes the activities of American filibusters acting as a
hindrance to the drawing up of the Gadsden Purchase Treaty
with Mexico, 1853.

1515   Rippy, J. Fred.   "Border Troubles Along the Rio
       Grande, 1848-1860."   Southwestern Historical Quarterly
       23 (Oct. 1919), 91-111.

1516   Rippy, J. Fred.   "The Boundary of New Mexico and the
       Gadsden Treaty."   Hispanic American Historical Review
       4 (Nov. 1921), 715-742.
Basically covers the activities of the boundary commission
arising out of the Treaty of Guadalupe Hidalgo and
especially the excitement on the border while the Gadsden
Treaty was being negotiated.

1517   Rippy, J. Fred.   "The Negotiation of the Gadsden
       Treaty."   Southwestern Historical Quarterly 27
       (1923-1924), 1-26.

1518   Rippy, J. Fred.   "A Ray of Light on the Gadsden
       Treaty."   Southwestern Historical Quarterly 24
       (1920-1921), 235-242.

1519   Rischin, Moses. "Continuities and Discontinuities in
       Spanish-speaking California." In Ethnic Conflict in
       California History. Edited by Charles Wollenberg.
       Los Angeles: Tinnon-Brown, 1970.

1520   Rister, Carl Coke. "Outlaws and Vigilantes of the
       Southern Plains, 1865-1885." Mississippi Valley
       Historical Review 19 (1933), 537-554.
A broad historical survey of the frontier and Mexican border
problem of outlawry. Includes Texas Ranger material.

1521   Rock, Michael J. "Anton Chico and Its Patent."
       Journal of the West 19:3 (July 1980), 86-91.
Illustrates how difficult it often was for former Mexican
citizens to get justice in their land rights.

1522   Romero, Matias. "The Garza Raid and Its Lessons."
       North American Review 155:430 (Sept. 1892), 324-337.
Catarino Garza, border journalist and anti-Diaz
revolutionary, invaded Mexico in the fall of 1891 with a
small force. The author was the Mexican Treasury Minister.

1523   Santee, J. F. "The Battle of La Glorieta Pass." New
       Mexico Historical Review 6 (1931), 66-75.
A crucial New Mexico battle between Union and Confederate
forces in the Civil War.

1524   Saunders, Lyle. "The Social History of
       Spanish-Speaking People in Southwestern United States
       Since 1846." First Congress of Historians from Mexico
       and the United States Proceedings (1950), 152-165.
       Mexico, D.F.: Editorial Cultura.

1525   Scott, Wayne W. "Spanish Land Grant Problems Were
       Here Before the Anglo." New Mexico Business 20 (July
       1967), 1-9.

1526   Scurry, W. R. "Operations on the Rio Grande, February
       21, 1862." Southern Historical Society Papers 18
       (1890), 318-319.
Describes the critical Civil War battle of Valverde in which
Texan Confederates defeated a New Mexican volunteer force
under Kit Carson despite their own heavy losses.

1527   Servin, Manuel P. "The Role of Mexican-Americans in
       the Development of Early Arizona." In An Awakened
       Minority: The Mexican Americans. Edited by Manuel P.
       Servin, pp. 28-44. Beverly Hills, Calif.: Glencoe
       Press, 1974.

1528   Shapiro, Harold A. "The Labor Movement in San
       Antonio, Texas, 1865-1915." Southwestern Social

Science Quarterly 36 (1955), 160-175.

1529   Springer, Frank H. "The Private Land Grant in New
        Mexico." In New Mexico Bar Association Fifth Annual
        Session *Report*, pp. 12-13. Santa Fe: New Mexico
        Printing Co., 1890.

1530   Spude, Robert L. "The Walker-Weaver Diggings and the
        Mexican Placero, 1863-1864." *Journal of the West* 14:4
        (Oct. 1975), 64-74.
Describes the pattern of anti-Mexican discrimination set by
early Anglo miners in central Arizona.

1531   Standart, (Sister) M. Collette, O.P. "The Sonoran
        Migration to California, 1848-1856: A Study of
        Prejudice." *Southern California Quarterly* 58 (Fall
        1976), 333-358.

1532   Stanger, Frank M. "A California Rancho Under Three
        Flags." *California Historical Society Quarterly* 17
        (Sept. 1938), 245-259.
Describes the history of Rancho Buri Buri on the San
Francisco peninsula under Spain, Mexico and the United
States. A typical pattern of subdivision, conflict, and
often loss.

1533   Steele, James W. "Among the New Mexicans." *Kansas
        Magazine* 1 (Feb. 1872), 105-112.

1534   Steele, Thomas J., S.J. "Italian Jesuits and Hispano
        Penitentes." *Il Giornalina* 5:1 (Feb. 1978), 11-17.
Consists largely of Jesuit reports from the New
Mexico-Colorado settlements on the Penitentes during the
second half of the nineteenth century. *Il Giornalino* is
published in Albuquerque.

1535   Steiner, Stan. "On the Trail of Joaquin Murieta."
        American West 18:1 (Jan.-Feb. 1981), 54-56, 66.
A piece of popular Sunday supplement history.

1536   Sunseri, Alvin R. "Anglo-American Attitudes Toward
        the Hispanos, 1846-1861." *Journal of Mexican American
        History* 3 (1973), 76-88.

1537   Tanner, John D., Jr. and Gloria R. Lothrop. "Don Juan
        Forster, Southern California Ranchero." *Southern
        California Quarterly* 52:3 (Sept. 1970), 195-230.
The recollections of an English-born Mexican land grant
recipient as given to Thomas Savage (for H. H. Bancroft) and
as corrected and amended by the editors. Forster was
related by marriage to the Pico family.

1538   Taylor, Morris F. "Capt. William Craig and the Vigil
        and St. Vrain Grant, 1855-1870." *Colorado Magazine* 45

(Fall 1968), 301-321.

1539   Taylor, Morris F. "The Leitensdorfer Claim in the
       Vigil and St. Vrain Grant." Journal of the West 19:3
       (July 1980), 92-99.
Illustrates the frequent complexity of land grant claims and
justice.

1540   Taylor, Morris F. "A New Look at an Old Case: The
       Bent Heirs' Claim in the Maxwell Grant." New Mexico
       Historical Review 43 (July 1968), 213-228.

1541   Taylor, Morris F. "Promoters of the Maxwell Grant."
       Colorado Magazine 42 (Spring 1965), 47-64.

1542   Taylor, Morris F. "The Two Land Grants of Gervacio
       Nolan." New Mexico Historical Review 47 (April 1972),
       151-184.

1543   Taylor, Morris F. "The Uña de Gato Grant in Colfax
       County." New Mexico Historical Review 51 (April
       1976), 121-143.

1544   Taylor, William B. and Elliot West. "Patron
       Leadership at the Crossroads: Southern Colorado in the
       Late Nineteenth Century." Pacific Historical Review
       42 (Aug. 1973), 335-357. Reprinted in The Chicano,
       edited by Norris Hundley, Jr. Santa Barbara, Calif.:
       American Bibliographical Center-Clio Press, 1975.
Describes southern Colorado rural social structure at the
end of the 19th century; argues the old patron-peon
relationship was modififed and finally disappeared as a
result of cultural and economic changes.

1545   Thompson, Jerry Don. "Mexican Americans in the Civil
       War: The Battle of Valverde." Texana 10:1 (Winter
       1972), 1-19.

1546   Tyler, Ronnie C. "Cotton on the Border, 1861-1865."
       Southwestern Historical Quarterly 73:4 (April 1970),
       456-471.

1547   Van Ness, John R. "Spanish American vs. Anglo
       American Land Tenure and the Study of Economic Change
       in New Mexico." Social Science Journal 13 (Oct.
       1976), 45-51.

1548   Vigil, Ralph H. "Willa Cather and Historical
       Reality." New Mexico Historical Review 50:2 (April
       1975), 123-138.
Discusses Cather's interpretation of Fr. Antonio Jose
Martinez of New Mexico in her Death Comes for the
Archbishop.

1549   Wagoner, Jay J. "The Gadsden Purchase Lands." New
       Mexico Historical Review 26 (Jan. 1951), 18-43.

1550   Waldrip, William I. "New Mexico During the Civil
       War." New Mexico Historical Review 28:3 (July 1953),
       163-182; 28:4 (Oct. 1953), 251-290.

1551   Walker, Henry Pickering. "Freighting from Guaymas to
       Tucson, 1850-1880." Western Historical Quarterly 1:3
       (July 1970), 291-362.

1552   Webster, Michael G. "Intrigue on the Rio Grande: The
       Rio Bravo Affair, 1875." Southwestern Historical
       Quarterly 74:2 (Oct. 1970), 149-164.
Part of the border problems and Texas expansionist ideas.

1553   West, Robert. "Validity of Certain Spanish Land
       Grants in Texas." Texas Law Review 2 (June 1924),
       435-444.

1554   Westphall, Victor. "Fraud and Implications of Fraud
       in the Land Grants of New Mexico." New Mexico
       Historical Review 49:3 (July 1974), 189-218.

1555   Westphall, Victor. "The Public Domain in New Mexico,
       1854-1891." New Mexico Historical Review 33:1 & 2
       (Jan. & April 1958), 24-52 & 128-143.

1556   "Why New Mexico Does Not Flourish." Nation 42 (Jan.
       28, 1886), 70-71.
Discusses the problems of Spanish and Mexican land grants.

1557   Wilcox, Sebron S. "The Laredo City Election and Riot
       of April, 1886." Southwestern Historical Quarterly 45
       (July 1941), 1-23.

1558   Williams, R. Hal. "George W. Julian and Land Reform
       in New Mexico, 1885-1889." Agricultural History 41
       (Jan. 1967), 71-84.
Julian was the incorruptible surveyor general appointed by
President Grover Cleveland in 1885.

1559   Wright, Doris M. "The Making of Cosmopolitan
       California: An Analysis of Immigration, 1848-1870."
       California Historical Society Quarterly 19 (Dec.
       1940), 323-343.
Includes a discussion of the Sonoran immigrants and the
Peruvian and Chilean miners as well. With charts on U.S.
and foreign-born population, on overland migration and
seaport arrivals.

V.
1900 TO WORLD WAR II _____

This section consists principally of materials on the Great Migration from Mexico between 1900 and 1929, on the relations of border-dwelling Mexican Americans with the Great Mexican Revolution of 1910, on World War I, the Great Depression, and the repatriation that occurred during the 1920s and 1930s.

1560   Anders, Evan. Boss Rule in South Texas: The
        Progressive Era. Austin: University of Texas Press,
        1982.
Includes the role of Manuel Guerra, merchant-rancher whose power in Starr County was based on his control of the Mexican American vote.

1561   Anderson, Rodney D. Outcasts in Their Own Land:
        Mexican Industrial Workers, 1906-1911. DeKalb:
        Northern Illinois University Press, 1976.
Describes conditions in Mexico that helped to initiate the beginnings of the Great Migration.

1562   Balderrama, Francisco E. In Defense of La Raza: The
        Los Angeles Mexican Consulate and Mexican Community,
        1929-1936. Tucson: University of Arizona Press, 1983.
Describes the role of the consulate as community advisor and leader in its dealing with problems of prejudice, discrimination, unemployment, school segregation, and labor strife during the very troubled early years of the Great Depression. A 1978 UCLA thesis.

1563   Barrera Fuentes, Florencio. Historia de la revolucion
        mexicana: la etapa precursora. Mexico, D.F.: Talleres
        Graficos de la Nacion, 1955.
Chapters VIII and XIII cover the role of the Southwest and of Mexican Americans in the Mexican revolution of 1910.

1564   Blaisdell, Lowell L. The Desert Revolution: Baja
        California, 1911. Madison: University of Wisconsin
        Press, 1962.
Includes material on the Mexican American role in the
struggle in Baja California.

1565   Bloch, Louis. Report on the Mexican Labor Situation
        in Imperial Valley. 22nd Biennial Report, 1925-1926.
        Sacramento: California State Bureau of Labor
        Statistics, 1926.

1566   Bogardus, Emory S. Immigration and Race Attitudes.
        New York: D. C. Heath & Co., 1928.
Discussion of nativist attitudes by an outstanding
sociologist and longtime expert on Mexican immigrants.

1567   Bogardus, Emory S. The Mexican Immigrant. Los
        Angeles: Council on International Relations, 1929.

1568   Bogardus, Emory S. The Mexican in the United States.
        Los Angeles: University of Southern California Press,
        1934. Reprints, San Francisco: R & E Research
        Associates, 1970; New York: Arno Press, 1970.
Especially valuable for a contemporary historical view.

1569   Bogardus, Emory S. The Survey of Race Relations on
        the Pacific Coast. Los Angeles: Council on
        International Relations, 1926.

1570   Braddy, Haldeen. Pershing's Mission to Mexico. El
        Paso: Texas Western College Press, 1966.
A popular history of the U.S. military penetration of Mexico
in 1916-1917 in search of Francisco Villa.

1571   Bresette, Linna E. Mexicans in the United States: A
        Report of a Brief Survey. Washington, D.C.: National
        Catholic Welfare Conference, 1929.
A 45-page report on the problems encountered by Mexicans.
Included in item 1583.

1572   Brophy, A. Blake. Foundlings on the Frontier: Racial
        and Religious Conflict in Arizona Territory,
        1904-1905. Tucson: University of Arizona Press, 1972.
The history of forty Anglo orphans placed with Mexican
families in Clifton, Arizona.

1573   Brown, Lyle C. The Mexican Liberals and Their
        Struggle Against the Diaz Dictatorship, 1900-1906.
        Mexico, D.F.: Mexico City College Press, 1956.
Includes materials on activities in the U.S. southwestern
border area.

1574   Byrkit, James. Forging the Copper Collar: Arizona's
       Labor-Management War, 1901-1921. Tucson: University
       of Arizona Press, 1982.
Includes material on the 1917 Bisbee deportation and the
role of Mexican miners.

1575   California, Legislature, Joint Immigration Committee.
       Increase in Mexican Population. Bulletin No. 316.
       Prepared by V. S. McClatchy. San Francisco:
       California Joint Immigration Committee, 1933.

1576   California, Mexican Fact-finding Committee. Mexicans
       in California. Report of Governor C. C. Young's
       Mexican Fact-finding Committee. Sacramento, Calif.:
       State Printing Office, 1930. Reprint, San Francisco:
       R & E Research Associates, 1970.
An exhaustive study with much valuable historical
information.

1577   Cardoso, Lawrence A. Mexican Emigration to the United
       States, 1897-1931: Socio-Economic Patterns. Tucson:
       University of Arizona Press, 1980.
Helpful for a fuller understanding of this early stage of
Mexican immigration. The second half of the work is devoted
to U.S. and Mexican reaction to the heavy immigration.

1578   Carrillo, Leo. The California I Love. Englewood
       Cliffs, N.J.: Prentice-Hall, 1961.
The personal story of a well-known Hollywood actor and
descendant of a prominent Californio family.

1579   Carreras de Velasco, Mercedes. Los mexicanos que
       devolvio la crisis 1929-1932. Tlatelolco, Mexico,
       D.F.: Secretaria de Relaciones Exteriores, 1974.
A Mexican view of the repatriation during the Great
Depression; an excellent study.

1580   Casey, Robert J. The Texas Border and Some
       Borderliners. Indianapolis, Ind.: Bobbs-Merrill Co.,
       1950.

1581   Cerwin, Herbert. These Are the Mexicans. New York:
       Reynal & Hitchcock, 1947.

1582   Chambers, Clarke A. California Farm Organizations; A
       Historical Study of the Grange, the Farm Bureau, and
       the Associated Farmers, 1929-1941. Berkeley:
       University of California Press, 1952.
Useful for an understanding of the California agricultural
strikes of the 1930s.

1583   Church Views of the Mexican American. Edited by
        Carlos Cortes. New York: Arno Press, 1974.
Includes: Elmer T. Clark, The Latin American Immigrant in
the South, 1924; Robert N. McLean and Charles A. Thomson,
Spanish and Mexican in Colorado, 1924; Vernon M. McCombs,
From Over the Border: A Study of the Mexicans in the United
States, 1925; Linna E. Bresette, Mexicans in the United
States: A Report of a Brief Survey, [1929]; Robert C. Jones
and Louis R. Wilson, The Mexican in Chicago, 1931; B. A.
Hodges, A History of the Mexican Mission Work Conducted by
the Presbyterian Church in the United States of America,
1931; Bertha Blair, Anne O. Lively and Glen W. Trimble,
Spanish-Speaking Americans: Mexicans and Puerto Ricans in
the United States, 1959.

1584   Clark, Elmer T. The Latin Immigrant in the South.
        Nashville, Tenn.: Cokesbury Press, 1924.
Includes a chapter on Mexicans in the U.S.; good for its
contemporary interpretation.

1585   Clendenen, Clarence C. The United States and Pancho
        Villa: A Study in Unconventional Diplomacy. Ithaca,
        N.Y.: Cornell University Press, 1961.
Is concerned with U.S.-Mexican border problems during the
1910 revolution.

1586   Coalson, George O. The Development of the Migratory
        Farm Labor System in Texas: 1900-1954. San Francisco:
        R & E Research Associates, 1977.
A reprint of the author's doctoral thesis.

1587   Cockcroft, James D. Intellectual Precursors of the
        Mexican Revolution. Austin: University of Texas
        Press, 1968.
Includes information on Mexican Americans and their
interaction with revolutionaries in the border region.

1588   Coles, Robert. The Old Ones of New Mexico.
        Albuquerque: University of New Mexico Press, 1973.
Includes forty black and white photographs and 73 pages of
text.

1589   Cordova, Alfred. Octaviano Larrazolo, A Political
        Portrait. Albuquerque: Department of Government,
        University of New Mexico, 1954.
The biography is an expansion of his 1952 publication, item
1590. Larrazolo played an important role in developing New
Mexico's 1910 state constitution.

1590   Cordova, Alfred and Charles Judah. Octaviano Ambrosio
        Larrazolo, the Prophet of Transition in New Mexico; an
        Analysis of His Political Life. Albuquerque:

Department of Government, University of New Mexico, 1952.
Division of Government Research Publication #32. Biography of an important New Mexico political figure, elected governor in 1918.

1591 Crocchiola, Stanley F. L. The Odyssey of Juan
      Archibeque. Pantex, Tex.: F. Stanley, 1962.
Archibeque was a Penitente leader in the very early 1900s.

1592 Croutch, Albert. Housing Migratory Agricultural
      Workers in California, 1913-1948. San Francisco: R &
      E Research Associates, 1975.

1593 Cuellar, Robert A. A Social and Political History of
      the Mexican-American Population of Texas, 1929-1963.
      San Francisco: R & E Research Associates, 1974.
A reprint of his 1969 thesis at the State University of Texas.

1594 Davila, Jose M. The Mexican Migration Problem. Los
      Angeles: Pan Pacific Progress, 1929.

1595 Davis, Edward E. The White Scourge. San Antonio,
      Tex.: Naylor Publishing Co., 1940.
Concerns the impact of Texas cotton farming expansion on migrant labor.

1596 Dawber, Mark A. Our Shifting Population. New York:
      Home Missions Council, 1941.
Includes a chapter on the Mexican immigrant. Good for contemporary view.

1597 Dillingham Commission. Report of the Immigration
      Commission: Immigrants in Industries. Washington,
      D.C.: U.S. Government Printing Office, 1911.

1598 Divine, Robert A. American Immigration Policy,
      1924-1952. New Haven, Conn.: Yale University Press,
      1957.
One chapter deals with the Mexican immigrant question in the 1920s and the U.S. debate over it. Also discusses the factors that go into making government policy.

1599 Dobie, James Frank. Coronado's Children. Garden
      City, N.Y.: Doubleday & Co., 1934.
Romantic historical legends about lost mines in the Southwest.

1600 Dobie, James Frank, ed. Puro Mexicano. Austin: Texas
      Folklore Society, 1935.
Includes corridos on Mexican immigrants in the United States and border folklore.

1601   Documents on the Mexican Revolution, Volume I: The
        Origins of the Revolution in Texas, Arizona, New
        Mexico and California, 1910-1911. Edited by Gene Z.
        Hanrahan. Salisbury, N.C.: Documentary Publications,
        1976-1978.

1602   Donnelly, Thomas C., ed. Rocky Mountain Politics.
        Albuquerque: University of New Mexico Press, 1940.
Each chapter is devoted to a particular state, e.g., "New
Mexico: An Area of Conflicting Cultures."

1603   Emerson, Dorothy. Among the Mescalero Apaches: The
        Story of Father Albert Brown, O.F.M. Tucson:
        University of Arizona Press, 1973.
Describes his fifty years of service to Indians and
Chicanos.

1604   Fabila, Alfonso. El problema de la emigracion de
        obreros y campesinos mexicanos. Mexico, D.F.:
        Talleres Graficos de la Nacion, 1928.
Thirty-eight pages devoted to the Mexican viewpoint on the
problem.

1605   Fernandez, Raul A. The United States-Mexico Border: A
        Politico-Economic Profile. Notre Dame, Ind.:
        University of Notre Dame Press, 1977.
An excellent border region study, looking at the area on
both sides of the line as a unit.

1606   Fincher, Ernest Barksdale. Spanish-Americans as a
        Political Factor in New Mexico, 1912-1950. New York:
        Arno Press, 1974.
Reprint of his 1951 New York University thesis; historical
analysis of the problems of Nuevo Mexicano political power.

1607   Fisher, Donald J. A Historical Study of the Migrant
        in California. San Francisco: R & E Research
        Associates, 1973.

1608   Foerster, Robert F. The Racial Problems Involved in
        Immigration from Latin America and the West Indies to
        the United States. Washington, D.C.: U.S. Department
        of Labor, 1925.

1609   Foley, Douglas E., et al. From Peones to Politicos:
        Ethnic Relations in a South Texas Town, 1900-1977.
        Austin: Center for Mexican American Studies,
        University of Texas Press, 1978.
Covers political, social, and economic conditions; race
relations.

1610   Ford, John Anson. Thirty Explosive Years in Los
        Angeles County. San Marino, Calif.: Huntington
        Library, 1961.

The history of Los Angeles during an era of great expansion, by a member of the Board of Supervisors (1934-1958). Includes material on the Mexican American in chapter 17. Some stereotyping.

1611   Galarza, Ernesto. Barrio Boy. Notre Dame, Ind.:
       University of Notre Dame Press, 1971.
An autobiographical story of Ernesto Galarza's early life in Mexico and the United States. Describes the emigration pattern.

1612   Gamio, Manuel. The Mexican Immigrant: His Life Story.
       Translated by Robert C. Jones. Chicago: University of
       Chicago, 1931. Reprint, New York: Arno Press, 1969.
Case studies of Mexican immigrants in the 1920s by an outstanding Mexican cultural anthropologist.

1613   Gamio, Manuel. Mexican Immigration to the United
       States. Chicago: University of Chicago Press, 1930.
       Reprint, New York: Arno Press, 1970.
Describes the origins and treatment of Mexican immigrants to the United States in the 1920s.

1614   Gamio, Manuel. Preliminary Survey of the Antecedents
       and Conditions of the Mexican Immigrant Population in
       the United States and the Formation of a Program for a
       Definite and Scientific Study of the Problems. New
       York: Social Science Research Council, 1928.

1615   Garcia, Mario T. Desert Immigrants: The Mexicans in
       El Paso, 1880-1920. New Haven, Conn.: Yale University
       Press, 1981.
A thoroughly documented and well organized history detailing the Mexican contributions to the development of El Paso as a communication and commercial center.

1616   Garis, Roy L. Immigration Restriction: A Study of the
       Opposition to and Regulation of Immigration into the
       United States. New York: Macmillan Co., 1927.
Little on the Mexican immigrant; no mention of the Box or Harris bills.

1617   Gomez-Quiñones, Juan. Sembradores: Ricardo Flores
       Magon y El Partido Liberal Mexicano: A Eulogy and
       Critique. Los Angeles: Aztlan Publications, 1973.

1618   Gonzales (Demireles), Jovita. Latin Americans. New
       York: Prentice-Hall, 1937.
Primarily concerned with Mexican Americans in Texas.

1619   Gray, James. The American Civil Liberties Union of
       Southern California and Imperial Valley Agricultural
       Labor Disturbances, 1930, 1934. San Francisco: R & E
       Research Associates, 1977.

Centers on the 1934 lettuce and melon strikes, on the ACLU role and that of Gen. Pelham D. Glassford.

1620   Hackett, Charles W. The Mexican Revolution and the
       United States, 1910-1926. New York: Gordon Press
       [n.d.]. Reprint, Boston: World Peace Foundation,
       1926.

1621   Harper, Allan G.; Andrew R. Cordova; and Kalervo
       Oberg. Man and Resources in the Middle Rio Grande
       Valley. Albuquerque: University of New Mexico Press,
       1943.

1622   Hernandez Alvarez, Jose. A Demographic Profile of the
       Mexican Immigration to the United States, 1910-1950.
       Berkeley: International Urban Research, University of
       California, 1966.

1623   Hidalgo, Ernesto. La proteccion de mexicanos en los
       Estados Unidos. Mexico, D.F.: Secretaria de
       Relaciones Exteriores, 1940.

1624   Hinojosa, Federico A. El Mexico de afuera, y su
       reintegracion a la patria. San Antonio, Tex.: Artes
       Graficas, 1940.
Seventy-one pages on the need for Mexicans in the U.S. to
maintain communications and ties with Mexico.

1625   Hoffman, Abraham. Unwanted Mexican Americans in the
       Great Depression: Repatriation Pressures, 1929-1939.
       Tucson: University of Arizona Press, 1974.
A well researched account of the repatriation of the 1930s,
especially in California.

1626   Hufford, Charles H. The Social and Economic Effects
       of the Mexican Migration into Texas. San Francisco: R
       & E Research Associates, 1975.
A 1929 master's thesis at Boulder, University of Colorado.
Good material on 1900-1928; but also some anti-Mexican
prejudices.

1627   Hutchinson, William H. Oil, Land, and Politics; The
       California Career of Thomas Robert Bard. 2 vols.
       Norman: University of Oklahoma, 1965.
Of some value for the study of the land issue in California.

1628   Hymer, Evangeline. A Study of the Social Attitudes of
       Adult Mexican Immigrants in Los Angeles and Vicinity.
       San Francisco: R & E Research Associates, 1975.
Reprint of a 1923 thesis.

1629   Jensen, Vernon H. Heritage of Conflict: Labor
       Relations in the Nonferrous Metals Industry Up to

1930. Ithaca, N.Y.: Cornell University Press, 1950.
Has material on the Clifton-Morenci and Bisbee strikes early
in the 20th century.

1630   Jones, Anita. Conditions Surrounding Mexicans in
        Chicago. San Francisco: R & E Research Associates,
        1971.
Reprint of her 1928 thesis describing Mexicans in Chicago
during the 1920s.

1631   Jones, Mary Harris. Autobiography of Mother Jones.
        Edited by Mary F. Parton. New York: Arno & The New
        York Times, 1969, a reprint.
Has some material on Mexican workers on the border,
especially copper miners. Mary Jones (1830-1930) was a
prominent radical (United Mine Workers) and Industrial
Workers of the World organizer from the 1890s to about 1915.
She was active in the Southwest.

1632   Jones, Robert Cuba. Unpublished Study of Mexicans in
        Chicago. Chicago: Pan-American Council, 1940.
By one of the early students of the Mexican American
experience.

1633   Jones, Robert Cuba and Louis R. Wilson. The Mexican
        in Chicago. Chicago: Comity Commission of Chicago
        Church Federation, 1931.

1634   Keffer, Frank M. History of San Fernando Valley.
        Glendale, Calif.: Stillman Printing Co., 1934.

1635   Kluger, James R. The Clifton-Morenci Strike: Labor
        Difficulties in Arizona, 1915-1916. Tucson:
        University of Arizona Press, 1970.
Describes this important strike and lockout in the copper
industry, involving Mexican and Mexican American workers.

1636   Knox, William J. The Economic Status of the Mexican
        Immigrant in San Antonio, Texas. San Francisco: R & E
        Research Associates, 1975.
Reprint of a 1927 University of Texas thesis; good for a
mid-1920s view of the San Antonio Mexican.

1637   Lahart, Edward. The Career of Dennis Chavez as a
        Member of Congress, 1930-1934. Albuquerque:
        University of New Mexico Press, 1958.
Early national career of the most famous Nuevo Mexicano
political leader (1888-1962), U.S. senator and leading Nuevo
Mexicano from the 1930s until his death.

1638   Leonard, Olen E. The Role of the Land Grant in the
        Social Organization and Social Processes of a
        Spanish-American Village in New Mexico. Ann Arbor:

University of Michigan Press, 1943. Reprint, Ann
      Arbor, Mich.: Edward Brothers, 1948.
An outstanding pioneering work on the social impact of the
land grant problem in New Mexico.

1639   Leonard, Olen E. and C. P. Loomis. Culture of a
        Contemporary Community. El Cerrito, New Mexico.
        Washington, D.C.: U.S. Bureau of Agricultural
        Economics, 1941.
Rural Life Study No. 1; available from Xerox University
Microfilms.

1640   Lewis, Tracy Hammond. Along the Rio Grande. New
        York: Lewis Publishing Co., 1916.
A journalist's account of the Rio Grande border area in
1916.

1641   Liggett, William V. My Seventy-Five Years Along the
        Mexican Border. New York: Exposition Press, 1964.
Describes pioneer life on the southwestern frontier.

1642   Lipschultz, Robert J. American Attitudes Towards
        Mexican Immigration, 1924-1952. San Francisco: R & E
        Research Associates, 1975.
A 1962 thesis which covers the development of restrictionist
attitudes in the 1920s and 1930s and their reversal in World
War II.

1643   Little, Wilson. Spanish-Speaking Children in Texas.
        Austin: University of Texas Press, 1944.
Sponsored by the Committee on inter-American Relations in
Texas. Deals primarily with education.

1644   Lowry, Edith E. They Starve That We May Eat. New
        York: Council of Women for Home Missions, 1938.
Traces the history of migrant agricultural workers in
seventy pages; includes photographs.

1645   Loyo, Gilberto. Emigracion de mexicanos a los Estados
        Unidos. Rome: Instituto Poligrafico dello Stato,
        1931.
Discusses briefly the labor exodus of Mexicans during the
1920s.

1646   McCombs, Vernon M. From Over the Border: A Study of
        the Mexicans in the United States. New York: Council
        of Women for Home Missions, 1925. Reprint, San
        Francisco: R & E Research Associates, 1970.
Excellent for a contemporary view. Included in item 1583.

1647   McLean, Robert N. That Mexican! As He Really Is.
        North and South of the Rio Grande. New York: Fleming
        H. Revell Co., 1928.
An interpretation of Mexican immigrants to the U.S., with

some background information.

1648   McLean, Robert N. and Charles A. Thomson. Spanish and
        Mexicans in Colorado: A Survey of the Spanish
        Americans and Mexicans in the State of Colorado. New
        York: Board of National Missions of the Presbyterian
        Church in the U.S.A., 1924. Reprinted in Church Views
        of the Mexican American. New York: Arno Press, 1974,
        item 1583.

1649   McNamara, Patrick Hayes. Mexican-Americans in Los
        Angeles County: A Study in Acculturation. San
        Francisco: R & E Research Associates, 1975.
A reprint of his 1957 M.A. thesis at St. Louis University.

1650   McWilliams, Carey. Factories in the Field: The Story
        of the Migratory Farm Labor in California. Boston:
        Little, Brown & Co., 1934. Reprint, Layton, Utah:
        Peregrine Smith, 1971.
A general history of California agricultural labor through
the 1930s. Some stress on the strikes in agriculture.

1651   Manuel, Herschel T. The Education of Mexican and
        Spanish-Speaking Children in Texas. Austin:
        University of Texas Press, 1930.
A pioneering work by an outstanding early authority in the
field.

1652   Marden, Charles F. Minorities in American Society.
        New York: American Book Co., 1952.
Chapter VI covers Mexican immigrants and other Spanish
Americans.

1653   Martinez, John R. Mexican Emigration to the United
        States, 1910-1930. San Francisco: R & E Research
        Associates, 1971.
A 1957 dissertation describing an important period of
immigration, largely from a Mexican economic viewpoint.

1654   Martinez de Alva, Ernesto. Vida rural. Mexico, D.F.:
        Talleres Graficos de la Nacion, 1933.
Includes a chapter on immigration and repatriates.

1655   Menefee, Selden Cowles. Mexican Migratory Workers of
        South Texas. Washington, D.C.: Superintendent of
        Documents, 1941. Reprinted as part of Mexican Labor
        in the United States. New York: Arno Press, 1974,
        item 2955.
A sixty-seven page WPA study on Crystal City, Texas in 1938.

1656   Menefee, Selden Cowles and Orin C. Cassmore. The
        Pecan Shellers of San Antonio: The Problem of
        Underpaid and Unemployed Mexican Labor. Washington,
        D.C.: U.S. Government Printing Office, 1940.

Reprinted as part of Mexican Labor in the United
States. New York: Arno Press, 1974, item 2955; and in
Migratory Workers of the Southwest. Westport, Conn.:
Greenwood Press, 1978, item 1660.
Details of an important 1938 strike by Mexican American
pecan shellers. A WPA study.

1657   Mexico, Secretaria de Gobernacion, Departamento de
        Migracion. El servicio de migracion en Mexico.
        Prepared by Andres Landa y Pina. Mexico, D.F.:
        Talleres Graficos de la Nacion, 1930.
Sixty pages; written by the head of the department.

1658   Mexico, Secretaria de Relaciones Exteriores. La
        migracion y la proteccion de mexicanos en el
        estranjero. Prepared by Andres Landa y Pina. Mexico,
        D.F.: Talleres Graficos de la Nacion, 1930.

1659   Mexico. Secretaria de Relaciones Exteriores. La
        proteccion de mexicanos en los Estados Unidos.
        Mexico, D.F.: Talleres Graficos de la Nacion, 1940.

1660   Migratory Workers of the Southwest: Consisting of
        "Migratory Cotton Pickers in Arizona" (1939), "The
        Pecan Shellers of San Antonio" (1940), and "Mexican
        Migratory Workers of South Texas" (1941). Westport,
        Conn.: Greenwood Press, 1978.
Reprint of three WPA studies.

1661   Monaghan, Jay. Schoolboy, Cowboy, Mexican Spy.
        Berkeley: University of California Press, 1977.
Includes autobiographical material on western frontier
experiences.

1662   Myers, John M. The Border Wardens. Englewood Cliffs,
        N.J.: Prentice-Hall, 1972.
One of the few works written on the Border Patrol;
pro-Border Patrol and anti-Mexican.

1663   The New Mexican Hispano. Edited by Carlos Cortes.
        New York: Arno Press, 1974.
Includes: Cleofas M. Jaramillo, Shadows of the Past, 1941;
Olen Leonard and G. P. Loomis, Culture of a Contemporary
Rural Community: El Cerrito, New Mexico, 1941; Irving
Rusinow, A Camera Report on El Cerrito: A Typical
Spanish-American Community in New Mexico, 1942; Fabiola
Cabeza de Baca, We Fed Them Cactus, 1954.

1664   Oxnam, G. Bromley. The Mexican in Los Angeles, Los
        Angeles City Survey, 1920. Los Angeles: Interchurch
        World Movement of North America, 1920. Reprint, San
        Francisco: R & E Research Associates, 1970.

1665 Panunzio, Constantine. How Mexicans Earn and Live: A
       Study of the Incomes and Expenditures of One Hundred
       Mexican Families in San Diego, California. Berkeley:
       University of California Press, 1933.
An early study of the Mexican American experience; of value
for the contemporary picture. Included in item 1671.

1666 Parker, Carleton H. The Casual Laborer and Other
       Essays. New York: Harcourt, Brace & Howe, 1920.
Includes in the appendix Parker's report on the 1913
Wheatland hop field riot.

1667 Patterson, Tom. A Colony for California: Riverside's
       First Hundred Years. Riverside, Calif.:
       Press-Enterprise Co., 1971.

1668 Peavy, John R. Echoes From the Rio Grande, 1905 to
       N-O-W. Brownsville, Tex.: Springman-King Co., 1963.

1669 Perales, Alonso S. En defensa de mi raza. 2 vols.
       San Antonio, Tex.: Artes Graficas, 1936, 1937.

1670 Perry, Louis B. and Richard S. Perry. A History of
       the Los Angeles Labor Movement, 1911-1941. Los
       Angeles: University of California Press, 1963.
Describes the vicissitudes of the Los Angeles trade union
development; excellent bibliography.

1671 Perspectives on Mexican-American Life. An anthology
       edited by Carlos Cortes. New York: Arno Press, 1974.
Contents: Elizabeth Fuller, The Mexican Housing Problem,
1920; Jay S. Stowell, The Near Side of the Mexican Question,
1921; Constantine Panunzio, How Mexicans Earn and Live: A
Study of the Incomes and Expenditures of One Hundred Mexican
Families in San Diego, California, 1933. The anthology
provides perspectives on Mexican-American life in the 1920s
and 1930s.

1672 Pesotta, Rose. Bread Upon the Waters. New York:
       Dodd, Mead & Co., 1945.
Includes a chapter titled "Mexican Girls Stand Their
Ground," dealing with the 1933 ILGWU strike in Los Angeles.

1673 Raat, William Dirk. Revoltosos! Mexico's Rebels in
       the United States, 1903-1923. College Station: Texas
       A & M University Press, 1981.
Includes materials on Mexican American relations to Mexico's
1910 revolution.

1674 Rak, Mary K. Border Patrol. Boston: Houghton Mifflin
       Co., 1938.
Good discussion of the Border Patrol's role in the

Southwest.

1675 Reisler, Mark. By the Sweat of Their Brow: Mexican
      Immigrant Labor in the United States, 1900-1940.
      Westport, Conn.: Greenwood Press, 1976.
Analyzes the evolution of U.S. policy on Mexican
immigration; describes the workers, their motives, their
successes and failures.

1676 Rosenblum, Gerald. Immigrant Workers: Their Impact on
      American Labor Radicalism. New York: Basic Books,
      1973.

1677 Saenz, Moises and Herbert I. Priestley. Some Mexican
      Problems. Chicago: University of Chicago Press, 1926.
A lecture program on social problems in Mexico with Saenz's
description of his government's program. Useful to
understand the heavy emigration to the U.S. in the 1920s.

1678 Samora, Julian and Richard A. Lamanna. Mexican-
      Americans in a Midwest Metropolis: A Study of East
      Chicago. Los Angeles: Mexican American Study Project,
      University of California, 1967.

1679 Sanchez, George I. Concerning Segregation of
      Spanish-Speaking Children in the Public Schools.
      Austin: University of Texas Press, 1951.

1680 Sandage, Shirley L. Child of Hope. Words by Shirley
      M. Sandage. Photos by Jo Moore Stewart. South
      Brunswick, N.J.: A. S. Barnes, 1968.
Describes migrant labor existence especially in the
Southwest of the United States. Includes an excellent
pictorial life of migrant family. Descriptive rather than
historical in perspective.

1681 Santibañez, Enrique. Ensayo acerca de la inmigracion
      mexicana en Los Estados Unidos. San Antonio, Tex.:
      Clegg Co., 1930.

1682 Schwartz, Harry. Seasonal Farm Labor in the United
      States; With Special Reference to Hired Workers in
      Fruit and Vegetable and Sugar Beet Production. New
      York: Columbia University Press, 1945.
Has considerable reference to Mexican migrant workers in the
context of the 1920s encouragement and 1930s repatriation.

1683 Serrano Cabo, Tomas. Cronicas: Alianza
      Hispano-Americana. Tucson, Ariz.: Alianza Hispano
      Americana, 1929.
A popular history of one of the earliest and long-lived
Mexican American organizations.

1684   Simmons, Ozzie G.   Anglo-Americans and Mexican
       Americans in South Texas.   New York: Arno Press, 1974.
Discussion of ethnic relations; reprint of his 1952 Harvard
thesis.

1685   Stambaugh, J. Lee and Lillian J. Stambaugh.   The Lower
       Rio Grande Valley of Texas.   San Antonio, Tex.: Naylor
       Publishing Co., 1954.

1686   Stein, Walter J.   California and the Dust Bowl
       Migration.   Westport, Conn.: Greenwood Press, 1973.
Discusses agricultural labor in California centering on
migratory workers from Oklahoma, Texas, and Arkansas in the
1930s.

1687   Sterling, William W.   Trails and Trials of a Texas
       Ranger.   Houston, Tex.: [Privately printed], 1959.

1688   Stimson, Grace H.   The Rise of the Labor Movement in
       Los Angeles.   Berkeley: University of California
       Press, 1955.

1689   Stoddard, Lothrup.   The Rising Tide of Color.   New
       York: Scribner's, 1921.
Presents a nativist view of and response to increased
Mexican immigration during the second decade of this
century.

1690   Stowell, (Rev.) Jay S.   The Near Side of the Mexican
       Question.   New York: George H. Doran Co., 1921.
       Reprinted in item 1671.
Views of a Methodist missionary in the Southwest on the
rising tide of immigration.

1691   Stowell, (Rev.) Jay S.   A Study of Mexicans and
       Spanish Americans in the United States.   New York:
       George H. Doran Co., 1920.

1692   Taylor, Paul S.   An American-Mexican Frontier: Nueces
       County, Texas.   Chapel Hill: University of North
       Carolina Press, 1934.
Ethnic interaction and the history of clashes circa 1900, by
an outstanding economist with an historical viewpoint.

1693   Taylor, Paul S.   Mexican Labor in the United States.
       2 vols.   New York: Arno Press and The New York Times,
       1970.   Reprint of 1928 to 1934 publications; includes
       items 1694-1700.

1694   Taylor, Paul S.   Mexican Labor in the United States:
       Bethlehem, Pennsylvania.   Berkeley: Publications in
       Economics, University of California, 1931.

1695   Taylor, Paul S. Mexican Labor in the United States:
       Chicago and the Calumet Region. Berkeley:
       Publications in Economics, University of California,
       1932.

1696   Taylor, Paul S. Mexican Labor in the United States:
       Dimmit County, Winter Garden, South Texas. Berkeley:
       Publications in Economics, University of California,
       1930.

1697   Taylor, Paul S. Mexican Labor in the United States:
       Imperial Valley. Berkeley: Publications in Economics,
       University of California, 1928.

1698   Taylor, Paul S. Mexican Labor in the United States:
       Migration Statistics, I-IV. 4 vols. Berkeley:
       Publications in Economics, University of California,
       1929-1934.

1699   Taylor, Paul S. Mexican Labor in the United States:
       Valley of the South Platte, Colorado. Berkeley:
       Publications in Economics, University of California,
       1929.

1700   Taylor, Paul S. The Migrants and California's Future.
       Washington, D.C.: U.S. Government Printing Office,
       1933.

1701   Taylor, Paul S. A Spanish-American Peasant Community,
       Arandas in Jalisco, Mexico. Berkeley: University of
       California Press, 1933.
Ninety-two pages. Describes the readjustment of migrants to
the U.S. on their return to Mexico.

1702   Taylor, Ralph C. Colorado, South of the Border.
       Denver, Colo.: Sage Books, 1963.
Essays and lectures on Colorado history; with maps.

1703   Tetreau, E. D. Seasonal Labor on Arizona Irrigated
       Farms. Tucson: University of Arizona, 1937.

1704   Texas, Legislature, Proceedings of the Joint Committee
       of the Senate and the House in the Investigation of
       the Texas State Ranger Force. Austin, [n.p.], 1919.
The archives of the Texas State Library in Austin has a copy
of this rare item.

1705   Texas, State Employment Service, Origins and Problems
       of Texas Migratory Farm Labor. Austin, [n.p.], 1940.
Includes good materials on Mexican workers in Texas.

1706   Thomas, Norman Mattoon. Human Exploitation in the
         United States. New York: Frederick A. Stokes, 1934.
A general survey by the long-time U.S. Socialist leader.

1707   Tijerina, Andres A. History of Mexican Americans in
         Lubbock County, Texas. Lubbock: Texas Technological
         University, 1979.

1708   Turner, Ethel Duffy. Revolution in Baja California:
         Ricardo Flores Magon's High Noon. Revised and edited
         by Rey Davis. Detroit, Mich.: Blaine Ethridge-Books,
         1981.
Includes material on Mexican American support.

1709   U.S., Bureau of Labor Statistics, Labor and Social
         Conditions of Mexicans in California. Washington,
         D.C.: U.S. Government Printing Office, 1931.
Bulletin #541; good for the contemporary picture and
background.

1710   U.S., Congress, House, Committee on Immigration and
         Naturalization, 66th Cong., 2nd sess. "Temporary
         Admission of Illiterate Mexican Laborers." Hearings.
         Washington, D.C.: U.S. Government Printing Office,
         1920.

1711   U.S., Congress, House, Committee on Immigration and
         Naturalization, 67th Cong., 1st sess. "Imported
         Pauper Labor and Serfdom in America: Statement of Hon.
         John C. Box." Hearings. Washington, D.C.: U.S.
         Government Printing Office, 1921.

1712   U.S., Congress, House, Committee on Immigration andnd
         Naturalization, 69th Cong., 1st sess. "Seasonal
         Agricultural Laborers From Mexico." Hearings.
         Washington, D.C.: U.S. Government Printing Office,
         1926.

1713   U.S., Congress, House, Committee on Immigration and
         Naturalization, 70th cong., 2nd sess. Hearings Before
         the Committee. Washington, D.C.: U.S. Government
         Printing Office, 1928.

1714   U.S., Congress, House, Committee on Immigration and
         Naturalization, 71st Cong., 2nd sess. Hearings Before
         the Committee. Washington, D.C.: U.S. Government
         Printing Office, 1930.

1715   U.S., Congress, House, Committee on Labor, 74th Cong.,
         1st sess. Labor Dispute Act. Hearings. Washington,
         D.C.: U.S. Government Printing Office, 1935.
San Joaquin cotton strike, 1933.

1716   U.S., Congress, Senate, Committee on Education and
       Labor, 76th Cong., 2nd sess. Hearings Pursuant to
       Senate Resolution 266 (74th Congress). Washington,
       D.C.: U.S. Government Printing Office, 1940.
Documents the history of the strike of cotton pickers in
California; by Paul Taylor and Clark Kerr, pp. 19945-20036.

1717   U.S., Congress, Senate, Immigration Commission, 61st
       Cong., 2nd sess. "Immigrants in Agriculture."
       Report. Washington, D.C.: U.S. Government Printing
       Office, 1911.

1718   U.S., Congress, Senate, Immigration Commission, 61st
       Cong., 2nd sess. "Immigrants in Industries."
       Reports. Washington, D.C.: U.S. Government Printing
       Office, 1911.

1719   U.S., Congress, Senate, Immigration Commission, 61st
       Cong., 3rd sess. Abstract of Reports of the
       Immigration Commission, Document No. 747. 2 vols.
       Washington, D.C.: U.S. Government Printing Office,
       1911.

1720   U.S., Congress, Senate, Industrial Relations
       Commission, 64th Cong., 1st sess. Industrial
       Relations, Final Report and Testimony Submitted to
       Congress by the Commission on Industrial Relations.
       Washington, D.C.: U.S. Government Printing Office,
       1916.
Includes testimony on the "stealing" of Mexican labor crews.

1721   U.S., Department of Agriculture, Soil Conservation
       Service. Notes on Community-Owned Land Grants in New
       Mexico. Regular Bulletin No. 48. Washington, D.C.:
       U.S. Government Printing Office, 1937.

1722   U.S., Department of Agriculture. The Spanish-American
       Villages. Tewa Basin Study. Albuquerque, N. Mex.:
       Economic Surveys Division Vol. XI, 1939.

1723   U.S., Department of Labor. Labor Unionism in American
       Agriculture, Department of Labor Bulletin No. 836. 4
       vols. Prepared by Stuart Jamieson. Washington, D.C.:
       U.S. Government Printing Office, 1945. Reprint, New
       York: Arno Press, 1974.
A detailed, thorough study focusing on the 1920s and 1930s.
Especially good for the strikes of the Southwest in which
Mexican labor was important.

1724   U.S., Farm Security Administration. Survey of
       Agricultural Labor Conditions in Placer County,
       California. Washington, D.C.: U.S. Government
       Printing Office, 1937.

1725   U.S., Treasury Department. Immigration Into the
       United States From 1820 to 1930. Washington, D.C.:
       U.S. Treasury Department, 1930.

1726   U.S., Works Progress Administration. Labor in
       California Cotton Fields. Oakland, Calif.: W.P.A.
       Federal Writers Project, 1939.

1727   U.S., Works Progress Administration. The Migratory
       Agricultural Worker and the American Federation of
       Labor to 1938 Inclusive. Oakland, Calif.: W.P.A.
       Federal Writers Project, 1939.

1728   Valdes, Daniel T. [Valdes y Tapia, Daniel]. The
       Spanish-Speaking People of the Southwest. Bulletin
       WE-4. Denver, Colo.: Works Progress Administration,
       1938.

1729   Valdes, Dennis N. El Pueblo Mexicano en Detroit: A
       Social History. Detroit, Mich.: College of Education,
       Wayne State University, 1982.

1730   Walter, Paul A., Jr. and M. A. Saxton. Social
       Pathology of New Mexico. Albuquerque: University of
       New Mexico, 1936.
Describes economic and social conditions and problems;
fourteen pages.

1731   Weigle, Marta, ed. Hispanic Villages of Northern New
       Mexico. Santa Fe, N. Mex.: Lightning Tree Press,
       1975.
Reprint of vol. II of the 1935 Tewa Basin, New Mexico study.

1732   Wertenbaker, Green Payton. San Antonio: City in the
       Sun. New York: McGraw-Hill Book Co., 1946.
Contains material on the pecan shellers' strike of 1938.

1733   West, Stanley A. The Mexican Aztec Society: A Mexican
       American Voluntary Association in Diachronic
       Perspective. New York: Arno Press, 1976.
A study of persons of Mexican origin in Bethlehem,
Pennsylvania and centering on the Mexican Aztec Society they
founded in 1937.

1734   Whisenhunt, Donald W., ed. The Depression in the
       Southwest. Port Washington, N.Y.: Kennikat Press,
       1980.
Lectures and essays on economic conditions in the 1930s in
the Southwest.

1735   White, Alfred E. Americanization, the Mexican Group.
       San Francisco: R & E Research Associates, 1971.
Reprint of a 1923 thesis at the University of California at
Berkeley. Good for the contemporary view.

1736   Woofter, T. J., Jr.   Races and Ethnic Groups in
       American Life. New York; McGraw-Hill Book Co., 1933.
Includes information on Mexicans in Chicago; valuable for
this early period.

1737   Young, David. Research Memorandum on Minority Peoples
       in the Depression. New York: Social Science Research
       Council, 1937.
Includes material on the repatriation of Mexican workers.

1738   Zeleny, Carolyn. Relations Between the
       Spanish-Americans and Anglo-Americans in New Mexico: A
       Study in Conflict and Accomodation in a Dual-Ethnic
       Situation. New York: Arno Press, 1974.
A comprehensive study of the New Mexican experience from the
sixteenth century through World War II. Discusses land
conflict, education, and economic, social and politial
relations of Hispano and Anglo.

V: Theses and Dissertations

1739   Albro, Ward S., III. "Ricardo Flores Magon and the
       Liberal Party: An Inquiry into the Origins of the
       Mexican Revolution of 1910." Tucson: University of
       Arizona, 1967.
Includes material on Ricardo Flores Magon's relations with
Mexican American communities in the Southwest.

1740   Allan, Robert A. "Migratory Mexican Labor in the
       United States, 1917-1924." Master's thesis. Hayward:
       California State University, 1971.

1741   Allwell, Patrick J. "Mexican Immigration into the
       United States." Master's thesis. Columbia:
       University of Missouri, 1928.
Excellent for a view of Mexican immigration at the height of
the 1920s exclusionist movement.

1742   Anderson, William W. "The Nature of the Mexican
       Revolution as Viewed from the United States,
       1900-1917." Austin: University of Texas, 1967.

1743   Armour, Basil Weldon. "Social Problems of the
       Mexicans in the Rio Grande Valley of Texas." Master's
       thesis. College Station: Texas A & M University,
       1932.

1744   Bauer, Edward J. "Delinquency Among Mexican Boys in
       South Chicago." Master's thesis. Austin: University
       of Texas, 1938.
Contains some good material on the history of the South
Chicago Mexican colony in the 1920s and 1930s.

1745   Beach, Frank L. "The Transformation of California,
       1900-1920. The Effects of the Western Movement in
       California's Growth and Development in the Progressive
       Period." Berkeley: University of California, 1963.

1746   Blake, Robert N. "A History of the Catholic Church in
       El Paso." Master's thesis. El Paso: University of
       Texas, 1948.

1747   Blazek, Leda F. "Food Habits and Living Conditions of
       Mexican Families on Four Income Levels in the Upper
       Rio Grande Valley . . ." Master's thesis. Austin:
       University of Texas, 1938.
Valuable for a picture of conditions in the mid-1930s.

1748   Broadbent, Elizabeth. "The Distribution of Mexican
       Population in the United States." Master's thesis.
       Chicago: University of Chicago, 1941.
Includes valuable statistical tables and maps, 1910-1930.

1749   Cameron, James W. "The History of Mexican Public
        Education in Los Angeles, 1910-1930." Los Angeles:
        University of Southern California, 1976.

1750   Castillo, Pedro G. "The Making of a Mexican Barrio:
        Los Angeles, 1890-1920." Santa Barbara: University of
        California, 1979.

1751   Chacon, Ramon. "The 1933 San Joaquin Cotton Strike."
        Master's project. Stanford, Calif.: Stanford
        University, 1972.
A description of the most important agricultural strike of
the 1930s.

1752   Chaffee, Porter. "A History of the Cannery and
        Agricultural Workers Industrial Union." Federal
        Writers Project, Oakland Library. Berkeley:
        University of California, ca. 1938.
The CAWIU was a leading communist-affiliated agricultural
union between 1931 and 1935.

1753   Chaffee, Porter. "Organization Efforts of Mexican
        Agricultural Workers." Federal Writers Project,
        Oakland Library. Berkeley: University of California,
        ca. 1938.
Includes a list of strikes in the 1930s led by Mexicans and
Mexican Americans.

1754   Christopulos, Diana K. "American Radicals and the
        Mexican Revolution, 1900-1925." Binghamton: State
        University of New York, 1980.

1755   Clark, Douglas M. "Wheatland Hop Field Riot."
        Master's thesis. Chico, Calif.: Chico State
        University, 1963.
The 1913 California agricultural labor riot that led to
greater awareness of migrant worker mistreatment.

1756   Connell, Earl M. "The Mexican Population of Austin,
        Texas." Master's thesis. Austin: University of
        Texas, 1925.
Valuable for its contemporary view.

1757   Cramp, Kathryn. "A Study of the Mexican Population of
        Imperial Valley, California." Manuscript. Berkeley:
        Bancroft Library, University of California, 1926.
Based largely on interviews in 1926; contains interesting
historical information on illegals, housing, etc.

1758   Culp, Alice B. "A Case Study of the Living Conditions
        of Thirty-Five Mexican Families of Los Angeles with
        Special Reference to Mexican Children." Master's
        thesis. Los Angeles: University of Southern
        California, 1921.

Presents a good picture of the Mexican's socio-economic position in southern California at the beginning of the 1920s.

1759   Davis, Ethelyn C. "Little Mexico: A Study of
        Horizontal and Vertical Mobility." Master's thesis.
        Dallas, Tex.: Southern Methodist University, 1936.
Studies Mexican American mobility in Dallas from the 1920s to 1933.

1760   Delgado, Anthony P. "Mexican Immigration to the Hull
        House and 18th Street Community Areas of Chicago,
        Illinois, 1900-1960." Master's thesis. Austin:
        University of Texas, 1978.

1761   Dewetter, Mardee. "Revolutionary El Paso, 1910-1917."
        Master's thesis. El Paso: University of Texas, 1946.

1762   Douglas, Helen Walker. "The Conflict of Cultures in
        First Generation Mexicans in Santa Ana, California."
        Master's thesis. Los Angeles: University of Southern
        California, 1928.
Illustrates well one aspect of Mexicans' problems in acculturation.

1763   Drake, Rollen H. "A Comparative Study of the
        Mentality and Achievement of Mexican and White
        Children." Master's thesis. Los Angeles: University
        of Southern California, 1927.
Valuable for a picture of the contemporary Anglo view of Mexicans and Mexican Americans.

1764   Edson, George T. "Mexican Labor in the California
        Imperial Valley." Typescript in Bancroft Library.
        Berkeley: University of California, ca. 1927.

1765   Edson, George T. "Mexicans in our Northcentral
        States." Typescript in Bancroft Library. Berkeley:
        University of California, ca. 1927.

1766   Edwards, Warrick Ridgely III. "United States-Mexican
        Relations, 1913-1916: Revolution, Oil, and
        Intervention." Baton Rouge: Louisiana State
        University and Agricultural and Mechanical College,
        1971.
U.S.-Mexican relations affected the daily lives of border Mexican Americans.

1767   Estrada, Richard M. "Border Revolution: The Mexican
        Revolution in the Ciudad Juarez, El Paso Area,
        1906-1915." Master's thesis. El Paso: University of
        Texas, 1975.

1768   Fearis, Donald Friend. "The California Farm Worker,
       1930-1942." Davis: University of California, 1971.

1769   Fellows, Lloyd W. "Economic Aspects of the Mexican
       Rural Population in California With Special Emphasis
       on the Need for Mexican Labor in Agriculture."
       Master's thesis. Los Angeles: University of Southern
       California, 1929.

1770   Felter, Eunice Beall. "The Social Adaptations of the
       Mexican Churches in the Chicago Area." Master's
       thesis. Chicago: University of Chicago, 1941.
Title somewhat confusing; describes church adaptations to
Mexican parishoners.

1771   Finney, Floy C. "Juvenile Delinquency in San Antonio,
       Texas." Master's thesis. Austin: University of
       Texas, 1932.

1772   Garcia, Richard Amado. "The Making of the
       Mexican-American Mind, San Antonio, Texas, 1929-1941:
       A Social and Intellectual History of an Ethnic
       Community." Irvine: University of California, 1980.

1773   Gerome, Frank A. "United States-Mexican Relations
       During the Initial Years of the Mexican Revolution."
       Kent, Ohio: Kent State University, 1968.

1774   Gilbert, James C. "A Field Study in Mexico of the
       Mexican Repatriation Movement." Master's thesis. Los
       Angeles: University of Southern California, 1934.

1775   Gilderhus, Mark T. "The United States and the Mexican
       Revolution, 1915-1920." Lincoln: University of
       Nebraska, 1968.

1776   Goldner, Norman. "The Mexican in the Northern Urban
       Area: A Comparison of Two Generations." Master's
       thesis. Minneapolis: University of Minnesota, 1959.
Includes some good material on 1920s-1930s urban Mexican
Americans.

1777   Gonzales (Mireles), Jovita. "Social Life in Cameron,
       Starr, and Zapata Counties." Master's thesis.
       Austin: University of Texas, 1930.

1778   Gonzales, Kathleen M. "The Mexican Family in San
       Antonio, Texas." Master's thesis. Austin: University
       of Texas, 1928.
Good for contemporary view.

1779   Gonzalez, Gilbert George. "The System of Public
       Education and its Function Within the Chicano

Communities, 1920-1930." Los Angeles: University of
California, 1974.

1780   Hagy, Jesse R. "The New Mexico Cattle Growers'
       Association, 1914-1934." Master's thesis.
       Albuquerque: University of New Mexico, 1951.

1781   Halcomb, Ellen L. "Efforts to Organize the Migrant
       Workers by the Cannery and Agricultural Workers'
       Industrial Union in the 1930's." Master's thesis.
       Chico, Calif.: Chico State University, 1963.

1782   Hanson, Stella E. "Mexican Laborers in the
       Southwest." Master's thesis. Pomona, Calif.: Pomona
       College, 1926.

1783   Hoffman, Nancy J. "Mexican Emigration to the United
       States, 1900-1910." Master's thesis. San Diego: San
       Diego State University, 1974.
Describes the first stage of migration to the United States,
before the 1910 Revolution loosed the floodtide.

1784   Hough, John. "Agricultural Labor Relations in the
       Imperial Valley from 1928 to 1934." Master's thesis.
       Los Angeles: University of Southern California, 1951.
Describes the conflict, especially with Mexican workers,
showing the trend to agribusiness.

1785   Howard, Donald Stephenson. "A Study of the Mexican,
       Mexican-American and Spanish-American Population in
       Pueblo, Colorado, 1929-1930." Master's thesis.
       Denver, Colo.: University of Denver, 1932.
Contains information on jobs, housing, and social problems.

1786   Humphrey, Norman D. "The Mexican Peasant in Detroit."
       Ann Arbor: University of Michigan, 1943.

1787   Humphrey, Norman D. "Patterns of Cultural Adjustment
       of the Mexican Relief Families." Master's thesis.
       Ann Arbor: University of Michigan, 1940.

1788   Hurt, Wesley. "Manzano: A Study of Community
       Disorganization." Master's thesis. Albuquerque:
       University of New Mexico, 1941.

1789   Johnson, Irma Yarbrough. "A Study of Certain Changes
       in the Spanish American Family in Bernalillo County,
       1915-1946." Master's thesis. Albuquerque: University
       of New Mexico, 1948.

1790   Johnson, Roberta M. "History of the Education of
       Spanish-speaking Children in Texas." Master's thesis.
       Austin: University of Texas, 1932.
Provides an historical approach to the educational problem.

1791   Kerr, Louise Año Nuevo. "The Chicano Experience in
        Chicago." Chicago: University of Illinois at Chicago
        Circle, 1976.

1792   Kienle, John E. "Housing Conditions Among the Mexican
        Population of Los Angeles." Master's thesis. Los
        Angeles: University of Southern California, 1912.
Valuable historically for its contemporary description.

1793   Kluckhohn, Florence. "Los Atarqueños: A Study of
        Patterns and Configurations in a New Mexico Village."
        Cambridge, Mass.: Radcliffe College, 1941.

1794   Laird, Judith Ann Fincher. "Argentine, Kansas: The
        Evolution of a Mexican-American Community, 1905-1940."
        Lawrence: University of Kansas, 1975.

1795   Landau, Saul. "The Bisbee Deportations: Class
        Conflict and Patriotism During World War I." Master's
        thesis. Madison: University of Wisconsin, 1959.
Describes vigilante response to a 1917 copper miners' strike
at Bisbee, Arizona.

1796   Langston, Edward L. "The Impact of Prohibition on the
        Mexican-U.S. Border: The El Paso-Ciudad Juarez Case."
        Lubbock: Texas Technical University, 1974.
Includes maps and a bibliography.

1797   Ledesma, Irene. "The New Deal Public Works Programs
        and Mexican-Americans in McAllen, Texas, 1933-36."
        Master's thesis. Edinburg, Tex.: Pan American
        University, 1977.

1798   Leis, Ward W. "The Status of Education for Mexican
        Children in Four Border States." Master's thesis.
        Los Angeles: University of Southern California, 1932.

1799   Leopard, Donald D. "Joint Statehood: 1906." Master's
        thesis. Albuquerque: University of New Mexico, 1958.
A part of the New Mexican quest for statehood.

1800   Lofstedt, Anna C. "A Study of the Mexican Population
        in Pasadena, California." Master's thesis. Los
        Angeles: University of Southern California, 1922.

1801   Lowenstein, Norman. "Strikes and Strike Tactics in
        California Agriculture: A History." Master's thesis.
        Berkeley: University of California, 1940.

1802   Lowerie, Samuel H. "Culture Conflict in Texas." New
        York: Columbia University, 1932.
A very useful early study.

1803   Luna, Jesus.   "Francisco I. Madero's Organization of
       the Mexican Revolution in San Antonio, Texas."
       Master's thesis.   Commerce: East Texas State
       University, 1969.

1804   Lunt, Olas A.   "Withdrawals of Spanish-speaking
       Students from an Arizona School System and the
       Implications Derived Therefrom."   Master's thesis.
       Flagstaff: Northern Arizona University, 1942.

1805   McEuen, William.   "A Survey of the Mexican in Los
       Angeles."   Master's thesis.   Los Angeles: University
       of Southern California, 1914.
Covers economic status, living conditions, and sociological
state--with photographs, especially of housing.

1806   Miller, Mary C.   "Attitudes of the San Diego Labor
       Movement Towards Mexicans, 1917-1936."   Master's
       thesis.   San Diego, Calif.: San Diego State
       University, 1974.

1807   Monroy, Douglas G.   "Mexicanos in Los Angeles,
       1930-1941: An Ethnic Group in Relation to Class
       Forces."   Los Angeles: University of California, 1978.

1808   Morrison, Ethel M.   "A History of Recent Legislative
       Proposals Concerning Mexican Immigration."   Master's
       thesis.   Los Angeles: University of Southern
       California, 1929.
Gives arguments both pro and con on legislation to establish
a quota for Mexicans (Harris and Box bills).

1809   Myers, Ellen H.   "The Mexican Liberal Party,
       1903-1910."   Charlottesville: University of Virginia,
       1970.
Includes material on the party's activities in the Southwest
and on border newspapers.

1810   Neal, Joe West.   "The Policy of the United States
       Toward Immigration from Mexico."   Master's thesis.
       Austin: University of Texas, 1941.

1811   Ohno, Kakujiro.   "History and Economic Significance of
       Mexican Labor in California."   Research report.   Los
       Angeles: University of Southern California, 1929.

1812   Ortegon, Samuel M.   "The Religious Status of the
       Mexican Population in Los Angeles."   Los Angeles:
       University of Southern California, 1932.

1813   Osborne, Marie A. S.   "The Educational Status of
       Intra-state Migrations in Texas, 1935-1940."   Master's
       thesis.   Austin: University of Texas, 1954.

1814   Parr, Eunice E. "A Comparative Study of Mexican and
       American Children in the Schools of San Antonio,
       Texas." Master's thesis. Chicago: University of
       Chicago, 1926.

1815   Parrish, Michael E. "Mexican Workers, Progressives,
       and Copper." La Jolla: University of California,
       1979.

1816   Peterson, Herbert. "Twentieth-Century Search for
       Cibola: Post World War I Mexican Labor Exploitation in
       Arizona." Tucson: University of Arizona, 1974.

1817   Pycior, Julie Leininger. "La Raza Organizes: Mexican
       American Life in San Antonio, 1915-1930 as Reflected
       in Mutualista Activities." Notre Dame, Ind.:
       University of Notre Dame, 1979.

1818   Reccow, Louis. "The Orange County Citrus Strikes of
       1935-1936: The Forgotten People in Revolt." Los
       Angeles: University of Southern California, 1971.
Focuses on early efforts of California Mexican American
agricultural workers to organize.

1819   Rocha, Rodolfo. "The Influence of the Mexican
       Revolution on the Mexican-Texas Border, 1910-1916."
       Lubbock: Texas Technological University, 1981.

1820   Rogers, Thomas G. "The Housing Situation of the
       Mexicans in San Antonio, Texas." Master's thesis.
       Austin: University of Texas, 1927.

1821   Romo, Ricardo. "Mexican Workers in the City: Los
       Angeles, 1915-1930." Los Angeles: University of
       California, 1975.
Published in 1983 under the title East Los Angeles: History
of a Barrio by the University of Texas Press. Argues the
importance of the urban experience.

1822   Rosales, Francisco A. "Mexican Immigration to the
       Urban Midwest During the 1920s." Bloomington: Indiana
       University, 1978.
Describes the development of the East Chicago, Indiana
Mexican community; covers regional differences of Mexican
immigrants and the importance of railroad employment.

1823   Rynearson, Ann Manry. "Hiding Within the Melting Pot:
       Mexican Americans in St. Louis." St. Louis, Mo.:
       Washington University, 1980.

1824   Sandos, James A. "The Mexican Revolution and the
       United States, 1915-1917: The Impact of Conflict in
       the Tamaulipas-Texas Frontier Upon the Emergence of
       Revolutionary Government in Mexico." Berkeley:

University of California, 1978.

1825 Santos, Joseph M. "Poverty and Problems of the
      Mexican Immigrant." Master's thesis. Stockton,
      Calif.: University of the Pacific, 1931.
Describes the Mexican's education, work, and socio-economic
problems.

1826 Sauter, Mary C. "Arbol Verde: A Cultural Conflict and
      Accomodation in a California Mexican Community."
      Master's thesis. Claremont, Calif.: Claremont
      Graduate School, 1933.
Describes the Mexican cultural background and shows the
contrast with Anglos in the Claremont colonia of Arbol
Verde.

1827 Sepulveda, Ciro H. "La Colonia del Harbor: History of
      Mexicanos in East Chicago, Indiana, 1919-1932." Notre
      Dame, Ind.: University of Notre Dame, 1976.

1828 Shapiro, Harold A. "The Workers of San Antonio,
      Texas, 1900-1940." Austin: University of Texas, 1952.

1829 Shelton, Cynthia J. "The Neighborhood House of San
      Diego: Settlement Work in the Mexican Community,
      1914-1940." Master's thesis. San Diego: California
      State University, 1975.

1830 Shinn, Vara Davis. "Social and Economic Status of the
      Mexican in Texas Since 1910." Master's thesis.
      Chicago: University of Chicago, 1930.

1831 Shuster, Stephen W., IV. "The Modernization of the
      Texas Rangers, 1930-1936." Master's thesis. Fort
      Worth: Texas Christian University, 1965.

1832 Simmons, Thomas E. "The Citizen Factories: The
      Americanization of Mexican Students in Texas Public
      Schools, 1920-1945." College Station: Texas A & M
      University, 1976.

1833 Skendzel, Eduardo A. "La colonia mexicana en
      Detroit." Master's thesis. Saltillo, Coahuila,
      Mexico: Universidad Autonoma de Coahuila, 1961.

1834 Steakley, Dan Lewis. "The Border Patrol of the San
      Antonio Collection District." Master's thesis.
      Austin: University of Texas, 1936.

1835 Suss, Stuart Allen. "Roots of a Revolution: Mexican
      Labor Agitation, 1906-1907." New York: New York
      University, 1975.

1836   Taylor, Juanita F. "A Comparison of First and Second
        Generation Mexican Parents." Master's thesis. Los
        Angeles: University of Southern California, 1943.

1837   Thomas, Dorothy E. "The Final Years of New Mexico's
        Struggle for Statehood, 1907-1912." Master's thesis.
        Albuquerque: University of New Mexico, 1941.

1838   Thomforde, Duane W. "Political Socialization in South
        El Paso." Master's thesis. El Paso: University of
        Texas, 1969.

1839   Van Gilder, Bert I. "The Sociological Aspects of
        Mexican Immigration to the United States." Master's
        thesis. Stockton, Calif.: University of the Pacific,
        1931.
Includes many photographs of the 1920s era.

1840   Walter, Paul A., Jr. "A Study of Isolation and Social
        Change in Three Spanish Speaking Villages of New
        Mexico." Stanford, Calif.: Stanford University, 1938.

1841   Weintraub, Harry. "The I.W.W. in California,
        1905-1931." Master's thesis. Los Angeles: University
        of California, 1947.
Includes material on the Wheatland farm workers riot, 1913.

V: Periodicals

1842   Airman, Duncan. "Hell Along the Border." American
       Mercury 5 (May 1925), 17-23.
An interesting 1920s view of Mexican border towns,
especially Ciudad Juarez.

1843   Allen, Ruth A. "Mexican Peon Women in Texas."
       Sociology and Social Research 16 (December 1931),
       131-142.
Based on a survey of Mexican farm women in central Texas;
evaluates their social position.

1844   Almaraz, Felix D., Jr. "The Making of a Boltonian:
       Carlos E. Castañeda of Texas--the Early Years." Red
       River Historical Review 1 (Winter 1974), 329-350.
Describes eminent historian Carlos Castañeda's struggle to
succeed in the field of Southwestern history.

1845   Alvarado, Ernestine M. "Mexican Immigration to the
       United States." In National Conference of Social Work
       Proceedings 47 (1920), 479-480. Chicago: University
       of Chicago Press.
A short descriptive article by a YWCA representative.

1846   Austin, Mary H. "Mexicans and New Mexico." Survey
       66:3 (May 1931), 141-144, 187-190.

1847   Axelrod, Bernard. "St. Louis and the Mexican
       Revolutionaries, 1905-1906." Missouri Historical
       Society Bulletin 28 (Jan. 1972), 94-108.
Covers part of the activities of the Flores Magon brothers
and their colleagues of the Partido Liberal in the American
Southwest.

1848   Aztlan 7:2 (Summer 1976).).
Entire issue is devoted to articles on the Chicano
experience in the Midwest.

1849   Bamford, Edwin F. "Industrialization and the Mexican
       Casual." Southwestern Political and Social Science
       Association Proceedings 5 (1924), 251-264. Austin,
       Tex.: The Southwestern Political and Social Science
       Association.

1850   Bamford, Edwin F. "The Mexican Casual Problem in the
       Southwest." Sociology and Social Research [Journal of
       Applied Sociology] 8:6 (July-Aug. 1924), 363-371.
A discussion of the employment and exploitation of Mexican

workers.

1851   Barnes, Elinor J.   "Arizona's People Since 1910."
        Arizona Review of Business and Public Administration
        13 (Jan. 1964), 3-10.

1852   Barrera, Mario.   "Class Segmentation and the Political
        Economy of the Chicano, 1900-1930."   New Scholar 6
        (1977), 167-181.

1853   Barton, Josef J.   "Land, Labor and Community in
        Nueces: Czech Farmers and Mexican Laborers in South
        Texas, 1880-1930."   A chapter in Ethnicity on the
        Great Plains.   Edited by Frederick C. Luebke.
        Lincoln: University of Nebraska Press, 1980.
The author inquires why Mexicans remained laborers while the
Czechs became landowners.

1854   Batten, James H.   "The Mexican Immigration Problem."
        Pan Pacific Progress 8 (1928), 39, 52.

1855   Batten, James H.   "New Features of Mexican
        Immigration: The Case Against Further Restrictive
        Legislation."   Pacific Affairs 3 (Oct. 1930), 955-966.

1856   Betten, Neil and Raymond A. Mohl.   "From
        Discrimination to Repatriation: Mexican Life in Gary,
        Indiana, During the Great Depression."   Pacific
        Historical Review 42:3 (Aug. 1973), 370-388.
Describes the changes that took place in treatment of the
Mexican industrial worker as the 1930s depression deepened.

1857   Bloch, Louis.   "Facts About Mexican Immigration Before
        and Since the Quota Restriction Laws."   Journal of the
        American Statistical Association 24 (March 1929),
        50-60.

1858   Boettcher, Ethel C.   "Eyewitness to a Penitente Rite."
        Greater Llano Estacado Southwest Heritage 10:1 (Spring
        1980), 12-15.
An early 1930s description of Good Friday activities by
Penitentes.

1859   Bogardus, Emory S.   "The Mexican Immigrant."   Journal
        of Applied Sociology 11 (May 1927), 470-488.

1860   Bogardus, Emory S.   "The Mexican Immigrant and
        Segregation."   American Journal of Sociology 36 (July
        1930), 74-80.

1861   Bogardus, Emory S.   "The Mexican Immigrant and the
        Quota."   Sociology and Social Research 12:4
        (March-April 1928), 371-378.
Describes both sides of the Mexican immigration quota issue

and gives some suggested solutions.

1862   Bogardus, Emory S.   "Mexican Repatriates."   Sociology
       and Social Research 18 (Nov.-Dec. 1933), 169-176.

1863   Bogardus, Emory S.   "Second Generation Mexicans."
       Sociology and Social Research 13 (Jan. 1929), 276-283.

1864   Box, John C., et al.   "Should Quota Law be Applied to
       Mexico."   Congressional Digest 7 (May 1928), 155-164,
       177.
By the congressional leader in the move to apply quota
legislation to Mexico.

1865   Bryan, Samuel.   "Mexican Immigrants in the United
       States."   Survey 28 (Sept. 7, 1912), 726-730.
Study with photographs of Mexican railroad workers.

1866   Burgess, T.   "On the American Side of the Rio
       Grande."   Missionary Review of the World 50 (Sept.
       1927), 689-692.

1867   Burnham, Frederick R.   "The Howl for Mexican Labor."
       In Alien in Our Midst.   Edited by Madison Grant and
       Charles S. Davison, pp. 44-49.   New York: Galton
       Publishing Co., 1930.
Opposes Mexican immigration as a source of cheap labor.

1868   Cadenhead, Ivie E., Jr.   "American Socialists and the
       Mexican Revolution of 1910."   Southwestern Social
       Science Quarterly 43 (1962), 103-117.

1869   Calcott, Frank.   "The Mexican Peon in Texas."   Survey
       44:13 (June 26, 1920), 437-438.
Describes the Mexican in Texas--with some stereotyping.

1870   Camblon, Ruth S.   "Mexicans in Chicago."   The Family 7
       (Nov. 1926), 207-211.

1871   Campa, Arthur L.   "Protest Folk Poetry in the Spanish
       Southwest."   Colorado Quarterly 20:3 (Winter 1972),
       355-363.

1872   Cardoso, Lawrence A.   "Labor Emigration to the
       Southwest, 1916 to 1920: Mexican Attitudes and
       Policy."   Southwestern Historical Quarterly 79 (April
       1976), 400-416.

1873   Cardoso, Lawrence A.   "La reparticion de braceros en
       epoca de Obregon, 1920-1923."   Historia Mexicana 26:4
       (April-June 1977), 576-595.

1874   Carlson, Alvar W.   "The Settling Process of Mexican
       Americans in Northwestern Ohio."   Journal of Mexican

American History 5 (1975), 24-42.
Describes the characteristics of the migrants who moved out
of the stream into permanent industrial employment, mostly
in smaller towns. Maps and tables of findings.

1875   Casillas, Mike. "Mexican Labor Militancy in the U.S.:
        1896-1915." _Southwest Economy and Society_ 4 (1978),
        31-42.

1876   Castillo, Pedro. "Urbanization, Migration, and the
        Chicanos in Los Angeles 1900-1920." In _Aztlan:
        historia contemporanea del pueblo chicano (1848-1910)_.
        Edited by David Maciel and Patricia Bueno. Mexico,
        D.F.: SepSetentas, 1975, item 99.

1877   Chavez, Fray Angelico. "The Archibeque Story." _El
        Palacio_ 54 (Aug. 1947), 179-182.
Archibeque was a leader of the Penitentes in the early
1900s.

1878   Clark, Victor S. "Mexican Labor in the United
        States." Bulletin #78 of the Bureau of Labor, pp.
        466-522. Washington, D.C.: U.S. Government Printing
        Office, 1908. Reprinted as part of _Mexican Labor in
        the United States_. New York: Arno Press, 1974, item
        2955.
An excellent pioneer work covering immigrants, migration,
occupations (farm, mine, misc.), standard of living, social
conditions, effects on Mexico and on the United States.

1879   "Commies Dominated LaFollette Committee." _The
        Associated Farmer_ 14:1 (July-Aug. 1953).

1880   Cosio Villegas, Daniel. "Border Troubles in United
        States-Mexican Relations." _Southwestern Historical
        Quarterly_ 72:1 (July 1968), 34-39.

1881   Crawford, Remsen. "The Menace of Mexican
        Immigration." _Current History_ 31 (Feb. 1930),
        902-907.

1882   Croxdale, Richard. "The 1938 San Antonio Pecan
        Shellers' Strike." In _Women in the Texas Workforce:
        Yesterday and Today_. Edited by Richard Croxdale and
        Melissa Hield, pp. 24-34. Austin: People's History in
        Texas, 1979.

1883   Cumberland, Charles C. "Border Raids in the Lower Rio
        Grande Valley, 1915." _Southwestern Historical
        Quarterly_ 57 (1954), 285-311.
Includes material on the Plan de San Diego, Texas.

1884   Cumberland, Charles C. "Mexican Revolutionary
        Movements from Texas, 1906-1912." _Southwestern_

Historical Quarterly 52 (1949), 301-324.

1885 Cumberland, Charles C. "Precursors of the Mexican
      Revolution of 1910." Hispanic American Historical
      Review 22 (1942), 344-356.

1886 Daniel, Pete. "Up From Slavery and Down to Peonage.
      The Alonzo Bailey Case." Journal of American History
      57 (Dec. 1970), 654-670.

1887 Davis, James J. "Selective Immigration." Forum 70
      (Sept. 1923), 1857-1865.

1888 Dawson, J. M. "Among the Mexicans in Texas; Waco
      Mission." Missionary Review of the World 50 (Oct.
      1927), 757-758.
Concerned with the heavy influx from Mexico.

1889 De La Cruz, Jesse. "Rejection Because of Race: Albert
      J. Beveridge and Nuevo Mexico's Struggle for
      Statehood, 1902-1903." Aztlan 7:1 (Spring 1976),
      79-97.

1890 De Leon, Arnoldo. "Blowout 1910 Style: A Chicano
      School Boycott in West Texas." Texana 2:2 (Spring
      1976), 124-140.

1891 De Leon, Arnoldo. "The Rape of Tio Taco: Mexican
      Americans in Texas, 1930-1937." Journal of Mexican
      American Studies 1 (Fall 1970), 4-15.

1892 De Leon, Arnoldo. "Los Tasinques and the Sheep
      Shearers' Union of North America: A Strike in West
      Texas, 1934." West Texas Historical Association
      Yearbook 55 (1979), 3-16.

1893 Dinwoodie, D. H. "Deportation: The Immigration
      Service and the Chicano Labor Movement in the 1930s."
      New Mexico Historical Review 52 (July 1977), 193-206;
      also in Immigration and Public Policy: Human Rights
      for Undocumented Workers and Their Families. Edited
      by Antonio Jose Rios-Bustamante. Los Angeles: Chicano
      Studies Center, University of California, 1977.

1894 Dobie, J. Frank. "Ranch Mexicans." Survey 66 (May
      1931), 167-170.

1895 Dowell, Edward H. "Restriction of Western Hemisphere
      Immigration." U.S. Senate. 70 Cong., 1st sess.,
      Hearing Before the Committee on Immigration on S.1437,
      Feb. 1, 1928, pp. 1-11.

1896   Elwes, Hugh C.   "Points About Mexican Labor."
       Engineering and Mining Journal 90 (Oct. 1, 1910), 662.

1897   Esquivel, Servando I.   "The Immigrant from Mexico."
       Outlook 125 (May 19, 1920), 131.

1898   Feingold, Gustave H.   "Intelligence of the First
       Generation of Immigrant Groups: A Study and a
       Critique." Journal of Educational Psychology 15 (Feb.
       1924), 65-82.
Good for its contemporary view and biases.

1899   Fergusson, Erna.   "New Mexico's Mexicans." Century
       116 (Aug. 1928), 437-444.

1900   Fields, Harold.   "Where Shall the Alien Work?" Social
       Forces 12 (Dec. 1933), 213-221.

1901   Fitch, John A.   "Arizona's Embargo on
       Strike-Breakers." Survey 37 (Oct. 1916-March 1917),
       143-146.

1902   Foscue, Edwin J.   "Agricultural History of the Lower
       Rio Grande Valley Region." Agricultural History 8
       (March 1934), 124-138.

1903   Francis, E. K.   "Multiple Intergroup Relations in the
       Upper Rio Grande Region." American Sociological
       Review 21 (1956), 84-87.

1904   Fuller, Elizabeth.   "The Mexican Housing Problem in
       Los Angeles." Sociology and Social Research 5:1 (Nov.
       1920), 1-11.
Gives a detailed description of the housing and furnishings,
from a survey of fifty homes.

1905   Fuller, Roden.   "Occupation of Mexican-born Population
       of Texas, New Mexico, and Arizona, 1900-1920."
       Journal of the American Statistical Association 23
       (March 1928), 64-74.

1906   Galarza, Ernesto.   "Life in the United States for
       Mexican People: Out of the Experience of a Mexican."
       National Conference of Social Work Proceedings 56
       (1929), 399-404.   Chicago: University of Chicago
       Press.

1907   Galarza, Ernesto.   "Without Benefit of Lobby." Survey
       66:3 (May 1, 1931), 181.
Discusses the dilemma of Mexican repatriates.

1908   Gamio, Manuel.   "Migration and Planning." Survey 66:3
       (May 1, 1931), 174-175.

1909   Garcia, Mario T.   "Americanization and the Mexican
       Immigrant, 1880-1930." Journal of Ethnic Studies 6
       (1978), 19-34.

1910   Garcia, Richard A.   "Class, Consciousness, and
       Ideology--The Mexican Community of San Antonio, Texas:
       1930-1940." Aztlan 9 (1978), 23-69.

1911   Garis, Roy L. "Lest Immigration Restriction Fail."
       Saturday Evening Post 198 (Oct. 10, 1925), 41.

1912   Garis, Roy L. "The Mexicanization of American
       Business." Saturday Evening Post 202 (Feb. 8, 1930),
       46, 51, 178, 181-187.
Part of the Post's campaign against Mexican immigration.

1913   Garnett, William E.   "Immediate and Pressing Race
       Problems of Texas."   Southwestern Political and Social
       Science Association Proceedings 6 (1925), 31-48.
       Austin, Tex.: The Association.

1914   Gerlach, Allen. "Conditions Along the Border--1915;
       The Plan de San Diego." New Mexico Historical Review
       43 (1968), 195-212.

1915   Gill, Mario. "Teresa Urrea, La Santa de Cabora."
       Historia Mexicana 6 (1957), 626-644.

1916   Goethe, C. M. "The Influx of Mexican Amerinds."
       Eugenics 2 (Jan. 1929), 6-9.

1917   Goethe, C. M. "Other Aspects of the Problem."
       Current History 28 (Aug. 1928), 766-768.
Critical of Mexican immigration.

1918   Goethe, C. M. "Peons Need Not Apply." World's Work
       59:11 (Nov. 1930), 47-48.
A brief article on the quota question by the president of
the Immigration Study Commission, Sacramento.

1919   Gomez-Quinones, Juan. "The First Steps: Chicano Labor
       Conflict and Organizing, 1900-1920." Aztlan 3:1
       (Spring 1972), 13-49.

1920   Gomez-Quinones, Juan. "Piedras Contra La Luna, Mexico
       en Aztlan y Aztlan en Mexico: Chicano-Mexicano
       Relations and the Mexican Consulates, 1900-1920." In
       Contemporary Mexico; Papers of the IV International
       Congress of Mexican History. Edited by James W.
       Wilkie, et al. Mexico, D.F.: 1975.

1921   Gomez-Quinones, Juan. "Research Notes on the
       Twentieth Century." Aztlan 1 (Spring 1970), 115-132.
Includes material on agricultural strikes of the 1930s, and

the irredentist movement and 1915 Plan de San Diego, Texas.

1922   Gompers, Samuel. "United States-Mexico-Labor-Their
       Relations." American Federalist 23 (Aug. 1916),
       633-652.
Views of the president of the American Federation of Labor.

1923   Gonzalez Navarro, Moises. "Los efectos sociales de la
       crisis del '29." Historia Mexicana 20:2 (April-June
       1970), 536-558.
The Mexican government's effort to resettle repatriates.

1924   Griswold del Castillo, Richard. "The 'Mexican
       Problem': A Critical View of the Alliance of Academics
       and Politicians During the Debate Over Mexican
       Immigration in the 1920's." The Borderlands Journal
       4:2 (Spring 1981), 241-251.

1925   Griswold del Castillo, Richard. "The Mexican
       Revolution and the Spanish Language Press in the
       Borderlands." Journalism History 4:2 (Summer 1977).

1926   Guinn, James M. "The Passing of the Rancho."
       Historical Society of Southern California Annual
       Publications 10 (1915-1916), 46-53.

1927   Gwin, J. Blaine. "Back and Forth to Mexico." Survey
       39 (Oct. 1917), 9-10.

1928   Gwin, J. Blaine. "Immigration Along Our Southwest
       Border." American Academy of Political and Social
       Science Annals 93 (Jan. 1930), 126-130.

1929   Gwin, J. Blaine. "Making Friends of Invaders: Mexican
       Refugees in Advance of the Returning Troops." Survey
       37 (Mar. 3, 1917), 621-623.

1930   Gwin, J. Blaine. "Social Problems of Our Mexican
       Population." National Conference of Social Work
       Proceedings 53 (1926), 327-332.

1931   Hager, William M. "The Plan of San Diego. Unrest on
       the Texas Border in 1915." Arizona and the West 5:4
       (Winter 1963), 327-336.

1932   Handman, Max. "Economic Reasons for the Coming of the
       Mexican Immigrant." American Journal of Sociology 35
       (Jan. 1930), 601-611.

1933   Handman, Max. "The Mexican Immigrant in Texas."
       National Conference of Social Work Proceedings 53
       (1926), 332-339; also: Southwestern Political and
       Social Science Quarterly 7 (June 1926), 33-40.

1934   Handman, Max S.   "San Antonio." Survey 66 (May 1,
       1931), 163-166.

1935   Hardy, Osgood. "Los Repatriados." Pomona College
       Magazine 21:2 (Jan. 1933), 71-73.

1936   Harris, C. H. and L. R. Sadler. "Plan of San Diego
       and the Mexican-United States War Crisis of 1916: A
       Reexamination." Hispanic American Historical Review
       58 (Aug. 1978), 381-408.
A study in depth of the controversial 1915 Mexican American
program for an uprising in Texas and its impact.

1937   Hayne, Coe. "Studying Mexican Relations at El Paso."
       Missionary Review of the World 50 (Feb. 1927),
       110-112.

1938   Heald, J. H. "Mexicans in the Southwest." Missionary
       Review of the World 42 (Nov. 1919), 860-865.

1939   Heflin, Reuben W. "The New Mexico Constitutional
       Convention." New Mexico Historical Review 21:1 (Jan.
       1946), 60-68.

1940   Henderson, Peter V. N. "Mexican Rebels in the
       Borderlands, 1910-1912." Red River Valley Historical
       Review 2 (Summer 1975), 207-219.

1941   Hernandez Alvarez, J. "Demographic Profile of the
       Mexican Immigration to the U.S., 1910-1950." Journal
       of Inter-American Studies and World Affairs 8 (July
       1966), 471-496.

1942   Hoffman, Abraham. "The Federal Bureaucracy Meets a
       Superior Spokesman for Alien Deportation." Journal of
       the West 14:4 (Oct. 1975), 91-106.
Describes U.S. government response to the complaining
letters of one J. C. Brodie of Superior, Arizona in the
early 1930s.

1943   Hoffman, Abraham. "Mexican Repatriation Statistics:
       Some Suggested Alternatives to Carey McWilliams."
       Western Historical Quarterly 3:4 (Oct. 1972), 391-404.
Argues that McWilliams' view of Mexican repatriation was
simplistic and that his totals for Los Angeles county are
estimates rather than exact figures.

1944   Hoffman, Abraham. "Stimulus to Repatriation: The 1931
       Federal Deportation Drive and the Los Angeles Mexican
       Community." The Pacific Historical Review 42:2 (May
       1973), 205-219.
Argues that the deportation drive helped lead to a mass
exodus from the Los Angeles Mexican community.

1945 Holmes, Samuel J. "An Argument Against Mexican
      Immigration." Commonwealth Club of California
      Transactions 21:1 (March 23, 1926), 21-27.

1946 Holmes, Samuel J. "Perils of the Mexican Invasion."
      North American Review 227:5 (May 1929), 615-623.
One contemporary report seeing a threat in Mexican
immigration at the end of the twenties.

1947 Hoover, Glenn E. "Our Mexican Immigrants." Foreign
      Affairs 8 (Oct. 1929), 99-107.
Anti-Mexican on a racist base.

1948 Hoover, Glenn E. "Resident Alien Problem of the
      Southwest." Institute of International Relations
      Proceedings 4 (1929), 193-194.

1949 Humphrey, Norman D. "Mexican Repatriates from
      Michigan--Public Assistance in Historical
      Perspective." Social Service Review 15:3 (Sept.
      1941), 497-513.

1950 Humphrey, Norman D. "Migration and Settlement of
      Detroit Mexicans." Economic Geography 19 (Oct. 1943),
      358-361.

1951 "Increase of Mexican Population in the United States,
      1920-1930." Monthly Labor Review 27 (July 1933),
      46-48.

1952 "The International Conference on Emigration and
      Immigration." Monthly Summary of the League of
      Nations 4 (March 1924), 75.

1953 "Is Mexican Labor Cheap?" Saturday Evening Post 207
      (July 21, 1934), 22.

1954 Johnson, Alvin S. "Mexico in San Antonio." The New
      Republic 7:86 (June 24, 1916), 190-191.
Discusses the "Mexican problem."

1955 Jones, Anita Edgar. "Mexican Colonies in Chicago."
      Social Service Review 2:4 (Dec. 1928), 579-597.
Describes the early experience in Chicago during the 1920s.

1956 Kelley, Edna E. "The Mexicans Go Home." Journal of
      Applied Psychology 19 (April 1935), 303.

1957 Kelley, Wilfrid D. "Settlement of the Middle Rio
      Grande Valley." Journal of Geography 54 (1955),
      387-399.

1958   King, Edith S. "My Mexican Neighbors." <u>Survey</u> (March
        3, 1917), 624-626.

1959   Kinnicutt, Francis H. "Immigration: Stalemate in
        Congress." <u>Eugenics</u> 3:7 (July 1930), 279.
Concerns the Harris Bill to put Mexican immigration under a
quota.

1960   Kiser, George C. "Mexican American Labor Before World
        War II." <u>Journal of Mexican American History</u> 2:2
        (Spring 1972), 122-142.
A general history of Mexican labor migration from the 19th
century; it includes the "first bracero program" of World
War I and the evolution of U.S. attitudes toward Mexican
workers.

1961   Kiser, George C. and David Silverman. "Mexican
        Repatriation During the Great Depression." <u>Journal of
        Mexican American History</u> 3 (1973), 139-164.
A broad survey of the repatriation which stresses its local
decentralized nature. The national government was pushed by
southwest farming interests and by relations with Mexico.

1962   "Labor and Social Conditions of Mexicans in
        California." <u>Monthly Labor Review</u> 32 (Jan. 1931),
        81-89.

1963   Larson, Robert W. "Statehood for New Mexico,
        1888-1912." <u>New Mexico Historical Review</u> 37:3 (July
        1962), 161-200.
The final stage of New Mexico's struggle for statehood.

1964   Lescohier, Don D. "The Vital Problem in Mexican
        Immigration." National Conference of Social Work
        <u>Proceedings</u> 54 (1927), 547-554.

1965   Levenstein, Harvey A. "The AFL and Mexican
        Immigration in the 1920s: An Experiment in Labor
        Diplomacy." <u>Hispanic American Historical Review</u> 48:2
        (May 1968), 206-219.
Recounts AFL efforts to get the Confederacion Regional de
Obreros Mexicanos to work for limiting Mexican worker
emigration.

1966   "'Little Mexico' in Northern Cities." <u>World's Work</u>
        48:5 (Sept. 1924), 466.
Brief reference to Mexicans in St. Paul and other industrial
centers.

1967   Longmore, T. Wilson and Homer L. Hitt. "A Demographic
        Analysis of First and Second Generation Mexican
        Population in the United States: 1930." <u>Southwestern</u>

Social Science Quarterly [Social Science Quarterly]
24:2 (Sept. 1943), 138-149.
A discussion of the 1930 census and changes since 1920.

1968 Loomis, Charles P., and Glen Grisham. "Spanish
      Americans: The New Mexico Experiment in Village
      Rehabilitation." Applied Anthropology 2:3 (1943),
      13-37.

1969 Lopez, Ronald W. "The El Monte Berry Strike of 1933."
      Aztlan 1 (Spring 1970), 101-114.
Describes an important Los Angeles strike of 1933 which led
to the founding of the Confederation of Unions of Mexican
Farm Laborers and Workers.

1970 McGinnis, John H. "Cities and Towns of the
      Southwest." Southwest Review 13 (Oct. 1927), 36-47.

1971 McGregor (pseud.). "Our Spanish-American Fellow
      Citizens." Harper's Weekly 56 (1914), 6-8.

1972 Machado, Manuel A., Jr. "The United States and the De
      La Huerta Rebellion." Southwestern Historical
      Quarterly 75 (Jan. 1972), 303-324.

1973 McLean, Robert N. "Goodbye, Vicente!" Survey 66 (May
      1, 1931), 182-183.

1974 McLean, Robert N. "The Mexican Returns." The Nation
      135 (Aug. 24, 1932), 165-166, 170-175.

1975 McLean, Robert N. "Mexican Workers in the United
      States." National Conference of Social Work
      Proceedings 56 (1929), 531-538.

1976 McLean, Robert N. "Tightening the Mexican Border."
      Survey 64 (April 1930), 28-29, 54-56.

1977 McWilliams, Carey. "The Forgotten Mexican." In his
      Brothers Under the Skin. Boston: Little, Brown & Co.,
      1944.

1978 McWilliams, Carey. "The Forgotten Mexican." Common
      Ground 3 (Spring 1943), 65-78.

1979 McWilliams, Carey. "Getting Rid of the Mexican."
      American Mercury 28 (March 1933), 322-324.

1980 McWilliams, Carey. "Mexicans to Michigan." Common
      Ground 2:1 (Autumn 1941), 5-18.
Describes the journey of Mexican migrants from the Texas
border.

1981   McWilliams, Carey.   "Thirty-six Thousand New Aliens in
       California."   Pacific Weekly (Aug. 24, 1936).

1982   Manuel, Herschel T.   "The Mexican Population of
       Texas."   Southwestern Social Science Quarterly 15
       (June 1934), 29-51.

1983   Marvin, George.   "Bandits and the Borderland."   Worlds
       Work 32 (Oct. 1916), 656-663.

1984   Marvin, George.   "Monkey Wrenches in Our Mexican
       Machinery."   Independent 120 (April 14, 1928),
       350-352.
Describes possible effects of extending the immigration
quota system to Mexico.

1985   Meaders, Margaret.   "Copper Chronicle: The Story of
       New Mexico 'Red Gold.'"   New Mexico Business 11
       (1958), 2-9.

1986   Meany, George.   "Peonage in California."   American
       Federalist 48 (May 1941), 3-5, 31.

1987   Medieros, Francine.   "La Opinion, A Mexican Exile
       Newspaper: A Content Analysis of Its First Years,
       1926-1929."   Aztlan 11:1 (Spring 1980), 65-87.
Describes the ambivalent attitude of La Opinion toward a
variety of problems affecting Mexicans in the United States.

1988   "Mexican Exodus."   Newsweek 14 (July 31, 1939), 11.
Mexican President Cardenas sent his Undersecretary of State
to the U.S. to arrange the return of 1.4 million Mexicans.

1989   "The Mexican Immigrant."   In Essentials of
       Americanization.   By Emory S. Bogardus, pp. 264-271.
       Los Angeles: University of Southern California Press,
       1920.

1990   "Mexican Immigration."   Commonwealth Club of
       California Transactions 21:1 (March 1926), 1-34.

1991   "Mexican Immigration."   In Survey of American Foreign
       Relations.   Edited by Charles P. Howland, pp. 202-233.
       New Haven, Conn.: Yale University Press, 1931.
Thoroughly covers Mexican immigration from 1900 to 1930.

1992   "Mexican Immigration and the Farm."   Outlook 147:14
       (Dec. 7, 1927), 423.
A call for a delay in setting a Mexican quota.

1993   "The Mexican 'Invaders' of El Paso."   Survey 36 (July
       8, 1916), 380-382.

1994   "Mexican Invaders Relieving our Farm-Labor Shortage."
        Literary Digest 66:3 (July 17, 1920), 53-54.

1995   "Mexican Labor Colony at Bethlehem, Pennsylvania."
        Monthly Labor Review 33 (Oct. 1931), 822-826.

1996   "Mexican Labor in the Imperial Valley, California."
        Monthly Labor Review 28 (March 1929), 477-483.

1997   "Mexicans and Indians." In Racial Factors in American
        Industry. Edited by Herman Feldman, pp. 104-131. New
        York: Harper & Bros., 1931.
Discusses immigration and attitudes toward the Mexican; his
economic position.

1998   "The Mexican Who Went Home." Los Angeles Times, March
        26, 1933.

1999   Mohl, Raymond A. "The Saturday Evening Post and the
        'Mexican Invasion.'" Journal of Mexican American
        History 3 (1973), 131-138.
Describes the Saturday Evening Post's vigorous nativist
campaign against Mexican immigrants. The Post strongly
supported the move to apply quotas to Mexico.

2000   Montalbo, Philip J. "Our Rights." LULAC News 5 (Feb.
        1938), 3-5.
Protests violations of the Guadalupe Hidalgo Treaty.

2001   Moore, C. B. "Mexican Immigration." Western Grower
        and Shipper (Feb. 1930), 11, 21.

2002   Morris, Austin P. "Agricultural Labor and National
        Labor Legislation." California Law Review 54:5 (Dec.
        1966), 1939-1989.
Discusses the NIRA and whether Congress intended to exclude
agricultural labor from its benefits; discusses the NLRA.

2003   Muls, Ernest E. "The Labor Movement in New Mexico."
        New Mexico Business Review 4 (1935), 137-140.

2004   Murphy, L. F. "Experiment in Americanization." Texas
        Outlook 23 (Nov. 1939), 23-24.

2005   Nelson-Cisneros, Victor B. "La clase trabajadora en
        Tejas, 1920-1940." Aztlan 6:2 (Summer 1975), 239-265.
A valuable work describing the economic and social
conditions of Mexicans in Texas, their virtual exclusion
from industrial employment in the period, and the complex
problem of agricultural union organization.

2006   Nelson-Cisneros, Victor B. "UCAPAWA and Chicanos in
        California: The Farm Worker Period, 1937-1940."

Aztlan 7:3 (Fall 1976), 453-477.

2007   Nelson-Cisneros, Victor B.   "UCAPAWA Organizing
       Activities in Texas, 1935-50."   Aztlan 9 (1978),
       71-84.

2008   "Next-Door Neighbors."   In Methodism's New Frontier,
       by Jay S. Stowell, chapter 4.   New York: Methodist
       Book Concern, 1924.
A good description of the Los Angeles Mexican community in
the early 1920s.

2009   Norman, Arthur M. Z.   "Migration to Southeast Texas:
       People and Words."   Southwestern Social Science
       Quarterly 37 (1956), 149-158.

2010   Nostrand, Richard L.   "The Hispano Homeland in 1900."
       Association of American Geographers Annals 70:3 (Sept.
       1980), 382-396.

2011   "Okies in Sombreros: Migrant Mexican Cropworkers."   In
       One Nation, by Wallace Stegner, pp. 95-116.   Boston:
       Houghton Mifflin Co., 1945.

2012   Oxnam, G. Bromley.   "The Mexican in Los Angeles from
       the Standpoint of the Religious Forces in the City."
       American Academy of Political and Social Science
       Annals 93 (Jan. 1921), 131-133.
Has some good information on economic and social conditions,
also on the work of Protestant groups among Mexicans.

2013   Pace, Anne.   "Mexican Refugees in Arizona, 1910-1911."
       Arizona and the West 16 (Spring 1974), 5-18.

2014   Park, Joseph F.   "The 1903 'Mexican Affair' at
       Clifton."   Journal of Arizona History 18 (1977),
       119-148.
An early copper mine strike by Mexican and Mexican American
workers at the Clifton-Morenci mines in Arizona.

2015   Phillips, Herbert.   "The School Follows the Child."
       Survey 66 (Sept. 1931), 493-495.
Describes educational efforts with migrant children.

2016   Pickens, William H.   "Bronson Cutting vs. Dennis
       Chavez: Battle of the Patrones in New Mexico, 1934."
       New Mexico Historical Review 46 (Jan. 1971), 5-36.
The victory of an Anglo New Deal liberal over a conservative
Hispano.

2017   Pinto, Alfonso.   "When Hollywood Spoke Spanish."
       Americas 32 (Oct. 1980), 3-8.
Describes the history of Spanish-language films and stars in
the 1930s.

2018   Putnam, Frank Bishop. "Teresa Urrea, 'The Saint of
        Cabora.'" Southern California Quarterly 45 (Sept.
        1963), 245-264.
Teresa Urrea (1873-1906), a border region mystic who became
the center of a cultist movement in the 1890s.

2019   Rausch, George J. "The Exile and Death of Victoriano
        Huerta." Hispanic American Historical Review 42 (May
        1962), 133-151.
Describes some effects of the 1910 Mexican revolution on the
border area.

2020   Redfield, Robert. "The Antecedents of Mexican
        Immigration to the United States." American Journal
        of Sociology 35 (Nov. 1929), 433-438.
Recapitulates some of Manuel Gamio's work on Mexican
immigration.

2021   Reisler, Mark. "Always the Laborer, Never the
        Citizen: Anglo Perceptions of the Mexican Immigrant
        During the 1920s." Pacific Historical Review 45:2
        (May 1976), 231-254.
Places the restrictionist side of the 1920s immigration
quota question in historical context.

2022   Reisler, Mark. "The Mexican Immigrant in the Chicago
        Area During the 1920s." Journal of the Illinois
        Historical Society 66 (Summer 1973), 144-158.

2023   Reisler, Mark. "Mexican Unionization in California
        Agriculture, 1927-1936." Labor History 14:4 (Fall
        1973), 562-579.

2024   "Results of Admission of Mexican Laborers Under
        Department Orders for Employment in Agricultural
        Pursuits." Monthly Labor Review 11 (Nov. 1920),
        221-223.
Describes the impact of what is sometimes referred to as the
"first bracero movement," during and at the end of World War
I.

2025   Richmond, Douglas W. "La guerra de Texas se renova
        (sic!): Mexican Insurrection and Carrancista
        Ambitions, 1900-1920." Aztlan 11:1 (Spring 1980),
        1-32.
Describes Mexican government activities among Mexicans in
Texas; contains material on the 1915 Plan de San Diego,
Texas.

2026   Roberts, Kenneth L. "The Docile Mexican." Saturday
        Evening Post 200:57 (March 10, 1928), 39-41, 165-166.

2027   Roberts, Kenneth L.   "Mexican Immigration in the
       Southwest." In The Alien in Our Midst. Edited by
       Madison Grant and Charles S. Davison, pp. 214-219.
       New York: Galton Publishing Co., 1930.
Argues against Mexican immigration.

2028   Roberts, Kenneth L.   "Mexicans or Ruin." Saturday
       Evening Post 200:54 (Feb. 18, 1928), 14-15, 142.
Argues the case of the southwestern farm operator.

2029   Roberts, Kenneth L.   "Wet and Other Mexicans."
       Saturday Evening Post 200:52 (Feb. 4, 1928), 10-11,
       137-138, 141-142, 146.
Includes some discussion of the Immigration Service and the
Border Patrol.

2030   Rodriguez, Richard and Gloria L. Rodriguez.   "Teresa
       Urrea: Her Life, as it Affected the Mexican-U.S.
       Frontier." El Grito 5:4 (1972), pp. 48-68. Reprinted
       in Voices: Readings From El Grito. Edited by Octavio
       Romano-V., pp. 179-199. Berkeley, Calif.: Quinto Sol,
       1973.
Teresa Urrea was a borderlands mystic and cult figure at the
end of the 19th century.

2031   Rodriguez, Theodore and W. G. Fennell.   "Agrarian
       Revolt in California." Nation 137 (Sept. 6, 1933),
       272.
A letter on the El Monte strike.

2032   Romo, Ricardo.   "Responses to Mexican Immigration,
       1910-1930." Aztlan 6:2 (Summer 1975), 173-194.
A broad description of Mexican immigration and the reaction
of various U.S. sectors to the heavy increase during World
War I and the 1920s.

2033   Romo, Ricardo.   "The Urbanization of Southwestern
       Chicanos in the Early 20th Century." New Scholar 6
       (1977), 183-207.
Argues for the continuity between 17th century Mexican
settlement in the Southwest and the more intense movement of
the 20th century. Romo points out that from the 1920s
onward Chicanos settled more and more in urban centers.

2034   Romo, Ricardo.   "Work and Restlessness: Occupational
       and Spatial Mobility Among Mexicans in Los Angeles,
       1918-1928." Pacific Historical Review 46 (May 1977),
       157-180.

2035   Rosales, Francisco A.   "The Regional Origins of
       Mexicano Immigrants to Chicago During the 1920s."
       Aztlan 7:2 (Summer 1976), 187-201.
Shows that immigrants came mostly from the Bajio region of

central Mexico plus some urban areas; explains the reasons
for their coming.

2036   Rosales, Francisco A. and Daniel T. Simon. "Chicano
       Steel Workers and Unionism in the Midwest, 1919-1945."
       Aztlan 6:2 (Summer 1975), 267-275.
Stresses Chicano labor union involvement in the 1930s,
especially in the Chicago area.

2037   Rowell, Chester H. "Why Make Mexico an Exception?"
       Survey 66 (May 1, 1931), 180.
Argues against excluding Mexico from immigration quotas.

2038   Rowell, Edward. "Patterns of Agricultural and Labor
       Migration Within California." Monthly Labor Review 47
       (Nov. 1938), 980-990.

2039   Rusinow, Irving. "Spanish Americans in New Mexico: A
       Photographic Record of the Santa Cruz Valley." Survey
       Graphic 27 (Feb. 1938), 95-99.

2040   Russell, John C. "Racial Groups in the New Mexico
       Legislature." American Academy of Political Science
       Annals 195 (Jan. 1938), 62-71.

2041   Sanchez, George I. "North of the Border." Texas
       Academy of Science Transactions 25 (1940).

2042   Sandos, James A. "International Water Control in the
       Lower Rio Grande Basin, 1900-1920." Agricultural
       History 54:4 (Oct. 1980), 490-501.

2043   Sandos, James A. "The Plan of San Diego: War and
       Diplomacy on the Texas Border, 1915-1916." Arizona
       and the West 14 (1972), 5-24.

2044   Sandoval, David A. "An Economic Analysis of New
       Mexico History." New Mexico Business 20:2 (Feb.
       1967), 1-34.

2045   Santiago, Hasel D. "Mexican Influences in Southern
       California." Sociology and Social Research 16
       (Sept.-Oct. 1931), 58-74.

2046   Scruggs, Otey M. "The First Mexican Farm Labor
       Programs, 1917-1921." Arizona and the West 2
       (Spring-Winter 1960), 319-326.
Describes the World War I exemptions made to Mexican
agricultural workers.

2047   Servin, Manuel. "The Pre-World War II
       Mexican-American: An Interpretation." California
       Historical Society Quarterly 45:4 (Dec. 1960),
       325-338.

Argues that the pre-World War II Mexican American had earned
a well-deserved reputation for hard work and sobriety and
that wartime Pachucos undid much of this positive image.

2048   Shapiro, Harold A.   "The Pecan Shellers of San
       Antonio, Texas." The Southwestern Social Science
       Quarterly 32 (March 1952), 229-243.
The 1938 pecan shellers' strike placed in historical
perspective.

2049   Sharpless, Richard E.   "Mexican and Puerto Rican Labor
       in Pennsylvania's Lehigh Valley." New Labor Review 3
       (June 1980), 112-127.
Covers the Mexican experience from the 1920s.

2050   "Should Quota Law be Applied to Mexico?"
       Congressional Digest (1928), 155-164.
Arguments pro and con on the issue of Mexican
immigration--free or quota--during the twenties.

2051   Simpich, Frederick.   "Along Our Side of the Mexican
       Border." National Geographic 38 (July 1920), 61-80.
A description of the border region and its problems, with
photographs.

2052   Simpich, Frederick.   "The Little Brown Brother Treks
       North." Independent 116 (Feb. 27, 1926), 237-239.
Discusses immigration from Mexico and the quota question.

2053   Slatta, Richard W.   "Chicanos in the Pacific
       Northwest: An Historical Overview of Oregon's
       Chicanos." Aztlan 6:3 (Fall 1975), 327-338.
A brief survey of Chicanos in Oregon, their economic
activities, and their problems.

2054   Slayden, (Hon.) James L.   "Some Observations on
       Mexican Immigration." American Academy of Political
       and Social Science Annals 93 (Jan. 1921), 121-126.

2055   Soil Conservation Service.   "Population of the Upper
       Rio Grande Watershed." SCS Regional Bulletin No. 43,
       1937.

2056   Soil Conservation Service.   "Rural Rehabilitation in
       New Mexico." SCS Regional Bulletin No. 50, 1935.

2057   Soil Conservation Service.   "Village Livelihood in the
       Upper Rio Grande Area and a Note on the Level of
       Village Livelihood in the Upper Rio Grande Area." SCS
       Regional Bulletin No. 44, 1937.

2058   Sonnichsen, C. L.   "Colonel William C. Greene and the
       Strike at Cananea, Sonora, 1906." Arizona and the

West (Winter 1971), 343-368.

2059   Spaulding, Charles B.   "The Mexican Strike at El
       Monte, California." Sociology and Social Research 18
       (July-Aug. 1934), 571-580.
An excellent contemporary account of the El Monte 1933 Berry
Strike which was a landmark for Chicano workers. Out of it
came the Confederation of Unions of Mexican Farm Laborers
and Workers.

2060   Stevenson, Emma R.   "The Emigrant Comes Home." Survey
       66 (May 1, 1931), 175-177.

2061   Stevenson, Philip.   "Deporting Jesus." Nation 143
       (July 18, 1936), 67-69.
Describes the events leading up to the deportation of Jesus
Pallares, a union organizer in New Mexico's coal fields.

2062   Stokes, Frank.   "Let the Mexicans Organize." Nation
       143 (Dec. 19, 1936), 731-732.
An unusual grower viewpoint during the strike-filled
mid-thirties.

2063   Stowell, Jay S.   "Danger of Unrestricted Mexican
       Immigration." Current History 28 (August 1928),
       763-766.

2064   Strauss, Melvin P.   "The Mexican-American in El Paso
       Politics." In Urbanization in the Southwest, edited
       by Clyde J. Wingfield, pp. 56-74. El Paso: Texas
       Western Press, 1968.

2065   Strout, Richard L.   "A Fence for the Rio Grande."
       Independent 120 (June 2, 1928), 518-520.

2066   Sturges, Vera L.   "Mexican Immigrants." Survey 46
       (July 2, 1921), 470-471.

2067   Sturges, Vera L.   "The Progress of Adjustment in
       Mexican and United States Life." In National
       Conference of Social Work Proceedings 47 (1920).
       Chicago: University of Chicago Press.

2068   Sullenger, T. Earl.   "The Mexican Population of
       Omaha." Journal of Applied Psychology 8 (May-June
       1924), 289-293.

2069   Survey 66:3 (May 1, 1931).
The entire issue is devoted to the Mexican American
experience.

2070   Sutton, Walter A.   "Texas Congressmen and the Mexican
       Revolution of 1910." Journal of the West 13:4 (Oct.
       1974), 90-107.

Describes the various activities of Texas congressmen attempting to influence President Woodrow Wilson's policy toward the contending factions in Mexico, 1913-1916. These activities were based on a Texas perception of the Mexican Revolution.

2071   Taylor, Paul S. "California Farm Labor: A Review." Agricultural History 42:1 (Jan. 1968), 49-53.

2072   Taylor, Paul S. "Contemporary Background of California Farm Labor." Rural Sociology 1:4 (Dec. 1936), 401-419.

2073   Taylor, Paul S. "Crime and the Foreign Born: The Problem of the Mexican." National Commission on Law Observance and Enforcement. Report on Crime and the Foreign Born. Washington, D.C.: U.S. Government Printing Office, 1931.

2074   Taylor, Paul S. "Employment of Mexicans in Chicago and the Calumet Region." Journal of the American Statistical Association 25 (June 1930), 206-207.

2075   Taylor, Paul S. "Mexicans North of the Rio Grande." Survey 66:3 (May 1, 1931), 135-140, 197, 200-202, 205. Describes migratory travels of farm laborers.

2076   Taylor, Paul S. "Mexican Women in Los Angeles Industry in 1928." Aztlan 11:1 (Spring 1980), 99-131. Part of Paul Taylor's 1928 research. It describes the Mexican population, the employment areas, and the impact of women working on their social attitudes.

2077   Taylor, Paul S. "Migratory Agricultural Workers on the Pacific Coast." American Sociological Review 3 (April 1938), 225-232.

2078   Taylor, Paul S. "More Bars Against Mexicans." Survey 64 (April 1930), 26-27.

2079   Taylor, Paul S. "Notes on Streams of Mexican Migration." American Journal of Sociology 36 (1930-1931), 287-288.

2080   Taylor, Paul S. "Some Aspects of Mexican Immigration." Journal of Political Economy 38:5 (Oct. 1930), 609-615. Material on Mexican railroad track workers. Also published in Monthly Labor Review 32:1 (Jan. 1931), 81-83.

2081   Taylor, Paul S. and Clark Kerr. "Uprising on the Farms." Survey Graphic 24 (Jan. 1935), 44.

2082   Taylor, Travis H. "Migratory Farm Labor in the United
       States." Monthly Labor Review 44 (March 1937),
       539-549.

2083   Teague, Charles C. "A Statement on Mexican
       Immigration." Saturday Evening Post 200:57 (March 10,
       1928), 169-170.
A part of the Post's anti-Mexican immigration campaign.

2084   Tenayuca, Emma and Homer Brooks. "The Mexican
       Question in the Southwest." The Communist 18 (March
       1939), 261.
Emma Tenayuca (Brooks) was a leader in the San Antonio Pecan
Shellers' strike of 1938 and a well known radical labor
speaker.

2085   Thomson, Charles A. "The Man from Next Door."
       Century 111 (Jan. 1926), 275-282.

2086   Thomson, Charles A. "Mexicans--An Interpretation."
       National Conference of Social Work Proceedings 55
       (1928), 499-503. Chicago: University of Chicago
       Press.

2087   Thomson, Charles A. "Restriction of Mexican
       Immigration." Journal of Applied Psychology 11
       (July-Aug. 1927), 574-578.

2088   Thomson, Charles A. "What of the Bracero?" Survey
       54:5 (June 1, 1925), 291-292.

2089   "Twenty-Eight Important Mexicans." Commonweal 47
       (Feb. 13, 1948), 436-437.
The 28 were undocumented workers killed in an airplane crash
while being returned to central Mexico by the I.N.S.

2090   U.S., Congressional Record, 68th Cong., 2nd sess.
       "Secretary of Labor: Importers Refuse to Repatriate
       Mexican Labor" 60 (Jan. 7, 1925), 1366-1367.

2091   U.S., Department of Labor, Bureau of Labor Statistics.
       "Increase of Mexican Labor in Certain Industries in
       the United States." Monthly Labor Review 32:1 (Jan.
       1931), 81-83.
Includes a chart on Mexican railroad workers, 1909-1929 and
one of steel and packing plant workers, 1912-1928.

2092   U.S., Department of Labor, Bureau of Labor Statistics.
       "Labor and Social Conditions of Mexicans in
       California." Monthly Labor Review 32:1 (Jan. 1931),
       83-89.

2093   U.S., Department of Labor, Bureau of Labor Statistics.
       "Mexican Labor Colony at Bethlehem, Pennsylvania."

Monthly Labor Review 33 (Oct. 1931), 74-78.

2094   U.S., Department of Labor, Bureau of Labor Statistics.
       "Results of Admission of Mexican Laborers, Under
       Departmental Orders, for Employment in Agricultural
       Pursuits." Monthly Labor Review 11 (1920), 1095-1097.

2095   U.S., Department of Labor, National Labor Board.
       "Leonard Commission Report." Mimeographed Release
       #3325. Written by J. L. Leonard, S. Lubin, and W.
       French. Washington, D.C.: National Labor Board, 1934.
A report on the January 1934 Imperial Valley lettuce strike.

2096   Varlez, Louis. "Migration Problems and the Havana
       Conference of 1928." International Labor Review 19
       (Jan. 1929), 3-8.

2097   Walker, Helen W. "Mexican Immigrants as Laborers."
       Sociology and Social Research 13:1 (Sept.-Oct. 1928),
       55-62.

2098   Walker, Helen W. "Mexican Journeys to Bethlehem."
       Literary Digest 77 (June 2, 1923), 103-104.
Describes the Pennsylvania Mexican steel workers' colony of
ca. 1000 in 1923.

2099   Walker, Helen W. "Mexican Miners Going Back Home."
       Survey 39 (Oct. 1917), 97-98.

2100   Walker, Kenneth P. "The Pecan Shellers of San Antonio
       and Mechanization." Southwestern Historical Quarterly
       69:1 (July 1965), 44-58.

2101   Wallace, Andrew. "Colonel McClintock and the 1917
       Copper Strike." Arizoniana 3:1 (Spring 1962), 24-26.

2102   Wallis, Wilson D. "The Mexican Immigrant of
       California." Pacific Historical Review 2 (Dec. 1921),
       444-454.

2103   Walter, Paul A., Jr. "Octaviano Ambrosio Larrazolo."
       New Mexico Historical Review 7 (April 1932), 97-104.
Larrazolo (1859-1930), a leading Nuevo Mexicano politician,
played an important role in the development of New Mexico's
1910 state constitution.

2104   Walter, Paul A., Jr. "The Spanish-Speaking Community
       in New Mexico." Sociology and Social Research 24:2
       (Nov.-Dec. 1939), 150-157.
Describes Nuevo Mexicano (Hispano) culture over historical
time with an emphasis on adjustment problems created by the
Great Depression.

2105   Ward, Stuart R.   "The Mexican in California."
        Commonwealth Club of California Transactions 21 (March
        1926), 4-10.
Basically questions who pays the social costs of cheap
labor.

2106   Watson, Morris P.   "The People of New Mexico."
        Outlook 73:6 (Feb. 7, 1903), 340-344.
A good contemporary view, with the usual bias.

2107   Weber, Devra Anne.   "The Organization of Mexicano
        Agricultural Workers: The Imperial Valley and Los
        Angeles, 1928-1934: An Oral Approach." Aztlan 3 (Fall
        1972), 307-347.
Has useful material on the Imperial Valley labor
organization and conflict and on the 1933 El Monte Berry
Strike which led to the organization of CUCOM.

2108   Weber, Francis J.   "Irish-Born Champion of the
        Mexican-American." California Historical Society
        Quarterly 49:3 (Sept. 1970), 233-249.
Describes the activities of John H. Cantwell, archbishop of
Los Angeles, from the 1920s to 1940s.

2109   Weeks, O. Douglas.   "The League of United
        Latin-American Citizens. A Texas Mexican Civic
        Organization." Southwestern Political and Social
        Science Quarterly 10 (Dec. 1929), 257-258.
Describes the organization of LULAC out of three earlier
groups and details its objectives.

2110   White, Owen P.   "A Glance at the Mexicans." American
        Mercury 3 (Feb. 1925), 180-187.

2111   Whittaker, William G.   "Samuel Gompers, Labor, and the
        Mexican American Crisis of 1916: The Carrizal
        Incident." Labor History 17:4 (Fall 1976), 551-567.

2112   Williams, Chester S.   "Imperial Valley Prepares for
        War." World Tomorrow 17 (April 26, 1934), 199-201.

2113   Wilson, Marjorie Haines.   "Governor Hunt, the 'Beast'
        and the Miners." Journal of Arizona History 15:2
        (Summer 1974), 119-138.
Describes the role of Governor George Hunt in the struggle
of Mexican World War I Arizona copper mine workers for
equality of pay with Anglo miners.

2114   Winter, Ella.   "California's Little Hitlers." New
        Republic 77 (Dec. 27, 1933), 188-190.
Describes police and vigilante attitudes and actions in
California's 1933 agricultural strikes.

2115   Woehlke, Walter V.   "Don't Drive Out the Mexicans."
       Review of Reviews 81:5 (May 1930), 66-68.
A pro-grower viewpoint on the immigration quota issue.

2116   Wollenberg, Charles.   "Huelga, 1928 Style: The
       Imperial Valley Cantaloupe Workers Strike." Pacific
       Historical Review 38:1 (Feb. 1969), 45-49, 52-58.
A valuable study of an important early strike which led to
the founding of the Mexican Mutual Aid Society of Imperial
Valley California.

2117   Wollenberg, Charles.   "Race and Class in Rural
       California: The El Monte Berry Strike of 1933."
       California Historical Quarterly 51:2 (Summer 1972),
       155-164.
A fairly brief account of the El Monte berry strike placing
it in the historical context of class and race relationships
in California agriculture.

2118   Wollenberg, Charles.   "Working on El Traque: The
       Pacific Electric Strike of 1903." Pacific Historical
       Review 42 (Aug. 1973), 358-359.
Describes the conditions and history of Mexican railroad
workers in the Southwest. The article then climaxes with
the Los Angeles 1903 strike, an early important Mexican
worker dispute.

2119   Zamora, Emilio, Jr.   "Chicano Socialist Labor Activity
       in Texas, 1900-1920." Aztlan 6:2 (Summer 1975),
       221-236.

2120   Zelman, Donald L.   "Mexican Migrants and Relief in
       Depression California." Journal of Mexican American
       History 5 (1975), 1-23.
Describes grower reaction to relief policies.

VI.
WORLD WAR II TO
THE 1980s

Books

Section VI covers the impact of the second World War on
Mexican Americans in the Armed Forces and on the home front,
the bracero program and related topics of Mexican
immigration, the Delano grape strike, and undocumented
workers. It includes the development of student and other
Chicano organizations, and the new post-war Raza leadership,
especially that of Cesar Chavez, Rodolfo "Corky" Gonzales,
Reies Lopez Tijerina, and Jose Angel Gutierrez. This
section ends in the 1980s--which have been declared "the
decade of the Hispanics."

2121   Alba, Pedro. Siete articulos sobre el problema de los
       braceros. Mexico, D.F.: [n.p.], 1954.

2122   Alexander, T. John. Spanish Surname Recent Migrant
       Families: Life Cycle, Family, Socioeconomic and
       Housing Status. San Francisco: R & E Research
       Associates, 1979.

2123   Allen, Steve. The Ground is our Table. Garden City,
       N.Y.: Doubleday & Co., 1966.
Covers Allen's involvement in the Delano grape strike.

2124   Allsup, Carl. The American G.I. Forum: Origins and
       Evolution. Austin: University of Texas Press, 1982.
The history of one of the largest and most important Chicano
organizations.

2125   Alvarez, Salvador E. The Legal and Legislative
       Struggle of the Farmworkers. Berkeley, Calif.: Quinto
       Sol, [n.d.].
Provides a documented account of legal and legislative
aspects of the United Farm Workers' efforts to organize.

2126   Alvirez, David. Efectos de la migracion a los Estados
       Unidos. Mexico, D.F.: Instituto de Investigaciones
       Sociales, Universidad Nacional Autonoma de Mexico,
       1972.

2127   Anderson, Henry Pope. The Bracero Program in
       California, With Particular Reference to Health
       Status, Attitudes, and Practices. Berkeley:
       University of California Press, 1961. Reprint: New
       York: Arno Press, 1976.
A rich source of first-hand information from interviews;
includes materials on border-crossing.

2128   Anderson, Henry Pope. Culture 'Exposure' and Cultural
       Change: The Bracero Program. Berkeley: School of
       Public Health, University of California, 1959.

2129   Anderson, Henry Pope. A Harvest of Loneliness: An
       Inquiry Into a Social Problem. Berkeley, Calif.:
       [n.p.], c.1964.
Provides statistics on the bracero, P.L. 78, and especially
health problems.

2130   Argoytia, Luis; Guillermo Martinez; and Luis Fernandez
       del Campo. Los braceros. Mexico, D.F.: Secretaria
       del Trabajo y Prevision Social, 1946.

2131   Baerresen, Donald W. The Border Industrialization
       Program of Mexico. Lexington, Mass.: D. C. Heath and
       Co., 1971.
Includes a description of the program and bibliographic
references.

2132   Ballis, George, et al. Basta! la historia de nuestra
       lucha. Delano, Calif.: Farm Workers Press, 1966.
Includes photographs of the Delano grape strike; pro-United
Farm Workers.

2133   Barrett, Edward L., Jr. The Tenney Committee.
       Ithaca, N.Y.: Cornell University Press, 1951.
Chapter VI discusses aspects of the Sleepy Lagoon case and
the 1943 Zoot-Suit riots in Los Angeles during World War II.

2134   Bergan, Frank and Murray Norris. Delano--Another
       Crisis for the Catholic Church. Fresno, Calif.:
       Rudell Publishing Co., 1968.
Presents an anti-United Farm Workers viewpoint of the Delano
Grape Strike.

2135   Blair, Bertha; Anne O. Lively; and Glen W. Trimble.
       Spanish-Speaking Americans. New York: National
       Council of Churches, 1959.

2136   Blawis, Patricia Bell. Tijerina and the Land Grants:
       Mexican Americans in Struggle for Their Heritage. New
       York; International Publishers, 1971.
A sympathetic view of Tijerina and the struggle of the
Alianza Federal de Pueblos Libres.

2137   Briggs, Vernon M., Jr. Mexican Migration and the U.S.
       Labor Market: A Mounting Issue for the Seventies.
       Austin: Center for the Study of Human Resources,
       University of Texas, 1975.
A brief study of the impact of immigration and border
policies on labor attitudes and employment.

2138   Briggs, Vernon M., Jr. The Mexico-United States
       Border: Public Policy and Chicano Economic Welfare.
       Austin: Center for the Study of Human Resources,
       University of Texas, 1974.
Discusses the impact of United States immigration policy; 28
pages.

2139   Briggs, Vernon M., Jr.; Walter Fogel; and Fred H.
       Schmidt. The Chicano Worker. Austin: University of
       Texas Press, 1977.
Discusses employment problems of the Mexican American,
primarily in the "new" Southwest.

2140   Bronder, Saul. Social Justice and Church Authority:
       The Public Life of Archbishop Robert E. Lucey.
       Philadelphia: Temple University Press, 1982.
Biography of a longtime supporter and advocate of Chicano
civil and social rights. Lucey was archbishop of San
Antonio and a founder of the Bishops Committee for the
Spanish Speaking.

2141   Browning, Harley L. and S. Dale McLemore. A
       Statistical Profile of Spanish Surname Populations of
       Texas. Austin: Population Research Center, University
       of Texas, 1964.

2142   Brusa, Betty War. The Bracero. New York: Pageant
       Press, 1966.
Descriptive rather than narrative; forty-one pages.

2143   Bullock, Paul. Occupational Distribution by Major
       Ethnic Groups and by Labor Market Areas, Selected
       Government Contractors, Los Angeles Metropolitan Area.
       Los Angeles: Institute of Industrial Relations,
       University of California, 1963.

2144   California, Department of Education. Racial and
       Ethnic Survey of California Public Schools Part One:
       Distribution of Pupils, Fall 1966. Sacramento,
       Calif.: State Printing Office, 1967.

2145   California, Department of Education. Racial and
       Ethnic Survey of California Public Schools Part Two:
       Distribution of Employees, Fall, 1966. Sacramento,
       Calif.: State Printing Office, 1967.

2146   California, Department of Employment. Employment
       Problems of the Mexican-American. Sacramento, Calif.:
       State Printing Office, 1963.

2147   California, Department of Employment. Mexican
       Nationals in California Agriculture, 1942-1959.
       Sacramento, Calif.: Department of Employment, 1959.
Covers the principal years of the bracero program.

2148   California, Department of Industrial Relations,
       Division of Fair Employment Practices. Californians
       of Spanish Surname: Population; Employment; Income;
       Education. Sacramento: California Department of
       Industrial Relations, 1964.

2149   California, Department of Industrial Relations,
       Division of Fair Employment Practices. Negroes and
       Mexican Americans in South and East Los Angeles,
       Changes Between 1960 and 1965 in Population,
       Employment, Income, and Family Status; An Analysis of
       a U.S. Census Survey of November 1965. Sacramento:
       California Department of Industrial Relations, 1966.

2150   California, Governor. Citizens Committee Report on
       the Zoot Suit Riots. Sacramento, Calif.: State
       Printing Office, 1943.
The Committee was headed by Bishop Joseph T. McGucken; Carey
McWilliams was also a member.

2151   California, Governor. Negroes and Mexican-Americans
       in California State Government. Sacramento, Calif.:
       State Personnel Board, 1965.

2152   California, Governor. Committee to Survey the
       Agricultural Labor Resources of the San Joaquin
       Valley. Final Report and Recommendations.
       Sacramento, Calif., 1951.
Contains charts, maps, and tables that are extremely useful.

2153   California, Legislature, Assembly, Interim Committee
       on Industrial Relations, Committee on Special
       Employment Problems. Special Employment Problems of
       the Mexican-American; Transcript of Proceedings.
       Sacramento, Calif., 1964.

2154   California, Legislature, Senate, Fact-Finding
       Subcommittee on Un-American Activities. Fourteenth
       Report. Sacramento, Calif.: 1967.

Contains a comprehensive chronological account of the early
years of the Delano grape strike.

2155   California, Legislature, Senate, Fact-Finding
       Subcommittee on Race Relations and Urban Problems.
       Remarks of Herman Gallegos. San Francisco: [n.p.],
       1963.

2156   Calles, Rudy. Champion Prune Pickers: Migrant
       Worker's Dilemma. Los Alamitos, Calif.: Hwong
       Publishing Co., 1979.

2157   Campa, Arthur L. Colorado's Youth Looks to the Skies.
       Denver, Colo.: Department of Education, 1949.

2158   Cantu, Mario. Hispanic Perspectives on the Reagan
       Administration's Economic Policies. Washington, D.C.:
       National Council of La Raza, 1981.

2159   Cardenas, Leo. Chicano 1969. San Antonio, Tex.:
       Commission for Mexican American Affairs, 1969.

2160   Carrillo, Emilia E. Bishop Has Kept His Word. New
       York: Carlton Press, 1966.
Concerns Bishop Sidney Metzger of El Paso, a longtime
supporter of Chicano rights.

2161   Carter, Thomas and Robert D. Segura. Mexican
       Americans in School: A Decade of Change. New York:
       College Entrance Examination Board, 1979.
Minor revision of an earlier work of the same name and a
different subtitle, item 3289; says there was little change.

2162   Castro, Tony. Chicano Power: The Emergence of Mexican
       America. New York: Saturday Review Press, 1974.
A topical approach to the history of the 1960s with emphasis
on the Chicano Movement.

2163   Chamberlain, Mark A., et al., eds. Our Badge of
       Infamy: A Petition to the United States on the
       Treatment of the Mexican Immigrant. Los Angeles,
       1959. Repinted as part of The Mexican-American and
       the Law. New York: Arno Press, 1974, item 3322.

2164   Chicago's Spanish-Speaking Population: Selected
       Statistics. Chicago: Chicago Department of
       Development and Planning, 1973.
Thirty-six pages; of value for updating the history of the
midwestern Chicano.

2165   Choldin, Harvey and Grafton Trout. Mexican Americans
       in Transition: Migration and Employment in Michigan
       Cities. East Lansing: Rural Manpower Center,

Agriculture Experiment Station, Michigan State
University, 1969.

2166   Clark, Charles T., et al. Del Rio, Border of Texas
        Industrialization. Area Economic Survey #21. Austin:
        Bureau of Business Research, University of Texas,
        1964.

2167   Clinchy, Everett Ross, Jr. Equality of Opportunity
        for Latin-Americans in Texas: A Study of the Economic,
        Social and Educational Discrimination Against
        Latin-Americans in Texas, and of the Efforts of the
        State Government on Their Behalf. Edited by Carlos
        Cortes. New York: Arno Press, 1974.
Reprint of a 1954 thesis. Covers the period from the
beginning of the 20th century, with some background history.
Chapter V is on the Texas Good Neighbor Commission.

2168   Cohen, Jerry and William S. Murphy. Burn, Baby, Burn:
        The Los Angeles Race Riot, August, 1965. New York: E.
        P. Dutton & Co., 1966.
Describes the 1965 Watts riots; a journalistic view.

2169   Cohen, Nathan E., ed. The Los Angeles Riots: A
        Socio-psychological Study. New York: Praeger
        Publishers, 1970.
Interpretation by the coordinator of the Los Angeles Riot
Study, University of California.

2170   Coles, Robert. Uprooted Children. Pittsburgh:
        University of Pittsburgh Press, 1969.
Describes the many problems of migrant children. By a child
psychologist.

2171   Compean, Mario, and Jose Angel Gutierrez. La Raza
        Unida Party in Texas: Speeches. New York: Pathfinder
        Press, 1970.
Fifteen pages, largely political rhetoric like any speech.
Of value to show the views of two of the principal leaders
of the Texas Raza Unida.

2172   Conference on the Culture of the American Southwest
        and Northern Mexico, April 3, 4, 5, 1952. Los
        Angeles: Occidental College. Rockefeller Foundation
        and the John Randolph Haynes and Dora Haynes
        Foundation, 1952.

2173   Cornelius, Wayne A. The Future of Mexican Immigrants
        in California: A New Perspective for Public Policy.
        Mimeographed. San Diego: United States-Mexican
        Studies, University of California, 1981.

2174   Cornelius, Wayne A. Illegal Migration to the United
        States: Recent Research Findings, Policy Implications

and Research Priorities. Cambridge: Center for
International Studies, Massachusetts Institute of
Technology, 1977.

2175   Cornelius, Wayne A. Immigration, Mexican Development
       Policy, and the Future of the U.S.-Mexican Relations.
       Mimeographed. San Diego: United States-Mexican
       Studies, University of California, 1981.

2176   Cornelius, Wayne A.; Leo R. Chavez; and Jorge G.
       Castro. Mexican Immigrants and Southern California: A
       Summary of Current Knowledge. San Diego: Center for
       U.S.-Mexican Studies, University of California, 1982.
A synthesis of recent research and studies about the
economic and social impact of Mexican immigration on the
urban centers of southern California.

2177   Corona, Bert. Bert Corona Speaks on La Raza Unida
       Party and the "Illegal Alien" Scare. New York:
       Pathfinder Press, 1972.
Views of one of the leaders of the (California) Mexican
American Political Association.

2178   Coyle, Laurie; Gail Hershatter; and Emily Honig.
       Women at Farah: An Unfinished Story. El Paso, Tex.:
       Reforma, 1979.
The bitter 1972-1974 strike by Chicanas et al. for union
representation.

2179   Craig, Ann L. Mexican Immigration: Changing Terms of
       the Debate in the United States and Mexico.
       Mimeographed. San Diego: United States-Mexican
       Studies, University of California, 1981.

2180   Craig, Richard B. The Bracero Program: Interest
       Groups and Foreign Policy. Austin: University of
       Texas Press, 1971.
Includes an extensive bibliography.

2181   Crow, John E. Mexican Americans in Contemporary
       Arizona: A Social and Demographic View. San
       Francisco: R & E Research Associates, 1975.
Briefly describes social conditions for Mexican Americans in
Arizona--with bibliographic references.

2182   Davidson, John. The Long Road North. Garden City,
       N.Y.: Doubleday & Co., 1979.
A personal account of undocumented Mexican workers; contains
good details.

2183   Davidson, R. Theodore. Chicano Prisoners: The Key to
       San Quentin. New York: Holt, Rinehart & Winston,
       1974.
A cultural anthropological study of Mexican American inmates

at San Quentin.

2184   Day, (Rev.) Mark.   <u>Forty Acres: Cesar Chavez and the</u>
       <u>Farm Workers</u>. New York: Praeger Publishers, 1971.
A personal account inside the Delano grape strike by a
priest-supporter from 1967 onward.

2185   De Toledano, Ralph.   <u>Little Cesar</u>. New York: Anthem
       Books, 1970.
Presents a very negative view of Cesar Chavez; sponsored by
the National Right to Work Committee.

2186   Dieppa, Ismael.   <u>The Zoot-Suit Riots Revisited; the</u>
       <u>Role of Private Philanthropy in Youth Problems of</u>
       <u>Mexican-Americans</u>. Los Angeles: University of
       Southern California, 1973.

2187   Dobrin, Arnold.   <u>The New Life: La Vida Nueva; the</u>
       <u>Mexican-Americans Today</u>. New York: Dodd, Mead & Co.,
       1971.
A picture of the Mexican American community from interviews
with its members.

2188   Ducoff, Louis J.   <u>Migratory Farm Workers in 1949</u>.
       Washington, D.C.: U.S. Department of Agriculture,
       1950.

2189   Dunne, John G.   <u>Delano: The Story of the California</u>
       <u>Grape Strike</u>. New York: Farrar, Straus & Giroux,
       1967; revised ed., 1971.
Eyewitness account of the Delano grape strike by a
sympathetic journalist.

2190   Duran, Patricia; Betty Flores; and Isabel Romo, comps.
       <u>Chicano Organizations</u>. Los Angeles: Chicano Studies
       Center, University of California, 1971.
Its twelve pages are good for a brief history of student
groups in the Los Angeles area.

2191   Endore, S. Guy.   <u>Justice for Salcido</u>. Los Angeles:
       Civil Rights Congress of Los Angeles, 1948. Reprinted
       as part of <u>The Mexican-American and the Law</u>. New
       York: Arno Press, 1974, item 3322.
The introduction is by Carey McWilliams who was deeply
involved in the issue of social justice for Chicanos.

2192   Endore, S. Guy.   <u>The Sleepy Lagoon Mystery</u>. Los
       Angeles: Sleepy Lagoon Defense Committee, 1944.

2193   Fanre, Lynn. <u>Chavez: One New Answer</u>. New York:
       Praeger Publishers, 1970.

2194   Fineberg, Richard A.   <u>Braceros By Any Other Name:</u>
       <u>Mexican Green Card Workers and Their Affect on U.S.</u>

Farm Labor. Santa Barbara, Calif.: McNally & Loftin,
1971.
Centers on Mexican permanent immigrant workers in the San
Joaquin Valley (California) in 1968.

2195   Fineberg, Richard A. Green Card Labor and the Delano
Grape Strike. San Francisco: United Church of Christ,
1968.
Thirty-four pages devoted to the use of Mexican green
carders during the Delano strike.

2196   Fishlow, David M., ed. Sons of Zapata: A Brief
Photographic History of the Farm Workers Strike in
Texas. Rio Grande City, Tex.: United Farm Workers
Organizing Committee, AFL-CIO, 1967.
Includes a brief text as well as photographs.

2197   Fogel, Walter. Education and Income of
Mexican-Americans in the Southwest. Los Angeles:
Mexican American Studies Project, University of
California, 1965.

2198   Fogel, Walter. Mexican-Americans in Southwest Labor
Markets. Los Angeles: Graduate School of Business,
University of California, 1967.

2199   Fogel, Walter. Mexican Illegal Alien Workers in the
United States. Los Angeles: Institute of Industrial
Relations, University of California, 1978.

2200   Fogelson, Robert M., comp. The Los Angeles Riots.
New York: N.Y. Times, 1969.
A collection of essays and reports on the 1965 Los Angeles
rioting.

2201   Fuller, Varden, et al. Domestic and Imported Workers
in the Harvest Labor Market. Berkeley: Giannini
Foundation of Agricultural Economics, University of
California, 1956.

2202   Fusco, Paul and George D. Horwitz. La Causa: The
California Grape Strike. New York: Macmillan Co.,
1970.

2203   Galarza, Ernesto. Farm Workers and Agri-business in
California, 1947-1960. Notre Dame, Ind.: University
of Notre Dame Press, 1977.
A general survey which stresses the 1947 National Farm Labor
Union strike at Di Giorgio and the important role of bracero
labor.

2204   Galarza, Ernesto. Merchants of Labor: The Mexican
Bracero Story. San Jose, Calif.: Rosicrucian Press,
1965.

Emphasizes the bracero in California, 1950-1964, placed in
an historical perspective.

2205   Galarza, Ernesto. Spiders in the House and Workers in
       the Field. Notre Dame, Ind.: University of Notre Dame
       Press, 1970.
Describes the 1947-1950 National Farm Workers Union strike
at Di Giorgio farms and lawsuits arising out of it--by an
outstanding farm labor expert and leader who was involved.

2206   Galarza, Ernesto. Strangers in Our Fields.
       Washington, D.C.: Joint United States-Mexico Trade
       Union Committee, 1956.
Recounts the abuses and exploitation of Mexican bracero
workers.

2207   Galarza, Ernesto. Tragedy at Chualar. Santa Barbara,
       Calif.: McNally & Loftin, 1977.
Gives the details of a serious farm labor accident near a
small California town just off Highway 101.

2208   Gallardo, Lloyd. Mexican Green Carders: Preliminary
       Report. Washington, D.C.: Bureau of Employment
       Security, United States Department of Labor, 1962.

2209   Galleo, Jose J. Justicia al obrero del campo.
       Chicago: Fabet Press Service, 1967.
Forty pages. Includes farmworker marches to Sacramento and
to Austin.

2210   Garcia, Juan Ramon. Operation Wetback: The Mass
       Deportation of Mexican Undocumented Workers in 1954.
       Westport, Conn.: Greenwood Press, 1980.
A 1977 University of Notre Dame thesis. A good
dispassionate presentation going back to World War I.

2211   Garcia y Griego, Manuel. The Importation of Mexican
       Contract Laborers to the United States, 1942-1964:
       Antecedents, Operation and Legacy. Mimeographed. San
       Diego: United States-Mexican Studies, University of
       California, 1981.

2212   Gardner, Richard. Grito! Reies Tijerina and the New
       Mexico Land Grant War of 1967. Indianapolis, Ind.:
       Bobbs-Merrill Co., 1970.
Probes all aspects of the Tierra Amarilla courthouse
confrontation; includes background material as well.
Sympathetic to Tijerina.

2213   Gerson, Louis L. The Hyphenate in Recent American
       Politics and Diplomacy. Lawrence: University of
       Kansas Press, 1964.

2214   Getty, Harry T. Interethnic Relationships in the
        Community of Tucson. New York: Arno Press, 1976.
Reprint of a 1950 thesis examining Tucson ethnic
relationships at the end of World War II.

2215   Grebler, Leo. Mexican Immigration to the United
        States: The Record and Its Implications. Los Angeles:
        Graduate School of Business Administration, University
        of California, 1966.
Advance Report No. 2 of the Mexican-American Study Project
emphasizes the pattern of assimilation.

2216   Gutierrez, Jose Angel. La Raza and Revolution. San
        Francisco: R & E Research Associates, 1972.
The empirical conditions for revolution in four south Texas
counties, by the national president of La Raza Unida.

2217   Guzman, Ralph. The Mexican-American Population; An
        Introspective View. Palm Springs, Calif.: Western
        Governmental Research Association, 1966.

2218   Hancock, Richard H. The Role of the Bracero in the
        Economic and Cultural Dynamics of Mexico; A Case Study
        of Chihuahua. Stanford, Calif.: Hispanic American
        Society, Stanford University, 1959.

2219   Haro, Carlos Manuel, ed. The Bakke Decision: The
        Question of Chicano Access to Higher Education. Los
        Angeles: Chicano Studies Center, University of
        California, 1976.
An early study of a famous case alleging reverse
discrimination on the part of the University of California
Medical School at Davis.

2220   Harward, Naomi. Socio-Economic and Other Variations
        Related to Rehabilitation of Mexican American
        Americans in Arizona. Tempe: Arizona State University
        Press, 1969.

2221   Hernandez, John W. The Rio Grande Environmental
        Project. Las Cruces: Water Resources Research
        Institute, New Mexico State University, 1973.

2222   Herrera-Sobek, Maria. The Bracero Experience:
        Elitelore Versus Folklore. Los Angeles: Latin
        American Center, University of California, 1979.
Describes Mexican writers' perceptions of the bracero
experience in the United States. Includes some corridos.

2223   Idar, Ed, Jr. and Andrew McLellan. What Price
        Wetbacks? Austin: American G.I. Forum of Texas, 1953.
A pamphlet on economic and social aspects of hiring
undocumented workers, published by the G.I. Forum and the

A.F. of L.

2224   Jackson, Ralph S., Jr. The Border Industrialization
       Program of Northern Mexico. Austin: Seminar in Latin
       American Commercial Law, University of Texas Law
       School, 1968.

2225   Jacobs, Paul and Saul Landau, with Eve Pell. To Serve
       the Devil. New York: Random House, 1971. 2 vols.
Includes material on the Chicano and a bibliography.

2226   Jenkinson, Michael. Tijerina: Land Grant Conflict in
       New Mexico. Albuquerque, N. Mex.: Paisano Press,
       1968.
A journalistic account of the Alianza Federal de Pueblos
Libres and its leader.

2227   Johansen, Sigurd. Rural Social Organization in a
       Spanish-American Culture Area. Albuquerque:
       University of New Mexico Press, 1948.
Covers the contemporary scene in northern New Mexico, with
an historical introduction.

2228   Jones, Lamar B. Mexican American Labor Problems in
       Texas. San Francisco: R & E Research Associates,
       1971.
Reprint of the author's 1965 University of Texas doctoral
dissertation. Stresses the clash of hand labor and
mechanization.

2229   Jones, Robert Cuba. Mexican War Workers in the United
       States: The Mexico-United States Manpower Recruiting
       Program, 1942-1944. Washington, D.C.: Pan American
       Union, 1945.

2230   Kelton, Elmer. These Are Braceros. San Angelo, Tex.:
       San Angelo Standard, 1958.

2231   Kibbe, Pauline Rochester. Latin-Americans in Texas.
       Albuquerque: University of New Mexico Press, 1946.
       Reprint, New York: Arno Press, 1974.
Discusses the contemporary problems of Mexicans in Texas;
little historical background. By the Executive Secretary of
the Texas Good Neighbor Commission.

2232   Kingrea, Nellie Ward. History of the First Ten Years
       of the Texas Good Neighbor Commission. Fort Worth,
       Tex.: Texas Christian University Press, 1954.
Describes the impact of the Commission on Mexicans and
Chicanos in Texas.

2233   Kirstein, Peter N. Anglo Over Bracero: A History of
       the Mexican Worker in the U.S. From Roosevelt to

Nixon. San Francisco: R & E Research Associates, 1977.
A 1973 St. Louis University thesis.

2234   Kostyu, Frank A. Shadow in the Valley: The Story of One Man's Struggle for Justice. Garden City, N.Y.: Doubleday & Co., 1970.
Discusses the difficulties of Rev. Ed Krueger of the Texas Migrant Ministry in the Rio Grande Valley of Texas; some material on Cesar Chavez.

2235   Kushner, Sam. The Long Road to Delano. New York: International Publishing Co., 1975.
Details of the Delano grape strike by a radical long time farm labor reporter.

2236   Landolt, Robert Garland. The Mexican-American Workers of San Antonio, Texas. New York: Arno Press, 1976.
Reprint of a 1965 doctoral thesis describing continued income and employment discrimination post-World War II.

2237   Lane, John Hart, Jr. Voluntary Associations Among Mexican Americans in San Antonio, Texas: Organizational and Leadership Characteristics. New York: Arno Press, 1976.
Reprint of a 1968 doctoral thesis describing the broad extent of Mexican American organizing.

2238   Levenstein, Harvey A. Labor Organizations in the United States and Mexico; A History of Their Relations. Westport, Conn.: Greenwood Press, 1971.
Contains materials on braceros and undocumented workers.

2239   Levy, Jacques E. Cesar Chavez: Autobiography of La Causa. New York: W. W. Norton & Co., 1975.
An extremely detailed account based on interviews with Chavez and other Causa leaders.

2240   Lewels, Francisco J., Jr. The Uses of the Media by the Chicano Movement: A Study in Minority Access. New York: Praeger Publishers, 1974.
An important study of Chicano politics and the mass media.

2241   Lewis, Jon. From This Earth . . . The Delano Grape Strike. San Francisco: [Privately printed], 1969.
A photographic account of the strike.

2242   Lewis, Sasha Gregory. The Slave Trade Today: American Exploitation of Illegal Aliens. Boston: Beacon Press, 1979.
A general work on undocumented workers stressing the Mexican immigrant. Includes an extensive bibliography, especially of newspaper articles, 1970-1979.

2243 Lindborg, Kristina and Carlos J. Ovando. _Five
      Mexican-American Women in Transition: A Case Study of
      Migrants in the Midwest_. San Francisco: R & E
      Research Associates, 1977.
Focuses on five Mexican-American women from migrant
backgrounds; based on open-ended interviews.

2244 London, Joan and Henry Anderson. _So Shall Ye Reap_.
      New York: Thomas Y. Crowell Co., 1970.
An excellent popular account of the Delano strike and Cesar
Chavez.

2245 Loomis, Charles P. and Nellie H. Loomis. _Skilled
      Spanish-American War-Industry Workers from New Mexico_.
      Washington, D.C.: Bureau of Agricultural Economics,
      U.S. Department of Agricultural Economics, U.S.
      Department of Agriculture, 1942.
Describes the history of 3,500 graduates from New Mexico's
vocational training program--of whom two-thirds eventually
went to the West Coast.

2246 Los Angeles County, Office of Superintendent of
      Schools. _Workshop in Education of Mexican and
      Spanish-Speaking Pupils_. Los Angeles, Calif.: County
      Superintendent of Schools, 1942.

2247 Mabry, Donald J. and Robert J. Shafer. _Neighbors--
      Mexico and the United States: Wetbacks and Oil_.
      Chicago: Nelson-Hall, 1981.
A provocative study of the possible inter-relationship of
Mexican oil and undocumented workers.

2248 McBride, John. _Vanishing Bracero, Valley Revolution_.
      San Antonio, Tex.: Naylor Publishing Co., 1963.
Describes the waning months of the second bracero program,
1950-1964.

2249 McElroy, Robert C. and Earle E. Gavett. _Termination
      of the Bracero Program: Some Effects on Farm Labor and
      Migrant Housing Needs_. Washington, D.C.: U.S.
      Government Printing Office, 1965.
A report of the U.S. Department of Agriculture following the
1964 end of the bracero program.

2250 Maciel, David R. _Al norte del Rio Bravo (pasado
      inmediato, 1930-1981)_. Mexico, D.F.: Siglo XXI, 1981.

2251 Macklin, Barbara J. _Structural Stability and Culture
      Change in a Mexican-American Community_. New York:
      Arno Press, 1976.
Reprint of a thesis describing the Toledo, Ohio Chicano
community at the end of the 1950s.

2252   McWilliams, Carey. Southern California Country. New
       York: Duell, Sloan & Pierce, 1946.
Describes racial and ethnic problems; especially good for
the period of World War II.

2253   Madsen, William. The Mexican-Americans of South
       Texas. New York: Holt, Rinehart & Winston, 1964.
Describes four communities in Hidalgo County, Texas,
1957-1961. A cultural anthropological perspective;
criticized for bias by some activists.

2254   Manpower Profiles. The Mexican American in Arizona.
       Phoenix: Arizona State Employment Service, 1968.

2255   Maram, Sheldon L. Hispanic Workers in the Garment and
       Restaurant Industries in Los Angeles County.
       Mimeographed. San Diego: United States-Mexican
       Studies, University of California, 1950.

2256   Marin, Christine. A Spokesman of the Mexican American
       Movement: Rodolfo "Corky" Gonzales and the Fight for
       Chicano Liberation, 1966-1972. San Francisco: R & E
       Research Associates, 1977.
A 1974 Arizona State University thesis describing the role
of the leader of the Crusade for Justice.

2257   Massy, Ellis L. Migration of the Spanish-Speaking
       People of Hidalgo County. Austin: University of Texas
       Press, 1953.

2258   Matthiessen, Peter. Sal Si Puedes. Cesar Chavez and
       the New American Revolution. New York: Random House,
       1969.
A popular account emphasizing Chavez's leadership role in
the Delano strike.

2259   Mexico, Ministro de Relaciones Exteriores. The Good
       Neighbor Policy and Mexicans in Texas. Mexico, D.F.:
       Secretaria de Relaciones Exteriores, 1943.

2260   Mittelbach, Frank G. and Grace C. Marshall. The
       Burden of Poverty. Los Angeles: Graduate School of
       Business Administration, University of California,
       1966.
Advance Report #5 of the Mexican American Study Project. A
brief description of the economic position of Mexican
Americans in the "new" Southwest.

2261   Mittelbach, Frank G. et al. Intermarriage of
       Mexican-Americans. Los Angeles: Graduate School of
       Business Administration, University of California,
       1966.
Advance Report #6 of the Mexican American Study Project.

2262   Moore, Joan W. with Robert Garcia. Homeboys: Gangs,
       Drugs, and Prison in the Barrios of Los Angeles.
       Philadelphia, Pa.: Temple University Press, 1978.
Describes the inter-related problems of barrio gangs,
Chicano convicts (pintos), and drugs. Has a good
bibliography.

2263   Moore, Joan W. Mexican-Americans: Problems and
       Prospects. Madison: University of Wisconsin Press,
       1967.
A 58-page work on Mexicans in the "new" Southwest. Prepared
for the Office of Economic Opportunity.

2264   Morales, Armando. Ando Sangrando. La Puente, Calif.:
       Perspectiva Publications, 1973.
An intensely personal account of the Los Angeles riots and
police conflict by a psychiatrist.

2265   Morgan, Patricia. Shame of a Nation, A Documented
       Story of Police-State Terror Against Mexican-Americans
       in the U.S.A. Los Angeles: Committee for Protection
       of Foreign Born, 1954. Reprinted as part of The
       Mexican-American and the Law. New York: Arno Press,
       1974, item 3322.

2266   Morin, Raul. Among the Valiant. Los Angeles: Borden
       Publishing Co., 1963.
Describes the experiences of Mexican American soldiers in
World War II.

2267   Nabokov, Peter. Tijerina and the Courthouse Raid.
       Albuquerque: University of New Mexico Press, 1969.
A complete and detailed first-hand journalistic account;
includes background materials on the loss of village lands.

2268   National Advisory Committee on Farm Labor. The Grape
       Strike. New York: The Committee, 1966.
A thirty-five page publication of the committee.

2269   Nelkin, Dorothy. On the Season: Aspects of the
       Migrant Labor System. Ithaca: New York State School
       of Industrial and Labor Relations, Cornell University,
       1970.
Discusses technical aspects of organizing agricultural
labor.

2270   Nelson, Eugene. Huelga: The First Hundred Days of the
       Great Delano Grape Strike. Delano, Calif.: Farm
       Worker Press, 1966.
A day by day account by a strike leader. With some
background history.

2271   Nelson, Eugene, comp. Pablo Cruz and the American
       Dream: The Experience of an Undocumented Immigrant

From Mexico. Salt Lake City, Utah: Peregrine Smith,
1975.
A 171-page first-person account, edited by an important
figure in California and Texas agricultural labor
organizing.

2272   Newman, Patty. ¡Do it up Brown! San Diego, Calif.:
       Viewpoint Books, 1971.
A definition, explanation, and guide to militant chicanismo,
its organizations, and leaders in the early 1970s.

2273   Newton, Horace E. _Mexican Illegal Immigration into_
       California, Principally Since 1945. San Francisco:
       R & E Research Associates, 1973.
A 1954 Claremont Graduate School master's thesis. Includes
Mexican push and California pull effects. Has a section on
migratory labor history.

2274   Norquest, Carrol. _Rio Grande Wetbacks; Mexican_
       Migrant Workers. Albuquerque: University of New
       Mexico Press, 1972.
A series of sociological tales of immigrant workers in
Texas, a cotton grower's reminiscences.

2275   North, David S. _Alien Workers: A Study of the Labor_
       Certification Programs. Washington, D.C.:
       TransCentury Corp., 1971.
A study of immigration and the U.S. labor market, prepared
for the U.S. Department of Labor.

2276   North, David S., et al. _The Border Crossers: People_
       Who Live in Mexico and Work in the United States.
       Washington, D.C.: TransCentury Corp., 1970.
Surveys immigration, emigration, and migration in the new
Southwest--a useful study.

2277   North, David S. and Marion F. Houston. _The_
       Characteristics and Role of Illegal Aliens in the U.S.
       Labor Market: An Exploratory Study. Washington, D.C.:
       Linton & Co., 1976.
A report for the U.S. Department of Labor, describing the
"typical" undocumented worker.

2278   North, David S. and William G. Weissert. _Immigrants_
       and the American Labor Market. Washington, D.C.: The
       TransCentury Corp., 1973.
Immigration and alien labor in the U.S.--a study for the
Manpower Administration, U.S. Department of Labor.

2279   Office of the Coordinator of Inter-American Affairs.
       Spanish-Speaking Americans in the War: The Southwest.
       Washington, D.C.: Coordinator of Inter-American
       Affairs and Office of War Information, 1943.

2280   Oliveira, Annette. <u>MALDEF: Diez Años</u>. San Francisco:
       MALDEF, c.1979.
Describes the first ten years' experience of the Mexican
American Legal Defense and Educational Fund.

2281   Ortega, Joaquin. <u>New Mexico's Opportunity: A Message
       to My Fellow New Mexicans</u>. Albuquerque: University of
       New Mexico Press, 1942.

2282   Ortiz, Martin. <u>The Mexican-American in the Los
       Angeles Community</u>. Los Angeles: Community Relations
       Educational Foundation, 1963.

2283   Parigi, Sam F. <u>A Case Study of Latin American
       Unionization in Austin, Texas</u>. Edited by Carlos
       Cortes. New York: Arno Press, 1976.
A 1964 dissertation in Economics on success and failure in
minority unionizing activities.

2284   Paz, Frank. <u>Mexican-Americans in Chicago</u>. Chicago:
       Chicago Council of Social Agencies, 1948.

2285   Pendas, Miguel and Harry Ring. <u>Toward Chicano Power:
       Building La Raza Unida Party</u>. New York: Pathfinder
       Press, 1974.

2286   Perales, Alonso S. <u>Are We Good Neighbors?</u> San
       Antonio, Tex.: Artes Graficas, 1948. Reprint, New
       York: Arno Press, 1974.
A documentary collection of testimony to discrimination
against Mexicans in Texas.

2287   Perez, Jean M. <u>Viva La Huelga: The Struggle of the
       Farm Workers</u>. New York: Pathfinder Press, 1973.
A brief study of the United Farm Workers.

2288   Pitrone, Jean M. <u>Chavez: Man of the Migrants</u>. New
       York: Pyramid Communications, 1971.
A pro-Chavez biography written for a juvenile audience by a
professional biographer.

2289   Plaut, Thomas R. <u>Net Migration into Texas and Its
       Regions: Trends and Patterns</u>. Austin: Bureau of
       Business Research, University of Texas, 1979.
A 54-page report covering the period from 1950 to 1970.

2290   Plunkett, Jim and Dave Newhouse. <u>The Jim Plunkett
       Story</u>. New York: Arbor House Publishing Co., 1981.
The personal life of an outstanding Mexican American
athlete.

2291   Poitras, Guy E., ed. <u>Immigration and the Mexican
       National: Proceedings</u>. San Antonio, Tex.: Border

Research Institute, Trinity University, 1978.
A variety of views presented at a conference held by the
Institute.

2292   Quinn, Anthony. _The Original Sin: A Self-Portrait_.
       Boston: Little, Brown & Co., 1972.
The autobiography of a Mexican immigrant who has become a
leading actor worldwide.

2293   Rasmussen, Wayne D. _A History of the Emergency Farm_
       Labor Supply Program, 1943-1947. Washington, D.C.:
       U.S. Government Printing Office, 1951.
Department of Agriculture Monograph No. 13.

2294   _La Raza and the Church in the 70's_. Milwaukee:
       [n.p.], 1971.
Report of the 1970 U.S. Catholic Conference at Lansing,
Michigan.

2295   Raza Unida Party. _Raza Unida Party Rules_. Houston,
       Tex.: Raza Unida Party Convention, 1974.
The rules as set down at the Raza Unida Party Convention,
September 2-22, 1974, Houston.

2296   Reid, Jesse T. _It Happened in Taos_. Albuquerque:
       University of New Mexico Press, 1946.
Describes the Taos County Project, circa 1940-1943.

2297   Rendon, Armando. _Chicano Manifesto_. New York:
       Macmillan Co., 1971.
A personal expression of the Chicano movement in its various
aspects.

2298   Rios-Bustamente, Antonio Jose, ed. _Immigration and_
       Public Policy: Human Rights for Undocumented Workers
       and Their Families. Los Angeles: Chicano Studies
       Center, University of California, 1977.

2299   Rodriguez, Armando M. _Speak Up, Chicano; the_
       Mexican-American Fights for Educational Equality.
       Washington, D.C.: U.S. Office of Education, 1968.
A strong argument for bicultural and bilingual education by
the (1971) president of East Los Angeles College.

2300   Rodriguez, Eugene, Jr. _Henry B. Gonzalez: A Political_
       Profile. New York: Arno Press, 1976.
Reprint of a 1965 St. Mary's University master's thesis;
strongly favorable and adulatory.

2301   Romero, Fred E. _Chicano Workers: Their Utilization_
       and Development. Los Angeles: Chicano Studies Center,
       University of California, 1979.
Includes graphs and bibliographic references. Chicano
Center Publication #8; describes background and development

of the Chicano and the labor market.

2302   Romero, Fred E.   The Spanish Speaking and the
       Comprehensive Employment and Training Act of 1973.
       Phoenix, Ariz.: Nuestro Associates & Progressive
       Enterprising Group, Inc., 1974.

2303   Ross, Stanley R., ed.   Views Across the Border; the
       United States and Mexico.   Albuquerque: University of
       New Mexico Press, 1978.
Covers a wide variety of border issues and problems from
undocumenteds to ecology, from politics to culture.

2304   Rubel, Arthur J.   Across the Tracks: Mexican Americans
       in a Texas City.   Austin: University of Texas Press,
       1966.
A study of Texas Chicano history as well as culture, social
activities and organizations.   Includes material on the
Texas Rangers.

2305   Runsten, David and Phillip LeVeen.   Mechanization and
       Mexican Labor in California Agriculture.   San Diego:
       United States-Mexican Studies, University of
       California, 1981.
A broad overview of California agriculture and its labor
with emphasis on the adjustment to the ending of the bracero
program.   Studies the impact of mechanization on fruit and
vegetable growing.   Includes a number of valuable tables and
graphs.

2306   Rusinow, Irving.   A Camera Report on El Cerrito; A
       Typical Spanish-American Community in New Mexico.
       Reprinted from U.S. Department of Agriculture, Bureau
       of Agricultural Economics.   Washington, D.C.: U.S.
       Government Printing Office, 1942.

2307   Salinas, Jose Lazaro.   La emigracion de los braceros:
       Vision objectiva de un problema mexicano.   Leon, Gto.,
       Mexico: Imprenta Cuauhtemoc, 1955.

2308   Sanchez, Guadalupe L. and Jesus Romo.   Organizing
       Mexican Undocumented Farm Workers of Both Sides of the
       Border.   San Diego: Program in United States-Mexican
       Studies, University of California, 1981.
Describes Arizona Farm Workers Union efforts at organizing
in the late 1970s; includes organizing strategies and
results.

2309   Santillan, Richard.   Chicano Politics: La Raza Unida.
       Los Angeles: Tlaquilo Publications, 1973.
A factual account of the beginnings of La Raza Unida Party;
little interpretation.

2310   Saunders, Lyle. The Spanish-Speaking Population of
       Texas. Austin: University of Texas Press, 1949.

2311   Saunders, Lyle and Olen E. Leonard. The Wetback in
       the Lower Rio Grande Valley of Texas. Austin:
       University of Texas Press, 1951.
A study in historical perspective of the problems and
discrimination faced by undocumented workers.

2312   Schmidt, Fred H. After the Bracero: An Inquiry Into
       the Problem of Farm Labor Recruitment. Los Angeles:
       Institute of Industrial Relations, University of
       California, 1964.
Suggests that the agricultural labor market might be
stabilized by recruiting in U.S. urban areas.

2313   Segalman, Ralph. Army of Despair: The Migrant Worker
       Stream. Washington, D.C.: Educational Systems, 1968.

2314   Shannon, Lyle W. and Elaine M. Krass. The Economic
       Absorption and Cultural Integration of Immigrant
       Mexican-American and Negro Workers. Iowa City: State
       University of Iowa Press, 1964.

2315   Shannon, Lyle W. and Magdaline Shannon. Minority
       Migrants in the Urban Community: Mexican-American and
       Negro Adjustment to Industrial Society. Beverly
       Hills, Calif.: Sage Publications, 1973.
Explores racial tensions between Blacks and Chicanos in
Racine, Wisconsin.

2316   Shockley, John S. Chicano Revolt in a Texas Town.
       Notre Dame, Ind.: University of Notre Dame Press,
       1974.
Analyzes the political upset in Crystal City, Texas, where
Mexican Americans in the 1960s twice rose up against Anglo
political domination. Describes the social structure.

2317   The Sleepy Lagoon Case--Concerning the Defense of
       Mexican Youths. Los Angeles: Sleepy Lagoon Defense
       Committee, 1943.

2318   Soukup, James R.; Clifton McClesky; and Harry
       Holloway. Party and Factional Division in Texas.
       Austin: University of Texas Press, 1964.
Includes material on ethnic aspects of Texas politics.

2319   The Spanish Land Grant Conflict in New Mexico.
       Albuquerque, N. Mex.: Alianza Federal, 1966.
A pamphlet describing views of the Alianza Federal de
Pueblos Libres on pueblo land grants.

2320   Status of Spanish-Surnamed Citizens in Colorado.
        Denver: Colorado Commission on Spanish-Surnamed
        Citizens, 1967.

2321   Stevenson, Coke R. and Ezequiel Padilla. The Good
        Neighbor Policy and Mexicans in Texas. Mexico, D.F.:
        Secretaria de Relaciones Exteriores, 1943.   Also
        reprinted as part of The Mexican American and the Law.
        New York: Arno Press, 1974, item 3322.
An important document by the governor of Texas and the
Mexican Minister of Foreign Relations.

2322   Survey on the Border Development Program. Mexico,
        D.F.: American Chamber of Commerce, 1969.

2323   Talbert, Robert H.   Spanish-Name People in the
        Southwest and West. Fort Worth: Potishman Foundation,
        Texas Christian University, 1955.
Prepared for the Texas Good Neighbor Foundation.

2324   Tanner, Myrtle L.   Handbook, Good Neighbor Commission
        of Texas. Austin, Tex.: Good Neighbor Commission,
        1954.
A handbook by the commission established to improve
Anglo-Mexican and Mexican American relations.

2325   Taylor, Ronald B.   Chavez and the Farm Workers.
        Boston: Beacon Press, 1975.
An even-handed account by a pro-Chavez reporter, with
historical background.

2326   Teller, Charles H.; Leo F. Estrada; and Jose
        Hernandez, eds.   Cuantos Somos: A Demographic Survey
        of the Mexican-American Population. Austin:
        University of Texas Press, 1978.
Mexican-American Monograph #2.

2327   Terzian, James P. and Kathryn Cramer. Mighty Hard
        Road: The Story of Cesar Chavez. Garden City, N.Y.:
        Doubleday & Co., 1970.
A high-school level account of Chavez and his United Farm
Workers movement.

2328   Texas Conference for the Mexican-American. Improving
        Education Opportunities of the Mexican-American:
        Proceedings. Edited by Dwain M. Estes and David W.
        Darling. San Antonio, Tex.: Southwest Educational
        Development Laboratory, 1967.

2329   Texas, Council on Migrant Labor. Texas Migrant Labor:
        The 1964 Migration. San Antonio, Tex.: The Council,
        1965.

2330   Texas, Education Agency. Report of Pupils in Texas
        Public Schools Having Spanish Surnames, 1955-56.
        Austin, 1957.

2331   Texas, Good Neighbor Commission. Texas: Friend and
        Neighbor. Austin, Tex.: Von Boeckmann-Jones Co.,
        1967.
Describes border relations between Mexico and Texas; a
non-critical view.

2332   Texas, Good Neighbor Commission. Texas Migrant Labor:
        The 1966 Migration. Austin, Tex.: [n.p.], 1967.

2333   Texas, Good Neighbor Commission. Texas Migrant Labor:
        The 1967 Migration. Austin, Tex.: [n.p.], 1968.

2334   Texas, University, School of Architecture. The Nature
        of the United States-Mexico Border Development.
        Austin, Tex.: [n.p.], 1967.

2335   Thomas, Howard E. and Florence Taylor. Migrant Farm
        Labor in Colorado: A Study of Migratory Families. New
        York: National Child Labor Committee, 1951. Reprinted
        as part of Mexican Labor in the United States. New
        York: Arno Press, 1974, item 2955.

2336   Tijerina, Reies Lopez. Mi lucha por la tierra.
        Mexico, D.F.: Fondo de Cultura Economica, 1978.
A personal account by the founder of the Alianza Federal de
Pueblos Libres.

2337   Tobias, Henry J. and Charles E. Woodhouse, eds.
        Minorities and Politics. Albuquerque: University of
        New Mexico Press, 1969.
Places the Alianza movement of New Mexico in the context of
other related movements.

2338   Topete, Jesus. Aventuras de un bracero. Mexico,
        D.F.: Editorial Amexica, 1949. Reprint, Mexico, D.F.:
        Editorial Grafica Moderna, 1961.

2339   Tuck, Ruth D. Not With the Fist: Mexican-Americans in
        a Southwest City. New York; Harcourt, Brace & Co.,
        1946. Reprint, New York: Arno Press, 1974.
A study of Mexican Americans in San Bernardino, California;
some stereotyping, but still useful for Anglo-Chicano
relations.

2340   Ulibarri, Horacio. Social and Attitudinal
        Characteristics of Migrant and Ex-Migrant Workers--New
        Mexico, Colorado, Arizona and Texas. Albuquerque:
        University of New Mexico Press, 1965.

2341   Ulloa, Irma I. Awakening of a Sleeping Giant: La Raza
        Unida Party in Perspective. Tempe: Arizona State
        University Press, 1974.

2342   U.S., Bureau of the Census. "Persons of Spanish
        Origin in the United States: March 1976." Current
        Population Reports, Series P-20, no. 310 (July).
        Washington, D.C.: U.S. Government Printing Office,
        1977.

2343   U.S., Commission on Civil Rights. Education and the
        Mexican American Community in Los Angeles County, a
        Report. Washington, D.C.: U.S. Government Printing
        Office, 1968.

2344   U.S., Commission on Civil Rights. The Mexican
        American. Prepared by Helen Rowan. Washington, D.C.:
        U.S. Government Printing Office, 1968.
Discusses problems in justice, education, employment, and
public policy.

2345   U.S., Commission on Civil Rights. Mexican American
        Report. Washington, D.C.: U.S. Government Printing
        Office, 1966.

2346   U.S., Commission on Civil Rights. Mexican Americans
        and the Administration of Justice in the Southwest.
        Washington, D.C.: U.S. Government Printing Office,
        1970.
An important evaluation of civil rights violations of
Chicanos; criticizes prejudicial law enforcement; includes
tables and statistics.

2347   U.S., Commission on Civil Rights. Spanish-Speaking
        Peoples. Staff Paper Submitted February 5, 1965.
        Washington, D.C.: U.S. Government Printing Office,
        1965.

2348   U.S., Commission on Civil Rights. The Tarnished
        Golden Door: Civil Rights Issues in Immigration.
        Washington, D.C.: U.S. Government Printing Office,
        1980.

2349   U.S., Congress, House, Committee on Agriculture, 83rd
        Cong., 2nd sess. Mexican Farm Labor; Hearings on
        House Joint Resolution 355. Washington, D.C.: U.S.
        Government Printing Office, 1954.

2350   U.S., Congress, House, Committee on Agriculture,
        Subcommittee on Equipment, Supplies, and Manpower,
        87th Cong., 1st sess. Extension of Mexican Farm Labor
        Program. Washington, D.C.: U.S. Government Printing
        Office, 1961.

2351   U.S., Congress, House, Committee on Agriculture,
        Subcommittee on Equipment, Supplies and Manpower, 84th
        Cong., 1st sess. _Mexican Farm Labor Program: Hearings
        on HR 3822_. Washington, D.C.: U.S. Government
        Printing Office, 1955.

2352   U.S., Congress, House, Committee on Agriculture,
        Subcommittee on Equipment, Supplies, and Manpower,
        91st Cong., 2nd sess. _The Migratory Labor Problem in
        the United States_. Washington, D.C.: U.S. Government
        Printing Office, 1970.

2353   U.S. Congress, House, Committee on the Judiciary, 87th
        Cong., 1st sess. _Migrant Farm Labor: A Serious
        National Problem_. Washington, D.C.: U.S. Government
        Printing Office, 1961.

2354   U.S., Congress, House, Committee on the Judiciary,
        Subcommittee No. 1, 91st Cong., 2nd sess. _Hearings to
        Amend the Immigration and Nationality Act, and For
        Other Purposes_. Washington, D.C.: U.S. Government
        Printing Office, 1970.

2355   U.S., Congress, House, Committee on the Judiciary,
        Subcommittee No. 1, 92nd Cong., 1st and 2nd sess.
        Illegal Aliens, Hearings. Washington, D.C.: U.S.
        Government Printing Office, 1971-1972.
Extensive hearings in five parts; Peter W. Rodino, Jr., was
chairman.

2356   U.S., Congress, House, Committee on the Judiciary,
        Subcommittee on Immigration, Citizenship and
        International Law, 94th Cong., 1st and 2nd sess.
        Hearings on Western Hemisphere Immigration.
        Washington, D.C.: U.S. Government Printing Office,
        1975-1976.

2357   U.S., Congress, House, Committee on Un-American
        Activities, 81st Cong., 1st sess. _Hearings Regarding
        Communist Infiltration of Minority Groups_.
        Washington, D.C.: U.S. Government Printing Office,
        1950.
Hearings growing out of the big red scare of the McCarthy
era.

2358   U.S., Congress, House, Conference Committee; 87th
        Cong., 1st sess. _Mexican Farm Labor Program;
        Conference Report to Accompany H.R. 2010_. Washington,
        D.C.: U.S. Government Printing Office, 1961.

2359   U.S., Congress, House, Select Committee Investigating
        National Defense Migration. _Hearings_ [of the Tolan
        Committee]. Washington, D.C.: U.S. Government
        Printing Office, 1941.

A critical congressional investigation headed by Representative John H. Tolan. It helped lead to the bracero program.

2360   U.S., Congress, Senate, Committee on Education and Labor, 76th Cong., 2nd sess. Hearings Pursuant to Senate Resolution 266 (74th Congress). Washington, D.C.: U.S. Government Printing Office, 1940.

2361   U.S., Congress, Senate, Committee on Labor and Public Welfare, 87th Cong., 2nd sess. Migrant Farm Workers in America. Washington, D.C.: U.S. Government Printing Office, 1962.

2362   U.S., Congress, Senate, Committee on Labor and Public Welfare, 82nd Cong., 2nd sess. Migratory Labor. Washington, D.C.: U.S. Government Printing Office, 1952.

2363   U.S., Congress, Senate, Committee on Labor and Public Welfare. 87th Cong., 1st sess. Migratory Labor. Washington, D.C.: U.S. Government Printing Office, 1961-1963.

2364   U.S., Congress, Senate, Committee on Labor and Public Welfare, 91st Cong., 2nd sess. Problems of Migrant Workers; Hearings. Washington, D.C.: U.S. Government Printing Office, 1970.

2365   U.S., Congress, Senate, Committee on Labor and Public Welfare, Subcommittee on Migratory Labor, 86th Cong., 2nd sess. The Migrant Farm Worker in America. Washington, D.C.: U.S. Government Printing Office, 1960.

2366   U.S., Congress, Senate, Committee on Labor and Public Welfare, Subcommittee on Migratory Labor Legislation, 90th Cong., 1st sess. Hearings. Washington, D.C.: U.S. Government Printing Office, 1969.

2367   U.S., Congress, Senate, Committee on Labor and Public Welfare, Subcommittee on Migratory Labor, 89th Cong., 2nd sess. Hearings on S. 1864, S. 1865, S. 1866, S. 1867, and S. 1868; Bills to Amend Migratory Labor Legislation. Washington, D.C.: U.S. Government Printing Office, 1966.

2368   U.S., Congress, Senate, Committee on Labor and Public Welfare, Subcommittee on Migratory Labor, 91st Cong., 1st and 2nd sess. Washington, D.C.: U.S. Government Printing Office, 1971.
In eight parts; Part II, the Migrant Subculture; Part V, Border Commuter Labor Problem.

2369   U.S., Congress, Senate, Committee on Labor and Public
       Welfare, Subcommittee on Migratory Labor, 91st Cong.,
       1st sess. The Migratory Farm Labor Problem in the
       United States. Washington, D.C.: U.S. Government
       Printing Office, 1969.

2370   U.S., Congress, Senate, Committee on Labor and Public
       Welfare, Subcommittee on Migratory Labor, 90th Cong.,
       1st sess. Migratory Labor Legislation. Washington,
       D.C.: U.S. Government Printing Office, 1967.

2371   U.S., Congress, Senate, Committee on the Judiciary,
       Subcommittee on Immigration and Naturalization, 94th
       Cong., 2nd sess. Hearings to Amend the Immigration
       and Nationality Act, and For Other Purposes.
       Washington, D.C.: U.S. Government Printing Office,
       1976.

2372   U.S., Congress, Senate, Subcommittee of the Committee
       on Education and Labor, 74th Cong., 2nd sess.
       Violation of Free Speech and Rights of Labor; Part 54,
       Agricultural Labor in California: Hearings Before the
       Subcommittee. Washington, D.C.: U.S. Government
       Printing Office, 1940.
The La Follette Committee report; contains important
materials on agricultural strikes in the 1930s, especially
the Corcoran cotton strike.

2373   U.S., Department of Agriculture, Economic Research
       Division, Economic and Statistical Analysis Division.
       Economic, Social and Demographic Characteristics of
       Spanish-American Wage Workers on U.S. Farms.
       Washington, D.C.: U.S. Government Printing Office,
       1963.

2374   U.S., Department of Agriculture, Interagency Committee
       on Migrant Labor. Migrant Labor . . . A Human
       Problem. Washington, D.C.: U.S. Government Printing
       Office, 1947.

2375   U.S., Department of Health, Education and Welfare. A
       Study of Selected Socio-Economic Characteristics of
       Ethnic Minorities Based on the 1970 Census. Vol. I:
       Americans of Spanish Origin. Washington, D.C.:
       Department of Health, Education and Welfare, 1970.
Has a section on characteristics of Mexican Americans as
well as graphs and tables.

2376   U.S., Department of Health, Education, and Welfare,
       Public Health Service. Domestic Agricultural Migrants
       in the United States, Maps and Statistics.
       Washington, D.C.: U.S. Government Printing Office,
       1960.

2377   U.S., Department of Health, Education, and Welfare,
        Office of Education. Mama Goes to Nursery School;
        School Bells for Migrants; Learn a lito Englich; se
        habla español. Washington, D.C.: U.S. Government
        Printing Office, 1968.

2378   U.S., Department of Justice. Final Report to the
        President of the United States by the Special Study
        Group on Illegal Immigrants from Mexico, U.S.
        Department of Justice. Washington, D.C.: U.S.
        Department of Justice, 1973.

2379   U.S., Department of Labor. Farm Labor Fact Book.
        Washington, D.C.: U.S. Government Printing Office,
        1959.

2380   U.S., Department of Labor, Bureau of Employment
        Security, Farm Placement Service. Information
        Concerning Entry of Mexican Agricultural Workers into
        the United States. Washington, D.C.: U.S. Government
        Printing Office, 1959.

2381   U.S., Department of Labor, Manpower Administration.
        Long-term Trends in Foreign-Worker Employment.
        Prepared by Kay Longcope. Washington, D.C.: U.S.
        Department of Labor, 1968.

2382   U.S., Department of State. Mexican Agricultural
        Workers. Washington, D.C.: U.S. Government Printing
        Office, 1949.

2383   U.S., Department of State. Temporary Migration of
        Mexican Agricultural Workers, Executive Agreement,
        Series 278. Washington, D.C.: U.S. Government
        Printing Office, 1943.
The World War II agreement between the United States and
Mexico.

2384   U.S., President, Committee on Migratory Labor.
        Mexican Farm Labor Program Consultants Report.
        Washington, D.C.: U.S. Government Printing Office,
        1959.

2385   U.S., President, Committee on Migratory Labor.
        Migratory Labor in American Agriculture; Report.
        Washington, D.C.: U.S. Government Printing Office,
        1951.
Good coverage of the history and practices.

2386   U.S., President, Select Commission on Western
        Hemisphere Immigration. Report of the Commission.
        Washington, D.C.: U.S. Government Printing Office,
        1968.

Chaired by Richard Scammon; materials on commuters and
greencarders.

2387   Vidal, Mirta. *Chicanas Speak Out: Women, New Voices
        of La Raza*. New York: Pathfinder Press, 1971.
Describes the role of women in the Chicano movement of the
late 1960s.

2388   Vidal, Mirta. *Chicano Liberation and Revolutionary
        Youth*. New York: Pathfinder Press, 1971.
Describes problems facing young Chicanos, especially racial
discrimination.

2389   Walter, Paul A., Jr. *Population Trends in New Mexico*.
        Albuquerque: University of New Mexico, 1947.

2390   Warburton, Amber Arthur; Helen Wood; and Marian M.
        Crane. *The Work and Welfare of Children of
        Agricultural Laborers in Hidalgo County, Texas*.
        Washington, D.C.: U.S. Department of Labor, 1943.
        Reprinted as part of *Mexican Labor in the United
        States*. New York: Arno Press, 1974, item 2955.

2391   Weintraub, Sidney and Stanley Ross. *The Illegal Alien
        From Mexico: Policy Choices for an Intractable Issue*.
        Austin: University of Texas Press, 1980.
A brief essay on undocumented immigration with discussion of
numbers, social costs, and other aspects of a serious issue
in U.S. politics.

2392   White, Florence M. *Cesar Chavez: Man of Courage*. New
        Canaan, Conn.: Garrard Publishing Co., 1973; also: New
        York: Dell Publishing Co., 1975.
An easy-to-read biography of Chavez, aimed at a juvenile
audience.

2393   Wiest, Raymond E. *Mexican Farm Laborers in
        California: A Study of Intragroup Social Relations*.
        San Francisco: R & E Research Associates, 1977.
Concerns primarily braceros and undocumented Mexican
workers.

2394   Williams, Dean L. *Political and Economic Aspects of
        Mexican Immigration in California and the U.S. Since
        1941*. San Francisco: R & E Research Associates, 1973.
A 1950 University of California at Los Angeles master's
thesis; covers a decade and centers on California.

2395   Williams, Robin Murphy. *Strangers Next Door: Ethnic
        Relations in American Communities*. Englewood Cliffs,
        N.J.: Prentice-Hall, 1964.
A general sociological study of racial discrimination with
some material on Mexican Americans.

2396 Woodhouse, Charles E., ed. Report on the Conference
      on Social Science Research in New Mexico.
      Albuquerque: University of New Mexico Press, 1963.

2397 Woods, (Sister) Frances J. Mexican Ethnic Leadership
      in San Antonio, Texas. Washington, D.C.: Catholic
      University of America Press, 1949. Reprint, New York:
      Arno Press, 1976.
A conservative viewpoint, but good for insights into aspects
of various kinds of organizations.

2398 Ximenes, Vicente Treviño and Shirley Driggs. New
      Mexico Housing at Mid-Century. Albuquerque:
      Department of Government, University of New Mexico,
      1954.

2399 Young, Jan. The Migrant Workers and Cesar Chavez.
      New York: Julian Messner, 1972.
Describes favorably Chavez and the farm worker movement he
led.

VI: Theses and Dissertations

2400 Andrade, Francisco M. "The History of 'La Raza'
      Newspaper and Magazine, and its Role in the Chicano
      Community from 1967 to 1977." Master's thesis.
      Fullerton: California State University, 1979.

2401 Arndt, Richard Werner. "La Fortalecita: A Study of
      Low-Income (Urban) Mexican Americans and the
      Implication for Education." Albuquerque: University
      of New Mexico, 1970.

2402 Bray, Nancy Gail Etheridge. "South Texas La Raza, a
      Fulcrum for Revolt? The Political Socialization
      Experience in Two Texas Towns." Master's thesis.
      Austin: University of Texas, 1975.

2403 Briegel, Kaye. "The History of Political
      Organizations Among Mexican Americans in Los Angeles
      Since the Second World War." Master's thesis. Los
      Angeles: University of Southern California, 1967.

2404 Brookshire, Marjorie Shepherd. "The Industrial
      Pattern of Mexican-American Employment in Nueces
      County, Texas." Austin: University of Texas, 1954.

2405 Brown, Jerald B. "The United Farm Workers Grape
      Strike and Boycott, 1965-1970 . . ." Ithaca, N.Y.:
      Cornell University, 1972.

2406 Busey, James L. "Domination and the Vote in a
      Southwestern Border Community: The 1950 Primary
      Campaign in El Paso, Texas." Columbus: Ohio State
      University, 1952.

2407 Campbell, Howard L. "Bracero Migration and the
      Mexican Economy 1951-1964." Washington, D.C.:
      American University, 1972.
Stage two of the bracero program, as seen from a Mexican
point of view. Includes background material and an
extensive bibliography.

2408 Campos, Atanacio. "Immigration: A Mexican American
      Dilemma." Master's thesis. Austin: University of
      Texas, 1978.

2409 Carney, John P. "Leading Factors in the Recent
      Reversal of U.S. Policy Regarding Alien Contract Labor
      Agreements." Master's thesis. Los Angeles:
      University of Southern California, 1954.
Gives the history of Mexican labor importation to 1942 with
the factors leading to the World War II policy.

2410   Carney, John P.   "Postwar Mexican Migration:
        1945-1955, with Particular Reference to the Policies
        and Practices of the United States Concerning its
        Control." Los Angeles: University of Southern
        California, 1957.
Has good general material on the bracero and undocumented to
c.1955; also a good chapter on the Border Patrol and
attitudes of various organizations in the U.S. toward
Mexican labor importation.

2411   Caselia, Eugene.   "The Trends in Legal Arrangements
        Regarding Importation of Mexican Agricultural Workers
        to the United States." Master's thesis. Albuquerque:
        University of New Mexico, 1952.

2412   (Castañeda) Shular, Antonia.   "Raza Unida: Culmination
        of an Historical Process." Master's thesis. Seattle:
        University of Washington, 1970.

2413   Clash, Thomas Wood.   "United States-Mexican Relations,
        1940-1946: A Study of United States Interests and
        Policies." Buffalo: State University of New York,
        1972.

2414   Cline, Donald L.   "Farm Labor in Arizona Since
        Termination of Public Law 78." Master's thesis.
        Tempe: Arizona State University, 1967.

2415   Copp, Nelson G.   "Wetbacks and Braceros: Mexican
        Migrant Laborers and American Immigration Policy,
        1930-1960." Boston: Boston University, 1963.

2416   Coronado, Richard J.   "A Conceptual Model of the
        Harvest Labor Market, the Bracero Program, and Factors
        Involved in Organization Among Farm Workers in
        California, 1946-1970." Notre Dame, Ind.: University
        of Notre Dame, 1980.

2417   Crowley, Donald W.   "The Impact of Serrano Vs. Priest:
        The Quest for Equal Opportunity." Riverside:
        University of California, 1979.

2418   Domer, Marilyn.   "The Zoot-Suit Riot: A Culmination of
        Social Tensions in Los Angeles." Master's thesis.
        Claremont, Calif.: Claremont Graduate School, 1955.
A study of inter-group relations from documentary and
newspaper sources.

2419   Driscoll, Barbara A.   "The Railroad Bracero Program of
        World War II." Notre Dame, Ind.: University of Notre
        Dame, 1980.
Discusses an important separate part of the wartime bracero
program.

2420   Dunbar, Robert L. "An Analysis of the Effects of
       Importing Farm Workers from Mexico." Master's thesis.
       Stockton, Calif.: University of the Pacific, 1963.
Somewhat belies its title; describes the bracero program,
with a final chapter on effects.

2421   Fields, Rona Marcia. "The Brown Berets: A Participant
       Observation Study of Social Action in the Schools of
       Los Angeles." Los Angeles: University of Southern
       California, 1970.

2422   Frank, Nyle C. "An Analysis of the March 1968 East
       Los Angeles High School Walkouts." Chapel Hill:
       University of North Carolina, 1968.

2423   Frisbie, William P. "Militancy Among Mexican
       Americans: A Study of High School Students." Chapel
       Hill: University of North Carolina, 1972.

2424   Garcia, Neftali G. "Mexican-American Youth:
       Orientations Toward Political Authority." Denton:
       North Texas State University, 1975.

2425   Garcia, Philip. "The Socioeconomic Attainment Process
       of Chicano Males Between the Ages of 25 and 64 Years
       for the Period 1960 to 1973." Los Angeles: University
       of California, 1980.

2426   Garcia, Richard A. "Political Ideology: A Comparative
       Study of Three Chicano Youth Organizations." Master's
       thesis. El Paso: University of Texas, 1970.
Describes the organizations and the conditions they
developed in, in El Paso.

2427   Geenens, Ronald Burke. "Economic Adjustments to the
       Termination of the Bracero Program." Fayetteville:
       University of Arkansas, 1967.

2428   Georgi, Peter H. "The Delano Grape Strike and
       Boycott: Inroads to Collective Bargaining in
       Agriculture." Senior thesis. Cambridge:
       Massachusetts Institute of Technology, 1969.
Presents the growers' case, strike, and boycott.

2429   Glass, Judith C. "Conditions Which Facilitate
       Unionization of Agricultural Workers: A Case Study of
       the Salinas Valley Lettuce Industry." Los Angeles:
       University of California, 1966.

2430   Gregory, Gladys G. "El Chamizal: A Boundary Problem
       Between the United States and Mexico." Austin:
       University of Texas, 1937.

2431   Gutierrez, Armando G.   "The Socialization of
       Militancy: Chicanos in a South Texas Town." Austin:
       University of Texas, 1974.

2432   Gutierrez, Jose Angel. "Toward a Theory of Community
       Organization in a Mexican American Community in South
       Texas." Austin: University of Texas, 1976.
Written by one of the founders and leaders of La Raza Unida
Party.

2433   Henderson, Julia J.   "Foreign Labor in the United
       States, 1942-1945." Minneapolis: University of
       Minnesota, 1945.
Summarizes the World War II experience.

2434   Housewright, George M.   "The Changing Economic Status
       in Texas of the Latin-American and the Negro:
       1950-1960." Fayetteville: University of Arkansas,
       1972.
Makes a comparison and argues that Mexican Americans moved
out of agricultural work in smaller numbers than Blacks.

2435   Hull, Frank L., Jr.   "The Effect of Braceros on the
       Agricultural Labor Market in California, 1950-1970:
       Public Law 78 and Its Aftermath." Urbana-Champaign:
       University of Illinois, 1973.

2436   Hulpe, John F.   "The Position of California Labor in
       Regard to the Bracero Program, 1942-1962." Master's
       thesis. San Francisco: California State University,
       1963.

2437   Jeffs, William G.   "The Roots of the Delano Grape
       Strike." Master's thesis. Fullerton: California
       State University, 1969.

2438   Jones, Solomon J.   "The Government Riots of Los
       Angeles, June, 1943." Master's thesis. Los Angeles:
       University of California, 1969.
Describes the zoot suit disturbances of the World War II
era.

2439   Kiser, George C.   "The Bracero Program: A Case Study
       of its Development, Termination, and Political
       Aftermath." Amherst: University of Massachusetts,
       1974.

2440   Kopala, Philip S.   "A Socio-psychological Study of
       Student Protest and Violence." Master's thesis.
       Austin: University of Texas, 1972.

2441   Kurtz, Donald V.   "Politics, Ethnicity, Integration:
       Mexican Americans in the War on Poverty." Davis:

University of California, 1970.

2442 Leff, Gladys R. "George I. Sanchez: Don Quixote of
      the Southwest." Denton: North Texas State University,
      1976.
The life of one of the important Mexican American
intellectual leaders in this century.

2443 Lepage, J. Preston. "A Study of the Relationship
      Between the Political Association of Spanish-speaking
      Organizations and Organized Labor in Texas." Master's
      thesis. Austin: University of Texas, 1965.

2444 McCain, Johnny. "Contract Labor as a Factor in United
      States-Mexican Relations, 1942-1947." Austin:
      University of Texas, 1970.
Includes material on undocumented workers.

2445 MacKaye, Margaret B. "A Historical Study of the
      Development of the Bracero Program, With Special
      Emphasis on the Coachella and Imperial Valleys."
      Master's thesis. Stockton, Calif.: University of the
      Pacific, 1958.

2446 Marin, Marguerite V. "Protest in an Urban Barrio: A
      Study of the Chicano Movement." Santa Barbara:
      University of California, 1980.
Presents a comparative study of five organizations in East
Los Angeles.

2447 Mason, John Dancer. "The Aftermath of the Bracero: A
      Study of the Economic Impact on the Agricultural Hired
      Labor Market of Michigan from the Termination of
      Public Law 78." East Lansing: Michigan State
      University, 1969.

2448 Mathis, William J. "Political Socialization in a
      Mexican American High School." Austin: University of
      Texas, 1973.

2449 Mazon, Mauricio. "Social Upheaval in World War II:
      'Zoot-Suiters' and Servicemen in Los Angeles, 1943."
      Los Angeles: University of California, 1976.

2450 Mindiola, Tatcho, Jr. "The Cost of Being Mexican
      American and Black in Texas, 1960-1970." Providence,
      R.I.: Brown University, 1978.

2451 Moberly, Alan L. "Fences and Neighbors: El Chamizal
      and the Colorado River Salinity Disputes in United
      States-Mexican Relations." Santa Barbara: University
      of California, 1974.

2452   Nava, Alfonso Rodriguez.   "A Political History of
       Bilingual Language Policy in the Americas."
       Claremont, Calif.: Claremont Graduate School, 1977.

2453   Negrete, Louis R.   "Chicano Movement Ideology in East
       Los Angeles, 1968-1972."   San Diego, Calif.: United
       States International University, 1976.

2454   Pfeiffer, David G.   "The Mexican Farm Labor Supply
       Program--Its Friends and Foes."   Austin: University of
       Texas, 1963.

2455   Prager, Kenneth.   "Sinarquismo: The Politics of
       Frustration and Despair."   Bloomington: Indiana
       University, 1975.
Describes a Mexican political movement that had an impact on
border Mexican Americans during World War II.

2456   Reilly, (Sister) De Prague.   "The Role of the Churches
       in the Bracero Program in California."   Master's
       thesis.   Los Angeles: University of Southern
       California, 1969.

2457   Restrepo, Carlos Emilio.   "The Transfer of Management
       Technology to a Less Developed Country: A Case Study
       of a Border Industrialization Program in Mexico."
       Lincoln: University of Nebraska, 1975.

2458   Rodriguez-Cano, Felipe.   "Analysis of the Mexican
       American Migrant Labor Force in the Stockbridge Area."
       Master's thesis.   East Lansing: Michigan State
       University, 1966.

2459   Rosen, Daniel A.   "Mexican-Americans and the Broadcast
       Media: A Study of San Antonio's Bilingual Bicultural
       Coalition on Mass Media."   Master's thesis.   Austin:
       University of Texas, 1976.

2460   Rosen, Gerald P.   "Political Ideology and the Chicano
       Movement: A Study of the Political Ideology of
       Activists in the Chicano Movement."   Los Angeles:
       University of California, 1972.

2461   Sabghir, Irving.   "Mexican Contract Labor in the
       United States, 1948-1953."   Cambridge, Mass.: Harvard
       University, 1956.
Includes the U.S.-Mexican agreement treaties in the
appendix.

2462   Salandini, (Rev.) Victor P.   "The Short-Run
       Socio-Economic Effects of the Termination of Public
       Law 78 on the California Labor Market for 1965-1967."

Washington, D.C.: Catholic University of America, 1969.
Concludes the result was minimal for California farmers and gave farm workers substantial gains.

2463   Santillan, Richard A. "The Politics of Cultural Nationalism: El Partido de la Raza Unida in Southern California: 1969-1978." Claremont, Calif.: Claremont Graduate School, 1978.

2464   Santoro, Carmela E. "United States-Mexican Relations During World War II." Syracuse, N.Y.: Syracuse University, 1967.

2465   Santos, Richard. "An Analysis of Earnings Among Persons of Spanish Origin in the Midwest." East Lansing: Michigan State University, 1977.

2466   Scruggs, Otey M. "A History of Mexican Agricultural Labor in the United States, 1942-1954." Cambridge, Mass.: Harvard University, 1958.
An excellent survey of the first half of the bracero period.

2467   Smith, Rosemary E. "The Work of the Bishops' Committee for the Spanish-speaking on Behalf of the Migrant Worker." Master's thesis. Washington, D.C.: Catholic University of America, 1958.
Describes the early activities of the Bishop's Committee which later became important in settling the Delano grape strike and other agricultural conflicts.

2468   Strauss, Julian. "The Bracero." Master's thesis. El Paso: University of Texas, 1956.

2469   Thompson, John M. "Mobility, Income and Utilization of Mexican American Manpower in Lubbock, Texas 1960-1970." Lubbock: Texas Technological University, 1972.

2470   Valerius, John B. "The Spanish-speaking Population of Texas: 1954-1955 Estimates and a Study of Estimation Methods." Master's thesis. Austin: University of Texas, 1956.

2471   Vargas y Campos, Gloria R. "El problema del bracero mexicano." Mexico, D.F.: Universidad Nacional Autonoma de Mexico, 1964.

2472   Walsh, (Brother) Albeus. "The Work of the Catholic Bishops' Committee for the Spanish Speaking in the United States." Master's thesis. Austin: University of Texas, 1952.

2473 Warkentin, Joel. "A Decade of Migratory Labor in the
      San Joaquin Valley, 1940-1950." Master's thesis.
      Berkeley: University of California, 1952.
Describes the problems and conditions of migrant workers
during World War II and immediate post-war years.

2474 Williams, David J. "Sinarquismo in Mexico and the
      Southwest." Master's thesis. Fort Worth: Texas
      Christian University, 1950.
Describes the impact of this right-wing Mexican organization
on Mexican Americans, especially during World War II.

2475 Wise, Donald E. "Bracero Labor and the California
      Farm Labor Economy: A Micro Study of Three Crops, 1952
      Through 1967." Claremont, Calif.: Claremont Graduate
      School, 1971.

2476 Woods, Cameron E. "Mexican Agricultural Labor in
      California: 1941-1945." Master's thesis. Fresno,
      Calif.: Fresno State University, 1950.

VI: Periodicals

2477   Adair, Douglas. "Cesar Chavez's Biggest Battle." The
       Nation 205 (Dec. 11, 1967), 627-628.
Describes the UFWOC's efforts to unionize the Giumarra
vineyards in Kern County, California.

2478   "Again, La Huelga; U.F.W. vs. Teamsters." Time 101
       (May 7, 1973), 79.

2479   Agenda: A Journal of Hispanic Issues 2:4 (Fourth
       Quarter 1981).
The issue is partly devoted to the theme of Hispanic
immigration and migration, pp. 2-26.

2480   Alexander, L. "Texas Helps Her Little Latins."
       Saturday Evening Post 234 (Aug. 5, 1961), 30-31.

2481   Alisky, Marvin. "The Mexican-Americans Make Themselves
       Heard." Reporter 36:3 (Feb. 9, 1967), 45-48.

2482   Allen, Gary. "The Grapes: Communist Wrath in Delano."
       American Opinion 9 (June 1966), 1-14.
A right wing interpretation of the Delano grape strike.

2483   Allsup, Carl. "Education is Our Freedom: The American
       G.I. Forum and the Mexican American School Segregation
       in Texas, 1948-1957." Aztlan 8 (1977), 27-50.
Describes the role of the G.I. Forum in fighting school
segregation in Texas, centering on the Delgado case.

2484   Almazan, Marco A. "The Mexicans Keep 'em Rolling."
       Inter-American 4 (Oct. 1945), 20-23, 36.

2485   Ames, Charles R. "Along the Mexican Border--Then and
       Now." Journal of Arizona History 18 (1977), 431-446.

2486   "Another Civil Rights Headache: Plight of
       Mexican-Americans, Los Angeles." U.S. News and World
       Report 60 (June 6, 1966), 46-48.
In broad terms surveys the rising concern of Los Angeles
Chicanos about their civil rights.

2487   Arias, Ronald. "The Barrio." Agenda 2 (July 1966),
       15-20.

2488   "Arizona Law Curbs Farm Union." U.S. News and World
       Report 72 (June 5, 1972), 102.
Details the provisions of state legislation designed to
weaken agricultural unionism. It bars picketing and bans
the secondary boycott.

2489 Arroyo, Luis L. "Chicano Participation in Organized
      Labor: The CIO in Los Angeles, 1938-1950. An Extended
      Research Note." Aztlan 6:2 (Summer 1975), 277-303.
An exploratory study of Chicano membership and leadership in
the CIO; includes the socio-economic conditions of Chicanos
in Los Angeles.

2490 "As Braceros Leave." Newsweek 32 (Jan. 28, 1965),
      42-45.

2491 Baer, Barbara and Glenna Matthews. "The Women of the
      Boycott." In America's Working Women: A Documentary
      History, 1600 to the Present. Edited by Rosalyn
      Baxardall, pp. 363-372. New York: Random House, 1976.

2492 Baker, Verne A. "Braceros Farm for Mexico." Americas
      5 (Sept. 1953), 3-5, 30-31.
Details the impact of bracero experience on Mexican
agriculture, principally in Sonora.

2493 Ball, C. D. and B. Fowler. "AFL-CIO Goes After Farm
      Workers." Farm Journal 84 (Oct. 1960), 33.

2494 Barnes, Peter. "Cesar Chavez and the Teamsters." New
      Republic 168 (May 19, 1973), 14-15.
Describes the ongoing conflict between the United Farm
Workers and the Teamsters Union.

2495 Barnes, Peter. "Chicano Power Liberating a Country."
      New Republic 169 (Dec. 1, 1973), 10-12.
Describes the successes of La Raza Unida in Zavala County,
Texas after 1969.

2496 Becker, Michael, et al. "San Diego-Tijuana: Plans
      Across the the Border." Cry California 2 (Summer
      1976), 29-35.

2497 Bergez, John. "The Grape Strike in Delano: A Three
      Part Case Study . . ." In Minorities in California
      History. Edited by George E. Frakes and Curtis B.
      Solberg, pp. 269-273. New York: Random House, 1971.

2498 Berman, J. J. and J. Hightower. "Chavez and the
      Teamsters." Nation 211 (Nov. 2, 1970), 427-431.

2499 Berman, P. and T. Mack. "Renaissance on the Rio
      Grande." Forbes 126 (Sept. 1, 1980), 38-40.

2500 Berni, Giorgio. "Border Industry: The Case of Ciudad
      Juarez, Chihuahua." Paper presented to the Conference
      on Economic Relations Between Mexico and the U.S.
      (April 1973), Austin, Tex.

2501   Biderman, B.   "America has D.P.'s of its Own."   New
       Republic 122 (April 24, 1950), 12-13.
Exposes the conditions under which migrant farm laborers
work and live in the lush valleys of the Southwest.

2502   "The Bishops and the Boycott."   America 129:1 (July 7,
       1973), 1.
Describes the Catholic bishops support for free elections in
the vineyards and lettuce fields.

2503   "Bishops For Chicanos."   America 124:21 (May 29,
       1971), 556-557.
Argues for the appointment of more Chicano bishops and
describes the adverse reaction to the naming of the Rev.
John J. Fitzpatrick as bishop of Brownsville diocese.

2504   "Bishops Support Cesar Chavez."   America 122:21 (May
       30, 1970), 574.
Cites the statements of Bishop J. Donnelly and the Bishops
Committee refuting charges that Chavez is a communist.

2505   "Bitter Fruit in the Vineyards."   Nations Business 58
       (Feb. 1970), 80-83.
A grower viewpoint of the Delano grape strike.

2506   Bogardus, Emory S.   "Current Problems of Mexican
       Immigrants."   Sociology and Social Research 25
       (Nov.-Dec. 1940), 166-174.
Lists fear of deportation, naturalization, unemployment and
relief, and the second generation adjustment.

2507   Bogardus, Emory S.   "Racial Distance Changes in the
       United States During the Past Thirty Years."
       Sociology and Social Research 44 (Nov.-Dec. 1959),
       127-135.
Discusses racial antagonism in historical perspective.

2508   Bonaparte, Ronald.   "The Rodino Bill: An Example of
       Prejudice Toward Mexican Immigration to the United
       States."   Chicano Law Review 2 (Summer 1975), 40-50.

2509   "Border Industries Foster New Jobs, More Exports."
       Mexican-American Review 36 (Feb. 1968), 14.

2510   "Braceros."   Fortune 43 (April 1951), 58-60.
Describes labor union unhappiness at the new agreement on
Mexican workers, i.e. the second bracero program.

2511   "Braceros and Wetbacks."   In Labor Organizations in
       the United States and Mexico, by Harvey Levenstein,
       chapter 13.   Westport, Conn.: Greenwood Publishing
       Co., 1971, item 2238.
Describes the first (1943) and second (1950) bracero
programs and U.S. union reaction to them.

2512   Breiter, Toni. "Bakke and Morales: An Update."
       Agenda 7:2 (March-April 1977), 15.

2513   Briggs, Vernon M., Jr. "Chicanos and Rural Poverty: A
       Continuing Issue for the 1970s." Poverty and Human
       Resources 7:1 (March 1972), 3-23.

2514   Briggs, Vernon M., Jr. "Mexican Migration and the
       U.S. Labor Market: A Mounting Issue for the
       Seventies." Studies in Human Resources Development 3
       (1975), 1-37.

2515   Briggs, Vernon M., Jr. "Mexican Workers in the United
       States Labor Market: A Contemporary Dilemma."
       International Labour Review 112:5 (Nov. 1975),
       351-368.

2516   "Bring Back the Braceros; Shortage of Domestic Farm
       Workers in California." Newsweek 65 (Mar. 8, 1965),
       78.

2517   Brody, Michael. "Chavez Country: Fresh Fields Lie
       Open to the United Farm Workers." Barron's 57 (Sept.
       5, 1977), 9, 16.
Discusses the expansion of the UFW outside of California,
especially in Texas and Florida. Also some of its problems.

2518   Buckley, William F., Jr. "Chavez Machine." National
       Review 23 (Aug. 10, 1971), 888-889.
A negative view of Cesar Chavez and the United Farm Workers
from a conservative commentator.

2519   "Building on the Border: U.S. Manufacturers Building
       Plants in North Mexico." Time (June 9, 1967), 106.
Describes the early development of the maquiladora program
on the border.

2520   Burma, John H. "The Present Status of the
       Spanish-Americans of New Mexico." Social Forces 28
       (Dec. 1949), 133-138.

2521   "A Business Boomlet on Mexico's Border." Business
       Week 2211 (Jan. 22, 1972), 36, 38.

2522   Bustamante, Jorge A. "Impact of Undocumented
       Immigration from Mexico on the U.S.-Mexican
       Economies." Fronteras 1976. Conference Proceedings
       (November 1976), 28-50, San Diego.

2523   Bustamante, Jorge A. "More on the Impact of the
       Undocumented Immigration from Mexico on the
       U.S.-Mexico Economies: Preliminary Findings and
       Suggestions for Bilateral Cooperation." Paper

presented to the Southern Economic Association (Nov.
1976), Atlanta, Georgia.

2524 Bustamante, Jorge A. and James Cockroft.
      "Mexico-United States: The Invisible Border." Boletin
      Informativo, Centro de Informacion Para Asuntos
      Migratorios y Fronterizos del Comite de Servicio de
      Los Amigos 5 (Spring 1982), 21-24.
An analysis of Mexican undocumented migration as of the
beginning of the 1980s.

2525 California, Governor's Committee to Survey the
      Agricultural Resources of the San Joaquin Valley.
      "Final Report and Recommendations." Sacramento,
      Calif.: Governor's Committee, 1951.
Presents problems posed by migrant farm workers.

2526 "California Passes Farm Labor Law." Monthly Labor
      Review 98:8 (Aug. 1975), 47.
Describes the 1975 California Agricultural Labor Relations
Act.

2527 "California Tries to Dam the Alien Tide." Business
      Week 2215 (Feb. 12, 1972), 34.

2528 "California: What Help for the Harvest? Discredited
      Bracero Program." Newsweek 64 (Nov. 2, 1964), 77.

2529 "California's Farm Law Gets Its First Test." Business
      Week 2397 (Sept. 8, 1975), 24-25.

2530 Camarillo, Alberto M. "Chicano Urban History: A Study
      of Compton's Barrio, 1936-1970." Aztlan 2:2 (Fall
      1971), 76-106.
Investigates the mobility and stability of Chicano families
in Compton, California; numerous statistical tables.

2531 Camarillo, Alberto M. "Research Note on Chicano
      Community Leaders: The G.I. Generation." Aztlan 2:2
      (Fall 1971), 145-150.
Questions the thesis that the World War II experience of
Chicanos led to their becoming community leaders and active
organizers.

2532 Camejo, Antonio. "A Report from Aztlan: Texas
      Chicanos Forge Own Political Power." In La Raza Unida
      Party in Texas. New York: Pathfinder Press, 1970.

2533 Carpenter, W. "Ferment in the Lettuce Fields."
      Nation 180:15 (April 9, 1955), Inside front cover.
A good description of the Imperial Valley lettuce fields and
working conditions.

2534   Carter, Harlon B.   "The Airlift." U.S. Immigration
       and Naturalization Service. Monthly Review 9:6 (Dec.
       1951), 72-74.
Airlifting undocumented workers from the U.S. to central
Mexico to prevent their immediate return.

2535   "Cesar's War." Time 91 (March 22, 1968), 23.
The Delano grape strike which began in 1965.

2536   Chambers, R. L. "The New Mexico Pattern." Common
       Ground 9:4 (Summer 1949), 20-27.
Describes a pattern of the race issue and discrimination.

2537   "Chance for Chavez." The Economist 256:6889 (Sept. 6,
       1975), 74.

2538   "Chavez: Again the Boycott." America 128:17 (May 5,
       1973), 402.

2539   "Chavez Blight Spreads East." National Business 60
       (May 1972), 32-35.
A grower view of UFW recruiting in the Florida citrus
groves.

2540   Chavez, Cesar. "The Organizer's Tale." Ramparts 5:2
       (July 1966), 43-50.

2541   "Chavez Escalates His Attack on Gallo." Business Week
       2365 (Jan. 27, 1975), 53-54.

2542   "Chavez vs. the Teamsters: Farm Workers' Historic
       Vote." U.S. News and World Report 79 (Sept. 22,
       1975), 32-33.

2543   "The Chicanos' Campaign for a Better Deal." Business
       Week 2178 (May 29, 1971), 48-53.

2544   Clapp, Raymond F. "Spanish-Americans of the
       Southwest." Welfare in Review 4 (Jan. 1966), 1-12.

2545   "C.M.A.U. (Congress on Mexican-American Unity)." La
       Causa (Los Angeles) (Feb. 28, 1970).
A Los Angeles Chicano umbrella organization with concerns
for community problems.

2546   Coalson, George O. "Mexican Contract Labor in
       American Agriculture." Southwestern Social Science
       Quarterly 33 (Dec. 1952), 228-238.
Concerns the first ten years of the bracero program,
1942-1951.

2547   Coburn, Judith. "Dolores Huerta--La Pasionaria of the
       Farmworkers." Ms. 5:5 (Nov. 1976), 11-16.
A lieutenant to Cesar Chavez, Dolores Huerta played an
important part in forming the United Farm Workers.

2548   Cohen, Irving J. "La Huelga! Delano and After."
       Monthly Labor Review 91:6 (June 1968), 13-16.

2549   Coles, Robert. "Our Hands Belong to the Valley: Texas
       Americans." Atlantic 235 (March 1975), 72-78.
Describes the Chicano experience in Texas; some emphasis on
the Texas Rangers.

2550   Coles, R. and T. Davey. "Working with Migrants:
       Efforts of Duke University Students." New Republic
       175 (Oct. 16, 1976), 14-16.

2551   "A Continuing Conversation with Cesar Chavez."
       Journal of Current Social Issues 9:5 (Spring 1971),
       30-31.

2552   "Contracts in the Coachella." Time 95 (April 13,
       1970), 21.
Early success of the United Farm Workers in the Coachella
Valley vineyards.

2553   "A Conversation with Cesar Chavez." The Journal
       [Journal of Current Social Issues] 9:3 (Nov.-Dec.
       1970), 3-9.
An informal interview by John Moyer of the United Church
Board for Homeland Ministries.

2554   Cook, Joy. "La Raza Unida Party." La Luz 1 (Aug.
       1972), 24-26.

2555   Coombs, S. W. "Bracero's Journey; U.S. Harvest
       Provides Seasonal Work for Mexican Farmers." Americas
       15 (Dec. 1963), 7-11.
A personal account of one bracero and the program's impact
on him. Includes many photographs.

2556   Cortez, Ruben. "Sleepy Lagoon and the 'Mexican Crime
       Campaign.'" Probe 2:4 (April 1969), 4, 10.
In 1942 the death of Jose Diaz and the ensuing trial of the
accused led to a Los Angeles journalistic "war against
Mexican crime."

2557   Coyle, Laurie, et al. "Women at Farah: An Unfinished
       Story." In Mexican Women in the United States.
       Edited by Magdalena Mora and Adelaida Del Castillo,
       pp. 117-143. Los Angeles: Chicano Studies Center,
       University of California, 1980.

2558   Crawford, W. Rex.   "The Latin-American in Wartime
        United States." American Academy of Political and
        Social Science Annals 223 (Sept. 1942), 123-131.

2559   Creagan, James F. "Public Law 78: A Tangle of
        Domestic and International Relations." Journal of
        Inter-American Studies 7 (1965), 541-556.
Public Law 78 is also known as the Migratory Labor Agreement
of 1951.

2560   "Crippling Farm Workers." New Republic 167 (Sept. 16,
        1972), 10.
Describes the growers' efforts to defeat the United Farm
Workers by passage of a California initiative, Proposition
22, in the 1972 elections.

2561   Daniel, Cletus E. "Radicals on the Farm in
        California." Agricultural History 49:4 (Oct. 1975),
        4.

2562   Davidson, Chandler and Charles M. Gaitz. "Ethnic
        Attitudes as a Basis for Minority Cooperation in a
        Southwestern Metropolis." Social Science Quarterly
        53:4 (March 1973), 738-748.
An examination of inter-ethnic attitudes in Houston, Texas.
Several tables.

2563   Davis, Thurston N. "Viva la Huelga." America 114:17
        (April 23, 1966), 589-590.

2564   "Deathtraps for Wetbacks: Trade in Illegal
        Immigrants." Time 92:15 (Oct. 11, 1968), 24-25.

2565   Deedy, J. "Boycott Lettuce." Commonweal 96 (June 30,
        1972), 346.
Concerns the Salinas lettuce strike by the United Farm
Workers.

2566   Degnan, James P. "Monopoly in the Vineyard." Nation
        202 (Feb. 7, 1966), 151-154.

2567   "The Delano Grape Story . . . From the Growers' View."
        Delano, Calif.: South Central Farmers Committee, 1968.

2568   "Democrats Invade the Lettuce Patch." Business Week
        2238 (July 22, 1972), 17-18.
A description of the Salinas lettuce strike; basically a
grower-Teamster view.

2569   Denny, Michael Wm. "Participant Citizenship in a
        Marginal Group: Union Mobilization of California Farm
        Workers." American Journal of Political Science 23:2
        (May 1979), 330-337.
Studies the impact of the UFW on its members and non-members

especially as to their political involvement.

2570   Dillman, C. Daniel. "Recent Developments in Mexico's
        National Border Program." Professional Geographer 22
        (Sept. 1970), 243-247.

2571   Dillman, C. Daniel. "Urban Growth Along Mexico's
        Northern Border and the Mexican National Border
        Program." Journal of Developing Areas 4:4 (July
        1970), 487-507.

2572   "Dispute in Delano." Commonweal 83 (Jan. 28, 1966),
        491.

2573   "Documents of the Chicano Struggle." International
        Socialist Review 31:4 (June 1970), 30-33, 44.
Proposals presented to the second annual Chicano Youth
Conference.

2574   Dodson, Jack E. "Minority Group Housing in Two Texas
        Cities." In Studies in Housing and Minority Groups.
        Edited by Nathan Glazer and Davis McEntire. Berkeley:
        University of California Press, 1960.
Compares Mexican Americans and Blacks in San Antonio, Texas.

2575   Dotson, Floyd. "Decrease of the Mexican Population in
        the U.S. According to the 1950 Census." New Mexican
        Sociological Review 17 (1955).

2576   Duberman, Martin. "Grapes of Wrath." New Republic
        157 (Dec. 2, 1967), 23-26.
A lengthy review of John G. Dunne's Delano: The Story of the
California Grape Strike.

2577   Dunne, John G. "Strike!" Saturday Evening Post 240:9
        (May 6, 1967), 32-68.
A popular history of the early part of the Delano grape
strike.

2578   Dunne, John G. "To Die Standing: Cesar Chavez and the
        Chicanos." Atlantic 227:6 (June 1971), 39-45.

2579   Dworkin, Anthony G. "No Siesta Mañana: The Mexican
        American in Los Angeles." In Our Children's Burden.
        Edited by Raymond W. Mack, pp. 389-439. New York:
        Random House, 1968.
Has a brief history of the Mexican American in Los Angeles.

2580   Dyer, Stanford P. and Merrell A. Knighten.
        "Discrimination After Death: Lyndon Johnson and Felix
        Langoria." Southern Studies 17 (1978), 411-426.
The famous Felix Langoria burial case of 1948 with emphasis
on young Senator Lyndon Johnson's role.

2581 Dymally, Mervyn M. "Afro-Americans and Mexican
      Americans: The Politics of Coalition." In Ethnic
      Conflict in California History. Edited by Charles
      Wollenberg, pp. 153-182. Los Angeles: Tinnon-Brown,
      1970.

2582 Eastman, Clyde. "Contrasting Attitudes Toward Land in
      New Mexico." New Mexico Business 24 (March 1971),
      3-20.

2583 Eckels, R. P. "Hungry Workers, Ripe Crops and the
      Non-Existent Mexican Border." Reporter 10 (April
      1954), 28-32.

2584 "Effects of Ending Bracero Program." America 116
      (April 15, 1967), 546.

2585 "End of La Causa?" The Economist 248:6788 (Sept. 29,
      1973), 59.

2586 "End of the Bracero Program." America 108 (June 22,
      1963), 878-879.

2587 Erenburg, Mark. "Obreros Unidos in Wisconsin; Migrant
      Farm Worker Organization." Monthly Labor Review 91
      (June 1968), 17-23.
Discusses the many barriers to unionization of agricultural
workers and cites an example of success in Wisconsin.

2588 Ericksen, Charles A. "Uprising in the Barrios;
      Concerning E. Los Angeles High School Walkouts."
      American Education 4 (Nov. 1968), 29-31; also
      Congressional Record, 91st Cong., 1st sess. (April 14,
      1969), Extension of Remarks, E2891-E2892.

2589 Erickson, Anna-Stina. "Economic Development in the
      Mexican Border Areas." Labor Developments Abroad, pp.
      1-8, June 1967. Washington, D.C.: U.S. Department of
      Labor, 1967.

2590 "Ethnic Dispute in San Antonio." Broadcasting 81:1
      (July 5, 1971), 49-50.

2591 Eulau, Heinz H. "Sinarquismo in the United States."
      Inter-American 3 (March 1944), 25-28.
Discusses the Mexican Sinarquismo movement and possible
connection with the 1943 zoot-suit riots in Los Angeles.

2592 Eulau, Heinz H. "Sleepy Lagoon Case; Court of Appeal
      Reverses Judgments." New Republic 111 (Dec. 11,
      1944), 795-796.

2593 "Fair Wages for Farm Workers." _America_ 124:19 (May
      15, 1971), 500.

2594 "Farm Labor Fights an Anti-Chavez Law." _Business_
      Week 2242 (Aug. 19, 1972), 21.

2595 "Farm Labor: New Phase." _Nation_ 216 (Jan. 29, 1973),
      133.
An alliance of the Teamsters union and the American Farm
Bureau Federation aimed at destroying the UFW union.

2596 "Farm Turmoil From a Model Law." _Business Week_ 2402
      (Oct. 13, 1975), 88.
Describes the conflict resulting from California's
Agricultural Labor Relations Act of 1975.

2597 "Farm Union Reaps First California Victory." _Business_
      Week 1911 (April 16, 1966), 158-160.
Covers the grape strikers' march to Sacramento and the
Schenley agreement.

2598 "Farm Workers and NLRB." _America_ 126:16 (April 22,
      1972), 414.

2599 "Farm Workers Drop Boycott Weapon." _U.S. News and_
      World Report 72 (April 17, 1972), 89.
The United Farm Workers ended its boycott against nine Napa
Valley (California) wineries.

2600 Farrell, Harry. "Salinas Valley Power Struggle." San
      Jose (California) _Mercury_, April 1, 1971.
The Salinas, California lettuce strike of the United Farm
Workers.

2601 "The Fate of PL 78." _Commonweal_ 78 (June 14, 1963),
      316-317.

2602 Fields, Rona M. "The Brown Berets." _The Black_
      Politician 3:1 (July 1971), 53-63.
Describes the history and objectives of the Brown Berets, a
militant community organization founded in 1967 in Los
Angeles.

2603 "Fight to Organize Farm Help." _Farm Journal_ 85 (April
      1961), 32-33.

2604 Fogel, Walter. "Job Gains of Mexican-American Men."
      Monthly Labor Review 91 (Oct. 1968), 22-27.

2605 Fragomen, Austin T., Jr. "President Carter's Amnesty
      and Sanctions Proposal." _International Migration_
      Review 11:4 (Winter 1977), 524-532.

2606   "From Delano to Sacramento." America 114 (April 2,
        1966), 430.
Cesar Chavez used the march to Sacramento to dramatize the
Delano grape strike.

2607   Fugita, Stephen S. "A Perceived Ethnic Factor in
        California Farm Labor Conflict: The Nisei Farmer."
        Explorations in Ethnic Studies 1 (1978), 50-72.

2608   Fugita, Stephen S. and David J. O'Brien. "Ethnic vs.
        Ethnic: Sizing up the Farm Workers Clash." Human
        Behavior 7 (May 1978), 35.

2609   Fuller, Varden. "A New Era for Farm Labor."
        Industrial Relations 6:3 (May 1967), 285-302.

2610   Galarza, Ernesto. "Big Farm Strike." Commonweal 48:8
        (June 4, 1948), 178-182.
Covers the 1947 Di Giorgio strike of the National Farm Labor
Union.

2611   Gallasch, H. F., Jr. "Minimum Wages and the Farm
        Labor Market." Southern Economic Journal 41:3 (Jan.
        1975), 480-491.

2612   "The Gallo Boycott." America 132:11 (March 22, 1975),
        204.

2613   Gamboa, Erasmo. "Chicanos in the Northwest: An
        Historical Perspective." El Grito 6:4 (Summer 1973),
        57-70.

2614   Gamboa, Erasmo. "Mexican Migration into Washington
        State: A History, 1940-1950." Pacific Historical
        Quarterly 72:3 (July 1981), 121-131.

2615   Gamio Leon, Carlos. "Braceros Bring Home New Ways."
        Americas 13 (May 1961), 28-30.
A discussion of the bracero experience by the son of Manuel
Gamio.

2616   Garaza, George J. "Good Neighbors--Texas Version?"
        Texas Outlook 27 (June 1943), 39.

2617   Garcia, Juan R. "History of the Chicanos in Chicago
        Heights." Aztlan 7:2 (Summer 1976), 291-306.
A general survey of the Chicano experience in Chicago
Heights from the early 1900s to the present. The entire
issue is devoted to the midwestern Mexican American.

2618   Garcia, Mario T. "A Chicano Perspective on San Diego
        History." Journal of San Diego History 18:4 (Fall
        1972), 14-21.

2619   Garcia, Richard A. "The Chicano Movement and the
       Mexican-American Community, 1972-1978: An
       Interpretative Essay." Socialist Review 8:4-5
       (July-Oct. 1978), 117-136.

2620   Givens, R. A. "Report on Migratory Farm Labor."
       Labor Law Journal 18 (April 1967), 246-248.

2621   Glass, Judith C. "Organization in Salinas." Monthly
       Labor Review 21 (June 1968), 24-27.

2622   "Going to Jail for the UFW." America 129:4 (Aug. 18,
       1973), 78.
Priests and nuns jailed for their support of the UFW
struggle against the combination of growers and the
Teamsters union.

2623   Gomez, David F. "Chicanos Besieged: The Bloody
       Fiesta." Nation 212:77 (March 15, 1971), 326-328.
Describes the tensions in Los Angeles barrios and the events
of the Chicano Anti-War Moratorium riot.

2624   Gomez, David F. "Chicanos: Strangers in Their Own
       Land." America 124 (June 26, 1971), 649-652.

2625   Gomez, David F. "Killing of Ruben Salazar: Nothing
       Has Really Changed in the Barrio." Christian Century
       88 (Jan. 13, 1971), 49-52.

2626   Gomez-Quiñones, Juan. "Preliminary Remarks Toward a
       Tentative History of the Chicano Student Movement in
       Southern California." Aztlan 1:2 (Fall 1970),
       101-102.

2627   Gonzales, Raymond J. "A Surprise Chicano View of
       Cesar Chavez." California Journal 8:4 (April 1977),
       110.
Discusses the UFW's influence in California politics and
generally Chicano electoral "clout."

2628   Good Neighbor Commission of Texas. "Texas Migrant
       Labor Report, 1971." Austin: Good Neighbor
       Commission, 1972.

2629   Good Neighbor Commission of Texas. "Texas Migrant
       Labor Report, 1972." Austin: Good Neighbor
       Commission, 1973.

2630   Good Neighbor Commission of Texas. "Texas Migrant
       Labor Report, 1973." Austin: Good Neighbor
       Commission, 1974.

2631 Good Neighbor Commission of Texas. "Texas Migrant
      Labor Report, 1974." Austin: Good Neighbor
      Commission, 1975.

2632 Good Neighbor Commission of Texas. "Texas Migrant
      Labor Report, 1975." Austin: Good Neighbor
      Commission, 1976.

2633 Graham, Otis L., Jr. "Illegal Immigration." Center
      Magazine 10:4 (July-Aug. 1977), 56-66.

2634 Graham, Otis L., Jr. "Illegal Immigration and the New
      Restrictionism." Center Magazine 12 (1979), 54-64.

2635 Grayson, George W., Jr. "Tijerina's Republic at San
      Joaquin del Rio de Chama." New Republic 157 (July 1,
      1967), 10-11.

2636 Grayson, George W., Jr. "Tijerina: The Evolution of a
      Primitive Rebel." Commonweal 86:17 (July 28, 1967),
      464-466.
An interview with Tijerina in the Santa Fe penitentiary
after the Tierra Amarilla courthouse affair.

2637 Green, George. "ILGWU in Texas, 1930-70." Journal of
      Mexican American History 1 (Spring 1971), 144-169.

2638 Greenburg, P. S. "Mañana: Colonias of South Texas."
      Newsweek 86 (Nov. 24, 1975), 16, 21-22.

2639 Greene, Sheldon L. "Operation Sisyphus, Wetbacks,
      Growers, and Poverty." Nation 209:13 (Oct. 20, 1969),
      403-406.
An early description of the problem of undocumented workers
from Mexico.

2640 Griffith, Beatrice W. "Viva Roybal--Viva America."
      Common Ground 10 (Autumn 1949), 61-70.

2641 Griffith, Winthrop. "Is Chavez Beaten?" New York
      Times Magazine (Sept. 15, 1974), 18-35.

2642 Grubbs, Donald H. "Prelude to Chavez: The National
      Farm Labor Union in California." Labor History 16:4
      (Fall 1975), 453-469.
A history of the NFLU from its origins in the Southern
Tenant Farmers Union in 1947 to its demise in 1964.

2643 Guade, J. "Agricultural Employment and Rural
      Migration in a Dual Economy." International Labour
      Review 106:5 (Nov. 1972), 475-490.

2644   Gutierrez, Armando. "Hispanics and the Sunbelt."
        Dissent 27 (Fall 1980), 492-499.
Good material on economic and political events of the 1970s.

2645   Guzman, Ralph. "Politics and Policies of the
        Mexican-American Community." In California Politics
        and Policies. Edited by Eugene P. Dvorin and Arthur
        I. Misner. Palo Alto, Calif.: Addison-Wesley, 1966.
Gives the history of Mexican American political action
groups: MAPA, PASO, LULAC, CSO, etc.

2646   Guzman, Ralph and Joan Moore. "The Mexican-Americans:
        New Wind from the Southwest." Nation 202 (May 30,
        1966), 645-648.
Gives a good account of the changes taking place in the
mid-1960s.

2647   Hansen, Niles M. "'Improving Economic Opportunity'
        for the Mexican Americans." Economic and Business
        Bulletin Temple University (Fall 1969), 1-14.

2648   Hawley, Ellis W. "The Politics of the Mexican Labor
        Issue, 1950-1965." Agricultural History 40:3 (July
        1966), 157-176.

2649   Hayes, Edward F., et al. "Operation Wetback: Impact
        on the Border States." Employment Security Review
        22:3 (March 1955), 16-21. Washington, D.C.: U.S.
        Department of Labor, 1955.
Describes the effects of deportation by states: California,
Arizona, New Mexico, and Texas.

2650   Higgins, George G. "La Causa: The Rank and File in
        Step." America 133 (July 5, 1975), 11-12.
A review of Ronald Taylor's Chavez and the Farmworkers.
Beacon Press, 1975, item 2325. Higgins argues that the UFW
represents the best interests of agricultural workers and
has already improved their standard of living.

2651   "Hope in California." America 132:20 (May 24, 1975),
        392.
Refers to California legislation to create the state
Agricultural Labor Relations Board.

2652   Hoult, Thomas F. "Native New Mexicans and Interethnic
        Accomodations." Sociology and Social Research 38
        (1954), 233-238.

2653   Howard, Al. "IAA Speaker Gives 'Inside' On Grape
        Strike." American Fruit Grower 88 (Dec. 1968), 91.

2654   Huck, J.   "Fiesta Flight: Returning Aliens to Mexico."
       Newsweek 88 (Oct. 18, 1976), 13.
Describes the Border Patrol program of flying undocumenteds
to the interior of Mexico.

2655   "Huelga . . . A Strike for Decent Living."   Nursing
       Outlook 18 (Feb. 1970), 40.

2656   "La Huelga! Delano and After."   Monthly Labor Review
       91:6 (June 1968), 13-16.
Includes material on farm worker strikes in Florida
following the UFW example.

2657   International Migration Review 5 (Fall 1971).
The entire issue is devoted to Mexican and Mexican American
migrants.

2658   Ireland, Robert E.   "The Radical Community, Mexican
       and American Radicalism."   Journal of Mexican American
       History 2:1 (Fall 1971), 22-32.
Largely Ricardo Flores Magon and the Partido Liberal
Mexicano. Little comparison.

2659   Issler, A. R.   "Good Neighbors Lend a Hand: Our
       Mexican Workers."   Survey Graphic 32 (October 1943),
       389-394.
Mexican nationals in California during the World War II 1943
harvest.

2660   Jacobs, Paul.   "The Forgotten People."   In his The
       State of the Unions, pp. 170-191. New York: Atheneum
       Press, 1963.
Describes the problems of Mexican and other migrant farm
workers.

2661   Jacobs, Paul.   "Huelga! Tales of the Delano
       Revolution."   Ramparts 5 (July 1966), 37-50.

2662   Jenkins, J. Craig.   "Push-Pull in Recent Mexican
       Migration to the U.S."   International Migration
       Review 11:2 (Summer 1977), 178-179.
Argues for weak pull and strong push factors.

2663   Johnson, Richard.   "The Rio Grande Frontier--Bridge or
       Barrier?"   In The Role of the Mexican American in the
       History of the Southwest: Conference of the
       Inter-American Institute, Pan American College, pp.
       46-52. Edinburg, Tex.: Pan American College, 1969.

2664   Jones, Lamar B.   "Alien Commuters in the United States
       Labor Market."   International Migration Review 4:3
       (Summer 1970), 65-86.

2665   "Justice Delayed." _America_ 132:17 (May 3, 1975), 333.
The UFW as possible effective defense against child labor in
agriculture.

2666   Kane, Tim D. "Structural Change in Chicano Employment
        in the Southwest, 1950-1970." _Aztlan_ 4:2 (Fall 1973),
        383-398.

2667   Kerby, Elizabeth. "Violence in Silver City: Who
        Caused the Trouble?" _Frontier_ 4:7 (May 1953), 5-10.
Vigilantism during the filming of _Salt of the Earth_ in Grant
County, New Mexico.

2668   Kerby, Phil. "The Los Angeles Schools." _Social
        Progress_ 59:5 (May-June 1969), 36-40.
Story of the March 1968 school walkout; also information on
the Brown Berets.

2669   Kerby, Phil. "Minorities Oppose Los Angeles School
        System." _Christian Century_ 85 (Sept. 4, 1968),
        1119-1122.

2670   Kerr, Louise Año Nuevo. "Mexican Chicago: Chicano
        Assimilation Aborted, 1939-1954." In _The Ethnic
        Frontier_. Edited by Melvin G. Holli and Peter Jones.
        Grand Rapids, Mich.: William B. Eerdmans Publishing
        Co., 1977.

2671   King, Allan G. "Unemployment Consequences of Illegal
        Aliens from Mexico." _Texas Business Review_ 53
        (March-April 1979), 43-45.

2672   Kirstein, Peter N. "American Railroads and the
        Bracero Program, 1943-1946." _Journal of Mexican
        American History_ 5 (1975), 57-90.

2673   Kistler, Alan J. "New Hope for the Farm Workers."
        American Federationist 82:9 (Sept. 1975), 1-5.

2674   Knowlton, Clark S. "Changing Spanish-American
        Villages of Northern New Mexico." _Sociology and
        Social Research_ 53:4 (July 1969), 455-474.
Examines the breakdown of the self-sufficient village
society in northern New Mexico and the inability of the
villagers to adjust to the dominent society. A broad
survey.

2675   Knowlton, Clark S. "The Guerrillas of Rio Arriba: The
        New Mexican Land War." _Nation_ 206:25 (June 17, 1968),
        792-796.
Reies Lopez Tijerina and the Alianza Federal de Pueblos
Libres.

2676   Knowlton, Clark S.   "Land Grant Problems Among the
       State's Spanish Americans." New Mexico Business 20:6
       (June 1967), 1-13.

2677   Knowlton, Clark S.   "Tijerina, Hero of the Militants."
       Texas Observer 61 (March 28, 1969), 1-4.

2678   Knowlton, Clark S.   "Violence in New Mexico: A
       Sociological Perspective." California Law Review 58
       (Oct. 1970), 1054-1084.
Describes land grants in New Mexico and their loss over the
years, culminating in the raid by Alianza Federal de Pueblos
Libres on the Tierra Amarilla courthouse. Includes material
on Tijerina's background and early life.

2679   Kopkind, Andrew. "The Grape Pickers' Strike." New
       Republic 154 (Jan. 29, 1966), 12-15.
Describes the early history of the Delano grape strike.

2680   "Labor Comes to Life in the Grape Fields." New
       Republic 154 (April 23, 1966), 6-7.

2681   La Brucherie, Roger A. "Aliens in the Fields: The
       Green Card Commuter Under the Immigration and
       Naturalization Act." Stanford Law Review 21:6 (June
       1969), 1750-1776.
A critical examination of the commuter concept and INS
policies regarding the practice of commuting.

2682   "The Latest Threat to Chavez: Mechanization."
       Business Week 2519 (Jan. 30, 1978), 69-70.

2683   Leary, Mary Ellen. "As the Braceros Leave." Reporter
       32 (Jan. 28, 1965), 43-45.

2684   Leibson, Art. "The Wetback Invasion." Common Ground
       9 (Autumn 1949), 11-19.

2685   Ligutti, L. G. "Chicago Mexicans Meet Synarchism;
       Reply with Rejoiner." Christian Century 61 (Dec. 13,
       1944), 450-1451.
Also see C. L. Venable in this section, item 2859.

2686   "The Little Strike that Grew to La Causa." Time 94:1
       (July 4, 1969), 16-21.
Article on Cesar Chavez, la huelga, and Mexican American
problems.

2687   Loomis, Charles P. "El Cerrito, New Mexico: A
       Changing Village." New Mexico Historical Review 33
       (Jan. 1958), 53-75.
Describes the negative effects of outside cultural and
economic contacts.

2688   Loomis, Charles P. "Wartime Migrations from Rural
       Spanish-Speaking Villages of New Mexico." _Rural
       Sociology_ 7 (Dec. 1942), 384-395.

2689   Loomis, Charles P. and Nellie H. Loomis. "Skilled
       Spanish-American War-Industry Workers from New
       Mexico." _Applied Anthropology_ 2:1 (1942), 33-36.

2690   Lopez, E. H. "Overkill at the Silver Dollar; Chicanos
       in Los Angeles." _Nation_ 211 (Oct. 19, 1970), 365-368.
Describes the shooting of Ruben Salazar in the Silver Dollar
bar.

2691   "Lost Generation, The Pachucos of Los Angeles." In
       One Nation. Edited by Wallace E. Stegner, Chapter 6.
       Boston: Houghton Mifflin, 1945.
Includes many photographs.

2692   Love, Joseph L. "La Raza: Mexican Americans in
       Rebellion." _Trans-Action_ 6:4 (Feb. 1969), 35-41.
Good article on Reies Lopez Tijerina.

2693   _La Luz_.
Vol. 7:2 (Feb. 1978) is largely devoted to immigration
issues.

2694   _La Luz_.
Vols. 8:4 (Oct.-Nov. 1979); 8:8 (Oct.-Nov. 1980); and 9:7
(Oct.-Dec. 1981) are largely devoted to Hispanic women and
their experiences.

2695   McCarthy, T. "Report from Los Angeles." _Commonweal_
       38 (June 1943), 243-244.
Describes the zoot-suit rioting of 1943.

2696   McCleskey, Clifton and Bruce Merrill. "Mexican
       American Political Behavior in Texas." _Social Science
       Quarterly_ 53:4 (March 1973), 785-798.
Examines such aspects as party identification, electoral
participation, and political awareness. A number of
statistical tables.

2697   McConahay, Mary Jo. "Hispanics: Fastest Growing
       Minority." _California Living Magazine_: San Francisco
       Chronicle (May 16, 1982), 6-10.

2698   McCully, John. "The Spanish-speaking People: North
       from Mexico." _Reporter_ 3 (Dec. 26, 1950), 25-28.

2699   McDonagh, Edward C. and Eugene S. Richards.
       "Mexicans." In their _Ethnic Relations in the United
       States_, chapter 8. New York: Appleton-Century-
       Crofts, 1953.

2700   "Machines Take Over Braceros Jobs." Business Week
       1897 (Jan. 8, 1966), 108-110.

2701   Mack, Toni. "Spanish Gold, AM and FM." Forbes 126
       (Nov. 10, 1980), 151, 154.
Article on Spanish language broadcasting and television.

2702   McNamara, Patrick H. "Rumbles Along the Rio: Mexican
       Americans Will Be Heard." Commonweal 89 (March 14,
       1969), 730-732.

2703   McTaggart, Fred. "In Texas: A Time of Terror and
       Tears." U.A.W. Solidarity 10 (July 1967), 10-11.
Describes farm labor organizing in the Texas border region
during the 1960s.

2704   McWilliams, Carey. "California and the Wetback."
       Common Ground 9:4 (Summer 1949), 15-19.

2705   McWilliams, Carey. "Los Angeles 'Pachuco' Gangs."
       New Republic 108 (Jan. 18, 1943), 76-77.

2706   McWilliams, Carey. "The Los Angeles Riot of 1943."
       In Violence in America. Edited by T. Rose, pp.
       168-180. New York: Random House, 1970.
A consideration of the World War II zoot suit riots.

2707   McWilliams, Carey. "Poverty Follows the Crops."
       Nation 162 (March 23, 1944), 343-344.

2708   McWilliams, Carey. "They Saved the Crops."
       Inter-American 11:8 (Aug. 1943), 10-14.
Describes the early success of the wartime bracero program.

2709   McWilliams, Carey. "Zoot-Suit Riots." New Republic
       108 (June 21, 1943), 818-820.

2710   Malley, Deborah De Witt. "How the Union Beat Willie
       Farah." Fortune 90:2 (Aug. 1974), 164-167.
The history of a Chicana strike against Farah Manufacturing
Company, 1972-1974.

2711   Mallory, Michael. "Human Wave of Mexicans Splashes
       Across Border." National Observer 10:41 (Oct. 16,
       1971), 4.
Brief article on undocumented Mexicans and "coyotes".

2712   Malone, Frank. "The Struggle to Organize the Farm
       Workers." Arizona 19 (Jan. 16, 1972), 6-14.

2713   Mangers, Dennis H. "Education in the Grapes of
       Wrath." National Elementary Principal 50:2 (Nov.
       1970), 34-70.

2714 "March of the Migrants." Life 60:17 (April 29, 1966),
      94-95.

2715 Marin, Christine. "Rodolfo 'Corky' Gonzales: The
      Mexican-American Movement Spokesman, 1966-1972."
      Journal of the West 14 (Oct. 1975), 107-120.

2716 Martin, Ray. "La Huelga: The Desperate Cry Along the
      Rio Grande." U.A.W. Solidarity 10 (March 1967), 3.

2717 Martinez, Douglas. "Overview: Hispanic Organizations:
      Meeting the Challenge of the 1980s." La Luz 8:6
      (Feb.-March 1980), 8-9, 43.
The entire issue of Feb.-March 1980 is devoted to Hispanic
organizations.

2718 Matthiessen, Peter. "Profiles: Organizer--I;"
      "Profiles: Organizer--II." New Yorker 45 (June 21,
      1969), 42-85; New Yorker 45 (June 28, 1969), 43-71.
Describes Cesar Chavez and his leadership role in labor
organizing.

2719 Mayer, Arnold. "The Grapes of Wrath, Vintage 1961."
      Reporter 24:3 (Feb. 2, 1961), 34-37.
Discusses the battle to renew the Mexican bracero program.

2720 Meister, Richard. "Still in Dubious Battle:
      California Farm Worker." Nation 191 (Sept. 24, 1960),
      178-180.

2721 "Mexican Wetbacks." Newsweek 32 (Oct. 25, 1948), 80.
Describes the El Paso border violation of October 1948.

2722 Middleman, Irene. "Two Reluctant Heroes: Billy
      Gallegos, James Lopez." La Luz 9:2 (Feb. 1981),
      10-13.
The brief history of two Mexican American hostages in the
1980 Iranian hostage crisis.

2723 "Migrant Workers Testify Before the Senate Committee."
      National Consumers League Bulletin (March 1953), 1,
      14.

2724 Miller, Michael V. "Grape Pickers in California." In
      Poverty: Views from the Left. Edited by Jeremy Larner
      and Irving Hower. New York: William Morrow & Co.,
      1968.
A good broad coverage of Cesar Chavez and the Delano strike.

2725 Miller, Michael V. and James D. Preston. "Vertical
      Ties and the Redistribution of Power in Crystal City."
      Social Science Quarterly 53:4 (March 1973), 772-784.
Good survey of Crystal City and its Chicano population to
ca. 1970. Community power is exemplified in the 1963

election of Los Cinco.

2726 Miller, Paul B. and John M. Glascow. "Job Crisis
      Along the Rio Grande." Monthly Labor Review 91:12
      (Dec. 1968), 18-23.
The problems of employment in the lower Rio Grande valley in
Texas, compounded by commuters, green carders and others.

2727 Mills, N. "United Farm Workers vs. the N.L.R.B."
      Commonweal 96 (April 28, 1972), 180-181.

2728 Mindiola, Tatcho. "The Cost of Being a Mexican Female
      Worker in the 1970 Houston Labor Market." Aztlan 11:2
      (Fall 1980), 231-247.
Looks at discrimination based on race and sex and finds
Chicanas near the bottom. A number of statistical tables.

2729 Minnesota, Governor. "The Mexican in Minnesota." A
      Report by the Governor's Interracial Commission, pp.
      49-64. Aug. 15, 1948.

2730 Mitchell, H. L. "Unions of Two Countries Act on
      Wetback Influx." American Federalist 61 (Jan. 1954),
      28-29.

2731 Mitchell, H. L. "Why Import Farm Workers?" American
      Federalist 56 (Feb. 1949), 20.

2732 Moles, Jerry A. "Who Tills the Soil? Mexican-
      American Workers Replace the Small Farmer in
      California: An Example from Colusa County." Human
      Organization 38 (Spring 1979), 20-27.

2733 "More of the Same for Farm Workers? Lettuce Dispute
      and New Arizona Law." America 127 (Aug. 19, 1972),
      79.
Possible results from Arizona legislation designed to weaken
the union bargaining position.

2734 Morgan, Thomas B. "The Texas Giant Awakens." Look
      27:20 (Oct. 8, 1963), 71-75.

2735 Muñoz, Carlos, Jr. "Chicano Militancy in California:
      A Quest for Identity and Power." In Racism in
      California. Edited by Roger Daniels and Spencer C.
      Olin, Jr., pp. 245-250. New York: Macmillan Co.,
      1972.

2736 Nabokov, Peter. "Reflections on the Alianza." New
      Mexico Quarterly 37:4 (Winter 1968), 343-356.
Views of Reies Lopez Tijerina and his Alianza Federal de
Pueblos Libres.

2737   National Advisory Committee on Farm Labor. "Farm
       Labor Organizing, 1905-1967." New York: National
       Advisory Committee on Farm Labor, 1967.
Forty page pamphlet on early farm labor organizing.

2738   "National Council of La Raza: Progress and Program."
       Mimeographed. Washington, D.C.: The Council, [ca.
       1980].

2739   "The National Frontier Program." Review of the
       Economic Situation of Mexico 47 (Jan. 1971), 19-22.
       Mexico, D.F.: Banco Nacional de Mexico.

2740   Navarro, Joseph. "La Causa and the History of Its
       Opposition." Probe 2:4 (April 1969), 10.

2741   Nelkin, Dorothy. "Invisible Migrant Workers."
       Society 9 (April 1972), 36-41.

2742   Nelson, Eugene, Jr. "New Farm Labor Agreement."
       Monthly Labor Review 96 (May 1973), 64.
Briefly describes a two-year contract between the Teamsters
union and the National Farm Labor Contractors Association.

2743   "A New Verdict." America 137:11 (Oct. 15, 1977), 228.
Describes the killing of Richard Morales by the police chief
of Castroville, Texas and the ensuing local developments.

2744   Nostrand, Richard. "El Cerrito Revisited." New
       Mexico Historical Review 57:2 (1982), 109-122.
Compares the village population over the past eighty years.
See Charles P. Loomis's earlier articles on El Cerrito.
Item 2687.

2745   Novak, Michael. "The Grape Strike." Commonweal 83:12
       (Dec. 24, 1965), 366-369.

2746   "Obreros Unidos in Wisconsin." Monthly Labor Review
       91:6 (June 1968), 17-23.
Describes the initial success of Obreros Unidos under the
leadership of Jesus Salas.

2747   O'Connell, Timothy. "Lettuce Boycott Reaches New
       York." America 124:6 (Feb. 13, 1971), 148-149.

2748   Orth, Maureen. "Zoot Suit: Luis Valdez Breaks the
       Rules, Again." Rolling Stone 357 (Nov. 26, 1981),
       25-26.
Describes the success of Luis Valdez's play, Zoot Suit.

2749   "The Other Texans: The Last Angry Americans." Look
       27:20 (Oct. 8, 1963), 68-70.

2750   "Pachuco Troubles--Zoot Suit Riots in Los Angeles."
       Inter-America 2 (Aug. 1943), 5-6.

2751   Padilla, Gilbert.   "Farm Workers Need Bargaining
       Rights."   Labor Today 6 (Aug.-Sept. 1967), 2-5.

2752   Pandya, Amit.   "The Simpson-Mazzoli Bill."
       Newsletter, Mexico-U.S. Border Program, American
       Friends Service Committee 12 (Spring 1982), 20-24.
An analysis of a Reagan administration immigration control
bill and its future impact.

2753   Pawlicki, Joseph F.   "Big Fish and Small Fry in the
       Valley."   America 133 (Dec. 6, 1975), 399-401.
Describes some typical Mexican American farm workers in
Mecca, Calif.

2754   Peñalosa, Fernando.   "The Changing Mexican-American in
       Southern California."   Sociology and Social Research
       45:4 (July 1961), 405-417.
Describes the Chicano population as 80% U.S.-born, 46%
skilled or semi-skilled, and 22% white collar.

2755   Peñalosa, Fernando.   "Recent Changes Among the
       Chicanos."   Sociology and Social Research 55:1 (Oct.
       1970), 47-52.
Discusses the beginnings of "el movimiento," the rise of
self-identification as Chicano, and the growing sense of
community.

2756   "The Pentagon Buys Lettuce."   America 124:3 (Jan. 23,
       1971), 58.
Examines the Pentagon's heavy purchase of lettuce from Bud
Antle of the Salinas Valley during the lettuce strike.

2757   Perez, Jose G.   "A Big Step Forward for the Raza Unida
       Parties."   International Socialist Review 34 (Jan.
       1973), 14-17.

2758   "Persons of Spanish Origin in the United States."
       Social Education 43 (Feb. 1979), 104-107.
Based on a 1977 population study.

2759   Phillips, N. D.   "Chicano Workers, Rio Grande Farmers
       Agree to Meet."   Christian Century 88 (Jan. 20, 1971),
       84-86.

2760   Pillsbury, Dorothy L.   "Adobe Pay Checks."   Common
       Ground 5 (Winter 1945), 87-91.
Describes World War II effects on the pay scale of Mexican
Americans and on family income.

2761   "A Plan to Slow the Flood of Illegal Aliens."
       Business Week (Aug. 11, 1975), 67.
Argues that an estimated 8 to 12 million undocumented
workers take high paying as well as low paying jobs.

2762   Portes, Alejandro. "Return of the Wetback." Society
       11:3 (March-April 1974), 40-46.

2763   Prado, Enrique L. "Sinarquism in the United States."
       New Republic 109 (July 26, 1943), 97-102.
An excellent survey of sinarquismo and its impact on the
Mexican barrios of the Southwest.

2764   "Proclamation of the Delano Grape Workers for
       International Boycott Day, May 10, 1969." El
       Malcriado 3:4 (April 15-30, 1969), 8-9. Delano,
       Calif.

2765   Proctor, Ben H. "The Modern Texas Rangers: A Law
       Enforcement Dilemma in the Rio Grande Valley." In The
       Mexican Americans: An Awakening Minority. Edited by
       Manuel P. Servin, pp. 212-226. Beverly Hills, Calif.:
       Glencoe Press, 1970. Also in Reflections of Western
       Historians. Edited by John A. Carroll, pp. 215-231.
       Tucson: University of Arizona Press, 1969.
A general history of the Texas Rangers with emphasis on the
workers' march to Austin during the 1966 agricultural
strike.

2766   Radtke, Theodore J. "The Wetback Situation in the Rio
       Grande Valley." Mimeographed Report of the Bishops'
       Committee for the Spanish-Speaking. Corpus Christi,
       Tex.: Bishops' Committee, Aug. 31, 1950.

2767   Ramirez, Henry M. "America's Spanish-speaking: A
       Profile." Manpower 4:9 (Sept. 1972), 30-34.

2768   Razee, Don. "Sorting Fact from Fiction Not Easy in
       Grape Boycott." California Farmer 229:9 (Nov. 2,
       1968), 5.
A grower viewpoint on the Delano grape strike.

2769   "Render Unto Cesar?" The Economist 247:6767 (May 5,
       1973), 53.

2770   Reyes, Robert J. "The Medal of Honor: A History." La
       Luz 9:2 (Feb. 1981), 18-23.
A brief history of the Medal of Honor and a list, with
photographs where available, of the 36 Hispanic recipients.

2771   "Rights for Farm Workers." America 120 (Apr. 26,
       1969), 492-493.

2772 Rios-Bustamante, Antonio J. "The Once and Future
      Majority." California History 60:1 (Spring 1981),
      24-25.
Forsees a Mexican-origin majority in California early in the
next century.

2773 Rochin, Refugio I. "The Short and Turbulent Life of
      Chicano Studies: A Preliminary Study of Emerging
      Programs and Problems." Social Science Quarterly 53:4
      (March 1973), 884-894.

2774 Rock, Michael J. "The Change in Tenure New Mexico
      Supreme Court Decisions Have Effected Upon the Common
      Lands of Community Land Grants in New Mexico." Social
      Science Journal 13 (Oct. 1976), 53-63.

2775 Rodney, James F. "The Effect of Imported Mexican Farm
      Labor in a California County." American Journal of
      Economics and Sociology 20 (Oct. 1961), 513-521.

2776 Rogers, C. R. "California's Farm Bill: A Breakthrough
      for Chavez." Christian Century 92 (June 25, 1975),
      620-621.
Examines the California Agricultural Labor Relations Act of
1975.

2777 Rosen, Gerald. "The Development of the Chicano
      Movement in Los Angeles from 1967-1969." Aztlan 4:1
      (Spring 1973), 155-183.

2778 Ross, Stanley and Sidney Weintraub. "Poor United
      States. So Close to Mexico." Across the Board 9:3
      (March 1982), 54-61.

2779 Roybal, Edward. "President Johnson and the Untold
      Story of the Mexican American Community."
      Congressional Record (daily edition), June 13, 1967.
      H7145-7156.

2780 Ruiz, Ramon E. "The New Mexican American." New
      Republic 159 (July 27, 1968), 11.
Discusses "Corky" Gonzales of Denver, Colorado and his
Crusade for Justice.

2781 "Rules for Admission of Mexican Workers as Railroad
      Track Laborers." Monthly Labor Review 57 (Aug. 1943),
      240-241.

2782 Salandini, (Rev.) Victor P. "Breakthrough in
      Coachella Valley." America 122 (May 2, 1970),
      470-471.
Describes the signing-up of three Coachella grape growers by
the UFWOC, United Farm Workers Organizing Committee.

2783 Salandini, (Rev.) Victor P. "The Delano Strike."
      Commonweal 83:23 (March 18, 1966), 683, 704-705.
A letter.

2784 Salandini, (Rev.) Victor P. "Union Organizing in the
      Fields." America 113 (Oct. 9, 1965), 400-401.
Describes the organizing efforts of AWOC, the Agricultural
Workers Organizing Committee, and the author's personal
involvement.

2785 Sanchez, George I. "Pachucos in the Making." Common
      Ground 4:1 (Fall 1943), 13-20.
Comments on the zoot-suit riots by the late dean of Mexican
American educators and scholars.

2786 Sanderson, R. K. and E. L. Barr, Jr. "Why Grape
      Growers Do Not Render Unto Cesar." Christian Century
      86 (June 11, 1969), 810-811.

2787 Santillan, Richard A. "El Partido de la Raza Unida:
      Revolt in the Barrios." Regeneracion 2:2 (1972),
      9-11.

2788 Santillan, Richard A. "El Partido la Raza Unida:
      Chicanos in Politics." The Black Politician 3:2 (July
      1971), 45-52.

2789 Santillan, Richard A. "Political Reapportionment and
      Hispanic Communities." Agenda: A Journal of Hispanic
      Issues 11:2 (Mar.—Apr. 1981), 18-19, 42.
Discusses Hispanic underrepresentation and its consequences
in recent history.

2790 Santillan, Richard A. "Third Party Politics: Old
      Story, New Faces." The Black Politician 3:2 (Oct.
      1971), 10-18.
Discusses California MAPA and La Raza Unida.

2791 Santillan, Richard A. "Viva La Raza Unida." The
      Black Politician 3:3 (Jan. 1972), 2-5, 36-38.

2792 Saunders, Lyle, and Olen E. Leonard. "The Wetback in
      the Lower Rio Grande Valley of Texas." Inter-American
      Education Occasional Papers (III). Austin: University
      of Texas, 1951.
Ninety-two page discussion of the role of undocumented
Mexican workers.

2793 Scheibla, Shirley. "Render Unto Cesar: How the U.S.
      Department of Labor Became an Arm of the UFW."
      Barrons 52 (July 10, 1972), 9.

2794 "Schenley Surrenders." Christian Century 83 (April
      27, 1966), 515-516.
Describes the first important Chavez victory in the Delano
grape strike.

2795 Schorr, Daniel L. "Reconverting Mexican Americans."
      New Republic 115:13 (Sept. 30, 1946), 412-413.
Examines post-war adjustment problems in San Antonio and
southern Texas; also the rise of discrimination against
Chicano veterans after World War II.

2796 Scott, R. F. "A History of the Mexican in Los
      Angeles: Zoot Suit Riots." Probe 2:5 (May-June,
      1969), 6-7.

2797 Scruggs, Otey M. "The Bracero Program under the Farm
      Security Administration, 1942-1943." Labor History 3
      (Spring 1962), 149-168.
Details the first stage of the bracero program before it was
put under the War Foods Administration.

2798 Scruggs, Otey M. "Evolution of the Mexican Farm Labor
      Agreement of 1942." Agricultural History 34:3 (1960),
      140-149.

2799 Scruggs, Otey M. "Texas and the Bracero Program,
      1942-1947." Pacific Historical Review 32 (Aug. 1963),
      251-264.

2800 Scruggs, Otey M. "Texas, Good Neighbors?"
      [Southwestern] Social Science Quarterly 43:2 (Sept.
      1962), 118-125.
Concerns the Mexican government's effort to reduce
discrimination against Mexicans in Texas during World War II
by withholding braceros.

2801 Scruggs, Otey M. "United States, Mexico and the
      Wetbacks, 1942-1947." Pacific Historical Review 30
      (May 1961), 149-164.

2802 Segal, Aaron. "Mexico and the Mexican-American." Con
      Safos 2:5 (1970), 16-20.

2803 Segur, W. H. and Varden Fuller. "California's Farm
      Labor Elections: An Analysis of the Initial Results."
      Monthly Labor Review 99:12 (Dec. 1976), 25-30.
Examines the first elections held under California's
Agricultural Labor Relations Act of 1975.

2804 Servin, Manuel P. "The Post-World War II
      Mexican-American, 1925-1965: A Non-achieving
      Minority." The Mexican-Americans: An Awakening

Minority, pp. 144-160. Beverly Hills, Calif.: Glencoe
Press, 1970.
Presents a rather negative view of Chicano achievements in
education, politics, and society.

2805 Severo, Richard. "The Flight of the Wetbacks." New
York Times Magazine (March 10, 1974), 17, 77-84.

2806 "Shabby Plot: United Farm Workers Struggle Against the
Teamsters and the Growers." Nation 216 (May 21,
1973), 644-645.
Describes Cesar Chavez's efforts to reach some juris-
dictional agreement with the Teamsters union in his struggle
with growers.

2807 Shockley, John S. "Chicano Revolt in a Texas Town."
Society 12 (July 1975), 88-89.
Briefly examines the Crystal City, Texas political upheaval
after 1963.

2808 Sillas, Herman. "Mexican Americans in California
Government." Black Politician 3:2 (July 1971), 64-68.

2809 Social Progress 59:5 (May-June 1969).
The entire issue is devoted to problems of Mexican
Americans.

2810 Social Science Quarterly 53:4 (March 1973).
The entire issue is devoted to the Chicano experience.

2811 Sosa Riddell, Adaljiza and Robert Aguallo, Jr. "A
Case of Chicano Politics: Parlier, California."
Aztlan 9 (1978), 1-22.
Examines the political activism by which the Chicano
majority won control of the city council of Parlier in 1971
and the ensuing confrontation.

2812 "Spanish-Americans in Politics." Congressional
Quarterly, Weekly Report (June 23, 1961), 1042-1043.

2813 "Statement on the Importation of Japanese, Chinese,
Filipino and Other Foreign Agricultural Workers Into
Areas Supplied by the Mexican Contract Labor Program."
Inter-American Labor Bulletin 7 (Aug. 1956), 4-6.

2814 Stilwell, Hart. "Portrait of the Magic Valley." New
Republic 116 (April 7, 1947), 14-17.
Discusses agricultural workers' conditions in the Rio Grande
valley.

2815 Stilwell, Hart. "The Wetback Tide." Common Ground
9:4 (Summer 1949), 3-14.
A solution to wetback problems. The entire issue is devoted
to the Mexican American.

2816   Stocker, Joseph A.   "People's Padre."   Catholic World
       165 (June 1947), 260-264.
Presents an ex-priest, Emmett McLaughlin, and his efforts
toward better housing for Mexican Americans.

2817   Stoltman, Joseph and John Ball.   "Migration and the
       Local Economic Factor in Rural Mexico."   Human
       Organization 30:1 (Spring 1971), 46-56.

2818   "The Struggle for Chicano Liberation."   International
       Socialist Review 32 (Nov. 1971), 25-37.
Centers on a discussion of Chicano movements in the 1960s.

2819   Sullivan, John R.   "Summer Brings the Mexicans."
       Commonweal 48 (July 2, 1948), 275-278.

2820   Survey 66 (May 1, 1931).
The entire issue is devoted to the Mexican American.

2821   Swadesh, Frances L.   "The Alianza Movement: Catalyst
       for Social Change in New Mexico."   American
       Ethnological Society. Proceedings (1968).   Seattle:
       University of Washington Press, 1968.
A reaction to Nancie Gonzalez's conclusions about Tijerina
and the Alianza in her The Spanish-Americans of New Mexico,
item 3637.

2822   Swadesh, Frances L.   "The Alianza Movement of New
       Mexico: The Interplay of Social Change and Public
       Commentary."   In Minorities and Politics.   Edited by
       Henry J. Tobias and Charles E. Woodhouse, pp. 53-84.
       Albuquerque: University of New Mexico Press, 1969.

2823   Snyder, Eldon E. and Joseph B. Perry.   "Farm Employer
       Attitudes Toward Mexican-American Migrant Workers."
       Rural Sociology 35:2 (June 1970), 244-251.

2824   Taylor, Ronald B.   "Chavez and the NLRA: Something is
       in the Wind."   Nation 220 (Feb. 22, 1975), 206-209.
A long discussion of the status of farm labor and its
problems in California; questions Chavez's leadership.

2825   Taylor, Ronald B.   "Huelga! The Boycott That Worked."
       Nation 211 (Sept. 7, 1970), 167-169.

2826   Taylor, Ronald B.   "Why Chavez Spurns the Labor Act."
       Nation 212 (April 12, 1971), 454-456.

2827   "TELACU: America's Leading Model in Massive Community
       Economic Development."   La Luz 9:3 (March 1981), 7-9.
A brief description and historical survey of the East Los
Angeles Community Union.

2828   "Temporary Halt on Boycott." America 124:14 (April
        10, 1971), 362.
On March 26, 1971 Cesar Chavez suspended the UFW lettuce
boycott for thirty days upon the signing of a UFW-Teamster
accord.

2829   Tercero, D. M. "Workers From Mexico: Labor Agreements
        Between Mexican and United States Government." Pan
        American Union Bulletin 78 (Sept. 1944), 500-506.

2830   Thornton, Richard V. "Tio Taco is Dead." Newsweek 75
        (June 29, 1970), 22-28.

2831   Tipton, Elis M. "What We Want is Action; Relations of
        Americans and Mexicans in San Dimas, California."
        Common Ground 7 (1946), 74-81.

2832   Torres, Isaias D. "The U.S. Supreme Court and Public
        Education for Undocumented Immigrants." La Red/The
        Net 58 (Sept. 1982), 2-4.
A brief description of the court history of the issue from
1974 through 1981.

2833   Trager, Lillian T. "Agricultural Workers in a
        California Town: Economics, Social Networks and
        Organizing for Change." Human Organization 34:1
        (Spring 1975), 105-107.

2834   Trillin, Calvin. "U.S. Journal: Crystal City, Texas."
        New Yorker 47 (April 17, 1971), 102-107.
Examines the Chicano political revolt emerging from the
issue of Chicana cheerleaders in high school.

2835   Tuck, Ruth D. "Behind the Zoot Suit Riots." Survey
        Graphic 32 (Aug. 1943), 313-316, 335-336.

2836   Tuck, Ruth D. "Sprinkling the Grass Roots." Common
        Ground 7 (Spring 1947), 80-83.
Describes the formation of Unity Leagues in California.

2837   "Tug-of-War Over the Farm Hands: Is Chavez Losing His
        Fight?" U.S. News and World Report 75 (Sept. 17,
        1973), 96-98.
Examines reverses suffered by the U.F.W. in the years after
its first big victory in 1970.

2838   Turner, Ralph H. and Samuel J. Surace. "Zoot-suiters
        and Mexicans: Symbols in Crowd Behavior." American
        Journal of Sociology 62 (July 1956), 14-20.
Describes stereotyping during the 1943 Zoot Suit riots of
World War II.

2839   "Unionizing the Farm." Business Week 1964 (April 22,
        1967), 164, 166.
Di Giorgio signs up with the UFWOC after a long conflict.

2840   "Unions Battle Over Vineyard Workers." U.S. News and
        World Report 74 (April 30, 1973), 62.
Continuation of the United Farm Worker-Teamster struggle to
represent agricultural workers.

2841   U.S., Commission on Civil Rights. "The Commuter on
        the United States-Mexican Border." Hearings, pp.
        983-1006. Washington, D.C.: U.S. Government Printing
        Office, 1968.
Hearings held at San Antonio, Texas December 9 to 14, 1968.

2842   U.S., Congress, Congressional Record, 88th Cong., 1st
        sess., 1963, 109, pt. 17: 23169-23177; 109, pt. 18:
        23217-23223. "Amendment of Title V of Agricultural
        Act of 1949."
One year extension of the Bracero program.

2843   U.S., Congress, Congressional Record, 82nd Cong., 1st
        sess., 1952, 97, pt. 6: 7538-7542. "Importation of
        Foreign Agricultural Workers."
A conference report on agricultural worker immigration.

2844   U.S., Congress, Congressional Record, 82nd Cong., 1st
        sess., 1952, 97, pt. 6: 7519-7526. "Supplying of
        Agricultural Workers From Mexico--Conference Report."

2845   U.S., Congress, House, Committee on Agriculture,
        Subcommittee on Equipment, Supplies, and Manpower,
        88th Cong., 1st sess. "Extend the Mexican Farm Labor
        Program." Hearings. Washington, D.C.: U.S.
        Government Printing Office, 1963.

2846   U.S., Congress, House, Committee on Agriculture,
        Subcommittee on Equipment, Supplies, and Manpower,
        87th Cong., 2nd sess. "Farm Labor Program." Hearing.
        Washington, D.C.: U.S. Government Printing Office,
        1962.

2847   U.S., Congress, House, Committee on Education and
        Labor, 91st Cong., 1st sess. "Employment of 'Green
        Card' Aliens During Labor Disputes." Hearings on H.R.
        12667. Washington, D.C.: U.S. Government Printing
        Office, 1969.

2848   U.S., Congress, Senate, Committee on Labor and Public
        Welfare, Sub-committee on Bilingual Education, 90th
        Cong., 1st sess. "Bilingual Education." Hearings. 2
        vols. Washington, D.C.: U.S. Government Printing
        Office, 1967.

2849   U.S., Department of Labor, Bureau of Employment
       Security. "The Farm Placement Program, 1955."
       Employment Security Review 22 (Jan. 1955), 1-44.

2850   U.S., Department of Labor, National War Labor Board,
       Non-Ferrous Metals Commission. "In re: Miami Copper
       Company . . . Feb. 5, 1944." In War Labor Reports,
       vol. 14, pp. 146-165. Washington, D.C.: Bureau of
       National Affairs, 1944.

2851   U.S., Department of State, "U.S. and Mexico Reach
       Agreement on Agricultural Workers." Department of
       State Bulletin 24:607 (Feb. 19, 1951).
The second bracero agreement.

2852   U.S., President, Inter-Agency Committee on Mexican
       American Affairs. "The Mexican-American: A New Focus
       on Opportunity." Testimony Presented at the Cabinet
       Committee Hearings on Mexican-American Affairs, El
       Paso, Texas, Oct. 26-28, 1967. Washington, D.C.: U.S.
       Government Printing Office, 1968.

2853   U.S., President, Select Commission on Western
       Hemisphere Immigration. "The Impact of Commuter
       Aliens Along the Mexican and Canadian Borders."
       Hearings Before the Commission. 3 vols. Washington,
       D.C.: U.S. Government Printing Office, 1968.
Excellent materials on commuters and greencarders; many
tables, statistics, and graphs.

2854   "U.S. Latins on the March." Newsweek 67 (May 23,
       1966), 32-36.

2855   Valdez, Armando. "Insurrection in New Mexico--Land of
       Enchantment." El Grito 1:1 (Fall 1967), 15-24.
Concerns Reies Lopez Tijerina and the Alianza Federal de
Pueblos Libres; with background materials.

2856   Van Arsdol, M. D. and L. A. Schuerman.
       "Redistribution and Assimilation of Ethnic
       Populations: The Los Angeles Case." Demography 8:4
       (Nov. 1971), 459-480.

2857   Vasquez, Amilcar. "Hispanics on the Frontline: A
       History." La Luz 9:2 (Feb. 1981), 7-9.
A broad overview of Hispanic participation in the Armed
Forces of the U.S.

2858   Velie, Lester. "Poverty at the Border." Reader's
       Digest 97 (Aug. 1970), 92-97.

2859 Venable, C. L. "Chicago Mexicans Meet Synarchism."
      Christian Century 61 (Oct. 11, 1944), 1183.

2860 Vigil, Maurilio E. "Jerry Apodaca and the 1974
      Gubernatorial Election in New Mexico: An Analysis."
      Aztlan 9 (1978), 133-150.

2861 "Violence and the UFW Strike." America 129:5 (Sept.
      1973), 106.
The deaths of Nagi Daifullah and Juan de la Cruz.

2862 Vizzard, James L., S.J. "The Extraordinary Cesar
      Chavez." Progressive 30 (July 1966), 16-20.

2863 Vizzard, James L., S.J. "The Long March of the
      Migrants." Jubilee 15 (May 1967), 36-40.

2864 Walsh, Edward J. "The Case of the United Farm
      Workers' Movement." In Research in Social Movements,
      Conflicts and Change, vol. 1. Edited by Louis
      Kriesberg. Greenwich, Conn.: Jai Press, 1978.

2865 Walsh, Edward J. "Farm Workers and Their Election:
      Milestone in California." Commonweal 102:11 (Aug. 15,
      1975), 325-326.
Examines the farm labor situation in California, especially
in context of Teamster-UFW rivalry.

2866 Walsh, Stewart. "Interview with Manuel Salas of
      Obreros Unidos." Wisconsin Review 4 (Fall 1968), 2-9.

2867 Walter, Paul A., Jr. "Population Trends in New
      Mexico." The Population of New Mexico, Publication
      #10. Albuquerque: Division of Government Research,
      University of New Mexico, 1947.

2868 "We Are Not Alone." Social Progress 59:5 (May-June
      1969), 14-15.
Surveys the Chicano movement; reprinted from El Grito del
Norte, March 28, 1969.

2869 West, Jonathan P. "The Mexican Visitor Industry." In
      The Economic Impact of Mexican Visitors to Arizona.
      Edited by Nat de Gennaro and Robert J. Ritchey, pp.
      5-20, 101-105. Tucson: Division of Business and
      Economic Research, University of Arizona.

2870 "Wetback Invasion in Texas." Nation 169 (Aug. 20,
      1949), 168.
Describes a rapid increase in the influx of undocumented
workers. Sees no solution to the problem.

2871   "Wetbacks." Time 57 (April 8, 1951), 24.
Presents the status of undocumented workers in the
Southwest.

2872   "Wetbacks, Cotton, and Korea." Nation 172 (May 5,
       1951), 408.
Describes the rapid increase in labor needs in the Southwest
as a result of the Korean conflict.

2873   "Wetbacks Hit Back." The Economist 270:7073 (March
       24, 1979), 52.

2874   "Wetbacks in Middle of Border War." Business Week
       1260 (Oct. 24, 1953), 62-66.
Covers the role of undocumented Mexican nationals in
southwestern agriculture and the problems of immigration
control.

2875   "Wetbacks Swarm In." Life 30 (May 21, 1951), 33-37.
Stresses Mexican immigrant disruption of the border economy
because of low wages.

2876   "Where Braceros Worked; California Vegetable Fields."
       Business Week (Jan. 16, 1965), 32-33.
Describes changes resulting from the end of the bracero
program.

2877   Whipple, Daniel S. and Deborah P. Klein. "Employment
       in Agriculture: A Profile." Monthly Labor Review 97:4
       (April 1974), 28-32.
Discusses migrant and seasonal workers and trends in
agricultural employment.

2878   Williams, D. A. "Chicanos on the Move." Newsweek 93
       (Jan. 1, 1979), 22-26.

2879   Williams, Doran. "The Starr County Strike." Social
       Progress 59:5 (May-June 1969), 25-29.
Covers the 1966 Texas UFWOC strike and the role of Captain
Allee of the Texas Rangers.

2880   Wolf, Jerome. "The Church and Delano." Commonweal
       84:6 (April 29, 1966), 168-169.
Discusses the issue of "disloyalty" of Church and other
officials, as seen by growers.

2881   Wollenberg, Charles. "Conflict in the Fields: Mexican
       Workers in California Agri-Business." In his Ethnic
       Conflict in California History, pp. 135-172. Los
       Angeles: Tinnon-Brown, 1970.

2882   Wollenberg, Charles. "Mendez v. Westminister: Race,
       Nationality and Segregation in California Schools."

California Historical Quarterly 53:4 (Winter 1974), 317–332.
Concerns a landmark Orange County school segregation case of 1945–47.

2883   Woodbridge, Hensley C.   "Mexico and U.S. Racism: How Mexicans View Our Treatment of Minorities." *Commonweal* 42 (June 22, 1945), 234–236.
Describes the attitudes of a number of leading Mexican periodicals and illustrates with some of their comments on U.S. discrimination.

2884   "Zoot Suit Riots."   *New Republic* 108:25 (June 21, 1943), 818–819.

2885   "Zoot Suits and Service Stripes."   *Newsweek* 21 (June 21, 1943), 35–36.

VII.
LABOR, IMMIGRATION,
AND THE BORDER
REGION _____

<u>Books</u>

   Section VII includes general works on the topics named in
the title and works on labor and immigration which seriously
overlap the chronological divisions of this bibliography.
It also embraces works on the Borderlands and Mexico's
border industrialization program and the maquiladoras.

2886 Alba, Francisco, et al. <u>Indocumentados, mitos y</u>
        <u>realidades</u>. Mexico, D.F.: El Colegio de Mexico, 1979.
The views of a number of specialists on the important issue
of undocumented workers in U.S.-Mexican relations.

2887 Anderson, Henry Pope. <u>Fields of Bondage</u>. Salinas,
        Calif.: H. Anderson, 1963.

2888 Arriola Woog, Mario. <u>El programa mexicano de</u>
        <u>maquiladoras. Una repuesta a las necesidades de la</u>
        <u>industria norteamericana</u>. Guadalajara: Instituto de
        Estudios Sociales, Universidad de Guadalajara, 1980.
The author sees the 1965 ending of the bracero program as
making the maquiladora program almost inevitable, with
resultant negative effects on the 1961 PRONAF program of
"Mexicanizing" the frontier zone.

2889 Biberman, Herbert. <u>Salt of the Earth: The Story of a</u>
        <u>Film</u>. Boston: Beacon Press, 1965. Reprint. New
        York: Arno Press, 1976.
Describes the making of a film about a Mexican American
miners' strike in New Mexico.

2890 Bishop, Charles E., ed. <u>Farm Labor in the United</u>
        <u>States</u>. New York: Columbia University Press, 1967.
Papers from an October 1965 conference on farm labor.

2891   Borderlands Sourcebook: A Guide to the Literature on
       Northern Mexico and the American Southwest. Edited by
       Ellwyn R. Stoddard, Richard L. Nostrand, and Jonathan
       P. West. Norman: University of Oklahoma Press, 1983.
Part one delineates the Borderlands area and discusses
borders and frontiers. Part two looks at the area from the
viewpoint of the various disciplines and geographic and
political subdivisions. Extensive bibliography in part
three.

2892   Briggs, Vernon M., Jr. Chicanos and Rural Poverty.
       Baltimore, Md.: Johns Hopkins University Press, 1973.
Describes the economic conditions of rural Chicanos as the
result of oppression; includes material on border crossers
and immigration.

2893   Brookings Institution--Colegio de Mexico. Structural
       Factors in Mexican and Caribbean Basin Migration: A
       Symposium, 28-30 June 1978. Washington, D.C.:
       Brookings Institution, n.d.

2894   Brooks, Melvin S. The Social Problems of Migrant
       Farm Laborers. Carbondale: Southern Illinois
       University Press, 1960.

2895   Bunker, Robert and John Adair. The First Look at
       Strangers. Newark, N.J.: Rutgers University Press,
       1959.
Based on a 1949-1951 ethnological study of Mexican
American-Indian relations in New Mexico.

2896   Cavanah, Frances, ed. We Came to America.
       Philadelphia, Pa.: Macrae Smith, 1954.
An anthology of firsthand accounts of immigrant experiences.

2897   Chavez, Cesar. Right to Work Laws; A Trap for
       America's Minorities. Delano, Calif.: United Farm
       Workers, AFL-CIO, 1968.
Views of the U.F.W.'s Chavez on a controversial legislative
area. An excellent brief history of early Mexican labor in
the United States. Basic.

2898   Coles, Robert. Migrants, Sharecroppers, Mountaineers.
       Boston: Little, Brown & Co., 1971.
Emphasis on the South and Southwest; includes bibliographic
references.

2899   Colquhoun, James. The Early History of the
       Clifton-Morenci District. London: W. Clowes & Sons,
       Ltd., 1935.
Good for the early story of copper mining in Arizona and the
role of Mexican miners.

2900   Cornelius, Wayne A. American in the Era of Limits:
       Nativist Reactions to the "New" Immigration. San
       Diego: United States-Mexican Studies, University of
       California, 1982.

2901   Cornelius, Wayne A. Building the Cactus Curtain:
       Mexican Migration and U.S. Responses, from Wilson to
       Carter. Berkeley: University of California Press,
       1980.
Describes the history of U.S. policy on undocumented
Mexicans since World War I.

2902   Cornelius, Wayne A. Illegal Mexican Migration to the
       United States: A Summary of Recent Research Findings
       and Policy Implications. Mimeographed. Revised and
       expanded version of briefing paper prepared for the
       National Security Council (1977).
Mexican American historiography.

2903   Cornelius, Wayne A. Mexican Migration to the United
       States: Causes, Consequences, and the U.S. Response.
       Cambridge, Mass.: Massachusetts Institute of
       Technology Press, 1978.
Studies the migration from a Mexican viewpoint. By an
outstanding specialist in Mexican migration studies.

2904   Cross, Harry E. and James A. Sandos. Across the
       Border: Rural Development in Mexico and Recent
       Migration to the United States. Berkeley: Institute
       of Government Series, University of California, 1982.
Presents Mexican migration to the United States as a
long-term historical development based on labor demand in
the U.S. Southwest and political turmoil and lack of
economic opportunity in Mexico. The authors argue that
Mexican policy has encouraged continued migration to the
U.S. Excellent bibliography.

2905   Cross, Ira B.; Carl Plehn; and Melvin Knight. Mexican
       Labor in the United States. Berkeley: University of
       California, 1931-1932.
University of California Publications in Economics, Vol.
VII. The early history of Mexican immigrant workers.

2906   Daniel, Cletus E. Bitter Harvest: A History of
       California Farmworkers, 1870-1941. Ithaca, N.Y.:
       Cornell University Press, 1981.
Based largely on original sources and oral interviews; an
excellent scholarly account.

2907   D'Antonio, William V. and William H. Form.
       Influentials in Two Border Cities: A Study in
       Community Decision-Making. Notre Dame, Ind.:
       University of Notre Dame Press, 1965.

2908   Demaris, Ovid. *Poso del Mundo: Inside the Mexican-American Border, From Tijuana to Matamoros*.
       Boston: Little, Brown & Co., 1970.
Describes social conditions, including crime, on both sides
of the border.

2909   Diez Canedo, Juan. *Undocumented Migration to the United States: A New Perspective*. Translated by
       Dolores E. Mills. Albuquerque: Latin American
       Institute, University of New Mexico, 1981.
Includes bibliographic references.

2910   Dinnerstein, Leonard and Frederick C. Jaher, eds. *The Aliens: A History of Ethnic Minorities in America*.
       New York: Appleton-Century-Crofts, 1970.
Essays, papers, and lectures stressing racial issues.

2911   Dunbar, Anthony and Linda Kravitz. *Hard Traveling: Migrant Farm Workers in America*. Cambridge, Mass.:
       Ballinger Publishing Co., 1976.
A popular account which has material on migrant life styles
and especially health.

2912   Ehrlich, Paul R.; Loy Bilderback; and Anne H. Ehrlich.
       The Golden Door: International Migration, Mexico, and the United States. New York: Ballantine Books, 1979.
Places the complex study of Mexican migration to the U.S. in
worldwide perspective.

2913   Elac, John Chala. *The Employment of Mexican Workers in U.S. Agriculture, 1900-1960*. San Francisco: R & E
       Research Associates, 1972.
Reprint of the author's excellent 1961 University of
California dissertation.

2914   Erb, Richard D. and Stanley R. Ross, eds. *United States Relations With Mexico: Context and Content*.
       American Enterprise Institute, 1981.
Eighteen essays by government and academic experts on border
concerns like immigration, trade, crime, and water use.

2915   *Estudios fronterizos: Reunion de universidades de Mexico y Estados Unidos*. Mexico, D.F.: Asociacion
       Nacional de Universidades e Institutos de Ensenanza
       Superior, 1982.
A collection of twelve papers on various borderland topics
presented at a conference held in La Paz, B.C. in late
February 1980.

2916   *Farm Labor Organizing, 1905-1967*. New York: National
       Advisory Committee on Farm Labor, 1967.
Includes good material on recent strikes, especially the
Delano grape strike.

2917   Farrell, James. _Give Us Your Poor (The Immigration_
       Bomb). San Francisco: Fulton-Hall Publishing Co.,
       1976.
A somewhat alarmist nativist view of world population
increase and its relation to immigration to the U.S.

2918   Fisher, Lloyd H. _The Harvest Labor Market in_
       California. Cambridge, Mass.: Harvard University
       Press, 1953.
An outstanding study of California agricultural labor and
the impact of mechanization.

2919   Foster, James C., ed. _American Labor in the_
       Southwest: The First 100 Years. Tucson: University of
       Arizona Press, 1982.
A collection of articles describing the important impact of
Mexican and Chicano labor on the economic development of the
Southwest.

2920   Fragomen, Austin T., Jr. _The Illegal Alien: Criminal_
       or Economic Refugee. Mimeographed. New York: Center
       for Migration Studies of New York, 1973.

2921   Frakes, George E. and Curtis B. Solberg, eds.
       Minorities in California History. New York: Random
       House, 1971.
Contains an excellent chapter on the Delano grape strike of
1965-1970.

2922   Friend, Reed E. and Samuel Baum. _Economic, Social and_
       Demographic Characteristics of Spanish-American Wage
       Workers on U.S. Farms. Washington, D.C.: U.S.
       Government Printing Office, 1963.

2923   Garcia y Griego, Manuel. _El volumen de migracion de_
       mexicanos no documentados a los Estados Unidos (nueva
       hipotesis). Mexico, D.F.: Centro Nacional de
       Informacion y Estadisticas del Trabajo, 1980.

2924   Goldfarb, Ronald L. _Migrant Farm Workers: A Caste of_
       Despair. Ames: Iowa State University Press, 1981.
Despite some stereotyping, this broad description of the
migrant experience contains excellent material for
understanding the many aspects of migrant farm workers'
problems. The author was appointed in 1975 to monitor
governmental services to migrants.

2925   Gomez-Quiñones, Juan. _Development of the Mexican_
       Working Class North of the Rio Bravo: Work and Culture
       Among Laborers and Artisans, 1600-1900. Los Angeles:
       Chicano Studies Center, University of California,
       1982.
A history of Mexican workers in the Southwest placed in
national and class context. Extensive bibliography.

2926   Gomez-Quiñones, Juan and Luis Leobardo Arroyo.
       Origenes del movimiento obrero chicano. Mexico, D.F.:
       Ediciones ERA, 1978. Reprint, New York: Arno Press,
       1978.
Essays giving background to understanding Chicano unrest at
Anglo injustice.

2927   Gonzalez Navarro, Moises. Poblacion y sociedad en
       Mexico, 1900-1970. 2 vols. Mexico, D.F.: Universidad
       Nacional Autonoma de Mexico, 1974.
Contains information on Mexican policy and attitudes
regarding emigration to the U.S.

2928   Gonzalez Salazar, Roque. La frontera norte:
       Integracion y desarrollo. Mexico, D.F.: El Colegio de
       Mexico, 1981.
A collection of sixteen essays by Mexican experts on the
problems of the northern border region. A Mexican
perspective on border development and the dominant U.S.
influence.

2929   Greer, Scott A. Last Man In; Racial Access to Union
       Power. Glencoe, Ill.: Free Press of Glencoe, 1959.
A comparison of union participation by Chicanos and Blacks
in Los Angeles.

2930   Halsell, Grace. The Illegals. New York: Stein & Day
       Publishers, 1978.
Journalistic account; mostly first-hand experience on the
border.

2931   Hansen, Niles M. The Border Economy: Regional
       Development in the Southwest. Austin: University of
       Texas Press, 1981.
Discusses the subregions of the borderlands and the role of
Mexican labor and undocumented immigrants in the economic
development of the Southwest.

2932   Hansen, Niles M. Location Preferences, Migration and
       Regional Growth: A Study of the South and Southwest
       United States. New York: Praeger Publishers, 1973.
By a specialist in regional economic development.

2933   Heaps, Willard A. Wandering Workers; the Story of
       American Migrant Farm Workers and Their Problems. New
       York: Crown Publishers, 1968.

2934   Hiestand, Dale L. Economic Growth and Employment
       Opportunities for Minorities. New York: Columbia
       University Press, 1964.
Emphasizes employment pattern changes, especially for women
and Blacks.

2935   Higham, John. Strangers in the Land. New Brunswick,
       N.J.: Rutgers University Press, 1955.
An outstanding general work on immigration to the United
States.

2936   Hill, George W. Texas-Mexican Migratory Agricultural
       Workers in Wisconsin. Madison: Agricultural
       Experiment Station, University of Wisconsin, 1948.

2937   Holland, Ruth. Forgotten Minority: America's Tenant
       Farmers and Migrant Workers. New York: Macmillan Co.,
       1970.
Discusses the historical reality and mythology of the farm
worker and especially the harsh lot of migrants.

2938   Hutchinson, Claude B. California Agriculture.
       Berkeley: University of California Press, 1946.
Has some information on early California agricultural labor.

2939   Hutchinson, E. P. Immigrants and Their Children,
       1850-1950. New York: John Wiley, 1956.
A comprehensive general work based on the 1950 census;
numerous statistical tables, some maps.

2940   Illinois, Legislative Investigative Commission.
       Illinois Study on Illegal Aliens. Springfield, Ill.:
       [n.p.], 1971.

2941   In Defense of the Alien: Proceedings, Annual Legal
       Conference on the Representation of Aliens. 3 vols.
       Staten Island, N.Y.: Center for Migration Studies,
       1979-1981.

2942   Jamieson, Stuart. Labor Unionism in American
       Agriculture. 4 vols. Washington, D.C.: U.S.
       Government Printing Office, 1945. Reprint, New York:
       Arno Press, 1976.
U.S. Department of Labor Bulletin No. 836. Includes
excellent material on early Mexican unionization efforts.

2943   Jorgenson, Janet M.; David E. Williams; and John H.
       Burma. Migratory Agriculture Workers in the United
       States. Grinnell, Iowa: Grinnell College, 1961.
The summarization of formal study reports from a project
financed by the Ford Foundation.

2944   Kiser, George C. and Martha W. Kiser, eds. Mexican
       Workers in the United States: Historical and Political
       Perspectives. Albuquerque: University of New Mexico
       Press, 1979.
Covers topics from World War I to the present, presenting
much material from a Mexican viewpoint. The bibliography is
especially rich in periodical materials.

2945   Kritz, Mary, ed. Immigration and Refugees.
       Lexington, Mass.: D. C. Heath & Co., 1982.
A collection of articles by leading specialists on the broad
aspects of immigration and refugee flow, with some emphasis
on implications for the United States.

2946   Ladman, Jerry. The Development of the Mexicali
       Regional Economy: An Example of Export Propelled
       Growth. Tempe: Bureau of Business Economic Research,
       Arizona State University, 1975.
An economist's study of border economic development.

2947   Lassey, William R. and Gerald Navratil. The
       Agricultural Workforce and Rural Development: Plight
       of the Migrant Worker. Bozeman: Agricultural
       Experiment Station, Montana State University, 1972.
A brief description of migrant agricultural worker
conditions in Montana.

2948   Loftis, Anne and Dick Meister. A Long Time Coming:
       The Struggle to Unionize America's Farm Workers. New
       York: Macmillan Co., 1977.
A thorough general survey, placing the United Farm Workers'
struggle in context.

2949   McWilliams, Carey, ed. The California Revolution.
       New York: Grossman Publishers, 1968.
A collection of lectures and essays on social and economic
changes in California, with bibliographic footnotes.

2950   McWilliams, Carey. Ill Fares the Land: Migrants and
       Migratory Labor in the United States. Boston: Little,
       Brown & Co., 1942. Reprint, New York: Arno Press,
       1976.
Discusses Mexican migrants as part of a national problem. A
detailed and thorough study.

2951   Maram, Sheldon. The Labor Market Impact of
       Undocumented Workers. Washington, D.C.: U.S.
       Department of Labor, 1981.

2952   Martinez, Oscar J. Border Boom Town: Ciudad Juarez
       Since 1880. Los Angeles: University of California
       Press, 1975.
An excellent history of a bordertown by an outstanding young
Chicano historian.

2953   The Mexican American in Arizona. Phoenix: Arizona
       State Employment Service, 1968.

2954   Metz, Leon. City at the Pass: An Illustrated History
       of El Paso. Woodland Hills, Calif.: Windsor
       Publications, 1980.
A broad survey with pictures and maps.

2955 Mexican Labor in the United States. Introduction by
      Carlos Cortes. New York: Arno Press, 1974.
Contents: Victor S. Clark, Mexican Labor in the United
States, 1908. Selden C. Menefree and Orin C. Cassmore, The
Pecan Shellers of San Antonio: The Problem of Underpaid and
Unemployed Mexican Labor, 1940. Selden C. Menefree, Mexican
Migratory Workers of South Texas, 1941. Amber Arthur
Warburton; Helen Wood; and Marian M. Crane, The Work and
Welfare of Children of Agriculture Laborers in Hidalgo
County, Texas, 1943. Howard E. Thomas and Florence Taylor,
Migrant Farm Labor in Colorado: A Study of Migratory
Families, 1951.

2956 Mexican Migration. Edited by Thomas Weaver and
      Theodore E. Downing. Tucson: Department of
      Anthropology, University of Arizona, c1976.
An economic study, with an excellent bibliography.

2957 Mexican Migration to the United States. With an
      introduction by Carlos E. Cortes; an original
      anthology. New York: Arno Press, 1976.
Contents: Paul S. Taylor, A Spanish-Mexican Peasant
Community, Arandas in Jalisco, Mexico, 1933. Lyle Saunders
and Olen E. Leonard, The Wetback in the Lower Rio Grande
Valley of Texas, 1951. American G.I. Forum of Texas and
Texas Sate Federation of Labor, What Price Wetbacks? [1953].

2958 Miller, Michael V. Economic Growth and Change Along
      the U.S.-Mexican Border. Austin: University of Texas,
      1982.
A case study of Brownsville, Texas, analyzing local
industrialization, its effects, and its beneficiaries.
Based on the author's surveys, interviews, and other data.

2959 Mines, Richard. Developing a Community Tradition of
      Migration: A Field Study in Rural Zacatecas, Mexico
      and California Settlement Areas. Mimeographed. San
      Diego: United States-Mexican Studies, University of
      California, 1981.

2960 Mines, Richard and Ricardo Anzaldua. New Migrants vs.
      Old Migrants: Alternative Labor Market Structures in
      the California Citrus Industry. San Diego: University
      of California, 1982.
Monograph #9 in U.S.-Mexican Studies program.

2961 Mitchell, Harry Leland. Mean Things Happening in the
      Land: The Life and Times of H. L. Mitchell, Co-Founder
      of the Southern Tenant Farmers Union. Montclair,
      N.J.: Allanheld, Osmun & Co., 1979.
H. L. Mitchell was involved with Ernesto Galarza in early
agricultural union organizing in California's Central
Valley.

2962   Moore, Truman E. The Slaves We Rent. New York:
       Random House, 1965.
Materials on the migrant labor system and problems of the
workers.

2963   Morin, Alexander. The Organizability of Farm Labor in
       the U.S. Cambridge, Mass.: Harvard University Press,
       1952.

2964   National Advisory Committee on Farm Labor.
       Agribusiness and Its Workers. New York: The
       Committee, 1963.
A forty-eight page pamplet describing some of the Mexican
migrants' problems.

2965   National Advisory Committee on Farm Labor. Farm Labor
       Organizing, 1905-1967; A Brief History. New York: The
       Committee, 1967.

2966   Norgren, Paul H. Toward Fair Employment. New York:
       Columbia University Press, 1964.

2967   Ojeda Gomez, Mario. La proteccion de los trabajadores
       emigrantes. Mexico, D.F., 1957.

2968   Padfield, Harland and William Martin. Farmers,
       Workers and Machines: Technological and Social Change
       in Farm Industries of Arizona. Tucson: University of
       Arizona Press, 1965.
Good for the impact of mechanization on agricultural
workers.

2969   Panunzio, Constantine. Immigration Crossroads. New
       York: Macmillan Co., 1927.
A pioneering work by a specialist in the sociology of the
immigrant.

2970   Pollitt, Daniel H. and Selma M. Levine. The Migrant
       Farm Worker in America. Washington, D.C.: U.S.
       Government Printing Office, 1960.
Prepared for the Subcommittee on Migratory Labor of the
Senate Committee on Labor and Public Welfare.

2971   Pourade, Richard F. The History of San Diego. 5
       vols. San Diego, Calif.: Union-Tribune Publishing
       Co., 1960-1965.

2972   Price, John A. Tijuana: Urbanization in a Border
       Culture. Notre Dame, Ind.: University of Notre Dame
       Press, 1973.

2973   Rakocy, Bill. _Images/ El Paso del Norte: 400 Years of
       Pictorial Borderland History_. El Paso, Tex.: Bravo
       Press, 1980.
Illustrated general history to the 1920s.

2974   Ramsdell, Charles. _San Antonio, a Historical and
       Pictorial Guide_. Austin: University of Texas Press,
       1959.
Popular history and historical photographs.

2975   Rapton, Avra. _Domestic Migratory Farmworkers:
       Personal and Economic Characteristics_. Washington,
       D.C.: Economic Research Service, U.S. Department of
       Agriculture, 1967.

2976   Rios-Bustamante, Antonio J., ed. _Mexican Immigrant
       Workers in the United States_. Los Angeles: Chicano
       Studies Center, University of California, 1981.
A collection of articles on the Mexican immigrant worker
under five subdivisions. Includes a section on women
workers.

2977   Roberts, Kenneth, et al. _The Mexican Migration
       Numbers Game: An Analysis of the Lesko Estimate of
       Undocumented Migration from Mexico to the United
       States_. Austin: University of Texas Press, 1978.
A thirty-three page research report critically analyzing the
methods of enumerating undocumented aliens.

2978   Rocha Alvarado, Arturo. _Cronica de Aztlan. A
       Migrant's Tale_. Berkeley, Calif.: Quinto Sol, 1977.
The bilingual odyssey of a farmworker from Texas to
Michigan.

2979   Ross, Stanley R. and S. Weintraub. _Temporary Alien
       Workers in the U.S_. Boulder, Colo.: Westview Press,
       1982.

2980   Ryan, Robert H.; Charles T. Clark; and L. L. Schkade.
       Bridge Into the Future, Eagle Pass, Texas. Austin:
       Bureau of Business Research, University of Texas,
       1964.
Presents an economic survey of the Eagle Pass area.

2981   Samora, Julian. _Los Mojados: The Wetback Story_.
       Notre Dame, Ind.: University of Notre Dame Press,
       1971.
A scholarly sociological viewpoint, by the director of the
U.S.-Mexican Border Studies Project at the University of
Notre Dame.

2982   Samora, Julian and Lyle Saunders. _Wetbacks: A
       Preliminary Report to the Advisory Committee, Study of_

Spanish-speaking People. Austin: University of Texas
Press, 1949.

2983 Scholes, William E. Next Move for the Migrants. New
      York: Friendship Press, 1966.

2984 Selby, Henry A. and Arthur D. Murphy. The Mexican
      Urban Household and the Decision to Migrate to the
      United States. Philadelphia: Ishi Publications, 1982.
Sees migration as part of a complex strategy to hold
families together. Based on more than 5,000 Mexican
households. Fifty-seven pages.

2985 Seligman, Mitchell A. and Edward J. Williams.
      Maquiladoras and Migration. Austin: University of
      Texas Press, 1982.
A systematic exploration of conflicting views on the billion
dollar border industries. Studies the impact of the Border
Industrialization program on Mexican migration and
undocumented immigration to the U.S.

2986 Selvin, David F. Sky Full of Storm: A Brief History
      of California Labor. Berkeley: Institute of
      Industrial Relations, University of California, 1966.
Eighty-six pages on the development of farm labor and grower
organizations, strikes, and related topics.

2987 Sepulveda, Cesar. La frontera norte de Mexico:
      historia, conflictos, 1762-1975. Mexico, D.F.:
      Editorial Porrua, 1976.

2988 Shotwell, Louisa Rossiter. The Harvesters: The Story
      of the Migrant People. Garden City, N.Y.: Doubleday &
      Co., 1961. Reprint, New York: Octagon Books, 1979.
Discusses the many economic and social problems faced by
migrant agricultural workers.

2989 Shotwell, Louisa Rossiter. This is the Migrant. New
      York: Friendship Press, 1958.

2990 Shryock, Henry S., Jr. Population Mobility Within the
      United States. Chicago: University of Chicago Press,
      1964.

2991 Sosnick, Stephen H. Hired Hands: Seasonal Farm
      Workers in the United States. Santa Barbara, Calif.:
      McNally & Loftin, 1978.
Describes recruiting and contracting, non-immigrant alien
workers, commuters, and undocumented workers, working
conditions. Includes material on the 1970-1974 UFW-Teamster
conflict.

2992   Stoddard, Ellwyn R.   Comparative United States-Mexico
       Border Studies. El Paso: University of Texas, 1970.
Border State Consortium for Latin America, Occasional Paper
#1, fifty-four pages.

2993   Stoddard, Ellwyn R.   Patterns of Poverty Along the
       U.S.-Mexico Border. El Paso: Center for
       Inter-American Studies, University of Texas, 1978.

2994   Stuart, James and Michael Kearney.   Causes and Effects
       of Agricultural Labor Migration from the Mixteca of
       Oaxaca to California. Mimeographed. San Diego:
       United States-Mexican Studies, University of
       California, 1981.

2995   Taft, Donald R. and Richard Robbins.   International
       Migrations; the Immigrant in the Modern World. New
       York: Ronald Press Co., 1955.
Taft was a sociologist with expertise in the area of
criminology. Includes map and diagrams; 670 pages.

2996   Taylor, Ronald B.   Sweatshops in the Sun: Child Labor
       on the Farm. Boston: Beacon Press, 1973.

2997   Toney, William T.   A Descriptive Study of the Control
       of Illegal Mexican Migration in the Southwestern U.S.
       San Francisco: R & E Research Associates, 1977.
Includes a description of economic and social conditions in
the Southwest.

2998   U.S., Congress, House, Committee on Education and
       Labor, 91st Cong., 1st sess. Employment of "Green
       Card" Aliens During Labor Disputes. Hearings on H.R.
       12667. Washington, D.C.: U.S. Government Printing
       Office, 1969.

2999   U.S., Congress, House, Select Committee on Population.
       95th Cong., 2nd sess. Legal and Illegal Immigration
       to the United States. Washington, D.C.: U.S.
       Government Printing Office, 1978.

3000   U.S., Department of Health, Education, and Welfare,
       Public Health Service. Domestic Agricultural Migrants
       in the United States, Maps and Statistics.
       Washington, D.C.: U.S. Government Printing Office,
       1960.
Publication No. 540.

3001   U.S., National Commission for Manpower Policy.
       Manpower and Immigration Policies in the United
       States. Washington, D.C.: U.S. Government Printing
       Office, 1978.
A special report describing past, current and projected

policies.   Includes appendices, tables, and figures; 275 pages.

3002   Vialet, Joyce. Illegal Aliens: Analysis and
       Background. Washington, D.C.: Congressional Research
       Service, Library of Congress, 1977.

3003   Wright, Dale. They Harvest Despair: The Migrant Farm
       Worker. Boston: Beacon Press, 1965.

3004   Zermeño, Andy. Don Sotaco. Delano, Calif.: Farm
       Workers Press, 1966.
An exposition of the issues of the Delano Grape strike via
cartoons.

VII: Theses and Dissertations

3005   Alvarez, Robert R., Jr. "Familia: Migration and
       Adaptation in Alta and Baja California, 1800-1975."
       Stanford, Calif.: Stanford University, 1979.
Describes migration based on economic incentive and familial
support systems. Considers migration as a traditional and
continuous process.

3006   Armstrong, John M., Jr. "A Mexican Community: A Study
       of the Cultural Determinants of Migration." New
       Haven, Conn.: Yale University, 1949.

3007   Becerra, Alejandro. "Report: Economic Welfare of
       Mexicans: in Mexico, the United States, and the United
       States-Mexico Border Area." Master's thesis. Austin:
       University of Texas, 1968.

3008   Berninger, Dieter G. "Mexican Attitudes Towards
       Immigration, 1821-1857." Madison: University of
       Wisconsin, 1972.
Concludes that immigration was a matter of secondary
concern, but that there was greater interest following the
Mexican-U.S. War, 1846-1847.

3009   Blevins, Audie Lee, Jr. "Rural to Urban Migration of
       Poor Anglos, Mexican Americans, and Negroes." Austin:
       University of Texas, 1970.

3010   Brunton, Anne M. "The Decision to Settle: A Study of
       Mexican-American Migrants." Pullman: Washington State
       University, 1971.
Describes the settlement of Mexican Americans in the Walla
Walla, Washington area. Details the life styles of the
former migrants.

3011   Bustamante, Jorge A. "Mexican Immigration and the
       Social Relations of Capitalism." Notre Dame, Ind.:
       University of Notre Dame, 1975.
Argues that U.S. immigration policy has been based on
capitalist class interests and on Mexican dependency upon
the United States.

3012   Cardenas, Gilbert. "Manpower Impact and Problems of
       Mexican Illegal Aliens in an Urban Labor Market."
       Urbana: University of Illinois, 1977.
Concludes that the manpower impact of undocumented workers
in San Antonio is somewhat exaggerated. They suffer from
the typical problems of undocumented workers.

3013   Cardenas, Gilbert. "A Theoretical Approach to the
       Sociology of Mexican Labor Migration." Notre Dame,

Ind.: University of Notre Dame, 1977.

3014   Carr, Charles Winn.   "Mexican Americans in the Texas
       Labor Movement."   Fort Worth, Tex.: Texas Christian
       University, 1972.

3015   Carrillo, Stella L.   "Importancia economica y social
       de la poblacion mexicana en Estados Unidos de
       Norte-america."   Master's thesis.   Mexico, D.F.:
       Universidad Nacional Autonoma de Mexico, 1963.

3016   Cothran, Mary Lessie.   "Occupational Patterns of Rural
       and Urban Spanish-Americans in Two South Texas
       Counties."   Master's thesis.   College Station: Texas
       A & M University, 1966.

3017   Cox, Annie M.   "History of Bisbee, 1877 to 1937."
       Master's thesis.   Tucson: University of Arizona, 1938.
The economic and social history of a border copper-mining
town.   Useful for the Mexican role in mining.

3018   Crain, Forrest Burr.   "The Occupational Distribution
       of Spanish-Name People in Austin, Texas."   Master's
       thesis.   Austin: University of Texas, 1948.

3019   Cummins, Densil H.   "Social and Economic History of
       Southwestern Colorado, 1860-1948."   Austin: University
       of Texas, 1951.

3020   Dearman, Cecil J.   "A Socio-Economic Study of
       Latin-American Farm Migrants in Texas."   Master's
       thesis.   College Station: Texas A & M University,
       1947.

3021   Dickerson, Ben E.   "An Analysis of the Incomes of
       Rural and Urban Spanish-Americans in Two South Texas
       Counties."   Master's thesis.   College Station: Texas
       A & M University, 1965.

3022   Donigan, Norma F.   "An Occupational Study of Dallas
       Migratory Mexicans . . ."   Master's thesis.   Dallas,
       Tex.: Southern Methodist University, 1950.

3023   Erenburg, Mark E.   "A Study of the Potential
       Relocation of Texas-Mexican Migratory Farm Workers to
       Wisconsin."   Madison: University of Wisconsin, 1969.
Concludes that relocation (in the 1960s) was a response to
technological changes and that it was impeded by feelings of
insecurity at leaving the Tejano culture area.

3024   Flynn, Walter J.   "Mexican Migration and American
       Policy."   Master's thesis.   Seattle: University of
       Washington, 1954.

3025 Fuller, (Levi) Varden. "The Supply of Agricultural
      Labor as a Factor in the Evolution of Farm
      Organization in California." Berkeley: University of
      California, 1940.

3026 Gildersleeve, Charles R. "The International Border
      City: Urban Spatial Organization in a Context of Two
      Cultures Along the United States-Mexico Boundary."
      Lincoln: University of Nebraska, 1978.
A study based on El Paso-Ciudad Juarez, Douglas-Agua Prieta,
and Nogales-Nogales. Includes geography and history of the
three areas.

3027 Graves, Ersilee Ruth Parker. "A History of the
      Interrelationships Between Imported Mexican Labor,
      Domestic Migrants and the Texas Agricultural Economy."
      Master's thesis. Austin: University of Texas, 1960.

3028 Hendrix, Dawn M. "An Analysis of Employment Factors
      Relevant to Selected Spanish-American Office Employees
      in Albuquerque, New Mexico." Master's thesis.
      Albuquerque: University of New Mexico, 1968.

3029 Hewes, Laurence I., Jr. "Some Migratory Labor
      Problems in California's Specialized Agriculture."
      Washington, D.C.: George Washington University, 1946.

3030 Hinojosa, Jose R. "Discretionary Authority Over
      Immigration: An Analysis of Immigration Policy and
      Administration Toward Mexico." Notre Dame: University
      of Notre Dame, 1980.
Analyzes U.S. immigration policy implementation with
emphasis on the congressional role. There is a chapter on
"commuter" policy and one on undocumented aliens.

3031 Jernigin, Richard T. "The Effect of Increased Mexican
      Migration on the Organization and Operations of the
      United States Immigration Border Patrol, Southwest
      Region." Master's thesis. Los Angeles: University of
      Southern California, 1957.

3032 Johns, Bryan T. "Field Workers in California Cotton."
      Master's thesis. Berkeley: University of California,
      1948.

3033 Kane, Tim D. "The Effect of Labor Market Change Upon
      the Employment of Low-Income Mexican Americans: The
      San Antonio Experience." Austin: University of Texas,
      1972.
Argues that in the 1960s Mexican Americans were deeply
affected by changing labor demands and that manpower
training failed to adjust to these changes.

3034   Krassowski, Witold.   "Naturalization and
       Assimilation-proneness of California Immigration
       Populations."   Los Angeles: University of California,
       1963.
Considers the Mexican case briefly.

3035   Leigh, Lawrence J.   "Migratory Labor: The Limits of
       National Response."   Master's thesis.   Salt Lake City:
       University of Utah, 1968.

3036   Lopez, Pedro.   "A Study of Unapprehended and
       Apprehended Aliens in El Paso: Characteristics and
       Reported Reasons for Coming to the U.S."   Master's
       thesis.   El Paso: University of Texas, 1977.

3037   Lyon, Richard M.   "The Legal Status of American and
       Mexican Migratory Farm Labor: An Analysis of the U.S.
       Farm Labor Legislation, Policy and Administration."
       Ithaca, N.Y.: Cornell University, 1954.

3038   McNaughton, Donald A.   "A Social Study of Mexican and
       Spanish-American Wage Earners in Delta, Colorado."
       Master's thesis.   Boulder: University of Colorado,
       1942.

3039   Martinez, Daniel.   "The Impact of the Bracero Programs
       on a Southern California Mexican-American Community."
       Master's thesis.   Claremont, Calif.: Claremont
       Graduate School, 1958.
Presents a brief history of foreign contract labor in
California and studies the bracero's impact on Cucamonga's
Mexican American community.

3040   Meador, Bruce Staffel.   "'Wetback' Labor in the Lower
       Rio Grande Valley."   Master's thesis.   Austin:
       University of Texas, 1951.

3041   Mendez, Amalia Alcantar.   "A Comparative Analysis of
       Motivational Characteristics of Mexican Immigrant and
       Mexican-American Males."   Master's thesis.   San Diego,
       Calif.: United States International University, 1974.

3042   Olson, Philip G.   "Agricultural Laborers: A Study of a
       Minority Group in a Small Arizona Community."
       Master's thesis.   Tucson: University of Arizona, 1956.

3043   Patton, James M.   "The History of Clifton."   Master's
       thesis.   Tucson: University of Arizona, 1945.
A study of an Arizona copper-mining development using
Mexican labor.

3044   Perry, Josef H. "Economic Characteristics of Texas
        Intrastate Migrants." Master's thesis. Austin:
        University of Texas, 1961.

3045   Portman, Robert. "A Study of Undocumented Mexican
        Workers on a Texas Ranch." Honors thesis. Hanover,
        N.H.: Dartmouth College, 1979.

3046   Privett, John D. "Agricultural Unionism Among
        Chicanos in Texas." Master's thesis. Austin:
        University of Texas, 1971.

3047   Provinzano, James. "Chicano Migrant Farm Workers in a
        Rural Wisconsin County." Minneapolis: University of
        Minnesota, 1971.
Describes migrant Mexican American economic and social
patterns in Centre County, and the efforts to establish a
union in order to end exploitation.

3048   Ramirez, Armando H. "The Socioeconomic Impact of the
        Illegal Aliens on the County of San Diego." Master's
        thesis. San Diego: San Diego State University, 1976.

3049   Ramirez, Emilia S. "Wetback Children in South
        Texas." Master's thesis. Austin: University of
        Texas, 1951.

3050   Rankin, Jerry L. "Mexican-Americans and Manpower
        Policy." Tucson: University of Arizona, 1971.

3051   Rohde, Joyce Alberta. "The Employment Status of
        Spanish-American Office Workers in Selected Firms of
        the Northern Rio Grande Valley." Master's thesis.
        Boulder: University of Colorado, 1957.

3052   Rungeling, Brian S. "Impact of the Mexican Alien
        Commuter on the Apparel Industry of El Paso, Texas (A
        Case Study)." Lexington: University of Kentucky,
        1969.
Argues that commuters in the apparel industry do take jobs
away from U.S. citizens. Commuters made up between
twenty-three and forty percent of the work force in 1968.

3053   Skrabanek, R. I. and Rapton, Avra. "Occupational
        Change Among Spanish Americans in Atascosa County and
        San Antonio, Texas." Paper. College Station: Texas
        A & M University, 1966.

3054   Solorzano, Rosalia. "Attitudes and Migration
        Patterns: A Comparative Study of the 'Marias' from
        Ciudad Juarez, Chihuahua, and Tijuana, Baja
        California, Mexico." Master's thesis. El Paso:
        University of Texas, 1979.

3055 Spellman, Carolyn J. "An Analysis of Viewpoints on
      Migrant Farm Labor Housing." Master's thesis. Chico,
      Calif.: Chico State University, 1950.

3056 Tiltti, John T. "Non-Border Search and Seizure:
      Authority of United States Border Patrol Agents Under
      Section 287-A of the Immigration and Nationality Act."
      Master's thesis. El Paso: University of Texas, 1978.

3057 Tomasek, Robert D. "The Political and Economic
      Implications of Mexican Labor in the United
      States . . ." Ann Arbor: University of Michigan,
      1958.

3058 Torres, Alexander J. "A Follow-up Study of Servo: A
      Project for Monolingual, Low-income Unemployed Mexican
      Americans." Master's thesis. San Diego, Calif.:
      United States International University, 1973.

3059 Tubbs, Lowell L. "A Survey of the Problems of
      Migratory Mexicans." Master's thesis. Austin:
      University of Texas, 1952.

3060 Vassberg, David Erland. "The Use of Mexicans and
      Mexican-Americans as an Agricultural Work Force in the
      Lower Rio Grande Valley in Texas." Master's thesis.
      Austin: University of Texas, 1966.

3061 Wagoner, Delmer W. "Recent Migration of Young Males
      into Houston, Texas." Master's thesis. Austin:
      University of Texas, 1957.

3062 Walton, Roger M. "A Study of Migratory Mexican
      Pea-Pickers in Imperial Valley." Master's thesis.
      Los Angeles: University of Southern California, 1940.

3063 Watt, Roberta. "History of Morenci, Arizona."
      Master's thesis. Tucson: University of Arizona, 1956.
Describes a border copper mining development in which
Mexicans and Chicanos played an important role.

3064 Wells, Miriam J. "From Field to Foundry:
      Mexican-American Adaptive Strategies in a Small
      Wisconsin Town." Madison: University of Wisconsin,
      1975.
Challenges some commonly held views of Anglo-Mexican
societal relations and describes the relative success of
Chicano adaptive strategies.

3065 Whiteford, Linda M. "Family Relations in 'Seco'
      County, Texas.: A Case Study of Social Change."
      Milwaukee: University of Wisconsin, 1979.
Describes changes in family work and social patterns, with

new socio-economic aspirations, in a fictitious town on the
Mexican border.

3066   Williams, Brett. "The Trip Takes Us: Chicano Migrants
        on the Prairie." Urbana-Champaign: University of
        Illinois, 1975.

3067   Wilson, Kay Dieckman. "The Historical Development of
        Migrant Labor in Michigan Agriculture." Master's
        thesis. East Lansing: Michigan State University,
        1978.

3068   Winn, Charles C. "Mexican-Americans in the Texas
        Labor Movement." Fort Worth: Texas Christian
        University, 1972.
Describes organizing efforts of the United Farm Workers in
Texas and the relation of unionization to the Movement.
Argues that racism does not play an important role in Tejano
participation in organized labor.

3069   Zamora, Oscar. "The JOBS Program and Mexican-
        Americans in the Southwest." Master's thesis.
        Austin: University of Texas, 1970.

3070   Zarrugh, Laura Hoffman. "Gente de mi tierra: Mexican
        Village Migrants in a California Community."
        Berkeley: University of California, 1974.

VII: Periodicals

3071 Abrams, E. and F. S. Abrams. "Immigration Policy: Who
      Gets in and Why." Public Interest 38 (1975), 3-29.

3072 Alarcon Acosta, Rafael G. "Undocumented Workers:
      Fifty-Seven Years of the Border Patrol." Boletin
      Informtivo, Centro de Informacion Para Asuntos
      Migratorios y Fronterizos del Comite de Servicio de
      Los Amigos 5 (Spring 1982), 7-8.
Cites recent instances of INS denial of civil and
constitutional rights to undocumented immigrants.

3073 "American DP's." America 107 (April 7, 1962), 9-10.

3074 Arnold, Frank. "A History of Struggle: Organizing
      Cannery Workers in the Santa Clara Valley." Southwest
      Economy & Society 2 (Oct.-Nov. 1976), 26-38.
Covers from the 1930s to the mid-1970s.

3075 Arroyo, Laura E. "Industrial and Occupational
      Distribution of Chicano Workers." In Essays on La
      Mujer. Edited by Rosaura Sanchez and Rosa Martinez
      Cruz, pp. 150-187. Los Angeles: Chicano Studies
      Center, University of California, 1977; also Aztlan 4
      (Fall 1973), 343-382.

3076 Arroyo, Luis L. "Notes on Past, Present and Future
      Directions of Chicano Labor Studies." Aztlan 6:2
      (Summer 1975), 137-149.
Discusses the writings of a number of Chicano scholars on
Mexican Americans as workers. Non-Chicano scholars are not
considered.

3077 Bach, Robert L. "Mexican Immigration and the American
      State." International Migration Review 12:4 (Winter
      1978), 536-558.

3078 Barnes, Elinor J. "Tracing Arizona Migration."
      Arizona Review of Business and Public Administration
      13 (Nov. 1964), 6-9.

3079 Beegle, J. Allan; Harold F. Goldsmith; and Charles P.
      Loomis. "Demographic Characteristics of the United
      States-Mexican Border." Rural Sociology 25 (1960),
      107-162.

3080 Begeman, Jean. "Wetbacks--Slaves of Today." New
      Republic 126:10 (March 10, 1952), 15-16.

3081 Bell, J. N. "Harvest of Hunger: America's Migrant
      Farm Workers." Good Health 175 (Sept. 1972), 106-107.

3082   Belsasso, Guido. "Undocumented Mexican Workers in
       the U.S.: A Mexican Perspective." In Mexico and the
       United States. Edited by Robert H. McBride, pp.
       128-157. Englewood Cliffs, N.J.: Prentice-Hall, 1981.
Covers both U.S. and Mexican policy on Mexicans who cross
into the United States without documents.

3083   Bernard, William S. "Economic Effects of
       Immigration." In Immigration, An American Dilemma.
       Edited by Benjamin M. Ziegler, pp. 50-70. Boston: D.
       C. Heath & Co., 1953.

3084   Bohning, W. R. "Legal and Illegal Migration to the
       United States." International Labour Review 119
       (March 1980), 255-260.

3085   "The Border Industries." In Review of the Economic
       Situation of Mexico (July 1970). Mexico, D.F.: Banco
       Nacional de Mexico, 1970.

3086   "Braceros." Americas 1 (March 1949), 14-17.

3087   Bradshaw, Benjamin Spencer. "Potential Labor Force
       Supply, Replacement, and Migration of
       Mexican-Americans and Other Males in the Texas-Mexico
       Border." International Migration Review 10:1 (Spring
       1976), 29-46.
A survey of both sides of the border. Concludes that the
age structure will continue to stimulate migration from both
areas.

3088   Brawner, Marlyn R. "Migration and Educational
       Achievement of Mexican-Americans." Social Science
       Quarterly 53:4 (March 1973), 727-737.
A comparison of school completion by Chicano children in
Racine, Wisconsin with counterparts in Texas. Argues that
the children of those who migrated have greater scholastic
success.

3089   Briggs, Vernon M., Jr. "La confrontacion del chicano
       con el inmigrante mexicano." Foro Internacional 18
       (Jan.-March 1978), 514-521.

3090   Briggs, Vernon M., Jr. "Illegal Aliens: The Need for
       a More Restrictive Border Policy." Social Science
       Quarterly 56:3 (Dec. 1975), 477-484.
Discusses the problem of undocumented workers and advocates
the U.S. helping Mexicans develop their economy and its
making the hiring of illegals a criminal act.

3091   Broadbent, Elizabeth. "Mexican Population in
       Southwestern United States." Texas Geographic
       Magazine 5:2 (1941), 16-24.

3092   Bullock, Paul. "Employment Problems of the
        Mexican-American." Industrial Relations 3 (May 1964),
        37-50.
A comparative study of Blacks, Mexican Americans, and
Anglos.

3093   Busey, James L. "The Political Geography of Mexican
        Migration." Colorado Quarterly 2 (Autumn 1953),
        181-190.
A good discussion of an imperceptible boundary, with a
gradual transition from Mexican to Anglo culture.

3094   Bustamante, Jorge A. "Emigracion indocumentada a los
        Estados Unidos." Foro Internacional 18 (Jan.-Mar.
        1978), 460-463.

3095   Bustamante, Jorge A. "The Historical Context of the
        Undocumented Immigration from Mexico to the United
        States." Aztlan 3:2 (Fall 1972), 257-281.
Looks at the historical processes of undocumented migration
to the U.S. from an "American" viewpoint. Does not consider
the "push" elements in Mexican society.

3096   Bustamante, Jorge A. "Our Documented Immigration from
        Mexico: Research Report." International Migration
        Review 11:2 (Summer 1977), 149-177.
Discusses the costs and benefits of undocumented migration,
as well as its nature and extent.

3097   Bustamante, Jorge A. "Structural and Ideological
        Conditions of Mexican Undocumented Immigration to the
        United States." American Behavioral Scientist 19:3
        (Jan.-Feb. 1976), 364-376.

3098   Bustamante, Jorge A. "The 'Wetback' as Deviant: An
        Application of Labeling Theory." American Journal of
        Sociology 77 (Jan. 1972), 706-718.
Describes the historical development of the undocumented
immigrant from Mexico and the labeling that straightjackets
his alternatives.

3099   Bustamante, Jorge A. and Geronimo G. Martinez.
        "Undocumented Immigration from Mexico: Beyond Borders
        but Within Systems." Journal of International Affairs
        33:2 (Fall-Winter 1979), 265-284.
A careful survey of undocumented migration with excellent
maps and numerous tables. Useful for the study of causes
and size of migration.

3100   Calderon, Liborio V. "Foreign Assembly Industries in
        Mexico: A Necessary Evil of an Undeveloped Society."
        Paper presented to the Conference on Economic
        Relations Between Mexico and the United States (April
        1973), Austin, Texas.

3101   Calderon, Miguel G. "El problema economico social de
        los braceros." In Mexico-Realizacion y esperanza.
        Mexico, D.F.: Editorial Superacion, 1952.

3102   California, Department of Industrial Relations,
        Division of Fair Employment Practices. "Californians
        of Spanish Surname." San Francisco: California
        Department of Industrial Relations, 1964.
A fifty-four page statistical study; describes changes of
status of Mexican Americans as compared to Anglos.

3103   Calles, Rudy. "Prune Heaven." Pacific Historian 23:1
        (1979), 58-65.
Describes the author's personal experience as a child
migrant worker. Has some excellent photographs.

3104   Cardenas, Gilbert. "Los Desarraigados: Chicanos in
        the Midwestern Region of the United States." Aztlan 7
        (1976), 153-186.
A broad consideration of the history and experience of
Mexican Americans in the Midwest. Includes a number of
valuable tables.

3105   Cardenas, Gilbert. "United States Immigration Policy
        Toward Mexico: An Historical Perspective." Chicano
        Law Review 2 (Summer 1975), 66-91.

3106   Cardenas, Leonard, Jr. "Trends and Problems of
        Urbanization in the United States-Mexico Border Area."
        Conference paper at Inter-American Institute, El Paso:
        University of Texas, June 14-15, 1968.

3107   Carter, Hugh and Bernice Doster. "Residence and
        Occupation of Naturalized Americans from Mexico."
        U.S. Immigration and Naturalization Service, Monthly
        Review 8:4 (Oct. 1950), 47-53.

3108   Castillo, Leonel L. "Dealing With the Undocumented
        Alien--An Interim Approach." International Migration
        Review 12:4 (Winter 1978), 570-577.
Views of the Commissioner of Immigration.

3109   Cazorla, Eugenio. "Employers and Aliens: The Labor
        Certification Process." Texas Bar Journal 38:1 (Jan.
        1975), 41-46.

3110   Chavira, Ricardo. "Immigration 'Reform' Squeezes
        Hispanic Americans." La Luz 9:4 (April-May 1981), 24.
The likelihood of I.D. cards, employer sanctions, and a
beefed-up Border Patrol and their effects on Hispanics.

3111   Chiswick, Barry R. "The Effect of Unemployment
        Compensation on a Seasonal Industry: Agriculture."

Journal of Political Economy 84:3 (June 1976),
591-602.

3112 Cleland, Robert Glass. "Aliens and Nomads." In his
      California in Our Time. New York: Alfred A. Knopf,
      1947.

3113 Cornelius, Wayne A. "Immigration, Mexican Development
      Policy, and the Future of U.S.-Mexican Relations." In
      Mexico and the United States. Edited by Robert H.
      McBride, pp. 104-127. Englewood Cliffs, N.J.:
      Prentice-Hall, 1981.

3114 Cornelius, Wayne A. "Mexican Migration to the United
      States: The View from Rural Sending Communities." In
      Migration and Development Study Group. Cambridge:
      Center for International Studies, Massachusetts
      Institute of Technology, 1976.

3115 Corwin, Arthur F. "Causes of Mexican Emigration to
      the United States: A Summary View." Perspectives in
      American History 7 (1973), 555-635.
Good for recent information on border crossers,
undocumenteds, and immigrants; also on U.S. and Mexican
policy regarding migrants.

3116 Culbert, James L. "Distribution of Spanish-American
      Population in New Mexico." Economic Geography 19
      (April 1943), 171-176.

3117 Davis, Kingsley and Clarence Senior. "Immigration
      from the Western Hemisphere." American Academy of
      Political and Social Science Annals 262 (March 1949),
      70-81.

3118 De Laittre, Karl. "The Mexican Laborer and You."
      Nation's Business 18 (Nov. 1930), 44, 104, 106, 108,
      110.
Describes the importance of Mexicans in Southwestern
economic development.

3119 DeWind, Josh; Tom Seidl; and Janel Shenk. "The New
      Braceros." NACLA Report on the Americas 11:8
      (Nov.-Dec. 1977), 4-9.
Describes the alien worker contract system, with some
emphasis on Caribbean agricultural workers.

3120 Dillman, C. Daniel. "Commuter Workers and Free Zone
      Industry Along the U.S.-Mexican Border." Association
      of American Geographers Proceedings 2 (1970), 48-51.

3121 Duncan, Cameron. "The Runaway Shop and the Mexican
      Border Industrialization Program." Southwest Economy

and Society 2 (Oct.-Nov. 1976), 4-25.

3122   Dunn, J. and J. Ullman. "These Proud Americans:
       Mexican American Migrant Workers." Saturday Evening
       Post 249 (Sept. 1977), 42-44.

3123   Ericson, Anna-Stina. "An Analysis of Mexico's Border
       Industrialization Program." Monthly Labor Review 93
       (May 1970), 33-40.
An informative article with tables and a map; discusses the
policy issues of the B.I.P.

3124   Estrada, Leobardo F. "A Demographic Comparison of the
       Mexican Origin Population in the Midwest and South-
       west." Aztlan 7 (1976), 203-234.
Compares and contrasts the Mexican American population of
the two areas. Some useful tables.

3125   Evans, John S. "Mexican Border Development and Its
       Impact Upon the United States." South Eastern Latin
       Americanist (June 1972), 4-9.

3126   Fallows, Marjorie. "The Mexican-American Laborers: A
       Different Drummer?" Massachusetts Review 8 (Winter
       1967), 166-167. Also in The Aliens: A History of
       Ethnic Minorities in America. Edited by Leonard
       Dinnerstein and Frederick C. Jaher. New York:
       Appleton-Century-Crofts, Inc., 1970.

3127   Federal Reserve Bank of San Francisco. "Factories on
       the Border." Monthly Review (Dec. 1971), 212-216.
Describes the dual plant system encouraged by the Mexican
Border Industrialization Program.

3128   Fernandez, Raul A. "The Border Industrial Program on
       the United States-Mexican Border." Review of Radical
       Political Economics 5:1 (Spring 1973), 37-52.

3129   Fisher, Lloyd H. "Harvest Labor Market in
       California." Quarterly Journal of Economics 65 (Nov.
       1951), 463-491.
Describes California agriculture broadly, especially the
utilization of the domestic labor force as it affects the
demand for foreign workers.

3130   Flannigan, James. "North of the Border--Who Needs
       Whom?" Forbes 119:8 (April 15, 1977), 37-41.
United States-Mexican relations and the immigration issue.

3131   Fogel, Walter A. "Immigrant Mexicans and the U.S.
       Work Force." Monthly Labor Review 98:5 (May 1975),
       44-46.
Argues that the inflow of undocumented workers reduces
incomes and employment security of American workers.

3132   Fogel, Walter A.   "Interstate Differences in the Labor
        Market Experiences of Minority Groups."   Annals of
        Regional Science (Dec. 1967), 243-255.

3133   Form, William; William D'Antonio; and Julius Rivera.
        "The Place of Returning Migrants in a Stratification
        System."   Rural Sociology 23 (Sept. 1958), 286-297.

3134   Fragomen, Austin T., Jr.   "The Undocumented Alien and
        His Aftermath."   International Migration Review 11:2
        (Summer 1977), 241-243.
A brief overview of the general problem of illegal alien
workers.

3135   Frazier, Charles.   "The Migrant Worker and the Bracero
        in the U.S."   In The Role of the Mexican American in
        the History of the Southwest: Conference of the
        Inter-American Institute, Pan American College, pp.
        24-34.   Edinburg, Tex.: Pan American College, 1969.

3136   Freithaler, William O.   "The Economic Development of
        the United States-Mexico Border Region."   Presented at
        the Annual Conference on Problems of Urbanization in
        Latin America.   El Paso, Texas, June, 1968.

3137   Frisbie, Parker.   "Illegal Migration from Mexico to
        the United States: A Longitudinal Analysis."
        International Migration Review 9:1 (Spring 1975),
        3-13.
Describes the various forces impelling migrants and argues
that push factors are more important than pull factors.

3138   Fuller, Varden.   "The Supply of Agricultural Labor as
        a Factor in the Evolution of Farm Organization in
        California."   In Violations of Free Speech and Rights
        of Labor.   Hearings before a Subcommittee of the
        Committee on Education and Labor, United States
        Senate, 76th Cong., 3rd sess.   Washington, D.C.: U.S.
        Government Printing Office, 1940.
Covers the labor force from mission Indians onward.

3139   Galarza, Ernesto.   "The Mexican American: A National
        Concern - Program for Action."   Common Ground 9:4
        (Summer 1949), 27-38.

3140   Galarza, Ernesto.   "They Work for Pennies."   American
        Federationist 59 (April 1952), 10-13.

3141   Gandara, Arturo.   "Chicanos y estranjeros ilegales: la
        conjuncion de sus derechos constitucionales frente al
        estado nortemericano."   Foro Internacional 18
        (Jan.-March 1978), 480-493.

3142   Garcia y Griego, Manuel.   "Estimating the Undocumented
        Population in the U.S."   La Red/The Net 58 (Sept.
        1982), 7-8, 17.
Includes a table showing a number of recent estimates and
points up the fact that there is little solid basis for any
estimate of the number of undocumented Mexicans in the U.S.

3143   Gilmore, N. Ray and Gladys W. Gilmore.   "The Bracero
        in California."   Pacific Historical Review 32 (Aug.
        1963), 265-282.
A brief history of agricultural labor in California,
centering on the second bracero program beginning in 1951.
Questions impact of the bracero program.

3144   Goethe, C. M.   "Immigration from Mexico."   In The
        Alien in Our Midst.   Edited by Madison Grant and
        Charles S. Davison, pp. 134-142.   New York: Galton
        Publishing Co., 1930.
Gives an anti-immigration viewpoint.   Goethe was the
president of the Immigration Study Commission.

3145   Gordon, Wendell.   "A Case for a Less Restrictive
        Border Policy."   Social Science Quarterly 56:3 (Dec.
        1975), 485-491.
Argues that estimates of undocumented aliens are grossly
inflated and that there is no proof they take jobs from
American citizens.

3146   Greene, Sheldon L.   "Immigration Law and Rural
        Poverty--The Problems of the Illegal Immigrant."   Duke
        Law Journal 3 (1969), 475-494.

3147   Gregg, Ralph.   "Medical Examination and Vaccination of
        Farm Laborers Recruited from Mexico."   Public Health
        Reports 65 (June 23, 1950), 807-809.

3148   Gregory, David D.   "A U.S.-Mexican Temporary Workers
        Program: The Search for a Co-Determination."   In
        Mexico and the United States.   Edited by Robert H.
        McBride, pp. 158-177.   Englewood Cliffs, N.J.:
        Prentice-Hall, 1981.

3149   Guerra Maram, Marti.   "The Media and the Undocumented
        Immigrant."   Proceedings of the Pacific Coast Council
        on Latin American Studies 8 (1981-1982), 143-152.
Criticizes media accuracy in covering undocumented worker
stories and issues.

3150   Hadley, Eleanor M.   "A Critical Analysis of the
        Wetback Problem."   Law and Contemporary Problems 21
        (1956), 334-357.
Describes the issue between 1944 and 1954; stresses the
conflict between growers' "needs" and national policy.

3151   Heer, David M.   "What is the Annual Net Flow of
       Undocumented Mexican Immigrants to the United States?"
       Demography 16:3 (Aug. 1979), 417-423.

3152   Hill, James E.   "El Chamizal: A Century-Old Boundary
       Dispute." Geographical Review 55 (1965), 510-522.

3153   Hinga, D.   "Rio Grande, River of Death." Colliers 118
       (Aug. 17, 1946), 24-26.
Describes the economic problems of Mexican immigrants.

3154   Hirschman, Charles.   "Prior U.S. Residence Among
       Mexican Americans." Social Forces 56 (1978),
       1179-1203.
Concludes that prior residence, often as an undocumented, is
a common step toward legal migration and also may lead to
impediments in acquiring higher socio-economic position.

3155   "Hit and Run, U.S. Runaway Shops on the Mexican
       Border." NACLA's Latin America and Empire Report 9:5
       (July-Aug. 1975).

3156   Hoffman, Abraham.   "An Unusual Monument: Paul S.
       Taylor's Mexican Labor in the United States Monograph
       Series." Pacific Historical Review 45:2 (April-June
       1976), 255-270.
Describes Taylor's seminal work and his methodology.

3157   Humphrey, Norman D.   "Employment Patterns of Mexicans
       in Detroit." Monthly Review 61 (1946), 913-923.

3158   "Illegal Mexican Immigrants to the United States."
       International Migration Review 12:4 (Winter 1978),
       469-613.
A special issue edited by Alejandro Portes.

3159   "Immigrant as Scapegoat." America 132:4 (Feb. 1,
       1975), 65.
Describes the conditions faced by the undocumented alien and
argues for a realistic, yet compassionate, response.

3160   "The In-Bond Industry." Review of the Economic
       Situation of Mexico 57:669 (Aug. 1981), 283-290.
       Mexico, D.F.: Banco Nacional de Mexico.
A comparative study placing Mexico's border industry in
world-wide context.

3161   Iwanska, A.   "Emigrantes o commuters?" America
       Indigena 33:1 (Summer 1973), 457-469.

3162   Jacobs, Paul.   "The Forgotten People." Reporter 20
       (Jan. 22, 1959), 13-20.
A general article on the poor economic status of farm

workers.

3163 Jenkins, J. Craig. "The Demand for Immigrant Workers:
      Labor Scarcity or Social Control?" _International_
      Migration Review 12:4 (Winter 1978), 514-535.

3164 Jones, Lamar B. "Labor and Management in California
      Agriculture, 1864-1964." _Labor History_ 11:1 (Winter
      1970), 23-40.

3165 Keely, Charles B. "Counting the Uncountable:
      Estimates of Undocumented Aliens in the United
      States." _Population and Development Review_ 3 (Dec.
      1977), 473-482.

3166 Keely, Charles B. "The Estimation of the Immigration
      Component of Population Growth." _International_
      Migration Review 8:3 (Fall 1974), 431-435.
A general consideration of all immigration as a component.

3167 Kelly, Willard F. "The Wetback Issue." _Immigration_
      and Naturalization Reporter 2:3 (Jan. 1954), 37-39.

3168 Kibbe, Pauline R. "The Economic Plight of Mexicans."
      In _Ethnic Relations in the United States_. Edited by
      Ed C. McDonagh and E. S. Richards, pp. 174-200. New
      York: Appleton-Century-Crofts, 1953.
A good account of post-war undocumented worker problems in
Texas.

3169 Knebel, Stanley M. "Restrictive Immigration
      Standards: Probable Impact on Mexican Alien Commuter."
      U.S. Department of Labor, _Farm Labor Developments_
      (Nov. 1968), 8-16.

3170 Korcik, William. "The Wetback Story." _Commonweal_ 54
      (June 13, 1951), 327-329.
Describes various problems facing the undocumented migratory
worker.

3171 Koziara, Karen S. "Collective Bargaining on the
      Farm." _Monthly Labor Review_ 91:6 (June 1968), 3-9.
Discusses mechanization, declining employment, unions and
collective bargaining.

3172 Leberthon, Ted. "At the Prevailing Rate." _Commonweal_
      67 (Nov. 1, 1957), 122-125.

3173 Longcope, Kay. "Long-term Trends in Foreign-worker
      Employment." _Farm Labor Developments_ (Feb. 1968),
      11-14.
A publication of the Manpower Administration of the
Department of Labor.

3174   Lopez, David T.   "Low-wage Lures South of the Border."
       American Federationist 76 (June 1969), 1-7.

3175   Lopez Malo, Ernesto.   "The Emigration of Mexican
       Laborers."   Ciencias Sociales 5 (Oct. 1954), 220-227.

3176   Lucey, (Rev.) Robert E.   "Badge of Infamy."   Extension
       53 (June 1958), 20-21.
Article on Mexican immigrant workers by the archbishop of
San Antonio.

3177   Lucey, (Rev.) Robert E.   "Migratory Workers."
       Commonweal 59 (Jan. 15, 1954), 370-373.
Archbishop Lucey describes the situation of migratory
workers as a scandal of greed and politics.

3178   La Luz 7:2 (Feb. 1978).
The entire issue is devoted to the problems of Mexican
immigration.

3179   McDonagh, Edward C.   "Attitudes Toward Ethnic Farm
       Workers in Coachella Valley."   Sociology and Social
       Research 40 (Sept. 1955), 10-18.

3180   McDonnell, (Rev.) Donald C.   "The Bracero Program in
       California."   In Ninth Regional Conference, Catholic
       Council for the Spanish Speaking, April 15-17, 1958,
       pp. 11-17.   San Antonio, Tex.: Schneider Printing Co.,
       1958.

3181   Maciel, David.   "Mexican Migrant Workers in the United
       States."   In American Labor in the Southwest: The
       First One Hundred Years.   Edited by James C. Foster.
       Tucson: University of Arizona Press, 1982.

3182   Madrid-Barela, Arturo.   "Alambristas, Braceros,
       Mojados, Norteños: Aliens in Aztlan."   Aztlan 6:1
       (Spring 1975), 27-42.
A discussion of three novels about border-crossers from
Mexico: Luis Spota, Murieron a mitad del rio; Edmund
Villasenor, Macho; Claud Garner, Wetback.

3183   Maitland, Sheridan T. and Stanley M. Knebel.   "Rural
       to Urban Transition."   Monthly Labor Review 21 (June
       1968), 28-32.

3184   Mano, D. K.   "Migrants."   National Review 28 (Oct. 29,
       1976), 1185-1186.
Describes some of the general problems of migrant
agricultural workers.

3185   Martinez, Oscar J.   "Chicanos and the Border Cities:
       An Interpretive Essay."   Pacific Historical Review 46
       (Feb. 1977), 85-106.

Discusses the unique functions of U.S.-Mexican border cities and argues that Chicanos are disadvantaged by them. Opposes massive deportations as a solution to the problem of undocumenteds.

3186 Martinez, Vilma S. "Illegal Immigration and the Labor Force: An Historical and Legal View." American Behavioral Scientist 19:3 (Jan.-Feb. 1973), 335-350.
The author was president of the Mexican American Legal Defense and Education Fund.

3187 Mejido, Manuel. "Las Fronteras." In his Mexico Amargo, pp. 189-239. Mexico, D.F.: Siglo Veintiuno Editores, S.A., 1973.
Discusses conditions in Mexican border towns and the illegal traffic in workers with its criminal element. Also some material on the border with Guatemala.

3188 "The Mexican-American." Economist 156 (June 18, 1949), 1139-1140.

3189 Mexican and Mexican American Migrants. A special issue of the International Migration Review 5 (Fall 1971). New York: Center for Migration Studies.
Includes bibliographical material.

3190 "Mexico--The Special Case." Center Magazine 10:4 (July-Aug. 1977), 67-80.

3191 "Migration of the Mexican Bracero." Review of the Economic Situation of Mexico 47 (Jan. 1971), 14-18. Mexico, D.F.: Banco Nacional de Mexico.

3192 "The Migratory Farm Worker." Monthly Labor Review 91:6 (June 1968), 10-13.
Surveys the characteristics of migrant farm workers and describes their problems.

3193 Mitchell, H. L. "Workers in Agriculture." American Federationist 63 (Aug. 1956), 26-29.

3194 Monroy, Douglas. "An Essay on Understanding the Work Experience of Mexicans in Southern California, 1900-1939." Aztlan 12:1 (Spring 1981), 59-74.
A general essay which concludes that the Mexican work experience generally was morally debilitating.

3195 Newman, Robert and Barton Smith. "Depressed Wages Along the U.S.-Mexican Border: An Empirical Analysis." Economic Inquiry 15 (Jan. 1977), 51-66.

3196 Nieto-Gomez, Ana. "Chicanas in the Labor Force." Encuentro Femenil 1 (1974).

3197   "North of the Border." Economist 263:6976 (May 14,
       1977), 96-98.
(Pages 24-26 in insert titled: The Third State, A Survey of
Texas.) Briefly describes migration and the Texas Chicano
community.

3198   Obledo, Mario G. "It's Not Too Late for a
       Barrier-free Border: An Analysis." La Luz 9:4
       (April-May 1981), 26.
The founder of the National Coalition of Hispanic
Organizations calls on Mexico and the United States to
recognize their interdependence and suggests some steps to
be taken.

3199   "Organizing Farm Workers." America 126:23 (June 10,
       1972), 604-605.
Centers on Arizona legislation aimed at emasculating farm
labor organizations and Cesar Chavez's response with a fast.

3200   Ortega, Joe C. "Plight of the Mexican Wetback."
       American Bar Association Journal 58 (March 1972),
       251-254.

3201   Panger, Daniel. "The Forgotten Ones." Progressive 27
       (April 1963), 20-23.
San Joaquin Valley, California, farm migrants.

3202   Peña, Devon Gerardo. "Las maquiladoras: Mexican Women
       and Class Struggle in the Border Industries." Aztlan
       11:2 (Fall 1980), 159-229.
An overview of the establishment of the Border
Industrialization Program by Mexico in 1965 and especially
the development of maquiladoras.

3203   Petersen, William. "A General Typology of Migration."
       American Sociological Review 23 (June 1958), 256-266.

3204   Piore, Michael J. "Impact of Immigration on the Labor
       Force." Monthly Labor Review 98:5 (May 1975), 41-44.
Considers all immigration (most of it undocumented) but
bases his views on a study of Puerto Ricans in Boston.

3205   Portes, Alejandro. "Illegal Immigration and the
       International System: Lessons from Recent Legal
       Mexican Immigrants to the United States." Social
       Problems 26:4 (April 1979), 425-438.

3206   Portes, Alejandro. "La inmigracion y el sistema
       internacional: algunas caracteristicas de los
       mexicanos recientemente emigrados a Estados Unidos."
       Revista Mexicana de Sociologia 41:4 (Oct.-Dec. 1979),
       1257-1277.

3207   Portes, Alejandro. "Labor Functions of Illegal
        Aliens." Society 14 (Sept.-Oct. 1977), 31-37.

3208   Portes, Alejandro. "Toward a Structural Analysis of
        Illegal (Undocumented) Immigration." International
        Migration Review 12:4 (Winter 1978), 469-484.

3209   Poston, Dudley L., Jr. and David Alvirez. "On the
        Cost of Being a Mexican American Worker." Social
        Science Quarterly 53:4 (March 1973), 697-709.

3210   Reubens, Edwin P. "Illegal Immigration and the
        Mexican Economy." Challenge 21 (Nov.-Dec. 1978),
        13-19.

3211   Reynoso, Cruz. "A Dissenting View to U.S. Immigration
        Study." La Luz 9:6 (Aug.-Sept. 1981), 20-21.

3212   Rischin, Moses. "Beyond the Great Divide: Immigration
        and the Last Frontier." Journal of American History
        55 (June 1968), 42-53.
Discusses the uniqueness of California's immigrant
population and briefly details its problems and prospects.

3213   Rischin, Moses. "Immigration, Migration and
        Minorities in California: A Reassessment." Pacific
        Historical Review 41 (Feb. 1972), 71-90.

3214   Rivera, George, Jr. and Juventino Mejia. "Mas aya del
        ancho rio: Mexicanos in Western New York." Aztlan 7:3
        (Fall 1976), 499-513.
A demographic study with brief historical background.
Considers occupations, self-identification, and feeling of
discrimination.

3215   Roberts, Shirley J. "Minority-Group Poverty in
        Phoenix: A Socio-Economic Survey." Journal of Arizona
        History 14 (Winter 1973), 347-362.

3216   Robinson, J. Gregory. "Estimating the Illegal Alien
        Population in the United States by the Comparative
        Trend Analysis of Age-Specific Death Rates."
        Demography 17:2 (1980), 159-176.

3217   Rooney, James F. "The Effect of Imported Mexican Farm
        Labor in a California County." American Journal of
        Economics and Sociology 20 (Oct. 1961), 513-521.
Includes a bibliography.

3218   Ross, Stanley R. "Key Issues in Mexican-United States
        Relations: The Border That Unites and Divides Us."
        Texas Business Review 53 (March-April 1979), 41-53.

3219   Rowan, Helen. "A Minority Nobody Knows." _Atlantic_
       219:6 (June 1967), 47-52.
Good on urban and political aspects of the Mexican American
experience.

3220   "Rural Workers in America." _Monthly Labor Review_ 91
       (June 1968), 1-32.
Includes a bibliography.

3221   Saloutos, Theodore. "The Immigrant Contribution to
       American Agriculture." _Agricultural History_ 50:1
       (Jan. 1976), 45-67.
Only briefly considers the Mexican contribution.

3222   Samora, Julian. "Mexican Immigration." In _Mexican_
       Americans Tomorrow. Edited by Gus Taylor, pp. 60-80.
       Albuquerque: University of New Mexico Press, 1975.

3223   Sanchez, Rosaura. "The Chicana Labor Force." In
       Essays on La Mujer. Edited by Rosaura Sanchez and
       Rosa Martinez Cruz, pp. 3-15. Los Angeles: Chicano
       Studies Center, University of California, 1977.

3224   Sepulveda, Ciro. "Research Note: Una colonia de
       obreros, East Chicago, Indiana." _Aztlan_ 7:2 (Summer
       1976), 327-336.
A brief overview of the midwestern Mexicano experience.
Includes a map.

3225   Servin, Manuel P. and Robert L. Spude. "Historical
       Conditions of Early Mexican Labor in the United
       States: Arizona--A Neglected Story." _Journal of_
       Mexican American History 5 (1975), 43-56.
Describes the employment of Mexican workers in gold, silver,
and copper mining down to World War I. Emphasizes the dual
wage system.

3226   Shannon, Lyle. "The Study of Migrants as Members of
       Social Systems." American Ethnological Society
       Proceedings (1968). Also in _Spanish-Speaking People_
       in the United States. Edited by June Helm, pp. 34-64.
       Seattle: University of Washington Press, 1968.

3227   Shannon, Lyle W. and Elaine M. Krass. "The Economic
       Absorption of Immigrant Laborers in a Northern
       Industrial Community." _American Journal of Economics_
       and Sociology 23:1 (Jan. 1964), 65-84.
A study of adjustments by rural Mexican Americans in Racine,
Wisconsin.

3228   Silva, Luciano V. "Characteristics of Mexican
       Immigration." _12th Annual Conference Journal_, pp.
       14-16. Los Angeles: Committee for the Protection of
       the Foreign Born, 1962.

3229   Silva, Luciano V. "Recent Developments in Mexican
        Immigration." 13th Annual Conference Journal, pp.
        17-20. Los Angeles: Committee for the Protection of
        the Foreign Born, 1963.

3230   Slade, Santiago. "From Michoacan to Southern
        California: The Story of an Undocumented Mexican."
        Southwest Economy and Society 3 (Fall 1977).

3231   Slatta, Richard W. "Chicanos in the Pacific
        Northwest: A Demographic and Socioeconomic Portrait."
        Pacific Northwest Quarterly 70 (1979), 155-162.

3232   Sloan, John W. and Jonathan P. West. "The Role of
        Informal Policy Making in U.S.-Border Cities." Social
        Science Quarterly 58:2 (Sept. 1977), 270-282,

3233   Smith, T. L. "Farm Labour Trends in the U.S.,
        1910-1969." International Labour Review 102 (Aug.
        1970), 149-169.

3234   Soto, Anthony. "The Bracero Story." Commonweal 71
        (Nov. 27, 1959), 258-260.
Describes the process by which Mexicans came to the United
States as braceros.

3235   Spradlin, T. Richard. "The Mexican Farm Labor
        Importation Program: Review and Reform." George
        Washington Law Review 30 (Dec. 1961), 84-122.

3236   Stegner, Wallace. "Okies in Sombreros: Migrant
        Mexican Crop Workers." In his One Nation, pp. 95-116.
        Boston: Houghton-Mifflin Co., 1945.

3237   Stocking, Collis. "Adjusting Immigration to Manpower
        Requirements." American Academy of Political and
        Social Sciences Annals 262 (March 1949), 114-123.

3238   Stoddard, Ellwyn R. "An Alternate Strategy for
        Resolving Illegal Mexican Alien Policies." Paper
        presented to the National Symposium on Immigration and
        Public Policy (April 1977), Houston, Texas.

3239   Stoddard, Ellwyn R. "Border and Non-border Illegal
        Mexican Aliens: A Commentary." Southwest Business and
        Economic Review 16 (May 1979), 21-27.

3240   Stoddard, Ellwyn R. "A Conceptualized Analysis of the
        'Alien Invasion': Institutionalized Support of Illegal
        Mexicans in the U.S." International Migration Review
        10:2 (Summer 1976), 157-189.
Carefully explores the many aspects of working toward a
satisfactory immigration policy in regard to undocumented

Mexicans.

3241   Stoddard, Ellwyn R.   "Illegal Mexican Aliens in
       Borderlands Society." Paper presented to the Society
       for the Study of Social Problems (Sept. 1978), San
       Francisco.

3242   Stoddard, Ellwyn R.   "Illegal Mexican Labor in the
       Borderlands: Institutionalized Support of an Unlawful
       Practice." Pacific Sociological Review 19 (April
       1976), 175-210.

3243   Stoddard, Ellwyn R.   "Northern Mexican Migration and
       the U.S.-Mexico Border Region." New Scholar 9 (Summer
       1982), in press.

3244   Stoddard, Ellwyn R.   "The Status of Borderland
       Studies: Sociology and Anthropology." Social Science
       Journal 12:3 (Oct. 1975)/ 13:1 (Jan. 1976), 29-54.
Describes the problems of the border region and its
literature. This double issue contains over 100 pages on
the status of the borderlands.

3245   Stoddard, Ellwyn R.   "The United States-Mexico Border
       as a Research Laboratory." Journal of Inter-American
       Studies 2 (July 1969), 477-488.

3246   Street, Richard S.   "The Economist as Humanist--the
       Career of Paul S. Taylor." California History 58:4
       (Winter 1979-1980), 350-361.
A brief description of the life and important work of Paul
S. Taylor in labor economics, especially in Chicano and
Mexican labor in the United States.

3247   Sturmthal, Adolph. "Economic Development, Income
       Distribution, and Capital Formation in Mexico."
       Journal of Political Economy 43 (June 1955), 185.
Describes some push factors in emigration.

3248   Swing, J. M. "A Workable Labor Program." Immigration
       and Naturalization Reporter 4 (Nov. 1955), 15-16.

3249   Szymanski, Albert. "The Growing Role of Spanish
       Speaking Workers in the U.S. Economy." Aztlan 9
       (1978), 177-208.
Compares the roles of Black and Spanish-speaking workers.
Numerous tables.

3250   Taylor, Paul S.   "Immigrant Groups in Western
       Agriculture." Agricultural History 41:1 (Jan. 1975),
       179-181.

3251   Taylor, Paul S.   "Songs of the Mexican Migration." In
       Puro Mexicano. Edited by J. Frank Dobie, pp. 241-245.

Austin: Texas Folklore Society, 1934.

3252 Taylor, Paul S. and Tom Vasey. "Historical Background
      of California Farm Labor." Rural Sociology 1:3 (Sept.
      1936), 281-295.
A broad historical survey with a number of excellent tables
and graphs.

3253 Thompson, A. N. "Mexican Immigrant Workers in
      Southwestern Agriculture." American Journal of
      Economics and Sociology 16 (Oct. 1956), 73-81.

3254 Thunder, J. A. "Feature X: System of Mexican Contract
      Laborers." America 89 (Sept. 1953), 599-600.
A letter from a border farmer pointing out that bracero
labor is of little use to small farmers and advocating an
"open border" policy.

3255 "Treatment of Immigrant Labor." United Nations
      Bulletin 7 (Nov. 1, 1949), 553-562.

3256 Turner, William. "No Dice for Braceros." Ramparts 7
      (Jan. 25, 1969), 37-40.

3257 Turner, William and John Beecher. "Bracero Politics:
      A Special Report: 'No Dice for Braceros,' by Turner;
      'To the Rear, March! -- 1965-1940,' by Beecher."
      Ramparts 4 (Sept. 1965), 14-32.

3258 U.S., Congress, Congressional Record. 89th Cong., 1st
      sess., March 9, 1965, 111, pt. 4; 4472-4484.
      "Agricultural Labor Shortage."

3259 U.S., Congress, Senate, Congressional Record, 91st
      Cong., 1st sess., March 26, 1979, 3300-3306.
      "Introduction of a Bill to Amend the Immigration and
      Nationality Act--Alien Commuter (Green Card) System."

3260 U.S., Congress, Senate, Congressional Record, 91st
      Cong., 1st sess., July 8, 1969, 7685-7686. "Mexican
      Nationalist Labor," by Walter Mondale.

3261 Valdez, Lorenzo. "Labor History in the Villages." El
      Cuaderno 3 (Spring 1974), 4.

3262 Van der Spek, Peter. "Mexico's Booming Border Zone: A
      Magnet for Labor Intensive American Plants."
      Inter-American Economic Affairs 29 (Summer 1975),
      33-47.

3263 Verdugo, Naomi. "The Bracero Program: A History of
      Foreign Contract Labor in California." Agenda: A
      Journal of Hispanic Issues 4:2 (Fourth Quarter 1981),
      9-13.

A summary history of Mexican immigration, the bracero program, and post-bracero developments.

3264   Vialet, Joyce. "Legislation Concerning Illegal Aliens." In Illegal Aliens: An Assessment of the Issues. Washington, D.C.: National Council on Employment Policy, 1976.

3265   Waddle, Paula. "The Legislative and Judicial Response to the Immigration of Undocumented Workers." South Texas Journal of Research and the Humanities 1 (Fall 1977), 177-210.

3266   Watanabe, Susume. "Constraints on Labor-Intensive Export Industries in Mexico." International Labour Review 109 (Jan.-June 1974), 23-45.
Includes information on the U.S.-Mexican border in-bond industries, the maquiladoras.

3267   Waters, Lawrence L. "Transient Mexican Agricultural Labor." Southwestern Social Science Quarterly 22 (1941), 49-66.

3268   Watson, Don. "An Historical Look at the IBT." El Malcriado (July 31, 1974); (Sept. 4, 1974).
A critical look at the Teamsters union development.

3269   West, Jonathan P. "Informal Policy Making Along the Arizona-Mexico International Border." Arizona Review 27 (Feb. 1978), 1-8.

3270   "Wetbacks: Can the States Act to Curb Illegal Entry?" Stanford Law Review 6 (March 1954), 287-322.

3271   Whalen, William A. "The Wetback Problem in Southwest Texas." Mexican Review 8:8 (Feb. 1951), 103-105.
Describes problems of the Immigration and Naturalization Service.

3272   Whitehead, Carlton J. and Albert S. King. "Differences in Managers' Attitudes Toward Mexican and Non-Mexican Americans in Organizational Authority Relations." Social Science Quarterly 53:4 (March 1973), 760-771.

3273   Wiest, Raymond E. "Wage-Labor Migration and the Household in a Mexican Town." Journal of Anthropological Research 29:3 (Autumn 1973), 180-209.

3274   Williams, J. Allen, Jr.; Peter G. Beeson; and David R. Johnson. "Some Factors Associated with Income Among Mexican Americans." Social Science Quarterly 53:4 (March 1973), 710-715.
Concludes that socioeconomic handicaps explain the lower

income of Chicanos.

3275   Wise, Donald E.   "The Effect of the Bracero on
       Agricultural Production in California."   Economic
       Inquiry 12 (Dec. 1974), 547-558.

VIII.
CIVIL RIGHTS
AND POLITICS

Books

Section VIII covers works on political organizations and their leaders, on educational and voting rights, on racism, prejudice, and discrimination, and general histories of the struggles of minorities and ethnic groups.

3276 Abelardo [Abelardo Delgado Barrientos]. The Chicano Movement: Some Not Too Objective Observations. Denver, Colo.: Migrant Council, 1971.
Views of an outstanding Chicano poet.

3277 Achor, Shirley. Mexican Americans in a Dallas Barrio. Tucson: University of Arizona Press, 1978.
A revision of the author's 1974 Southern Methodist University thesis describing politics and social conditions. Good bibliography.

3278 Almanza, Arturo S. Mexican-Americans and Civil Rights. Los Angeles: County Commission on Human Relations, 1964.

3279 Alvarado, Roger, et al. Why a Chicano Party? Why Chicano Studies? New York: Pathfinder Press, 1970.

3280 Ambrecht, Biliana C. Politicizing the Poor: The Legacy of the War on Poverty in a Mexican-American Community. New York: Praeger Publishers, 1976.
Deals with East Los Angeles economic conditions and political participation by Advisory Council members.

3281 Aragon de Shepro, Theresa. Chicanismo and Mexican American Politics. Seattle: Centro de Estudios

Chicanos, University of Washington, 1971.
A brief survey of Chicano history with emphasis on the
development of political chicanismo.

3282   Baird, Frank L., ed. Mexican Americans: Political
       Power, Influence, or Resource. Lubbock: Texas
       Technological University Press, 1977.
A series of lectures and essays on Chicano suffrage and
politics.

3283   Barron, Milton L. American Minorities. New York:
       Alfred A. Knopf, 1957.
One section addresses the problems of Hispanics and their
political weakness.

3284   Baruch, Dorothy. The Glass House of Prejudice. New
       York: William Morrow & Co., 1946.

3285   Belenchia, Joanna M. Latinos and Chicago Politics.
       Evanston, Ill.: Center for Urban Affairs, Northwestern
       University, 1979.

3286   Blauner, Robert. Racial Oppression in America. New
       York: Harper & Row Publishers, 1972.

3287   Brace, Clayton, et al. Federal Programs to Improve
       Mexican American Education. Washington, D.C.: U.S.
       Office of Education, 1967.

3288   Brown, George H., et al. The Condition of Education
       for Hispanic Americans. Washington, D.C.: U.S.
       Government Printing Office, 1980.
An excellent statistical study.

3289   Carter, Thomas P. Mexican Americans in School: A
       History of Educational Neglect. New York: College
       Entrance Examinations Board, 1970.
A valuable discussion of public education and its relations
to Chicanos. See item 2161.

3290   Caughey, John W. Their Majesties the Mob. Chicago:
       University of Chicago Press, 1960.
Describes cases of vigilantism against Mexican Americans in
California and other parts of the West.

3291   Chalmers, David M. Hooded Americanism. Garden City,
       N.Y.: Doubleday & Co., 1965.
Includes the Matias and Fidel Elduayen case in Los Angeles
in 1922.

3292   Cole, K. W., ed. Minority Organizations: A National
       Directory. Garrett Park, Md.: Garrett Park Press,
       1978.
A list of 3,000 organizations with brief descriptions or

comments.   Also has useful geographical and functional
indexes.

3293   Cooke, W. Henry.   People of the Southwest: Patterns of
       Freedom and Prejudice.   New York: Anti-Defamation
       League of B'nai B'rith, 1951.
A thirty-six page pamphlet.

3294   Cornelius, Wayne A.   Mexican Migration to the United
       States: The Limits of Government Intervention.
       Mimeographed.   San Diego: United States-Mexican
       Studies, University of California, 1981.

3295   Daniels, Roger and Harry H. L. Kitano.   American
       Racism: Exploration of the Nature of Prejudice.
       Englewood Cliffs, N.J.: Prentice-Hall, 1970.
An in-depth study which includes material on Mexican
Americans.

3296   Dinnerstein, Leonard and Frederic C. Jaher, eds.
       Uncertain Americans: Reading in Ethnic History.   New
       and revised edition.   New York: Oxford University
       Press, 1977.
An updating of item 2910.

3297   Dinnerstein, Leonard; David M. Reimers; and Roger L.
       Nichols.   Natives and Strangers: Ethnic Groups and the
       Building of America.   New York: Oxford University
       Press, 1979.

3298   Documents of the Chicano Struggle.   New York:
       Pathfinder Press, 1971.
A collection emphasizing voting rights and politics.

3299   Garcia, F. Chris, comp.   La Causa Politica: A Chicano
       Politics Reader.   Notre Dame, Ind.: University of
       Notre Dame Press, 1974.
A collection of essays on politics and the vote.

3300   Garcia, F. Chris, ed.   Chicano Politics.   New York:
       MSS Information Corp., 1973.
Describes political activism including that of Cesar Chavez,
Fernando Peñalosa, and George Rivera.

3301   Garcia, F. Chris.   The Political Socialization of
       Chicano Children.   New York: Praeger Publishers, 1973.

3302   Garcia, F. Chris and Rudolph O. de la Garza.   The
       Chicano Political Experience: Three Perspectives.
       North Scituate, Mass.: Duxbury Press, 1977.
Presents a socio-political study of Chicano political
experiences.

3303   Garner, Van Hastings. Conflict and Resistance: The
        Chicano in the Twentieth Century. St. Charles, Mo.:
        Forum Press, 1974.
Volume one in Forums in History.

3304   Garza, Edward D. LULAC: League of United Latin
        American Citizens. San Francisco: R & E Research
        Associates, 1972.
A 1951 master's thesis, describing the history, structure,
and objectives of LULAC.

3305   Gonzalez, Isabel. Stepchildren of a Nation: The
        Status of Mexican-Americans. New York: American
        Committee for Protection of Foreign Born, 1947.
        Reprinted as part of The Mexican-American and the Law.
        New York: Arno Press, 1974, item 3322.

3306   Gutierrez, Jose Angel. A Gringo Manual on How to
        Handle Mexicans. Crystal City, Tex.: Wintergarden,
        1973.
A long essay on race discrimination, especially in Texas, by
the principal founder of La Raza Unida.

3307   Gutierrez, Jose Angel. El Politico: The
        Mexican-American Elected Official. El Paso, Tex.:
        Mictla Publications, 1972.
Views of one of the principal founders and later president
of La Raza Unida.

3308   Guzman, Ralph C. The Political Socialization of the
        Mexican American People. New York: Arno Press, 1976.
Reprint of the author's 1970 thesis. Describes
organizational efforts, leadership, voting patterns, and
ideologies. By a leading activist scholar in the field.

3309   Hein, Marjorie. Strictly Ghetto Property: The Story
        of Los Siete de la Raza. Berkeley, Calif.: Ramparts
        Press, 1972.

3310   Hernandez, Jose Amaro. Mutual Aid for Survival: The
        Case of the Mexican American. Melbourne, Fla.:
        Krieger Publishing Co., 1983.
A valuable study of community organization, political
thought and behavior, and social welfare with emphasis on
the political side of mutualist societies.

3311   Hirsch, Herbert and Armando Gutierrez. Learning to be
        Militant: Ethnic Identity and the Development of
        Political Militance in a Chicano Community. San
        Francisco: R & E Research Associates, 1977.

3312 Hispanic Americans and the Crisis in the Nation.
      Philadelphia, Penn.: Office of Church and Society,
      1969.
Twelve pages on contemporary problems, with recommendations
for solving them.

3313 House, John W. Frontier on the Rio Grande: A
      Political Geography of Development and Social
      Deprivation. New York: Oxford University Press, 1982.
Interprets the international nature of the border zone, its
people, politics, resources, and economy. Contrasts
development and deprivation in this area that is neither the
United States nor Mexico.

3314 Howard, John R., ed. Awakening Minorities: American
      Indians, Mexican Americans, Puerto Ricans. Chicago:
      Aldine Publishing Co., 1970.
A collection of essays including two on Chicano political
activism.

3315 Key, V. O. Southern Politics in State and Nation.
      New York: Alfred A. Knopf, 1949.
Discusses the Mexican American role in Texas politics.

3316 Kurtz, Donald V. The Politics of a Poverty Habitat.
      Cambridge, Mass.: Ballinger, 1973.
Centers on the California border town of San Ysidro;
describes the relationship of ethnicity and politics.

3317 Larralde, Carlos. Carlos Esparza: A Chicano
      Chronicle. San Francisco: R & E Research Associates,
      1977.
The life story of an important Tejano literary figure who
supported the liberation movement of Juan Cortina in the
third quarter of the nineteenth century.

3318 Lemert, Edwin M. Administration of Justice to
      Minority Groups in Los Angeles County. Berkeley:
      University of California Press, 1948.

3319 Loomis, Nellie Holmes. Spanish-Anglo Ethnic Cleavage
      in a New Mexican High School. Ann Arbor, Mich.:
      University Microfilms, 1955.

3320 McEntire, Davis. Residence and Race: . . . Report to
      the Commission on Race and Housing. Berkeley:
      University of California Press, 1960.
Includes materials on discrimination against Mexican
Americans in housing, with maps, diagrams, tables, and an
excellent bibliography.

3321   Masuoka, Jitsuichi. _Race Relations: Problems and_
       Theory. Chapel Hill: University of North Carolina
       Press, 1961.
Devotes a chapter to Mexican American civil rights problems.

3322   _The Mexican-American and the Law_. New York: Arno
       Press, 1974.
An anthology containing eight works on the various problems
of Mexican-Americans and the U.S. legal system. They range
from dispassionate analyses to fervent demands for justice.

3323   Minnesota. Governor's Human Rights Commission. _The_
       Mexican in Minnesota: A Report to Governor C. Elmer
       Anderson by the Governor's Interracial Council. St.
       Paul, Minn.: Governor's Human Rights Commission, 1953.
       Reprint, San Francisco: R & E Research Associates,
       1979.

3324   Moore, Joan W. and Frank Mittelbach. _Residential_
       Segregation in the Urban Southwest. Los Angeles:
       Mexican American Study Project, University of
       California, 1966.

3325   _La otra cara de Mexico: el pueblo chicano_. Compiled
       by David R. Maciel. Mexico, D.F.: Ediciones El
       Caballito, 1970.

3326   Peñalosa, Fernando. _Class Consciousness and Social_
       Mobility in a Mexican-American Community. San
       Francisco: R & E Research Associates, 1971.
As they existed in the early 1960s in Pomona, California.
Bibliography.

3327   Pendas, Miguel. _Chicano Liberation and Socialism_.
       New York: Pathfinder Press, 1976.

3328   _La Raza Unida_. Lansing, Mich.: Raza Unida Party,
       1973.

3329   _La Raza Unida Party in Texas_. New York: Pathfinder
       Press, 1970.
A Merit pamphlet.

3330   Rodriguez, Olga, ed. _The Politics of Chicano_
       Liberation. New York: Pathfinder Press, 1977.

3331   Rodriguez, Roy C. _Mexican-American Civic_
       Organizations: Political Participation and Political
       Attitudes. San Francisco: R & E Research Associates,
       1978.
The background chapter (II) is of historical value. The
remainder describes political attitudes and preferences of
Tejanos.

3332   Roeder, Sandra. A Study of the Situation of Mexican
       Americans in the Southwest. Washington, D.C.:
       Community Relations Service, U.S. Department of
       Justice, 1967.

3333   Rose, Arnold M., ed. Race Prejudice and
       Discrimination. New York: Alfred A. Knopf, 1951.
Several essays treat the Mexican American experience.

3334   Rose, Peter I. They and We: The Story of Racial and
       Ethnic Relations in the U.S. New York: Random House,
       1963.

3335   Ross, Fred W. Community Organization in
       Mexican-American Communities. Los Angeles: American
       Council on Race Relations, 1947.
Ross was the leading developer of Unity Leagues in southern
California; later he was also deeply involved in the United
Farm Workers.

3336   Ross, Fred W. Get Out if You Can, the Saga of Sal si
       Puedes. San Francisco: California Federation for
       Civic Unity, 1953.
A pamphlet by an expert in community organizing which
describes problems of Mexican American civil rights in San
Jose, California.

3337   Sanchez, David. Expedition Through Aztlan. La
       Puente, Calif.: Perspectiva Publications, 1978.
The story of the Brown Berets organization by its founder.

3338   Schrieke, Bertram J. O. Alien Americans: A Study of
       Race Relations. New York: Viking Press, 1936.
Includes some material on Mexican American problems.

3339   Shelton, Edgar Greer, Jr. Political Conditions Among
       Texas Mexicans Along the Rio Grande. San Francisco:
       R & E Research Associates, 1974.
A 1946 Austin, University of Texas master's thesis; concerns
politics, government, and suffrage.

3340   Simpson, George Eaton and J. M. Yinger. Racial and
       Cultural Minorities: An Analysis of Prejudice and
       Discrimination. 3rd ed. New York: Harper & Row,
       1965.
Includes some materials on Mexican Americans. Bibliography
and bibliographic footnotes.

3341   Sowell, Thomas. Race and Economics. New York: David
       McKay Co., 1975.
Primarily concerns Blacks, but has some material on
discrimination against Mexicans.

3342   Stocker, Joseph. The Invisible Minority . . . Pero No
        Vencibles. Washington, D.C.: National Education
        Association, 1966.

3343   Tijerina, Reies Lopez. From Prison. Edited by Ed
        Ludwig and James Santibañez. Baltimore: Penguin
        Books, 1971.

3344   Tyler, Gus, ed. Mexican-Americans Tomorrow; Economic
        and Educational Perspectives. Albuquerque: University
        of New Mexico Press, 1975.
Results of a 1972 conference at Aspen, Colorado, sponsored
by the Weatherhead Foundation.

3345   U.S., Commission on Civil Rights. The Civil Rights
        Status of Spanish-Speaking Americans in Kleberg,
        Nueces and San Patricio Counties. Washington, D.C.:
        U.S. Government Printing Office, 1967.

3346   U.S., Commission on Civil Rights. Mexican American
        Education Study. Report #1: Ethnic Isolation of
        Mexican Americans in the Public Schools of the
        Southwest. Washington, D.C.: U.S. Government Printing
        Office, 1971.

3347   U.S., Commission on Civil Rights. Political
        Participation of Mexican Americans in California.
        Washington, D.C.: U.S. Government Printing Office,
        1971.
Ninety pages describing political conditions and Chicano
exercise of the franchise.

3348   U.S., Commission on Civil Rights. The Spanish
        Speaking People in the U.S. Prepared by Julian
        Samora. Washington, D.C.: U.S. Commission on Civil
        Rights, 1962.

3349   U.S., Congress, Senate, Special Committee on Aging,
        91st Cong., 1st sess. "Availability and Usefulness of
        Federal Programs and Services to Elderly
        Mexican-Americans." Hearings, Part V. Washington,
        D.C.: U.S. Government Printing Office, 1969.

3350   Valdes y Tapia, Daniel [also Daniel T. Valdes].
        Hispanos and American Politics: A Sociological
        Analysis and Description of the Political Role,
        Status, and Voting Behavior of Americans with Spanish
        Names. New York: Arno Press, 1976.
Reprint of the author's 1964 dissertation at the University
of Colorado. Role of ethnicity in voting patterns.

3351   Vander Zanden, James W. American Minority Relations;
        The Sociology of Race and Ethnic Groups. New York:

Ronald Press, 1963; revised 2nd ed., 1966.
A study of the race issue in the United States; has a
detailed bibliography.

3352   Vento, Adela Sloss. Alonso S. Perales: His Struggle
       for the Rights of Mexican-Americans. San Antonio,
       Tex.: Artes Graficas, 1977.

3353   Vigil, Antonio S. The Coming of the Gringo and the
       Mexican American Revolt: An Analysis of the Rise and
       Decline of Anglo America. New York: Vantage Press,
       1970.
A broad survey, placing Chicano-Anglo conflict in the
Southwest in historical perspective.

3354   Vigil, Antonio S. The Ugly Anglo: An Analysis of
       White Extremism in Latin American Relations. Jericho,
       N.Y.: Exposition Press, 1967.
Discusses racial discrimination and the position of
minorities in the United States.

3355   Vigil, Maurilio E. Chicano Politics. Washington,
       D.C.: University Press of America, 1977.
A general survey; includes bibliographical references.

3356   Villarreal, Roberto E. Chicano Elites and Nonelites.
       San Francisco: R & E Research Associates, 1979.
Discusses politics, suffrage, social conditions, and ethnic
identity in Beeville, Texas.

3357   Wagley, Charles and Marvin Harris. Minorities in the
       New World. Six Case Studies. New York: Columbia
       University Press, 1967.
The sections on Indians in Mexico has some material on
migration to the U.S.

3358   Webster, Staten W. Mexican Americans: Our
       Second-Largest Non-Anglo Minority Group. Scranton,
       Penn.: Intent Educational Publishers, 1972.
Describes the Mexican Americans' problems in the U.S.
educational system.

3359   Weschler, Louis F. and John F. Gallagher. Cases in
       American National Government and Politics. Englewood
       Cliffs, N.J.: Prentice-Hall, 1966.
Includes material on the Chicano.

3360   Wiley, Tom. Politics and Purse Strings in New
       Mexico's Public Schools. Revised and enlarged 2nd ed.
       Albuquerque: University of New Mexico Press, 1968.
Describes the organization, management, and financing of
public education in New Mexico.

3361   Wiley, Tom. Public School Education in New Mexico.
       Albuquerque: University of New Mexico Press, 1965.
First edition of Politics and Purse Strings in New Mexico's
Public Schools, item 3360 listed above.

3362   Wilkinson, J. Harvie, III. From Brown to Bakke: The
       Supreme Court and School Integration, 1954-1978.
       Fairlawn, N.J.: Oxford University Press, 1979.

3363   Wollenberg, Charles. All Deliberate Speed:
       Segregation and Exclusion in California Schools,
       1855-1975. Berkeley: University of California Press,
       1976.
A general survey including material on Mexican Americans.
Bibliographic references.

3364   Wright, Kathleen. The Other Americans: Minorities in
       American History. 3rd ed. Los Angeles: Lawrence
       Publishing Co., 1969.

VIII: THESES AND DISSERTATIONS

3365   Arriaga, Adrian A.   "Mexican American City Officials
       in Texas." Master's thesis. College Station: Texas
       A & M University, 1973.

3366   Ashton, Price R. "The Fourteenth Amendment and the
       Education of Latin-American Children in Texas."
       Master's thesis. Austin: University of Texas Press,
       1949.

3367   Bareno, John Meza. "The Mexican-American Political
       Experience in Colton, California." San Diego, Calif.:
       United States International University, 1978.
A study of the political characteristics of Chicanos in
Colton and especially their leaders. Concludes that the
community is concerned about its political ineffectiveness
and seeks ways to improve its political and socio-economic
position.

3368   Batista y Calderon, Judith. "A Study of
       Counter-Prejudice in a Mexican-Spanish Community in
       the Surroundings of Des Moines, Iowa." Master's
       thesis. Des Moines, Iowa: Drake University, 1948.

3369   Benavides, Alfredo H. "Mexican-Americans and Public
       Service Institutions in a Midwestern Community: An
       Analysis of Mutual Images and Interactions." East
       Lansing: Michigan State University, 1978.
Concludes that the Chicano community lacks a clear
understanding of public and social welfare institutions,
their purposes, and operational methods. Argues that
relations between public agencies and the community are
largely negative.

3370   Briegel, Kaye L. "Alianza Hispano-Americana,
       1894-1965: A Mexican-American Fraternal Insurance
       Society." Los Angeles: University of Southern
       California, 1974.
Discusses the development of this important mutualist
organization.

3371   Bryant, Jill M. "Patterns of Conflict Between
       Government and Minority Groups: A Cross-National
       Study." Master's thesis. San Diego: San Diego State
       University, 1975.

3372   Buehler, Marilyn H. "Political Efficacy, Political
       Discontent, and Voting Turnout Among Mexican-Americans
       in Michigan." Notre Dame, Ind.: University of Notre
       Dame, 1975.
Argues that Michigan Chicanos in 1969 did not differ
significantly from other Americans in indexes of political

activity and effectiveness. Finds that feelings of
discrimination may lead to feelings of political
powerlessness.

3373   Cardenas, Blandina. "Defining Equal Access to
       Educational Opportunity for Mexican-American Children:
       A Study of Three Civil Rights Actions Affecting
       Mexican-American Students . . ." Amherst: University
       of Massachusetts, 1974.
Argues that there are areas of conflict between typical
school programs and the cultural-social-economic position of
most Mexican Americans, and studies three actions by HEW and
schools.

3374   Cardenas, Isaac. "Equality of Education Opportunity:
       A Descriptive Study on Mexican American Access to
       Higher Education." Amherst: University of
       Massachusetts, 1974.

3375   Chandler, Charles R. "The Mexican-American Protest
       Movement in Texas." New Orleans: Tulane University,
       1968.
Places the protest movement in Texas in historical
perspective. Includes the 1966 "March on Austin" and the
Starr County farm workers strike.

3376   Chavez, David J. "Civic Education of the Spanish
       American." Master's thesis. Socorro: New Mexico
       Institute of Mining and Technology, 1923.

3377   Ciuccio, Victor A. "Political Change in a
       Mexican-American Community." University Park:
       Pennsylvania State University, 1975.

3378   Cobas, Jose A. "Disaffection in the Barrio: A Study
       of Political Attitudes Among Chicano Adolescents."
       Austin: University of Texas, 1975.
Includes information on political development in Crystal
City, Texas.

3379   Cuellar, Alfredo, Jr. "A Theory of Politics: The Idea
       of Chicano Revisionism." Claremont, Calif.: Claremont
       Graduate School, 1976.

3380   Daniel, Cletus E. "Labor Radicalism in Pacific Coast
       Agriculture." Seattle: University of Washington,
       1972.
Covers the early history of farm labor organizing down to
the mid-1930s. Valuable for the role of the I.W.W. and the
communist C.A.W.I.U.

3381   Davis, James Alston. "'Do People Like Me Have Any
       Control Over Politics?' A Study of the Locus of
       Political Control As Perceived by Mexican-American

Adolescents of South Texas." Miami, Florida:
University of Miami, 1977.

3382   De Leon, Arnoldo. "White Racial Attitudes Toward
       Mexicanos in Texas, 1821-1900." Fort Worth: Texas
       Christian University, 1974.
Argues that the negative attitudes towards Mexicans that
most whites brought with them to Texas were used to justify
the denial of equality and civil rights and led to feelings
of Anglo superiority.

3383   Dickens, Edwin L. "The Political Role of the Mexican
       Americans in San Antonio, Texas." Lubbock: Texas
       Technological University, 1969.
Examines cultural, social, and personal aspects of the
political role in historical context and concludes Chicano
leaders have been politically more successful on the
personal level.

3384   Garcia, Alejandro. "The Contribution of Social
       Security to the Adequacy of Income of Elderly
       Chicanos." Waltham, Mass.: Brandeis University, 1980.

3385   Geilhufe, Nancy Lanelle. "Ethnic Relations in San
       Jose: A Study of Police-Chicano Interaction."
       Stanford, Calif.: Stanford University, 1972.
A case study of mutual suspicion and hostility between the
police and Chicanos in San Jose, California. Argues that
problems and perceptions of the two groups are different and
lead to conflict.

3386   Girsch, David W. "A Study of Prejudices and Attitudes
       of the Mexican-American." Master's thesis. Chico,
       Calif.: Chico State University, 1971.

3387   Grossman, Mitchell. "Multi-Factional Politics in San
       Antonio and Bexar County, Texas." Austin: University
       of Texas, 1959.

3388   Hamilton, James. "Mexican-American Problems and
       Trends in Corpus Christi, Texas." Master's thesis.
       San Antonio, Tex.: St. Mary's University, 1970.

3389   Harris, Leroy E. "The Other Side of the Freeway; A
       Study of Settlement Patterns of Negroes and
       Mexican-Americans in San Diego, California."
       Pittsburgh, Pa.: Carnegie-Mellon University, 1974.

3390   Kenneson, Susan Reyner. "Through the Looking-Glass: A
       History of Anglo-American Attitudes Towards the
       Spanish-Americans and Indians of New Mexico." New
       Haven, Conn.: Yale University, 1978.

3391   Lawrence, Penelope D.   "Citizen Participation: A Study
       of Ten Mexican-American Groups in the City of San
       Diego."   Master's thesis.   San Diego, Calif.: San
       Diego State University, 1977.

3392   Lopez, Manuel M.   "Patterns of Residential
       Segregation: The Mexican-American Population in the
       Urban Southwest, 1970."   East Lansing: Michigan State
       University, 1977.
Studies racial segregation comparatively in fifty-six
Southwestern cities.   Suggests that segregation is based
more on race or ethnicity than on income or other
socio-economic factors.

3393   McEachren, Mary A.   "The Cultural Context of Mexican
       American Brokers, Their Strategies and Effectiveness
       in Three Southern California Communities."   Santa
       Barbara: University of California, 1977.

3394   Madla, Frank L., Jr.   "The Political Impact of Latin
       Americans and Negroes in Texas Politics."   Master's
       thesis.   San Antonio, Tex.: St. Mary's University,
       1964.

3395   Marin, Eugene Acosta.   "The Mexican American Community
       and Leadership of the Dominant Society in Arizona: A
       Study of Their Mutual Attitudes and Perspectives."
       San Diego, Calif.: United States International
       University, 1973.

3396   Miller, Michael V.   "Conflict and Change in a
       Bifurcated Community: Anglo - Mexican-American
       Political Relations in a South Texas Town."   Master's
       thesis.   College Station: Texas A & M University,
       1971.

3397   Miyares, Marcelino.   "Models of Political
       Participation of Hispanic Americans."   Evanston,
       Ill.: Northwestern University, 1974.
Studies Chicano, Puerto Rican, and Cuban political
participation in Chicago, Ill.   Explains limited
participation on the basis of education, age, and income.

3398   Mosqueda, Lawrence J.   "Chicanos, Catholicism, and
       Political Ideology."   Seattle: University of
       Washington, 1979.
Evaluates the impact of the Catholic Church on Chicano
political attitudes and behavior.   Finds that the influence
is non-uniform and sometimes contradictory.

3399   Muñoz, Carlos.   "The Politics of Chicano Urban
       Protest: A Model of Political Analysis."   Claremont,

Calif.: Claremont Graduate School, 1973.

3400 Nathan, Paul. "Mexico Under Cardenas." Chicago:
      University of Chicago, 1953.
Includes material on activities in defense of the rights of
Mexicans in the U.S. during the depression years.

3401 Pacheco, Henry J. "Chicano Political Behavior."
      Claremont, Calif.: Claremont Graduate School, 1977.

3402 Pachon, Harry P. "Ethnicity, Poverty and Political
      Participation: Select Case Studies of Mexican-
      Americans in East Los Angeles." Claremont, Calif.:
      Claremont Graduate School, 1973.

3403 Padilla, Fernando V. "Legislative Gerrymandering of
      California Chicanos." Santa Barbara: University of
      California, 1977.
Argues that Chicanos' political impotence in California,
despite their numbers as compared to Colorado and New
Mexico, indicates that until recent reapportionment of the
state legislature Chicanos were gerrymandered out of
political power.

3404 Paris, Phillip L. "The Mexican American Informal
      Policy and the Political Segregation of Brown
      Students: A Case Study in Ventura County, California."
      Los Angeles: University of Southern California, 1973.
Discusses the reasons for revolutionary attitudes and the
manner in which they occur.

3405 Parker, Benny L. "Power-in-Conflict: A Chicano
      Political Party's Definition of Social Disequilibrium
      and Anglo Power Relationships as Expressed Through a
      Situational Analysis of Public Address in Crystal
      City, Texas, in 1972." Carbondale: Southern Illinois
      University, 1975.
A study of power and rhetoric based largely on speeches by
Jose Angel Gutierrez, head of La Raza Unida. Concludes that
political power was used to protect both the Chicano
community and individual members.

3406 Penrod, Vesta. "Civil Rights Problems of Mexican
      Americans in Southern California." Master's thesis.
      Claremont, Calif.: Claremont Graduate School, 1948.
Discusses citizenship, community segregation, school
segregation, employment and the FEPC.

3407 Peregrino, Santiago. "The Political Ideology of the
      Mexican-American in Southeast City: El Paso."
      Master's thesis. El Paso: University of Texas, 1970.

3408   Post, Donald E. "Ethnic Competition for Control of
        Schools in Two South Texas Towns." Austin: University
        of Texas, 1974.
Describes the history of a power struggle in south Texas
centering on control of the school system. Largely the
conflict in Crystal City led by Jose Angel Gutierrez.

3409   Ruby, Carrie L. "Attitudes Toward Latin-Americans as
        Revealed in Southwestern Literature." Master's
        thesis. Austin: University of Texas, 1953.

3410   Russell, John C. "State Sectionalism in New Mexico."
        Stanford, Calif.: Stanford University, 1939.

3411   Salces, Luis Mario. "Spanish American Politics in
        Chicago." Evanston, Ill.: Northwestern University,
        1978.

3412   Sandoval, Raymond E. "Intrusion and Domination: A
        Study of Chicano Power in a Southwestern Community,
        1870-1974." Seattle: University of Washington, 1980.
A history of land resources as a basis for political power.

3413   Scott, Robin Fitzgerald. "The Mexican-American in the
        Los Angeles Area, 1920-1950: From Acquiescence to
        Activity." Los Angeles: University of Southern
        California, 1971.
Studies the impact of prejudice in an historical perspective
and emphasizes the depression of the 1920s as important in
shaping Chicano attitudes and the World War II experience as
bringing new viewpoints.

3414   Seligman, Irving S. "The Political Alienation of the
        Mexican American in San Antonio, Texas." Master's
        thesis. San Antonio, Tex.: St. Mary's University,
        1968.

3415   Shepro, Theresa Aragon. [Also Aragon de Shepro,
        Teresa] "The Nature of Chicano Political
        Powerlessness." Seattle: University of Washington,
        1978.
Examines dependency as the main cause of Chicano political
powerlessness and argues for inconsistency between goals and
behavior. Analyzes recent Chicano political history,
especially el movimiento.

3416   Soto, John A. "Mexican American Community Leadership
        for Education." Ann Arbor: University of Michigan,
        1974.

3417   Taylor, Jacqueline J. "Ethnic Identity and Upward
        Mobility of Mexican-Americans in Tucson." Tucson:

University of Arizona, 1973.

3418   Tirado, Michael D.   "The Mexican American Minority's
       Participation in Voluntary Political Associations."
       Claremont, Calif.: Claremont Graduate School, 1970.

3419   Torres-Gil, Fernando M.   "Political Behavior: A Study
       of Political Attitudes and Political Participation
       Among Older Mexican-Americans."   Waltham, Mass.:
       Brandeis University, 1976.
Fits the elderly Chicano into 1970s Chicano politics; finds
them politically aware but inactive.   Argues that
generational conflict is not a major factor, but rather
cultural habits, e.g. deference.

3420   Torres-Raines, Rosario.   "Casas Ricas y Pobres: The
       Effects of Housing Market Expenditures on Residential
       Segregation of Mexican Americans in Texas and
       California."   Denton: Texas Woman's University, 1978.

3421   Trujillo, Larry D.   "The Quest for Chicano Community
       Control: A Case Study."   Berkeley: University of
       California, 1978.
Studies the 1971-1972 Chicano political revolt in Parlier,
California and the historical background to it.   Questions
whether the political victory meant community control.

3422   Vadi, Jose M.   "Mobilization Problems of Chicanos in a
       Southern California City."   Madison: University of
       Wisconsin, 1977.
Covers various aspects of the political mobilization of
Chicanos in South Pomona.   Argues that Chicanos have had
difficulty in channeling their discontent into political
demands.   Includes a consideration of Black-Chicano
political coalition.

3423   Vega, Anthony M.   "Cultural Differences,
       Powerlessness, and Distributive Justice: A Study of
       Attitudes and Participation in the Chicano Movement."
       Master's thesis.   Fullerton: California State
       University, 1971.

VIII: Periodicals

3424   Acuña, Rodolfo F. "Bird in a Cage: Subjugation of the
        Chicano in the U.S." In The Reinterpretation of
        American History and Culture. Edited by William H.
        Cartwright and Richard L. Watson, Jr. Washington,
        D.C.: National Council for the Social Sciences, 1974.

3425   Almaguer, Tomas. "Class, Race and Chicano
        Oppression." Socialist Revolution (July-Sept. 1975),
        71-99.

3426   Almaguer, Tomas. "Historical Notes on Chicano
        Oppression: The Dialectics of Racial and Class
        Domination in North America." Aztlan 5:1 (Spring &
        Fall 1974), 27-56.

3427   Almaguer, Tomas. "Toward the Study of Chicano
        Colonialism." Aztlan 2:1 (Spring 1971), 7-21.
Argues that the U.S. socio-economic system is the basic
cause of Chicano oppression and that only fundamental
societal change can end Chicano colonialism.

3428   Althoff, Phillip. "The Political Integration of
        Mexican-Americans and Blacks: A Note on a Deviant
        Case." Rocky Mountain Social Science Journal 10 (Oct.
        1973), 79-84.

3429   Alvarez, Rodolfo. "The Psycho-historical and
        Socioeconomic Development of the Chicano Community in
        the United States." Social Science Quarterly 53:4
        (March 1973), 920-942.
An excellent broad survey of the Mexican American
experience, based largely on the theme of political and
economic subjugation.

3430   "Americanos de Habla Hispana: Sus Problemas de
        Potencial Humano y de Oportunidades." Washington,
        D.C.: Department of Labor, [ca. 1974].
A section in the President's 1973 Manpower Report.

3431   "Another Civil Rights Headache--Plight of Mexican
        Americans." U.S. News & World Report 60 (June 6,
        1966), 46-48.
Describes Chicano-Black antagonism.

3432   Aragon de Valdez, Theresa. "Organizing as a Political
        Tool for the Chicana." Frontiers: A Journal of Women
        Studies 5:2 (Summer 1980), 7-13.

3433   Barrera, Mario; Carlos Muñoz; and Charles Ornelas.
        "The Barrio as Internal Colony." Urban Affairs Annual
        Review 6 (1972), 465-498.

3434 Bennett, Michael and Cruz Reynoso. "California Rural
      Legal Assistance: The Survival of a Poverty Law
      Practice." Chicano Law Review 1 (1972), 1-79.
Describes the early history of the CRLA, especially in the
political sphere, and its difficulties with Governor Ronald
Reagan.

3435 Bongartz, Roy. "The Chicano Rebellion." Nation 208
      (March 3, 1969), 271-274.
Efforts of Chicano students to destroy the traditional
stereotypes of the Mexican-American.

3436 "Boycott on the Ballot." Economist 245:6739 (Oct. 21,
      1972), 56-57.

3437 Briegel, Kaye. "The Development of Mexican American
      Organizations." In The Mexican-Americans: An
      Awakening Minority. Edited by Manuel P. Servin, pp.
      160-178. Beverly Hills, Calif.: Glencoe Press, 1970.

3438 Browning, Harley L. and S. Dale McLemore. "The
      Spanish Surname Population of Texas." Public Affairs
      Comment 10:1 (Jan. 1964). Austin: Institute of Public
      Affairs, University of Texas.

3439 Buehler, Marilyn H. "Voter Turnout and Political
      Efficacy Among Mexican-Americans in Michigan."
      Sociological Quarterly 18 (1977), 504-517.

3440 Burma, John H. "The Civil Rights Situation of Mexican
      Americans and Spanish Americans." In Race Relations:
      Problems and Theory. Edited by J. Masouka and P.
      Valien, pp. 155-167. Chapel Hill: University of North
      Carolina Press, 1961.

3441 Burma, John H. and Janet Jorgensen. "The Push of an
      Elbow: Civil Rights and our Spanish-Speaking
      Minority." Frontier 11:9 (July 1960), 10-12.

3442 Burnhill, James. "The Mexican People of the
      Southwest." Political Affairs 32 (Sept. 1953), 43-52;
      (Dec. 1953), 50-63.

3443 Burns, Haywood. "From Brown to Bakke and Back: Race,
      Law and Social Change in America." Deadalus 110:2
      (Spring 1981), 219-231.
The history of civil rights from 1954 to the present.

3444 Cabrera, Y. Arturo. "The Chicano Voice is Being
      Heard." C.T.A. Journal 65 (Oct. 1969), 26-27.
Notes the emergence of militant Chicanos and explains their
motivation and objectives.

3445   California, Advisory Committee to the U.S. Commission
        on Civil Rights. "Report on California
        Police-Minority Relations." Sacramento, August 1963.

3446   California, Fair Employment Practice Commission.
        "Si-Se Puede." Sacramento: Government Publications
        Section, 1964.

3447   Casavantes, Edward. "Pride and Prejudice: A Mexican
        American Dilemma." Civil Rights Digest 3:1 (Winter
        1970), 22-27.

3448   "La causa chicana: una familia unida." Social
        Casework 52 (May 1971), 259-324.

3449   Chavez, Jennie V. "Women of the Mexican-American
        Movement." Madamoiselle 74:12 (April 1972), 82,
        150-152.

3450   "The Chicano Experience in the United States." Social
        Science Quarterly 53:4 (March 1973), 652-942.
The entire issue is devoted to the Chicano.

3451   "Civil Rights." La Luz 8:6 (Feb.-March 1980), 10-14,
        41, 43.
Describes the goals and activities of LULAC, the G.I. Forum,
National IMAGE, the National Council of La Raza, and other
Hispanic organizations.

3452   Comer, John C. "Correlates of Recognition and
        Approval of Ethnic Organizations in a Non Reinforcing
        Environment: Mexican Americans in Omaha, Nebraska."
        Journal of Political and Military Sociology 8 (1980),
        113-120.

3453   Comer, John C. "Street-Level Bureaucracy and
        Political Support: Some Findings on Mexican
        Americans." Urban Affairs Quarterly 14 (1978),
        207-228.

3454   "Convention for the Protection of Human Rights and
        Fundamental Freedoms." The American Journal of
        International Law, Official Documents 45 (April 1951),
        25-39.

3455   Cooke, W. Henry. "The Segregation of Mexican-American
        School Children in Southern California." School and
        Society 67 (June 5, 1948), 417-421.

3456   Corona, Bert N. "The Chicano, a National Oppressed
        Minority." New Generation Magazine 53:4 (Fall 1971),
        1-6.
The entire issue is devoted to problems of the Spanish-

speaking.

3457   Corona, Bert N.   "An Interview with Bert Corona (by
       John C. Hammerback)."   Western Journal of Speech
       Communication 44:3 (Summer 1980), 214-220.
Corona discusses the role of oratory and communication
skills in the movimiento.   Includes a brief biographical
sketch.

3458   Coronado, Greg.   "Spanish-Speaking Organizations in
       Utah."   In Working Papers Toward a History of the
       Spanish Speaking in Utah.   Edited by Paul Morgan and
       Vince Mayer.   Salt Lake City: American West Center,
       University of Utah, 1973.

3459   Crosthwait, (Rev.) Joseph H.   "The Status of Our
       Spanish-Speaking People."   Ninth Regional Conference,
       Catholic Council for the Spanish Speaking, April
       15-17, 1958.   San Antonio, Tex.: Schneider Printing
       Co., 1958.

3460   Cuellar, Alfredo.   "The Chicano Movement."   In From
       the Barrio: A Chicano Anthology.   Edited by Luis O.
       Salinas and Lillian Faderman, pp. 3-10.   San
       Francisco: Canfield Press, 1973.
Explains the development of the Chicano movement and the
concept of Chicanismo.

3461   Dahlke, H. Otto.   "Race and Minority Riots."   Social
       Forces 30 (May 1952), 419-425.
A general discussion of race riots.

3462   Davis, Junetta and Reg. Westmoreland.   "Minority
       Editorial Workers on Texas Daily Newspapers."
       Journalism Quarterly 51:1 (Spring 1974), 132-134.

3463   De La Cruz, Jesse and Ellen Cantarow.   "My Life."
       Radical American 12 (1978), 26-40.

3464   "Demandas de la Raza."   Social Progress 59:5 (May-June
       1969), 11-13.
Demands made during the Poor People's Campaign, 1968.

3465   Dodson, Jack E.   "Minority Group Housing in Two Texas
       Cities."   In Studies in Housing and Minority Groups.
       Edited by Nathan Glazer and David McIntire, pp.
       84-109.   Berkeley: University of California Press,
       1960.
Describes the housing conditions of Chicanos and Blacks in
Houston and San Antonio.

3466   Dominguez, Adolfo G.   "El chicanismo: Su origen y
       actualidad politica."   Cuadernos Americanos 30:178:2

(March-April 1971), 64-76.
A sweeping survey which concludes that chicanismo is a
movement in search of its identity.

3467   Dorsey, Emmet E. "The Political Role of Mexican-
        Americans." In Minority Problems. Edited by Arnold
        M. Rose and Caroline B. Rose, pp. 202-204. New York:
        Harper & Row, 1965.

3468   Edgel, Ralph L. "New Mexico Population." New Mexico
        Business 11:10 (Oct. 1958), 2.

3469   "Few Spanish-speaking Children in High Schools in the
        Southwest." School and Society 94 (Nov. 12, 1966),
        377.

3470   Flores, Felipe V.; Robert F. Kane; and Felix
        Velarde-Muñoz. "Rights of Undocumented Children to
        Attend Public Schools in Texas." Chicano Law Review 4
        (1977), 61-93.

3471   Flores, Guillermo. "Race and Culture in the Internal
        Colony: Keeping the Chicano in His Place." In
        Structure of Dependency. Edited by Frank Bonilla and
        Robert Girling. East Palo Alto, Calif.: Nairobi
        Bookstore, 1973.

3472   Forbes, Jack D. "Race and Color in Mexican-American
        Problems." Journal of Human Relations 16 (1968),
        55-68.
Includes the history of Anglo color prejudice.

3473   Friedlander, Judith. "Struggles on the Rio Puerco:
        Environmental Stress and Ethnic Conflict in Northern
        New Mexico". Revue Francaise d'Etudes Americaines
        [France] 5 (1980), 67-77.

3474   Frisbie, Parker. "Militancy Among Mexican American
        High School Students." Social Science Quarterly 53:4
        (March 1973), 865-883.
Discusses various high school "blowouts" and boycotts and
argues that these arose from a perception of discrimination
and a belief that mobilization could bring positive results.

3475   Garcia, F. Chris. "The Continuation of a Long
        Journey: Mexican-Americans in U.S. Politics,
        1965-1980." In The Chicano Community and California
        Redistricting, pp. 14-36. Claremont, Calif.: Rose
        Institute, Claremont College, 1981.

3476   Garcia, Flaviano Chris. "Manitos and Chicanos in
        Nuevo Mexico Politics." Aztlan 5:1&2 (Spring & Fall,
        1974), 177-188.
Discusses the political position of Nuevo Mexicanos and

points out that this derives from a well established culture and set of institutions unique in New Mexico.

3477 Garcia, F. Chris. "New Mexico: Urban Politics in a State of Varied Political Cultures." In Politics in the Urban Southwest. Edited by Robert D. Wrinkle. Albuquerque: Division of Government Research, University of New Mexico, 1971.

3478 Garcia, F. Chris. "Orientations of Mexican American and Anglo Children Toward the U.S. Political Community." Social Science Quarterly 53:4 (March 1973), 814-829.
Finds that Chicano children's early attachment to the U.S. weakens as they grow older, probably as the result of rejection by American society.

3479 Garcia, John A. "An Analysis of Chicano and Anglo Electoral Patterns in School Board Elections." Ethnicity 6:2 (June 1979), 168-183.

3480 Garcia, Jose Z.; Cal. Clark; and Janet Clark. "Public Impacts on Chicanos and Women: A State Case Study." Policy Studies Journal 7 (1978), 251-257.

3481 Gonzales, Raymond J. "Why Chicanos Don't Vote." California Journal 6:7 (July 1975), 245-246.
Describes the factors in voting apathy among Mexican Americans and explains why there have been few Chicano politicos with a statewide basis of power.

3482 Gonzalez, Henry B. "The Mexican-American: An Awakening Giant." Employment Service Review 4:7 (July 1967), 10-13.

3483 Gonzalez, Isabel. "Stepchildren of a Nation: The Status of Mexican Americans." (Report prepared for a conference, Oct. 25-26, 1947). New York: American Committee for Protection of Foreign Born, 1947.

3484 Griffith, Beatrice. "A Mexican American Runs for Political Office." In Race Prejudice and Discrimination. Edited by Arnold Rose. New York: Alfred A. Knopf, 1951.
Refers to Edward Roybal in Los Angeles, California.

3485 Guernica, Antonio Jose. "TELACU: Community Change Through Economic Power." Agenda 7:6 (Nov.-Dec. 1977), 14-16.

3486 Gutierrez, Armando and Herbert Hirsch. "The Militant Challenge to the American Ethos: 'Chicanos' and 'Mexican Americans.'" Social Science Quarterly 53:4 (March 1973), 830-845.

Concerns differences in attitudes, values, and self-perception of Crystal City students who identified themselves as Chicanos and Mexican Americans. Includes background history of the Texas Rangers and of Crystal City.

3487 Gutierrez, Jose Angel. "An Interview with Jose Angel Gutierrez (by Richard J. Jensen)." <u>Western Journal of Speech Communication</u> 44:3 (Summer 1980), 203-213.
Gutierrez describes the objectives of his rhetoric as redefining Chicano culture to create positive images and using the Anglo "devil" to unite Mexican Americans.

3488 Guzman, Ralph. "The Function of Anglo-American Racism in the Political Development of Chicanos." <u>California Historical Quarterly</u> 50:3 (Sept. 1971), 321-337.
Explores the political implications stemming from stereotypical views of Chicanos; argues that mutual images have held back Chicanos politically and socio-economically.

3489 Guzman, Ralph. "The Hand of Esau: Words Change, Practices Remain in Racial Covenants." <u>Frontier</u> 7:8 (June 1956), 7, 16.
Describes unchanged housing discrimination against Chicanos in the Los Angeles area.

3490 Guzman, Ralph. "How El Centro Did It." <u>Frontier</u> 7:4 (Feb. 1956), 13, 16.
Describes a successful court suit against school segregation in El Centro, California.

3491 Guzman, Ralph. "Rights Without Roots: A Study of the Loss of Citizenship by Native-Born Americans of Mexican Ancestry." Mimeographed. Los Angeles: Fund for the Republic, Inc. and Southern California Chapter American Civil Liberties Union, 1955.

3492 Guzman, Ralph and Joan Moore. "The Mexican-Americans: New Wind from the Southwest." <u>Nation</u> 202:22 (May 30, 1966), 645-648.
Describes some of the changes in Chicano attitudes and goals, resulting in part from the national attention given to the Delano grape strike.

3493 Hall, Martin. "Roybal's Candidacy and What It Means: The Awakening of New Forces in California." <u>Frontier</u> 5 (June 1954), 5-7.

3494 Hartmire, Wayne C. "The Church and the Emerging Farm Workers Movement. A Case Study." <u>National Farm Workers Ministry</u>, 1967.

3495 Hernandez, Jose, et al. "Census Data and the Problem of Conceptually Defining the Mexican American

Population." Social Science Quarterly 53:4 (March
1973), 671-687.
Enumerates and explores the various difficulties involved in
a census definition of Mexican Americans and looks at some
results, e.g., underenumeration.

3496 Herrera, Juan M. "A View from Within: 'Years of
       Shout' Seem Over in Chicano Politics." California
       Journal 4:5 (May 1973), 155-158.
An insightful look at Chicano politics on the national scene
and especially in California.

3497 Hill, Gladwin. "The Political Role of Mexican-
       Americans." In Minority Problems. Edited by Arnold
       M. Rose and Caroline B. Rose. New York: Harper & Row,
       1965.
Describes Anglo American reaction and response to Mexican
American control in local politics.

3498 "History of LULAC." La Luz 6:5 (May 1977), 15-19.

3499 James, Laurence P. "The Great Underground Manhunt,
       Or, One Mexican Versus the State of Utah." Journal of
       the West 18:2 (April 1979), 11-20.
The story of Rafael Lopez and the search for him in a
Bingham, Utah copper mine.

3500 Jenkins, J. C. and C. Perrow. "Insurgency of the
       Powerless: Farm Worker Movements (1946-1972)."
       American Sociological Review 42 (April 1977), 249-268.

3501 Jensen, Richard J. and John C. Hammerback. "Radical
       Nationalism Among Chicanos: The Rhetoric of Jose Angel
       Gutierrez." Western Journal of Speech Communication
       44:3 (Summer 1980), 191-202.
Briefly recounts the career of Gutierrez and explains how he
used his rhetoric to unite Chicanos in the movimiento.

3502 Johnson, Dallas. "They Fenced Tolerance In." Survey
       Graphic 36:7 (July 1947), 398-399.
The ending of school segregation in Mendota, Calif.

3503 Kennedy, Paul. "Conference Sifts U.S.-Mexican
       Issues." New York Times (Feb. 21, 1965).

3504 Knowlton, Clark S. "An Approach to the Economic and
       Social Problems of Northern New Mexico." New Mexico
       Business Review (June 1964).

3505 Knowlton, Clark S. "A Comparison of Spanish American
       and Mexican American Leadership Systems of Northern
       New Mexico and El Paso." A paper presented to the
       Texas Academy of Science, Dec. 10, 1965.

3506   Kucharsky, David E. "La Causa Chicana." Social
        Casework 52 (May 1971), 59-334.

3507   Lamare, James W. "The Political World of the Rural
        Chicano Child." American Politics Quarterly 5 (Jan.
        1977), 83-109.

3508   Lamb, Blaine P. "The Convenient Villian: The Early
        Cinema Views the Mexican-American." Journal of the
        West 14:4 (Oct. 1975), 75-81.
Describes briefly the plots of a number of early Hollywood
films that centered on stereotypes of Mexicans.

3509   Lara-Braud, Jorge. "Problems We Face in the Lower Rio
        Grande Valley." Social Progress 59:5 (May-June 1969),
        22-24.
Socio-economic facts from a one-day conference (Nov. 2,
1968), of forty Spanish-speaking Protestants at La Feria,
Texas.

3510   Limon, Jose E. "Stereotyping and Chicano Resistance:
        An Historical Dimension." Aztlan 4:2 (Fall 1973),
        257-270.
Describes Chicano reaction to stereotyping, centering on
John K. Turner's Barbarous Mexico appearing as a series of
articles in 1909-1910.

3511   Lopez, Victor M. "Equal Protection for Undocumented
        Aliens." Chicano Law Review 5 (1982), 29-54.

3512   Lucey, (Rev.) Robert E. "Justice for the Mexicans."
        Commonweal 49 (Nov. 1948), 117.
Archbishop Robert Lucey of San Antonio speaking for Mexican
Americans at the El Paso meeting of the Bishops' Committee
for the Spanish-Speaking.

3513   Lucey, (Rev.) Robert E. "The Spanish Speaking of the
        Southwest and the West." Report on the Conference of
        Leaders. Washington, D.C.: Social Action Department,
        National Catholic Welfare Conference, 1943.

3514   La Luz 8:6 (Feb.-March 1980).
The entire issue is devoted to Hispanic organizations and
their histories.

3515   McGovney, D. O. "Race Discrimination in
        Naturalization." Iowa Law Bulletin 8 (1923), 129-211.

3516   Macias, Ysidro R. "The Chicano Movement." Wilson
        Library Bulletin 44:7 (March 1970), 731-735.

3517   Mack, Raymond. "Riot, Revolt and Responsible Action."
        Sociology Quarterly 10 (Spring 1969), 147.

3518   McNeely, John. "Mexican-American Land Issues in the
       United States." In The Role of the Mexican American
       in the History of the Southwest: Conference of the
       Inter-American Institute, Pan American College, pp.
       35-45. Edinburg, Tex.: Pan American College, 1969.

3519   McWilliams, Carey. "America's Disadvantaged
       Minorities: Mexican-Americans." Journal of Negro
       Education 20 (Summer 1951), 301-309.

3520   McWilliams, Carey. "The Mexican Problem." Common
       Ground 8:3 (Spring 1948), 3-17.

3521   Marin, Christine. "Go Home, Chicanos: A Study of the
       Brown Berets in California and Arizona." In An
       Awakened Minority: The Mexican-American. Edited by
       Manuel Servin, pp. 226-246. Beverly Hills, Calif.:
       Glencoe Press, 1974, 2nd ed.

3522   Marrett, Cora Bagley. "The Brown Power Revolt: A True
       Social Movement?" Journal of Human Relations 19:3
       (1971), 356-366.

3523   Martinez, Arthur D. "Addressing a Chicano Political
       Drought." La Luz 9:7 (Oct.-Nov.-Dec. 1981), 20.

3524   Martinez, Frank. "Oregon's Chicanos' Fight for
       Equality." Civil Rights Digest 5 (Winter 1972),
       17-22.
Principally the history of Oregon state senate bill 677, on
farm labor and unionization.

3525   Martinez, Thomas M. "Advertising and Racism: The Case
       of the Mexican-American." El Grito 2:4 (Summer 1969),
       3-13.
Argues that advertising has presented the Mexican American
regularly in objectionable and demeaning stereotypes.
Includes a list of advertisers who thus promote racism.

3526   Miller, Tom. "Pistol Justice: White Cops and Chicano
       Corpses." Nation 227 (Nov. 4, 1978), 470-472.
Describes a proneness to police violence along the
U.S.-Mexico border. Describes four specific cases.

3527   "Minorities, Pocho's Progress." Time 89:17 (April 28,
       1967), 24-25.
Mainly in Los Angeles; includes material on Dr. Francisco
Bravo.

3528   Moore, Joan W. "Colonialism: The Case of the Mexican
       Americans." Social Problems 17 (Spring 1970),
       463-472.

3529 Morales, Armando. "Chicano-Police Riots." In
      Chicanos: Social and Psychological Perspectives.
      Edited by Nathaniel Wagner and Marsha Haug, pp.
      184-202. St. Louis: C. V. Mosby Co., 1971.
Covers the 1970 Los Angeles rioting.

3530 Morales, Armando. "Justice and the Mexican-American."
      El Grito 1:4 (Summer 1968), 42-48.

3531 Munoz, Carlos, et al. "The Barrio as Internal
      Colony." In People and Politics in Urban Society.
      Edited by Harlan Hahn. Beverly Hills, Calif.: Sage
      Publications, 1972.

3532 Murphy, Betty. "Community Development: There Aren't
      Any Miracles." Vista Volunteer 4 (Jan. 1968), 12-19.

3533 Nabakov, Peter. "La Raza, the Land and the Hippies."
      Nation 210 (April 20, 1970), 464-468.
Describes Reies Lopez Tijerina's activities as leader of the
land grant movement in New Mexico (the Alianza Federal de
Pueblos Libres) and the entrance of hippies into the area.

3534 National Council for the Spanish-Speaking. "National
      Council for the Spanish-Speaking. Its Needs . . .
      Its Goals . . . Its Programs." National Council for
      the Spanish Speaking, 1964.

3535 Navarro, Armando. "The Evolution of Chicano
      Politics." Aztlan 5:1&2 (Spring & Fall 1974), 57-84.
A broad overview of the development of Chicano politics,
arguing that from the beginning resistance has been central
to the movement.

3536 Neighbor, Howard D. "Are Resident Aliens Entitled to
      Representation?" National Civic Review 67 (Dec.
      1978), 519-522.

3537 "New Accent on Civil Rights: The Mexican American."
      Civil Rights Digest 2:1 (Winter 1969), 16-23.

3538 Olivarez, Elizabeth. "Women's Rights and the Mexican
      American Woman." YWCA Magazine (Jan. 1972), 14-16.

3539 Ortega, Joe. "The Privately Funded Legal Aid Office:
      The MALDEF Experience." Chicano Law Review 1 (1972),
      80-84.
Describes the scope of the Mexican American Legal Defense
Education Fund's concerns and activities.

3540 Ortego (y Gasca), Philip D. "The Mexican-Dixon Line."
      El Grito 1:4 (Summer 1968), 29-31.

3541 Ortego (y Gasca), Philip D. "The Minority on the
      Border: Cabinet Meeting in El Paso". Nation 205 (Dec.
      11, 1967), 624-627.
Describes the meeting as largely show which did not address
the real issues.

3542 "Other Texan-Mexicanos." Look 27 (Oct. 8, 1963),
      58-70.

3543 Paredes, Americo. "Texas' Third Man: The Texas-
      Mexican." Journal of the Institute of Race Relations
      [London] 4:2 (May 1963), 49-58.

3544 Parra, Ricardo; Victor Rios; and Armando Gutierrez.
      "Chicano Organizations in the Midwest: Past, Present
      and Possibilities." Aztlan 7:2 (Summer 1976),
      235-253.
A survey of the development of Chicano organizations in the
Midwest, centering on LULAC, the American G.I. Forum, La
Raza Unida, and civil rights and youth groups.

3545 Payne, William. "Mexican American Farmers in South
      Texas." Civil Rights Digest 2:2 (Spring 1969), 37-38.
Describes their economic and social position.

3546 Penalosa, Fernando and Edward C. McDonagh. "Social
      Mobility in a Mexican American Community." Social
      Forces 44 (June 1966), 498-505.

3547 Penalosa, Fernando and Edward C. McDonagh. "A
      Socioeconomic Class Typology of Mexican-Americans."
      Sociological Inquiry 36 (Winter 1966), 19-30.

3548 Pinkney, A. "Prejudice Toward Mexican and Negro
      Americans: A Comparison." Phylon 24 (Winter 1963),
      353-359.

3549 Pritchett, Howard E. "The Political Influence of the
      Mexican-American Community in the Imperial Valley of
      California." New Scholar 1 (April 1969), 79-94.

3550 Raigoza, Jaime. "The East Los Angeles Cityhood
      Measure." Campo Libre 1:1 (Winter 1981), 1-23.

3551 Rangel, Jorge C. and Carlos M. Alcala. "Project
      Report: De Jure Segregation of Chicanos in Texas
      Schools." Harvard Civil Rights-Civil Liberties Law
      Review 7 (March 1972), 307-391.

3552 Rees, L. and P. Montague. "Ford and La Raza: They
      Stole Our Land and Gave Us Powdered Milk." Ramparts 9
      (Sept. 1970), 10-18.

3553   Rendon, Armando. "How Much Longer--The Long Road?"
       Civil Rights Digest 1 (Summer 1968), 34-44.

3554   Rendon, Armando. "La Raza - Today Not Mañana." Civil
       Rights Digest 1 (Spring 1968), 7-17.

3555   "Revolt in the Southwest?" Economist 227:6511 (June
       8, 1968), 53-54, 59-60.
Describes the rising tide of Chicano political activism in
the Southwest, including UFW union organizing in California
and Texas.

3556   Rivera, George, Jr. "Nosotros Venceremos: Chicano
       Consciousness and Change Strategies." Journal of
       Applied Behavioral Science 8:1 (Jan.-Feb. 1972),
       56-71.

3557   Rivera, Julius. "Justice, Deprivation and the
       Chicano." Aztlan 4 (Spring 1973), 123-135.
Argues that U.S. society has failed to provide justice for
Chicanos, especially in the areas of health, housing, and
education. Tables.

3558   Rodriguez, Armando M. "Speak Up, Chicano." American
       Education 4:5 (May 1968), 25-27.

3559   Rogers, John. "Poverty Behind the Cactus Curtain."
       Progressive 30 (March 1966), 23-35.

3560   Rose, Arnold M. and Caroline B. Rose. "Mexicans and
       Other Latins." In America Divided. Edited by Arnold
       and Caroline Rose, pp. 50-53. New York: Alfred A.
       Knopf, 1953.

3561   Ross, Malcolm. "Those Gringos." Common Ground 2
       (Winter 1948), 3-13.

3562   Roybal, Edward R. "Hispanics: A Political
       Perspective." Social Education 43 (Feb. 1979),
       101-103.

3563   Sanchez, George I. "The American of Mexican Descent."
       Chicago Jewish Forum 20 (Winter 1961-1962), 2.

3564   Sedillo, Pablo. "The Forum of National Hispanic
       Organizations--First Steps Towards Unity." Agenda
       10:1 (Jan.-Feb. 1980), 4-7.

3565   Segade, Gustavo V. "Identity and Power: An Essay on
       the Politics of Culture and the Culture of Politics in
       Chicano Thought." Aztlan 9 (1978), 85-100.
A study at San Diego State University, of the student
movement and leaders, especially radicals.

3566   Servin, Manuel P.   "The Mexican-American Awakens: An
        Interpretation." Journal of the West 14:4 (Oct.
        1975), 121-130.
Discusses the movimiento, and especially the roles of
post-World War II organizations.

3567   Shaw, Ray. "Overlooked Minority." Wall Street
        Journal 167:86 (May 3, 1966), 1, 28.
Tells how prejudice blights the lives of Mexican Americans.

3568   Sheldon, Paul. "Mexican American Formal
        Organizations." In Mexican Americans in the United
        States. Edited by John Burma, pp. 267-272.
        Cambridge, Mass.: Schenkman, 1970.
Briefly describes the CMAA, CSO, AGIF, MAPA, PASSO.

3569   Smith, W. Elwood and Douglas E. Foley. "Mexican
        Resistance to Schooling in a South Texas Colony."
        Education and Urban Society 10 (1978), 145-176.

3570   Social Science Quarterly 53:4 (March 1973).
The entire issue concerns the Chicano experience, with
emphasis on political and economic subordination.

3571   Sosa Riddell, Adaljiza. "Chicanas and el Movimiento."
        Aztlan 5:1&2 (Spring & Fall 1974), 155-165.
Argues that Chicanas should have complete equality with
Chicanos in the movimiento, in order to end a divisive
situation.

3572   Steiner, Stan. "No One Hears Our Silence."
        Progressive 34 (May 1970), 37-39.

3573   "Summary of Conference on Latin-American Relations in
        Southwestern United States." New York: Division of
        Racial Minorities, National Council of the Protestant
        Episcopal Church, 1959.

3574   Tirado, Miguel D. "Mexican American Community
        Political Organization: The Key to Chicano Political
        Power." Aztlan 1 (Spring 1970), 53-78.
Covers 1910 to 1970 in an excellent broad historical
overview.

3575   Torres, Louis R. and Jesus S. Treviño. "The Legacy of
        Sleepy Lagoon." Chisme-Arte 1:3 (Summer 1977), 3-7.

3576   Trillin, Calvin. "U.S. Letter: McFarland." New
        Yorker 43 (Nov. 4, 1967), 173-181.
Describes the work of the California Rural Legal Assistance
organization.

3577 U.S., Congress, Congressional Record, 91st Cong., 1st
      sess., April 14, 1969, 2893-2894. "Speak Up Chicano -
      The Mexican-American Fights for Educational Equality,"
      by Armando Rodriguez. Extension of Remarks. Also,
      American Education (May 1968), item 3558.

3578 U.S., Congress, House, Congressional Record, 91st
      Cong., 1st sess., April 22, 1969, 2928-2930.
      Gonzalez, Henry B. "Rights of Mexican-Americans."

3579 U.S., Congress, Senate, Congressional Record, 91st
      Cong., 1st sess., Feb. 17, 1969, S1606-S1607. "The
      Mexican American: Quest for Equality."
A report by the National Advisory Committee on Mexican
American Education.

3580 Villarreal, Jose Antonio. "Mexican-Americans in
      Upheaval." West 21 (Sept. 18, 1966), 30, 39.

3581 Walker, Helen W. "Mexican Immigrants and American
      Citizenship." Sociology and Social Research 13:5
      (May-June 1929), 465-471.

3582 Watson, James Bennett and Julian Samora.
      "Subordinate Leadership in a Bicultural Community: An
      Analysis." American Sociological Review 19 (Aug.
      1954), 413-421.

3583 Weeks, O. Douglas. "The Texas-Mexican and the
      Politics of South Texas." American Political Science
      Review 24:3 (Aug. 1930), 606-627.
Surveys political organization and leadership and describes
the Mexican American voter. A great deal of sociological
stereotyping underlies the entire article.

3584 Welch, Susan; John Comer; and Michael Stenman.
      "Political Participation Among Mexican Americans: An
      Exploratory Examination." Social Science Quarterly
      53:4 (March 1973), 799-813.
Based on four Nebraska Chicano communities, this study finds
Chicanos are similar to other Nebraskans in interest in
politics but tend to participate less. Five tables.

IX.
CULTURE

Books

Section IX includes the topics of acculturation, assimilation, and naturalization; the history of Chicano literature, the Church, religion, and education; folk arts, music, and corridos; family and barrio life; and Anglo views of the Mexican and Mexican American.

3585 Acosta, Adalberto J. Chicanos Can Make It. New
York: Vantage Press, 1971.
A personal account of Chicano success.

3586 Action Research: In Defense of the Barrio: Interviews
with Ernesto Galarza, Guillermo Flores and Rosalio
Muñoz. Edited by Mario Barrera and Geralda Vialpando.
Los Angeles: Aztlan Publications, 1974.
Excellent material on civic associations and community
organization by leaders in the field; thirty-six pages.

3587 Ahlborn, Richard. The Sculpted Saints of a Borderland
Mission. Tucson, Ariz.: Southwest Mission Research
Center, 1974.

3588 Andersson, Theodore and Mildred Boyer, eds. Bilingual
Schooling in the United States: History, Rationale,
Implications, and Planning. 2 vols. Austin: Tex.:
Southwest Education Development Laboratory, 1970.
Revised ed., Detroit: Blaine Ethridge, 1976.
A major basic survey of bilingualism; includes an essay on
Mexican bilingualism. Has an extensive bibliography.

3589 Arciniega, Tomas A. The Urban Mexican American. Las
Cruces: ERIC-CRESS, New Mexico State University, 1971.

3590   Aspects of the Mexican-American Experience. With an
        introduction by Carlos E. Cortes. New York: Arno
        Press, 1976.
Contents: Merton E. Hill, The Development of an
Americanization Program, 1928; The Survey 66:3 (May 1,
1931); George I. Sanchez, ed., First Regional Conference on
the Education of Spanish-Speaking People in the Southwest
(Dec. 13-14-15, 1945), 1946; John Ryland Scotford, Within
These Borders, 1953; Belden Associates, The Mexican-American
Market in the United States, 1962; Arnold R. Rojas, The
Vaquero, 1964. This original anthology shows the many
aspects of the Chicano experience.

3591   Bacigalupa, Andrea. Santos and Saints' Days. Santa
        Fe, N. Mex.: The Sunstone Press, 1972.
This thirty-two page book includes reproductions of Nuevo
Mexicano folk art.

3592   Barker, George Carpenter. Pachuco: An American-
        Spanish Argot and Its Social Functions in Tucson,
        Arizona. Tucson: University of Arizona Press, 1950;
        reprint, 1974.
Includes materials on social life and customs of Chicanos.

3593   Barker, George Carpenter. Social Functions of
        Language in a Mexican-American Community. Tucson:
        University of Arizona Press, 1972.
A reprint of the author's 1947 University of Chicago thesis.
Anthropological Papers No. 22.

3594   Barker, Ruth Laughlin. Caballeros. New York: D.
        Appleton Co., 1931. Reprint, New York: Arno Press,
        1976.
Offers a personal, romantic interpretation of Anglo-Mexican
relations and Hispano culture, including village arts and
crafts.

3595   Barrera, Mario; A. Camarillo; and F. Hernandez. Work/
        Family/ Sex Roles/ Language: NACS Selected Papers.
        Berkeley, Calif.: Tonatiuh-Quinto Sol, 1980.

3596   Barrett, Donald N. and Julian Samora. The Movement of
        Spanish Youth from Rural to Urban Settings.
        Washington, D.C.: National Committee for Children and
        Youth, 1963.
Author Barrett is a specialist in population problems.

3597   Barrio, Raymond. Mexico's Art and Chicano Artists.
        Guerneville, Calif.: Ventura Press, 1975.

3598   Beals, Ralph L. Culture Patterns of Mexican-American
        Life. Los Angeles: Southwest Council on the Education
        of Spanish-Speaking People, Pepperdine College, 1951.
An interpretation by an outstanding anthropologist,

specialist in Mexican Indian cultures.

3599 Beals, Ralph L. and Norman D. Humphrey. No Frontier
      to Learning: The Mexican Student in the United States.
      Minneapolis: University of Minnesota Press, 1967.

3600 Bean, Frank D. and W. Parker Frisbie, eds. The
      Demography of Racial and Ethnic Groups. New York:
      Academic Press, 1978.
Based on presentations at a 1977 population research
conference at Austin, Texas. Valuable for materials on race
relations.

3601 Blicksilver, Edith, ed. The Ethnic American Woman:
      Problems, Protests, Lifestyle. Dubuque, Iowa:
      Kendall/Hunt Publishing Co., 1979.
An anthology of eighty-five items about women of more than
twenty ethnic groups and including four Chicanas.

3602 Boatright, Mody C., comp. Mexican Border Ballads and
      Other Lore. Dallas, Tex.: Southern Methodist
      University Press, 1967.

3603 Bodine, John J. A Tri-Ethnic Trap. American
      Ethnological Society, Proceedings, 1968 Annual Spring
      Meeting. Seattle: University of Washington Press,
      1968.
Describes Mexicans, Indians, and Anglos in Taos, New Mexico.
A revision of the author's 1967 Tulane University thesis.

3604 Briggs, Charles L. The Woodcarvers of Cordova, New
      Mexico. Knoxville: University of Tennessee Press,
      1980.
Mostly contemporary wood-carving, but includes background
history. Numerous photographs, bibliography.

3605 Brody, Eugene B., et al. Minority Group Adolescents
      in the United States. Baltimore, Md.: Williams &
      Wilkins, 1968.
Studies in mental health by various specialists in the
field.

3606 Brown, Lorin W. with Charles Briggs and Marta Weigle,
      eds. Hispanic Folklife of New Mexico. Albuquerque:
      University of New Mexico Press, 1978.
A 1930s WPA federal writers' oral history project.

3607 Bruce-Novoa, Juan D. Chicano Authors: Inquiry by
      Interview. Austin: University of Texas Press, 1980.
Covers novelists and poets only; includes history of the
Chicano literary renaissance.

3608 Buss, Fran Leeper. La Partera: Story of a Midwife.
      Ann Arbor: University of Michigan Press, 1980.
Story of a Nuevo Mexicana midwife, in her own words.

3609 Cabrera, Y. Arturo. Emerging Faces--the
      Mexican-Americans. Dubuque, Iowa: William C. Brown
      Co., 1971.
Discusses Raza concerns about politics, economics, and
especially education.

3610 Caine, Allen T. Social Life in a Mexican-American
      Community: Social Class or Ethnic Grouping? San
      Francisco: R & E Research Associates, 1974.
Discusses the question of social class versus ethnic
identity as determinant in the community.

3611 Campa, Arthur L. Hispanic Culture in the Southwest.
      Norman: University of Oklahoma Press, 1979.
The distillation of a lifetime's study by the principal
expert in Hispanic folklore of the Southwest.

3612 Campa, Arthur L. Treasure of the Sangre de Cristos:
      Tales and Traditions of the Spanish Southwest.
      Norman: University of Oklahoma Press, 1963.
Discusses the cultural roots of Nuevo Mexicanos.

3613 Carranza, Eliu. Pensamientos on Los Chicanos: A
      Cultural Revolution. Berkeley: California Book Co.,
      1969; 2nd ed., 1971.
Concerns the Americanization of Mexicans largely through the
U.S. education system.

3614 Carrillo-Beron, Carmen. Traditional Family Ideology
      in Relation to Focus of Control: A Comparison of
      Chicano and Anglo Women. San Francisco: R & E
      Research Associates, 1974.
Compares sex roles in typical Anglo and Mexican American
families.

3615 Casavantes, Edward J. A New Look at the Attributes of
      the Mexican-American. Albuquerque, N. Mex.: Southwest
      Cooperative Education Laboratory, 1969.
Describes the problem of distinguishing between
socio-economic and ethnic factors.

3616 Castañeda, Alfredo, ed. Mexican Americans and
      Educational Change. New York: Arno Press, 1974.
Papers from a symposium on Chicano educational problems at
the University of California, Riverside, May 21-22, 1971.

3617 Castañeda Shular, Antonia; Tomas Ibarra-Frausto; and
      Joseph Sommers. Literatura chicana: texto y contexto.

Englewood Cliff, N.J.: Prentice-Hall, 1972.
Includes the history of the Chicano literary movement as
well as many historical items, e.g.: Plan de San Diego, Juan
Cortina's Proclamation, Plan de Santa Barbara.

3618   Chicano Educational Conference, St. Edward's
       University, 1974. Proceedings of the Chicana
       Educational Conference. Edited by Imelda I. Ramos.
       Austin, Tex.: Educational Research Corporation for the
       Advancement of Mexican American Women, 1975.
Proceedings of the Conference held Feb. 23, 1974.

3619   The Chicano Experience. Edited by Stanley West and
       June Macklin. Boulder, Colo.: Westview Press, 1979.
A collection of papers and addresses on Chicano problems in
American society.

3620   The Chicano Heritage. Edited by Carlos Cortes. New
       York: Arno Press, 1976.

3621   Church Views of the Mexican American. New York: Arno
       Press, 1974.
An original anthology of seven works, 1924-1959: E. T.
Clark, The Latin Immigrant in the South, 1924; R. N. McLean
and C. A. Thompson, Spanish and Mexican in Colorado, 1924;
V. M. McCombs, From Over the Border, 1925; L. E. Bresette,
Mexicans in the United States, 1929; R. C. Jones and L. R.
Wilson, The Mexican in Chicago, 1931; B. A. Hodges, A
History of the Mexican Mission Work Conducted by the
Presbyterian Church in the United States of America, 1931;
and B. Blair, A. O. Liveley, and G. W. Trimble,
Spanish-speaking Americans, 1959.

3622   Clark, Margaret. Health in the Mexican American
       Culture: A Community Study. Berkeley: University of
       California Press, 1959; 2nd ed., 1970.
A health survey in Sal si Puedes, a barrio of San Jose,
California; the author's 1957 thesis.

3623   Cotera, Martha P. The Chicana Feminist. Austin,
       Tex.: Information Systems, 1977.

3624   Dickey, Dan Wm. The Kennedy Corridos: A Study of the
       Ballads of a Mexican American Hero. Austin: Center
       for Mexican American Studies, University of Texas,
       1978.
Includes a short bibliography of Mexican American corridos.

3625   Dickey, Roland F. New Mexico Village Arts; Drawings
       by Lloyd Lozes Goff. Albuquerque: University of New
       Mexico Press, 1949; reprint, 1970.
Describes the folk arts and the art "industry" of New
Mexico.

3626   Edmonson, Munro S. Los Manitos-A Study of
       Institutional Values. New Orleans: Middle American
       Research Institute, 1957.
Describes social conditions and problems of acculturation.

3627   Education and the Mexican American. New York: Arno
       Press, 1974.
An anthology of five works, 1930-1951: A. Reynolds, The
Education of Spanish-speaking Children in Five Southwestern
States, 1933; G. I. Sanchez, Concerning Segregation of
Spanish-speaking Children in the Public Schools, 1951; H. T.
Manuel, The Education of Mexican and Spanish-speaking
Children in Texas, 1930; W. Little, Spanish Speaking
Children in Texas, 1944; and G. I. Sanchez, The Education
of Bilinguals in a State School System, 1934.

3628   Elsasser, Nan; Kyle MacKenzie; and Yvonne Tixier y
       Vigil. Las Mujeres: Conversations from an Hispanic
       Community. Old Westbury, N.Y.: Feminist Press, 1981.
A series of oral histories presenting essentially a Nuevo
Mexicana perspective on the Chicana experience.

3629   Espinosa, Jose E. Saints in the Valleys: Christian
       Sacred Images in the History, Life, and Folk Art of
       Spanish New Mexico. Albuquerque: University of New
       Mexico Press, 1960; revised ed., 1967.
A useful survey of a distinctive Nuevo Mexicano folk art,
the carving of santos.

3630   Ewing, T. W. A Report on Minorities in Denver: The
       Spanish-speaking People in Denver. Denver, Colo.:
       Mayor's Interim Survey Committee on Human Relations,
       1947.

3631   Frierman, Jay D. The Ontiveros Adobe: Early Rancho
       Life in Alta California. Pacific Palisades, Calif.:
       Greenwood and Associates, 1982.
Describes Hispanic cultural life in southern California.

3632   Garcia Cisneros, Florencio. Santos of Puerto Rico and
       the Americas. Detroit: Blaine Ethridge Books, 1979.
A general survey of the art of carving and painting wooden
santos in Latin America, by a specialist in Latin American
art.

3633   Gastil, Raymond D. Cultural Regions of the United
       States. Seattle: University of Washington Press,
       1975.
A comparative study of thirteen socio-cultural regions
identified by the author.

3634   Gil, C. B. The Many Faces of the Mexican American: An
       Essay Concerning Chicano Character. Seattle:

University of Washington, 1982.
A publication of the university's Centro de Estudios
Chicanos.

3635   Gomez-Quiñones, Juan. On Culture. Los Angeles:
       Chicano Studies Center, University of California,
       1972.

3636   Gonzalez, Carlos. An Overview of the Mestizo
       Heritage: Implications for Teachers of Mexican-
       American Children. San Francisco: R & E Research
       Associates, 1976.
Generally equates mestizo with Mexican American and makes
recommendations for reducing conflict between school and
home.

3637   Gonzalez, Nancie L. The Spanish-Americans of New
       Mexico: A Heritage of Pride. Albuquerque: University
       of New Mexico Press, 1969.
Largely a socio-cultural history of Nuevo Mexicanos, plus
recent political events. Criticized by some for bias.

3638   Griffith, Beatrice. American Me. Boston: Houghton
       Mifflin Co., 1948.
Covers various aspects of Mexican American life in southern
California, especially palomillas, zoot suits, World War II,
and the immediate postwar period.

3639   Gutierrez, Felix and Jorge Reina Schement.
       Spanish-Language Radio in the Southwestern United
       States. Austin: Center for Mexican American Studies,
       University of Texas, 1979.

3640   Hall, Elizabeth Boyd (White). Popular Arts of Spanish
       New Mexico. Santa Fe: Museum of New Mexico Press,
       1974.
A comprehensive survey of New Mexican folk arts, with
illustrations, photographs, and a brief bibliography.

3641   Haseldon, Kyle. Death of a Myth. New York:
       Friendship Press, 1964.
Concerns the church affiliations of Mexican Americans.

3642   Heller, Celia S. Mexican American Youth: Forgotten
       Youth at the Crossroads. New York: Random House,
       1966.
A sociological study which includes material on educational
experience and delinquency as well as the obstacles to
acculturation and upward mobility.

3643   Hernandez, Deluvina. Mexican American Challenge to a
       Sacred Cow. Los Angeles: Mexican American Cultural
       Center, University of California, 1970.
Attacks earlier sociological studies of Mexican Americans;

especially critical of stereotypical assumptions of two UCLA
School of Education studies.

3644   Hispano Culture of New Mexico. With an introduction
       by Carlos E. Cortes. New York: Arno Press, 1976.
Contents: Aurora Lucero-White, Los Hispanos: Five Essays on
the Folkways of the Hispanos, 1947; Aurora Lucero-White, The
Folklore of New Mexico, Vol. I--Romances, Corridos, Cuentos,
Proverbios, Dichos, Adivinanzas, 1941; Aurora Lucero-White;
Eunice Hauskins; and Helene Mareau, Folkdances of the
Spanish Colonials of New Mexico, 1940; Mela Sedillo, Mexican
and New Mexican Folkdances, 1950; F. M. Kercheville and
George E. McSpadden, A Preliminary Glossary of New Mexican
Spanish. (Reprinted from the University of New Mexico
Bulletin, Language Series 5:3 (1924).

3645   Houghland, Willard. American Primitive Art. New
       York: Kleijkamp & Monroe, 1947.
Stresses the art of santo-making in New Mexico.

3646   Huerta, Jorge A. Chicano Theater: Themes and Forms.
       Ypsilanti, Mich.: Bilingual Press/Editorial Bilingüe,
       1982.
Excellent for the history of the Mexican American theater in
the context of U.S. theater development.

3647   Institute of Texan Cultures. Los Mexicanos Texanos.
       San Antonio: University of Texas, 1971.
Thirty-two pages; also in English with the title The Mexican
Texans.

3648   Jimenez, Francisco, ed. The Identification and
       Analysis of Chicano Literature. New York: Bilingual
       Press, 1979.
Includes both history and criticism of Chicano authors and
their works. The articles themselves describe the
development of the various categories in Chicano literature.

3649   Jimenez, Francisco, ed. Mosaico de la vida: prosa
       chicana, cubana, y puertorriqueña. New York: Harcourt
       Brace Jovanovich, 1981.
Includes introductory essays placing each selection in
historical context; also bibliographic references.

3650   Jordan, Lois B. Mexican Americans: Resources to Build
       Cultural Understanding. Littleton, Colo.: Libraries
       Unlimited, 1973.

3651   Karpas, Melvin R. Mexican-American and Cultural
       Deprivation. Chicago: Juvenile Delinquency Research
       Projects, Chicago Teachers College, 1964.

3652   Keyes, Charles F., ed. _Ethnic Change_. Seattle:
       University of Washington Press, 1981.

3653   Kluckhohn, Florence R. et al. _Variations in Value_
       Orientations. Evanston, Ill.: Row, Peterson, 1961.
Includes excellent material on social patterns in New
Mexico.

3654   Kruszewski, Z. Anthony; Richard L. Hough; and Jacob
       Ornstein-Galacia. _Politics and Society in the_
       Southwest: Ethnicity and Chicano Pluralism. Boulder,
       Colo.: Westview Press, 1982.
A series of articles emphasizing the heavy flow of
undocumented Mexicans across the border and pointing out
increasing Chicano participation in the majority society as
well as the powerful forces preserving cultural and language
ethnicity.

3655   Kubler, George. _Santos; an Exhibition of the_
       Religious Folk Art of New Mexico. Forth Worth, Tex.:
       Amon Carter Museum of Western Art, 1964. Also,
       Philadelphia: University of Pennsylvania Press, 1964.

3656   Leal, Luis, et al., eds. _A Decade of Chicano_
       Literature (1970-1979): Critical Essays and
       Bibliography. Santa Barbara, Calif.: Editorial La
       Causa, 1982.
Studies by ten specialists in the genres of Chicano
literature reviewing the trends in their areas of expertise
during the decade of the seventies. These were originally
papers presented at a conference held at the University of
California at Santa Barbara in 1980.

3657   Leon-Portilla, Miguel. _Culturas en peligro_. Mexico,
       D.F.: Alianza Editorial Mexicana, 1976.
Chapters 6, 7, and 8 deal with the Chicano, migration, the
frontier, cultural differences, and the Treaty of Guadalupe
Hidalgo. By a leading Mexican historian.

3658   Lopez, Richard Emilio. _Anxiety, Acculturation and the_
       Urban Chicano: The Relationship Between Stages of
       Acculturation and Anxiety Level of EOP Students.
       Berkeley: California Book Co., 1970.

3659   Lopez, Ronald W., et al. _Chicanos in Higher_
       Education: Status and Issues. Los Angeles: Chicano
       Studies Center, University of California, 1976.

3660   Lopez, Thomas R., Jr. _Prospects for the Spanish_
       American Culture of New Mexico. San Francisco: R & E
       Research Associates, 1974.
A cultural history, from the 16th century to the 1960s,
based on the author's University of New Mexico thesis.

3661   Lucas, I. The Browning of America: The Hispanic
       Revolution in the American Church. Chicago: Fides
       Claretian Publications, 1981.

3662   Major, Mabel; Rebecca W. Smith; and Thomas M. Pearce.
       Southwest Heritage, A Literary History with
       Bibliography. Rev. 2nd ed. Albuquerque: University
       of New Mexico Press, 1948.
A relatively brief history with an extensive bibliography,
pp. 165-192.

3663   Malarin, Mariano. The Dictionary of Mariano Malarin,
       Whose Life Spanned Two Cultures. Cupertino, Calif.:
       California History Center, De Anza College, 1980.
Edited by Albert Shumate; thirty-seven pages.

3664   Manuel, Herschel T. Spanish-Speaking Children of the
       Southwest. Austin: University of Texas Press, 1965.
Problems of the Spanish-speaking child in an English-
speaking environment.

3665   Marshall, Wes, et al. Fiesta: Minority Television
       Programming. Tucson: University of Arizona Press,
       1974.
A history of the development of Mexican American television.

3666   Martinez, Arthur D. and B. Lopez de Martinez. Who's
       Who? Chicano Officeholders, 1981-1982. 4th ed.
       Silver City, N. Mex.: n.p., 1982?
Includes officials at local, state, and national levels;
also some bibliographical material and photographs.

3667   Martinez, Julio A., ed. Chicano Scholars and Writers:
       A Bibliographical Directory. Metuchen, N.J.:
       Scarecrow Press, 1979.
An extremely useful tool, also containing limited
biographical information.

3668   Mendoza, Vicente T. Lirica narrativa de Mexico. El
       corrido. Mexico, D.F.: Instituto de Investigaciones
       Esteticas, Universidad Nacional Autonoma de Mexico,
       1964.
A collection of corridos, four or five concerning the
Mexican American of the Southwest.

3669   Mills, George T. The People of the Saints. Colorado
       Springs, Colo.: Taylor Museum, 1967.
A brief pamphlet on Nuevo Mexicano religious art.

3670   Montenegro, Marilyn. Chicanos and Mexican Americans:
       Ethnic Self-Identification and Attitudinal
       Differences. San Francisco: R & E Research
       Associates, 1976.

Includes charts and a good bibliography.

3671   Morton, John A. <u>The Mexican American in School and
       Society</u>. Los Angeles: Institute for American Studies,
       Los Angeles State University, 1956.

3672   Murguia, Edward. <u>Assimilation, Colonialism, and the
       Mexican American People</u>. Austin: Center for Mexican
       American Studies, University of Texas, 1975.
Describes social conditions that act as a deterrent to
assimilation.

3673   Murphy, James M. <u>The Spanish Legal Heritage in
       Arizona</u>. Tucson: Arizona Pioneers' Historical
       Society, 1966.

3674   Myers, Gustavus. <u>History of Bigotry in the United
       States</u>. New York: Capricorn Books, 1960.
Describes the nativist movement in the United States,
placing anti-Mexican feeling in historical perspective.

3675   Newcomb, Rexford. <u>Spanish Colonial Architecture in
       the United States</u>. New York: J. J. Augustin, 1937.

3676   Ortega, Joaquin. <u>The Intangible Resources of New
       Mexico</u>. Santa Fe, N. Mex.: Archaeological Institute
       of America, 1945.
A brief fifteen page pamphlet.

3677   Ortego (y Gasca), Philip D., ed. <u>We are Chicanos: An
       Anthology of Chicano Literature</u>. New York: Pocket
       Books, 1973.

3678   Osorio, Josina, ed. <u>A Bridge Between Two Peoples</u>.
       Moscow: University of Idaho, 1981.
Report of a conference held at the University of Idaho in
April 1981. Presentations on Chicano literature and
culture.

3679   Padilla, Amado M., ed. <u>Acculturation: Theory, Models
       and Some New Findings</u>. Boulder, Colo.: Westview
       Press, 1980.

3680   Paredes, Americo and Raymund Paredes, eds.
       <u>Mexican-American Authors</u>. Boston: Houghton Mifflin
       Co., 1976.
A collection of short stories, poems, and corridos, many of
which have historical value in explaining the Chicano
experience.

3681   Paz, Octavio. <u>The Labyrinth of Solitude; Life and
       Thought in Mexico</u>. New York: Grove Press, 1961.
A fundamental work reflecting on the Mexican historical
experience; includes the Chicano in Chapter 1 titled "The

Pachuco and Other Extremes."

3682 Peon, Maximo (pseud.). Como viven los mexicanos en
       los Estados Unidos. Mexico, D.F.: B. Costa-Amic,
       1966.
A critical personal account.

3683 Pettit, Arthur G. Images of the Mexican American in
       Fiction and Film. College Station: Texas A & M
       University Press, 1980.
Places the Mexican American in the context of U.S.
literature and motion pictures. Includes an excellent
bibliography.

3684 Picon-Salas, Mariano. A Cultural History of Spanish
       America. Berkeley: University of California Press,
       1965.
Background to understanding the Spanish cultural
contribution.

3685 Poggie, John L., Jr. Between Two Cultures: The Life
       of an American-Mexican. Tucson: University of Arizona
       Press, 1973.
American by culture, Mexican by nationality, Ramon Gonzales
searches for identity.

3686 Powell, Philip W. Tree of Hate: Propaganda and
       Prejudices Affecting United States Relations With the
       Hispanic World. New York: Basic Books, 1971.
A historical overview of ethnic and cultural conflict.

3687 Quirarte, Jacinto. Mexican American Artists. Austin:
       University of Texas Press, 1973.
A history of Mexican American art and artists by the
outstanding specialist in the field.

3688 Reid, John T. Spanish American Images of the United
       States, 1790-1960. Gainesville: University Presses of
       Florida, 1977.
Describes the changing images of the United States held by
Spanish Americans from 1790-1960.

3689 Reyes, Ignacio. A Survey of the Problems Involved in
       the Americanization of the Mexican-American. San
       Francisco: R & E Research Associates, 1972.
Reprint of a 1957 University of Southern California master's
thesis.

3690 Reynolds, Annie. The Education of Spanish-Speaking
       Children in Five Southwestern States. Washington,
       D.C.: U.S. Government Printing Office, 1933.
U.S. Department of the Interior Bulletin 1933, No. 11.

3691   Ridge, Martin, ed. The New Bilingualism: An American
       Dilemma. New Brunswick, N.J.: Transaction Books,
       Rutgers--the State University, 1982.
Based on a conference at the University of Southern
California, it explores the aspects and problems of
bilingualism and biculturalism.

3692   Robinson, Cecil. Mexico and the Hispanic Southwest in
       American Literature. Tucson: University of Arizona
       Press, 1977.
Revision and update of With the Ears of Strangers, item
3693.

3693   Robinson, Cecil. With the Ears of Strangers: The
       Mexican in American Literature. Tucson: University of
       Arizona Press, 1963.
An accurate, objective literary history with insights on the
development of stereotypes.

3694   Romanell, Patrick. Making of the Mexican Mind; a
       Study in Recent Mexican Thought. Notre Dame, Ind.:
       University of Notre Dame Press, 1952.
Helpful toward understanding Mexican American culture.

3695   Rosenquist, Carl M. and Edwin I. Megargee.
       Delinquency in Three Cultures. Austin: University of
       Texas Press, 1969.
Covers juvenile delinquency in San Antonio, Texas.

3696   Salinas, Luis O. and Lillian Faderman, comps. From
       the Barrio: A Chicano Anthology. San Francisco:
       Canfield Press, 1973.
Socio-political essays, fiction and poetry in two parts: My
Revolution and My House.

3697   Saunders, Lyle. Spanish-Speaking Americans and
       Mexican-Americans in the United States. New York:
       Bureau for Intercultural Education, 1944.

3698   Schermerhorn, Richard A. These Our People; Minorities
       in American Culture. Boston, Mass.: D. C. Heath &
       Co., 1949.
Includes material on the acculturation of Mexicans.

3699   Shevky, Eshref and Marilyn Williams. The Social Areas
       of Los Angeles, Analysis and Typology. Berkeley:
       University of California Press, 1949.
Demographic profile, with distribution and characteristics
of Los Angeles Mexican Americans.

3700   Soto, Antonio R. The Chicano and the Church. Denver,
       Colo.: Marfel Associates, 1975.
Early account of Church-Mexican American relations by a
leading specialist in the area.

3701   Steele, Thomas J. _Santos and Saints: Essays and
        Handbook_. Albuquerque, N. Mex.: Calvin Horn, 1974.
        Reprint, Santa Fe, N. Mex.: Ancient City Press, 1982.
An excellent study which includes bibliographic references.
The 1982 edition has an updated bibliography.

3702   Steinberg, Stephen. _The Ethnic Myth: Race, Ethnicity,
        and Class in America_. New York: Atheneum Publishers,
        1981.
Argues that many traits considered to be ethnic may in fact
be related more to class or other social factors.

3703   Swadesh, Frances Leon. _Hispanic Americans of the Ute
        Frontier from the Chama Valley to the San Juan Basin,
        1694-1960_. Boulder: University of Colorado Press,
        1966.
A tri-ethnic research project thesis, University of
Colorado.

3704   Tatum, Charles M. _Chicano Literature_. Boston, Mass.:
        Twayne Publishers, 1982.
The first two chapters describe the historical development
of Chicano literature.

3705   Thurston, Richard G. _Urbanization and Sociocultural
        Change in a Mexican-American Enclave_. San Francisco:
        R & E Research Associates, 1974.
Reprint of the author's 1957 thesis, University of
California at Los Angeles. Based heavily on interviews, it
includes material on cultural developments.

3706   Tireman, Lloyd S. _Teaching Spanish-Speaking Children_.
        Albuquerque: University of New Mexico Press, 1948.
        Reprint, New York: Arno Press, 1976.
A pioneering effort in this field.

3707   Tireman, Lloyd S. and Mary Watson. _A Community School
        in a Spanish-Speaking Village_. Albuquerque:
        University of New Mexico Press, 1948. Reprint, New
        York: Arno Press, 1976.
Describes an experimental school in a New Mexican Hispano
community.

3708   Tushar, Olibama Lopez. _The People of "El Valle." A
        History of the Spanish Colonials in the San Luis
        Valley_. [Denver, Colo.?] Olibama Lopez Tushar, 1975.
A study of the homes, occupations, folk customs, and leisure
activities of Hispanics in southern Colorado. See also item
3377.

3709   Ulibarri, Sabine R. _Cultural Heritage of the
        Southwest, the Mexican American. A New Focus on_

Opportunity. Washington, D.C.: U.S. Government
            Printing Office, 1967.
Testimony presented at the Cabinet Committee Hearings on
Mexican American Affairs, El Paso, Texas, 1967.

3710   U.S., Commission on Civil Rights. Toward Quality
       Education for Mexican Americans. Report VII: Mexican
       American Education Study. Washington, D.C.: U.S.
       Government Printing Office, 1974.

3711   U.S., Commission on Civil Rights. The Unfinished
       Education: Outcomes for Minorities in Five
       Southwestern States. Report II: Mexican American
       Educational Series. Washington, D.C.: U.S. Government
       Printing Office, 1971.

3712   U.S., Congress, House, Committee on Education and
       Labor, General Subcommitee on Education, 91st Cong.,
       2nd sess. Hearings on H.R. 14910. Washington, D.C.:
       U.S. Government Printing Office, 1970.
Hearings held Feb.16-May 6, 1970 on Ethnic Heritage Study
Centers.

3713   U.S., Department of Labor, Employment Standards
       Administration, Women's Bureau. Women of Spanish
       Origin in the United States. Washington, D.C.: U.S.
       Government Printing Office, 1976.

3714   Urbanski, Edmund S. Hispanic America and Its
       Civilizations: Spanish Americans and Anglo Americans.
       Translated by Frances K. Hendricks and Beatrice
       Berler. Norman: University of Oklahoma Press, 1978.
An excellent comparative study; includes a short
bibliography.

3715   Urzua, Roberto; Martha P. Cotera; and Emma G. Stupp,
       eds. Library Services to Mexican Americans. Las
       Cruces: ERIC-CRESS, New Mexico State University, 1978.

3716   Van Stone, Mary R. Spanish Folk Songs of New Mexico.
       Chicago: R. F. Seymour, 1926.

3717   Villanueva, D. Chicano Sports Heroes: Athletes and
       Athletics in the Spanish Speaking Community.
       Englewood Cliffs, N. J.: Prentice-Hall, 1975.

3718   Vogt, Evon Zartman and Ethel M. Albert, eds. People
       of Rimrock; a Study of Values in Five Cultures.
       Cambridge, Mass.: Harvard University Press, 1966.
A study of New Mexican social life and customs.

3719   Walter, Paul A., Jr. Race and Cultural Relations.
       New York: McGraw-Hill Book Co., 1952.
Has material on the Spanish-speaking American's problems; a

also historical background.

3720   Waugh, Julia (Nott). *The Silver Cradle; Mexicans in San Antonio*. Austin: University of Texas Press, 1955.

3721   Wells, Gladys. *Factors Influencing the Assimilation of the Mexican in Texas*. San Francisco: R & E Research Associates, 1974.
Reprint of a 1941 master's thesis at Southern Methodist University.

3722   Wilder, Mitchell A. *New Mexican Santos*. Colorado Springs, Colo.: Taylor Museum, 1968.
A brief publication on New Mexican folk art; illustrated.

3723   Wilder, Mitchell A., ed. *Santos: The Religious Folk Art of New Mexico*. Colorado Springs, Colo.: Taylor Museum, 1943.

3724   Wilson, Michael and Deborah Rosenfelt. *Salt of the Earth*. Old Westbury, N.Y.: Feminist Press, 1978.
Film script of a southwest copper strike, with commentary.

3725   Wolf, Bernard. *In This Proud Land: The Story of a Mexican-American Family*. Philadelphia: J. P. Lippincott Co., 1978.
Describes the life experiences of a Mexican American migrant family of Texas. High school level.

3726   Wroth, William. *Christian Images in Hispanic New Mexico*. Colorado Springs, Colo.: Taylor Museum, 1982.
A study, with photographs, of Hispanic santos and bultos from New Mexico and southern Colorado.

IX: Theses and Dissertations

3727 Adorno, William. "The Attitudes of Selected Mexican
      and Mexican-American Parents in Regards to
      Bilingual/Bicultural Education." San Diego, Calif.:
      United States International University, 1973.

3728 Allen, Joseph E. "A Sociological Study of Mexican
      Assimilation in Salt Lake City, 1947." Master's
      thesis. Salt Lake City: University of Utah, 1947.

3729 Arnold, Charles A. "The Folk-lore, Manners, and
      Customs of the Mexicans in San Antonio, Texas."
      Master's thesis. Austin: University of Texas, 1928.

3730 Baird, Janet Rae. "An Analysis of Mexican-American
      Culture Taught in Kansas Migrant Programs." Lawrence:
      University of Kansas, 1973.

3731 Barraza Flores, Jose. "Establishing a Barrio Myth."
      Master's thesis. Tempe: Arizona State University,
      1973.
Public planning and Mexican American sociology.

3732 Barton, May. "Methodism at Work Among the Spanish
      Speaking People of El Paso, Texas." El Paso:
      University of Texas, 1950.

3733 Berrios, Lizardo S. "Socialization in a Mexican
      American Community: A Study in Civilizational
      Perspective." New York: New School for Social
      Research, 1979.
Based in part on a study in southwest Texas. Finds
assimilation and acculturation taking place, especially as
the result of federal civil rights legislation and Chicano
activism. Includes historical background.

3734 Buckner, Dellos. "Study of the Lower Rio Grande
      Valley as a Culture Area." Master's thesis. Austin:
      University of Texas, 1929.

3735 Cabrera, Y. Arturo. "A Study of American and
      Mexican-American Culture Values and Their Significance
      in Education." Boulder: University of Colorado, 1964.

3736 Campa, Arthur Leon, Jr. "Ivory Towers and Ethnic
      Revival: Chicanos in Academe." Boulder: University of
      Colorado, 1980.
Explores factors in the relation of Chicano educational
expectations and attitudes of ethnicity to parental
education levels and income as well as other variables.
Includes some Chicano cultural history and relations with
the U.S. school system.

3737   Chavez, John R. "The Lost Land: The Chicano Image of
        the Southwest." Ann Arbor: University of Michigan,
        1980.

3738   Clements, Harold McCutcheon. "An Analysis of Levels
        of Living of Spanish-American Rural and Urban Families
        in Two South Texas Counties." Master's thesis.
        College Station: Texas A & M University, 1963.

3739   Corona, Bert C. "Study of Adjustment and
        Interpersonal Relations of Adolescents of Mexican
        Descent." Berkeley: University of California, 1955.

3740   Crampton, Helen Mickelsen. "Acculturation of the
        Mexican-American in Salt Lake County, Utah." Salt
        Lake City: University of Utah, 1967.
Argues that Mexican Americans' achievement of acculturation
responds primarily to educational and language improvement.

3741   Degarmo, Elvinia Reyes. "An Exploratory Study of
        Mexican-American Women in an Urban Community."
        Berkeley: University of California, 1975.

3742   Flores, Raymond J. "The Socio-economic Status Trends
        of the Mexican People Residing in Arizona." Master's
        thesis. Tempe: Arizona State University, 1951.
Contains good information on jobs, housing, immigration, and
the church in the post-World War II period.

3743   Foppe, Regina E. "The Response of the Roman Catholic
        Church to the Mexican Americans in West Texas, 1839
        into Post-Vatican II." Master's thesis. Lubbock:
        Texas Technological University, 1976.

3744   Friesden, Maria S. "The Influence of the Early
        Cultures of New Mexico on the Contemporary Fashions of
        that Area." Columbus: Ohio State University, 1961.

3745   Garcia, Homer Dennis Calderon. "Chicano Social Class,
        Assimilation, and Nationalism." 2 vols. New Haven,
        Conn.: Yale University, 1980.
Finds that Mexican American social and economic success is
hindered more by dominant Anglo society repression than by
home socio-economic status.

3746   Garza, Roberto J. "Chicano Studies: A New Curriculum
        Dimension for Higher Education in the Southwest."
        Stillwater: Oklahoma State University, 1975.
Finds that Chicano Studies programs have a positive effect
on self-concepts of undergraduate Mexican American students.

3747   Gibson, Delber Lee. "Protestantism in Latin American
        Acculturation." Austin: University of Texas, 1959.
Argues that Protestantism is a cause for and evidence of

acculturation. In studying a sample in Austin, Texas Gibson found that those already attracted to Anglo values were more likely to convert to Protestantism.

3748   Ginn, Mabelle D. "Social Implications of the Living
        Conditions in a Selected Number of Families."
        Master's thesis. Los Angeles: University of Southern
        California, 1947.
Includes much material on housing; based mostly on
interviews in Belvedere, California.

3749   Goldkind, Victor. "Factors in the Differential
        Acculturation of Mexicans in a Michigan City." East
        Lansing: Michigan State University, 1963.

3750   Gonzalez, Juan L., Jr. "Social Mobility Among
        Mexican-American Agricultural Workers in Northern
        California." Berkeley: University of California,
        1980.

3751   Guerra, Fermina. "Mexican and Spanish Folklore and
        Incidents in Southwest Texas." Master's thesis.
        Austin: University of Texas, 1941.
Includes the founding of ranches; ranch life, tales.

3752   Guerra, Irene. "The Social Aspirations of a Selected
        Group of Spanish-Name People in Laredo, Texas."
        Master's thesis. Austin: University of Texas, 1959.

3753   Gutierrez, Felix F. "Spanish-Language Radio and
        Chicano Internal Colonialism." Stanford, Calif.:
        Stanford University, 1976.
Includes a descriptive analysis of 485 radio stations
broadcasting in Spanish; uses an internal colonialism model.

3754   Haney, Jane Bushong. "Migration, Settlement Pattern,
        and Social Organization: A Midwest Mexican-American
        Case Study." East Lansing: Michigan State University,
        1978.
Useful for social, political, and economic patterns and for
the history of Chicanos in Flint and Lansing, Michigan.

3755   Harding, Jacobina Burch. "A History of the Early
        Newspapers of San Antonio, 1823-1874." Master's
        thesis. Austin: University of Texas, 1951.

3756   Harrison, David C. "A Survey of the Administrative
        and Educational Policies of the Baptist, Methodist,
        and Presbyterian Churches Among Mexican-American

People in Texas." Master's thesis. Austin:
University of Texas, 1952.
Covers from the colonial period to 1950.

3757   Howard, Raymond G. "Acculturation and Social Mobility
       Among Latin-Americans in Resaca City." Master's
       thesis. Austin: University of Texas, 1952.

3758   Huerta, Jorge A. "The Evolution of Chicano Theatre."
       Santa Barbara: University of California, 1974.

3759   Hunt, Thomas Lynn. "The Equity and Impact of Medicare
       and Medicaid With Respect to Mexican Americans in
       Texas." Austin: University of Texas, 1978.

3760   Hurtado, Juan. "An Attitudinal Study of the Social
       Distance Between the Mexican and the Church." San
       Diego, Calif.: United States International University,
       1976.
Finds Mexicans closer to the Church than Chicanos, women
than men, less educated than more educated. A majority
showed an undercurrent of dissatisfaction with the Church as
an institution. Sees the Church as basically an Anglo
organization.

3761   Jackson, Robena E. "East Austin: A Socio-Historical
       View of a Segregated Community." Master's thesis.
       Austin: University of Texas, 1979.

3762   Jensen, James M. "The Mexican-American in an Orange
       County Community." Master's thesis. Claremont,
       Calif.: Claremont Graduate School, 1947.
Studies the Anaheim Mexican American community; more
statistical than descriptive.

3763   Jones, Dixie Lee Franklin. "The Plight of the Migrant
       Child in the Lower Rio Grande Valley." Master's
       thesis. Austin: Unversity of Texas, 1969.

3764   Jordan, Anne Harwell. "A Guide to Publishing for
       Americans of Mexican Descent: And, Foreign Printers in
       Sixteenth Century Mexican Society." Master's report.
       Austin: University of Texas, 1972.

3765   Juarez, Rumaldo Zapata. "Education Status
       Orientations of Mexican American and Anglo American
       Youth in Selected Low-Income Counties of Texas."
       Master's thesis. College Station: Texas A & M
       University, 1968.

3766   Jurado, Pete. "The Chicano Aggregation: A Barrio
       Gang." Graduate manuscript. El Paso: University of
       Texas, 1976.

3767   Kazan, Phyllis M.   "Mexican American Kinship
        Interaction; A Study of 20 Families in Austin, Texas."
        Master's thesis.   Austin: University of Texas, 1966.

3768   Keefe, Susan E.   "Women in Power: Anglo and Mexican
        American Female Leaders in Two Southern California
        Communities."   Santa Barbara: University of
        California, 1974.

3769   King, Marianna.   "Accounting for Chicano Gangs."
        Master's thesis.   Fullerton: California State
        University, 1979.
Discusses social structures and development of palomillas
(urban gangs).

3770   Kurtz, Norman.   "Gatekeepers in the Process of
        Acculturation."   Boulder: University of Colorado,
        1966.
Studies the role of persons who act as links between a rural
Mexican culture and the urban Anglo culture.

3771   Lacy, James M.   "Attitudes of Anglo-American Writers
        Towards the Spanish-Americans of the Southwest."
        Chicago: University of Chicago, 1956.

3772   Landman, Ruth H.   "Some Aspects of the Acculturation of
        Mexican Immigrants and Their Descendants to American
        Culture."   New Haven, Conn.: Yale University, 1954.

3773   Laquest, Katherine W.   "A Social History of the
        Spaniards in Nacogdoches."   Master's thesis.   Waco,
        Tex.: Baylor University, 1941.

3774   Larralde, Carlos Montalvo.   "Chicano Jews in South
        Texas."   Los Angeles: University of California, 1978.

3775   Lasswell, Thomas.   "A Study of Status Stratification
        in Los Angeles."   Los Angeles: University of Southern
        California, 1952.
Indicates that anti-Mexican discrimination is on the decline
since World War II.

3776   Leach, Joseph L.   "The Establishment of the Texan
        Tradition."   New Haven, Conn.: Yale University, 1948.
Shows anti-Mexican attitudes and development of the Texan
stereotypical character.

3777   Lopez, Olibama.   "The Spanish Heritage of the San Luis
        Valley."   Denver, Colo.: University of Denver, 1942.
Describes Mexican American culture in Colorado. See also
item 3708.

3778   Lovey, Ida S.   "Certain Mexican Social Values: A
        Comparative Inquiry Into Tradition and Change."

Master's thesis. Chicago: Roosevelt University, 1962.

3779   McConville, J. Lawrence. "A History of Population in
       the El Paso-Ciudad Juarez Area." Master's thesis.
       Albuquerque: University of New Mexico, 1966.

3780   McCrary, Mallie E. "These Minorities in our Midst:
       With Emphasis on Latin-Americans in Texas." Master's
       thesis. Austin: University of Texas, 1953.
Concerns largely primary education problems of
Spanish-speaking Mexican children.

3781   McGarry, (Sister) Francesca. "A Study of Cultural
       Patterns Among Three Generations of Mexicans in San
       Antonio, Texas." Master's thesis. Austin: University
       of Texas, 1957.

3782   McLeod, Joseph A., Jr. "Baptists and Racial and
       Ethnic Minorities (including Mexican Americans) in
       Texas." Denton: North Texas State University, 1972.

3783   McNamara, Patrick H. "Bishops, Priests and Prophecy:
       A Study in the Sociology of Religious Protest." Los
       Angeles: University of California, 1968.
Reviews the relations of the Catholic Church and the Mexican
American.

3784   Marston, Miriam. "The History of Alianza Patriota
       Revolucionaria Americana." Master's thesis. El Paso:
       University of Texas, 1950.

3785   Martinez, Ruth L. "The Unusual Mexican--A Study in
       Acculturation." Master's thesis. Claremont, Calif.:
       Claremont Graduate School, 1942.
Studies status achievement by educated Mexican Americans in
San Bernardino County; good on cultural background and
acculturation factors.

3786   Matthiasson, Carolyn W. "Acculturation of
       Mexican-Americans in a Midwestern City." Ithaca,
       N.Y.: Cornell University, 1968.

3787   Meador, Bruce S. "Minority Groups and Their Education
       in Hays County, Texas." Austin: University of Texas,
       1959.
Includes material on problems of the undocumented immigrant.

3788   Meier, Harold C. "Three Ethnic Groups in a
       South-western Community." Master's thesis. Boulder:
       University of Colorado, 1955.

3789   Montes, Mary. "School-Community Relations: A View
       from the Barrio." Claremont, Calif.: Claremont
       Graduate School, 1974.

Focuses on Chicano efforts to change the school system as it affects them. Studies the conditions affecting Chicano entrance into the educational power structure.

3790 Moyers, Robert A. "A History of Education in New Mexico." Nashville, Tenn.: George Peabody College for Teachers, 1941.

3791 Murray, John M. "A Socio-Cultural Study of 118 Mexican Families Living in a Low-rent Public Housing Project in San Antonio, Texas." Washington, D.C.: Catholic University of America, 1955.

3792 Nostrand, Richard L. "The Hispanic-American Borderlands: A Regional Historical Geography." Los Angeles: University of California, 1968.
Provides a good historical geographical study from 1950 to 1960; describes the history and pattern of settlement. Has good Mexican American 1960 population maps of the Southwest by counties. The basis of item 134.

3793 Nuñez, Thomas D. "Occupational Choice and Social Mobility of Mexican-Americans: A Study of the Vocational Aspirations of Mexican-American High School Seniors." Master's thesis. Fresno, Calif.: Fresno State University, 1968.

3794 Officer, James E. "Sodalities and Systemic Linkage: The Joining Habits of Urban Mexican-Americans." Tucson: University of Arizona, 1964.

3795 O'Neill, Elizabeth F. S. "Mexican-American Children in the Process of Acculturation." Master's thesis. Stockton, Calif.: University of the Pacific, 1968.

3796 Ortego (y Gasca), Philip D. "Backgrounds of Mexican American Literature." Albuquerque: University of New Mexico, 1971.
Examines the broad history of Chicano literature as it has led up to the contemporary literary renaissance. Argues for an American literature that includes the Hispanic as well as Anglo American contributions.

3797 Painter, Norman W. "The Assimilation of Latin Americans in New Orleans, Louisiana." Master's thesis. New Orleans, La.: Tulane University, 1959.
Includes Mexican Americans among sixty-seven case studies.

3798 Parsons, Theodore W., Jr. "Ethnic Cleavage in a California School." Stanford, Calif.: Stanford University, 1966.
Finds that the U.S. school system encourages ethnic cleavage which reaches 100% by the eighth grade. This cleavage reflects adult patterns and is reinforced by mutual

stereotypes.

3799   Portes, Alejandro. "Assimilation of Latin American
       Minorities in the U.S." Durham, N.C.: Duke
       University, 1975.
An unpublished research proposal.

3800   Press, Ernest. "The Mexican Population of Laramie."
       Master's thesis. Laramie: University of Wyoming,
       1946.

3801   Pruneda, Manuela C. "Acculturation, Self-concept and
       Achievement of Mexican American Students." Commerce:
       East Texas State University, 1973.

3802   Ramirez, Sara Leonil. "The Educational Status and
       Socio-economic Backgrounds of Latin-American Children
       in Waco, Texas." Master's thesis. Austin: University
       of Texas, 1957.
Studies the relationship of acculturation, self-concept and
academic achievement among Chicano grade and high school
students in Waco, Texas.

3803   Ramos, Juan. "Spanish-Speaking Leadership in Two
       Southwestern Cities: A Descriptive Survey." Waltham,
       Mass.: Brandeis University, 1968.
Describes three categories of leaders in San Antonio and
Phoenix; provides some insight in the structure and
operation of ethnic leadership and in its variations.

3804   Reich, Alice Higman. "The Cultural Production of
       Ethnicity: Chicanos in the University." Boulder:
       University of Colorado, 1977.

3805   Remy, Martha C. M. "Protestant Churches and Mexican
       Americans in South Texas." Austin: University of
       Texas, 1970.
Describes the Chicano Protestant as cut off from his Mexican
culture by his religious beliefs; finds the new social and
political activism of South Texas Chicanos a kind of secular
fundamentalism.

3806   Rendon, Armando. "The Chicano Press: Status and
       Trends of Chicano Newspapers and Magazines."
       Washington, D.C.: Antioch Graduate School, 1975.

3807   Reynolds, Clarence L. "Decision-Making and Cultural
       Change: The Status of Spanish American Small Farms in
       Northern New Mexico." Dallas, Tex.: Southern
       Methodist University, 1974.

3808   Reynolds, Diane A. Trombetta. "Economic Integration
       and Cultural Assimilation: Mexican-Americans in San

Jose." Stanford, Calif.: Stanford University, 1974.
Studies the interrelation of economic achievement and
retention of ethnicity. Finds the efforts to preserve
aspects of both cultures and the greatest degree of
assimilation in language and dress.

3809   Rivera, George F., Jr.   "El Barrio: A Sociological
       Study of Acculturation in a Mexican American
       Community." Buffalo: University of New York, 1971.
Investigates the importance of structural and cultural
variables in understanding the process of acculturation
among Mexican Americans.

3810   Romano-V., Octavio. "Don Pedrito Jaramillo: The
       Emergence of a Mexican-American Folk-saint."
       Berkeley: University of California, 1964.
Describes the character, life-style, and experiences of
Pedrito Jaramillo (1829-1907), folk-healer.

3811   Rubalcava, Luis A. "Assimilation Among Urban
       Chicanos: A Structural and Cultural Analysis." Ann
       Arbor: University of Michigan, 1980.
A study based on Detroit Chicanos; it finds that economic
and social attainment did not weaken attachment to Mexican
cultural values. Includes a sketch of Chicano history in
Michigan and especially Detroit.

3812   Samora, Julian. "The Acculturation of the Spanish
       Speaking People of Fort Collins, Colorado, in Selected
       Culture Areas." Master's thesis. Fort Collins:
       Colorado Agricultural and Mechanical College, 1947.

3813   Samora, Julian. "Minority Leadership in a Bi-Cultural
       Community." St. Louis, Mo.: Washington University,
       1953.

3814   San Miguel, Guadalupe, Jr. "Endless Pursuits: The
       Chicano Educational Experience in Corpus Christi,
       Texas, 1880-1960." Stanford, Calif.: Stanford
       University, 1979.
Stressing the period between 1930 and 1960, this work
studies the struggle against discrimination and racism in
the public school system.

3815   Sanchez, Armand J. "Self-concept of Mexican-American
       Youth: The Stability of Self-concept of Mexican-
       American Youth in Relation to Identification with
       Mexican Cultural Values." Master's thesis. Fresno,
       Calif.: Fresno State University, 1967.

3816   Sanchez, George I. "The Education of Bilinguals in a
       State School System." Berkeley: University of
       California, 1934.

3817 Sanchez, Luisa Guerrero G. "The Latin-American of the
      Southwest: Backgrounds and Curricular Implications."
      Austin: University of Texas, 1954.

3818 Sandoval, Joe R. "Use of Welfare Services by
      Mexicans: A Study of Cultural Influence on Public
      Assistance Recipients of Madera County, California."
      Master's thesis. Fresno, Calif.: Fresno State
      University, 1967.

3819 Sandoval, T. Joe. "A Study of Some Aspects of the
      Spanish Speaking Population in Selected Communities in
      Wyoming." Master's thesis. Laramie: University of
      Wyoming, 1946.

3820 Savage, Fred. "Baptist Missions Among Foreign
      Language Groups in El Paso." Master's thesis. El
      Paso: University of Texas, 1955.

3821 Saxton, Russell Steele. "Ethnocentrism in the
      Historical Literature of Territorial New Mexico."
      Albuquerque: University of New Mexico, 1980.

3822 Schmidt, Patricia B. "Organizations for the
      Achievement of Latin-Americans in Texas." Master's
      thesis. New Orleans, La.: Tulane University, 1966.

3823 Scott, Helen Browne. "Educational Attainment and
      Aspirations of Rural and Urban Spanish-Americans in
      Two South Texas Counties." Master's thesis. College
      Station: Texas A & M University, 1969.

3824 Sjoberg, Gideon. "Culture Change as Revealed by a
      Study of Relief Clients of a Suburban New Mexico
      Community." Master's thesis. Albuquerque: University
      of New Mexico, 1947.

3825 Smith, Clara G. "The Development of the Mexican
      People in the Community of Watts, California." Los
      Angeles: University of Southern California, 1956.

3826 Smith, Courtland L. "The Salt River Project in
      Arizona: Its Organization and Integration with the
      Community." Tucson: University of Arizona, 1968.

3827 Soto, Antonio R. "A Study of an Ethnic Minority
      Within the Roman Catholic Church." Berkeley:
      University of California, 1978.

3828 Spence, Allyn G. "Variables Contributing to the
      Maintenance of the Mexican-American Social Structure
      in Tucson." Master's thesis. Tucson: University of
      Arizona, 1968.

3829   Stern, Gwen Louise. "Ethnic Identity and Community
        Action in El Barrio." Chicago: Northwestern
        University, 1976.

3830   Stewart, Arleen. "'Las Mujeres de Aztlan': A
        Consultation With Elderly Mexican-American Women in a
        Socio-historical Perspective." Berkeley: California
        School of Professional Psychology, 1973.

3831   Takesian, Sarkis A. "A Comparative Study of the
        Mexican-American Graduate and Dropout." Los Angeles:
        University of Southern California, 1967.

3832   Trueax, Alice. "Mexican-American Students in Schools
        of the Southwest." Graduate manuscript. Fresno,
        Calif.: Fresno State University, 1965.

3833   Valerio, Luis G. "The Socio-Psychological Development
        of the Mexican American: Historical and Sociological
        Events as Determinants." Greeley: University of
        Northern Colorado, 1974.
A broad historical suvey of Chicano cultural heritage, with
the impact of Indian cultures and the continuing pervasive
influence of the Catholic Church. Also discusses the
attributes of contemporary Mexican American students.

3834   Vallejos, Thomas. "Mestizaje: The Transformations of
        Ancient Indian Religious Thought in Contemporary
        Chicano Fiction." Boulder: University of Colorado,
        1980.

3835   Van Ness, John R. "Hispanos in Northern New Mexico:
        The Development of Corporate Community and
        Multicommunity." Philadelphia: University of
        Pennsylvania, 1979.
Finds that the emergence of corporate communities in early
New Mexico enabled settlers to meet political, economic and
religious needs. After the U.S. takeover these communities
acted to defend the inhabitants against socio-economic
changes.

3836   Viramontes, Maria de la Cruz. "Creating a Stereotype:
        A Study of the Chicano." Master's thesis. Fullerton:
        California State University, 1974.

3837   Weaver, Thomas. "Social Structure, Change, and
        Conflict in a New Mexico Village." Berkeley:
        University of California, 1965.

3838   Wessel, David S. "The Quetzalcoatl Prophecy and
        Interpretation of 'Reality is a Great Serpent' Chicano
        Expression." East Lansing: Michigan State University,
        1977.
Investigates the use of the Feathered Serpent as part of

Chicano artistic and aesthetic expression in literature, the
theatre, sculpture, and painting.

3839 Wilson, Foster W.   "Demographic Characteristics of
      Texas White Persons of Spanish Surname."   Master's
      thesis.   College Station: Texas A & M University,
      1966.

3840 Winnie, William W., Jr.   "The Hispanic Peoples of New
      Mexico."   Master's thesis.   Gainesville: University of
      Florida, 1955.

3841 Zeltmann, Judith B.   "Factors Affecting Mexican-Anglo
      Intermarriage in Nogales and Tucson, Arizona."
      Master's thesis.   Tucson: University of Arizona, 1964.

3842 Zurfluh, Hattie E.   "The Spanish Heritage in Texas."
      Master's thesis.   Waco, Tex.: Baylor University, 1933.
Covers briefly all aspects of Spanish heritage from
agriculture to the dance; a useful survey.

IX: Periodicals

3843   Alisky, Marvin. "Mexican Heritage--Texas, New Mexico,
       Arizona and California." In The Role of the Mexican
       American in the History of the Southwest: Conference
       of the Inter-American Institute, Pan American College,
       pp. 3-11. Edinburg, Tex.: Pan American College, 1969.

3844   Altus, William. "The American-Mexican: The Survival
       of a Culture." Journal of Social Psychology 29 (May
       1949), 211-220.
Sees language, religion, and propinquity to Mexico as
factors encouraging the survival of Mexican culture.

3845   Apodaca, Maria L. "The Chicana Woman: An Historical
       Materialist Perspective." Latin American Perspectives
       4: 1 & 2 (Winter & Spring 1977), 70-89.

3846   Aragon, Jane L. "The Cofradias of New Mexico: A
       Proposal and a Periodization." Aztlan 9 (1978),
       101-118.
Covers the cofradias as agents of community unity and
survival from the colonial period to the early 20th century.
Includes a good brief bibliography.

3847   Arce, Carlos H. "A Reconsideration of Chicano Culture
       and Identity." Deadalus 110:2 (Spring 1981), 177-191.
Concerns itself with problems of assimilation and cultural
indentification and argues the need for further
socio-psychological study. A good reference list is
included.

3848   Armas, Jose. "La familia de la raza." De Colores 3:2
       (1977), 4-54.

3849   Atkins, James A. "A Cultural Minority Improves
       Itself." In his Human Relations in Colorado,
       1868-1959. Denver, Colo.: Office of Instructional
       Services, 1961.

3850   Austin, Mary. "Catholic Culture in Our Southwest."
       Commonweal 8:21 (Sept. 26, 1928), 510-512, I: El
       Dorado on the Rio Grande; 8:22 (Oct. 3, 1928),
       544-546, II: The Work of the Brown Gowns; 8:23 (Oct.
       10, 1928), 572-575, III: Salvaging the Old Crafts.

3851   "Authentic Pachuco." Time 44 (July 10, 1944), 72.

3852   Aztlan 13 (Spring & Fall 1982).
Entire issue is devoted to Mexican American folk art and
folklore.

3853 Bagdikian, Ben H. "The Invisible Americans."
      Saturday Evening Post 236:45 (Dec. 21-28, 1953),
      28-33.
Story of the culture of poverty; includes Mexican Americans.

3854 Barker, Ruth L. "Where Americans Are Anglos." North
      American Review 228 (1929), 568-573.

3855 Bean, Frank D. "Components of Income and Expected
      Family Size Among Mexican Americans." Social Science
      Quarterly 54:1 (June 1973), 100-116.
Finds rural and urban attitudes toward family size and age
at marriage important, but not necessarily decisive factors.

3856 Bernal, Ignacio. "The Cultural Roots of the Border:
      An Archaeologist's View." In Views Across the Border.
      Edited by Stanley R. Ross, pp. 25-32. Albuquerque:
      University of New Mexico Press, 1978.

3857 Boettcker, Joe E. "Penitente Memorial Act."
      Southwest Heritage 10 (Summer 1980).

3858 Bogardus, Emory S. "Gangs of Mexican-American
      Youths." Sociology and Social Research 28:1 (1943),
      55-66.
Discusses the zoot suiter and argues that the rioting of
1943 did not result from criminal activities.

3859 Borah, Woodrow W. and Sherburne F. Cook. "Marriage
      and Legitimacy in Mexican Culture: Mexico and
      California." California Law Review 54 (May 1966),
      946-1008.

3860 Borderlands Journal 4:1 (Fall 1980).
The entire issue is devoted to various aspects of Mexican
American health topics.

3861 Braddy, Haldeen. "Pachucos and Their Argot."
      Southern Folklore Quarterly 42 (1960), 255-271.

3862 Broom, Leonard and Eshref Shevky. "Mexicans in the
      United States." Sociology and Social Research 36
      (Jan.-Feb. 1952), 150-159.
Discusses social and cultural origins, isolation and
integration in the U.S. and assimilation and urbanization.

3863 Brown, Robert L. "Social Distance Perception as a
      Function of Mexican-American and Other Ethnic
      Identity." Sociology and Social Research 57:1 (Oct.
      1972), 273-286.

3864 Buzan, Bert C. and Diana Buder Phillips.
      "Institutional Completeness and Chicano Militancy."

Aztlan 11:1 (Spring 1980), 33-64.
Discusses Chicano attitudes and action in Crystal City and
in Corpus Christi, Texas. Includes a number of analytical
tables.

3865 Cafferty, Pastora. "Spanish-Speaking Americans:
      Economic Assimilation or Cultural Identity." In
      Pieces of a Dream: The Ethnic Workers' Crisis with
      America. Edited by Michael Wenk; S. M. Tomasi; and
      Geno Baroni, pp. 191-262. Staten Island, N.Y.: Center
      for Migration Studies, 1972.

3866 Campa, Arthur L. "Culture Patterns of the
      Spanish-Speaking Community." In _The Spanish-Speaking_
      People of the Southwest, pp.20-36. Dallas, Tex.:
      Council of Spanish-American Work, 1966.

3867 Campa, Arthur L. "Folklore and History." _Western_
      Folklore 24:1 (Jan. 1965), 1-6.

3868 Campa, Arthur L. "Individualism in Hispanic Society."
      In _The Spanish-Speaking People of the Southwest_, pp.
      11-20. Dallas, Tex.: Council of Spanish-American
      Work, 1966.

3869 Campa, Arthur L. "Manana is Today." In
      Southwesterners Write. Edited by T. M. Pearce and A.
      P. Thomason, pp. 291-304. Albuquerque: University of
      New Mexico Press, 1946.

3870 Campa, Arthur L. "Protest Folk Poetry in the Spanish
      Southwest." _Colorado Quarterly_ 20:3 (Winter 1972),
      355-363.

3871 Candelaria, Cordelia, ed. "Chicanas en el ambiente
      nacional/ Chicanas in the National Landscape." A
      special issue of _Frontiers: A Journal of Women's_
      Studies 5:2 (Summer 1980).
Multiple oppression of Chicanas is the main theme of these
twelve articles, which range from history to literature.

3872 Caplan, Stanley W. and Ronald Ruble. "A Study of
      Culturally Imposed Factors." _Journal of Educational_
      Research 58:1 (Sept. 1964), 16-21.

3873 Cardenas, Gilbert. "Who Are the Midwestern Chicanos:
      Implications for Chicano Studies." _Aztlan_ 7:2 (Summer
      1976), 141-152.
A brief survey of the articles on Midwestern Chicanos
appearing in vol. 7:2 of _Aztlan_.

3874 Cardoso, Lawrence A. "Protestant Missionaries and the
      Mexican: An Environmentalist Image of Cultural

Differences." New Scholar 7: 1&2 (1978), 223-236.

3875 Carlson, Alvar W. "Corrales, New Mexico: Transition
      in a Spanish-American Community." Red River Valley
      Historical Review 4:2 (Spring 1979), 88-99.
Covers from the 18th century to the present.

3876 Carroll, Charles D. "Miguel Aragon, a Great Santero."
      El Palacio 50 (March 1943), 49-64.

3877 Casas, J. Manuel; Bruce E. Wampold; and Donald R.
      Atkinson. "The Categorization of Ethnic Stereotypes
      by University Counselors." Hispanic Journal of
      Behavioral Sciences 3:1 (March 1981), 83-90.

3878 Chance, John K. "On the Mexican Mestizo." Latin
      American Research Review 14:3 (1979), 153-168.
A history of the term.

3879 Chandler, Charles R. "Value Orientations Among
      Mexican Americans in a Southwestern City." Sociology
      and Social Research 58:3 (April 1974), 262-269.

3880 Chavarria, Jesus. "A Brief Inquiry into Octavio Paz'
      Laberinto of Mexicanidad." The Americas 27:4 (April
      1971), 381-388.
Concerns especially the pachuco.

3881 Chavez, Cesar. "The Mexican American and the Church."
      El Grito 1:4 (Summer 1968), 9-12.

3882 Cheyney, S. and M. Candler. "Santos: An Enigma of
      American Native Art." Parnassus 7 (May 1935), 22-24.

3883 Christian, Jane McNab and Chester C. Christian.
      "Spanish Language and Culture in the Southwest." In
      Language Loyalty in the United States. Edited by
      Joshua A. Fishman. The Hague: Mouton & Co., 1966.
      Reprint, New York: Arno Press, 1978.

3884 Common Ground 8 (Spring 1948).
The bulk of this issue is devoted to the Mexican American.
Includes seven pages of photographs.

3885 Crews, Mildred T. "Saint-Maker from Taos." Americas
      21:3 (March 1969), 33-37.
Describes the life and work of Patrocinio Barela; numerous
photographs of his wood carvings.

3886 Cromwell, Ronald E. and Rene A. Ruiz. "The Myth of
      Macho Dominance in Decision Making Within Mexican and
      Chicano Families." Hispanic Journal of Behavioral
      Sciences 1:4 (Dec. 1979), 355-374.

3887   Curti, Josafat. "The Chicano and the Church."
       Christian Century 92:9 (March 12, 1975), 253-257.
More on the Mexican American's situation in the United
States than on his relations with the church.

3888   De Anda, Jose. "Mexican Culture and the
       Mexican-American." El Grito 3 (Fall 1969), 42-48.
Argues that Mexican Americans need to know their Indian and
Spanish cultural roots.

3889   De Leon, Arnoldo. "Growing Up Tejano." La Luz 6:10
       (Oct. 1977), 13.

3890   Delucchi, Mary P. "El Teatro Campesino de Aztlan:
       Chicano Protest Through Drama." Pacific Historian
       16:1 (Spring 1972), 15-27.
Describes the historical development and organization of the
"teatro campesino;" also its role in the movimiento.

3891   Demos, George D. "Attitudes of Mexican-Americans and
       Anglo Groups Toward Education." Journal of Social
       Psychology 57 (Aug. 1962), 249-256.
Holds that there are significant differences in attitudes
toward education that may be due to ethnic group membership.

3892   Dickerson, R. E. "Some Suggestive Problems in the
       Americanization of Mexicans." Pedagogical Seminary
       26:3 (Sept. 1919), 288-297.

3893   Donnelly, Thomas C. "New Mexico: An Area of
       Conflicting Cultures." In Rocky Mountain Politics.
       Edited by Thomas C. Donnelly, pp. 218-251.
       Albuquerque: University of New Mexico Press, 1940.

3894   Dozier, Edward P. "Peasant Culture and Urbanization:
       Mexican Americans in the Southwest." In Peasants in
       the Modern World. Edited by Philip K. Bock.
       Albuquerque: University of New Mexico Press, 1969.

3895   D'Silva, Fabio. "Mexican-Americans and Voluntary
       Associations." Research Reports in the Social
       Sciences 2:1 (Spring 1968). Social Science Training
       and Research Lab., University of Notre Dame.

3896   Dubois, Cora. "The Dominant Value Profile of American
       Culture." American Anthropologist 57 (1955), 1232.

3897   Duran, Percy. "Latino Success Stories--Plunkett and
       Flores Aren't Alone." La Luz 9:1 (Dec. 1980-Jan.
       1981), 24, 25.

3898   Dworkin, Anthony G. "Stereotypes and Self-Images Held
       By Native-born and Foreign-born Mexican-Americans."

Sociology and Social Research 49:2 (Jan. 1965),
214-260.
Based on a survey of 200 East Los Angelenos.

3899 Fairchild, Halford H. and Joy A. Cozens. "Chicano,
      Hispanic, or Mexican American: What's in a Name?"
      Hispanic Journal of Behavioral Sciences 3:2 (June
      1981), 191-198.

3900 Faught, Jim D. "Chicanos in a Medium-sized City:
      Demographic and Socioeconomic Characteristics."
      Aztlan 7:2 (Summer 1976), 307-326.
Delineates a profile of the Chicano population in South
Bend, Indiana which dates heavily from post-1965. Includes
various tables and charts.

3901 Felice, Lawrence G. "Mexican American Self-Concept
      and Educational Achievement: The Effects of Ethnic
      Isolation and Socioeconomic Deprivation." Social
      Science Quarterly 53:4 (March 1973), 716-726.
Argues the school socio-economic climate influences
educational achievement and that desegregation would
positively benefit Mexican American students.

3902 Fergusson, Erna. "The New New Mexico." New Mexico
      Quarterly Review 19 (Winter 1949), 417-426.

3903 Fitzpatrick, Joseph P. "Mexicans and Puerto Ricans
      Build a Bridge." America 94 (Dec. 31, 1955), 373-375.

3904 Ford, Georgiana B. "A Legend: Its Influence Upon
      Mexican Nationality." Out West 37 (Jan.-June 1917),
      320-329.
Importance of the Virgin of Guadalupe in Mexican culture and
nationalism.

3905 Francesca, (Sister) Mary. "Variations of Selected
      Cultural Patterns Among Three Generations of Mexicans
      in San Antonio, Texas." American Catholic Social
      Review 19 (1958), 24-34.

3906 Frank, Eva A. "The Mexicans Simply Won't Work."
      Nation 125 (1927), 155-167.
Examines Anglo-Latin differences in cultural values in
Mexico.

3907 Garth, Thomas R. and E. Candor. "Musical Talent of
      Mexicans." American Journal of Psychology 49 (1937),
      298-301.

3908 Garza, Roberto J. "Cultural Contributions of the
      Mexican Americans." In The Role of the Mexican
      American in the History of the Southwest: Conference
      of the Inter-American Institute, Pan American College,

pp. 53-60. Edinburg, Tex.: Pan American College,
1969.

3909 Gecas, Viktor. "Self-Conceptions of Migrant and
      Settled Mexican Americans." Social Science Quarterly
      54:3 (Dec. 1973), 579-595.
Finds that ethnic identity was less important than gender,
religion, and family in both groups. Includes six useful
statistical tables based on surveys in the state of
Washington.

3910 Gleason, Philip. "The Melting Pot: Symbol of Fusion
      or Confusion." American Quarterly 16 (Spring 1964),
      20-46.

3911 Gomez-Quiñones, Juan. "On Culture." Revista
      Chicano-Riqueña 5:2 (Spring 1977), 29-47.

3912 Gomez-Quiñones, Juan and Luis Leobardo Arroyo. "On
      the State of Chicano History: Observations on Its
      Development, Interpretations, and Theory, 1970-1974."
      Western Historical Quarterly 7:2 (April 1976),
      155-185.

3913 Gonzales, Eugene. "The Mexican-American in
      California." California Education 3 (Nov. 1965),
      19-22.

3914 Gonzales (de Mireles), Jovita. "Latin Americans." In
      Our Racial and National Minorities: Their History,
      Contributions and Present Problems. Edited by Francis
      J. Brown and Joseph Roucek, pp. 497-509. New York:
      Prentice-Hall, 1937.

3915 Gonzalez, Henry B. "Hope and Promise: Americans of
      Spanish Surname." American Federationist 74-75 (June
      1967), 13-16.

3916 Grebler, Leo. "The Naturalization of Mexican
      Immigrants in the United States." International
      Migration Review 1 (Fall 1966), 17-32.
Sees isolation as an important factor in low levels of
naturalization; compares the rate of Mexicans with all
immigrants. Includes seven useful tables making various
comparisons.

3917 Griswold del Castillo, Richard. "Chicanos' Cultural
      Vitality Under Pressure." Center Magazine 13 (1980),
      47-52.

3918 Gutierrez, Felix. "Spanish-Language Media in America:
      Background, Resources, History." Journalism History
      4:2 (Summer 1977), 39-41, 65-66.

3919   Hammerback, John C. and Richard J. Jensen. "The
       Rhetorical Worlds of Cesar Chavez and Reies Tijerina."
       Western Journal of Speech Communication 44 (1980),
       166-176.
Studies and compares the rhetoric and content of the
speeches of these two movimiento leaders. Concludes that
despite differences of style they share similar perception
of their roles.

3920   Hayden, Robert G. "Spanish-Americans of the
       Southwest: Life Style Patterns and Their
       Implications." Welfare in Review 4 (April 1966),
       14-25.

3921   Heist, Elizabeth H. "Border Music of the 1970's in
       the Southwestern United States." In Popular Music in
       Mexico. Edited by Claes af Geijerstam. Albuquerque:
       University of New Mexico Press, 1976.

3922   Heller, Celia S. "Chicano is Beautiful." Commonweal
       91 (1969-1970), 454-458.
Describes a spirit of optimism and militancy among Chicano
youths, which Heller sees as coming out of the post-World
War II generation.

3923   Hernandez, Jose; Leo Estrada; and David Alvirez.
       "Census Data and the Problem of Conceptually Defining
       the Mexican-American Population." Social Science
       Quarterly 53:4 (March 1973), 671-687.
Concerns the problem of precisely who was identified in the
1970 census as Mexican American.

3924   Hernandez, Luis. "The Culturally Disadvantaged
       Mexican-American Student." Journal of Secondary
       Education Part I: 42:2 (Feb. 1967), 59-65; Part II:
       42:3 (March 1967), 123-138.

3925   Herrera-Sobek, Maria. "The Acculturation Process of
       the Chicana in the Corrido." Proceedings of the
       Pacific Coast Council on Latin American Studies 9
       (1982), 25-34.
Uses the corrido to show process of acculturation among
Mexican American women, as seen by Mexican males rather than
an idealized concept.

3926   Hewes, Gordon H. "Mexicans in Search of 'The
       Mexican.'" American Journal of Economics and
       Sociology 13 (Jan. 1954), 209-223.

3927   Huerta, Jorge A. "Chicano Theater-A Background."
       Aztlan 2:2 (Fall 1971), 63-78.
A brief broad survey covering from 1598 to the present
times, emphasizes the important role of Luis Valdez.

3928   Huerta, Jorge A. "Concerning Teatro Chicano." Latin American Theatre Review 6:2 (1973), 13-20.

3929   Humphrey, Norman D. "Cultural Background of the Mexican Immigrant." Rural Sociology 13 (1948), 239-256.
Describes the town life and background "typical" of the Mexican who migrated to the United States.

3930   Humphrey, Norman D. "The Detroit Mexican and Naturalization." Social Forces 22 (1943-1944), 332-335.

3931   Humphrey, Norman D. "The Integration of the Detroit Mexican Colony." American Journal of Economics and Sociology 3 (Jan. 1944), 155-166.

3932   Humphrey, Norman D. "The Mexican Image of Americans." Annals of the American Academy of Political and Social Science 295 (Sept. 1954), 116-125.
Argues that the Mexican view of Americans is influenced by the class, social, and economic position of the viewer.

3933   Humphrey, Norman D. "Mexican Middleton." Common Ground 6 (1946), 20-28.

3934   Humphrey, Norman D. "The Stereotype and the Social Types of Mexican American Youth." Journal of Social Psychology 22 (1945), 69-78.
Describes "types" of Detroit Mexicans, which Humphrey finds divergent from popular stereotypes of Mexican youths (as in the Los Angeles zoot suiter).

3935   Jacobs, Sue-Ellen. "Top-Down Planning: Analysis of Obstacles to Community Development in an Economically Poor Region of the Southwestern United States." Human Organization 37 (1978), 246-256.

3936   Jaramillo, Mari-Luci. "How to Succeed in Business and Remain Chicana." La Luz 8:7 (Aug.-Sept. 1980), 33-35.
Ambassador to Honduras Jaramillo argues that Chicanas should capitalize on their individual personalities and styles rather than try to change.

3937   Jimenez, Francisco. "Chicano Literature: Sources and Themes." Bilingual Review 1:1 (Jan.-April 1974), 4-15.
Traces the heritage base of Chicano literature and argues that Chicano authors are redefining their culture and history.

3938   Jimenez, Francisco. "Dramatic Principles of the Teatro Campesino." Bilingual Review 2:1&2 (Jan. & Aug. 1975), 99-111.

Describes the Teatro Campesino as eclectic in form, content
and objectives.

3939   Jimenez, Francisco. "An Interview with Jose Antonio
       Villarreal." Bilingual Review 3:3 (Jan.-April 1976),
       66-72.
An in-depth interview with the author of Pocho and The Fifth
Horseman; includes his experience growing up in Santa Clara,
California.

3940   Jimenez Nuñez, Alfredo. "Los hispanos de Nuevo
       Mexico: contribucion a una antropologia de la cultura
       hispana en USA." Anales de Antropologia 14 (1977),
       439-442.

3941   Johansen, Sigurd. "The Social Organization of Spanish
       American Villages." Southwestern Social Science
       Quarterly 23 (Sept. 1942), 152-159.

3942   Johnson, J. B. "The Allelujas: A Religious Cult in
       Northern New Mexico." Southwest Review 22 (Jan.
       1937), 131-139.

3943   Jones, Robert Cuba. "Mexican-American Youth."
       Sociology and Social Research 32:4 (March-April 1948),
       793-797.
Argues for the need to end discrimination and prejudice
against Mexican Americans and describes some of the steps
being taken.

3944   Juston, Neal. "Mexican-American Achievement Hindered
       by Culture Conflict." Sociology and Social Research
       56:4 (July 1972), 471-479.
Based on students in Tucson, Arizona, this study of third
and fourth generation Chicanos seems to indicate a
considerable degree of acculturation.

3945   Kapp, Joe and Jack Olsen. "A Man of Machismo."
       Sports Illustrated (July 20, 1970).

3946   Kennedy, Diane. "The Chicano Press." Missouri
       Library Association Quarterly 30 (Sept. 1969),
       221-224.
A brief enumeration and description.

3947   Knowlton, Clark S. "Changes in the Structure and
       Roles of Spanish-American Families of Northern New
       Mexico." Southwestern Sociological Association
       Proceedings (1965), 15-48.

3948   Knowlton, Clark S. "The Spanish Americans in New
       Mexico." Sociology and Social Research 45:4 (July
       1961), 448-454.
Finds the breakdown in village culture and economy is

rapidly leading to assimilation, partly as the result of a
move to industrial centers.

3949 Kurtz, Norman R. "Gatekeepers: Agents in
      Acculturation." Rural Sociology 33:1 (March 1968),
      64-70.
The acculturation of Mexican Americans in Denver, Colorado.

3950 Leal, Luis. "Mexican American Literature: A
      Historical Perspective." Revista Chicano-Riqueña 1:1
      (1973), 32-44.

3951 Le Viness, W. Thetford. "Three Cultures of New
      Mexico." Americas 18 (June 1966), 8-15.
Describes the state of New Mexican Indian culture and the
history of its impact on Mexican and Anglo settlers.

3952 Lopez, Lino M. "Spanish-Americans in Colorado."
      America 91 (Sept. 18, 1954), 585-587.
A brief but insightful description of Colorado Chicanos and
the transition from Mexican to Anglo cultural norms.

3953 Lucey, (Rev.) Robert E. "The Catholic Church in
      Texas." In The Catholic Church, U.S.A. Edited by
      Louis J. Putz, C.S.G., pp. 225-231. Chicago: Fides
      Publishers Association, 1956.

3954 McDonagh, Edward C. "Status Levels of Mexicans."
      Sociology and Social Research 33:6 (July-Aug. 1949),
      449-459.
Discusses the legal status of Mexicans, recounts cases of
discrimination encountered by veterans, and touches on the
zoot suit riots of 1943. Finds Mexican Americans near the
bottom in status ranking.

3955 Maciel, David R. and Angelina Casillas. "Aztlan en
      Mexico: Perspectivas Mexicanas sobre el Chicano."
      Aztlan 11:1 (Spring 1980), 133-135.
Briefly describes Mexican scholarly interest in the Chicano,
his history and experience.

3956 McKenney, J. Wilson. "The Dilemma of the Spanish
      Surname People of California." California Teachers
      Association Journal 61 (March 1966), 17.

3957 McNamara, Patrick H. "Catholicism, Assimilation, and
      the Chicano Movement: Los Angeles as a Case Study."
      In Chicanos and Native Americans: The Territorial
      Minorities. Compiled by Rudolph O. de la Garza; Z.
      Anthony Kruszewski; and Tomas A. Arciniega, pp.
      124-130. Englewood Cliffs, N.J.: Prentice-Hall, 1973.

3958   Madrid-Barela, Arturo. "Towards an Understanding of
        the Chicano Experience." Aztlan 4:1 (Spring 1973),
        185-193.
A brief interpretive essay on the Mexican and Chicano
experience, emphasizing the internal colonial model.

3959   Manuel, Herschel T. "The Mexican Population of
        Texas." Southwest Review 17 (1932), 290-292.

3960   Martinez, A. "Literacy Through Democracy of
        Education." Howard Education Review 40 (May 1970),
        280-282.

3961   Martinez, Oscar J. "Chicano Oral History: Status and
        Prospects." Aztlan 9 (1978), 119-131.

3962   Mazon, Mauricio. "Illegal Alien Surrogates: A
        Psycho-historical Interpretation of Group Stereotyping
        in Time of Economic Stress." Aztlan 6:2 (Summer
        1975), 305-324.
A study in depth of American reaction to undocumented
Mexican migration to the United States. Includes an
analysis of pending legislation.

3963   Meier, Matt S. "Maria Insurgente." Historia Mexicana
        23:3 (Enero-Marzo 1974), 466-482.
Describes the development of the Virgin of Guadalupe as a
nationalistic Mexican symbol.

3964   Metzgar, Joseph V. "The Ethnic Sensitivity of Spanish
        New Mexicans: A Survey and Analysis." New Mexico
        Historical Review 49 (Jan. 1974), 49-73.

3965   "Mexican Artistic Invasion." Literary Digest 93:13
        (June 25, 1927), 27.

3966   Meyer, Doris. "Felipe Maximiliano Chacon: A Forgotten
        Mexican-American Author." New Scholar 6 (1977),
        111-126.

3967   Miller, Michael V. "Mexican Americans, Chicanos, and
        Others: Ethnic Self-Identification and Selective
        Social Attributes of Rural Texas Youth." Rural
        Sociology 41:2 (Summer 1976), 234-247.
A study of self-identifying terms, arguing that differences
were based on a wide variety of factors and finding a large
minority rejecting any ethnic label.

3968   Miranda, Gloria E. "Gente de Razon Marriage Patterns
        in Spanish and Mexican California: A Case Study of
        Santa Barbara and Los Angeles." Southern California
        Quarterly 63:1 (Spring 1981), 1-21.
Covers late 1700s and early 1800s.

3969 Morrissey, Richard S. "The Shaping of Two Frontiers."
      Americas 3:1 (Jan. 1951), 3-6, 41-42.
A comparison of the northern Spanish-Mexican frontier and
its western Anglo-American counterpart.

3970 Nall, Frank. "Role Expectations: A Cross Cultural
      Study." _Rural Sociology_ 27 (March 1952), 28-41.
Finds three different role orientations within the Mexican
American group and much greater uniformity in the Anglo
American group studied.

3971 Negrete, Louis R. "The Education of Mexican Students
      in the United States." _Campo Libre_ 1:1 (Winter 1981),
      35-84.

3972 Nostrand, Richard L. "'Mexican American' and
      'Chicano': Emerging Terms for a People Coming of Age."
      Pacific Historical Review 42:3 (Aug. 1973), 389-406.

3973 Olmo, Frank Del. "Voices for the Chicano Movement."
      Quill 40 (Dec.1971), 8-14.
A general review of the Chicano Press Association.

3974 Olvera, Joe. "Chicano Literature: Talent Awaiting
      Recognition." _La Luz_ 8:8 (Oct.-Nov. 1980), 20-21.
A brief survey of Chicano literature, listing a number of
active Chicano publishing houses.

3975 Ortego (y Gasca), Philip D. "The Chicano
      Renaissance." _Social Casework_ 52 (May 1971), 294-307.
Describes the Chicano literary movement.

3976 Ortego y Gasca, Philip D. "The Hispanic Woman: A
      Humanistic Perspective." _La Luz_ 8:8 (Oct.-Nov. 1980),
      6-9.
A broad survey of leading Hispanic women from Sor Juana Ines
de la Cruz to Emma Tenayuca and beyond.

3977 Padilla, Ron. "Apuntes para la documentacion de la
      cultura chicana." _El Grito_ 5:2 (Winter 1971-1972),
      3-43.
A in-depth study of bibliographic work on Chicano topics.

3978 Palfi, Marion. "Mexican-Americans." _Common Ground_ 8
      (1948), 52-61.

3979 Paredes, Americo. "Los Estados Unidos, Mexico, y el
      machismo." _Journal of Inter-American Studies_ 9:1
      (Jan. 1967), 65-84.

3980 Paredes, Raymund A. "Chicano Literature: An
      Historical Perspective." _UCLA Librarian_ 34:4 (April
      1981), 26-27.

3981 Paredes, Raymund A. "The Mexican Image in American
      Travel Literature, 1831-1869." New Mexico Historical
      Review 52 (Jan. 1977), 5-29.

3982 Paredes, Raymund A. "The Origins of Anti-Mexican
      Sentiment in the United States." New Scholar 6
      (1977), 139-165.
Emphasizes the early development of anti-Mexicanism. This
entire issue of the New Scholar is devoted to the Chicano.

3983 Pearce, T. M. "Southwestern Culture: An Artificial or
      a Natural Growth?" New Mexico Quarterly 1:3 (Aug.
      1931), 195-209.

3984 Pino, Frank, Jr. "A Chicano Perspective on American
      Cultural History." Journal of Popular Culture 13
      (Spring 1979), 488-500.

3985 Ramirez, Manuel, "Cognitive Styles and Cultural
      Democracy in Education." Social Science Quarterly
      53:4 (March 1973), 895-904.

3986 Ramirez, William L., ed. "Libraries and the
      Spanish-speaking." Wilson Library Bulletin 44 (March
      1970), 714-767.

3987 "La Raza Looks to its People." Economist 266:7018
      (March 4, 1978), 25-26.

3988 Reeve, Frank D. "New Mexico: Yesterday and Today."
      New Mexico Quarterly Review 16 (Summer 1946), 133-152.

3989 Rios, Francisco A. "The Mexican in Fact, Fiction, and
      Folklore." In Voices. Edited by Octavio I. Romano-V.
      Berkeley, Calif.: Quinto Sol, 1971.
Describes Mexican Americans and Mexicans as interpreted by
Anglo American writers.

3990 Robinson, Cecil. "Spring Water with a Taste of the
      Land: The Mexican Presence in the American Southwest."
      American West 3:3 (1966), 6-15, 95.

3991 Rodriguez, Jacobo. "Alienation of a New Generation of
      Chicanos." Aztlan 4:1 (Spring 1973), 147-154.
Argues for the rationality of giving undocumented aliens in
the U.S. permanent resident visas.

3992 Romano-V., Octavio I. "Charismatic Mexican Folk
      Healing and Folk Sainthood." American Anthropologist
      67 (Oct. 1963), 1151-1173.

3993   Romano-V., Octavio I. "Minorities, History and the
       Cultural Mystique." El Grito 1:1 (Fall 1967), 5-11.
The views of an outstanding early sociologist-leader in
Chicano studies.

3994   Sanchez, George I. "New Mexicans and Acculturation."
       New Mexico Quarterly Review 11 (Feb. 1941), 61-68.
Stresses the 1846 to 1902 failure to educate the Nuevo
Mexicano.

3995   Sanchez, George I. "Spanish in the Southwest." In
       Southwest Intercollegiate Conference. Summary of
       Proceedings of the Southwest Conference on "Social and
       Educational Problems of Rural and Urban
       Mexican-American Youth." Los Angeles: Occidental
       College, 1963.

3996   Sandoval, Moises. "Spanish-speaking vs. Church II."
       National Catholic Reporter 11:13 (Jan. 24, 1975), 16.
A broad survey of Chicano attitudes, largely centered on
Catolicos por la Raza, PADRES, and the Mexican American
Cultural Center in San Antonio, Texas.

3997   Schermerhorn, Richard A. "Mexicans and Spanish-
       Speaking Americans: A Mixed Culture." In his These
       Our People, Minorities in American Culture, pp.
       175-198. Boston: D. C. Heath & Co., 1949.

3998   Sedaño, Michael V. "Chicanismo: A Rhetorical Analysis
       of Themes and Images . . ." Western Journal of Speech
       Communication 44 (Summer 1980), 177-190.

3999   Sena Rivera, Jaime. "Chicanos: Culture, Community,
       Role: Problems of Evidence, and a Proposition of Norms
       Towards Establishing Evidence." Aztlan 1:1 (Spring
       1970), 37-51.

4000   Senter, Donovan. "Acculturation Among New Mexican
       Villagers in Comparison to Adjustment Patterns of
       Other Spanish-Speaking Americans." Rural Sociology 10
       (1945), 31-47.
Argues that Nuevo Mexicanos have been subject to less
conflict and stress than other Mexican Americans in the
process of acculturation.

4001   Servin, Manuel P. "California's Hispanic Heritage: A
       View into the Spanish Myth." Journal of San Diego
       History 19 (Winter 1973), 1-9.

4002   Shepperson, Wilbur S. "The Foreign-Born Response to
       Nevada." Pacific Historical Review 39 (Feb. 1970),
       1-18.
Includes a Mexican viewpoint.

4003   Simmons, Ozzie G. "The Mutual Images and Expectations
       of Anglo Americans and Mexican Americans." _Deadalus_
       90:2 (Spring 1961), 286-299. Also pp. 289-304 in
       Minorities in a Changing World. Edited by Milton L.
       Barron. New York: Alfred A. Knopf, 1967.
This entire issue of _Daedalus_ is devoted to ethnic groups in
the U.S.

4004   Smith, Griffin, Jr. "The Mexican Americans: A People
       on the Move." _National Geographic_ 157:6 (June 1980),
       780-808.
A broad-ranging article, from Texas to California and from
employment to culture. Includes many excellent photographs.

4005   Sommers, Vita S. "The Impact of Dual Cultural
       Membership on Identity." _Psychiatry_ 27 (1964),
       332-344.

4006   Soto, Shirlene A. "The Emerging Chicana: A Review of
       the Literature." _Southwest Economy and Society_ 2:1
       (Oct.-Nov. 1976), 39-45.

4007   Spilka, Bernard and Lois Gill. "Some Non-Intellectual
       Correlates of Academic Achievement Among Spanish-
       American Students." _School Counselor_ 12 (May 1965),
       213-221.

4008   Stoddard, Ellwyn R. "The Adjustment of Mexican
       American Barrio Families to Forced Housing
       Relocation." _Social Science Quarterly_ 53:4 (March
       1973), 749-759.
Found relocated El Paso Chamizal families made varying
adjustments, some more successful than others; also
discovered the importance of "mini-neighborhoods."

4009   Summer, Margaret L. "Mexican-American Minority
       Churches." _Practical Anthropology_ 10 (May-June 1963),
       115-121.
Discusses various implications of Mexican American
conversion to Protestantism.

4010   Swadesh, Frances L. "Property and Kinship in Northern
       New Mexico." _Rocky Mountain Social Science Journal_
       2:1 (1965), 209-214.

4011   Tatum, Charles. "Some Examples of Chicano Prose
       Fiction of the Nineteenth and Early Twentieth
       Centuries." _Revista Chicano-Riqueña_ 9:1 (1981),
       58-67.

4012   Terrones, Ed. "Some Thoughts of a Macho on the
       Chicana Movement." _Agenda_ 7:6 (Nov.-Dec. 1977),
       35-36.

4013 Tireman, Lloyd S. "New Mexico Tackles the Problem of the Spanish-speaking Child." Journal of Education 114 (1931), 300-301.

4014 Tuck, Ruth D. "Mexican-Americans: A Contributory Culture." California Elementary School Principals' Association Yearbook 17 (1945), 106-109.

4015 Ulibarri, Sabine R. "Cultural Heritage of the Southwest, The Mexican Americans. A New Focus on Opportunity." Testimony presented at the Cabinet Committee Hearings on Mexican American Affairs. Washington, D.C.: U.S. Government Printing Office, 1967.

4016 U.S., Congressional Record, 91st Congress, 1st sess., 1969, 2891. Extension of Remarks. "Mexican American Education: Search for Identity."

4017 U.S., Department of Health, Education, and Welfare, Office of Education. "Viva la Raza; Mexican American Education: Search for Identity." Washington, D.C.: U.S. Government Printing Office, 1968.

4018 Urquides, M. "Tucson's Tale of Two Cultures." NEA Journal 56 (Feb. 1967), 62.

4019 Vaca, Nick. "George I. Sanchez Memorial Lecture." Unpublished paper presented at a conference sponsored by the Mexican American Studies Center, April 24, 1972. Austin: University of Texas.

4020 Valdez, Luis. "The Tale of the Raza." Ramparts 5:2 (July 1966), pp. 40-43.
A partial and somewhat theatrical and lyrical description of the movimiento by the founder of the teatro campesino.

4021 Vigil, Diego. "Adaptation Strategies and Cultural Life Style of Mexican American Adolescents." Hispanic Journal of Behavioral Sciences 1:4 (Dec. 1979), 375-392.

4022 Vivas, Gustavo E. "Our Spanish-Speaking U.S. Catholics." America 91 (May 15, 1954), 187-188.
Describes the growing problem of the U.S. church ministering to the needs of a rapidly expanding Mexican population.

4023 Vollmar, Edward R., S.J. "La Revista Catolica." Mid-America, An Historical Review 58:2 (April-July 1976), 85-96.
Briefly describes the history of La Revista Catolica, a Spanish language publication of the Society of Jesus in the Southwest; began its life in Albuquerque in 1875 and ended

in El Paso in 1962.

4024 Wagner, Henry R. "New Mexico Spanish Press." New
      Mexico Historical Review 12:1 (Jan. 1937), 1-40.

4025 Walter, Paul A., Jr. "Spanish-Speaking Americans."
      In his Race and Culture Relations. New York:
      McGraw-Hill Book Co., 1952.

4026 Welch, Susan; John Comer; and Michael Steinman.
      "Interviewing in a Mexican-American Community . . .
      Potential . . . Bias." Public Opinion Quarterly 37:1
      (Spring 1973), 115-126.

4027 Wells, Miriam J. "Oldtimers and Newcomers: The Role
      of Context in Mexican Assimilation." Aztlan 11:2
      (Fall 1980), 271-295.
Studies the impact of socio-economic contexts on the
assimilation of Mexicans in the Wisconsin town of Riverside.
Points out differences in Catholic and Protestant attitudes
toward newly arrived Mexicans.

4028 "What is a Chicano?" Wilson Library Bulletin 46 (Feb.
      1972), 492-493.

4029 Wilder, Mitchell A. "Santos (Religious Folk Art of
      New Mexico)." American West 2:4 (Fall 1965), 37-46.

4030 Williams, J. Allen, Jr.; Nicholas Babchuk; and David
      R. Johnson. "Voluntary Associations and Minority
      Status: Comparative Analysis of Anglo, Black and
      Mexican Americans." American Sociological Review 38:5
      (Oct. 1973), 637-646.

4031 Williams, Linda. "Type and Stereotype: Chicano Images
      in Film." Frontiers: A Journal of Women Studies 5:2
      (Summer 1980), 14-17.

4032 Wolf, Eric R. "The Virgin of Guadalupe: A Mexican
      National Symbol." Journal of American Folklore 71
      (1958), 34-39.

4033 Womack, John Jr. "The Chicanos." New York Review of
      Books 19 (Aug. 31, 1972), 12-18.
A review of the historical literature to date.

4034 Wroth, William. "Hispanic Southwestern Craft
      Traditions and the Taylor Museum Collection." Journal
      of the West 19:3 (July 1980), 100-106.
Considers European, Indian, Mexican and Anglo influences.
With photographs.

4035 Yinger, J. M. and G. E. Simpson. "Integration of
      Americans of Mexican, Puerto-Rican, and Oriental

Descent." Annals of the American Academy of Politial
and Social Sciences 304 (March 1956), 124-127.
Sees Mexican integration proceeding more rapidly in school
than in employment and housing.

4036 Zurcher, L. A., et al. "Value Orientation Role
Conflict, and Alienation from Work, a Cross-Cultural
Study." American Sociological Review 30 (Aug. 1965),
539-548.

X.
BIBLIOGRAPHIES
AND GUIDES

4037 Adams, Ramon F. Six Guns and Saddle Leather. Norman:
      University of Oklahoma Press, 1954; revised and
      enlarged ed., 1969.
An annotated bibliography of the western frontier.

4038 Altus, David M. Bilingual Education: A Selected
      Bibliography. Las Cruces: ERIC-CRESS, New Mexico
      State University, 1970.
Valuable for bilingual materials in historical context.

4039 Altus, David M. Migrant Education: A Selected
      Bibliography. Las Cruces: ERIC-CRESS, New Mexico
      State University, 1971.

4040 American Council of Race Relations. Mexican
      Americans: A Selected Bibliography. Chicago: The
      Council, 1949.
A brief early bibliography of over 100 items.

4041 Anderson, Frank G. Southwest Archeology: A
      Bibliography. New York: Garland Publishing Co., 1982.

4042 Arroyo, Luis Leobardo. A Bibliography of Recent
      Chicano History Writings, 1970-1975. Los Angeles:
      Chicano Studies Center, University of California,
      1975.
This forty-five page bibliography focuses on recently
published articles, books, and theses. It is organized
basically by chronological periods.

4043 Barnes, Thomas C.; Thomas H. Naylor; and Charles W.
      Polzer. Northern New Spain: A Research Guide. Tucson:
      University of Arizona Press, 1981.
Provides lists of guides to document collections by area and
states, useful to help researchers find their way through
these collections in the United States, Mexico, and Europe.

Includes lists of colonial officials, government
organization, weights, measures, and coinage.

4044   Barrios, Ernest, et al., eds. Bibliografia de Aztlan:
        An Annotated Chicano Bibliography. San Diego, Calif.:
        Centro de Estudios Chicanos, San Diego State
        University, 1971.
Over 300 items, topically arranged; contains a section on
history.

4045   Beauchamp, Martha. Bilingualism with Reference to
        American Minority Groups. Washington, D.C.: Education
        and Public Welfare Division, Library of Congress,
        1967.

4046   Beebe, Ronald. Spanish Influence in the American
        Tradition: A Selected Bibliography. Washington, D.C.:
        Legislative Reference Service, Library of Congress,
        1964.

4047   Beers, Henry P. Spanish and Mexican Records of the
        American Southwest: A Bibliographical Guide to Archive
        and Manuscript Sources. Tucson: University of Arizona
        Press, 1979.
Excellent for bilbiographies, archives, and historical
sketches.

4048   Benitez, Mario A. and Lupita G. Villarreal. The
        Education of the Mexican-American: A Selected
        Bibliography. Washington, D.C.: National
        Clearinghouse for Bilingual Education, 1979.

4049   Bogardus, Emory S., comp. The Mexican Immigrant: An
        Annotated Bibliography. Los Angeles: Council of
        International Relations, 1929. Reprinted in Mexican
        American Bibliographies. Edited by Carlos E. Cortes.
        New York: Arno Press, 1974, item 4155.
An early Mexican American bibliography of about 200 items.

4050   Bolton, Herbert E. Guide to Materials for the History
        of the United States in the Principal Archives of
        Mexico. Washington, D.C.: Carnegie Institute, 1913.
Describes sources for the colonial and Mexican periods of
southwestern history in Mexican national, state and local
archives. Long a standard work.

4051   Bonilla, Rosalinda Sosa. The Education of the Mexican
        American: An Annotated Bibliography. Kingsville:
        Texas A & I University, 1979.
A doctoral thesis.

4052   Boorkman, C. J. Chicano Bibliography. New York:
        Gordon Press, 1974.

4053   Borderlands Sourcebook: A Guide to the Literature on
       Northern Mexico and the American Southwest. Edited by
       Ellwyn R. Stoddard; Richard L. Nostrand; and Jonathan
       P. West. Norman: University of Oklahoma Press, 1983.
Part three discusses resources for Borderlands study.
Includes a massive composite bibliography--the work of fifty
scholars from various disciplines. Invaluable for
borderlands research.

4054   Briggs, Marvin D. A Guide to the Mexican-American in
       the Southwest. Master's thesis. Fullerton:
       California State University, 1969.

4055   Bustamante, Jorge and Francisco Malagamba, eds.
       Mexico-Estados Unidos: bibliografia general sobre
       estudios fronterizos. Mexico, D.F.: El Colegio de
       Mexico, 1980.

4056   Caballero, Cesar and Kenneth Hedman, eds. Chicano
       Studies Bibliography. Mimeographed. El Paso:
       Library, University of Texas, 1973.

4057   Cabello-Argandoña, Roberto; Juan Gomez-Quiñones; and
       Patricia Herrera Duran. The Chicana: A Comprehensive
       Bibliographical Study. Los Angeles: Chicano Studies
       Center, University of California, 1976.
Nearly 500 entries. Encompasses a broad range of materials
in various disciplines; includes films and serials as well
as books, articles, and official reports. Partially
annotated.

4058   California, Fresno State College, Library. Afro and
       Mexican Americana: Books and Other Materials in the
       Library of Fresno State . . . Fresno, Calif.:
       Library, Fresno State College [now University], 1969.

4059   California, Historical Records Survey. Inventory of
       the State Archives of California, Department of
       Industrial Relations, Division of Immigration and
       Housing. San Francisco: Northern California
       Historical Records Survey Project, 1941.
Lists documents on immigration and housing by topics down to
1940.

4060   California Library Association. California Local
       History: A Centennial Bibliography. Edited by Ethel
       Blumann and Mabel W. Thomas. Stanford, Calif.:
       Stanford University Press, 1959.

4061   California, Los Angeles State University, Chicano
       Research Library. The Chicana: A Preliminary
       Bibliographic Study. Los Angeles: California State
       University, 1973.
A partially annotated bibliography of the Chicana.

4062 California, Los Angeles State University, Library. A
      Library Guide to Mexican-American Studies.
      Mimeographed. Los Angeles: J. F. Kennedy Memorial
      Library, California State University, 1969.

4063 California, San Diego State University, Library.
      Chicano Bibliography. Mimeographed. San Diego,
      Calif.: State University Library, n.d.

4064 California, San Jose State University, Library.
      Bibliografía de materiales tocante al Chicano: A
      Bibliography of Materials Relating to the Chicano in
      the Library, California State University, San Jose.
      Compiled by Milton Loventhal, with Robert L. Lauritzen
      and Christine Simpson. 2nd ed. San Jose: California
      State University, 1972.

4065 California, State College at San Bernardino, Library.
      Black and Brown Bibliography: History. Mimeographed.
      San Bernardino: State College Library, 1970.

4066 California, University of California at Santa Barbara,
      Library. Chicanos: A Selective Guide to Materials in
      the University of California at Santa Barbara Library.
      Mimeographed. Santa Barbara: University of California
      Library, [1972].
A revision and expansion of the 1969 U.C.S.B. library guide
to Mexican American materials, item 4067.

4067 California, University of California at Santa Barbara,
      Library. Mexican Americans: A Selective Guide to
      Materials. Mimeographed. Santa Barbara: University
      of California Library, 1969.

4068 Campa, Arthur L. "A Bibliography of Spanish Folk-lore
      in New Mexico." Albuquerque: University of New Mexico
      Bulletin, Language Series 2:3 (Sept. 1930).
An early listing of New Mexico and Colorado folklore
materials.

4069 Campbell, Walter S. The Book Lover's Southwest: A
      Guide to Good Reading. Norman: University of Oklahoma
      Press, 1955.
A general guide; Campbell also writes under the name Stanley
Vestal.

4070 Cardenas, Gilbert. Selected Bibliography Pertaining
      to La Raza in the Midwest and Great Lakes States,
      1924-1973. Revised ed. Notre Dame, Ind.: Notre Dame
      University, 1973.
Stresses works on migrant labor; 240 unannotated items,
listed alphabetically. One of the few bibliographies on the
midwestern Chicano.

4071   Carranza, Sharon M. An Annotated, Multi-Media
       Bibliography of Elementary and Intermediate Grade
       Level Materials in English and in English and Spanish
       on the Mexican-American. Master's thesis. San Jose,
       Calif.: San Jose State University, 1975.

4072   Castillo, Guadalupe and Herminio Rios. "Toward a True
       Chicano Bibliography: Mexican-American Newspapers:
       1848-1942." El Grito 2 (Summer 1970), 17-24.
Lists 193 Mexican American papers, most published in the
Southwest.

4073   Chapa, Evey, et al. La Mujer Chicana: An Annotated
       Bibliography. Austin: Chicana Research and Learning
       Center, University of Texas, 1976.
An annotated eighty-six page compilation of works on the
Chicana, arranged topically.

4074   Charles, Edgar B., ed. Mexican American Education, a
       Bibliography. Bethesda, Md.: ERIC-CRESS, 1968.

4075   Charno, Steven M., ed. Latin American Newspapers in
       United States Libraries: A Union List. Austin:
       University of Texas Press, 1969.

4076   Chavarria, Jesus. "A Precis and a Tentative
       Bibliography on Chicano History." Aztlan 1:1 (Spring
       1970), 133-141.
Outlines a chronological periodization of Chicano history
with a corresponding brief bibliography.

4077   Chavez, (Fray) Angelico. Archives of the Archdiocese
       of Santa Fe, 1678-1900. Washington, D.C.: Academy of
       American Franciscan History, 1957.
Lists some three thousand church and mission documents; has
author and subject index.

4078   Chavez, Arnold. Handbooks for Chicano Studies.
       Doctoral thesis. Greeley: University of Northern
       Colorado, 1975.

4079   Chicano: A Selected Bibliography. Compiled by Barbara
       Flynn, et al. San Bernardino, Calif.: Inland Library
       System, 1971.
A general work covering many aspects of the Mexican American
experience; ninety-three pages.

4080   Chicano Periodical Index: A Cumulated Index to
       Selected Periodicals Published Between 1967 and 1978.
       Boston: G. K. Hall, 1981.
Covers some eighteen Chicano journals; items briefly
annotated. Organized topically, with author and title
index.

4081   Clark, Carter B. "Research Tools, Guides and
       Bibliographies of New Mexico History. A Selected
       List." _Arizona and the West_ 24:2 (Summer 1982),
       153-168.

4082   Clark y Moreno, Joseph A. "A Bibliography of
       Bibliographies Relating to Studies of Mexican
       Americans." _El Grito_ 5:2 (Winter 1971-1972), 47-79.
A revision of his earlier "Bibliographies Relating to
Mexican American Studies." _El Grito_ 3:4 (Summer 1970),
25-31. Contains over 500 items concerning history,
politics, sociology, and so forth.

4083   Colley, Charles C., comp. _Documents of Southwestern
       History: A Guide to the Manuscript Collections of the
       Arizona Historical Society_. Tucson: Arizona
       Historical Society, 1972.
Lists over 1000 documents and includes bibliographic
references and guides. Especially valuable for the history
of Mexicans and Mexican Americans in early Arizona.

4084   Cordova, Marcella C. and Rose Marie Roybal.
       _Bibliografia de la chicana/ Bibliography on the
       Chicana_. Lakewood, Colo.: [privately printed], 1973.
A bibliography of 300 items on Mexican American women,
partially and briefly annotated.

4085   Corwin, Arthur F. "Historia de la emigracion
       mexicana, 1900-1970. Literatura e investigacion."
       Historia Mexicana 22:2 (Oct.-Dec. 1972), 188-220.
A lengthy bibliographic essay. Very similar to item 4086.

4086   Corwin, Arthur F. "Mexican Emigration History,
       1900-1970: Literature and Research." _Latin American
       Research Review_ 8:2 (Summer 1973), 3-24.
Describes bibliography of Mexican immigration to the U.S.;
includes Mexican as well as U.S. scholars' research and
writing.

4087   Cotera, Martha P. _Mexican American Literature: A
       Primary List_. Austin, Tex.: Southwest Educational
       Laboratory, 1970.

4088   Cowan, Robert E. and Robert G. Cowan, comps. _A
       Bibliography of the History of California, 1510-1930_.
       3 vols. San Francisco: J. H. Nash, 1933; 2nd ed., 4
       vols. in 1, Los Angeles: Torrez Press, 1964.
A useful reference to California history materials;
selective and annotated, with indexes (and supplementary
updating in the 1964 edition).

4089   Cowan, Robert Granniss. _Ranchos of California: A List
       of Spanish Concessions, 1775-1822, and Mexican Grants,_

1822-1846. Fresno, Calif.: Academy Library Guild, 1956.
Useful for historical study of California land grants, grantees, and claimants.

4090 Coy, Owen C. Guide to County Archives of California. Sacramento: California State Printing Office, 1919.
A valuable guide to vital statistics of and genealogical information on Californios, as well as to other records.

4091 Cumberland, Charles C. "The United States-Mexican Border: A Selective Guide to the Literature of the Region." Rural Sociology, Supplement 25:2 (June 1960), 1-236. Reprinted in Mexican American Bibliographies, edited by Carlos E. Cortes. New York: Arno Press, 1974, item 4155.
An excellent bibliography, arranged topically and stressing the period between 1821 and 1958. Includes an essay on the 1958 state of research and writing on the border area.

4092 De Leon, Arnoldo. Apuntes Tejanos. Ann Arbor, Mich.: University Microfilms International, 1978.
A list of newspaper articles from various Texas newspapers, 1855-1900; material on Cortina, J. A. Navarro, Cart War, El Paso Salt War, Teresa Urrea, Pedro Jaramillo.

4093 Denver Public Library. Hispanic Heritage. Mimeographed. Denver, Colo.: Public Library, 1969.
A brief bibliography.

4094 Diaz, Albert J. A Guide to the Microfilm of Papers Relating to New Mexico Land Grants. Albuquerque: University of New Mexico Press, 1960.
A useful source for materials on grants, supporting documents, and claims. Includes a selective bibliography.

4095 Dobie, James Frank. Guide to Life and Literature of the Southwest. Austin: University of Texas Press, 1943. Revised and enlarged, Dallas, Tex.: Southern Methodist University, 1952.

4096 Duran, Daniel Flores. Latino Materials: A Multimedia Guide for Children and Young Adults. Edited by Patricia G. Schuman. Santa Barbara, Calif.: American Bibliographical Center-CLIO Press, 1979.
Part 3 covers books, journals, and films about Mexican Americans.

4097 Elliot, Claude. Theses on Texas History: A Check List of Theses and Dissertations in Texas History Produced in the Departments of History of Eighteen Texas Graduate Schools and Thirty-three Graduate Schools Outside Texas, 1907-1952. Austin: Texas State Historical Association, 1955.

Excellent for unpublished sources on Mexican American
history, primarily in Texas.

4098   Ellis, L. Tuffly and Barbara J. Stockley, eds. and
        comps. "A Checklist of Theses and Dissertations in
        Texas Studies, 1964-1974." Southwestern Historical
        Quarterly 78 (Jan. 1975), 313-324.

4099   ERIC Clearinghouse on Rural Education and Small
        Schools. Mexican-American Education: A Selected
        Bibliography. Las Cruces: Education Resources
        Information Center, New Mexico State University, 1975.

4100   Flores, M. G., comp. and L. Gutierrez-Witt, ed.
        Mexican American Archives at the Benson Collection: A
        Guide for Users. Austin: Mexican American Library,
        University of Texas, 1981.

4101   Fodell, Beverly. Cesar Chavez and the United Farm
        Worker: A Selective Bibliography. Detroit, Mich.:
        Wayne State University Press, 1974.
Lists books, articles, reports, etc. regarding Chavez, the
United Farm Workers, and labor. Some are briefly annotated.
Chapters 1 and 2 are devoted to published articles.

4102   Garcia-Ayvens, Francisco; Darien Fisher; and Hilda
        Villarreal. ¿Quien Sabe?: A Preliminary List of
        Chicano Reference Materials. Los Angeles: Chicano
        Studies Research Center, University of California,
        1981.
A heavily annotated list of 100 reference works on the
Chicano; includes author, title, and subject indexes.
Includes works on Mexico; a large number are in Spanish.

4103   Garza, Ben, et al. Chicano Bibliography.
        Mimeographed. Davis: Library, University of
        California, 1969.

4104   Genealogical Society, Church of Jesus Christ of
        Latter-day Saints. Genealogical Record Sources in
        Mexico. Salt Lake City, Utah: The Genealogical
        Society, 1970.
A listing of genealogical source materials, organized by
states and towns. Mostly parish registers. Also includes
10,000-20,000 microfilm rolls of "other material."

4105   Gilbert, W. H. Mexican-Americans and Mexicans in the
        U.S. Since 1943: Selected References. Washington,
        D.C.: Legislative Reference Service, 1965.

4106   Gomez-Quiñones, Juan, comp. Selected Materials for
        Chicano Studies. Austin: Center for Mexican American
        Studies, University of Texas, 1973.

4107 Gomez-Quiñones, Juan and Alberto Camarillo, comps.
      Selected Bibliography for Chicano Studies. 3rd ed.
      Los Angeles: Chicano Studies Center, University of
      California, 1975.
Unannotated list of 900 items; topically arranged, it has a
strong emphasis on history.

4108 Gomez-Quiñones, Juan and Luis L. Arroyo. "On the
      State of Chicano History: Observations on Its
      Development, Interpretations, and Theory, 1970-1974."
      Western Historical Quarterly 2 (Apr. 1976), 155-185.
An important survey of the state of Chicano historiography.

4109 Gomez-Quiñones, Juan and Victor Nelson Cisneros.
      Selective Bibliography on Chicano Labor Materials.
      Los Angeles: Chicano Studies Center, University of
      California, 1974.
Organized both topically and by type of material; includes
dissertations. Includes materials on women workers, workers
in industry, and agricultural workers.

4110 Grove, Pierce S.; Becky J. Barnett; and Sandra J.
      Hanson, eds. New Mexico Newspapers: A Comprehensive
      Guide to Bibliographical Entries and Locations.
      Albuquerque: University of New Mexico Press, 1975.
Has a section on "Spanish-American" newspapers; includes
maps and indexes.

4111 Gutierrez, Lewis A. Bibliography of La Mujer Chicana.
      Austin: Center for the Study of Human Resources,
      University of Texas, 1975.

4112 HAPI (Hispanic American Periodicals Index). Los
      Angeles: Latin American Center, University of
      California, 1977-1981 (4 vols.).
Surveys Latin American periodicals; includes some articles
on Mexican Americans.

4113 Harding, Susan, comp. Bibliography on Mexican
      American Affairs. Washington, D.C.: Legislative
      Reference Service, 1968.

4114 Harrigan, Joan, comp. Materiales tocante los Latinos.
      Denver: Colorado Department of Education, 1967.

4115 Harrigan, Joan, comp. More Materials tocante los
      Latinos: A Bibliography of Materials on the
      Spanish-American. Denver: Colorado Department of
      Education, 1969.
Primarily materials for use in public schools.

4116 Heathman, James E., and Cecilia J. Martinez, comps.
      Mexican American Education--A Selected Bibliography.
      Las Cruces: Education Resources Information Center,

New Mexico State University, 1969.
Especially good for bilingual materials.

4117   Hispanic American in the United States, A Selected
       Bibliography, 1963-1974. Washington, D.C.: Department
       of Housing and Urban Development, 1974.
Available from Public Documents Distribution Center, Pueblo,
Colorado.

4118   Historical Records Survey. Arizona. Inventory of the
       County Archives. Phoenix, Ariz.: Historical Records
       Survey, 1938.
Prepared by the Works Progress Administration.
Mimeographed.

4119   Historical Records Survey. California. Guide to
       Depositories of Manuscript Collections in the United
       States; California. Los Angeles: Southern California
       Historical Records Survey Project, 1941.
Describes manuscript holdings in seventy-four California
depositories including the Los Angeles County Museum of
History and the Bancroft Library. Heaviest in 19th century.

4120   Historical Records Survey. California. Inventory of
       the County Archives of California. San Francisco: The
       Northern California Historical Records Survey Project,
       1937.
Prepared by the Works Projects Administration.
Mimeographed.

4121   Historical Records Survey. Colorado. Guide to Vital
       Statistics Records in Colorado. Vol. 2, Church
       Archives. Denver: Colorado Historical Records Survey,
       1942.
Provides a guide to vital statistics in church records from
1850 to 1940. Organized by counties.

4122   Historical Records Survey. Colorado. Inventory of
       the County Archives of Colorado. Denver: The Colorado
       Historical Records Survey, [193?].
Prepared by the Works Projects Administration.
Mimeographed.

4123   Historical Records Survey. New Mexico. Guide to
       Public Vital Statistics Records in New Mexico.
       Albuquerque: Historical Records Survey, 1942.
Covers from 1697 to the beginnings of the 1940s. Useful for
genealogical information on Nuevo Mexicanos.

4124   Historical Records Survey. New Mexico. Inventory of
       the County Archives of New Mexico. Albuquerque, N.
       Mex.: The Historical Records Survey, 1937.
Prepared by the Works Progress Administration.
Mimeographed.

4125   Historical Records Survey. Texas. <u>Inventory of the</u>
       <u>County Archives of Texas</u>. San Antonio: The Texas
       Historical Records Survey, 1942.
Prepared by the Works Projects Administration.
Mimeographed.

4126   Hoskin, Beryl M.; Doreen Cohen; and Alice E. Whistler.
       <u>The California Experience: An Annotated List of</u>
       <u>California Bibliographies Based on the Collection in</u>
       <u>the Michel Orradre Library, University of Santa Clara</u>.
       Sacramento: California Library Association, 1977.
A list of 164 California bibliographies stressing the
colonial period; annotated and indexed.

4127   Institute of Latin American Studies. <u>Seventy Five</u>
       <u>Years of Latin American Research at the University of</u>
       <u>Texas . . . 1893-1958 . . .</u> Austin: Institute of
       Latin American Studies, University of Texas, [n.d.]
Includes both Ph.D. and Masters' theses in Southwestern
history.

4128   Jamail, Milton H. <u>The United States-Mexican Border: A</u>
       <u>Guide to Institutions, Organizations and Scholars</u>.
       Tucson: Latin American Area Center, University of
       Arizona, 1981.
Lists local, regional, and national organizations and some
200 specialists in border studies.

4129   Janeway, W. Ralph. <u>Bibliography of Immigration in the</u>
       <u>U.S. 1900-1930</u>. Columbus, Ohio: H. L. Hendrick, 1934.

4130   Jenkins, Myra Ellen. <u>Guide to the Microfilm Edition</u>
       <u>of the Mexican Archives of New Mexico, 1821-1846</u>.
       Santa Fe: New Mexico Records Center, 1969.
Useful for history of New Mexican land grants, government,
and military activities.

4131   Jones, Oakah L. "The Spanish Borderlands: A Selected
       Reading List." <u>Journal of the West</u> 8 (Jan. 1969),
       137-142.
Brief, but useful for the colonial borderlands.

4132   Jones, Robert Cuba. <u>Mexicans in the United States: A</u>
       <u>Bibliography</u>. Washington, D.C.: Pan American Union,
       1942. Reprinted in <u>Mexican American Bibliographies</u>.
       New York: Arno Press, 1974, item 4155.
An early bibliography of some 200 items by a pioneer in the
field. Unannotated.

4133   Jones, Robert Cuba. <u>Selected References on Labor</u>
       <u>Importation Program Between Mexico and the United</u>
       <u>States</u>. Washington, D.C.: Pan American Union, 1948.

Covers 1900 to 1948, arranged topically.

4134   Jordan, Anne Harwell. A Guide to Publishing for
       Americans of Mexican Descent; and Foreign Printers in
       Sixteenth Century Mexican Society. Austin: University
       of Texas, 1972.
Has materials on Chicano periodicals and publishers.
Includes bibliographies.

4135   Jordan, Lois B. Mexican Americans: Resources to Build
       Cultural Understanding. Littleton, Colo.: Libraries
       Unlimited, 1973.
Selective and annotated; includes audio-visual as well as
printed materials. Also brief bibliographical sketches of
prominent Mexican Americans.

4136   Kielman, Chester Valls. The University of Texas
       Archives: A Guide to the Historical Manuscript
       Collections in the University of Texas Archives.
       Austin: University of Texas Press, 1967.
Over 2,400 collections arranged alphabetically and
annotated, with name and topic index. Heavy on 19th and
20th centuries, but goes back to 16th century.

4137   Kramer, Debora. Mexican Americans: Selected
       References. Washington, D.C.: Legislative Reference
       Service, 1964.

4138   Lange, Arthur W., et al.. comps. The Spanish and
       Mexican Influence in the Cultural Development of the
       Southwest. A Compilation of Reading Materials for Use
       in the High Schools of Laredo Independent School
       District. 3 vols. Mimeographed. Laredo, Tex.:
       Laredo Independent School District, 1969-1971.

4139   Leggett, Delia C. and Carlos Arce, eds. Chicanos in
       Higher Education: A Bibliography. Ann Arbor: Survey
       Research Center, Institute for Social Research,
       University of Michigan, 1978.

4140   Library of Congress. Mexican Americans in the U.S.:
       Housing, Education, Migrant Labor, etc. Washington,
       D.C.: Legislative Reference Service, 1964.

4141   Lo Buglio, Rudecinda A. "Survey of Pre-statehood
       Records: A New Look at Spanish and Mexican California
       Genealogical Records." Spanish-American Genealogist
       35-38 (1980), 625-681.
Lists California archives of Spanish and Mexican era
documents, with a bibliography. Very useful information.

4142   Loeb, Catherine. "La Chicana: A Bibliographic
       Survey." Frontiers: A Journal of Women Studies 5:2

(Summer 1980), 59-74.

4143 Lomeli, Francisco A. and Donald W. Urioste. <u>Chicano Perspectives in Literature: A Critical and Annotated Bibliography</u>. Albuquerque, N. Mex.: Pajarito Publications, 1976.
Covers 127 titles dating from the 1890s to the present; comprehensive.

4144 Los Angeles County. Department of Social Services. <u>A Selected Guide to Literature on the Mexican-American</u>. Los Angeles: [n.p.] [1969].

4145 MacCurdy, Raymond E. <u>A History and Bibliography of Spanish-Language Newspapers and Magazines in Louisiana, 1808-1949</u>. Albuquerque: University of New Mexico Press, 1951.

4146 Maciel, David R., comp. <u>Mexico. A Selected Bibliography of Sources for Chicano Studies</u>. Los Angeles: Chicano Studies Center, University of California, 1973.
A basic guide for study of the Mexicans' experience in Mexico, as it later affected them in the United States.

4147 Martinez, Gilbert T., comp. <u>Bibliography on Mexican Americans</u>. Mimeographed. Sacramento, Calif.: Sacramento Unified School District, 1968.
Covers the broad spectrum of Chicano studies with emphasis on the social sciences. Unannotated list of 600 items.

4148 Martinez, Julio A., ed. and comp. <u>Chicano Scholars and Writers: A Bio-bibliographical Directory</u>. Metuchen, N.J.: Scarecrow Press, 1979.
A very comprehensive work of nearly 600 pages.

4149 Massa Gil, Beatriz. <u>Bibliografia sobre migracion de trabajadores mexicanos a Los Estados Unidos</u>. Mexico, D.F.: Biblioteca del Banco de Mexico, 1959.
A bibliography of United States sources: pamphlets, articles, and government documents published between 1950 and 1958.

4150 Mecham, John L. "The Northern Expansion of New Spain, 1522-1822. A Selected Descriptive Bibliographical List." <u>Hispanic American Historical Review</u> 7 (1927), 233-276.

4151 Meier, Matt S. "Dissertations." <u>Journal of Mexican American History</u> 1:2 (Spring 1971), 170-190.
A list of 300 theses and dissertations useful for the study of Mexican American history.

4152 Meier, Matt S. and Feliciano Rivera. <u>Bibliography for Chicano History</u>. San Francisco: R & E Research Associates, 1972.
A bibliography of books, periodical articles, and theses in chronological and topical divisions.

4153 Mellor, Earl F. <u>Directory of Data Sources on Racial and Ethnic Minorities</u>. Washington, D.C.: U.S. Department of Labor, 1975.
Lists data sources published by federal agencies.

4154 Messinger, Milton A. <u>The Forgotten Child: A Bibliography, With Special Emphasis on Materials Relating to the Education of Spanish-Speaking People in the United States</u>. Austin: University of Texas Press, 1967.

4155 <u>Mexican American Bibliographies</u>, edited by Carlos E. Cortes. New York: Arno Press, 1974.
A reprint of five bibliographies: Emory S. Bogardus, <u>The Mexican Immigrant: An Annotated Bibliography</u>, 1929; Robert C. Jones, <u>Mexicans in the United States: A Bibliography</u>, 1942; Lyle Saunders, <u>Spanish-Speaking Americans and Mexican-Americans in the United States: A Selected Bibliography</u>, 1944; George I. Sanchez and Howard Putnam, <u>Materials Relating to the Education of Spanish-Speaking People in the United States: An Annotated Bibliography</u>, 1959; Charles C. Cumberland, <u>The United States-Mexican Border: A Selective Guide to the Literature of the Region</u>, 1960.

4156 <u>Mexican-American History: A Critical Selective Bibliography</u>, edited by Ruben Cortez and Joseph Navarro. Santa Barbara, Calif.: Mexican-American Historical Society, 1969.
Includes works on Spain, Mexico, and Indians, as well as Chicano history.

4157 <u>Mexican-American Study Project Revised Bibliography</u>. Los Angeles: Graduate School of Business, University of California, 1967.
Advance Report No. 3 of the Mexican-American Study Project series; with a bibliographical essay by Ralph Guzman.

4158 <u>Mexican-Americans, a Selected Bibliography--Revised and Enlarged</u>. Mimeographed. Houston, Tex.: Libraries, University of Houston, [ca. 1974].

4159 <u>Mexican-Americans in the United States: Housing, Education, Migrant Labor, etc</u>. Washington, D.C.: Legislative Reference Service, 1964.

4160 Mexico and the Mexican American. Whittier, Calif.:
      Whittier College, 1968.
A bibliography based on materials in the Whittier College
Library. Covers a wide range of materials relating to the
Chicano, mostly in the Southwest. One of many college and
university library bibliographies of the late 1960s.

4161 Mickey, Barbara H. A Bibliography of Studies
      Concerning the Spanish-Speaking Population of the
      American Southwest. Greeley: Museum of Anthropology,
      Colorado State College, 1969.

4162 Millares Carlo, Agustin. Repertorio bibliografico de
      los archivos mexicanos y de los europeos y
      norteamericanos de interes para la historia de Mexico.
      Mexico, D.F.: Universidad Nacional Autonoma de Mexico,
      1959.
A general guide to archival materials concerning Mexican
history in Mexico, the United States, and Europe.

4163 Miller, Wayne C. "Mexican Americans: A Guide to the
      Mexican American Experience." In his A Comprehensive
      Bibliography for the Study of American Minorities. 2
      vols. New York: New York University Press, 1976, pp.
      911-953. The bibliographic essay appears also in his
      Handbook of American Minorities. New York: New York
      University Press, 1976, pp. 213-225.
An excellent bibliographic compilation of some 600 items,
annotated and arranged by topics.

4164 National Chicano Research Network. Guide to Hispanic
      Bibliographic Services in the United States. Ann
      Arbor: Survey Research Center, University of Michigan,
      1980.
Includes information on seventy bibliographic service
centers.

4165 Navarro, Eliseo A., comp. The Chicano Community: A
      Selected Bibliography for Use in Social Work
      Education. New York: Council on Social Work
      Education, 1971.
An annotated bibliography covering racism, economics,
politics, education, literature, society, and family life.

4166 The New York Times Index, 1851-1908, 1913-Present.
Especially valuable for locating materials with contemporary
viewpoints.

4167 Newman, Bud. "Southwest Archives. Mexican Records."
      Password 24:3 (Fall 1979), 131-132.
Describes the microfilm collection of North American
archives in the University of Texas at El Paso.

4168   Nogales, Luis G., et al., eds. The Mexican American:
       A Selected and Annotated Bibliography. Stanford,
       Calif.: Stanford University Press, 1971.
An annotated selection of over 400 works, mostly
sociological; enlarged and revised version of the 1969
Stanford bibliography.

4169   Oczon, Annabelle M. "Land Grants in New Mexico: A
       Selective Bibliography." New Mexico Historical Review
       57:1 (Jan. 1982), 81-87.
Unannotated, it includes theses and articles. The entire
issue is devoted to the land grant issue in New Mexico.

4170   Ortego, Philip D. Selective Mexican American
       Bibliography. El Paso, Tex.: Border Regional Library
       Association, 1972.
Topically organized, valuable for the history of folklore
and literature. Unannotated.

4171   Padilla, Ray. "Apuntes para la documentacion de la
       cultura chicana." El Grito 5:2 (Winter 1971-1972),
       1-46.

4172   Paul, Rodman W. and Richard W. Etulain, comps. The
       Frontier and the American West. Arlington Heights,
       Ill.: AHM Publishing Corp., 1977.
Subdivided by topics in frontier history.

4173   Peña, Devon G. Maquiladoras: A Select Annotated
       Bibliography and Critical Commentary on the United
       States-Mexico Border Industry Program. Austin: Center
       for the Study of Human Resources, University of Texas,
       1981.
Includes a twenty-nine page introductory essay on the
origins and significance of the B.I.P.

4174   Pino, Frank. Mexican Americans: A Research
       Bibliography. 2 vols. East Lansing: Latin American
       Studies Center, Michigan State University, 1974.
A multi-disciplinary guide, computer generated. Organized
by areas, topics, and disciplines.

4175   Pomerance, Deborah and Dianne Ellis. Ethnic
       Statistics: A Compendium of Reference Sources.
       Arlington, Va.: Data Use and Access Laboratories,
       1978.
A valuable tool to locate statistical sources.

4176   Portillo, Cristina, et al., comps. Bibliography of
       Writings on La Mujer. Berkeley: Chicano Studies
       Library, University of California, 1976.
A listing of materials on the Chicana located in the Chicano
Studies Library; fifty-three pages.

4177   Quintana, Helena, comp. with Richard A. Moore. A
       Current Bibliography of Chicanos, 1960-1973.
       Albuquerque: College of Education, University of New
       Mexico, 1974.
A selective annotated work, especially good for Chicano
culture.

4178   Rader, Jesse L. South of Forty, From the Mississippi
       to the Rio Grande: A Bibliography. Norman: University
       of Oklahoma Press, 1947.

4179   Reed, Robert D. How and Where to Research Your
       Ethnic-American Cultural Heritage: Mexican Americans.
       Saratoga, Calif.: [the author], 1979.

4180   Revelle, Keith. Chicano! A Selected Bibliography of
       Materials by and about Mexico and Mexican Americans.
       Oakland, Calif.: Oakland Public Library, 1969.
Covers 1939 to 1968; includes newspapers, reports and
speeches in addition to books and periodical articles.
Briefly annotated.

4181   Riemer, Ruth. An Annotated Bibliography of Material
       on Ethnic Problems in Southern California. Los
       Angeles: Hayes Foundation and Department of
       Anthropology, University of California, 1947.
A sixty page mimeographed bibliography of race relations.

4182   Rios, Herminio. "Toward a True Chicano
       Bibliography--Part II." El Grito 5:4 (Summer 1972),
       38-47.
Lists 185 Mexican American newspapers published between 1881
and 1958.

4183   Rittenhouse, Jack De Vere. The Santa Fe Trail: A
       Historical Bibliography. Albuquerque: University of
       New Mexico Press, 1971.
Covers from the Mexican era to the 1880s. Includes maps and
illustrations.

4184   Robinson, Barbara J. and J. Cordell Robinson. The
       Mexican American: A Critical Guide to Research Aids.
       Greenwich, Conn.: JAI Press, 1980.
An outstanding annotated guide to Chicano bibliographies,
guides, directories, dictionaries, and other sources for
research.

4185   Rocq, Margaret M. California Local History, a
       Bibliography and Union List of Library Holdings.
       Stanford, Calif.: Stanford University Press, 1970.
Revised and enlarged for the California Library Association,
it has over 17,000 items; it also lists special collections.

4186   Ruesink, David C. and Brice T. Batson, comps.
       Bibliography Relating to Agricultural Labor. College
       Station: Texas A & M University Press, 1969.
Primarily concerned with Texas; 93 pages of items published
between 1964 and 1969.

4187   Saldaña, Nancy. Mexican-Americans in the Midwest: An
       Annotated Bibliography. East Lansing: Rural Manpower
       Center, Michigan State University, 1969.

4188   Sanchez, George I. and Howard Putnam. Materials
       Relating to the Education of Spanish-Speaking People
       in the United States: An Annotated Bibliography.
       Austin: Institute of Latin American Studies,
       University of Texas, 1959. Reprinted in Mexican
       American Bibliographies. New York: Arno Press, 1974,
       item 4155.
Especially good for bilingual education.

4189   Saunders, Lyle, comp. A Guide to Materials Bearing on
       Cultural Relations in New Mexico. Albuquerque:
       University of New Mexico Press, 1944.
Has a section on Spanish Americans and Mexicans, pp.
322-354; it covers labor, immigration, social conditions and
other aspects of the Mexican and Mexican American
experience.

4190   Saunders, Lyle. Spanish-Speaking Americans and
       Mexican-Americans in the United States: A Selected
       Bibliography. New York: Bureau of Intercultural
       Education, 1944. Reprinted in Mexican-American
       Bibliographies. New York: Arno Press, 1974, item
       4155.
An early bibliographic guide to various aspects of the
Mexican American experience. Unannotated.

4191   Schramko, Linda Fowler. Chicano Bibliography:
       Selected Materials on Americans of Mexican Descent.
       Revised. Mimeographed. Sacramento, Calif.:
       Sacramento State College Library, 1970.
Lists by topical subdivisions ca. 1000 items in the college
library.

4192   Simmen, Edward; Jane Talbot; and Gilbert Cruz.
       Chicano Bibliography. Austin, Tex.: Pemberton Press,
       1977.

4193   Slobodek, Mitchell. A Selective Bibliography of
       California Labor History. Los Angeles: Institute of
       Industrial Relations, University of California, 1964.
An extensive annotated selection covering the period from
the Treaty of Guadalupe Hidalgo to the 1960s. Has a section
on the Spanish and Mexican backgrounds.

4194   Southwestern Historical Quarterly. Cumulative Index.
        2 vols. Austin: Texas State Historical Association,
        1950 and 1960.
A cumulative index to volumes 1 to 60 (1897 to 1957) which
contains many articles on Mexicans and Mexican Americans.
Especially useful for Texas and to a lesser extent the
entire Southwest.

4195   Spanish Archives of New Mexico, 1621-1821. Santa Fe:
        New Mexico Records Center, 1968.
Useful for study of the social and economic history of the
colonial epoch.

4196   Steck, Francis Borgia. A Tentative Guide to
        Historical Materials on the Spanish Borderlands.
        Philadelphia: Catholic History Society of
        Philadelphia, 1943. Reprint, New York: Lenox Hill,
        1971.
Covers the colonial and Mexican periods; includes Florida
and the Gulf coast.

4197   Streeter, Thomas W. Bibliography of Texas, 1795-1845.
        5 vols. Cambridge, Mass.: Harvard University Press,
        1955-1960.
Three parts in five volumes: 1. Texas imprints, 1817-1845;
2. Mexican imprints, 1808-1845; 3. U.S. and European
imprints, 1795-1845.

4198   Swadesh, Frances L. 20,000 Years of History: A New
        Mexico Bibliography. Santa Fe, N. Mex.: Sunstone
        Press, 1973.
An annotated bibliography with an introductory chapter on
New Mexico's ethnohistory.

4199   Talbot, Jane and Gilbert R. Cruz, comps. with Edward
        Simmen. A Comprehensive Chicano Bibliography,
        1960-1972. Austin, Tex.: Jenkins Publishing Co.,
        1973.
A topically subdivided general bibliography of 3167 items;
includes sections on history, culture, politics, migrant
labor, etc.

4200   Tatum, Charles M. A Selected and Annotated
        Bibliography of Chicano Studies. 1st ed. Lincoln:
        Society of Spanish and Spanish-American Studies,
        University of Nebraska, 1976.
A bibliography of 300 items stressing Mexican American
culture and arranged topically.

4201   Tatum, Charles M. A Selected and Annotated
        Bibliography of Chicano Studies. 2nd ed. Lincoln:
        Society of Spanish and Spanish-American Studies,
        University of Nebraska, 1979.
Expanded to 526 items; includes a section on the Chicana.

Heavy on Chicano literature.

4202   Tatum, Charles M.   "Toward a Chicano Bibliography of
        Literary Criticism." ATISBOS: Journal of Chicano
        Research (Winter 1976-1977), 35-59.
Useful for literature and cultural history.

4203   Taylor, Virginia H.   Index to Spanish and Mexican Land
        Grants. Austin, Tex.: General Land Office, 1976.
Limited to land grants in the province of Texas between the
Rio Grande and Nueces rivers.

4204   Teschner, Richard V.   Spanish-Surnamed Populations of
        the United States; A Catalog of Dissertations. Ann
        Arbor, Mich.: Xerox University Microfilms, 1974.

4205   Teschner, Richard V.   Supplement No. 1 to
        Spanish-Surnamed Populations of the United States; A
        Catalog of Dissertations. Ann Arbor, Mich.:
        University Microfilms International, 1977.

4206   Texas, University, Austin.   Catalogue of the Texas
        Collection in the Barker Texas History Center.
        Boston: G. K. Hall, 1978. 14 vols.
Lists over 100,000 items, subdivided topically and stressing
the 19th and 20th centuries.

4207   Texas, University, Libraries. Mexican Americans: A
        Selected Bibliography. Houston, Tex.: University of
        Houston Libraries, 1972.
Divided by areas: history, sociology, etc.; 151 pages.

4208   Tompkins, Dorothy L.   Poverty in the United States
        During the Sixties; a Bibliography. Berkeley:
        University of California Press, 1970.
A 542-page bibliography with sections on Mexican Americans
and migrant workers.

4209   Trask, David F.; Michael C. Meyer; and Roger D. Trask,
        comps. and eds. A Bibliography of United States-Latin
        American Relations Since 1810. A Select List of
        Eleven Thousand Items. Lincoln: University of
        Nebraska Press, 1968.

4210   Trejo, Arnulfo D.   Bibliografia Chicana: A Guide to
        Information Sources. Detroit: Gale Research Co.,
        1975.
A broad work, selective and annotated, covering all areas of
the Chicano experience after 1848. Includes lists of
Chicano periodicals.

4211   Trueba, Henry T.   Mexican American Bibliography:
        Bilingual-Bicultural Education. ERIC, 1973.
Lists topically about 300 items on bilingual education.

Unannotated and unindexed.

4212   Tucker, Mary. Books of the Southwest: A General
       Bibliography. New York: J. J. Augustin, 1937.
An early list of works on the Southwestern experience.

4213   Tully, Marjorie F. An Annotated Bibliography of
       Spanish Folklore in New Mexico and Southern Colorado.
       Albuquerque: University of New Mexico Press, 1950.

4214   Tuterow, Norman E., ed. and comp. The
       Mexican-American War: An Annotated Bibliography.
       Westport, Conn.: Greenwood Press, 1981.
Contains nearly 5,000 items, mostly U.S. materials, plus a
chronology of the war, various statistical and other lists,
and twenty-one maps. An outstanding, well-organized
bibliography.

4215   Twitchell, Ralph Emerson. The Spanish Archives of New
       Mexico. 2 vols. Cedar Rapids, Iowa: Torch Press,
       1914.
A useful annotated guide to materials in various archives,
mostly from the 1700s; includes lists of land grants.

4216   U.S., Cabinet Committee on Opportunities for Spanish
       Speaking People. The Spanish Speaking in the United
       States: A Guide to Materials. Washington, D.C.: U.S.
       Government Printing Office, 1971; also Detroit, Mich.:
       Blaine Ethridge Books, 1975.
About 1300 items, emphasizing social and economic problems
of Mexican Americans; a revision of the 1969 Inter-Agency
Committee on Mexican American Affairs bibliography, item
4220.

4217   U.S., Commission on Civil Rights. Bibliography of
       Books and Periodicals on Mexican Americans.
       Washington, D.C.: U.S. Government Printing Office,
       1969.

4218   U.S., Department of Housing and Urban Development.
       Hispanic Americans in the United States: A Selective
       Bibliography, 1963-1974. Washington, D.C.: U.S.
       Government Printing Office, 1974.

4219   U.S., Inter-Agency Committee on Mexican American
       Affairs. A Guide to Materials Relating to Persons of
       Mexican Heritage in the United States. Washington,
       D.C.: U.S. Government Printing Office, 1968.
Includes books, articles, government documents, theses, and
audio-visual materials.

4220   U.S., Inter-Agency Committee on Mexican American
       Affairs. The Mexican American: A New Focus on
       Opportunity; A Guide to Materials Relating to Persons

of Mexican Heritage in the United States. Washington,
D.C.: U.S. Government Printing Office, 1969.

4221 U.S., Legislative Reference Service of the Library of
Congress. Migrant Labor Law and Relations: Selected
References, 1960-1969. Washington, D.C.: U.S.
Government Printing Office, 1969.

4222 Urzua, Roberto; Martha P. Cotera; and Emma Gonzalez
Stupp, eds. "Chicano Libraries, Special Collections,
Projects: An Overview." In Library Services to
Mexican Americans: Policies, Practices and Prospects.
Las Cruces: New Mexico State University, 1978.

4223 Valdes, Dennis N. Materials on the History of Latinos
in Michigan and the Midwest: An Annotated
Bibliography. Detroit, Mich.: College of Education,
Wayne State University, 1982.

4224 Wagner, Henry Raup. The Spanish Southwest, 1542-1794;
An Annotated Bibliography. Berkeley, Calif.: J. J.
Gillick & Co., 1924. Reprint, Albuquerque, N. Mex.:
Quivira Society, 1937. New York: Arno Press, 1967.
Long the standard bibliography of Spanish language materials
on Mexico's northern frontier in the colonial era.

4225 Wallace, Andrew. Sources and Readings in Arizona
History; A Checklist of Literature Concerning
Arizona's Past. Tucson: Arizona Pioneers Historical
Society, 1965.
Divided into fifteen topical sections, the first four of
which are particularly useful for background to Mexican
Americans in Arizona.

4226 Washington, Superintendent of Public Instruction.
Listing of Resource Material Concerned with the
Spanish-speaking. Mimeographed. Olympia, Wash.:
Superintendent of Public Instruction, 1971.

4227 Weber, David J. "Mexico's Far Northern Frontier,
1821-1845: A Critical Bibliography". Arizona and the
West 19 (Autumn 1977), 225-266.
Covers some 160 secondary works.

4228 Weigle, Marta, comp. A Penitente Bibliography.
Albuquerque: University of New Mexico Press, 1976.
The outstanding bibliography of the Penitente organization;
162 pages, 1,233 items, annotated.

4229 Winnie, William, Jr.; John Stegner; and Joseph
Kopachevsky, comps. Persons of Mexican Descent in the
United States: A Selective Bibliography. Fort
Collins: The Center for Latin American Studies,
Colorado State University, 1970.

About 1,000 items alphabetically organized, especially
valuable because they emphasize Colorado; from 1891 to 1970.

4230   Wolf, T. Philip, comp. A Bibliography of New Mexico
       State Politics. Albuquerque: Division of Government
       Research, University of New Mexico, 1974.
Annotated and edited by Wolf, a specialist in New Mexico
government and politics.

4231   Woods, Richard D. Reference Materials on
       Mexican-Americans: An Annotated Bibliography.
       Metuchen, N.J.: Scarecrow Press, 1976.
An excellent reference tool of 387 annotated items, arranged
alphabetically, with some emphasis on Texas materials.

4232   Woods, Richard D. and Grace Alvarez-Altman. Spanish
       Surnames in Southwestern United States: A Dictionary.
       Boston: G. K. Hall, 1979.
Woods specializes in Mexican American bibliographic study
with emphasis on literature and literary history.

4233   Wright, Doris M. A Guide to the Mariano Guadalupe
       Vallejo documentos para la historia de California,
       1780-1875. Berkeley: University of California Press,
       1953.
Guide to manuscripts in the Bancroft Library, University of
California, Berkeley.

XI.
COLLECTIONS, ARCHIVES, AND LIBRARIES

The following are the principal libraries, archives, and collections which researchers in Mexican American history may find helpful in their research. They are preceded by five works which describe archives and collections from a somewhat broader perspective and in greater detail.

4234 Cardoso, Lawrence A. "Archival Sources in Mexico for the Study of Chicano History." New Scholar 7: 1 & 2 (1978), 255-258.
Describes in some detail part of the holdings in the Archivo Historico de la Secretaria de Relaciones Exteriores that have Chicano materials. These are collections on the Mexican Revolution, the Flores Magon brothers, and government cultural efforts in the United States.

4235 Day, James, comp. Handbooks: Texas Archival and Manuscript Depositories. Austin: Texas Library and Historical Commission, 1966.
Lists, alphabetically by location, the various archives throughout the state with a brief description of each and its holdings.

4236 Everton, George B. and Gunnar Rasmuson. Handy Book for Genealogists. Logan, Utah: Everton Publishers, 1965.
Includes a useful list of the Historical Records Survey. Organized alphabetically by states.

4237 Lo Buglio, Rudecinda A. "The Archives of Northwestern Mexico." Spanish-American Genealogist 35-38 (1980), 598-624.
A compilation of Southwestern archives, with an introductory essay and a bibliography.

4238   Smith, Jessie Carney. <u>Minorities in the United
       States: Guide to Resources</u>. Nashville, Tenn.: Peabody
       Library School, Peabody College for Teachers, 1973.
Includes a chapter on Mexican American library collections
and a brief bibliography. Does not distinguish between
Mexican and Chicano materials.

4239   Arizona Historical Society
       Tucson, Arizona
Has Mexican period materials, including land grants. See
item 4083.

4240   Arizona State Museum
       Southwestern Mission Research Center
       University of Arizona
       Tucson, Arizona
A private organization located on the University of Arizona
campus. Has a collection of colonial period materials,
especially those dealing with missionary activity, put on
computer. Publishes a newsletter largely devoted to recent
bibliography of the Spanish Southwest.

4241   Arizona State University
       Arizona Collection
       Tempe, Arizona
Contains history and statehood materials.

4242   Arizona State University
       Hayden Library
       Chicano Studies Collection
       Arizona State University
       Tempe, Arizona
Contains materials on history, labor, politics, and
literature--emphasis on Arizona.

4243   Baylor University
       Oral History Project
       Box 6307
       Waco, Texas

4244   California Arts Committee
       Chicano Cultural Center
       2004 Park Blvd.
       San Diego, California
Emphasizes materials on art, music, and theatre.

4245   California, State Archives
       Sacramento, California
Includes Spanish and Mexican era materials: documents, land
grants, diseños.

4246   California State University, Fullerton
       Library, Oral History Program
       Fullerton, California

4247   California State University, San Diego
       Library
       San Diego, California
Has extensive pamphlet files on California history,
especially San Diego history.

4248   Chicago Public Library
       El Centro de la Causa
       731 W. 17th Street
       Chicago, Illinois
Contains materials on Mexican American history, sociology,
and literature.

4249   De Golyer Foundation Library
       Dallas, Texas
Includes materials on frontier life and on genealogy of
Mexican families in the Southwest.

4250   El Paso Public Library
       La Raza Collection
       501 N. Oregon
       El Paso, Texas
Covers history, literature, and culture of the Mexican
American.

4251   El Paso Public Library
       Southwest Collection
       El Paso, Texas
Materials on Texas, the Mexican border region, and the
Arizona-New Mexico area.

4252   Federal Records Center
       Bell, California
Has archives of the Surveyor General of Arizona.

4253   Federal Records Center
       Denver, Colorado
Includes land grant materials for Colorado, New Mexico, and
Arizona.

4254   Federal Records Center
       San Francisco, California
Has archives of the Surveyor General of California.

4255   Genealogical Society of the Church of Jesus Christ of
          Latter-Day Saints
       Salt Lake City, Utah
Has microfilms of Texas mission registers, of Santa Fe
Archdiocesan archives and of Mexican genealogical studies.

4256   Henry E. Huntington Library
       San Marino, California
Has documents of the Spanish and Mexican periods in New
Mexico, California missions, California land cases; also
maps and map reproductions.

4257   Hispanic Urban Center
       1201 East 1st Street
       Los Angeles, California
Contains materials on discrimination, education, and
desegregation.

4258   Historical Society of New Mexico
       Albuquerque, New Mexico
Has materials and microfilms of documents from the Spanish
period in New Mexico.

4259   Historical Society of Southern California
       200 East Avenue
       Los Angeles, California
Has reproductions of Los Angeles Pueblo records.

4260   Los Angeles County Museum of Natural History (Library)
       Los Angeles, California
Includes southern California newspapers from 1852 to 1900.

4261   Los Angeles Public Library
       Central Library
       630 W. 5th Street
       Los Angeles, California
Useful for materials on Mexican American history, music, and
art.

4262   Los Angeles Public Library
       Chicano Research Center
       4801 E. Third Street
       Los Angeles, California
Emphasizes history, political science, and sociology.

4263   Mexican American Legal Defense and Education Fund
       Policy Studies Library
       28 Geary Street
       San Francisco, California
Includes materials on civil rights, education, and
immigration.

4264   Mexico, Archivo General de la Nacion
       Mexico, D.F.
Has extensive materials on Spanish and Mexican periods for
the northern frontier, especially after 1700, and
particularly in the areas of politics and administration.

4265   Mexico, Archivo Historico de Hacienda
       Mexico, D.F.
Materials here complement those in the Archivo General de la
Nacion, focusing on the economy. Includes northern mission
information.

4266   Mexico, Archivo Historico Militar Mexicano
       Mexico, D.F.
Holdings heaviest in the Mexican period (1821-1848) although
there is material from the late colonial period as well.

4267   Mexico, Biblioteca Nacional
       Mexico, D.F.
Includes materials on the Franciscan and Jesuit missions in
the northern frontier region.

4268   Mexico, Instituto Nacional de Antropologia e Historia
       Mexico, D.F.
Has considerable archival materials dealing with the
northern frontier.

4269   Mexico, Museo Nacional
       Mexico, D.F.
Houses Franciscan mission materials and other collections
dealing with northern Mexico.

4270   Mexico, Secretaria de Relaciones Exteriores
       Mexico, D.F.
Includes materials on conflict with the United States over
the northern frontier region.

4271   Museum of New Mexico
       History Library
       Santa Fe, New Mexico
Contains New Mexican history materials.

4272   New Mexico State Record Center and Archives
       New Mexico Archives Collection
       Santa Fe, New Mexico
Spanish, Mexican, and territorial history materials;
includes land grant records.

4273   New Mexico State University
       ERIC Clearinghouse on Rural Education and Small
         Schools (CRESS)
       Las Cruces, New Mexico
Emphasizes education and migrancy.

4274   Newberry Library
       Chicago, Illinois
Has various materials on the Abiquiu area in northwestern
New Mexico, and on California.

4275   Northwestern University
        Quincy College Library
        Fraborese Collection
        Evanston, Illinois
Has materials on the Spanish borderlands.

4276   Oakland Public Library
        Latin American Library
        1900 Fruitvale Avenue
        Oakland, California
Covers history, literature, and folklore.

4277   Pan American University
        Pan American University Library
        Learning Resource Center
        1201 West University Drive
        Edinburg, Texas
Includes history, emphasizing south Texas and Mexico, and
bilingual education.

4278   Rosenberg Library
        Galveston, Texas
Has papers of the secretary to Stephen Austin, Col. Samuel
Williams.

4279   San Diego State University
        Love Library, Room 120
        Coleccion Chicana
        San Diego, California
Emphasizes undocumented workers, bilingual education, and
Chicano literature.

4280   Stanford University
        Chicano Reference Library
        590 S. The Nitery
        Stanford, California
Valuable for materials on politics, culture, society, and
bilingual education.

4281   Stanford University
        Special Collections
        Ernesto Galarza Collection
        Stanford, California
Contains labor, agribusiness, and education materials from
Dr. Galarza's long career.

4282   Texas State Library
        Archives Division
        Austin, Texas
Has Nacogdoches archives and other Nacogdoches records and
manuscripts; also Texas and Mexican manuscripts and records.

4283   Tucson Museum of Art
        Archives of Arizona Art

Tucson, Arizona
Includes art relating to the Mexican American.

4284   University of Arizona
       Library
       Tucson, Arizona
Has materials for the north Mexican border region of Sonora,
1800 to 1870.

4285   University of California, Berkeley
       Bancroft Library
       Berkeley, California
Has extensive collections related to northern Mexico plus a
huge microfilm collection. Covers history, culture, land
grants, and early Californiana. An outstanding library for
Chicano materials.

4286   University of California, Berkeley
       Chicano Studies Library
       110 Wheeler Hall
       Berkeley, California
Covers literature, social history, and bilingual education;
includes a very extensive Chicano Dissertation Collection
and a comprehensive collection of over 250 Chicano
newspapers.

4287   University of California, Los Angeles
       Special Collections
       Carey McWilliams Collection
       Los Angeles, California
Contains materials on migrant labor and Mexican Americans.

4288   University of California, Los Angeles
       Chicano Studies Research Library
       1112 Campbell Hall
       Los Angeles, California
Contains materials on the history of the Southwest,
immigration, and labor.

4289   University of California, Santa Barbara
       University Library
       Coleccion Tloque Nahuaque
       Santa Barbara, California
Includes history, literature, and bilingual education
materials.

4290   University of Michigan
       National Chicano Research Network Library
       6085 Institute for Social Research
       Ann Arbor, Michigan
Emphasizes ethnic identity, family, and education.

4291   University of New Mexico
       Zimmerman Library

Ethnic Studies Section
Albuquerque, New Mexico
Includes history, literature, folklore, and bilingual
education.

4292   University of New Mexico
        Zimmerman Library
        New Mexico Collection
        Albuquerque, New Mexico
Has documents from the Spanish and Mexican periods; strong
in microfilms of U.S.-Mexican diplomatic relations.

4293   University of Texas at Arlington
        Division of Archives and Manuscripts
        Archives on History of Labor in Texas and the
           Southwest
        Arlington, Texas
Contains valuable materials, especially interviews with
Chicano leaders; over 100 archival collections and forty
oral history interviews.

4294   University of Texas, Austin
        Barker Texas History Center
        Austin, Texas
An outstanding collection of materials on the Mexican
American; includes manuscripts and newspapers as well as
books. See item 4206.

4295   University of Texas, Austin
        Nettie Lee Benson Latin American Collection
        Sid Richardson Hall
        Austin, Texas
Includes the Texas Collection of materials as well as other
documents relating to the northern frontier of Mexico.

4296   University of Texas, Austin
        University of Texas Archives
        Austin, Texas
Includes the Bexar Archives, Texas provincial records and
correspondence, map collections, and manuscript collections.

4297   University of Texas at El Paso
        Institute of Oral History
        Liberal Arts 339
        El Paso, Texas
Stresses El Paso and border history, 1900 to present.

4298   University of Texas at El Paso
        University Library
        El Paso, Texas
Materials on history, sociology, education, literature, and
the arts.

4299 U.S., Department of the Interior
        Bureau of Land Management
        Washington, D.C.
Records relating to private land grants in the western
states, their surveys and mapping.

4300 U.S., Library of Congress
        Washington, D.C.
The manuscript division has numerous collections covering
aspects of Mexico's northern frontier history, especially
between 1600 and 1900. The Lowery Collection focuses on
pre-1800 materials from Arizona, California, New Mexico, and
Texas.

4301 U.S., National Archives
        Washington, D.C.
Has records of U.S.-Mexico relations, especially State
Department documents. Also is the repository of government
land records.

4302 Wayne State University
        Archives of Labor History and Urban Affairs
        Detroit, Michigan
Notable for United Farm Workers Organizing Committee
materials, 1966-1971.

XII.
JOURNALS _____

Many useful Mexican American history studies have
appeared in print only in periodicals or journals. A
helpful introduction to these articles is:

4303 "Hispanic American Periodicals for Libraries," an
      annotated list by Richard D. Woods and Ann H. Graham
      in The Serials Librarian 4:1 (Fall 1979), 85-98.

Also of great utility are the two volumes of the Chicano
Periodical Index published by G. K. Hall & Co.:

4304 Chicano Periodical Index: A Cumulative Index to
      Selected Chicano Periodicals Published Between 1967
      and 1978. Boston: G. K. Hall & Co., 1981.

4305 Chicano Periodical Index, 1979-1981. Boston: G. K.
      Hall & Co., 1982.

They cover the leading Mexican American publications, with a
complete subject index under 1000 headings and a
supplemental author-title index.

There follows a list of journals and periodicals which
regularly publish or have published materials dealing with
the Chicano historical experience. Many are rich in their
variety of Mexican American materials, including, in
addition to historical studies, some descriptive, critical,
and cultural approaches to topics like civil rights,
education, the family, and ethnicity. Some specialize in
the Mexican ethnic group; others are broader in their
coverage.

4306   Agenda: A Journal of Hispanic Issues
         National Council of La Raza
         Washington, D.C., bimonthly
Publishes articles on history, politics, social justice,
education, the arts, and culture.

4307   America
         America Press, Inc.
         New York, N.Y., weekly
A journal of social and political commentary published by
the Jesuits of the United States and Canada. Often carries
articles and comments on current events relating to the
Mexican American.

4308   Americas
         Pan American Union
         Washington, D.C., monthly
Publishes occasional articles on the Chicano experience.

4309   Arizona and the West
         University of Arizona
         Tucson, Arizona, quarterly
Concerns itself primarily with the period after 1900; many
articles relate to Mexican Americans, directly or
peripherally.

4310   Arizona Quarterly
         Tucson, University of Arizona
Has material on the political history of Arizona, of
importance to the Chicano experience.

4311   Atisbos: Journal of Chicano Research
         Stanford University
         Stanford, California, irregular
         [Soon to move to the University of Arizona, Tempe]
Publishes articles on the Chicano experience; aims to
provide Chicano scholars with a forum for their research on
Mexican Americans.

4312   Aztlan, International Journal of Chicano Studies and
         Research
         Mexican American Cultural Center
         University of California, Los Angeles, California
Specializes in scholarly articles, mostly in English, on
Chicano history, the social sciences, literature, and art.

4313   The Bilingual Review/ La Revista Bilingüe
         Department of Foreign Language
         Eastern Michigan University
         Ypsilanti, Michigan
Serves as a bibliographic and research resource for
scholars, primarily in the area of literature.

4314   The Borderlands Journal
        Department of Behavioral Sciences
        Texas Southmost College
        Brownsville, Texas, semi-annual
Specializes in topics related to the U.S.-Mexican frontier
region. Formerly the South Texas Journal of Research and
Humanities.

4315   Bronce
        California Migrant Ministry Newsletter
        Oakland, California, monthly
Articles regarding Chicanos in the areas of the social
sciences.

4316   California History
        San Francisco, California, quarterly
Especially rich in articles on the Mexican period and the
post-Guadalupe Hidalgo Treaty era. Formerly titled
California Historical (Society) Quarterly.

4317   Campo Libre: Journal of Chicano Studies
        Centro de Publicaciones
        California State University, Los Angeles, California,
            semi-annual
Publishes scholarly articles in history and the social
sciences.

4318   Caracol: La Revista de la Raza
        San Antonio, Texas, monthly, bilingual
Publishes short articles, interviews, and reviews.

4319   Chicano Law Review
        University of California
        Los Angeles, California, annual
Concerns itself with current legal issues affecting
Chicanos.

4320   Chicano Student Movement
        Chicano Student Movement
        Los Angeles, California, bimonthly
Presents an activist Chicano student perspective.

4321   Chismearte
        Los Angeles, California, quarterly
Publishes articles on literature and art, especially those
relating to the Chicano's social struggle.

4322   Colorado Magazine
        Colorado Historical Society
        Denver, Colorado, quarterly
Useful for articles touching on the Colorado Chicano
experience.

4323   Comexas News Monitoring Service
        Comite de Mexico y Aztlan
        Oakland, Calif., monthly
Maintains an indexed news-monitoring service covering seven
important newspapers of the Southwest.

4324   Commonweal
        Commonweal Publishing Co.
        New York, N.Y., weekly
A review of politics, literature, and the arts. It
frequently comments on matters of interest to La Raza.

4325   Con Safos: Reflections of Life in the Barrio
        Los Angeles, California, irregular
Emphasizes history, politics, and literature, as they affect
the urban Chicano.

4326   ¡Coraje!
        Tucson, Arizona
Published by the Mexican American Liberation Committee.

4327   El Cuaderno
        Dixon, New Mexico
Emphasizes local Chicano history, folklore, and literature.

4328   La Cucaracha
        Pueblo, Colorado, irregular
Covers Colorado news and issues of special interest to
Mexican Americans.

4329   De Colores: Journal of Chicano Expression and Thought
        Pajarito Publications
        Albuquerque, New Mexico, quarterly
Publishes historical articles, interviews, and some literary
works.

4330   Encuentro Femenil
        San Fernando, California, semi-annual
Describes itself as the first Chicana feminist journal.
Began publication in 1973.

4331   Entrelineas
        Kansas City, Missouri, irregular
Includes current events, Chicano literary works, and book
reviews.

4332   Frontera: Borderlands Review
        Department of Geography
        California State University
        Northridge, California

4333   El Grito: A Journal of Contemporary Mexican American
        Thought
        Berkeley, California, quarterly

Published articles of high quality on history, politics, the
social sciences, and literature.

4334   El Grito del Sol
       Tonatiuh International, Inc.
       Berkeley, California, quarterly
Basically a literary journal, El Grito del Sol publishes
articles on the Chicano experience as well as literary
works. Successor to El Grito.

4335   Hispanic American Historical Review
       Duke University Press
       Durham, North Carolina
Includes Mexican American materials, primarily in the
context of Mexican history.

4336   El Independiente
       Independent Publishing Co.
       Albuquerque, New Mexico, weekly
Emphasizes current civil rights and other legal problems of
Mexican Americans.

4337   Inside Eastside
       Los Angeles, California, irregular
Covers materials of interest to the East Los Angeles Chicano
community.

4338   International Migration Review
       Center for Migration Studies of New York
       Staten Island, N.Y., quarterly
Stresses historical, social, sociological, and legislative
aspects of migration and ethnic group relations. A degree
of European emphasis.

4339   Journal of American Ethnic History
       Immigration History Society
       Department of Social Sciences
       Georgia Institute of Technology
       Atlanta, Georgia, semi-annual
The journal focuses on ethnic and immigration history in
North America. The Society also publishes a newsletter.

4340   Journal of Arizona History
       Arizona Historical Society
       Tucson, Arizona, quarterly
Includes the Mexican American experience after the Guadalupe
Hidalgo Treaty. Formerly titled Arizoniana.

4341   Journal of Comparative Cultures
       National Bilingual Education Association
       Cypress, California, annual
Concerns itself with social, especially educational, topics
of interest to ethnic minorities, particularly Chicanos.

Formerly called the <u>Journal of Mexican American Studies</u>.

4342   <u>Journal of Ethnic Studies</u>
       College of Ethnic Studies
       Western Washington University
       Bellingham, Washington, quarterly

4343   <u>Journal of Mexican American History</u>
       Santa Barbara, California, irregular
Published scholarly articles related to many aspects of
Chicano history.

4344   <u>Journal of the West</u>
       1915 South Western Avenue
       Los Angeles, California, quarterly
Many issues include articles dealing with the Mexican
American experience.

4345   <u>La Luz</u>
       360 South Monroe Street
       Denver, Colorado, monthly
Features a variety of popular articles about Hispanics with
emphasis on Chicanos and their role in American life. A
national perspective.

4346   <u>Magazin</u>
       San Antonio, Texas, irregular
Includes material on Chicano history and folklore, as well
as contemporary news.

4347   <u>El Malcriado</u>
       Delano, California
The United Farm Worker publication; it stresses news items
of interest to members of the union.

4348   <u>Monthly Labor Review</u>
       U.S. Department of Labor
       Washington, D.C., monthly
Especially useful for articles on southwestern and migrant
labor since 1900.

4349   <u>The Nation</u>
       The Nation Associates, Inc.
       New York, N.Y., weekly
A journal of political and social commentary; it often
carries editorial comment and articles on problems of
Mexican Americans.

4350   <u>New Mexico Historical Review</u>
       Historical Society of New Mexico
       Albuquerque, New Mexico, quarterly
For half a century it has published numerous excellent
articles on colonial and nineteenth century New Mexican and
southwestern history. The <u>New Mexico Historical Review</u> also

publishes excellent topic and reference guides to articles
in the journal's fifty-eight volumes.

4351   New Mexico Magazine
         Bataan Memorial Building
         Santa Fe, New Mexico, monthly
Provides broad coverage of southwestern culture; includes
popular history and book reviews.

4352   New Scholar
         University of California, San Diego
         La Jolla, California, bi-annual
A activist journal with Chicano and third world interests.
Many excellent articles on Chicano politics and history.

4353   Nuestro: The Magazine for Latinos
         Nuestro Publications
         New York, N.Y., monthly, bilingual
Devotes itself to cultural and political coverage on a
national level.

4354   Pacific Historical Review
         University of California Press
         Berkeley, California, quarterly
Journal of the Pacific Coast Branch of the American
Historical Association; carries articles on the history of
Mexican Americans and their concerns.

4355   El Paisano
         Tolleson, Arizona
A monthly, published by the United Farm Workers Organizing
Committee of Arizona.

4356   Perspectives: A Civil Rights Quarterly
         U.S. Commission on Civil Rights
         Washington, D.C., quarterly
Useful articles on the Mexican American civil rights
experience. Formerly called Civil Rights Digest.

4357   La Raza
         P.O. Box 31004
         Los Angeles, California, irregular
Focuses on news, especially politics affecting Mexican
Americans.

4358   La Raza Habla
         Chicano Affairs Office
         New Mexico State University
         Las Cruces, New Mexico
Began publication in 1976.

4359   La Red/ The Net
         Institute for Social Research
         University of Michigan

Ann Arbor, Michigan, monthly
Publishes short articles on Chicano topics in the social sciences; carries book reviews and information on current research and recent publications.

4360   Red River Valley Historical Review
       Red River Valley Historical Association
       Southeastern Oklahoma State University
       Durant, Oklahoma, quarterly

4361   Regeneracion
       P.O. Box 54624
       Los Angeles, California, irregular
An activist journal emphasizing news events of concern to Chicanos.

4362   La Revista Catolica
       El Paso, Texas
A Spanish-language periodical published by the Jesuit order between 1875 and 1962. The 19th century issues, especially, included frequent references to Mexicans and Mexican Americans.

4363   Revista Chicano-Riqueña
       Gary, Indiana, quarterly, bilingual
A quality journal promoting cultural pluralism and especially devoted to Chicano and Puerto Rican literature.

4364   Rural Sociology
       Rural Sociological Society
       Brigham Young University
       Provo, Utah, quarterly
The official journal of the Rural Sociological Society, it has published articles on the Chicano in a rural context.

4365   Social Science Quarterly
       University of Texas
       Austin, Texas, quarterly
Includes articles on Mexican American topics in history and the social sciences. Formerly Southwestern Social Science Quarterly.

4366   Sociology and Social Research
       University of Southern California
       Los Angeles, California, quarterly
Has published and publishes useful articles on the Mexican American experience in the 20th century.

4467   Somos
       San Bernardino, Calif., monthly
News and essays with a strong emphasis on California.

4368   Southern California Quarterly
       Historical Society of Southern California

Los Angeles, California
Publishes scholarly articles on Western history, especially
California.

4369 Southwestern Historical Quarterly
Texas State Historical Association
University of Texas
Austin, Texas, quarterly
Over the years has published articles on Mexican American
history, especially for the period 1821 to 1900.

4370 El Tecolote
San Francisco, California, monthly
Expresses its views on Chicano and Latin American political
and social problems.

4371 Texas Historical Association Quarterly
Sid Richardson Hall 2/306
University Station
Austin, Texas, quarterly
Includes materials on the Mexican American experience,
especially in Texas.

4372 Western Historical Quarterly
Utah State University
Logan, Utah
Publishes some articles on Chicano history.

AUTHOR INDEX

In the list below, the numbers after each name
refer to item numbers in the <u>Bibliography</u>

A

Abbott, Carl. 1
Abelardo [Abelardo Delgado
    Barrientos]. 3276
Abrams, E. 3071
Abrams, F. S. 3071
Achor, Shirley. 3277
Acosta, Adalberto J. 3585
Acuña, Rodolfo [Rudolph] F.
    2, 3, 4, 5, 6, 1364,
    3424
Adair, Douglas. 2477
Adair, John. 2895
Adam, V. G. 443
Adams, Alexander B. 7
Adams, David Bergen. 413
Adams, Eleanor B. 444
Adams, Emma H. 980
Adams, Ramon F. 4037
Adorno, William. 3727
Aguallo, Robert, Jr. 2811
Aguirre, Yjinio F. 835,
    1365
Ahlborn, Richard. 3587
Airey, Guy. 1266
Airman, Duncan. 1842
Akers, Toma. 1267
Alarcon Acosta, Rafael G.
    3072
Alba, Francisco. 2886
Alba, Pedro. 2121
Alba, Victor. 236
Albert, Ethel M. 3718
Albrecht, Elizabeth. 1366
Albro, Ward S., III. 1739
Alcala, Carlos M. 3551
Alcaraz, Ramon. 527
Alessio Robles, Vito. 237,
    528

Alexander, Gladys M. 776
Alexander, L. 2480
Alexander, T. John. 2122
Alford, Harold J. 8
Alisky, Marvin. 2481, 3843
Allan, Robert A. 1740
Allen, Gary. 2482
Allen, Joseph E. 3728
Allen, R. H. 1268, 1367
Allen, Ruth A. 1843
Allen, Steve. 2123
Allsup, Carl. 2124, 2483
Allwell, Patrick J. 1741
Almaguer, Tomas. 1269,
    3425, 3426, 3427
Almanza, Arturo S. 3278
Almaraz, Felix D., Jr. 202,
    238, 836, 837, 838,
    1368, 1844
Almazan, Marco A. 2484
Almonte, Juan Nepomuceno.
    529, 839
Almquist, Alan J. 1092
Alsberg, Henry G. 9
Althoff, Phillip. 3428
Altus, David M. 4038, 4039
Altus, William. 3844
Alvarado, Ernestine M. 1845
Alvarado, Roger. 3279
Alvarez, Jose Hernandez.
    3073
Alvarez, Robert R., Jr.
    3005
Alvarez, Rodolfo. 3429
Alvarez, Salvador E. 2125
Alvarez-Altman, Grace. 4232
Alvirez, David. 2126, 3923
Ambrecht, Biliana C. 3280

SUBJECT INDEX _____

In the list below, the numbers after each name

refer to item numbers in the <u>Bibliography</u>

A

Acculturation. 37, 656,
1158, 1296, 1309, 1344,
1649, 1735, 1762, 1789,
1826, 1832, 1909, 1989,
2004, 2047, 2067, 2261,
2314, 2441, 2856, 2910,
3034, 3581, 3590, 3613,
3626, 3642, 3654, 3658,
3672, 3679, 3685, 3689,
3698, 3721, 3728, 3733,
3740, 3745, 3747, 3749,
3757, 3770, 3772, 3785,
3786, 3795, 3797, 3799,
3801, 3802, 3807, 3808,
3809, 3811, 3812, 3837,
3862, 3865, 3892, 3896,
3910, 3916, 3944, 3948,
3949, 3957, 3994, 4000,
4021, 4027, 4035
Activism. 2481, 2543, 2561,
2623, 2646, 2702, 2735,
2749, 2811, 2854, 3308,
3314, 3327, 3328, 3330,
3343, 3353, 3375, 3377,
3399, 3412, 3419, 3441,
3444, 3449, 3464, 3466,
3482, 3486, 3487, 3492,
3496, 3501, 3522, 3566,
3580, 3864, 3922. See
also Civil Rights; Raza
Unida; Politics and
Government.
Student. 2422, 2423, 2424,
2426, 2440, 2448, 2453,
2573, 2588, 2626, 3435,
3474, 3565, 3864, 3922.
See also Brown Berets.
AFL-CIO. 2196, 2493, 2784

Agricultural Labor Relations
Act (California).
2526, 2529, 2596, 2597,
2651, 2673, 2776, 2803,
2865
Agricultural Labor Relations
Board (California).
See Agricultural Labor
Relations Act.
Agriculture. 203, 234,
1268, 1353, 1367, 1582,
1902, 2938, 3111
Alamo. 650, 662, 687, 742,
911, 917, 924, 953,
975, 976
Albuquerque, New Mexico.
1335, 1358
Alianza Federal de Mercedes.
See Alianza Federal de
Pueblos Libres.
Alianza Federal de Pueblos
Libres. 2136, 2226,
2267, 2319, 2336, 2337,
2675, 2676, 2678, 2736,
2821, 2822, 2855, 3533
Alianza Hispano-Americana.
1683
Alianza Patriota Revolu-
cionaria Americana.
3784
Alta California. See California, Colonial.
American G.I. Forum. 1593,
2124, 2483, 3451, 3544,
3568
Anglo Views of Mexicans.
549, 559, 576, 593,
606, 635, 644, 674,

About the Compiler

MATT S. MEIER is the Donohoe Professor of History at the University of Santa Clara, California. He is the author of the *Bibliography for Chicano History* and *The Chicanos: A History of Mexican Americans*, and co-author of the *Dictionary of Mexican American History* (Greenwood Press, 1981).